THE NOBLE CAT

THE NOBLE CAT

Aristocrat of the Animal World

Howard Loxton

Portland House
New York

For Sara and Sayaka, Thomas and Matthew, Ryozo and Sachiko-neko, and in memory of Nike.

This United States edition published in 1990 by Portland House, a division of dilithium Press, Ltd, distributed by Outlet Book Company, Inc., a Random House Company, 225 Park Avenue South, New York 10003, in association with David Bateman, Auckland, New Zealand.

© 1990 David Bateman Ltd

Printed and bound in Hong Kong
Production: Paul Bateman
Design: Errol McLeary
Jacket design: Suellen Allen/Errol McLeary

ISBN 0-517-02325-3

87654321

ACKNOWLEDGMENTS

This book is not entirely my own work. Angela Sayer Rixon, an experienced breeder and judge, responsible for developing the Foreign Spotted Shorthair in Britain, an international show judge and herself a well-known author, has written the whole section on cat breeds and contributed the material on cat genetics. Dr Graham Meadows, a British-trained veterinarian who has practiced in several countries of the world, handling both domestic and zoo animals, and has been involved in zoo administration as well as having his own radio and television programs, has written the section on feline illnesses and their treatment. They have both advised on the overall text as have Will Thompson, an international show judge from the United States, past editor of *All Cats*, and Peter Jackson, Chairman of the International Union for the Conservation of Nature's Survival Commission's Cat Specialist Group and former Director of the Worldwide Fund for Nature's Project Tiger. To all four of them I extend my gratitude. Their guidance has made this a better book; if any error survives the blame must all be mine.

I owe a debt also to the many previous writers on cats, from Herodotus through the medieval bestiarists to the contemporary scientists whose research is expanding our knowledge and understanding of the cat family — some of whom will be found listed in the bibliography, but especially to Dr Paul Leyhausen, Dr David Macdonald, Dr Roger Tabor, and the late Frank Manolson, MRCVS, a prince of feline veterinarians, who taught me so much about cat care; also the other vets, zoo keepers, naturalists, breeders and cat owners who have shared their knowledge and stories over the years.

Margaret Forde not only copy-edited the text and compiled the index but also contributed the philatelic pages. My thanks to her and to the photographers, artists, cat breeders, designer and my picture researcher, Jan Croot; also the publishers, who first conceived the idea of the book and their production team.

My last — but probably greatest — debt is to the cats themselves, wild and domesticated, that have added color and companionship to life. I hope this book does them some service.

Howard Loxton

I am grateful to the following for all their help, advice and support: Associate Professor Boyd Jones, Massey University, Palmerston North, New Zealand; Dr Stewart Bickerstaff and other colleagues; Becky Trethowan, Sheryl Jamieson, Twink McCabe, Dianne and Nigel Davidson, Jill and Claire Dawson, Iris Kerridge, Mark Ryan, and the Auckland SPCA for assistance with my photographs; Sandra Perry and Peg Barningham for help in selecting the breed photographs; and the many owners and breeders who allowed me to photograph their cats.

Graham Meadows

INTRODUCTION

Despite millennia of separate development and enormous differences in size, the various members of the cat family are closely related and easily recognized as members of the same family. The kitten on the hearth is probably the least changed from the wild form of all the animals that have been domesticated, if one can describe as domestication the way in which the cat has infiltrated our homes. Its behavior displays in microcosm that of all the cats. Each species has its own special characteristics, according to the particular way in which it has adapted to its environment, but comparisons aid understanding of them all, and if we are to save the endangered species and ensure that our pets live happy and healthy lives, we need to understand them.

Not much is known about some of the more secretive cat species and it is only in recent years that scientists have turned their attention to a study of domestic pets and feral cats. Our knowledge about cats is growing, but research appearing in specialist publications is not readily available to the general reader and often not easy for the lay person to understand. To ensure that this book is useful to all I have tried not to take any prior knowledge of cats for granted, while the experienced cat owner or safari veteran will, I hope, find much that will confirm their own observation.

The natural history of the cats and the care of domestic pets is only a part of the cat story. The members of the cat family have had an important role in our cultural life. From prehistoric times, the strength and elegance of the cats has drawn both fear and admiration. The power of the big cats has made them both a symbol of kingship and a prey of the hunter. The domestic cat has been both venerated and persecuted. This book also sets out to celebrate those other facets of the human-cat interaction.

As any cat owner knows, it is not only men and women that can be exploiters; cats can be very demanding, but we must accept responsibility both for the cats we take into our homes and for the survival of their relatives in the wild. The future of both is in our hands.

CONTENTS

THE PHYSICAL CAT

DOMESTIC VARIETIES

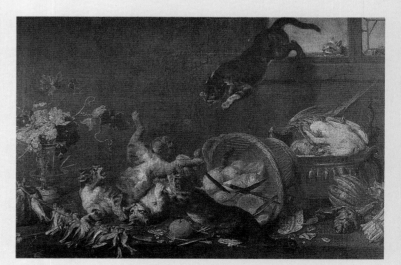

THE LIFE OF CATS

CATS AND PEOPLE

CARING FOR CATS

THE PHYSICAL CAT

THE EVOLUTION OF THE CAT FAMILY

The domestic cat belongs to a family well established before the coming of the early hominids.

In the timescale of the history of life, it was only recently that the domestic cat became a companion of humans, but the cat family was around long before the development of *Homo sapiens*. Fossils in rock strata laid down over millions and millions of years have enabled scientists to reconstruct much of the pattern of the evolution of life on earth. A fossil, the record of a once living animal or plant, may be the actual remains of a living thing, its form preserved by replacement minerals which fill the space which it once occupied, or an impression such as that of a footprint or other track left on wet clays and similar surfaces.

To be preserved the remains or marks must be rapidly covered by sediments or other material. When land creatures die they are often eaten by other animals, or are broken down by bacteria, so that nothing remains to become a fossil. Sometimes, if animals fall into a lake or river, they become buried by sediment before they decay, or are carried down by river currents to the sea and preserved under the sediments carried down after them. A few may be trapped beneath cave falls, buried in sand storms or, like the remains of Pompeii and Herculaneum, smothered by the ash of a volcanic eruption, but only a very small proportion of creatures die under such circumstances. Sea creatures and those that live in lakes and boggy terrain are more likely to be covered before being scavenged or decaying.

The greatest number of fossils come from strata that were once the bed of the sea, forced up later by the movements of the earth to become the territories where the fossils are eventually discovered. Our knowledge of prehistoric marine life is consequently more detailed than that of terrestrial forms, but the accumulated fossil evidence which has been found enables scientists to establish a comprehensive picture of the way in which life on earth has developed. New discoveries are continually adding greater detail.

Fossils were the key to establishing Darwin's theory of the evolution of species. There are still some people who, often for religious reasons, refuse to accept the idea that the millions of modern life forms have evolved from earlier forms, rather than being newly and individually created, but scientists now generally believe that a clear pattern of development can be seen, even though some stages are uncertain because the necessary evidence is missing.

There are no fossil records of the Earth's earliest living organisms. They were probably too small to leave any trace and the early rocks in which they could have been present have been subjected to temperature changes and pressures so great that any traces are likely to have been destroyed. The earliest signs of life are organisms similar to primitive bacteria, first identified from 3800 million years ago. It was not until about 1450 million years ago that the first single-celled plants and animals appeared. The development

of skeletons led to fishes (530 million years ago), amphibians which carried animal life onto the land (370 million years ago) and then to the reptiles (340 million years ago).

The very first mammals developed about 200 million years ago, about the same time as the first dinosaurs came into being. Mammals (with the exception of the very primitive monotremes which still lay eggs) differ from most reptiles in that the egg in which their young develop hatches within the body of the female mammal — but there is another important difference, mammals are 'warm-blooded'. They developed fur, a hairy coat that enables them to retain heat and control their own body temperature. Unlike reptiles they can be active even when the temperature drops — at night, for instance, when reptile activity slows down. Mammals also have teeth with which they chew; reptiles use them only to get their food and then swallow it — a difference of great significance to paleontologists for early mammals are now known largely through finds of jaws and teeth (which survive particularly well).

The very earliest mammals still laid eggs. They were tiny creatures (smaller than a modern rat) that probably came out foraging at night, feeding perhaps on worms, insects and grubs. Pointed cusps on their cheek teeth enabled them to crack beetle carapaces, while later some used their gnawing teeth to eat nuts and fruit. Their only enemies were the ostrich dinosaurs which hunted them at evening as the light faded. They spread everywhere, except to what are now Australasia and South America, in a world that was dominated by dinosaurs, some of whom, some scientists believe, may also have developed ways of regulating their body temperature. Then the dinosaurs began to disappear. They and many other species became extinct. We do not know why, perhaps it was due to climatic change or a dramatic alteration of sea level. It has been suggested that it was the result of tidal waves and dust-clouds following the impact of a giant meteor. The decline of the dinosaurs took five million years with up to 100,000 years separating the disappearance of different species, so some such sudden disaster was probably not the cause.

Among the survivors were the mammals. During the Paleocene Era (65–53 million years ago) they were able to colonize numerous environmental 'niches', particular habitats and ways of life, which had once been occupied by the dinosaurs. Some became plant eaters, others remained carnivorous and developed into accomplished hunters. One early group, the fish-eating creodonts, were rather like modern wolves and bears, but their line became extinct. Another group of much smaller forest-living mammals, the miacids which developed about 60 million years ago, were the actual ancestors of the wolves and bears and the rest of the group of animals we know as carnivores which includes the now

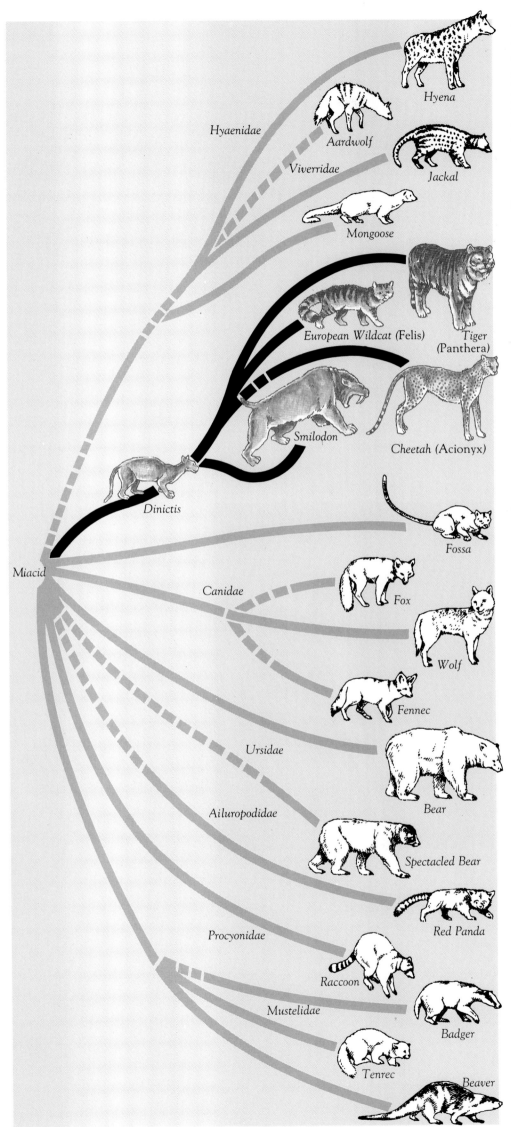

The carnivorous mammals all developed from the miacids which appeared about 60 million years ago, different branches becoming the modern hyena, civet, weasel, panda, raccoon, bear and dog families as well as that of cats. The earliest cats date from the Eocene, 50 million years ago. The sabre-tooths and false sabre-tooths developed in the Oligocene 34–32 million years ago, some surviving until about 13,000 years ago. The modern genera began to appear about 3 million years ago. Among the existing species Cougar and Lynx date from the Upper Pliocene (2 million years ago), the Wildcats from the very early Pleistocene (1.6 million years ago) and the big cats from the Ice Ages. The domestic cat is almost certainly descended from the Wildcat.

almost vegetarian pandas, the weasels, badgers, skunks, otters, civets, genets, mongooses, hyenas and the whole of the cat family.

The first miacids were short-legged, long-bodied animals, looking rather like modern pine martens. Adept climbers of trees, they probably had retractile claws, like those of modern cats. Fossils dating from 50 million years ago include an animal which must have looked very like members of the modern cat family. It has been given the name *Dinictis* and was about the size of a lynx. It had cat-like teeth, though the canines (the long fang-like teeth on either side of the central incisors) were larger than in modern cats, and it had a much smaller brain.

These early 'cats' began to spread around the world, developing a variety of forms to suit particular ecological niches. None reached Antarctica or Australasia and it was much later before the cats reached South America, although a separate but parallel development among the marsupials produced some similar-looking prehistoric animals.

When the very first primitive mammals developed, over 200 million years ago, the continents of the world formed a single great land mass, known now as Pangea. This separated during the Jurassic and Cretaceous Periods. The placental mammals evolved in Asia during the Late Cretaceous, spreading to western North America and some on to South America. Marsupials, or pouched mammals, may have evolved in South America and then spread north and to the still connected Antarctica and Australasia. In the early Cenozoic North America seems to have become the main centre of placental mammal evolution, from which they spread to Asia, Europe and Africa. *Dinictis* is thought to have developed in Asia and spread from there, but came into existence too late to reach the now separate southern continents.

From *Dinictis* feline evolution went in two separate directions. In one branch were the machairodonts — some paleontologists think *Dinictis* should actually be included among them — in which the canine teeth became even larger. In the other branch, developing later in the late Miocene and Pliocene 15–1 million years ago, the canines were smaller. It was these, the Felidae, which eventually produced our modern cats.

The machairodonts, which began to diverge in the Oligocene (34–23 million years ago) include *Eusmilus* and *Hoplophoneus*, two of the earliest sabre-toothed cats. Both these began as Old World species. Protective flanges on their lower

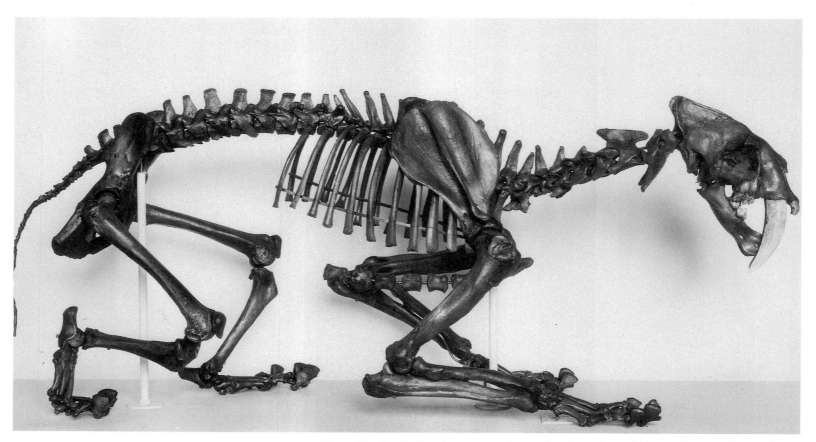

Above *The fossilized skeleton of the sabre-toothed Smilodon, which could lower itself to stalk like a modern big cat. About the same size as today's lion or tiger, its name means 'knife-tooth'. The canine teeth (below) were 6 in (15 cm) long and delivered a stabbing blow powered by the muscles of the neck, not the jaw.*

jaws made it impossible for them to use their long canine teeth unless the mouth was already wide open. The New World genus *Smilodon*, which ranged across North America and spread southward to Argentine and Brazil after the Panamanian land bridge was re-established, was more advanced. Its sabre-teeth extended beyond the lower jaw when it was closed and so could be used without gaping the mouth. In all the sabre-tooths these vicious teeth were used not to bite but to inflict a stabbing blow. The sabre-tooths' lower jaws were comparatively weak but the neck muscles and those used to bring the head down could deliver considerable force. They were able to attack large slow-moving animals such as elephants and mammoths.

Bones of a South American species, *Smilodon neogaenus*, have been found in the pampas lands of Argentina in considerable numbers. Its predations are thought to have been responsible for the extinction of many of the earlier large South American mammals. The sabre-tooths themselves were not to survive. They were still living in California only 13,000 years ago, but the most recent date established for fossils in Europe is much earlier — 30,000 years ago for a Lesser Scimitar Cat *Homoptherium latidens* discovered in Robin Hood's Cave, in Derbyshire, England.

The Californian sabre-tooth *Smilodon californicus* was preserved in considerable numbers when animals became trapped in pools of tar at what is now Rancho La Brea in the middle of Los Angeles, California. These pools became one of the richest of all fossil deposits. From 40,000 to 4000 years ago crude oil seeped up to the surface creating sticky pools of tar or asphalt in which thousands of creatures became trapped — in the three years 1912–15, 750,000 bones were excavated! They include those of plant eaters such as horses, mammoths, bison, camels, and giant ground sloths which sauntered into the tar or perhaps became trapped when drinking water

on its surface. There are even a few wolves, foxes, Californian lions, cougars and bobcats, but the majority are dire-wolves, vultures and sabre-tooths. The sabre-tooths, like all mammals, were more intelligent than the creatures that came before them, but they were still comparatively stupid compared with the feline forms. The Felidae were much more intelligent hunters and, except for a few unfortunates, they seem to have been able to avoid getting trapped.

One of the earliest of the Felidae was *Nivramus*, which, lacking the long canine teeth, killed its prey with a bite to the neck. Long before the Rancho La Brea tar captured its first victims the felines had developed into fast, intelligent hunters like the modern species of cat. There are fossils about 12 million years old that are very like the bones of modern smaller cats. By 3 million years ago the three extant cat genera were already established, though then with more diversity than exists today. When man first came on the scene he formed part of their prey. At Swartkrans, in the Transvaal, South Africa, anthropologist Dr Raymond Dart discovered a fissure filled with the bones of baboons and of an early hominid *Australopithecus africanus* (the African southern ape), which was an upright-walking intermediary stage between ape-like primates and man. These were not complete skeletons, just heads, hands and feet. In just such sites today leopards climb into trees with their kill to keep it from scavengers and, as they eat, heads and extremities fall down below. These bones are the remnants of leopard meals and among them is

Sabre-tooth cats survived alongside the early Panthera *species, but compared with them were slow and cumbersome. They also had relatively smaller brains. The American Smilodon (**below** foreground) once prowled the Hollywood hills, and thousands of years ago, in the centre of modern Los Angeles (**right**) at Rancho La Brea, a natural eruption of tar trapped some of them. The more intelligent Californian Lions (Panthera atox, on mammoth) and more recent types of cat were too clever to be caught but dim-witted Smilodon charged in after supposedly sitting prey and ended up trapped as well.*

the skull of an Australopithecine child with fractures spaced to match the canine teeth of a leopard which probably dragged it off with its upper teeth in the eye sockets and the lower ones in the back of the head.

People still form the occasional meal for one of the larger cats but it is human hunters and human destruction of natural habitat that have hastened the extinction of some of the once widespread feline species and threaten the extinction of even those that remain. However at fault we may be, we do not carry all the blame. Great shifts in climatic conditions with the successive ice ages of the Quaternary Period (since 1.6 million years ago and continuing) have put pressure on species to move, or adapt, or to die.

The larger cats seem to have developed after the spread of grasslands during the Miocene to exploit the browsing herds just as they do in Africa today. Others have developed to exploit other habitats, such as forests and mountainsides. Once, lions ranged across Europe and Asia and through Alaska into North America as well as Africa. The Cave Lion *Panthera atrox* is among the Rancho La Brea finds, and its remains have also been found in Alaska. Its close European relation *Panthera leo spelaea* was established in Britain 500,000 years ago. It has been found on

the banks of the Thames in deposits dating from just before the last Ice Age, 100,000 years ago, when the British climate was much warmer than today, and probably survived in Britain for a further 50,000 years. In Greece it is thought to have been extant in Macedonia until 480 BC when lions attacked the baggage train of the invading Persian ruler Xerxes. The tiger spread right across Asia, including Japan, the lynx had already reached America, and before the Ice Ages the leopard already ranged over the combined Old World territories of both the lion and the tiger.

The origin of the domestic cat

Although taxonomists differ about the finer degrees of relationship between the members of the cat family, they generally agree that at generic level the living cats form two main groups: the *Panthera* (most of the big cats) and *Felis* (most of the small cats); plus *Acinonyx* for the Cheetah and *Neofelis* for the Clouded Leopard, because they show differences which separate them from the others.

While there are several small cat species that bear a resemblance to the typical spotted or tabby

When Sir Edwin Landseer carved the lions that flank Nelson's Column in London's Trafalgar Square (above) he was reflecting the power and dominance of the British Empire, but they are doubly appropriate for nearby were found the bones of Cave Lions (top) which hunted along the banks of the River Thames before the onset of the last Ice Age.

domestic cat it seems certain that our pets are descended from the Wildcat *Felis silvestris*. Most people would probably mistake a Scottish Wildcat *F.s.grampia* for a heavily-built domestic tabby, but the evidence seems to suggest that it seems more likely that it was the African form *F.s.lybica*, rather than one of the northern subspecies, that was first domesticated. Although mummified Egyptian pets which have been studied include some Jungle Cats *F.chaus*, the vast majority appear to be African Wildcats. That subspecies domesticates fairly easily, whereas European Wildcats are rarely possible to tame. It seems clear that domestic stock spread outwards from Egyptian sources. Since the subspecies of *Felis silvestris* can interbreed (in Scotland hybridization is now considered a threat to the survival of the pure wild species) it is possible that other cats may have played some part in the domestic cat's make-up but this could only be incidental. Every indication is that the ancestry of your family pet places it as a development from the African Wildcat.

Close relatives of the cats

Separate from the cat family, but clearly coming from the same miacid stock and much closer relatives than the bears or the dogs and wolves which took longer to appear, are the members of the family Viverridae which include the many kinds of genets, civets and linsangs, the mongooses and the meerkat. The Aardwolf and the hyenas which form the family Hyaenidae are also near relatives. Found only in Africa and Asia, mainly in the south, they all share very similar skull structures, including short jaws with a strong bite, and are skilled and formidable predators. Civets and genets, though long-tailed, have cat-like heads and bodies and some are patterned with spots and tail stripes. They are forest dwellers and nocturnal in their habits. Mongooses look less like cats and the hyenas might be more readily associated with dogs both from their appearance and because they are pack animals — nevertheless their evolutionary links are closer to the cats.

Genet.

The marsupial cats

The marsupials are an Order within the mammal group. Most mammals carry their offspring in the womb for a considerable period, facilitated by thin layers of tissue (the placenta) through which food and wastes can be diffused between the blood of the mother and that of the embryo. They are the placental mammals. The marsupials have no placenta and are born at an earlier stage of development as tiny, worm-like creatures which crawl up to a pouch (the Latin *marsupium* means pouch) to be suckled and continue their development. They probably developed first in South America (where many mouse like forms exist today), then spread through Antarctica to Australia.

Modern marsupials include the koala, kangaroo, opossums, bandicoots and wombats. Some of them have been given the name 'cat', but none is a member of the cat family. The Tiger Cat *Dasyurus maculatus* of Tasmania and east and south-east Australia hunts in the forest much as small cats elsewhere in the world and looks slightly similar. New Guinea has its Marsupial Cat *D.albopunctatus*, and there are several other species in the genus including the Western and Eastern Quolls, *D.geoffroii* and *D.viverrinus* (also known as the Western and Eastern Native Cats), were both perhaps once widespread in Australia but are now confined respectively to Western Australia and Papua and to Tasmania, for the Eastern Quoll has probably become extinct on the mainland.

A Miocene form from South America, of which fossils have been found in Australia, was the Marsupial Lion *Thylacoleo*. The size of a leopard, it had stabbing incisor teeth with blade-like slicing teeth behind them. Its skeleton shows links with the opossums and phalangers rather than the marsupial 'cats' but fine scratches on the teeth show it to have been a carnivore.

The African Wildcat, the subspecies from which the domestic cat is most likely to have developed.

THE CAT'S BODY

The flexibility of the cat's skeleton enables it to adopt the most contorted attitudes.

The cat family have all the typical features of mammals. These include a bone skeleton which gives the animal its basic shape and envelops and protects its internal organs. The limbs are placed beneath the body and the bones to which the front limbs are attached (the pectoral girdle) are fused, which gives an upright gait. Females have mammary glands which secrete milk to nourish the offspring in the first phase of their life. They have a four-chambered heart and are 'warm-blooded' so that, except when very young or in extreme conditions, they can maintain their body temperature at an even level (about 38.6°C, 101.5°F in most domestic cats, rather higher than in humans and Rex cats are said to be even a little higher) which makes it possible for them to remain active in cold weather.

Temperature control is helped by the most noticeable feature of mammals, their hair or fur, which provides a degree of insulation. Like other mammals, cats have sweat glands — perspiring is one way of lowering body temperature when overheated — but the cats' almost complete covering of fur leaves only those on the paw pads discharging directly to the surface and effective for heat loss. These are the only ones in cats which produce a watery sweat similar to that of humans. You can sometimes see a trail of damp paw prints made by a cat that is sweating from the heat, or from fright; as you have probably experienced, mammals also sweat when frightened. Evaporation of saliva spread on the fur by grooming is a more effective means of keeping cool, and when very hot, cats will pant as another way of losing heat.

Most mammals have larger brains (in proportion to their size) than non-mammals and cats are no exception. The brain of the domestic cat is in many ways very like that of humans, and cats have been widely used in laboratory experiments to find out more about the brain.

There is little sexual dimorphism (different forms) among the members of the cat family, apart from the obvious differences of the reproductive organs and a tendency for males to be of larger size. The only markedly noticeable characteristic is the development of the mane in the male lion, and even that is not very obvious in some geographical races. However, most people familiar with domestic cats will probably be able to recognize the somewhat heavier look and wider jowl which develops in the unneutered male domestic cat. When he is allowed to roam freely they will often be accompanied by battle scars gained in establishing his territory and defending it and his females from competing toms.

The cat's skeleton

As carnivores, the meat-eating group of mammals, cats have evolved a skeleton specialized to make them efficient hunters and they have a well-developed muscular system. The cats have about one-fifth more bones than are in the human body; the extra ones are mostly in the spine and tail, and the proportions of one bone to another show many differences from ours. Between species there are also differences, for some are long-legged and others have shorter limbs.

People have rigid collar bones between their shoulder blades and breastbone but in cats these are reduced, or even missing, leaving the forelegs connected to the chest only by muscles. This makes it possible for the shoulder blades, which are placed to the cat's sides, rather than on its back like ours, to match the movement of the legs, which can move up, down, forwards, backwards and to some degree sideways as well. The forelegs are usually carried slightly flexed but extra support can be given by locking the backward-hinged elbow to make the leg rigid. A longer stride is provided by walking and running on the equivalent of only our finger and toe bones, a posture known as digitigrade. The cat's equivalent of our wrist or ankle is the joint you can see angled well above the ground; what would be the sole of our foot is the part of the back leg that the cat puts down when it sits. The cat's hind legs are not so flexible as the fore and have limited sideways movement, but they are very powerfully muscled and provide the main propulsion for locomotion and for leaps.

The vertebrae are more loosely connected than in most animals, making the spine extremely flex-

The difference between the skeletons of the various members of the cat family reflect their conformation but, apart from some variation in the skull, especially in the Cheetah, they are too small to be noticed by most non-scientists. All cats have lithe bodies and powerful musculature.
From top to bottom *Domestic cat, Jaguar, Lioness.*

A drawing by George Stubbs (1724–1806) of a leopard with its skin removed. Stubbs went to great lengths to understand the anatomy of the animals he painted. The powerful structure of the animal's body becomes even more apparent when the obscuring pattern and texture of the fur is missing.

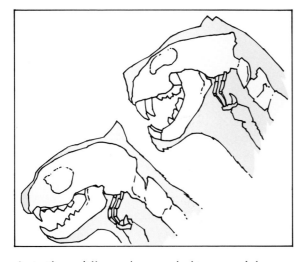

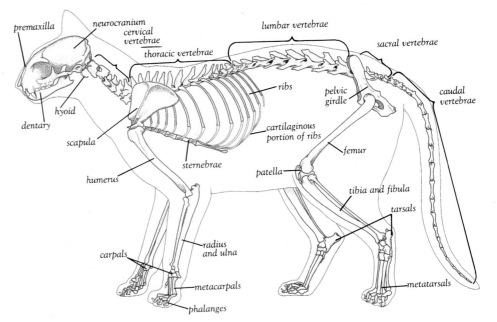

A significant difference between the big cats and the smaller cats which taxonomists use to place species within the main genera, or groups of species (Panthera and Felis) is a group of bones which link the larynx to the skull. In Panthera, the big cats, one section within these two chains of bones is cartilage which is elastic and allows sufficient mobility in the vocal apparatus to lengthen the air column. Combined with a pad of elastic tissue at the end of the vocal folds this enables the animal to roar. In Felis, the smaller Old World and New World species, the whole chain is bony and inflexible (ossified) so that these cats cannot make such full-throated roars and vocalization becomes more like a scream.
On the other hand, Felis can purr continuously, vocalizing on both incoming and outgoing breath. The actual mechanism that produces purring is not properly understood, but it is thought to be the vibration of additional membranes close to the vocal chords.

The domestic cat's skeleton is made up of about 144 bones, including, in most domestic cats, 21 in the tail alone. The pelvis is clearly a different shape from that of humans. The spine is particularly supple, the forelegs able to rotate much more than our legs and the leg bones differently arranged. Cats walk on their toes — we walk on the flat of the foot right up to the heel bone, the metatarsals flat on the ground. Hooved animals like the horse and deer walk on the ends of their toes.

ible. Those at the top of the neck are shaped to enable the head to turn and move very freely. The chest and ribcage are comparatively narrow, making it easier to negotiate tight spaces and to balance on branches or narrow walkways.

Internal organs

Although their skeletal structure and strong muscles give the cats the power to chase and overwhelm prey, they cannot sustain such energetic activity for very long. As predators they can never be certain of success in making a kill so must be able to eat as much as possible when they do get a meal. Their digestive system therefore has to be able to process considerable quantities taken at one time and this requires considerable space for the digestive organs at the expense of that available for the heart and lungs. Consequently, although they can put on great spurts of energy, cats are soon exhausted and short of oxygen.

The domestic cat and other small felines which catch small prey such as mice may eat many little meals much more frequently than the big cats who kill large prey but, although food usually passes through their bodies in about 24 hours, considerable space is still taken up by their digestive system.

Domestic cats breathe faster than we do, making 25 to 30 inhalations every minute when at rest, and more for young cats or for cats that are hot or exerting themselves — as high as 40 per minute for kittens. The pulse is also faster than ours: 110–140 beats per minute for adults and 150–200 for small kittens.

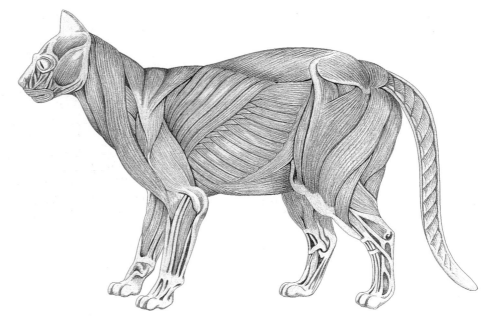

The cat has over 500 different skeletal muscles attached to the bones, plus smooth muscles which create the movement necessary for the functioning of the organs of the body.

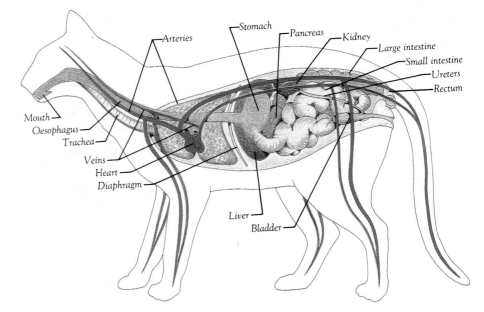

The cat's body systems are very like our own, although proportionally more space is occupied by the digestive system. The rate of breathing can be easily seen by the expansion and contraction of the upper body and the heartbeat heard by putting an ear against the fur.

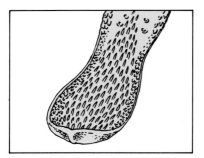

Above The coarse, backward-pointing papillae on the tongue can rasp off flesh as well as being an efficient brush and comb. Even the tongue of a domestic cat can feel quite rough. An over-affectionate big cat can scrape wool off a sweater or take the skin off an unprotected face when greeting an unwary human.

Most of the cat family have a dental pattern of one molar, two premolars (three in the upper jaw), one canine and three incisors on each side of the mouth. Exceptions are the Lynx, Serval (far right), Cheetah and Pallas's Cat which lack the extra premolar. Kittens have only 26 milk teeth, shed by domestic cats at about four months, the adult set being complete by six months old.

Below The premolars and molars, known as carnassials, are the most effective shearing teeth so cats bite with the head to one side to cut through meat.

Below right Many insects add variety to the feline diet.

Teeth and claws

Felines have 30 teeth when mature (with the exception of the Lynx and Pallas's Cat which both have only 28). The milk teeth in kittens and cubs number only 26. At the front of the jaw, both top and bottom, is a row of six small incisors which do a little nibbling where other teeth and the scraping tongue are ineffective. These are flanked by the long sharp canine teeth, which curve slightly inward and are used for holding and killing prey and for tearing its flesh. Then come three premolars on each side of the upper jaw (two in the Lynx and Pallas's Cat) and two below, although their pointed cusps make them look like more. They are followed by the single molars, the upper one rather small. All these rear teeth are cutting teeth, used to shear up food into digestible portions.

This arrangement of teeth reflects the cats' specialization as hunters. They are designed to grasp and cut rather than chew and grind, though they can still be very effective at crunching bone. The tongue is also very efficient at stripping flesh off bones. Its surface is covered with backward-facing horny spikes, called papillae, which also make a useful comb for grooming the coat. Newborn kittens, in whom this surface is not developed, have a rim of spikes around the edge of the tongue which helps them to hold on to their mother's nipple, the tongue encircling it like a tube.

The cats' hind paws have four claws, the forepaws five, and in the domestic cat, and most members of the family, the front claws are fully retractable, being drawn back into sheaths which protect their sharp points from wear. Cheetahs lose the ability to draw their claws right in from about 15 weeks old and also lack the claw sheaths of other cats, while in the Fishing Cat the sheaths are not large enough to completely enclose the claws.

The rear claws are worn down by walking but even so can inflict a nasty wound when they strike with the full force of which the back legs are capable. The fifth claw on the front paw is placed rather like our thumb and helps the cat to grip when climbing or holding prey. Both

The cat family are all meat eaters. They may occasionally eat vegetables, especially grass, which domestic cats appear to use as an emetic to get rid of swallowed fur, cooked rice, which is regularly fed to pets in the Far East, and whatever takes a particular animal's fancy, but their digestive systems and stomach acids are best equipped to deal with meat. Their teeth are designed for biting and shearing, not for chewing or grinding, and when pieces of flesh have been stripped from a carcass they will be swallowed in pieces to be broken down by the gastric juices.

paws have soft pads which enable the cat to move almost silently, though on a hard surface the claws of Siamese cats, which seem to project slightly more than in other domestic breeds, can sometimes be heard making contact as they walk.

In domestic cats polydactylism — having extra toes — is quite a common condition. Usually there is only one extra and it makes no difference to the cat's way of life. Genetically it is a dominant characteristic which means that as well as occurring when both parents are polydactyl, when only one parent is extra-toed its normal offspring can still pass the extra toe on to their kittens.

Cats are often seen 'sharpening' their front claws. This is not actually honing their points but is a way of removing the blunted outer surface of the claw to expose a new sharp point on the layer beneath. Cats often use their teeth to remove dead surface pieces from both front and back claws to keep them in good condition.

House pets, whose claws do not get sufficient wear, often need regular trimming. This is quite different from the removal of the claws which involves cutting away the growing cells and the whole or part of the terminal bone of the toe.

De-clawing of pet cats

It is difficult for those who really care about cats to imagine circumstances in which this operation is justified. It is not a simple cutting back of the claws but, to ensure that the claws do not regrow, requires the severance of the ligaments and a section of bone from which each claw grows — imagine cutting the bone out of the end of each of your own fingers. It is comparatively simple surgery, though if it does go wrong malformed claws could regrow.

Such surgery, although resorted to by some owners who think more of their furnishings than of the well-being of the cat, is outlawed by many cat organisations *which will not accept declawed cats in shows*. It inevitably reduces the cat's ability to climb, grip and walk on slippery surfaces, but more importantly it deprives it of a set of important defensive weapons. No cat which goes outdoors should ever be declawed. Many American and Australasian vets are prepared to perform it and there are those who claim there is no cruelty involved but imagine yourself without finger nails, unable to scratch or do the things you use them for, then think how much more useful a cat's claws are in its life. Removal of the front claws only, does leave the animal with some defense but is still to be deplored.

A cat needs to exercise its claws and should be trained to a scratching post from kittenhood. Patience is infinitely preferable to surgery.

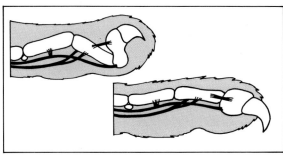

Above Most cats like to eat grass occasionally, not necessarily as an emetic. Perhaps it provides roughage in the diet, like bran for people.

Above *Claws are formed of keratin, a protein which also forms the outer layer of skin. They are rooted in the terminal bone of the toe and grow continuously from just below the outer fold of skin. For protection and to give a silent footfall they are normally retracted within the sheath by an upper ligament which joins the toe bone from which it grows to the next bone. To extend the claw, to provide extra grip on a surface or as a weapon, the muscles tighten the tendons below the bone, straightening the toe and pushing out the claw. The claws of cats which do not walk on hard surfaces and subject them to normal wear may have to be trimmed to prevent them growing too long and curling back into the pads of the feet. Cheetahs are not able to retract their claws, their toe structure being more like that of dogs.*

Below Most cats have four toe pads and four claws on their hind paws, five on the forepaws. This fifth helps the front paws to hold prey and to climb.

Left *Polydactylism, having an extra toe, is not uncommon in cats. It certainly has no ill effect upon the animal and may give it added stability and grip when running and climbing.*

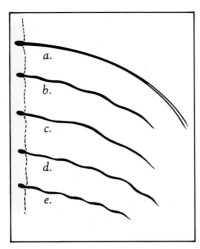

Above *Hair types in the domestic cat: a. Guard hairs, long and stiffened by a solid inner structure, form the coarser outer coat, protecting the fur beneath. They are erectile and stand up when a cat feels threatened. b. Awn hairs are a thinner form of guard hair with a thickened bristle-like tip; they help to provide both insulation and protection. e. Down or wool hairs are much more numerous; fine, soft and crinkly with a series of air spaces through their centre, they form the insulating undercoats. c.d. There is often a whole range of intermediate hairs, usually called awned down hairs, which are woolly but with thickened tips. Down hairs are usually much shorter than guard hairs but in some types of long-haired cats breeders have now achieved down hairs that are almost as long.*

Hairs of different colors create a coat pattern but changes of color along each hair also create different effects. a. A light-colored hair dark at the very tip produces the chinchilla coat. b. A longer tipping gives shaded fur. c. Pigment down the hair with white roots produces the smoke type. d. Dark hairs striped or 'ticked' with a band of light color along their length are known as agouti and usually have a pale root. They make up the guard hairs of the light parts in a tabby coat and the Abyssinian's coat.

Fur and whiskers

The cats have a loose skin, which reduces the risk of deep wounds in fights. Except in a few exceptional breeds of domestic cat, it is covered with a dense growth of fur everywhere except for the paw pads, nose and teats. The fur is generally made up of three main kinds of hair: down hairs (also called wool hairs), which form a soft underfur; awn hairs, which are thicker; and guard hairs, which form the coarse top coat. Most domestic cats have about twelve times as many wool and awn hairs as guard hairs on the back and twice that ratio on the belly, although there are breeds in which the proportion is radically changed (see Rex and Sphynx breeds in *Domestic Varieties*).

Guard hairs are thick, long, straight and taper evenly to a point. Down hairs are finer, crinkly and an even width throughout their length. Awn hairs grow thicker toward the tips before tapering abruptly and are bent towards the end. There are also intermediate hairs: awned down hairs which are thin and crinkly at the base, thickening to a straighter, bristly tip.

The guard hairs grow from a single socket, or follicle, and are surrounded by a cluster of down and awn hairs, groups of which grow from single follicles set less deeply in the skin. Muscles within the base of the guard hairs make them 'stand on end' (erectile) in response to temperature or emotional changes. Raising the fur traps a layer of warm air close to the skin, increasing the degree of insulation.

Hair growth is not continuous. Each follicle has a resting phase when the base of each fully developed hair becomes detached. When growth recommences the new hairs push the old ones out. House cats shed fur right through the year but, in temperate climates, hair growth will respond to seasonal change. A thick coat develops for the winter and after a generally dormant period the new growth commences in the spring, molting the old coat to provide a thinner summer cover. Sometimes shedding may be caused by illness. Adjuncts of the hair follicles

Rex cats have a fur in which growth is genetically retarded. The Cornish has no guard hairs and although the Devon has guard hairs they are almost indistinguishable from down hairs. Many Devon Rex have no whiskers or only rudimentary ones.

are the sebaceous glands which produce an oily secretion that lubricates and waterproofs the fur and is spread by the cat's tongue when it washes itself. This sebaceous fluid, or sebum, contains cholesterol which is converted by sunlight into Vitamin D, then licked off and ingested by the cat. The eccrine glands are another form of sweat gland that produce a fluid that may carry pheromones involved in sex attraction.

Sebaceous glands are most productive on the back, or dorsal region, on the lips and beneath the chin. The sebum they produce sometimes causes a greasy stain around the root of the tail, commonly known as 'stud tail' because it most frequently occurs in uncastrated tom cats.

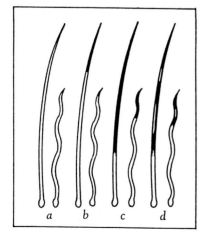

In the big cats the fur extends right down the nose, leaving only the tip as bare leather, but in the smaller cats the upper surface of the nose leather is also exposed.

Right *Temperature affects the color of the fur. Dark-furred cats that spend hours by a fire or sunbathe excessively may lighten on the areas most exposed to heat. Point-patterned cats, such as Siamese, whose coats have darkened will often get a pale coat back in a hot summer. The positioning of their points is itself affected by body temperature.*

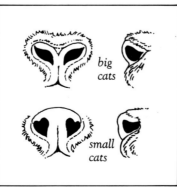

There are no sweat glands on a cat's nose and its ridged pattern is different for every individual, as with our fingerprints.

A cat's coat color is genetically determined but changes of temperature affect the production of pigmentation and produce a change to a winter coat in the Northern Lynx. To a lesser degree this may also be seen in Siamese and other pointed-patterned cats whose points (darker coloring of tails, ears, feet) become more clearly defined in hot, sunny weather, due to the lightened body fur, even though age may have brought a general darkening. Persistent sitting by a fire may cause a lightening of dark coats on the side habitually turned towards the heat and black cats often develop a brownish tinge in warm weather. This 'rustiness' is partly a result of the effect of moisture from washing helping to produce a bleaching effect. It can be very inconvenient if the cat happens to be entered for a show!

Most cats have comparatively short fur. Wild species in which distribution includes a wide climatic range, such as the Cougar, have noticeably longer and softer fur in colder climes and shorter and more bristly hair in tropical regions. Siberian Tigers have a longer coat than those of the Indian subcontinent, especially in winter when it may be over 2 ins (5 cm) on the back and 2½ ins (6 cm) on the belly.

The Snow Leopard, an inhabitant of high mountain regions, has dense and rather woolly hair, long compared with other species: from 1¼ in (3 cm) on the back to 2¾ in (6.5 cm) on the belly. The Lynx also has longish fur, but the longest coat, comparatively speaking, belongs to Pallas's Cat of the rocky steppes of Asia. It has been suggested that Pallas's Cat may have had some part to play in the development of the long-haired domestic breeds which possibly originated within its range, but taxonomists have given no credence to this idea.

The Sand Dune Cat has dense mats of fur on the feet; at ¾ in (2 cm) long they completely hide the paw pads. This fur mat helps the cat to keep a better grip on shifting sand and loose stones

Left *Siamese kittens show no patterning when they are born. Only their nose leather is any indication of what color points they will develop as they get older. Some self-color kittens have noticeable tabby markings which fade as the kittens grow.*

Long-haired domestic cats can produce a distinctive mane — but not exclusive to the male — and 'breeches', like those of the Lynx. Lynx also develop side whiskers in winter which can begin to look like manes in some individuals.

The adult male lion's mane is the only obvious form of sexual differentiation in the cat family.

and probably gives extra insulation against the high temperatures such surfaces can build up. The Lynx's paws are also heavily furred to enable it to move across the crusty winter snow. This gives it an advantage over the deer it hunts which step through the surface layer, hampering their movements and sometimes injuring themselves. Even Lynx have problems negotiating heavy falls of loose snow and they tend to avoid such areas.

Distribution of fur on the body usually follows a pattern of short on the back and longer on the belly. As well as dense fur on the feet, Lynx grow 'breeches' of fur to increase protection from winter cold. Long-haired domestic cats also tend to have furry breeches and long fur between the

Below left *Dense fur on the paws of the Lynx both insulates against the cold and spreads weight over a larger surface. On crisp snow this makes its movement easier than that of the small deer on which it preys which sink into the snow. This advantage is lost when snow is soft and deep.*
Below *Jaguars are one of the species in which melanistic (dark-coated) individuals appear. Black leopards are also fairly common. Although the ground color becomes nearly black, the spotted pattern can still be seen in certain lights.*

Right *A cat usually has about 12 whiskers growing from the pads on each upper lip. They are important sensory organs which register both direct touch and changes to air pressure caused by the proximity of objects. Twice as thick as guard hairs, they also extend three times deeper into the epidermis and are served by a dense network of nerves which are stimulated by the slightest pressure. The eyebrows are also sensitive and there are a few similar hairs at the rear of the cheeks, although these are less noticeable. These whisker-type hairs are known as vibrissae.*

This Siamese kitten pictured at age 36 hours, 4 weeks and 15 weeks shows how its patterning develops as it grows older.

toes. Only male lions, among the wild species, develop a heavy mane. It can spread from the top of the head along the upper part of the spine and down to the lower chest. Although tigers do not have such a magnificent mane males often have a ruff of longer hair growing from in front of the ears to beneath the chin; Bobcats and Lynx also have this beard.

Long-haired domestic cats can sometimes develop ruffs which are almost as magnificent as the lion's mane, though usually emerging more evenly from the rest of the coat and more likely to be lighter in color. That of the lion is darker, even nearly black. Even on short-haired cats the lie of the fur on the chest can sometimes suggest a stylized presentation of the lion's mane.

Lynx and Caracals have noticeable tufts of hair at the tips of their ears and most cats develop a feathering of hair inside the ears.

All cats have facial whiskers. These are akin to guard hairs but are twice as thick and they extend much deeper into the skin and have a protective covering around the follicle to give them further strength. They are well supplied with nerves which carry information about air movements as well as any physical contact with objects, enabling the brain to interpret spacial information. The arrangement of each cat's whiskers, like its nose skin pattern, is particular to that individual. Hairs similar to the whiskers form the eyelashes and groups, known as carpel hairs, on the back of the forelegs which are also very touch sensitive.

Camouflage

The striped and spotted fur of the cat family gives them effective camouflage when moving through vegetation or in dappled shade, merging with the pattern of shadows and breaking up their body shape. Even a lion's unmarked coat can be extremely difficult to spot against the dry sandy-brown savanna, in long grass or in the shade of a thorn thicket, and the cubs are spotted to make it even harder for predators to find them when their mother has to leave them to go hunting. Spotted patterns are usually associated with forest animals and striped coats with those that need to conceal themselves in grassland. Because the cat family has spread through different habitats or been forced to retreat before the encroachment of human beings their coats do not always follow that rough division: tigers, for instance, may be found in forest land. Nevertheless, they are still well served by their camouflage.

It has been suggested that the juvenile coat of the Cheetah, with long pale fur along its back and a dark belly, is an exception to the rules of camouflage since it makes it more conspicuous against green grass in the nest. However, as the cheetahs grow, begin to play in the grass and later to follow their mother when she goes out hunting, it actually works effectively among the grasses and even in the nest it may be a protection. The cub's coat could warn off predators, for it mimics that of the Honey Badger *Mellivora capensis*, a very aggressive little animal that puts up such a battle it is hardly worth tackling.

The cheetah cub's gray fur matures to reveal the same spotted pattern as its mother's, which has been beneath the long hair all the time. In lions and other cats which have plain coats, cubs and kittens frequently start with spotted or tabby coats and then lose the patterning as they reach adult, though many young lions still tend to have spotted undersides.

Below *Most young members of the cat family show spots or stripes on their coats, an atavistic echo of a shared patterned origin. Overlaying their patterned coat, these cheetah cubs have long gray fur which is lost as they grow older.*

*Patterns on the coat break up the surface of the animal, making its shape more difficult to identify and allowing it to mingle with shadow patterns through which it passes, like the tiger (**top**). The unpatterned coat of the lion (**above left**) is difficult to spot against the terrain in which it mainly lives, and in the open plains of East Africa the dark mane can easily be mistaken for a clump of savanna grass. Even without cover a spotted coat (**above right**) can blur the distinction between an animal and its surroundings.*

MOVEMENT

Walking and running

The fastest of all the cats, and the fastest land mammal, is the Cheetah. Cheetahs have recorded a speed of more than 60 mph (96 kph), and an excess of 65 mph (100 kph) has been claimed. Even if such speeds are genuine, however, they are only over comparatively short distances of a few hundred yards and the antelopes they pursue can often keep going well after the Cheetah has been winded. Nevertheless even

the domestic cat can put on quite a spurt for very short distances, which gives it the necessary speed to dash for cover when threatened. Its hunting pattern does not require long chases. All the cat family will approach prey as closely as they can in cover before starting the chase or wait in ambush to make a final bound or drop.

As important to the cats as their burst of speed is the ability to stop and freeze, even in mid-step, for movement is always more noticeable than a still object. Cats can move smoothly from one gait to another, but although they can jump and twist their bodies with great agility they are not good at rapidly changing direction. If you watch a domestic cat closely you will see that it will often have to pull up almost to a halt, or at least dramatically brake its speed, if it suddenly decides

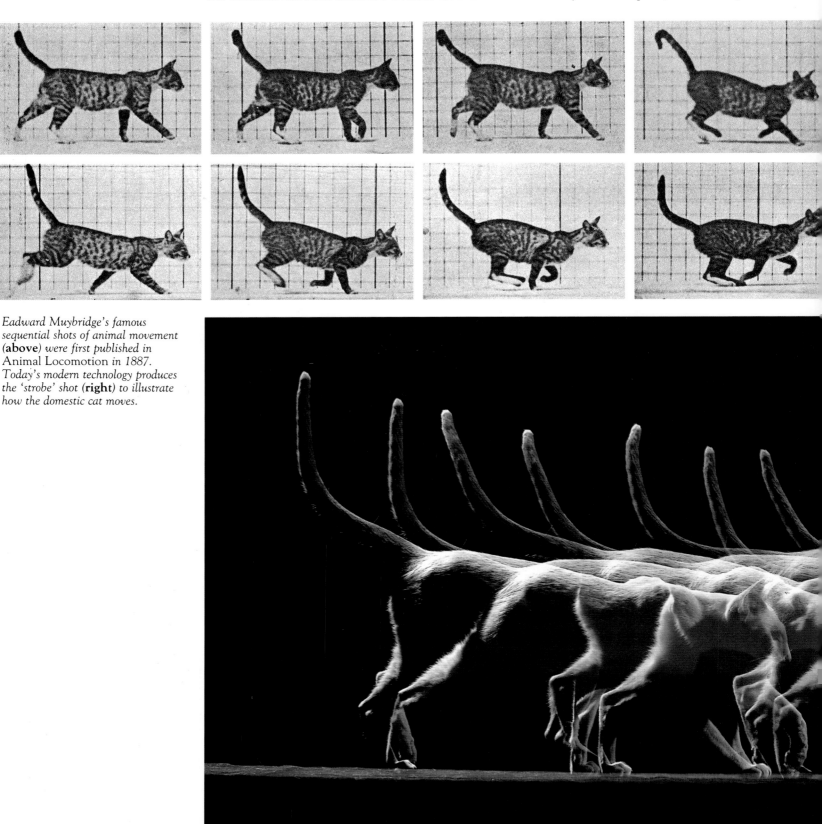

Eadward Muybridge's famous sequential shots of animal movement (**above**) *were first published in* Animal Locomotion *in 1887. Today's modern technology produces the 'strobe' shot* (**right**) *to illustrate how the domestic cat moves.*

to alter course. This gives prey which can turn in shorter distances a chance to zigzag or double back and escape.

Cats will not usually expend any more energy than they have to. Effort goes into necessary activity; with kittens and cubs that includes play, and in a mature cat we perhaps rightly consider play a kittenish characteristic. Lions may spend a great deal of their day simply resting and their normal gait is quite slow, less perhaps than 2 mph (4 kph), although they can sustain a faster trot for quite some time, or progress for a while in a series of bounds through long grass.

Photographs taken by Eadward Muybridge, an Englishman working in California, were the first to reveal exactly how a feline moves. His techniques, originally developed in connection with

a bet made by the Governor of California about the way in which horses gallop, played their part in the development of cinematography.

At the walk, the domestic cat moves first the legs on one side and then those on the other. The movement of the back leg is followed by the foreleg, with each foot being placed neatly ahead of the one on the other side so that their paw prints form almost a straight line. When speed is increased to a trot, the hind legs — and cats are usually right-footed so that is the side that leads — move quickly to catch up with the diagonally opposite forelegs and then move together, right foreleg with left hind leg and vice versa. To increase speed further, the cat pushes off with both back legs at the same time, giving a much stronger forward movement, but still

A tiger takes this stream in one easy leap.

Below left, right and opposite below *Leaping the space between two benches, this cat takes off from the very edge, limiting the distance and obtaining maximum push off, then stretching out its body as it touches down with its forelegs and draws its back legs in to finish the landing.*

places the front paws down separately, though in rapid succession so that it maintains a steady momentum rather than just a series of jumps. However, a cat may proceed in jumps if there is any obstruction or it needs to see over grass and herbage.

Jumping

Not all the cat family are designed as efficient jumpers. The Lynx and Cougar have proportionally longer legs, especially the hind ones, which give them particularly powerful springs; a cougar leap of nearly 40 ft (12 m) has been recorded, six times the largest cougar's body length. The lion, whose leg to body ratio is much less, cannot match this size for size but it has achieved a similar distance, about four and a half times what a large lion's body measures. Siberian Tigers are said regularly to spring 16–23 ft (5–7 m) when chasing prey and can leap as much as 33 ft (10 m) when travelling downhill, while one Snow Leopard was seen to jump a ditch more than 50 ft (15 m) wide while running uphill. A galloping Leopard is reported to have cleared a 22 ft (6.6 m) ravine, though for this species 10 ft (3 m) would be more usual from a standing position. Many of the smaller cats also show excellent jumping skills.

The average domestic cat can jump five times its own height with ease, and some can show amazing skill at landing on awkward narrow spaces, such as a window sill. If they are

negotiating familiar territory with an action performed many times before, they will go straight into the jump from their walk or run. With an easily managed height, they usually give themselves plenty of clearance and then, if there is something they could not see from below on a ledge or tabletop, they can adjust their balance and landing to avoid the obstruction. It is rare for a cat to knock something over, but leaving something near the edge of a surface that you know is regularly used by a cat is inviting breakage and could endanger the cat if it and a shattered object land on the floor together.

If a wall looks rather more than an easy leap a cat will jump almost to the top and then appear to run vertically up the final stretch, bouncing as it were up the last couple of feet, its front claws

giving it just sufficient purchase to enable it to do so.

Jumping down, even from quite a low position, a cat will take advantage of a vertical surface to reduce the downward fall by stretching its body as far as possible before jumping or even extending the body down the wall and pushing off from it in a reversal of the upward process. This lessens the impact on the forelegs when it lands. If possible it will take a great drop by leaping forwards so that the back legs have more chance of landing at the same time as the front, helping to break the fall. After a heavy landing a cat will often lick the paw pads that took the brunt of the shock.

A cat reaches down as far as possible before leaping from the tailboard of a truck.

Overleaf *Strobe photographs show the precise movements of cats leaping upwards and jumping down.*

Climbing

All cats can climb, but not all regularly do. Lions in Lake Manyara National Park, in Tanzania and at Ishasha in the Ruwenzori National Park, Uganda, have become famous as tree climbers, though they have been observed in trees in other places too. At Manyara they seem to be trying to avoid the dense undergrowth while still finding cool shade and an escape from the torment of biting flies; at Ruwenzori they seem to be using the trees as vantage posts to see over the tall grasses. Females and young tigers have been known to take to a tree to escape a pack of dogs — the Caracal does too — but, although tigers have climbed up a tree to pull down a man who had thought himself quite safe, climbing is rare behavior for them. Both tigers and cheetahs may, however, jump up onto a fallen or leaning tree trunk.

Leopards, on the other hand, are great tree climbers, often carrying a kill up into the branches to eat or to cache food away from scavengers and thieves. Cougars climb well too. Jaguars are not quite as expert but will take to the trees to hunt some of the animals that share their forests and the Margay regularly hunts among the branches.

Above *Cats find it difficult to run down a tree head first so have to come down backwards, turning as soon as possible to jump to the ground. The Margay, which has especially maneuverable hind limbs that can rotate 180° inward, does seem to be able to climb down head first, sometimes spiralling around a tree, though it also jumps down from considerable heights. Its foot has a soft sole with mobile metatarsal bones to catch hold of a branch in mid leap or fall and pull itself on with a single paw.*
Left *Leopards are rapid and efficient climbers.*

Although most of the other small forest cats are likely to be at home in the trees, they find climbing much easier than trying to come down to earth again.

Shinning up a tree trunk, a small cat, such as the domestic cat, will probably jump the first stage, or may stretch up to get its first grip by anchoring its front claws in the bark. It can then walk up with its back legs, stretch out in turn with each of the front legs to secure a firm hold again and so climb as far as it needs to go. Leaping from branch to branch, it may be able to descend far enough to jump down to the ground, but coming down the trunk again will usually be tackled backwards because the incurving claws mean that the cat can only hang from them when they are uppermost. The descent is supported by the claws of one front paw at a time plus any purchase the back legs can find on protrusions from the rough surface of the tree. Since tree trunks are usually slightly tapered, the descent is not entirely vertical and for a short distance a cat may run down head first, but it will then leap outwards as soon as possible.

Most of the time cats make a good four-point landing and unless seriously handicapped have an almost infallible righting mechanism.

Above *A lion takes refuge in a tree.*

Tigers (**below left**) *are water enthusiasts and are strong swimmers; they regularly cool off in streams and pools. Few domestic cats like getting their feet wet but all cat species can swim if they have to. However, the Turkish Van* (**below**) *is a breed that also seems to really enjoy the water.*

Swimming

Cats can swim with a 'dog-paddle' movement but most will not take to water except by accident or when it becomes unavoidable, as at times of flood. Fishing Cats, however, will happily wade in shallows and swim in deeper water, and Lynx cross quite broad rivers. Lions regularly cross some rivers and have been seen on an island in Lake Victoria 650 ft (200 m) from shore. Tigers really like the water and can swim strongly for three of four miles, and Jaguars are also excellent swimmers who enjoy the water.

Most domestic cats shun water, although there is one report of a cat regularly diving into the sea for fish, and the breed originating near Lake Van in Turkey swim in their native streams and are said to enjoy a swim when kept as pets.

THE CAT'S SENSES

Five senses are not enough for cats and they seem to have abilities that lie unused or atrophied in most of us. Even without any apparent extrasensory apparatus, they are extremely well equipped and outstrip us in many areas. That is not to say that there is nothing that we do better. We see more sharply in the best part of our range and probably better distinguish color, our hearing extends to deeper notes and we have a quicker response to temperature change. But in all the things that matter for a cat's life in the wild its specialized sensitivities outshine our own.

Sight

Sight is one area where everyone knows that cats see better — after all, any child can tell you that cats see in the dark. Well, of course, they don't. Vision is impossible without light; even infra-red photography, which enables film or television cameras to record images in what appears to be the dark, are using light, though at the extreme end of the spectrum beyond what our eyes, or those of cats, can register.

Cats probably do not see exactly the same spectrum as we do but they make much more efficient use of the amount of light that reaches them. In only a glimmer of light, too little for us to distinguish anything, a cat will still be able to see, but in pitch darkness it is as blind as we are.

Domestic cats can utilize up to 50 percent more available light than people and see in only one-sixth of the illumination level we need. Most nocturnal animals share this ability to register the maximum in poor light. It is achieved by a number of features of which the most noticeable is the tapetum lucidum, a layer of cells backing the retina of the eye. These cells form a reflective surface from which any light not absorbed on its passage through the eye is bounced back

to give a second stimulus to the light-sensitive cells contained within the retina. This is not totally efficient, for even then not all the light is used and can be seen as the eye-shine that is reflected when a light is shone into the animal's eyes.

Cats' eyes differ from ours in several other ways which make them better equipped as night hunters. In proportion to body size they are very much larger; and a lion's eyes are actually bigger — 1½ in (3.75 cm) to our nine-tenths of an inch (2.5 cm). The eyeball is more spherical than ours with the cornea (the transparent surface which covers the front of the eye) and the lens set nearer to its centre. This gives them a wider curve and a short focal length, which means that they can see through a wider angle — about 280°, though on each side about 80° of this is only peripheral vision registered by one eye only. (We have about 180° angle of vision but only some 70° is binocular.)

The iris of the cat's eye opens and closes to a greater extent than ours. Its muscles can expose a pupil diameter of half an inch (1.25 cm) in the domestic cat (larger in the bigger animals) to allow the maximum amount of light to enter, just as one 'opens up' a camera to photograph when there is less light available, and narrow down to almost nothing when the light is very bright. In the domestic cat the pupil may narrow to an almost closed slit with only tiny openings at the top and bottom admitting light; in the lion and most other *Panthera* species the pupil contracts to a tighter circle as do our pupils. The Cheetah's narrowed pupils are also round as are the Cougar's, differentiating it from the other *Felis*, while the Clouded Leopard is halfway between with the closed pupil a vertical oblong.

This wide variation in aperture enables the cats to let in as much light as possible when it is scarce and to reduce the amount to the minimum in very bright conditions and avoid dazzle; as with a camera, the smaller the hole the greater the clarity of vision.

The lens of the cat's eye is large and, for its size, not well muscled; it may not be able to alter its shape at all, only that of the pupil. This gives

Below *Cats' eyes 'shine' because light is reflected by the surface at the back of the eye known as the tapetum lucidum.*

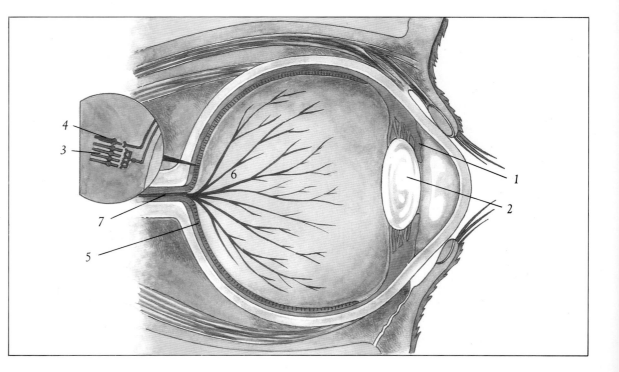

Light passing into a cat's eye passes through the aperture of the iris (1) and is focussed by the lens (2) before hitting the light-sensitive rods (3) and cones (4) of the retina (5). Light which passes beyond them is reflected back by the tapetum lucidum (6) to reactivate the rods and cones and increase the signal carried to the optic nerve (7), but some may still pass out of the eye to create 'eye-shine'.

it generally less clarity of vision than we have, with poor focus on close objects. The optimum range for the domestic cat's eye to focus is about 7–20 ft (2–6 m).

The retina, where light signals are collected for transmission to the optic nerve, carries two kinds of receptors: rods, which respond to brightness, and cones, which respond to color. The ratio is about 25:1, compared with 4:1 in our eyes, which means that cats have much less color awareness. At one time it was believed that cats could not see color at all but it is now thought that they can differentiate between blue and green, and probably are more sensitive than we are at the ultra-violet end of the spectrum. However, it is uncertain to what extent they possess red-sensitive cones, red probably appearing gray.

Crepuscular and nocturnal animals have less use for color perception than those who live mainly in full light. Cones are less sensitive to poor light; our own color vision becomes reduced to a grayness when light fades. A hunting cat has more need of strong brightness signals. Not only do the high proportion of rod sensors reflect this, they are also connected in groups so that in dim light each fiber in the optic nerve gets a multiple charge to make the most of available light. The drawback is that these multiple signals are drawn from a wider area of the retina than the single cones and consequently from a wider field of view. The image therefore lacks sharpness, which, coupled with the softer focus of its lens, makes it much more difficult for a cat to distinguish uncontrasted stationary objects. The cat has a greater concentration of cones in the centre of the field of view, providing more resolution in that area but still not giving an image as clear as with human vision. A change in the image is more noticeable and a moving shape more easily seen than a still one, which is probably why a cat rarely pounces on stationary prey but waits until the moment when it moves, as you may observe when it is after a fly.

At very close quarters, when eating for instance, a cat's vision is very poor indeed; you will find your own is too if you just bring your palm up to your nose, although a few inches

The pupils of a domestic cat's eyes narrow to slits when viewing a well-lit scene, increasing the definition.

A cat's eyes open wide to make the most efficient use of reduced light levels.

While the muscles in the domestic cat overlap and pull the iris to a slit, those of the big cats, like this tiger cub, are like those in human eyes and contract the iris down to a small circle.

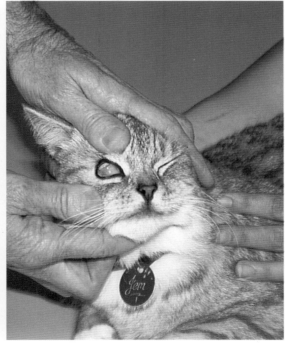

Left *A domestic cat's eyes with the nictitating membrane (haw) raised. This protects the eye from dust and excessive glare and helps spread tears across the cornea. It is often, but not always, raised as a reaction to illness and, strangely, may also appear after a cat has eaten a grasshopper.*

Far left *The keen eyesight of the cat family was demonstrated by tests with a tame lynx. It could see a mouse at a distance of 250 ft (75 m, more than three times the length of a tennis court), a hare at 1000 ft (300 m, three times the length of a football pitch) and a roe deer, only 30 in (75 cm) high, at 1500 ft (500 m, five football pitches away).*

away you probably see better than a cat. Often a cat has difficulty in precisely locating a morsel of food put down for it outside its usual feeding bowl, but then other senses come into play and do the locating for it.

Prey animals have their eyes on the side of the head so that they get as close to an all-round view as possible. Cats, as do all predators, have them set well forward which gives much more overlap between the two eyes and consequently a greater area of three-dimensional vision. To see behind it must turn its head, made easier by the very flexible neck.

The optic nerves connect each eye with the opposite side of the brain. In albino and Siamese domestic cats (Siamese have a partially albino genetic make-up) some of these connections are made to the wrong side; consequently their vision is not as good as with some other cats, although with most Siamese you are unlikely to be aware of it. It has been suggested that this may be a reason for the squint (crossed-eyes) which was once a feature of the breed.

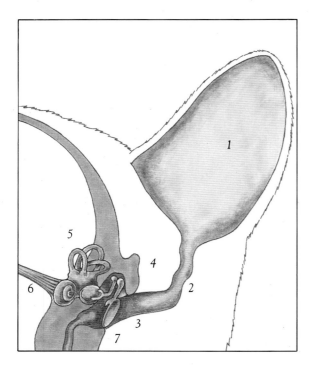

Above. *In the ear the pinna (1) is composed mainly of cartilage covered in skin. Sounds collected by the hairless inner surface are directed down the external ear canal (2) to the ear drum (3), which separates it from the middle ear containing the muscles and structures called ossicles (4) that tense the ear drum. The inner ear contains the structures responsible for hearing (5), and balance and orientation (6), and has nerve connections to the brain and other parts of the body. The Eustachian tube (7) connects the middle ear to the back of the nose and mouth, and drains fluids and equalizes the air pressure inside the drum to that of the air outside it.*

Hearing

Hearing is almost as important to predators as sight, especially at night and when hunting small creatures. In the cat family it is particularly acute. The Cheetah perhaps relies much more on sight in locating prey, for the chase is more important in its hunting, but the smaller cats especially can locate rodents and similar prey by their high-pitched squeaks and rustling as they move over leaves or touch plant stems.

The cats cannot hear quite such low notes as we do; dogs can but they can also hear wavelengths much higher than our capacity. The visible, external part of the ear (the pinna) collects and channels the sound waves in the air down the auditory canal to the receptive parts of the ear which are mainly set within the skull. Sounds strike the ear drum, making it vibrate. A series of small bones amplify these pulses and transfer them to a maze of tubes and spirals where they

A cat will locate a potential prey by the tiny noises it makes as it moves, or a thrown ball of paper by the slight crackling as the crumples adjust after landing.

A kitten rushes off, responding to a familiar sound. Cats readily recognise sounds related to their interests; a friend's footsteps, the engine of the family car. They will identify the sound of the door of the cupboard where their food is kept and appear almost immediately; open the cupboard next to it and the sound will be ignored.

The pitch or frequency of sound is measured in hertz (cycles per second). Most adult humans have a range slightly beyond that of the seven octaves of the standard piano, already less than a baby can hear. Dogs hear higher notes, cats higher still, well into the range of bats, whose calls are beyond the hearing of most people. A domestic cat's hearing does not begin to fade until about 40,000 hertz and some seem to be able to register as high as 60,000.

are separated into their different components and translated into signals to the brain.

The pinna can move through 180° to pick up and concentrate on any sound source — it is easy to see the direction of a cat's aural focus by the position of its ears. The pointing of the ears towards a sound does not necessarily improve the cat's sound location but it does help it to pick up faint sounds. Direction finding and exact placement of a sound is based, like binocular vision, on receiving and comparing information from two sources. The domestic cat can differentiate the origin of a sound to within about 5° of arc — at a distance of a yard that means about three inches (8 cm at 1 m). Try this out when playing with a cat. Most enjoy chasing a small ball of crumpled paper, probably partly because the paper makes soft crackling noises as the crumples move, continuing for a moment after each impact. Throw it, and a cat will pinpoint its position exactly, even though it may not have

been able to see it land — much more fun than a fluffy ball that is much harder to locate by sound.

Cats will hear sounds at distances which make them insignificant to us and have very accurate recognition of sound patterns. The individual sound of the family motor car will be recognized long before you can hear it and familiar footsteps will be recognized long before they reach your door. That is why a cat is so often waiting for you inside the door when you reach home. Cats have an excellent internal clock and, if you come and go at regular hours, the cat may have been expecting you — indeed, a cat allowed outdoors may even come to meet you as you walk down the street — but in a very irregular household you may often see a cat prick up its ears from apparent sleep and bound down four flights of stairs long before you hear the sound of a key put in the lock.

Cats identify all kinds of sounds. Those made by potential prey or which mean danger in the natural world must be the most important that they learn.

The sudden mechanical sounds coming from inanimate objects such as a vacuum cleaner or a hair-dryer seem to disturb them. They may keep their distance or even try to attack, though they will center their attention on the moving, sucking end of the vacuum rather than on the motor itself. However, they seem oblivious to general motor noises such as refrigerators and air conditioners. In fact, apart from loud bangs, most noises that do not have any particular significance to them seem to be ignored, but no domestic cat is likely to miss the sound of the opening of the door of the particular cupboard in which its food is kept. Cats certainly learn to recognize the sound patterns of their names, and probably those of some of the household, though recognizing a name does not necessarily mean they come when called! One of the writer's cats seemed to identify the name of a well-known hamburger chain and would become excited even before anyone left for the shop. This ruled

Are lions musical?

Whether cats listen for pleasure as well as information is uncertain. They will certainly recognize particular notes and will probably not respond to a familiar call if it is given at a different pitch. Some seem to like certain music: John Wesley noted in his journal that a lion in Edinburgh was fond of music and that one lion and one tiger out of a group in the Tower of London menagerie appeared to respond to the playing of a flute. A Mozart flute concerto is likely to be more to their taste than the deep bass of *Boris Godounov*; notes at the bottom of their range seem to cause some discomfort.

As a cat falls it first turns its head to an upright position and then its body follows so that it is in position for a four-point landing. However, if a cat is deeply asleep on a window ledge and rolls off without waking, it may be too late to bring the righting mechanism into operation and the cat may be injured. It is advisable, therefore, to protect window ledges or discourage cats from sleeping on them.

out any possibility of smelling the hamburgers or even recognizing any identifiable sound from their particular plastic boxes and paper bags. There can certainly be cases of *Pas devant les chats!*, but there is no evidence to suggest any understanding of a pattern of words linked for sense rather than a response to particular sound codes and emotional tones.

Balance

Most cats have an almost unerring sense of balance. This is not solely due to physique and fine motor control but involves a particularly delicate organ within the inner ear which consists of several tunnels part-filled with fluid and chambers lined with tiny hairs. In the larger chambers, tiny particles of chalk rest on whichever hairs are presently below them; the resulting message to the brain signals gravitational up-down. In the canals, flaps of tissue into which the hairs project respond to the sloshing around of the fluid as the head moves about. The messages transmitted by the hairs enable the brain to read direction and acceleration of any movement.

Cats are not alone in having this organ, the 'vestibular apparatus'; we have something very similar. Whether the cat's apparently better balancing skills are due to some small anatomical difference, to better connections and responses or whether it is simply that most of us fail to use them properly is a matter of conjecture. You have only to look at any high-wire act to see that people can achieve considerable skill in this direction too.

Cats have a special advantage in their remarkable ability to land on their feet, which many people thought was directly related to their fine sense of balance. It is not infallible and it does not mean that cats cannot injure themselves in a fall. They cushion their landing by arching the back and extending the legs, so that the shock will be absorbed as they bend them, but the speed with which they fall will depend upon their size and weight. If the distance is too short, from a small child's arms for instance, they may have no time to turn the body, although they can usually right themselves during 1–1½ ft (30–45 cm) of fall. If they are falling from a great height they may land properly but the impetus could still crash their head against the ground and crack their palate, if it does no worse injury, or damage the limbs because they are not able to absorb enough of the shock of landing. A New York study of 132 such falls in 1984 showed, however, that heights of seven or more storeys usually resulted in less serious injury. The cat had time to stretch out its body to offer more resistance to the air and to prepare a more spread out landing. In shorter falls the cat is possibly reacting to the acceleration of fall with tension. The greater height allows it to reach terminal velocity and then relax before impact.

A British researcher, Donald McDonald, carried out experiments (using low heights and a rubber mattress as a landing pad) with a 15-year-old deaf cat which was still able to right itself.

The animal had been born deaf so did not achieve balance through the normal use of the ears. Was it was possible that the critical part still functioned? When the cat was blindfolded it proved totally unable to right itself in falling and significantly was very slow to do so after landing. Sight was obviously the important factor for this cat. Another experiment with a cat completely lacking the inner ear showed clear righting ability, but no attempt to right itself when blindfolded. The situation is confused by the fact that kittens appear to have an inherent righting reflex even before their eyes are open, when they still cannot walk properly. It is thought that the combination of information from the eyes and from the vestibular apparatus in the ear produces an orienting signal from the brain to the neck muscles which turns the cat's head to the upright and horizontal. The rest of the body then twists to line itself up accordingly.

One quality which can be related directly to the efficiency of the vestibular organ is that a cat rarely suffers motion sickness in vehicles or at sea. It may vomit up its dinner if it bolts it down too quickly but, except for some young cats who quickly grow out of it, trips away are thankfully free of this handicap, one from which dogs unfortunately frequently suffer.

Smell

Outside the stimulus to appetite of cooking aromas and the warning smells of decay and putrefaction, people are mainly aware of smell as a way of recognizing strongly scented substances and a matter of likes and dislikes rather than a source of information as important as our eyes. No doubt there are many unconscious ways in which we react to the pheromones (scent signals) with which we are surrounded but, while losing our senses of smell and taste (which are so closely linked as to be almost indivisible) would take away some pleasure, it would not seem too serious a loss in practical terms, apart from being unable to identify food that had gone off or smell smoke and dangerous gases. To a cat, however, smell is perhaps the most important sense for recognition of things and conveys all kinds of overt information — about sex for instance — which we are rarely aware of using in our own lives. Instead of reading our own and other people's sexual aromas we tend to cover them up with manufactured perfumes which their advertisers have told us are seductive! A female cat in oestrus signals her condition by producing special pheromones that are recognized by toms over a very wide area.

You only have to watch a domestic cat about its ordinary daily business to see how much use it makes of scent. It recognizes friends, human and animal, by their smell; not only by smelling them but smelling places where they have been or have deliberately left a scent mark. It will sniff your clothes, your briefcase, your shopping to see where you have been and whom you might have met; it will check out all kinds of foods to make sure that they smell right before it will attempt to taste them; it will smell prey, and

danger, like the dog next door; it will scent a potential mate and it will revel in some smells simply because it enjoys them.

Smells are registered in the cavities which lie behind the nose. Here a thick, spongy membrane, the olfactory mucosa, carries many million olfactory cells which respond to the more volatile airborne substances carried as the cat inhales. In people this membrane covers an area only about half the 3–6 sq in (20–40 sq cm) that it covers in the cat. Cats also have a specialized scent organ that we lack, though several other animals also have it. This is Jacobson's organ, or the vomeronasal organ. It is placed between

Cats move confidently along the tops of fences and other narrow supports. The tail usually plays a part in maintaining balance but there is no evidence that Manx or Japanese Bobtail cats are at any disadvantage because their tails are reduced or lacking.

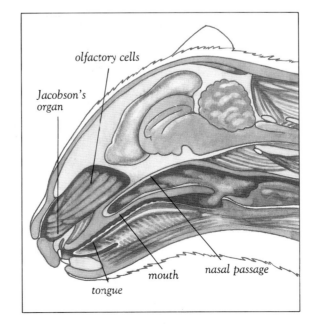

Smell and taste are very closely linked; both are registered in the same part of the brain. Smell is undoubtedly the most important to the cat, conveying messages of many kinds. While taste is largely concentrated on the edges of the tongue, smell enters through both mouth and nose. The tongue transfers tiny solid particles in the air to the Jacobson's (or vomeronasal) organ and scents breathed through the nose stimulate olfactory cells in the olfactory mucosa before passing through the nasal passage which opens into the mouth.

olfactory cells

Jacobson's organ

nasal passage

mouth

tongue

the nose and palate and two canals lead to it from behind the upper incisor teeth. The cat first traps particles on its tongue and then flick transfers them to the duct. You will often see a cat with its mouth open, its upper lip curled back and a look of apparent distaste on its face. This is known as the 'flehmen' reaction, a German word that is almost impossible to translate, perhaps the nearest English is 'grimacing', and it indicates not dislike but enthusiastic interest. The technique is more obvious in snakes — their constant flickering of the tongue is picking up tiny chemical molecules and transferring them to their vomeronasal organ.

The big cats show flehmen most noticeably when investigating sexual signals in the air, but some cats will sit on a window ledge taking in a deep smell picture of all kinds of things, not just sexual and marking odors. They are especially 'turned-on' by certain plants: Catnip or Catmint *Nepeta cataria*, which grows wild and in gardens in Europe and North America, valerian *Valerian officinalis*, a European medicinal herb of damp places, the Asian shrub Matatabi (silver vine) *Actinidia polygame* and Cat Thyme *Tenerium manum*.

Smells are another form of information, but however much a domestic cat may use its nose to find things out it seems even more to use it for aesthetic pleasure. Scents seem to provide its poetry, or at least its second-hand thrills!

Taste

Taste and smell are very closely linked, two aspects of the way in which the brain receives information about chemical phenomena. While the nose handles volatile molecules, taste is registered on the tongue. Taste buds on the tip, sides and base of the tongue, and on the inside of the mouth and lips, react to substances which dissolve in water or saliva during the licking and eating processes. Jacobson's organ seems to handle the whole range from volatile to solid and soluble molecules. There are no taste buds associated with the papillae on the central surface of the tongue, which make it feel so rough. These are for rasping food and collecting liquids.

Cats respond to salt, sour and bitter tastes but do not show any interest in sweet tastes. They are very sensitive to the taste of water. Protein-based chemicals appear to activate the taste buds, while animal fats are registered as smell sensations, so that it is the smell of rabbit that it prefers to beef, or vice versa, rather than literally its taste. Respiratory infections which affect the sense of smell can therefore interfere with a cat's appetite. Strong-smelling foods may then tempt it to eat but this ploy does not always succeed.

Other nerves on many other moist surfaces of the body also react to differing chemical contacts but they do not produce the sensations of taste or smell.

Touch

Touch does not only mean a response to pressure on or by the paws and other surfaces. It also embraces the sensations of pressure, heat and coldness and the registering of pain. The whole skin surface is responsive to touch but especially the pads of the paws and the nose leather, which have no fur covering. The tongue and the rest of the face are also highly sensitive. The paws, which can be rapidly withdrawn, are often used to explore an object, especially to see if it is animate and a danger.

Pressure sensitive pads are scattered across the skin making tiny lumps among the hairs — from 45 per sq in (7 per sq cm) to 160 per sq in (25 per sq cm) in the most responsive areas.

Touch does not require direct contact with the skin. Pressure on every hair is transmitted to sensors in the hair follicles. Those linked to guard hairs are more responsive and those of the stiff vibrissae most of all. The vibrissae — the whiskers, eyebrows and the long stiff hairs on the back of the front legs — are likely to be important not only for sensing objects which they touch but also because they respond to air currents and changes of pressure caused by the presence of adjacent things. In dim light especially, the vibrissae will supplement the failing near-sight when the inefficiency of the cat's eyes at very close quarters is aggravated by poor illumination.

As well as supplying information, touch is also a pleasurable sensation for cats. Domestic cats, and many tamed wild species, enjoy being stroked, some enjoying really strong pressure being exerted. Some domestic pets intensely dislike their paw pads being touched while others seem to love it, especially if combined with massage between the toes. The contentedness which comes with stroking and massage may hark back to the feeling of security generated by maternal grooming but, at the same time, cats will react instantly to some unexpected or single contact, even when contented.

Although *Felis silvestris* has adapted to a wide range of climatic conditions, lions seem to have been partly forced out of Europe by cold. Domestic cats certainly prefer warm places, but their sensitivity to temperature change seems to be much less than our own. You are much more likely to smell a cat's fur burning than the cat to feel any uncomfortable heat from having draped its tail into a gas or candle flame, or even too close to the bar of an electric fire and, strangely, singed fur does not seem to be a warning smell to most domestic cats. They do not show any sign of pain until their skin temperature reaches about 126°F (52°C), whereas people find a temperature of 112°F (44°C) too hot for comfort. It takes a little time for a localized high temperature to penetrate the fur, so the fur itself is already higher than 126°F by the time the skin reaches that temperature.

Cats do seem to be more sensitive to a mild drop in temperature than to a rise, but still much less so than a person. From a comfortable 84°F (29°C) you will probably notice a drop of 2.7°F (1.5°C) but experiments showed that most cats will take a drop of nearly 16°F (8.8°C) before

A cat uses its tongue as a washcloth and comb, moistening paws to groom those places the tongue cannot reach.

Right *A cat's vibrissae are a valuable spatial guide, operating through direct contact and their sensitivity to changes of air pressure caused by objects.*

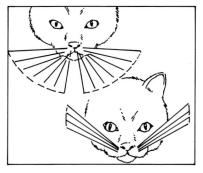

Above *A cat will also move its whiskers forwards to investigate a surface, for instance checking the lie of fur or feathers on prey, but will draw them back close to the cheeks when defensive.*

A tap with a paw is frequently the first check for any danger.

they react. Some house cats may curl up on top of a heater or radiator too hot for us to comfortably touch, then, getting an urge to go outdoors will, with no apparent sign of shock, walk off into a sub-zero temperature. Not all, however; one of the writer's cats, whose favourite spot was on top of the boiler, would rarely venture beyond the doorstep if the day was cold, though this may have had more to do with what was happening outside than the temperature itself.

Although domestic cats will accept high temperatures on their outer skin, when it comes to food they do not seem to be prepared to take hot pieces in the mouth, frequently rejecting pieces that you might find acceptable. This is another occasion when the paws may be used first to test food, or the heat sensors in the nose leather (which can respond to changes of as little as half a Fahrenheit degree) may be brought close to register temperature. Since a cat must either rasp meat off with the surface of its tongue, swallow chunks whole or take it into its mouth to shear it up into swallowable pieces, it is obviously wiser to check temperature first before exposing the tender surfaces of the mouth to contact.

In nature a fresh kill will be at the animal's body temperature so perhaps this care over hot food is a learned reaction, following at least one instance of something being too hot.

Although the occasional pet develops a taste for ice cream, very cold food is also usually rejected. Licking still-frozen food could do the tongue serious damage; putting out frozen salt licks was once used as a way of catching ermine,

their tongues freezing to the block and trapping them most painfully. Any food straight from the refrigerator should be allowed to come to room temperature before being fed to a cat; cold food has less of a smell to tempt it!

Time Sense

Cats have a very accurate sense of time and tend to be creatures of habit. Tigers and jaguars with large territories patrol them in a regular sequence and return to a particular location at predictable intervals. Domestic pets expect their meals at regular times and will let you know if they are kept waiting. If they sleep in your bedroom the more people-oriented breeds will probably tell you when it is bedtime if you stay up late, or remind you that this is the time when they expect you to play a particular game with them. If they ask for dinner early or try to make you stir when you have a Sunday morning lie-in it is more likely greed or self interest coming to the fore than a failure of their inner clock.

There are many indicators which identify a time, from sun position and daylight levels to particular human activities, but a cat will often anticipate the obvious signals. It is not you switching the television off that says it is bedtime to the cat — the cat comes to tell you that the late night movie is interrupting his or her routine.

One famous example which illustrates this is Willy, recorded by Gustave Eckstein in *A Cat that knows Monday*. Promptly at 7.45 each Monday evening he would appear at a traffic

intersection, cross with the lights as people crossed, cut through a hedge and along a brick wall to a window sill of a dining room for nurses where he settled down to watch a weekly game of Bingo. Any other night he might go out much earlier and come in for supper at any time from eight to midnight but on Mondays he ate at 7.30 precisely and got home at 9.45, as soon as the Bingo game had finished. It is not his accuracy that is surprising but that he found something so fascinating in watching humans putting crosses on little bits of paper!

Supper time was a moveable feast for Willy but breakfast certainly was not, for he liked to prowl at night and sleep indoors by day and his owners left the house at 8.10 in the morning to catch a streetcar into work. If he was five minutes early he would take his time over the last stretch home, perhaps have a few minutes lying in the sun, but if he was cutting it fine he would come rushing back to be there before they went out and locked the door.

Extra sense

Cats have a very strong sense of place and direction as well as of time. Even when exploring somewhere for the first time they have a marked ability to find their way home which becomes stronger as they mature. When very small, kittens use scent to find their way back to the nest, and scent markers seem to be one way in which cats retrace a location.

As with any other ability, homing skill is not equal in all cats, but most apparent 'strays' are less likely to be animals that have lost their way than pets who have been deliberately rejected, themselves decided to move on or who have, accidentally or not, hitched a lift to some new territory and do not think 'home' worth the effort of going back to. What is surprising is that many who find themselves in distant and strange terrain, whether as accidental stowaways or because they have been taken to a new home, *are* able to find their way back. A tabby called McCavity, for instance, was taken to Cumbernauld in Scotland but three weeks later was back at his old home 500 miles (800 km) south in Cornwall.

There are no familiar landmarks to orientate these journeys; no scent trail left on the ground to retrace. How do the cats do it? Sensitivity to minute scent particles carried enormous distances, magnetic forces, ley lines, have all been suggested. Experiments conducted with students by Dr Robin Baker of Manchester University showed that humans also seem to have an uncanny ability to identify at least the direction of the base from which they started. Some of his subjects who were blindfolded claimed to have been able to reconstruct the route because they could match timing and vehicle turns with road patterns, or by the feel of the sun on their faces, but it became clear that after the blindfold was removed, subjects found it much more difficult to guess correct directions. Did the clue lie in the earth's magnetism? To test this, electromagnets were fitted around some subjects' heads to interfere with this phenomenon (some being activated without the subject knowing). The conclusions seemed positive. Humans have a magnetic sense which is used in orientation. The further from base the more accurate were the results in this experiment; women appear to use this magnetic sense more than men and it apparently does not function when we are asleep.

Homing pigeons are also known to use this kind of magnetic orienteering and cats would appear to use it to give them a basic direction and then probably rely on other more local signs when they are closer to home. Over long distances such skills alone would not be enough. The cat must also have the motivation to want to return, for on a long journey they must find food or people to feed them and may encounter many opportunities to adopt another home.

Even more amazing than this homing ability is that of cats who have been left behind when human associates have moved and who appear to have gone off in search of them, sometimes right across a continent.

Examples include a French cat which left home and succeeded in finding a young man who had left home to do his military service, covering 75 miles (120 km) through the Vosges mountains before he reached the man's barracks 11 days later. In 1949 an American cat left in Chicago, Illinois, traced its owner in Boston, Massachusetts — 950 miles (1520 km) — in only eight days, a speed record that must have involved hitching on trucks or railroad cars.

Unless you are prepared to credit a cat with asking the Post Office for the forwarding address or calling enquiries to check out long distance telephone numbers how could they possibly know where 'their' people are? Yet, there are numerous cases well authenticated. Because it is always possible that a different but superficially identical cat could be welcomed by cat owners as the pet they left behind, researchers have been highly sceptical of such claims and insisted that there be incontestable distinguishing marks, physical abnormalities, specific previous injuries, specific behavior patterns or interaction with other animals that would rule out any possibility of its simply being a case of looking and behaving alike.

Among cases authenticated by Drs Joseph Rhine and Sara Feather of Duke University are one cat that was left behind in California and appeared 14 months later in Oklahoma, and Beau Chat, a pet in Louisiana who went missing while the family were looking for a house in

Southampton's Cat

One famous cat who went looking for his 'master' belonged to Henry Wriothesley, third Earl of Southampton. In 1601 the Earl, for a time the friend of William Shakespeare, the probable addressee of the poet's sonnets and one of the golden boys of the time, was imprisoned in the Tower of London for his part in the Earl of Essex's rebellion against Elizabeth I. The cat, presumably resident at the Earl's London home, Southampton House, not his Gloucestershire mansion, found its way across the city to the Tower. That, perhaps, is not surprising, the distance would not have been great, but he also contrived to climb over the battlements and roofs, managed to identify the chimney of the very chamber in which the Earl was detained, and climbed down it to join him. Is the story true? The first written record is by the antiquarian Thomas Pennant and dates from many years later, but a painting contemporary with Southampton's imprisonment shows a black and white bicolored cat sitting beside him, and a view of the White Tower, the castle keep, inserted in the upper corner.

John de Critz the Elder painted Henry Wriothesley as a prisoner in the Tower of London c.1601–3.

Texarkana, Texas. Father stayed in Texas and the family came home but there was still no sign of Beau Chat. Five months later, when they were all settled at Texarkana he turned up in the school yard where mother taught and one child was a pupil. Another cat, from New York, made a 2300 miles (3700 km) and five-month trek right to California to join its owner.

Such feats are inexplicable through normally accepted senses and abilities. Dr Rhine coined the name 'psi' to cover paranormal events and called this behavior 'psi-trailing'. In his research into parapsychology he also claimed to have found firm evidence of both precognition and telepathy in cats. Before dismissing such suggestions it is worth considering the remarks of the leading animal ethologist and Nobel Prizewinner, the late Nikko Tinbergen, who declared of extrasensory perception, 'if one applies the term to perception by processes not yet known to us, extrasensory perception among living creatures may well apply widely.' We still have a great deal to learn about our own and animal senses and abilities.

Sleep and dreaming

Cats spend much of their time asleep or resting. Those that live in hot climates lie up in shade during the hottest part of the day, and some cats may sleep for as many as 18 hours out of 24, exerting themselves only when absolutely necessary. Domestic cats who are left alone all day will probably sleep most of the hours when people are out. In the past it was more usual for house cats to be put out at night, because that was when they were most active, but most pets today will also sleep at night when their humans do — and often on their beds if they get the chance!

A cat's natural sleeping pattern is not a single long stretch, however, as with humans, but a series of shortish periods — hence the expression 'catnaps'. If a cat is bored, and especially when it is well fed and warm, these may be very frequent and extended.

Like ours, cats' sleep varies in level through four stages which can be recognized by the different patterns produced in an electroencephalogram of the electrical activity within the brain. From drowsiness, sleep becomes deeper until, at its deepest, the body is completely relaxed and the brain in lowest gear. You can lift a cat's limb in this state and it will be totally without tension. You can probably carry the cat without its even waking, especially if your touch and smell are familiar so that no sense of threat or danger is registered. At this deep stage a cat may dream, a state linked with rapid eye movements beneath not only a closed outer lid but a raised nictitating membrane. Experiments made in Lyons, France, by Professor Michel Jouvet have shown that brain-damaged cats who do not exhibit the extreme relaxed condition may move, even stand and appear to stalk prey, when they are dreaming, but in normal cats there is no outward sign of their dreams. Yet cats will often twitch their paws and whiskers, even make a chattering with the jaws, similar to their reaction when watching birds through a window, which most owners tend to interpret as acting out their dreams. Apparently they are doing nothing of the kind. These movements are not linked with brain activity. It is thought that they may simply be some way of discharging surplus electrical energy in the muscle systems.

Kittens go straight into deep sleep for the first month of their lives but adult cats usually have deep sleep periods lasting only six or seven minutes, followed by a 20–30 minute period of light sleep when their senses appear to be able to register external stimuli, responding out of sleep if they signal danger.

A cat in a deep sleep appears oblivious to everything.

THE FAMILY OF CATS

Every member of the cat family, from the largest lion to the smallest kitten curled up on a comfortable chair, is easily identified as being a cat. It does not take a zoologist to recognize the obvious similarities, but there are specific features which they all share that show how closely the different species are linked.

They all have lithe and muscular bodies with long legs, short faces with large eyes, very similar dentition and most are solitary hunters.

Cross-breeding shows how very close some species are. Koshien Zoo, in Japan, has bred 'leopons' from a leopard and a lioness and numerous zoos have produced 'tigons' (born of a male tiger and a lioness) and 'ligers' (male lion and tigress). Although these are usually infertile, a female liger at Munich was successfully mated back to a lion and the cub reared to adulthood. At Chicago Zoo offspring of a jaguar with a leopardess which were then mated to a lion successfully produced a further generation.

The African and European Wildcats can mate to produce fertile kittens and both can mate successfully with domestic cats. Hybridization is probably possible between others of the smaller cats.

This very closeness of the cats to each other makes it difficult to work out their exact relationships. Taxonomists — who seek to define scientifically the links between different types of animal, arranging them according to their relationships into family, genus, species and subspecies — do not agree on the way in which each kind of cat has developed from the ancestral cat forms described from earlier evolutionary periods. Some feel that they are so close that they should all be in the same genus, others divide them into two major groups — *Felis* and *Panthera*, with the

Cheetah and the Clouded Leopard each usually placed in a genus of its own, *Acinonyx* and *Neofelis*. A number of American authorities also place *Lynx* in a separate genus and the German scientist Paul Leyhausen, well known for his studies of the domestic cat, considers the differences sufficient to classify the family into 14 genera, while R.F. Ewer assigns them to no fewer than 19. Others have classified many of the cats into subgenera within the genera they propose. Fortunately there is wide agreement on the specific level.

To avoid confusion common names and the broad division into four genera are used here, together with specific names. Readers who want to investigate the various taxonomic proposals should consult the scientific works listed in the bibliography.

Wildcat *Felis silvestris*

The Wildcat has often been considered as two or more individual species for there are notable differences between what are now usually regarded as subspecies, of which up to 23 have been identified by some taxonomists, 11 of them in Africa. One of these, the African Wildcat *Felis silvestris lybica* is the most likely origin of the domestic cat, which taxonomically probably belongs within the species as *Felis silvestris catus*.

Wildcats are usually somewhat larger than the domestic form but the European Wildcat or Forest Cat *Felis silvestris silvestris* and especially the Scottish Wildcat *Felis silvestris grampia* are very similar to a heavily-built tabby, the main differences being a broader head and a shorter tail that is blunt rather than pointed at the tip, though juveniles have a tapering tail. Since Wildcats interbreed with feral domestic cats hybrids can confuse the clear distinction between them. Larger brain size has sometimes been suggested as a way of distinguishing the domestic from the wild cat.

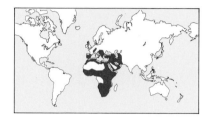

WILDCAT
Body length: *20–30 in (50–75 cm), males larger than females; tail: 8–14 in (21–35 cm); the Scottish race among the smallest, the Carpathian the largest.*
Distribution: *Southern Europe north to the Tatras and Carpathians, Scotland, throughout Africa and western Asia.*

Right *Wildcat seen here in its African form* Felis silvestris lybica, *domesticated in Egypt.*

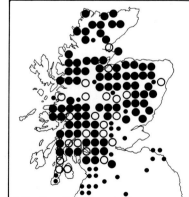

Evidence of the recovery of the Wildcat in Scotland is this mapping of the authenticated sightings of animals or of tracks and feeding remains, prepared by the Biological Research Records Centre from records supplied by the Mammal Society. Each symbol represents a sighting in that area, not an exact location.
- *pre 1900*
- *1900-59*
- *1960-85*

Left *The Scottish Wildcat is distinguished from the domestic cat by its bulk and the blunt end to its tail.*

Coat color of the Wildcat varies according to area and habitat. The European cats are yellowish gray, darker on the back with much paler underparts. In Africa and Asia fur color ranges in general from light sandy or light gray in dry regions to an ochre-brown in wet areas, although very different forms can appear side by side. The European cat has a pattern of stripes over the head merging into a longitudinal line to the base of the tail with stripes running down from it to the belly and stripes across the legs. The tail is ringed and has a black tip and the nose is pink.

In Africa *Felis silvestris lybica* may have a pattern of stripes or these may be replaced by spots, or be very indistinct, and there may be spots on the chest. Its tail is long and tapering, unlike that of the Scottish Wildcat. The Asiatic Steppe Wildcat, or Desert Cat, *Felis silvestris ornata*, which ranges south from the Soviet Union to central India (though not into the Ganges valley), is usually smaller than the other two main subspecies and has small spots of brown, gray or black instead of the body stripes. Among other forms are *Felis silvestris chutuchta* of the southern Gobi, which has unbroken stripes, and the Ordos Cat *Felis silvestris vellerosa* of south-eastern Mongolia, which is unmarked and has much longer fur.

There are differences in temperament as well as physical differences between the subspecies: while the African Wildcat often lives close to human settlements, and its kittens can become very tame house pets, the European form keeps well away from people. Even kittens taken from the wild when very young have proved untameable. An exception was one that Scottish naturalist David Stephen obtained before its eyes had opened and which was tame from the time they did. A sister from the same litter, which had already-open eyes when taken, proved 'a spitfire' all her life.

The Wildcat in its various forms lives in an enormous range of habitats from northern forests to sandy plains, reed beds to rocky steppe, almost everywhere except waterless deserts and equatorial forests. Its prey is equally varied from mice to fawns and small antelopes (though mostly much smaller rodents), birds, fish, lizards, snakes and insects. It is solitary and mainly active at dusk (crepuscular) or at night, but will hunt during the day in dull weather in Africa. In Europe it enjoys sunning itself, frequently in a tree, though it usually spends the day holed up in a rock crevice, a hollow tree or deep cover.

The kittens, which are more heavily marked than adults, usually begin to go out hunting with their mother at about 12 weeks and become independent at five months, maturing when about one year old.

Wildcats were once widespread over most of Europe, but cooling of the climate seems to have reduced their northern range and the species has been unknown in Scandinavia and most of Russia since the middle ages. It was hunted for sport and for its fur in earlier times and ruthlessly destroyed in the nineteenth century because it was considered a threat to game birds, so that it disappeared from large areas of central and western Europe. Interruption of field sports

Jungle Cat

during the two World Wars gave surviving populations some respite and their numbers have partially recovered in Scotland, Switzerland and West Germany. It is now a protected species in Spain, Germany and Czechoslovakia.

Jungle Cat *Felis chaus*

Sometimes known as the Reed Cat, Marsh Cat or Swamp Cat (in Egypt and Iraq it often lives in the reed beds of the riverside), *Felis chaus* has been found among the cats mummified by the ancient Egyptians. It is sometimes suggested that this is the cat shown in Egyptian tomb paintings of fowling in the marshes and that it was trained as a hunting cat. The Egyptian race has been identified as a subspecies, *Felis chaus nilotica*.

The Jungle Cat looks like a larger and particularly long-legged African Wildcat. Its fur is uniformly sandy or yellowish gray to a tawny red or grayish brown with a yellowish underside and sometimes a darker patch in the middle of the back. Adults are only indistinctly speckled or spotted with darker color, often with none noticeable on the body and only slight stripes on the limbs and darker rings and tip on the tail. Kittens are dark with distinct stripes or spots. The backs of the ears are reddish to black with black and slightly tufted tips and there are faint tabby facial markings.

The Jungle Cat is found in woodlands and open country as well as in marshes and by rivers and will lie up in dry places among reeds and thickets, in disused burrows, among rocks and even in buildings. It does not shun humans and will hunt in village fields. Mainly crepuscular (active at twilight) and nocturnal, it can also be seen by day. Prey range from hares and other small mammals, even porcupines, to the fawns of cheetal deer, pheasants, frogs, fish and snakes. Jungle Cats run, climb and swim well, and can jump high into the air, although they usually move slowly and carefully. Kittens purr and adults use a harsh mew to attract a mate.

Kittens suckle for two months and are independent at five, reaching maturity at about 18 months.

The species ranges from Lower Egypt through the Middle East to Asia Minor and through the southern Soviet Republics to Chinese Turkestan and Nepal and south to Sri Lanka and Cambodia, perhaps as far as Yunnan, and from sea level to 8000 ft (2400 m) in the Himalayas. An isolated subspecies, which has not been scientifically described, has also been located in the Tassili of southern Algeria.

Serval *Felis serval*

Placed by some taxonomists in a subgenus *Leptailurus*, the Serval is a long-legged, slender African cat, with a more elongated skull than most other felines. It is similar in size to the Caracal but has a shortish tail, large rounded ears which lack tufts and a distinctly different coat. It could not be mistaken for the Caracal even in those areas where distribution overlaps.

The tawny or yellowish fur is densely spotted with black markings which vary considerably over its range. In the generally drier bush, grasslands and open savanna country the spots are large, sometimes developing into streaks along the back, but in the moister zones of dense savanna, open woodlands and forests the spots are smaller and more closely spaced, sometimes appearing to merge along the back. This smaller-spotted form was formerly classed as a separate species, the Servaline Cat *F.servalina*, and is said to be slightly smaller. The spots along the tail give way to complete rings at about midway and the tail has a dark tip. The dark backs of the ears carry flashes of white. There are dark stripes above the eyes and running from their outer corners. Melanistic (black-coated) forms occur, especially in the moister areas around the edges of the rain forest, and have frequently been sighted on Mount Kenya and Kilimanjaro.

A solitary animal, the Serval is less nocturnal than the Caracal and is often seen in daylight. It is nonetheless mainly a night hunter preying upon mice, rats and other rodents, hares, lizards, birds up to the size of a guinea fowl and even small antelopes.

The German zoologist and behaviorist Paul Leyhausen filmed a serval which, having caught a rat, was careful to carry it without hurt. It then repeatedly pushed the rat into a crevice and fished it out again with a paw, something he had observed servals do as a game, pushing a piece of bark or other playthings into a hole.

The Serval can be very swift over short distances, with a bounding run, and can leap to catch birds nearly 10 ft (3 m) from the ground. It climbs well and will take refuge in trees if threatened by larger predators.

Kittens, usually two or three, which are colored like the adults, are born in a rock hole, a porcupine's or similar burrow or in thick scrub and are suckled for up to seven months. They become independent before the end of a year and are able to breed at two years.

Servals can purr and have a high-pitched cry usually repeated seven or eight times in succession.

Once very common in suitable terrain in north-west Africa and south of the Sahara, they have been hunted in East Africa for their meat and fur, which was used for traditional cloaks or *carosses* as well as in the fur trade, and in farming areas for taking domestic fowl. The Serval has disappeared from many areas in the north and west and the far south, especially south of the Orange Free State. The northern subspecies *Felis serval constantina* was listed as endangered in 1980 and the species is now on CITES Appendix II. It is protected in some countries and is found in most of the national parks and reserves within its range. It has bred successfully in zoos.

Caracal *Felis caracal*

This cat is sometimes considered as belonging to a separate genus, *Caracal*, or placed in a subgenus of its own, and has also been called

Top left *Jungle cat*;
Top and centre right *Serval*;
Centre left *Prater's Jungle Cat*;
Left *Caracal*;
Above *Serval kitten*.

the Desert or African Lynx. However, although closely related to the Lynx, it is smaller and has a much longer tail. Its long, slender body is set on long slim legs, the hind longer than the fore, the tail one-third to half the body length. The fur is dense and fairly short, the upperside uniformly colored from sandy to reddish brown, sometimes with gray or black hairs spreading through it, and lightening to the underside of both body and tail. Chin, throat and belly are white and the eyes are ringed with white. There are vertical black or dark brown stripes on the forehead, and from eye to nose, with spots at the corners of the mouth and on whisker pads. The underside of the body and inside of the legs may be paler spotted with a stripe on the back of the thighs. The narrow, pointed ears are dark on the back and have 1¾ in (4.5 cm) long tufts, usually black but sometimes white. Young caracals are grayer and darker than adults. Melanistic (black-coated) forms occur.

A solitary, mainly crepuscular and nocturnal animal, though also seen by day, it runs rather like a cheetah, is fast for its size and can leap 6 ft (2 m), often knocking birds down with its paws. It can climb trees, to which it sometimes carries a kill. Prey include birds up to the size of guinea fowl, rodents, hyraxes, small antelopes, the fawns of larger ones and even poisonous snakes. In Iran and India it was once trained to catch hares and birds.

The Caracal lives in the dry woodlands and savannas of Africa, the hilly steppes and mountain ranges of Arabia and stony, broken scrub in India. Its distribution ranges from central India north to Turkmenistan and west through Africa except for true desert and rain forest areas. It has now disappeared from many parts of India, the Middle East and the Near East and the Russian subspecies *Felis caracal michaelis* was classified as rare in 1978. All the Asian forms are now on CITES Appendix I and others on Appendix II.

Kittens, usually two or three, although there may be as many as six, are born in borrowed burrows, rock holes or thick scrub. They suckle for six months, remain with their mother for about one year and reach sexual maturity at two.

Caracals are not very vocal but have a loud bark, rather like a lower-key version of the cry of a leopard, with which they call to their mate.

CARACAL

Body length: *24–36 in (60–90 cm); tail up to 12 in (30 cm).*
Distribution: *Africa, except rain forest belt and true desert, Sinai, to southern USSR and central India.*

Opposite *Caracal in the Serengeti.*
Left *Caracal and kitten.*

Black-footed Cat *Felis nigripes*

The smallest wild cat, less than half the size of the African Wildcat, to which it is probably closely related, the Black-footed Cat occupies a similar ecological niche in southern Africa to that of the Sand Cat in the north. The coat is sandy to dark ochre, whitish on the cheeks, throat, underbody and inside of the legs. It is boldly patterned with dark brown or black spots on the whitish areas and stripes on the cheeks, throat, forelegs and haunches. The tail is ringed near the end and has a black tip. It is the soles of the feet which are black and give the cat its name. Females are usually more conspicuously marked and juveniles seem much darker because their spots are closer together.

Generally described as nocturnal, the Black-footed Cat has been frequently seen both early and late in the day in Kruger National Park, and in captivity has been more active during the day than most other small cats. Its prey ranges from mice to ground-squirrel-sized mammals, birds and reptiles.

It is a particularly solitary species, and even mating meetings are very brief, for the female's heat is said to last only five to ten hours. Young are thought to be born usually at the bottom of a burrow, but kittens have been found under a bush and in a thick clump of palms. Kittens bred by Paul Leyhausen in captivity showed an unusual reaction to danger. Instead of scattering to cover, as domestic kittens do, they froze until their mother made a very quiet staccato sound, accompanied by a raising and lowering of flattened ears, signalling all clear, at which they ran back to her. Young, especially, purr and the adult has a rather loud call, like that of a high-pitched tiger.

The Black-footed Cat is an inhabitant of dry, open country and semi-desert from southern Angola to the south-east of Cape Province and possibly as far north as Zimbabwe, although it now appears to be extinct in Natal. The nominate form is found in Cape Province; those of the Karoo and the rest of its range are a subspecies *Felis nigripes thomasi*, which is slightly larger and has darker coloring.

Sand Cat *Felis margarita*

There are four subspecies of this small cat, which live in the Sahara and Libyan deserts and in the deserts of the Near East across to the Karakum and possibly Afghanistan. The African subspecies is often known as the Sahara Sand Cat and Sand Dune Cat is another name. The form in Pakistan *F.m.scheffeli* was not discovered until 1966 and was declared endangered by the IUCN in 1978, but Sand Cats have been hunted for the fur trade, for captive study and for pets and are generally rare throughout their range.

Sand is this cat's color as well as its habitat, darkest on the spine, and with the lower half of the face and the underside whitish. It is marked like the African Wildcat, though often very indistinctly, and with a reddish streak across the cheeks. Dark ear tips, cheek and forehead markings, thigh stripes and at least one ring or spot in front of a black tail tip are visible, even when other markings are indistinguishable, and

BLACK-FOOTED CAT
Body length: *14–16 in (37–40 cm); females smaller; tail 6–7 in (15–18 cm).*
Distribution: *Steppe and dry savanna in South Africa, Botswana, Namibia.*

Below right *Sand Cat. The darker markings of such young cats usually pale as they become older and the fur becomes longer on the soles of the paws.*

Below *Black-footed cat.*

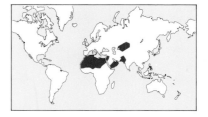

SAND CAT
Body length: *18–23 in (45–57 cm); tail 9–14 in (23–35 cm).*
Distribution: *Sahara and Libyan deserts, south to northern Niger, parts of Arabia, Soviet Central Asia, Pakistan.*

in the young markings are very clear. The face is broad and made to look even wider by its large, low-set ears.

The Sand Cat is highly adapted to its environment. The soles of the feet have long dark fur which hides the pads and helps movement over loose sand, probably also providing insulation from the hot surface of sand and rocks if it has to break its usually nocturnal habits. The flattened appearance of the Sand Cat's head and ears help it to conceal itself when stalking prey amongst desert rocks.

During the heat of the day it hides in a burrow dug into a dune or under scrub. It is able to survive without drinking water, getting enough liquid from its prey which include jerboas and other rodents, birds, reptiles and even locusts.

The Sand Cat wanders widely but rarely climbs and is a poor jumper. It has a very loud, often repeated, mewing call, needed perhaps because populations are low and dispersed. Litters of two to four young are usually born in late March or early April and stay with their mother for at least four months, by which time they are three-quarters adult size. They are able to breed at about one year old.

Chinese Desert Cat *Felis bieti*

Another small cat closely allied to the Wildcat but, despite its name, not a cat of sandy deserts for it lives in rocky steppe and even mountain forests in southern Mongolia from Gansu to Sichuan. It has similarities to the Desert Cat with comparable, though not identical, rather fugitive markings on a yellowish-gray coat and long fur making hairy pads on the soles of the feet, but this feature is not so pronounced as in the Sand Cat. The ear tips have tufts of hair about three-quarters of an inch (2 cm) long.

Very little is known about this cat which was first discovered in 1889 when a scientific expedition, led by Prince Henri d'Orléans, was turned back from an attempt to reach Lhasa. In the markets of Sichuan a member of the expedition found two unusual feline skins. Nothing else was known until 1925 when a skull turned up which was considered to be from the same species. Since then there have been other sightings, including one at 10,000 ft (3000 m).

Pallas's Cat *Felis manul*

This cat is named for Peter Simon Pallas, the German naturalist, who discovered and described it from the area around the Caspian Sea, where he was also probably the first European to see and describe a cat with a Siamese form of coat pattern. Also known as the Manul, it is about the size of a large domestic cat but with a massive body and short, stout legs. The head is short and broad, the width accentuated by a longer cheek ruff and the large, low-set, widely-spaced ears. Some features suggest a close link with the European Wildcat but cranial differences have led other zoologists to connect it with

the Lynx. It has sometimes been placed in a separate genus *Otocolobus*.

Pallas claimed that these cats liked to mate with domestic cats and suggested that they might be an ancestor of the long-haired breeds, such as Angoras and Persians, though this is not now considered very likely.

The Pallas's Cat's coat is longer and more dense than that of other wild *Felis* species and this provides some insulation from the snow and frozen ground of its habitat in steppe land, deserts and rocky plateaux up to more than 13,000 ft (4000 m) from the eastern Caspian shore to Sichuan and Ladakh.

The coat varies from a light gray to yellowish buff with each individual hair tipped with white to give a frosted, silvery look. Fur on the underparts and towards the end of the tail is particularly long. Lips, chin and throat are white, and two dark streaks run from the corner of each eye down the cheeks. 'Eyebrows' appear pencilled in across the flattened head. The tail is ringed and has a dark tip and there may be faint stripes along the back and across the legs.

A solitary and secretive animal that can sometimes be seen by day but usually hunts at night, it hides in a borrowed burrow, in a cave, a rock fissure or a hole under a rock. The placing of its ears creates a low silhouette, for hunting in country where there may be little vegetation for cover, and the forward and high placement of the eyes exposes less of the cat when it raises its head to look over a rock. It feeds mainly on pikas (mouse hares) and other small animals.

The young (born in litters of five or six to captive specimens) have a thick woolly coat but

CHINESE DESERT CAT
Body length: *27–37 in (68–94 cm)*;
tail 11–14 in (29–35 cm).
Distribution: *south-western China.*

PALLAS'S CAT
Body length: *20–26 in (50–65 cm)*;
tail 8–12 in (20–30 cm).
Distribution: *Iran to western China, central Kazakhstan, Altai and Inner Mongolia to Tibet and Ladakh.*

Pallas's Cat.

do not have the frosting they gain as adults. They are said to produce a scream reminiscent both of the barking of a small dog and of the call of an owl and apparently do not spit and hiss but make a shrill sound through scarcely opened lips.

Captive animals are said to remain very wild and vicious, but there are reports of some being kept as half-tamed pets and of at least one that became very tame, although still disliking strangers.

Pallas's Cat is distributed over a very wide range but possibly present in only a few isolated locations, although at various times it has been common on the southern slopes of the Tannu Ola in the Mongolian Republic and in some other places. It is now considered threatened in the USSR and Ladakh (northern India) and it is protected in both countries and listed on CITES Appendix II.

African Golden Cat *Felis aurata*

This is a cat of the high deciduous forest of central and west Africa and the edge of the savanna in Guinea, up to 12,000 ft (3600 m) in Uganda. It is frequently placed in a subgenus, *Profelis*, together with the Asian Golden Cat, and some taxonomists promote it to full generic status.

The African Golden Cat is considerably larger than the African Wildcat, robustly built with rather long legs ending in large paws, and a smallish head with large, rounded ears set fairly high. Coat color varies from a deep golden brown, usually with a reddish tinge, through fawn to gray-brown or even a bluish or blackish gray. The fur on the underparts is longer and lighter, sometimes almost white, as are the chin and chest. The whole body may be spotted in dark brown or dark gray or spotting may be limited to the underparts and inside of the legs. The back is usually darkened, the back of the ears are black and there is a black tip to the tail which may also have up to a dozen faint rings around it. Some melanistic cats have been recorded.

The wide color range can exist side by side, though the red and gray forms were once thought to be distinct species. It has been suggested that the fur changes from red to gray with age but this is only conjecture. Spots tend to be more noticeable from Gambia to Togo while those from Cameroun to western Kenya are darker.

The Golden Cat is said to hunt by both night and day, catching rock hyraxes, rodents, birds and probably small antelopes by careful stalking and a final rush. It is mainly terrestrial but can climb well. It is very seldom reported. To some tribespeople in the area of its distribution it seems endowed with magical properties, which may lead them to keep sightings secret. The pygmies of Cameroun valued its tail as a charm to bring success in elephant hunting and its fur forms part of chiefs' ceremonial robes. Very little is known about this animal, which may now be under threat because of the destruction of its habitat. It is listed in CITES Appendix II.

Above *Asian Golden Cat (Fontainier's Cat).*
Below *African Golden Cat.*

AFRICAN GOLDEN CAT
Body length: 28–37 in (72–94 cm); tail 6–8 in (15–20 cm).
Distribution: *Equatorial Africa from Gambia to western Kenya, not Nigeria.*

ASIAN GOLDEN CAT
Body length: *29–42 in (73–105 cm); tail 17–22 in (43–50 cm).*
Distribution: *Nepal and Tibet, through Assam, Burma, Thailand, Vietnam, Cambodia, southern China and Malaysia to Sumatra.*

Asian Golden Cat *Felis temmincki*

This species, also known as Temminck's Golden Cat, is the most closely related to the African Golden Cat, together with which it is sometimes placed in a separate genus, *Profelis*. It lives in similar habitat, up to altitudes of more than 10,000 ft (3000 m), often where the forest is broken by rocky ground, earning it the Chinese name of Rock Cat (*shilului*). Once, perhaps, its ancestors lived in a great rain forest that encompassed the terrain of both, but now there is a distance of more than 4000 miles (6500 km) between its ranges in Africa and Asia. The scientific name of this Asian cat forms another link, for it was the Dutch naturalist Temminck who described and named the African Golden Cat.

Generally larger than the African cat, though of similar conformation, the coat of the Asian Golden Cat varies from a golden red to a dark brown or gray. The face is marked with white and black streaks across the cheeks and running over the temple. The ears are short and rounded with a gray flecked area in the middle of their black backs and the underside of the end of the tail is white. In the southern part of its range there are no other markings, or only faint spots on the sides and belly, but in the north some are heavily spotted and striped all over. This led to one subspecies, known as Fontainier's Cat *F.t.tristis* being wrongly classed as a form of Leopard Cat *F.bengalensis*. Melanistic individuals occur, including one which was in the Basel Zoo, Switzerland.

Although probably mainly a terrestrial hunter for hares, birds, lizards, small deer, it can certainly climb and, in the foothills of the Himalayas in the north of Assam, was said to raise its kittens in a hollow tree. Tribespeople near Assam's north-western frontier, however, claimed that it never climbed at all. Some specimens have been tamed — one picked up as a kitten made a very affectionate pet before being given to London Zoo — and, although rare in zoos, they have bred in captivity. However, not much is known about them in the wild; it is said they hunt in pairs and that the male helps rear the young.

An extremely retiring animal, the Asian Golden Cat ranges from the foothills of the Himalayas in Nepal, through southern China and the Malay Peninsula to Sumatra. It was hunted for its fur but is now protected over much of its range, although destruction of its habitat is still putting it in danger and it is listed on CITES Appendix I.

Leopard Cat *Felis bengalensis*

This, and the following four species, are often grouped in a subgenus, *Prionailurus*, which some zoologists consider so different from the other *Felis* species as to warrant being considered a separate genus. They are probably the closest of the modern cat species to the ancient common ancestor of the whole cat family.

The most common wild cat of southern Asia, the Leopard Cat is about the size of a domestic cat (although longer in the leg), and looks much like one with particularly large eyes and slightly pronounced whisker pads. Coat color ranges from reddish to grayish but is usually a light tawny sand paling to white underparts. The white rises up onto the cheeks or streaks them, and there are white stripes running from the inner corners of the eyes up over the head. The face is patterned with broken black bands; the backs of the ears are black with white 'thumb-marks' on them, and there are usually several narrow black bands running over the head and down the spine where they are frequently broken down into streaks and spots. Both body and legs are covered with dark spots. There is considerable variation in the shape of the markings which may appear more like broken bands.

Leopard Cats are found over a wide area, from the Ussuri region of Siberia to Bali and from Kashmir to the Sea of Japan. As many as ten subspecies have been identified, some of which show clear differences in coat, and many of which were once considered separate species. However, despite the name, its spots are not in the open rosette form seen on the true Leopard.

You may find Leopard Cats referred to by a variety of names in old books when different forms were thought to be separate species. These included the Sumatran Cat *F.b.sumatranus*, which tended to have fewer and smaller markings, the Java Cat *F.b.javanensis*, which is rather dull in color, the Borneo Cat *F.b.borneoensis*, which is brighter and redder in tone. There are five or six subspecies in China, where they are known as the 'money cats' because the spots look

LEOPARD CAT
Body length: *17–24 in (44–60 cm)*;
tail 13–15 in (32–37 cm).
Distribution: *Kashmir, Baluchistan, northern India, through Burma and Malaya to Java, Bali, Borneo and the central Philippines, northward on the continent to North Korea to south-eastern Siberia and Quelpart and Tsushima islands.*

Above *Leopard Cat.*
Left *Leopard Cat kittens.*

like a scattering of coins. The Philippines have a small subspecies *F.b.minuta* and the much larger Amur and Far Eastern Forest Cat *F.b.eruptilur* may have a head and body length up to 3 ft (90 cm).

A good climber, the Leopard Cat hunts in trees and on the ground for hares, rodents, birds, reptiles, small deer — and fish. It swims well and has thus been able to colonize small offshore islands. It makes a den in hollow trees, under exposed tree roots or in small caves. Habitat varies considerably from taiga pine forest to the scrub in river valleys and behavior may differ in different territories. It has been described as fierce and untameable, but some have been kept as domestic pets. It does not seem to be afraid of man and often lives close to settlements. Although generally solitary, during the mating season several males may come together to court the same female and males may participate in the rearing of the young — usually two or three, though litter size can vary from one to four. In Siberia and India kittens seem to be produced in May but some authorities claim that in southeast Asia breeding may occur throughout the year.

Rusty-spotted Cat *Felis rubiginosus*

This is another species in the group sometimes separated as *Prionailurus*. It is smaller than a domestic cat and is a native of the southern part of Sri Lanka, where it lives in humid mountain forest, and of southern India, where its habitat tends to be more open country, dry grassland and scrub, often around seasonally dry waterways and near human settlements. It has been reported from Gujarat and from central India but is found mainly on the western side of the southern states of Tamil Nadu and Andhra Pradesh.

The Rusty-spotted Cat is a descriptive name. The coat is a broken gray above tinged with a rusty red, which is stronger on the tail, and marked with broken lines of brown blotches. The underside of the body and inside of the legs are white and also covered with large spots. There are dark streaks on the face and running over the head to the nape of the neck with white lines on each side of the nose.

It is a mainly nocturnal hunter, preying on small mammals and birds. Although it can be fairly easily tamed if captured when a very young kitten, not much is known about its habits or its breeding behavior.

Fishing Cat *Felis viverrinus*

Another candidate for the genus or subgenus *Prionailurus*, the Fishing Cat also has a gray-brown coat with rows of dark brown spots, but it is larger than the Leopard Cat or the Rusty-spotted Cat. Dark lines run over the head and down the neck, and the black backs of the high-set, rounded ears have white spots. The head is rather big and broad and the tail comparatively short. The forefeet have slightly webbed paws with claws which cannot be fully withdrawn into

Top *Rusty-spotted Cat.*
Above *Tsushima Cat.*

A recent discovery: the Tsushima Cat

The second 'new' endemic wild cat to be discovered in Japan in recent years (the Iriomote Cat is the other) is a local form of the Siberian subspecies of the Leopard Cat, *Felis bengalensis manchuricus* or *F.b.eruptilur*. It lives in bushy forest edges and paddy fields near the coast of this small island, coming quite close to villages. It is larger than the continental subspecies but smaller than the Iriomote Cat. The island's habitat, with ravines cutting into steep mountains, is quite unlike that of Iriomote. The cat's skull measurements are comparable to those of the Korean Leopard Cat but there are no Leopard Cats in South Korea or elsewhere in Japan. It seems likely that the present population — less than 100 — are descendants of a relic population, separated from the other Leopard Cats long, long ago.

RUSTY-SPOTTED CAT
Body length: *16–18 in (40–45 cm);*
tail 7–10 in (18–25 cm).
Distribution: *Southern India and Sri Lanka.*

their sheaths. Its scientific name reflects its superficial resemblance to the civet family, especially the Large Indian Civet *Viverra zibetha*.

The Fishing Cat (a direct translation of its Bengali name, *mach-bagral*) lives in mangrove swamps, reed beds and marshy creeks and its webbed paws help it to scoop fish out of the water as it crouches on a sandbank or rock or wades in shallow water. It swims well and is not intimidated by deep water. Several observers have seen it dive, so it may catch fish in its jaws as well. It also eats frogs, small mammals, birds, snakes and crustaceans.

Captive Fishing Cats have bred successfully, a male at Frankfurt Zoo helping with rearing the kittens from the time of birth. Young at Philadelphia Zoo were weaned at 53 days and reached adult size in 8½ months, but not much is known about reproduction in the wild. This is said to be an easy species to tame.

The Fishing Cat ranges from Sri Lanka and the southern tip of India up the west coast to Mangalore, and from Sind in the north, across to Nepal, Bangladesh and through Assam and Burma to south-east Asia to Sumatra, possibly Bali, and to Taiwan. Its distribution is rather fragmented. It will live close to habitation, so is less disturbed by settlement than many species, but is widely trapped for its fur, although it does not fetch high prices. It is protected in India, where it is considered threatened in some places and is on CITES Appendix II.

Flat-headed Cat
Felis planiceps

This is another Asian species of the group sometimes classified as the species or subspecies *Prionailurus*. It is about the size of the domestic cat but does not look very like one, having a rather longer body set on short legs, a short tail and a slightly flattened head. Its fur is longish, thick and soft.

The main coat color is deep brown but the fur is tipped with white which gives it a silvery tinge. The underparts are white, spotted and blotched with brown. The inside of the legs, and top of the head are reddish brown, the lower part of the face lighter in color. Dark marks on the cheeks and yellow lines between eye and ear

FISHING CAT
Body length: *29–34 in (72–86 cm)*;
tail 10–12 in (23–30 cm).
Distribution: *Pakistan to Sri Lanka, Java and Taiwan.*

Below and bottom *Fishing Cat.*

Iriomote Cat *Felis iriomotensis*

This cat, which is about the same size as a domestic cat, lives only on the island of Iriomote, one of the furthest south of the Japanese Ryukyu group, east of Taiwan. Occasionally trapped by local people, who considered its flesh a delicacy, it was not known to the scientific world until 1967.

From skins and skulls Dr Yoshimori Imaizumi, of the Tokyo National Museum, decided that this was not just a new species but a new genus and gave it the scientific name *Mayailurus*, believing it to be a representative of the Metailurinae, a prehistoric branch of the cat family, previously known only from fossils. Later opinion is that it is related to the Leopard Cat and should be included in the subgenus (or genus) *Prionailurus*. This and the preceding three species may differ considerably from the other cats usually classed as *Felis*. They are considered to be the closest to the common ancestor of all modern cats and the Iriomote Cat is probably the most primitive of them all. The discovery of a fossil cat resembling the Iriomote Cat on the nearby Miyako Island by Dr Hasequawa, suggests that it may have been a separate species since at least the Pleistocene.

About the size of a domestic cat, it is long in the body and short in the leg, with a shortish tail. It has a dark brown coat with darker spotting in lengthwise rows that may merge into bands. The ears are rounded with the black backs carrying white spots.

It lives in lowland subtropical rain forest where it hunts at night for small rodents, water birds, and water prey such as crabs and mud-skippers. It is strictly territorial (territories being about a square mile or two square kilometres) and no

FLAT-HEADED CAT
Body length: *16–22 in (40–55 cm); tail 5–7 in (13–17 cm).*
Distribution: *India, Sri Lanka to southern China, Sumatra, Java and Bali.*

IRIOMOTE CAT
Body length: *24 in (60 cm); tail c.8 in (20 cm).*
Distribution: *known only on Iriomote Shima.*

pattern the face. Kitten fur is gray, changing first to light and then to darker brown.

As in the Fishing Cat, the claws are not fully retractile. A captive kitten enjoyed playing in water, captured frogs and took pieces of fish from the water while ignoring live birds, though an adult has been seen stalking chickens.

This is a very rare and elusive cat and not much is known about it. It seems likely that it lives along river banks, probably taking fish, frogs, birds and small mammals. It is reported from southern Thailand, Malaya, Borneo and Sarawak. It is thought to be endangered in Thailand and Indonesia and is on CITES Appendix I.

Top *Flat-headed Cat.*
Right *Iriomote Cat.*

social contact has been observed outside mating. However, little is known about the animal's behavior.

The Iriomote Cat is now totally protected but the destruction of habitat by agriculture, together with the setting of traps to catch Ryukyu wild boar continue to put it very much at risk. Its numbers have fallen considerably since 1974. The most recent estimate was that about 100 animals survive. It is on CITES Appendix II.

Marbled Cat *Felis marmorata*

The Marbled Cat is a little larger than the average domestic cat and has a more rounded head than the other members of the genus *Felis*. It is placed by some taxonomists in a subgenus, *Pardofelis*, with the Bay Cat.

This little known and rarely seen species has a dense coat that looks somewhat like that of the Clouded Leopard. When first described it was thought, despite the difference in size, to be the same animal, the size given in earlier descriptions of that animal being thought perhaps erroneous. The fur may be a brownish gray to a bright yellow ochre or russet, marked with large irregular dark blotches on the sides of the body, each outlined in black, and solid spots on the legs and underparts. Short, rounded ears are black with gray bars and there are narrow stripes over the head and neck that merge to form a broken stripe along the back. The long bushy tail is also spotted, tipped with black and black on its upper side.

This cat can be found from Nepal to Borneo. It seems to be a nocturnal hunter, mainly after birds which it hunts in the trees, but probably includes squirrels, rats, lizards and frogs amongst its prey. In Nepal it lives high on forest slopes but in Borneo it is more frequently found in low country. Human intrusion into and destruction of its habitat has made it very rare in much of its range. It is now protected in both India and Thailand and may occur in national parks within its range. It is classed as endangered under United States law and is on CITES Appendix I.

Bay Cat *Felis badia*

This species, also called the Bornean Red Cat, is known only from a few locations in Borneo and rarely seen. It is classed, with the Marbled Cat, in the subgenus *Pardofelis*.

The Bay Cat is a little larger than *F.marmorata* and looks somewhat like a smaller version of Temminck's Cat, so that some taxonomists have placed it in the same subgenus instead of grouping it with *F.marmorata*.

Its fur is bright chestnut, becoming paler on the underparts with some faint spotting on the belly and legs. Some individuals with bluish to blackish gray fur have also been reported. The underside of the long tail has a white tip continuing as a streak halfway and marked with a black spot.

This cat lives in dense forest and frequents rocky areas on the forest edges. It probably hunts small mammals but little is known about it.

Lynx *Felis lynx*

The lynx is often placed in a subgenus with its close relative the Bobcat (as subgenus *Lynx*), or given a genus to itself, while the North American and Spanish subspecies are sometimes treated as full species.

The Lynx is the only extant member of the cat family which is found in both the Old World and the New World. It was once widespread in suitable habitats throughout most of mainland Europe, northern Asia, the Near East and southward in North America as far as the southern United States. As climate change or felling removed the wood cover from many areas it withdrew to those territories that remained

BAY CAT
Body length: *20–24 in (50–60 cm);*
tail 14–16 in (35–40 cm).
Distribution: *Borneo.*

MARBLED CAT
Body length: *18–21 in (45–53 cm);*
tail 19–22 in (45–53 cm).
Distribution: *Nepal to Malay Peninsula, Vietnam, Sumatra, Borneo.*

thickly forested. It has been widely hunted both for its fur and because it has been considered a predator of domestic animals and game so that today it has disappeared from most areas where people have settled in any numbers.

The Lynx is the largest of the European cats, males often more than five times heavier than the average domestic cat, although size can vary considerably. It is a very sturdy looking animal set on solid looking legs, the rear noticeably longer than the front, with large paws, a fairly small head and a very short tail.

The coat is long and thick with tufts on the ear tips; 'sideboards', which become especially noticeable in winter, may develop to almost a full ruff. Long fur on the feet aids movement over soft snow.

Color ranges from a sandy gray to a tawny red with white underparts, with some degree of spotting. In North America *F.l.canadensis* may have a rather frosted appearance, so that the spots become hardly noticeable. Lynx in Kashmir and Tibet, *F.l.isabellinus*, a race of the European Lynx, look unspotted when in their thick winter coat but show indistinct spots on the underparts in summer. The Pardel or Spanish Lynx *F.l.pardina* of the Balkans, the Caucasus and Czechoslovakia, the Guadalquivir Delta and the Cota Doñana reserve in Spain, which has a yellowish-red coat and white underparts, is clearly spotted in black, less heavily in the Pyrenees. Northern Eurasian Lynxes *F.l.lynx* look much like the North American race. The Northern Lynx and the Pardel Lynx can interbreed freely and in territories between the extreme forms there is a variety of levels of spotting, the spotting becoming less distinct from south to north.

Lynx generally live in tall coniferous forest with dense undergrowth but have adapted to other kinds of terrain. In south-west Spain and Portugal they live in much more open woodland and in the bush of the delta swamps. In Mongolia they have made their habitat among the rocky outcrops of the Altai. In Kashmir and Tibet, lynx have been seen on the harsh unforested slopes above the Upper Indus to an altitude of 10,000 ft (3000 m), but they rarely range very far above the tree line and their habitat does not normally extend beyond the taiga, although they have been reported in tundra areas.

Lynx can climb well and are good swimmers. They have acute vision and will stalk prey over long distances or wait patiently in ambush before making a final, typically felid bound from as close as possible. They are usually solitary animals and nocturnal hunters but cooperative hunting has occasionally been observed, with rabbits being driven towards a waiting ambush or a pair of lynxes stalking from both sides of joint prey.

In North America the Snowshoe Hare is the most important prey animal but lynx will also take small rodents, ducks and ground-dwelling birds, young deer, fish and larger cattle, if they can be ambushed from above in winter when

Female Lynx with kittens of the North American F.l.canadensis.

LYNX

Body length: *32–52 in (80–130 cm); tail 2–10 in (5–25 cm).*
Distribution: *Scandinavia to Siberia, Kashmir and Tibet; Alaska and Canada to northern United States; Spain and Portugal, possibly Sardinia, reintroduced Switzerland, eastern Europe.*

Lynx, here in Spanish form F.l.pardina.

they are at a disadvantage in the snow or when they have sustained injury. Elsewhere other hares, rodents, chamois, roe deer, even young wild boar, wildcats, badgers, foxes and dogs may all feature in their diet. In Sweden even reindeer have been taken. Home range varies considerably according to the type and availability of prey.

Both males and females seem to go beyond their territories in the mating season, which may be as early as January in Spain, later further north. In the Carpathians, according to the naturalist G.K. Werner, a male will claim a particular mating territory where females compete for his attention while other males roam the periphery for those females that are kept out by his mates. More commonly, perhaps, males seek out females. The breeding male makes a high-pitched wail which ends in a softer moan, the female answering with a vibrato siren-like howl. They also make a variety of hissing and chattering sounds.

A litter, usually of two or three kittens, is produced in the early summer and reared in a lair in a hollow tree, rock cleft or similar site. They may take meat at one month but are not fully weaned until five months old. When winter comes they have still not got their adult teeth or fully developed their claws so that, although they will have been accompanying their mother on hunting expeditions for some time, they are not yet able to survive alone. They stay with their mother until the next mating season, when they are usually chased away by suitors. Siblings often stay together for a time after separating from their mother. Females reach sexual maturity at 21 months, males at 33 months.

The Lynx still survives over much of Canada to the tree line but has been exterminated in the south-east. It ranges into northern Washington, northern Idaho and western Montana and, at times when the population in Canada peaks and territories are occupied, may be found in North Dakota and Minnesota. There are small populations in New England and Utah and sightings have been claimed in Oregon, Wyoming and Colorado.

Always rare in western Europe, the Lynx has not lived in Britain since the last Ice Age, but once ranged from Scandinavia right down to the Mediterranean. Today populations survive in Norway, Sweden, Finland and across the Baltic to Poland, in Spain and Portugal, Czechoslovakia, Greece, Romania and the USSR. It spreads across Siberia to Sakhalin, and south beyond the Himalayas and a few survive in northern Iraq.

Lynx were given protection in Romania and Czechoslovakia in the 1930s which not only stabilised but built up the population. More recently there have been reintroductions in Germany, Switzerland, Sweden, Austria, Italy and Yugoslavia and, with protection, the species is recolonizing.

In Norway it is still possible to hunt the Lynx, though the WWF is campaigning to have this banned. Across the frontier in Sweden a WWF program is in operation for the reintroduction of 300 pairs of Lynx.

Lynx have been reintroduced in Switzerland and have become established, now numbering 50–100 individuals in the Alps and Jura, but Swiss hunters claim that they compete for deer and other game and sheepowners complain of losses, so a radio-monitoring study is under way to provide evidence of their behavior. Hunting is still permitted in the United States and Canada where they continue to be exploited for their fur and for 'sport', so that they are disappearing from parts of their range. In Spain hunting is also permitted except in the Cota Doñana Nature Reserve in the Guadalquivir delta, where the extremely threatened Spanish form has its best chance of survival. All lynx are on CITES Appendix II except for the Pardel Lynx which was moved to Appendix I in October 1989.

The Lynx does not easily coexist with wolves. When wolves moved into parts of eastern Slovakia during World War Two the lynxes moved out. Lynx will also avoid an encounter with a Wolverine, a large member of the weasel family which shares the Lynx's climbing ability and large hairy feet adapted to snow, and roams the tundra overlapping with it. They may even give up a kill if a Wolverine approaches, although the other animal may be smaller. The same discretion is shared by bears who equally avoid pitting themselves against it, such is the strength and viciousness of this competitor.

Canadian Lynx and Snowshoe Hare cycles

In Canada the numbers of lynx appear to fluctuate dramatically, a phenomenon first brought to notice by the considerable variation in the number of furs collected by the Hudson's Bay Company, which ranged from as few as 2000 to as many as 36,000 in a single year. The peak years, which varied according to location, occurred, on average, slightly more frequently than every ten years. Overall statistics do not exist but an indication is given by a study made in central Alberta which showed a low population density of 2.3 per 40 sq miles (100 sq km) in the winter of 1966/67 rising to 10 five years later.

The cause of the falls in population seem to be food shortage, leading to a reduced pregnancy rate and the death from starvation of a great number of the kittens that are born. There is a direct link with a similar variation in the population of the main prey of the Lynx in Canada, the Snowshoe Hare *Lepus americanus*, which has a similar fluctuation caused by disease.

Lynx seem so habituated to catching this one species that many make no attempt to catch other prey, even though small rodents, for instance, may be plentiful.

Bobcat *Felis rufus*

This North American cat is like a slightly smaller version of the Lynx, but it occurs in a wider range of habitats. The coat is shorter, the legs thinner, the feet smaller and the ear tufts considerably reduced or even nonexistent, but the markings can be very similar to the more sandy and spotted ones of the Lynx and it has the same cheek whiskers.

The Bobcat is not so wary of people as the Lynx and settlement has not restricted its territory. When hunting it may come quite close to homes and farmsteads, sometimes preying on domestic animals and poultry, although its usual diet is rabbits, rodents, birds and the occasional deer, larger prey being taken in winter when fewer small mammals are available.

It can be found in British Columbia, Nova Scotia and from the Canadian border southward through the United States to Mexico, though it has been hunted out in heavily settled parts of several eastern and mid-western states. including the region of the southern Great Lakes, the upper Mississippi Valley and much of the valley of the Ohio River. Habitat ranges from dense forest to sage brushland and semi-desert, from bare mountain to subtropical swamp forest.

A more than ten-fold increase in the value of pelts led to around 92,000 being killed annually by the late 1970s. In central Mexico the local subspecies *F.r.escuinapae* became so rare that it was listed as endangered in 1980. Since then conservation concern has led to the ending of bounties for killing Bobcats. Hunting of a regulated number during a fixed season is still permitted in some states but it is now protected in eleven. In some areas where they were previously exterminated, such as New Jersey, they are now being re-established. They are listed in CITES Appendix II.

Although secretive and mainly nocturnal, the Bobcat can be a diurnal hunter in wintertime and will sunbathe during the day in places where it feels secure. Dens are made within a rockpile, cave or fissure, in a tree hollow, in dense thicket or among close fallen trees.

Mating is usually from February to June but has been recorded as early as November and as late as August. Usually silent, Bobcats sometimes make loud screams, hisses and other sounds during courtship. The den is lined with grass and moss for the birth of kittens after a gestation of about two months. Only one litter of one to six (usually three) is born each year, usually either in the spring or in late summer–early autumn. They are weaned after about two months and leave the den site to travel with their mother at from three to five months, beginning to hunt alone after another four months but probably not leaving their mother until her next mating.

BOBCAT
Body length: *26–42 in (65–105 cm)*;
tail 4–8 in (10–20 cm).
Distribution: *Southern Canada to Baja California and central Mexico.*

Bobcat

Females may be sexually mature at about one year but males do not mate until later.

Cougar *Felis concolor*

This is the largest species in the genus *Felis*, averaging at about the same size as the Leopard, although size varies greatly. The smallest occur in the tropics and the largest at the extreme north and south parts of their range. It once ranged from British Columbia to the Straits of Magellan and still has the widest distribution of any New World mammal — except for *Homo sapiens*.

The Cougar has several other common names: Puma (from the Quechuan name), Mountain Lion, Panther — and many more that were used in earlier times, such as Catamount, Painter and Mountain Devil. Spanish colonists in Argentina and Central America called it the American Lion (*leon americana*) and the Portuguese in Brazil the Red Jaguar (*onca vermilha*) and early North American settlers called it 'lion', but it has no link with the big cats. It has the felid purr and a catlike scream, though it differs from most of the genus *Felis* in that its eyes contract to a smaller circle instead of to a slit. Some taxonomists make it a subgenus on its own and others even make it a full genus as *Puma concolor*.

The Cougar has a long narrow body, carried on very strong legs, the rear ones longer and especially powerful, pushing up the rump. Tail and neck are also long and the head is small with a short face and small, rounded ears.

The fur comes in two main color phases, both variable. One ranges from bluish or slaty gray to silver gray, the other from buff through tawny reds to a rusty brown. Color is darkest on the back, lighter on the shoulders and flanks and whitish on the underparts. Throat, chin and upper lip are white, the sides of the muzzle and backs of the ears black, with the end of the tail darkening to blackish. Melanistic cougars sometimes appear. Fur tends to be short and bristly when near the equator, becoming longer and softer when further north or south.

Cougar cubs have a yellowish-tan ground color and are boldly patterned with rows of black spots and rings around the tail which gradually fade as they grow. In some tropical adults a fugitive pattern remains but usually it disappears completely.

Cougar can flourish in habitats ranging from montane coniferous forest to swamps and from sea level to heights of 15,000 ft (4500 m), anywhere that offers them sufficient cover and prey. They are mainly solitary except at mating, although female territories often overlap, and in turn are overlapped by males, though there are also many transients trying to find an unoccupied area. Individual animals can use territories as large as 250 sq miles (650 sq km), though usually much less, and there may be distinct summer and winter ranges as the Cougar follows its prey from summer to winter grazing grounds. Deer are the main prey together with smaller animals, including insects, according to local species.

There is no fixed breeding season. One to six, but usually three or four cubs, are born in a cave

or a den under a fallen tree. They may be weaned at three months, or they can suckle longer. They accompany their mother hunting and even after they have learned to kill stay with her for several months. Sometimes a family may stay together for a further year. They breed when about three years old.

Cougar have been extensively hunted since Europeans arrived in the Americas. Most north of Mexico were eliminated before 1900, except for some parts of the mountainous West, southern Texas and Florida. The Florida Panther *F.c.coryi*, which once ranged from eastern Texas to Florida and parts of South Carolina, is now one of the most endangered of all cats; it is estimated that only 20–50 individuals survive.

Cougars have the full feline vocal range, like that of the domestic cat, but even their purr is much louder.

Above *Cougar, also known as the Puma, Mountain Lion and several other names. Its young are heavily spotted.*
Below: *Florida Cougar* Felis concolor coryi, *designated official Florida State Mammal in 1982, is threatened with extinction, largely due to the huge increase in human population and given protection only comparatively recently.*

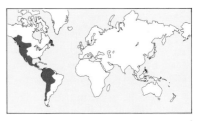

COUGAR
Body length: *3–6 ft (1–2 m); tail 21–37 in (53–92 cm).*
Distribution: *Southern Yukon and Nova Scotia, western United States to Mexico and south, though not now to the tip of the continent. Isolated populations in Texas and Florida; sparse in north-western South America.*

OCELOT
Body length: *22–39 in (55 cm–1 m); tail 12–18 in (30–45 cm).*
Distribution: *Arizona and Texas to northern Argentina.*

MARGAY
Body length: *18–27 in (45–70 cm); tail 13–20 in (33–51 cm).*
(F.w.pirrensis of Panama has a 4 in (10 cm) longer tail than most.)
Distribution: *Mexico to Paraguay and northern Argentina.*

Ocelot *Felis pardalis*

The Ocelot has been put in the subgenus *Leopardus* with the following four species which together are sometimes treated as a genus. It lives in a wide range of habitat from tropical rain forest to the chaparral of Texas, dry scrub to riverine marsh. Much smaller than the Cougar, it has a coat ranging from a pale tawny yellow to gray or rusty gray, white underneath, marked with a very variable pattern consisting of chains of darker blotches and spots, each outlined in black. There are black streaks on the face, bars on the legs and rings on the tail. All ocelots present a very handsome appearance and the wide appeal of their fur led to the killing of huge numbers for the fur trade.

They appear to live in couples, sharing a territory, but individuals usually hunt separately for birds, mammals from mice to small deer, fish and reptiles, including snakes. Sometimes observed in daytime, the Ocelot is more generally nocturnal, increasingly so in areas near human habitation. It swims, jumps and climbs well but lives mainly on the ground, though it may sleep out the heat of the day on a tree branch.

Mating takes place at night, with yowling like that of the domestic cat. Two kittens are born, or less frequently up to four.

Capture for the pet market, as well as for their fur has reduced populations further but some of the ten subspecies are under even greater danger from loss of habitat. Clearing Texan brush for agriculture endangers the remaining *F.p.albescens* in Texas. Illegal hunting still continues, despite controls and, coupled with deforestation in Central America, Amazonia and Ecuador, threatens those populations. All subspecies were moved to CITES Appendix I in October 1989.

Margay *Felis wiedi*

The Margay, sometimes spelled Marguey (which means tiger cat), is also known as the Long-tailed Spotted Cat. It looks like a smaller version of the Ocelot, and has very similar markings, but it is slimmer, with proportionally longer legs and tail. It is much more arboreal than the Ocelot, perhaps exclusively so, and is a nocturnal hunter, feeding on birds and small mammals.

Hunted for their fur and captured for the pet trade, they are now rare or extinct in many areas of their range which extends from Panama to Paraguay and northern Argentina. One specimen found in Texas in the first half of the nineteenth century may have been a lone wanderer, and any that survive in the forests of Mexico are extremely rare. The Central American subspecies *F.w.nicaraguae* and *F.w.salvinia* were placed on CITES Appendix I and in 1989 all of the possible ten subspecies were moved from Appendix II to join them.

Margay.

Tiger Cat.

TIGER CAT
Body length: *16–22 in (40–55 cm);
tail 10–16 in (25–40 cm).
Distribution: Costa Rica, Panama
and eastern South America across to
the Andes (but not the western coast)
south to Paraguay.*

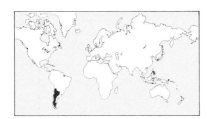

KODKOD
Body length: *15–19 in (38–48 cm);
tail 7–9 in (18–23 cm).
Distribution: Central to southern
Chile and parts of Argentina.*

GEOFFROY'S CAT
Body length: *18–28 in (45–70 cm);
tail 10–14 in (26–35 cm).
Distribution: Bolivian Andes to
Uruguay and far south of Brazil, and
southward through Argentina (not
Tierra del Fuego).*

Right *Geoffroy's Cat*

Tiger Cat *Felis tigrinus*

This smaller spotted cat, often mistaken for a margay, is also known as the Oncilla and as the Little Spotted Cat. Grouped with the Ocelot and Margay in the subgenus *Leopardus* and with a similarly attractive coat, it has been heavily hunted.

It is very variable in color, usually pale buff or rich ochre, with rows of dark spots which become black-bordered blotches on the upper parts. Underparts are lighter and more lightly spotted and the tail has ten or twelve rings and a black tip. A high proportion — about one-fifth — of Tiger Cats are melanistic.

Although found mainly in forests, the Tiger Cat seems to live less in the trees than the Margay, but little is known about it in the wild. Captive litters have consisted of one to two young who do not open their eyes until 17 days old and do not begin to take solid food until nearly five weeks. A male seemed very aggressive both to domestic cats and to a female Tiger Cat.

The Tiger Cat is found from Costa Rica to the Andes and south through eastern and central South America to northern Argentina. Heavily hunted both for its fur and for the pet trade, it is rare throughout its range. First the Costa Rican subspecies *F.t.oncilla* and now all the subspecies are on CITES Appendix I.

Geoffroy's Cat *Felis geoffroyi*

Another spotted South American cat, placed in the subgenus *Leopardus* by those who recognize it, Geoffroy's Cat lives in open woodland and scrub up to an altitude of 11,000 ft (3300 m) from the Andes in southern Bolivia across to Paraguay and south through Argentina. Its coat is very variable, from a bright ochre to silvery gray, always with fine black spotting and streaks on the cheeks, crown and between the shoulders. Spots at the base of the tail become rings towards

its tip. Spots on the upper parts of limbs may form rosettes or wavy lines. Melanistic individuals are not uncommon.

Geoffroy's Cat climbs and swims well; a nocturnal hunter, it may sleep during the day in trees. Prey include small mammals, birds, reptiles and fish.

Exploitation for its fur has made heavy inroads on this species but they are still more numerous than other cats in most of their range. Nevertheless they are listed in CITES Appendix II.

Kodkod *Felis guigna*

This is the smallest of the New World cats. Also known as the Guiña, and placed in the subgenus *Leopardus*, it is much like Geoffroy's Cat in appearance, but found on the other side of the Andes in central Chile and in some places around high Andean lakes of Argentina. Its two subspecies differ in size and pattern. *F.g.tigrillo* is larger, paler and has no spots on the feet and is found to the north of the range. *F.g.guigna*, found to the south, is smaller, more brightly colored and has spotted feet. Both types include melanistic individuals.

The Kodkod lives in forests and is a nocturnal hunter. Raids on domestic poultry houses have been reported but its main prey is probably small mammals. It has been described as an expert climber hunting in the trees but other observers say it is mainly terrestrial.

Mountain Cat *Felis jacobita*

This little-known South American cat, also called the Andean Highland Cat, is often placed in its own subgenus *Oreailurus*. It lives in the high arid and semi-arid zones of the Andes from southern Peru through Chile and Bolivia to northern Argentina, mainly in dry habitats around 1600 ft (500 m) but also up to an altitude of 16,000 ft (5000 m), and sometimes perhaps hunting

PAMPAS CAT
Body length: *22–28 in (56–70 cm);*
tail 11–13 in (29–32 cm).
Distribution: *Southern Peru,*
northern Chile, southern Bolivia,
northern Argentina.

MOUNTAIN CAT
Body length: *up to 29 in (72 cm);*
tail up to 18 in (45 cm).
Distribution: *Southern Peru,*
northern Chile, southern Bolivia,
northern Argentina.

JAGUARUNDI
Body length: *22–31 in (55–77 cm);*
tail 13–24 in (33–60 cm).
Distribution: *Southern Texas to*
northern Argentina.

Below *Jaguarundi*

above the snow line. Rare throughout its range, little is known about it but it is believed to hunt small mammals such as chinchillas and the similar but larger viscachas. Its fine, soft coat is about 1½ in (4 cm) long on the back and shades from a silvery gray above to white on the underparts. The back is marked with brown or orangey stripes and spots giving way to black spots below with brown rings around the bushy tail, which has a white tip.

It has been declared endangered and is protected in Peru and listed on CITES Appendix I.

Pampas Cat *Felis colocolo*

This species is sometimes placed in a subgenus *Lynchailurus*. It is known in Argentina as Gato Pajero ('grass cat'), with the race there once considered a separate species as *F.pajeros*, but, despite its names, the Pampas Cat is not limited to grassy plains. Its range also extends to the mountains of Ecuador and Peru across to central Brazil and south through Chile and Argentina to Patagonia where it lives on the edges of rain forests as well as among the high grasses. It is found throughout the Peruvian Andes and appears to be quite common even in heavily settled parts of Chile, though it is said to be aggressive and difficult, if not impossible, to tame.

Ground color of the fur ranges from creamy yellow through brown to silvery gray with oblique stripes across the face and body.

A mainly terrestrial, nocturnal hunter, prey includes small mammals, such as guinea pigs, and ground birds, especially tinamous. It may also raid domestic fowl sheds.

Jaguarundi *Felis yagouarundi*

The adult Jaguarundi does not look much like any other of the cat family and from its appearance might quite reasonably be thought a closer relative of the weasels, polecats and otters —

indeed, its German name is Weasel Cat (*Weisel Katze*). It has a very long slender body on very short legs with a small flattened head, short round ears and a long tail. Its fur is a uniform color all over but may be either a dark brownish gray or a chestnut red. These are not geographical races, and kittens of both types can occur in the same litter. The kittens look much more typically feline than their parents.

Jaguarundi were, until recently, found from southern Arizona and the valley of the Rio Grande in Texas, through Central America to Paraguay and northern Argentina. They live mainly in dense lowland forest and bush, such as the Texas chaparral, but not up in the mountains. Jaguarundi fur has no market value and it has not been hunted commercially, but all the subspecies of the southern United States and Central America are now listed on CITES Appendix I, since it would be difficult to identify the almost indistinguishable subspecies in trade.

Only a few individuals are thought to survive in Texas and none in Arizona, but it is possible that an attempt to introduce them in Florida may have been successful.

Although an agile climber, it is mainly a ground hunter for birds and small mammals from mice and guinea pigs to small fawns. It sleeps through the middle of the day but is more often seen in daytime than other cats. Jaguarundi appear to be solitary animals in Mexico but live as pairs in Paraguay. A litter may be of one to four kittens.

Lion *Panthera leo*

Some taxonomists place lions in a subgenus *Leo* or even a genus of its own *Leo leo*, while other authorities consider the genus *Panthera* invalid and place the whole genus within *Felis*. The appearance of lions is so distinctive that they are unlikely to be confused with any of the other cats. They are large, muscular and imposing but when they roll on their backs or lick a paw their affinity with the domestic cat is easy to see.

The lion's shortish coat may range from a light buff, touched with silvery gray, to a dark orange brown; undersides are lighter, whitish in females. The backs of the ears are marked with black and there is a black or dark brown tuft at the end of the tail. Cubs are spotted and spots sometimes persist, especially on the underparts of young adults. White lions also occur. Only the males, who are generally larger, have manes. The mane begins to grow at about 18 months old and takes five or more years to develop fully. It varies regionally from a neck mane and a short facial surround to hair up to 10 in (25 cm) long on the top of the head, cheeks, neck, shoulders and breast, sometimes continued on the elbows and belly. Mane color also varies from yellow to black but everywhere in old age it becomes darker from back to front. Asiatic Lions are usually smaller than the African subspecies.

The lion is the only wild feline to live in social groups with a shared territory — the pride — and regularly to hunt on a cooperative basis. Lions may hunt by day or night but they rarely exert themselves unnecessarily. Although adults may occasionally become frolicsome, splashing about in pools after a cooling rainstorm, they are usually active for only about four hours a day, resting through the heat of the day in shade, sometimes up trees. Prey are mainly mid- to large-size mammals, especially antelopes in Africa, deer in the Gir Forest, where domestic cattle also provide a significant proportion of their diet. However they will sometimes take hippos, crocodiles and snakes and are not averse to scavenging other predators' kills.

Cubs are born in litters of one to four (usually two to three) and open their eyes at six to nine days (although zoo records include cubs born with their eyes open or opening much earlier). They are weaned at six months and should be competent hunters by two years. Although sexually mature earlier, a lioness will not usually breed until about two and a half and lions are not fully adult until about four.

LION
Body length: *up to 10 ft (3 m); tail up to 42 in (1.05 m).*
Distribution: *East and Central Africa to the Kalahari and the Gir Forest in India.*

Above *A white and a normal lion cub shortly after rejoining their pride.*
Left *Lion and lioness.*
Right *A lion leaps a stream in the Masai Mara Game Reserve.*

Lions use a loud roar, which can carry over 5 miles (8 km), as one way to mark and claim territory. A deep growl is a more intimate form of contact, not necessarily aggressive although it is also used in warning — a coughing sound usually preceding an attack. A softer growl is used by females to communicate with cubs who will greet her with a high whimper. Lions purr when pleased, but because of the different development of the hyoid bone this is not on both inward and outward breaths as in the smaller cats.

Once the most widely distributed of terrestrial mammals the lion now survives only in Africa and in one forest in India. The African Lion *P.l. leo* has been exterminated in north, south (except for Kruger National Park) and much of west Africa; even in East and Central Africa it is now rare outside reserves. Despite protection in most countries where it occurs it is still hunted in some places. It is listed on CITES Appendix II. The Asiatic Lion *P.l. persica* is carefully managed in the Gir Forest in Gujarat. An attempt to found another colony at Chandrabhaga in Uttar Pradesh failed but there are still plans to re-establish the lion elsewhere in India, perhaps in Rajasthan. The African species is sometimes divided into up to seven subspecies of which the nominate form *P.l.leo* is used for the now extinct Barbary Lion of North Africa. The Cape Lion *P.l.melanochaita* of the far south is also extinct.

Lions of the Gir Forest

At the turn of the century Lord Curzon, then Viceroy of India, declined an invitation to a lion shoot in the Gir when he heard that only a dozen were left and suggested that the animal should be protected. The Nawab of Junagadh imposed a ban on shooting and in 1900 the lion became a protected animal in the Gir. In the confusion after Partition in 1947 land-hungry peasants invaded the area with their cattle. Competition for grazing so reduced the deer population that lions increasingly killed cattle, becoming more diurnal in their hunting, but they were frequently driven from the kills and the meat taken.

In 1966 part of the forest was set aside as the Gir Lion Sanctuary but three years later the population was only 177 and falling. Gujarat State then turned a much wider area into a protected reserve and began to relocate villagers and their flocks outside the area. Vegetation has now recovered, the deer are thriving and lion numbers have increased to 230. This seems to be about the maximum population that the area can support. Over the years some lions needing veterinary care and some captured cubs have been removed to Sakkarbagh Zoo where there is a breeding stock of pure Asian lions, unhybridized with the African subspecies. Salem and Bihar, a Gir lion and lioness produced the first four pure Gir cubs born outside India in 1975 in East Berlin.

A pride of lions in Gir National Park, India.
Far left *A lioness lead her cubs off to a kill.*

LEOPARD
Body length: 3 ft–6 ft 4 in (91-190 cm); tail 23-43 in (58-110 cm). Distribution: *Africa through the Middle East to Malaysia, Korea and Siberia.*

Top *Leopard of the Chinese race.*
Above *Black leopard. In the melanistic form the spotted pattern can still be seen in certain lights or on paler areas of the coat.*
Below *Leopard in Sri Lanka.*

Leopard *Panthera pardus*

The Leopard, or Panther as it is sometimes called, is an elegant, long-bodied cat with a proportionally smaller head, sturdy legs of medium length and a long tail, more sinuous in its movements than the heavier-bodied lion and tiger. As with other *Panthera*, some taxonomists place it in a subgenus of its own, while others include it under *Felis*.

The close, soft coat of the Leopard is short and sleek in tropical areas, longer in colder climates. The ground color varies from straw or a grayish yellow through to a chestnut brown, with the underside from chin to belly and the inside legs paling to cream or white. The upper parts are patterned with rosettes formed from spots, sometimes with a darkened center, and with solid black spots on head, neck and underside which on the throat and breast may merge as stripes and on the tail as rings. A white spot on the back of the ears grows larger and gains color with age. Cubs are grayer, with rosettes appearing solid and more closely patterned. Melanistic leopards are fairly common and can occur in the same litter as normal coats. They still carry the rosette pattern which is visible in certain lights. They are more frequently found in wet habitats, especially in parts of India and south-east Asia.

Leopards are found in a wide range of habitat, from desert to savanna and forest. Once found through most of Africa and through the Middle East to Java, they are still fairly common in some parts of central and east Africa and there are scattered populations in west Africa and many parts of Asia. In India it often seems to prefer to live near villages where it preys on dogs, goats, calves and chickens. Depredations on domestic stock may be outweighed by their control of baboons, cave rats and other animals that destroy crops. Other prey includes almost anything from antelopes to rodents, hares, frogs and even dung beetles. Around the Kariba Lake of Zambia and Zimbabwe they catch fish. They are strong swimmers and climb well, often carrying carcasses 20 ft (6 m) up into a tree.

The leopard can be a very secretive animal and is a stealthy hunter. As an Indian hunter quoted by zoologist C.A.W. Guggisberg metaphorically remarked, 'Where the leopard walks, he brushes out his tracks with his tail!' Where itself hunted, it is nocturnal and seldom seen but in reserves it has often become used to vehicles and may be seen hunting in daylight.

Although usually solitary, there have been reports of males staying with mates and even helping to rear cubs, and groups of up to six have occasionally been seen.

Up to six cubs (but usually three) are born in a cave, hollow tree or thicket. They are weaned at three months, but stay with their mother until 18 months or two years old and reach sexual maturity and full size at two and a half to three years old.

Leopards have a call, described as 'grunt-ha! grunt-ha!' by naturalist C.T. Astley Maberly, and a variety of other grunts, coughs and a sound like someone sawing wood, but they are usually silent.

Leopards have been heavily hunted for their fur, and loss of habitat and natural prey has increased predation on stock (and sometimes attacks on people) leading to further killings. They are now protected through most of their range and on CITES Appendix I, but a number of subspecies are now very rare in some or all areas: *P.p.orientalis* (southern Siberia, Manchuria, Korea),*P.p.nimr* (Arabia, Jordan, Israel), *P.p.jarvisi* (Sinai), *P.p.tulliana* (Asia Minor), *P.p.panther* (north-western Africa).

All leopards south of Cameroun, the Central African Republic and the Sudan are considered threatened and in those countries and northwards it is endangered.

Snow Leopard *Panthera uncia*

Again sometimes singled out as a separate genus, *Uncia*, or alternatively included within the genus *Felis*, the Snow Leopard is also called the Ounce. It has a long low body and smallish head. Its thick, long coat of pale gray to gray-brown fur sometimes has a creamy tinge, the underparts white and marked overall with large irregular rings or rosettes that may merge to form a black streak down the middle of the back.

The Snow Leopard inhabits a great arc of high Asia from Mongolia through China, USSR, Afghanistan, Pakistan, India, Nepal and Bhutan from the Hindu Kush to the west of Sichuan and the Altai Mountains, and lives right up to the snow line. It hunts through rocky grasslands between the tree line and the snow line, sometimes following prey down into the forests below at seasonal migration. Goats, sheep, deer, boar and pikas are sometimes supplemented by domestic livestock as its habitat has been increasingly exploited for pasture, in turn leading to hunting by villagers to prevent their losses. However, the high price paid for its fur has been the main threat to its survival. It is often active during daylight, especially very early and very late. Generally considered solitary, except when mating or rearing a family, it does not appear to be unsociable and it has been suggested that some pairs may hunt cooperatively, one chasing prey to where the other waits in ambush.

A litter of one to five (usually two or three) is born, usually April to June, in a rock shelter which the mother lines with her fur. Weaning begins at two months and by three months cubs begin to follow their mother. They hunt with her for at least their first winter, reaching maturity at two years old.

The Snow Leopard does not roar; it lacks the pad of fibro-elastic tissue which forms part of the vocal folds of the other big cats — one reason why it is sometimes given a genus of its own instead of being placed in *Panthera*.

Despite being protected through most of their range Snow Leopards are still illegally trapped and hunted.

They are on CITES Appendix I.

Below *Snow Leopard*   **Above** *Chinese Leopard*

SNOW LEOPARD
Body length: *3ft 3 in–4 ft 3 in (100–130 cm); tail 32–39 in (80–100 cm).*
Distribution: *High mountains of Central Asia.*

Tiger *Panthera tigris*

Like the other *Panthera*, the tiger is sometimes placed in a subgenus of its own or with all cats in the genus *Felis*. The Tiger includes the largest of all cats, its Siberian subspecies *P.t.altaica*. There is considerable variation among the different Tiger types, the smallest, until it became extinct in the 1970s, was *P.t.balica* of Bali.

Tigers are comparatively long-bodied and very solidly built, the belly being more level with and carried closer to the ground than in the lion, the tail only about half the head and body length. Although they have the weight and power of the lion combined with much greater agility, they seem more devious animals which prefer to avoid any challenging confrontation.

Fur is longer in colder climates and in Siberia and Manchuria there is thick underfur in winter. Males usually develop long cheek fur which forms

5000. The Caspian Tiger *P.t.virgata* and Balinese Tiger were probably already extinct; only five Javan Tiger *P.t.sondaica* survived — its habitat has been destroyed and it too is now extinct; a few Chinese Tiger *P.t.amoyensis* remained only in the Yangtze Valley, most exterminated on government orders as enemies of 'agricultural and pastoral progress'. The Siberian Tiger was down to about 300 in the USSR and northern China, the Sumatran Tiger *P.t.sumatrae* then stood at 500–1000 but was declining rapidly. The Indochinese *P.t.corbetti*, once ranging from Burma to the China Sea, was down to about 2000 and the Bengal Tiger *P.t.tigris*, already killed off in Pakistan early in this century, numbered less than 2000 in India and a little over half that number in the border states from Nepal through to Burma. It was then that the Indian Government initiated Project Tiger to save its own tigers from extinction, but the whole species must still

TIGER
Body length: *4ft 6 in–9 ft (140–280 cm); tail 24–38 in (60–95 cm).*
Distribution: *South-eastern Siberia to Sumatra, India and the Caucasus.*

a distinct ruff. Coat color varies from orange to a reddish ochre, in one strain even white, paling to white on the throat, belly and inside of the legs. It is overlaid with black or dark brown stripes, mainly vertical modifying to horizontal on the lower legs. Stripes are frequently very broken, often forming whorls on the cheeks and by the eyes. They are more dispersed on the forelegs and front of the body. There are bold white flashes, ringed with black, on the backs of the ears and a white area around each eye.

Tiger habitat ranges from mangrove swamp and tropical forest to savanna and rocky mountainside. Tigers are found from India to Siberia and south to the Malayan Archipelago but their distribution is frequently interrupted. Many areas, such as the Tibetan plateau, were never home to tigers, and hunting for sport, for their skins, to prevent depredations on livestock or because people feared them has reduced distribution further and cut populations drastically.

In 1972 it was estimated (although these figures are guesses without firm scientific base) that the entire Asian tiger population was down to about

be considered in danger. Although tigers are bred successfully in zoos, in the wild they are likely to survive only in reserves and parks, despite now being protected throughout their range. All tigers have been on CITES I since 1987.

Tigers are mainly nocturnal, hunting medium to large mammals. They will hunt by day in places like the jungles of Malaya, shaded from direct sun, rarely troubled by people and with their favourite prey, wild pig, readily available. Pig are popular through much of their range, together with deer and antelopes, but they will also take a wide range of animals from fish and turtles to young elephants. Older animals will take domestic livestock which are easier prey, and in some areas man-eaters have been a problem. A tiger will cover a kill with grass or other litter and return to it for further meals over several days.

Generally tigers are thought to be solitary hunters but they are not unsociable. One who has made a kill may allow others to share it. There have been many reports of tigers hunting in pairs and in Manchuria, Korea and India

Above *A captive tiger at London Zoo.*

Opposite *Tiger in the Kanha Tiger Reserve of Madhya Pradesh, India.*

Above *Nineteenth-century Japanese painting of a tiger by Ohashi Suiseki.*
Below *White Bengal Tiger in Florida Zoo.*

CLOUDED LEOPARD
Body length: *24–39 in (60 cm–1 m)*
tail 22–36 in (55–90 cm).
Distribution: *Nepal to southern*
China and Taiwan, through
Malaysia to Indonesia and Borneo.

Clouded Leopard.

families and larger groups have been reported together.

Young are born in a cave, dense vegetation or a similar den, in litters of from one to six (usually two or three). Weaned at six months, they stay with their mother until two or more years old, though only about half survive that long.

Clouded Leopard *Neofelis nebulosa*

Most authorities place the Clouded Leopard in a genus on its own, though Paul Leyhausen also puts the Tiger into *Neofelis*. It is about the size of a small leopard but not closely related and looks quite different. Long bodied and short limbed with broad, hard-padded paws, it has a very long tail and a relatively large head with the largest canine teeth of any living cat.

The coat ranges from a pale yellowish brown to a gray earth brown. Its 'cloud' pattern, reminiscent of that of the Marbled Cat, consists of large and small blotches, darker than the ground color and edged with black, with thicker edging towards the rear. These patches become smaller dark solid blotches on the limbs, streaks on the sides of the head and irregular spots over the head and elongated along the back, joining to ring the end of the tail.

The Clouded Leopard lives in forested country from the Himalayas across Assam and southern China to Taiwan and south through the Malay Peninsula to Borneo. It climbs well and spends the day in trees and hunts, mainly at night and on the ground, for birds, monkeys, goats, pigs and deer, though often dropping on them from a tree.

Kittens, born in litters of two to four, are at first a uniform yellowish gray. They are weaned by five months, and by six have acquired the adult patterning.

Clouded Leopards are now protected over most of their range but are threatened by loss of habitat, especially in Thailand and Malaysia, and were until recently hunted for their skins. They are listed on CITES Appendix I.

Jaguar *Panthera onca*

The only New World member of *Panthera* and the largest of the American cats, the Jaguar's big bones, heavy chest and well-muscled forelegs make this cat heavier and more powerful than the Cougar or the Old World Leopard, which looks somewhat similar. The coat of rather bristly fur ranges from yellow to tawny with whitish underparts. It is spotted in dark brown or black on the head and neck, blotched on the limbs and patterned elsewhere with rosettes with further spots within them, sometimes merging to form a solid line along the spine and making rings on the tail. Melanistic animals are frequent and can occur in the same litter as spotted cubs.

As recently as the beginning of this century Jaguars ranged from southern California and Arizona as far south as the Rio Negro in Argentina. Its distribution is defined more by the presence of suitable prey than by climate; it could be found from the mangrove swamps of the Mexican west coast and the steaming Amazon jungle to the near-desert of Central Mexico, the pampas of Argentina and the high Andes of Peru. It has now been exterminated in the United States, through most of Mexico, much of Central America and at the other end of its range from Uruguay and all but the far north of Argentina.

The spread of ranching in South America offered domestic cattle as an easy prey and consequently jaguar were widely hunted to reduce their depredations and for sport. However, it was the demand for its fur that led to 15,000 jaguars being killed each year in the Amazonian region of Brazil alone during the 1960s. It is now considered endangered and on CITES Appendix I.

The Jaguar is usually a solitary hunter, although small prides have been reported in remote areas. It appears to be gregarious only at breeding times, when groups of eight or more have been seen. In areas where it has been hunted by man it is almost exclusively nocturnal, lying up by day, sometimes making its den in the ruins of the ancient civilizations of Central and South America.

Prey varies according to terrain. It includes deer, tapirs and the pig-like peccaries. Jaguar are

JAGUAR
Body length: *3 ft 3 in-6 ft (100-180 cm); tail 18-30 in (45-75 cm).*
Distribution: *Mexico to northern Argentina.*

Jaguar cubs.

good swimmers and find an easy prey in capybara, which live on river banks, and they also fish. They climb well and take monkeys and other tree-living animals, though their weight prevents their climbing to higher branches where monkeys and sloths flee to keep out of reach.

Cubs with a long woolly coat are born in litters of one to four and stay with their mother for about two years, reaching maturity at three or four years old.

Cheetah *Acinonyx jubatus*

The Cheetah also warrants a genus on its own. It is a large, slim, long-legged cat with a short and comparatively small head with short ears. The paws are rather narrow, more like those of dogs than most of the cats, and the claws are blunt, only slightly curved and not fully retractile. The coat is tawny on the back, fading to white on the belly and chin. The fur on the neck and shoulders is thicker than elsewhere and forms an incipient mane which is barely noticeable in adults but can be clearly seen in cubs. Most of the body is patterned with spots, sometimes very small ones set between larger ones, which merge into rings at the end of the tail which has a bushy white tip. The face has a black stripe from the inner corner of each eye down to the edge of the mouth, where it broadens into a blob. The back of the ears is black tipped with white. In a small area of Zimbabwe a variant form, the King Cheetah, once classed as a separate species *A.rex*, has spots joining up to form stripes and angles.

Cheetah used to be found from Morocco south through Africa and across to India wherever there was suitable open country, ranging from semi-desert to open bush, but it has been hunted for its fur and for its depredations on livestock, captured to be trained for use as a hunting leopard. It is now extinct in most of the northern parts of its range.

In Asia it is now found only in reserves in Iran and possibly in the adjoining USSR. In Africa a few may still survive in Libya but in West Africa it has largely disappeared and in the East it survives only in reserves and parks. The main population is now in southern Africa and especially in Namibia and Zimbabwe.

It usually hunts in the cool of evening, early morning or by moonlight. Prey is mainly gazelles, impala and other small antelopes (black buck and axis deer in Asia), hares, ostriches and guineafowl, which it chases with bursts of speed which can reach 60 mph (100 kph) over short distances. Hunting in groups, cheetahs will also bring down zebra and wildebeest. More frequently they hunt alone or in pairs but small family groups are often seen, usually three or four related males or a female with cubs.

Cubs are born in litters of two to four, hidden in thick scrub or dense grass. They soon find their feet. Weaned at about three months in the wild, they have already been following their mother since about six weeks and families move frequently; nevertheless cub losses seem to be very high. Juveniles become independent from

Jaguar in the tropical forest of South America.

about 18 months and are sexually mature by two years old.

Cheetahs are fairly vocal, with a whole series of 'prrps' and 'peeps' for communicating with cubs, a loud yowl that can be heard a mile (2 km) away, and a steady feline purr.

As well as being hunted out, the Cheetah seems much less adaptable than the Leopard to human disruption, although it has shown itself playful and friendly when tamed, and has been widely used for hunting other animals in former times. The Asiatic subspecies *A.j.venaticus* (= hunting) is particularly endangered but the whole species is included on CITES Appendix I.

CHEETAH
Body length: *3 ft 3 in–5 ft (100–150 cm); tail 24–36 in (60–90 cm).*
Distribution: *Libya, Baluchistan, Iran, east and southern Africa.*

Top right *A cub still in juvenile coat;* **below right** *an adult;* **below** *a normally coated cheetah with the variant form known as the King Cheetah (left).*

DOMESTIC VARIETIES

THE CAT FANCY

Cat fanciers, those who breed and show cats, come from all walks of life, but share a love of beautiful felines bred to exacting official standards. For centuries cats were kept as pets or for controlling rats and mice in kitchen, cellar and barn. Inevitably they multiplied and unwanted kittens were destroyed. Selection began when people decided to keep one or two, choosing those they considered to be the most attractive, or to have the best potential as hunters.

In the mid-nineteenth century, people began to take a pride in owning beautiful and unusual pets, and to enter them into friendly competition with other owners. Clubs were formed and basic standards for points of perfection were drafted to determine the ideal conformation of each type. Fanciers began to take special care in the mating of their cats and the concept of breeds came into existence. Written pedigrees became fashionable as a means of authenticating breeding stock and, long before the science of genetics embraced cat breeds, colors and patterns, fanciers realized the value of the detailed pedigree in predicting the result of certain matings; 'pedigreed' became synonymous with the term 'pure bred'. Without the enthusiasm of those fanciers there would be fewer pedigreed breeds, no new breeds and no cat shows.

A pedigree is a written record of ancestry. Every cat *could* have a pedigree if sufficient of its ancestry is known, but to be officially acknowledged by cat fanciers, the ancestry must be acceptable to the appropriate feline association and the forebears must have been correctly registered beforehand. Lineage is paramount once a breed is accepted by a registering body.

Early cat shows

The first cat show recorded was at St Giles Fair, Winchester, England, in the year 1598, but it could have borne little resemblance to the cat shows of today. The benched show, with cats exhibited in individual cages, began with a splendid event staged by Mr Harrison Weir on July 13th 1871 at the Crystal Palace, Paxton's magnificent glass hall built for the Great Exhibition of 1851 which had been re-erected in Sydenham, south London. It was a memorable affair with about 160 cats entered for competition and display. Its success produced a 'cat fever'; the showing of pedigreed cats became the vogue. In 1873 a show was held at the Alexandra Palace, in north London, and another in Birmingham. The number of entries rose and an 1875 show in Edinburgh drew 560 exhibits. A Crystal Palace show that same year had 325 exhibition pens and included a special class for Wild or Hybrid between Wild and Domestic Cats which was won by an ocelot.

The early cat shows attracted mainly short-coated cats, entered in classes divided by color; subsequently various imported cats began to make their mark. British cats were also exported to form the bases for breeding in other countries and, in 1895, the first properly benched American cat show was staged in New York's Madison Square Gardens. This was soon followed by many other shows spread across several states. The love of pedigreed cats and competition among owners and breeders to produce fine examples has spread throughout the world. Enthusiasts have formed clubs and established regulatory bodies which lay down rules for competitive shows and the recognition of new breeds and varieties.

Cat organizations

In Britain, the National Cat Club was formed in 1887 with Harrison Weir as its first President. The club instituted a stud book to record full details of winning cats' ancestries and set up a system for the official registration of pedigreed cats. Various clubs were formed throughout the British Isles and most agreed to run their shows under rules laid down by the National Cat Club.

In 1898 another body, the Cat Club, was created and the cat fancy split its loyalties until 1910, when a special meeting of delegates from 19 clubs met in Westminster, London, and resolved to form a new official registering body to be called the Governing Council of the Cat Fancy (GCCF). This organization still exists today. It is run by an executive committee and more than 60 affiliated area and breed clubs send their delegates to Council meetings.

For many years the GCCF remained the sole body for the registration of cats and the licensing of cat shows in Britain. Then, in 1983, a group of breeders, judges and show organizers resolved to form an alternative body called the Cat Association of Britain (CA) run entirely by its members which now operates in parallel with the older organization.

Elsewhere developments have been more diverse. In North America cat fanciers have the

Previous pages *Seal Point Balinese kittens.*
Above right *Frances Simpson, an important figure in the Cat Fancy at the turn of the century, judging at the Richmond Cat Show in 1901.*
Below *Harrison Weir with the Persian kitten winner of the First Prize trophy at the first Crystal Palace Show.*

choice of nine registering bodies (full details of which, along with those of other countries, are listed on pages 327-8). The oldest American registry for cats is the American Cat Association (ACA), started in 1899. Today it is a fairly small organization but it is interesting to note that one of the earliest ACA clubs was the Lady Beresford Cat Club which honored an early influential English breeder of long-haired cats.

The Cat Fanciers' Association (CFA) is the world's largest registry of pedigreed cats and is a body governed by a board of directors. There are CFA shows being held somewhere in the United States almost every weekend throughout the year and the body has clubs in Canada, Japan, France, Switzerland and Brazil, with applications for clubs from many countries throughout the cat-loving world. The CFA publishes an impressively large and immaculately produced annual yearbook, crammed with information, advertisements, articles and photographs, many in full color. Cats are pictured from all over the world.

In Europe many countries have at least two registering bodies, of which one is generally affiliated to the Fédération Internationale Féline (FIFe), an exceptionally well-organized incorporated and chartered body, established in 1949, which unites some 150,000 fanciers. FIFe, which claims to be the largest feline organization in the world, has affiliates in many countries, including some outside Europe. It is managed by an executive board, one member from each member country, each elected to serve for a term of three years, and has three commissions: the judges' commission, responsible for the study of new breeds and their standards, the modification of existing standards for recognized breeds and the regulation of the stud book; the show commission, responsible for the efficient management of licensed shows and the application of show rules and regulations; and the disciplinary commission which listens to complaints and deals with problems from member countries and arbitrates in disputes.

There are several registering bodies in Australia and New Zealand, some based on GCCF rules, as is the sole body in the Republic of South Africa.

Modern cat shows

Cat shows put cats in competition to determine the best example of each breed or variety. They educate the public about cat breeds, types and colors and help develop a greater awareness of the needs of and best care for all cats. Show hall layouts and methods of judging and benching vary according to the organization licensing them.

Shows may be all-breed competitions or specialist shows for Longhairs, Shorthairs or specific breeds or varieties. Some small shows are really social gatherings without Championship status and some shows are designed for the assessment and authentication of new breeds, new color varieties or coat types within an existing breed. Most cat shows also have sections for non-pedigree or part-pedigree pet cats.

In Britain shows are normally one-day affairs; in Europe and the United States two-day shows are common. Some American shows, and those of the CA in Britain, consist of several 'rings', each of which is a small complete show within the main show. A qualified judge presides over each ring and, at some, stewards bring cats to him or her for appraisal before an audience; at others the owners present their cats for evaluation. Each exhibit is first judged in its breed or variety class, then for Best of Breed and then for Best Cat, Best Kitten, Best Neuter, Best Pet and finally for Best Exhibit. Exhibitors can often join the audience to watch their entries being thoroughly assessed and discussed by the judge.

All GCCF-licensed shows in Britain, including the largest in the world held annually in London by the National Cat Club, the club which started it all in 1887, are staged under GCCF rules. Well over 2000 cats, kittens, neuters and non-pedigree pets take part each year in the NCC show. Each is judged in one 'open' breed or variety class and a miscellany of specialist and club classes for which it may be entered. Despite the size and prestige of the show, there is no climax to the one-day event such as a Best Exhibit or Supreme Winner. The hall is cleared of exhibitors before the judging is carried out in anonymity, with each cat sitting in its consecutively numbered pen with a plain white blanket, white toilet tray and water bowl, and no decoration of any kind which could identify the owner.

The GCCF also holds one special show each season billed as the 'Supreme'. It is unlike any other cat show in the world as the participants must qualify by winning open breed classes at previous shows. The climax comes with the

Above *The National Cat Club badge designed by Louis Wain.*
Below left *The poster for an early American cat show.*

awarding of Supreme rosettes to the best cat, kitten and neuter in the pedigree section, and the best non-pedigree kitten and neuter.

Recently CFA has instituted a very prestigious National Invitational Show which is the culmination of Regional Qualifying shows held in October of each year at which cats compete to qualify for the National Invitational. At the National Invitational, a panel of judges evaluate the exhibits with overall results being tabulated by computer. The Best Cat, Kitten and altered (neutered) (Premiership) exhibits are announced along with runners-up and Best of Breed or variety. Substantial cash prizes plus prestige accrue to the winners.

Exhibitors in Britain, Australia and New Zealand find their satisfaction in the pleasure of competition and the cups and certificates that acknowledge the excellence of their cats. The National Shows in Australia and New Zealand are outstanding major feline events with large entry and great public and civic interest.

In most European shows, ring judging is common but the rings are isolated from the main exhibition hall and judges work in private, with the exhibits brought to them by skilled stewards.

In most open-ring shows, cats may accrue either points or certificates to achieve titles on one day. This reduces the need for cats to attend a great number of shows, imposing less stress on the cats and reducing the risk of picking up infections. In closed-ring shows and in those where the cat has only one 'open' or breed class, cats must attend several shows to achieve championship titles.

Whatever the mode of judging, the criteria are the same. Each judge must be an expert in the breed or variety in which he or she officiates. In most associations judges follow rigorous training procedures and sit demanding examinations in order to qualify. American bodies such as CFA, ACFA and TICA, the worldwide FIFe and Britain's CA insist that judges achieve a very high standard of pass marks, as well as being noted breeders and exhibitors of cats themselves. GCCF judges do not have to qualify academically, but breeders of long standing, who have stewarded for leading judges, apply to their breed clubs for nomination to the official judging lists.

Entering a cat show

A cat must be registered with the relevant registration body prior to showing. If not bred by the exhibitor it must be officially transferred to his or her ownership before entry. Breeders are best qualified to guide a novice through the intricacies of entering their first show, not only with the paperwork but with the preparation and grooming necessary for a particular breed or variety.

Cats must become accustomed to being benched in show pens (cages), to being handled by strangers and to the noise and attention of the many visitors. Keeping them for periods in a cage at home, encouraging visitors to handle them and even playing noisy tapes are some of

Top *At this ring-judged show the public can watch as judges work at six separate judging tables, each backed by a set of temporary pens to which cats are brought.*
Above left *Graham Meadows 'vetting in'. At British shows, and those run on similar lines, all entries must pass a medical check.*
Above right *Angela Sayer-Rixon judging at a ring-judge show.*
Left *At GCCF type shows exhibitors and public leave the hall during open-class judging and the judges move along the benches of pens which must be unadorned.*
Opposite *A group of Champions.*

the methods exhibitors use to achieve this. There must also be rigorous grooming to ensure the coat looks its best; all breeders have their own ways of doing this without actually modifying the cat's appearance so much that it falls into the area of 'intent to deceive' — that is, makes the animal appear to be other than it really is through use of dyes, powders, plucking of undesirable spots of white, etc.

Applications for entry should be made well before the show. Sometimes entries are required three months in advance to give sufficient time to process the entries and organize the judging sequences. It also takes time to get a cat into peak condition with the coat at its optimum quality, texture and sheen. Cats should be kept in the best possible conditions at all times, but with a show cat, a little extra care can make the difference between winning and losing.

FELINE GENETICS

Every living thing that reproduces sexually, with components from two parents rather than dividing or budding to produce complete new individuals, can inherit characteristics from both, including features which may not be apparent in the parent but that nonetheless have been passed on to them as possibilities from previous generations. These characteristics are determined by genes, control mechanisms carried rather like beads on two strings along the rod-like bodies, called chromosomes, of which the cat has 38 in every cell of its body. The chromosomes are arranged in 19 pairs, sometimes both halves of a pair carrying identical genes, sometimes not.

In normal cell division (*mitosis*), which creates new cells for growth, the full set of genes is replicated for each new cell. A rare mistake in the process, or the effects of radiation, can bring about minute chemical changes which produce a variation, or mutation, but the new set of chromosomes usually carries genes identical with the old. In *meiosis*, the division which produces eggs and sperm, each cell carries only 19 chromosomes and during division individual genes may cross from one chain of chromosomes to the other, giving a random selection of those the parent has inherited from his or her parents. At conception each parent contributes half their chromosomes with their attached genes, producing a new combination in the fertilized cell or *zygote*.

Genes for particular features are arranged in a particular order along the chromosomes. When a gene has a matched partner for a comparable characteristic — hair length for instance — these are known as *allele*. Some genes, known as dominant genes, have a stronger influence than others which are called recessive genes. If a kitten receives identical alleles from both parents for a particular characteristic it is said to be *homozygous* for that characteristic. If it receives a particular gene from one parent and an alternative from the other, it is said to be *heterozygous* for that characteristic. A cat homozygous for any feature will express that feature regardless of the characteristic's dominance or recessivity but the appearance of a heterozygous characteristic depends upon the dominance or recessivity of the particular characteristic involved.

Some characteristics are sex-linked. In the cat these include the red factor (called yellow by some geneticists and symbolized by O for orange). The sexes differ in their chromosomes. A female cat has 19 pairs which match, a male has only 18 matching pairs. His final pair consists of one of medium size, the X chromosome, and one much smaller, the Y chromosome. Males have the XY chromosome pair and females have the XX pair.

Every ovum must carry an X chromosome but sperm can carry either an X or Y. When an ovum is fertilized it is a matter of chance whether the sperm with which it fuses carries X or Y

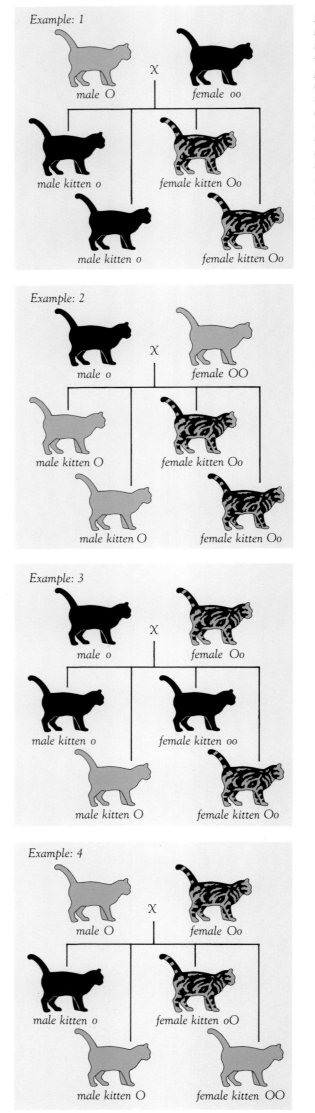

Example: 1

male O   X   female oo

male kitten o   female kitten Oo

male kitten o   female kitten Oo

Example: 2

male o   X   female OO

male kitten O   female kitten Oo

male kitten O   female kitten Oo

Example: 3

male o   X   female Oo

male kitten o   female kitten oo

male kitten O   female kitten Oo

Example: 4

male O   X   female Oo

male kitten o   female kitten oO

male kitten O   female kitten OO

Some characteristics are carried on the X chromosome, of which females have two and males only one. The red factor, which must be present to produce red or cream coats, is the best known example in cats. Sex-linked inheritance of red coat color can produce a variety of possible litters. The black color in these examples, which are applicable to any breed, could also be any of the dilute forms of black and the red could also be the dilute cream. An orange female kitten can be born when both parents show that color whether Orange (O) x Orange (O) or Orange x Tortoiseshell (Oo).

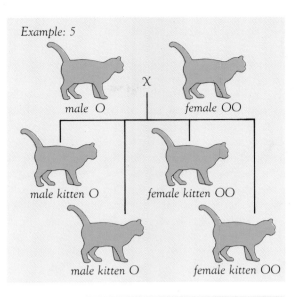

Example: 5

male O   X   female OO

male kitten O   female kitten OO

male kitten O   female kitten OO

Inheritance of features that are not sex-related. In these examples the appearance or phenotype of the cats is either agouti (tabby) or non-agouti but any gene pair in which one is a dominant gene will operate in the same way. The genetic makeup or genotype of each cat or kitten is indicated by the symbols AA (agouti), Aa (carrying non-agouti) and aa (non-agouti). In all there are six possible crosses. Only when the genotype is aa can the cat express the non-agouti appearance. A knowledge that an agouti phenotype carries an Aa genotype can be deduced from pedigree records, siblings and previous matings.

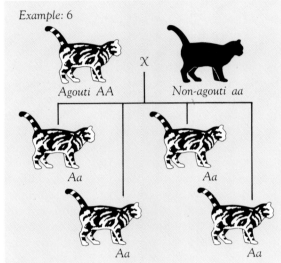

Example: 6

Agouti AA   X   Non-agouti aa

Aa   Aa

Aa   Aa

Example: 7

Agouti Aa   X   Agouti Aa

AA   Aa

Aa   aa

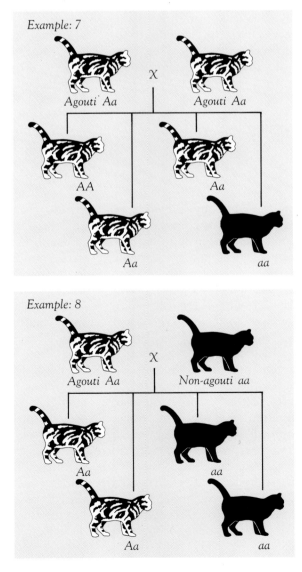

Example: 8

Agouti Aa   X   Non-agouti aa

Aa   aa

Aa   aa

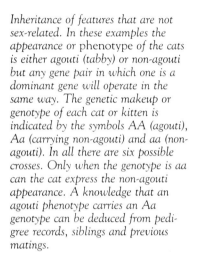

chromosomes. If the sperm carries an X then the zygote will be XX and the resulting kitten female. If it is fertilised by a Y-bearing sperm the zygote will be XY and the kitten will be male.

The red color in the cat can only be carried on the X chromosome and as the male cat has only one X he can be either O (orange) or o (non-orange) according to the genes. The female, having two X chromosomes can be OO (orange) Oo (tortoiseshell) or oo (non-orange). The tortoiseshell is the heterozygote, her coat exhibiting the influence of both orange areas, O, and non-orange areas, o.

Dominant characteristics

Cat breeders are mainly concerned with the genetic factors affecting coat length, pattern and color. It is important for them to understand which factors are dominant or recessive:
White is dominant to all other colors
Black is dominant to blue (dilute)
Tabby (agouti) is dominant to non-tabby (non-agouti)
Shorthair is dominant to longhair
Full coat is dominant to rex coat
Manx (taillessness) is dominant to normal tail

Not all genes affect only one characteristic. There are also *polygenes* which, although not individually having great effect, can act together to modify length of coat and strength of color in fur or eyes when they are then known as modifiers.

Not all genes operate at birth. For instance, all kittens in the cat family are born with blue eyes which only take on their adult coloration at two to four months of age. Tabby markings may also appear which later fade — including the spotted patterns of lion cubs — and the colored parts of Siamese and similar coats appear only gradually as the kitten matures.

In some cats one gene, though not dominant in the normal sense of predominating over its heterozygote partner, has the effect of masking a characteristic, as in the melanistic black leopard and jaguar or the merging of the tabby pattern in the domestic cat into the black ground color when a non-agouti gene eliminates the ticking on its coat. This effect is known as *epistasis*.

Melanistic animals are the most obvious example of genetic effect in the wild species. The King Cheetah are one example of a local race with a different coat and there are clearly different races in other species which perhaps reflect some local adaptation which has proved advantageous and been preserved naturally.

Once the basic rules of inheritance are understood and the dominance or recessivity of any specific characteristics have been determined it is simple to work out the characteristics to be expected from virtually any crosses between cats whose ancestry and genetic makeup is known. But there is more to breeding healthy cats than this. While no breeder can safeguard against aberrant mutations she or he must watch out for a genetic history which includes harmful elements such as hereditary diseases. Unfortunately certain desirable attributes are sometimes linked with undesirable conditions. For instance the gene which eliminates the tail in Manx cats can cause further malformations and, if inherited from both parents, can be lethal. The Siamese gene also brings with it a defect in the nerve connections between eyes and brain which gives them poor binocular vision. Best known perhaps is a linkage between the gene for true white (the blue-eyed white) and deafness.

Conformation

Conformation refers to the physical appearance of each cat of each breed. The agreed-upon standard of perfection of each association provides a word description of the perfect cat of each of the breeds. It is this standard that breeders work to achieve. By inbreeding and line breeding they seek to 'set' desirable traits (small, well-rounded ears on a Persian, for example) while eliminating undesirable traits (large, pointed ears on the Persian).

From time to time, what is termed as a 'prepotent' male of a breed will appear who is able to set his stamp upon his progeny independent of the blood lines of the females to whom he is bred. However this is the exception. Most breeders feel themselves fortunate to be able to produce an occasional top show winner in any breed. Because of the permutations and combinations of the genetic crosses, relatively few 'great' show cats are produced each year. This is the challenge to the knowledgeable breeder of today. What combination will produce tomorrow's beautiful show cat?

Coats and colors

Coat and color pattern in the domestic cat depend on the presence of pigment granules in the cells of the epidermis. These consist of melanin, found as two compounds: *eumelanin*, which produces black and brown pigmentation, and *phaenomelanin*, which gives rise to red and yellow pigmentation. Eumelanin is converted in a series of slow stages from the amino acid *tyrosine*, through the action of an enzyme containing copper. Cats with a diet deficient in copper may be unable to develop their true genetic coat color. Phaenomelanin is derived from the amino acid *tryptophan*.

Melanin is manufactured in specialized cells called melanocytes which pass pigment to the skin, hair and eyes of the cat. The number, action and distribution of the melanocytes is genetically determined. The cells are formed during the kitten's embryonic stage and spread through its body to their designated positions in the early stages of development. The amazing number of permutations in which distribution and clumping of melanocytes occur gives rise to the large variety of patterns and colors seen in domestic cats today.

The original, or wild-type, coat in the cat has been termed *agouti*. In its basic form, agouti refers to a cat with the basic black hairs banded with yellow, producing a typical 'ticked' effect — also seen in other wild creatures such as rats, mice and rabbits. This agouti effect is due to the presence of both types of melanin in the hair shaft.

In the wild, the ancestors of today's cats were short-coated with black pigmented areas making patterns of stripes or spots against the paler, ticked hairs of the basic overall coat. The designs created by these areas of solid pigment — known as *tabby patterns* — are quite variable in the cat. They fall into several basic types: *ticked tabby*, of which the best example is seen in Abyssinian cats, the longitudinally striped *mackerel tabby*, and the intricately marked *classic tabby* (also known as the marbled or blotched tabby) and the *spotted tabby*.

The first natural mutation to occur in the cat was probably the simple non-agouti gene which gave rise to totally black coat color. This black or melanistic mutation has also occurred in other feline species. Even so, in certain light, the basic tabby pattern can be detected on these 'black'-coated cats. The pattern appears as black on black.

A dilution of black to blue was brought about by a simple mutant gene inherited as a recessive and affecting the clumping of the pigment granules within the hair shafts in such a way that the cat appears to be light or dark slate-gray in color. The same dilution factor also works on other colors, changing orange (red) to cream, for example.

Another mutant gene occurred which reduced the color of the normal black pigmentation; this time to brown or chocolate. The effect of this gene is best seen in the Havana Brown or the Oriental Chestnut. When a cat also carries the blue dilutant, the color expresses itself as lilac.

The mutation which gave rise to orange or red coloring in the cat (as already mentioned) affected a gene linked to the X chromosome; the correlation it produces is therefore sex-linked. When the black dilutant is also carried the red becomes cream. The orange gene is independent of other color and pattern factors so can be inherited along with them. This can give rise to many varied and interesting coat patterns, particularly in female cats. These are known as the tortoiseshell patterns.

A group of the most popular of pedigree cats have coat patterns and subtle colors produced by a related set of alleles known as the *albino series*. This group consists of silver, Burmese, albino and Siamese cats. Each mutant allele in the series removes more of the pigment from the coat. The gene for silver takes out most of the yellow pigment, especially in any agouti area, but leaves the black pigment. The gene for Burmese takes out even more yellow and modifies the black areas to dark brown. The albino gene gives rise to a cat without any pigmentation, causing the coat to appear white. The Siamese gene takes out the color from the body areas, leaving color only in the extremities (the 'points': feet and lower legs, tail, face mask and ears — not to be confused with the standard of points by which a breed is described). Even in these the color is reduced, bringing black down to a dark brown (seal). Coloring will be further reduced by the presence of the previously mentioned genes for dilute colorations.

It is quite a different gene that produces truly white cats. Its effect is to prevent the migration of the melanocytes throughout the body of the embryo kitten. Without these cells there is no pigmentation, and so the cat's coat is white. Some geneticists point out that many white kittens are born with a small patch of color on the head. This small spot of color indicates the true color of the kitten which is 'masked' by the overall white coat.

Therefore we have white cats (the spot of color disappears with maturity) which are really black, blue, red, cream, or even tortoiseshell, in which color is completely masked by the expressed overall white coat. It is probable that a very similar gene is responsible for white markings on otherwise colored cats. The clumping of melanocytes and their uneven distribution produces a colored cat with a white throat, chest, underbody or paws, or any or all of these.

Length of coat

One of the most significant of the cat's mutations was that of the gene for long hair. This, perhaps more than any other factor, was responsible for the rapid rise in popularity of pedigreed cats at the turn of last century. Pedigreed long-haired breeds have long, full, silky coats produced by careful genetic selection over many years. The ordinary domestic longhair has a slightly shorter, less full and coarser coat. Selective breeding for any trait brings about the manipulation of many *polygenes*. These factors exert individual minute effects on characteristics. Length and texture of cats' coats are due to the multiple effects of polygenes.

Several mutations have occurred in the cat which affect the structure of the coat hairs and the balance among them, producing such variations as the Devon and Cornish Rex, the American Wirehair, and the 'hairless' Sphynx.

Eyes

The eye color of the cat is very variable and is also due to the genetic distribution of melanin. In some breeds the gene which influences the coat pattern or color may also determine the color of the eyes. An example is the Siamese or Himalayan patterned cats, which all have blue eyes (in varying degrees of blueness), regardless of the color of the points. Differences in the intensity of eye color are due to polygenes. The blue may range from an almost transparent bluish-gray to the preferred dark, almost electric, sapphire blue.

Pedigree form. Each column shows the previous generation of antecedents.

Creating new breeds

Although an occasional mutation may occur, such as the tightly folded ears of the Scottish Fold or the curled coat of the Rex, which breeders can exploit to create a new kind of cat, most new 'breeds' are, in fact, merely variations of existing breeds or breed types.

To maintain breed purity, cats are usually bred with the best possible examples of their type, especially looking out for a match which provides good type for any characteristic which may be defective in the other parent. However, a new color, coat pattern or hair length can be introduced by outcrossing the basic type to suitable cats exhibiting the desired characteristic for the modification sought. Selected kittens from these litters are then back-crossed to the very best specimens of the basic breed until cats of the proposed standard (ideal description) are produced in sufficient numbers which breed true — produce kittens which always maintain the new characteristics — to be classified. In this way it is feasible to produce every known and accepted kind of cat in every possible coat pattern and color.

The road to acceptance of a new breed or color is a long one requiring hard work and dedication on the part of knowledgeable breeders.

Registration bodies differ in their exact requirements for a new breed; in general they will require evidence that it is distinctly different from any variety already recognized, has bred true over a minimum number of generations (enough to produce at least 100 viable examples of the new variety in the case of the CFA) and has no harmful defects or other handicaps. Some bodies ban outcrossing and will only allow registration of pure-bred stock of the breeds they recognize. Numbers and quality are two of the requirements. There must also be a proven interest in proliferating the new color or breed. Ultimately, much depends upon public acceptance.

Hotspotz Tickety Boo, a hybrid cross between a Sorrel Abyssinian and an Oriental. This was the first step in obtaining a cinnamon color when crossed with a similar hybrid. Tickety Boo has also produced the first generation of Ocicat, when crossed with a Siamese. The Ocicat, named after the Ocelot, is a powerful spotted cat, noted for its wild appearance.

New Zealand Cat Fancy Incorporated
Standard Pedigree Form For Registered Cats

Name: PIZZICATO COSI FANTUTTE   Breeder: TWINK McCABE

Reg. No. PR2971/5   Date of Birth 20-10-88   Address 20, CHATHAM AVE, RD3 ALBANY, AUCKLAND, N.Z.

Sex FEMALE   Breed SIAMESE   Breed No. 24C   Colour LILAC POINT

PARENTS	GRANDPARENTS	GREAT GRANDPARENTS	GREAT GREAT GRANDPARENTS
Reg.No. F.17847-1	Reg.No. V5023	BRONZE GRAND CHAMPION	GR. CH ARWEN QUICKSILVER (24)
	GRAND CHAMPION	BENWELL BELLINI (24)	BR.CH BENWELL BELLADONNA (24)
GRAND CHAMPION	TARAQUIN ROWAN (24)	GRAND CHAMPION	CH RAHDEN TUTANKHAMEN (24B)
NAENGNOI SHANSI		ZOLIKIMA SERAPHINA (24B)	CH KIMRUKA KUCHING MANIS (24)
(IMP. AUST)	Reg.No. V6055	GRAND CHAMPION	GR.CH ASHRIDGE JOUDAN (24A)
		BLUE COMANCHE (24A)	CH KELBERRY BLUE CASHONA (24A)
(24B)	NAENGNOI AMETHYST (24C)	NAENGNOI OPAL (24)	CH VELETIPS MILO (24A)
			KATALEENA MING (24B)
Reg.No. PR2687-1	Reg.No. S.16485-1	CHAMPION	GR CH REYNARDS TARKA (24)
	KALAMUNDA	KALOKE TOLTEC (24)	KALOKE PIBO (24)
CHAMPION	VICE REGAL (24)	KALAMUNDA SHIRALEE (24)	CH SEADOG PELE (IMP UK) (24)
PIZZICATO ARIA			HEADINGLEY VICERENE (24)
	Reg.No. PR2495-1	HOWZAT HANDY ANDY (24)	MONTPELIER KATHAN DU (24)
			HOWZAT DOLCE VITA (24)
(24C)	HOWZAT TUTU (24)	CHNLA MACAROON (24B)	HIGHFIELDS JOSHUA (24C)
			CHNLA KATRINA (24B)

(All Ancestors to have Breed Numbers inserted in brackets)

I/We hereby certify that the above particulars are true and correct to the best of my/our knowledge and belief.

Signed   Date 10th April 1990

Cat coat colors and patterns

A limited range of the possible variations of color and pattern is recognized by the Cat Fancy. The various bodies differ in what they accept in a particular breed but additions are made as new types are established. Particular colors are complemented by matching nose leather and eye colors.

Colors Breed standards are agreed upon written description of the perfect cat both in 'type' (conformation), coat length, pattern, and color of coat, eyes, paw pads and nose leather. These are voted on by the several associations made up of serious breeders whose basic desire is to produce an animal of beauty for esthetic enjoyment and companionship. Breed standards require particular eye colors with each coat color. Eye colors are listed separately, leather colors detailed here. Individual registration bodies may differ slightly and should be consulted for their particular standards.

White Leather: pink
Black Leather: black
Blue (which is the cat fancy name for a range of shades of gray) Leather: blue
Chocolate Leather: chocolate or pinkish brown, eye rims chocolate
Cinnamon (a lighter shade of chocolate, Orientals only) Leather: cinnamon brown or pink (eye rims cinnamon) or tan to pinkish beige
Lilac or Lavender Leather: lavender, pink or lavender-pink
Fawn (Orientals only) Leather: mauvish pink
Red Leather: pink or brick red
Cream Leather: pink
Ruddy (see agouti below)
Sorrel (see agouti below)

Other colors In America **Champagne** and **Platinum** are used to describe the slightly modified cream and lilac of the Burmese, while the glowing coats of the Tonkinese are called different types of **Mink**. Other colors which have been developed include: **Caramel** (leather taupe or pinkish-taupe); **Beige** (leather pale pink); **Apricot** (leather pink); **Indigo** (leather slate gray).

The **Silver** range of colors, seen in the tipped, shaded and smoke cats, is due to a dominant gene that produces an apparently white coat with tipping of various depths.

A.O.C. (Any Other Color) covers those colors not specifically recognised for a particular breed. In New Zealand a whole range of potential colors combining silver coats with Siamese pattern have been called **Pastel-points**.

Patterns Both arrangement of color on the body and banding along individual hairs affect a cat's appearance.

Agouti is a pattern on the hairs themselves, each being ticked with bands of the basic color along its length. It is part of the make-up of all tabbies but in the Abyssinian and Somali affects a whole range of colors, as in the modification of black to the Usual or Ruddy Abyssinian and of red to Sorrel.

There are four distinct tabby patterns, but the Ticked and Spotted are not recognized in Longhairs (Persians) and long coats tend to diffuse the full effect of the other two patterns, although they should still show correct markings which should be symmetrical in all forms and should be clearly defined on a base coat of a paler color. All have distinct facial markings: an 'M' on the forehead, unbroken lines running back from the eyes and narrow lines on the cheeks. There is a residual tendency to near-white agouti in the area of the lips and lower jaw on some shorthair varieties but this must not extend to the neck. Tabby patterns have also been created with a golden base color to the coat.

Ticked tabby has three bands of agouti on each hair with non-agouti at the tip. Non-agouti color extends well up the back of the hind legs and is allowed along the spine if the coat is fully ticked. Light tabby marks may appear on the underbody but not on upper parts; legs, tail and face should show distinct tabby marks with the tail tip non-agouti. Shorthair and Oriental cats should have a dark necklace on the chest. The Abyssinian has been selectively bred for minimal markings; only parts of the face markings, the dark hock-marking and the non-agouti tail tip are present.

Spotted tabby has round spots distributed throughout the coat. They may vary in size but must be distinct from ground color with the spine line broken into spots and a broken necklace on the chest. Legs may be barred and/or spotted with spotting on the paws preferred.

Classic tabby (also known as *Blotched* or *Marbled*) has three well-separated lines down the spine and a large oyster-shaped patch surrounded by one or more unbroken lines on each flank (the 'bullseye'). The tail should be ringed, the legs barred with spotted toes, and the abdomen spotted (vest buttons). Lines running over the top of the head should form butterfly-shaped shoulder markings.

Mackerel tabby has an unbroken line down the spine with broken narrow lines running alongside. From these, narrow lines run vertically down the body to form the mackerel pattern on the ribs. Broken stripes are acceptable. These and those ringing the tail should be as narrow as possible. Legs should be evenly barred with narrow bracelets, the underbody spotted and several necklaces appear on the chest.

Bi-colors are white-coated cats patched with any one of the solid colors permitted for the type, leaving not more than half and preferably less than one-third white and with color on the top of the head, ears, cheeks, back, tail and flanks but with a white inverted 'V' on the muzzle preferred. The white areas should be free of any pattern or contrasting markings.

Tortoiseshell consists of a mixture of red and black, or their dilute forms (blue and cream, lilac and cream, chocolate and cream). In the United States this looks like a black cat patched with color. In Britain Shorthairs have well-defined patches but Longhairs have mingled colors as do Burmese (not recognized in this color in the US) and pointed cats. Tortoiseshell cats have mottled nose leather outlined with the name color and

1. White.
2. Black.
3. Blue.
4. Chocolate.
5. Cinnamon.
6. Lilac/Lavender.
7. Fawn.
8. Red.
9. Cream.
10. Ruddy.
11. Sorrel.
12. Patched tabby.
13. Mackerel tabby.
14. Spotted tabby.
15. Blotched tabby.
16. Bi-color.
17. Tortoiseshell.
18. Tortoiseshell and white.

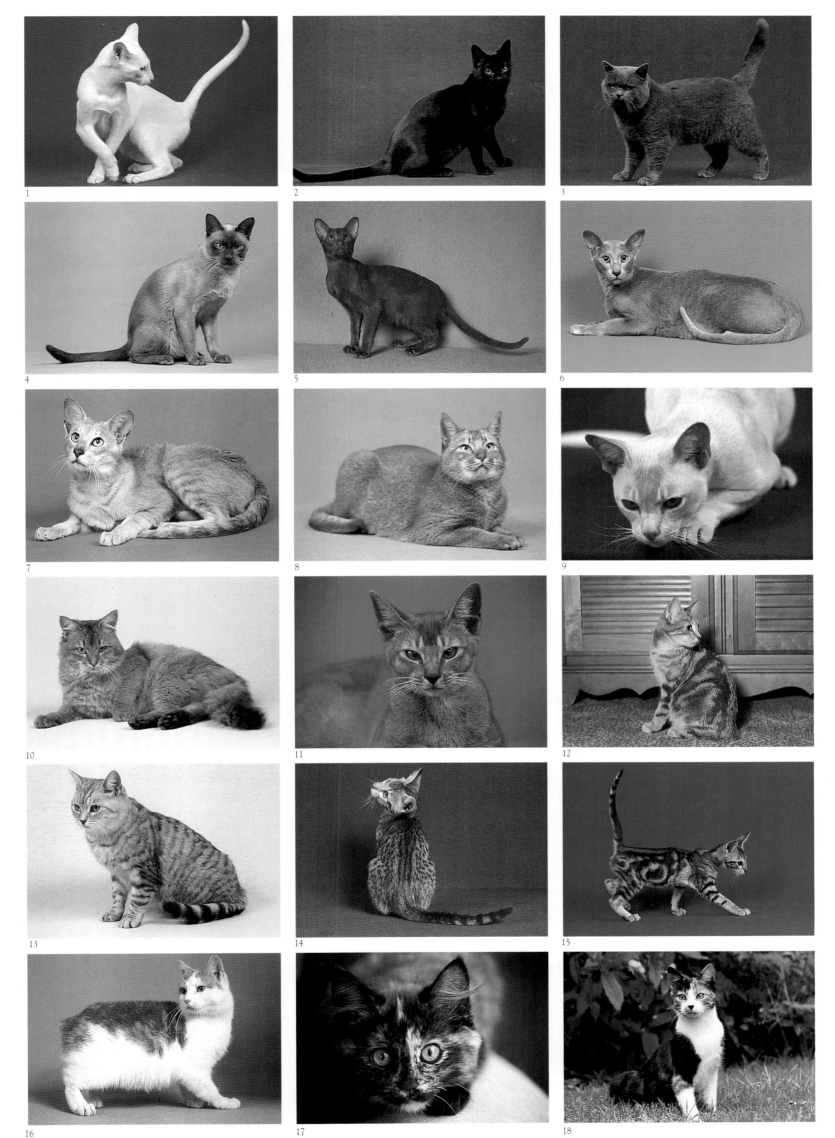

name color eye rims. In the multi-colored cats the leather color matches the color of the hair contiguous to it both on the leather and the paw pads.

Blue-cream is the dilute form of the tortoiseshell.

Tri-colors are like bi-colors but have color patches consisting of one of the tortoiseshell mixtures; they are known as *Calico* in the United States, *Tortie and White* in Britain.

Patched tabby has markings of the Classic of Mackerel tabby but with additional clear patches of red, light red or cream. They are presently recognized only with the tabby markings in brown, blue and silver and also described as Torbies or Tortie-tabbies. Golden Torbies have the same golden base color to the fur as the Golden Tabbies.

Chinchilla or Silver Tipped fur has the ends of each hair tipped with a darker color giving a sparkling silvery appearance. Black on white is known as Chinchilla; red tipping is called **Shell Cameo**. Tipped cats have red nose leather outlined with their name color and name color eye rims.

Golden Tipped coats are analogous to the Silver-shaded range but the undercoat has a warm-toned golden shade.

Shaded Silver is similar to the Chinchilla, but darker as the tipping extends further down each hair and the undercoat has the palest tint according to the name color. British bodies recognize a **Pewter** as well as a Shaded Silver but it is identical except that the eyes are orange or copper. **Red** tipping is also known as **Shaded Cameo**.

Golden Shaded are analogous to Shaded Silver but with a golden or rich warm apricot undercoat.

Smoke is the darkest of the tipped furs, the color extending well down each hair, and appearing as a solid color cat when still but with the undercoat and roots of the fur pale silver, and showing through in contrast when the cat is in motion. In oriental varieties ghost markings which give a watered silk or moire effect are preferred. **Red Smoke** is also identified as **Cameo Red**.

Pointed pattern originally appeared only on Siamese cats. Feet, lower legs, tail, ears (the points) and face (or mask) are of the name color and contrast with a pale body which should be of even tone and as free of pattern and heavy color as possible (most darken with age). Except in kittens, when the mask is incomplete, the point color should cover the entire face including the whisker pads, and be connected to the color on the ears by fine traced lines from above the eyes. The top of the head should be of the paler body color. Points may be of solid, tabby or tortoiseshell colors (although they are not all recognized in all breeds), but diluted so that black appears as seal and so forth. Seals have fawn bodies, Blues cold white, Chocolates ivory white, Lilacs glacial white and Reds (which retain the tabby pattern) pale cream. Tabby points are usually known as lynx points in North America. Pointed patterns are now seen in other breeds as well.

Van was originally the pattern of the Turkish Van but is now seen in both Persian and Short-hair cats. It consists of a white coat with solid or tortoiseshell patches of color confined to the extremities — head, tail and legs, although one or two small colored patches may be permitted on the body. In the Van Tortoiseshell and White the red and cream areas should ideally be separated from other colored areas.

Harlequin coats have a random combination of one or of two colors with white in clearly defined patches as in the Van varieties but include additional colors.

Eye colors
Breed standards require eye colors to match or complement the coat color.

Long-haired and Short-haired breeds
In most colors, eyes should be deep gold, orange or copper but:
White Blue, orange or one eye of each
Himalayans (Colourpoints) Blue
Shaded Silvers Brilliant copper or blue-green, except for Cameos which should be copper
Silver tabby Green, hazel or copper
Silver Patched tabby Copper or hazel
Cream tabby Only brilliant copper in longhairs

Foreign Shorthairs (Oriental Shorthairs)
Siamese Blue
Abyssinians Gold or green
Orientals Brilliant green with yellow tones permissible in Cameos and Torties

19. Blue cream.
20. Smoke.
21. Chinchilla.
22. Golden Shaded.
23. Harlequin.
24. Pointed pattern.

Red and Cream Persian (Long-haired) Cats.

THE BREEDS OF CATS

Cats come in a wide range of patterns and colors and a variety of conformations and each has its own personality and appeal. The alley cat and the mongrel domestic pet can be as attractive, intelligent and affectionate as any show bench champion but pedigreed cats have been developed to create or to preserve particular physical characteristics — and some breeders would claim certain personality traits for them.

Fashions for particular breeds come and go, the standards laid down for the same breed by different organizations often vary slightly in detail, and even within them there will be occasional differences in interpreting those standards.

So many new breeds have been established since cat shows began that it might seem impossible to create new ones. Yet new color varieties are still being bred and chance mutations may result in a new breed. Undoubtedly breeders are trying to create new combinations of color, coat and form to add to the range of cats recognized by breed societies all around the world.

Cat breeds can be divided into three broad groups: Shorthairs, Longhairs and Foreign Short-hairs (the 'Oriental' cats). This grouping has been used here. However, crossings between these main types have produced varieties which combine the characteristics of one type with those of another. These have been placed with the breed whose characteristic conformation they retain. The Cymric, for instance, although a cat with long fur, is placed with the short-haired group following the Manx from which it was developed.

Standards of points

For every breed to which they grant recognition the various cat bodies each draw up their own 'standards' or descriptions of the ideal form of the cat, together with any unacceptable faults. Various aspects — head, body, eyes, coat, color, etc. — are accorded a particular number of 'points' according to their importance to the overall quality of the cat, together totalling 100. These maximums for each feature — which may vary from breed to breed as well as between associations — are used by judges at cat shows. Some organizations have a fixed list of points or fractions of a point to be deducted for each feature in which a cat falls short of the ideal standard.

Black-tipped British Shorthair.

THE SHORT-HAIRED CATS

Wild cats and the first domestics all had short-haired fur, which is perhaps why the long-haired Persians originally attracted so much attention. Many believe a short coat allows the cat's natural form to show more clearly than when adorned with luxuriant fur and that the solid form of the shorthair has a more direct appeal than the overt sensuality of the slinky foreign and oriental cats.

The shorthairs are closer to the farm and working cats which formed the original European stock. Their short fur is easier to groom than that of long-haired cats and they are not usually so demanding of attention.

British Shorthair

It has been suggested that the Romans introduced domestic cats to northern Europe to protect their granaries from rodents, so probably the forebears of the British Shorthair arrived in the British Isles with Roman colonists nearly 2000 years ago. Today's British Shorthair may be descended from those cats but it is a refined breed which conforms to a strict standard of points, and differs considerably from the ordinary domestic cat of the British farm or fireside.

The breed is quite a large cat but must never look coarse or overweight. It is cobby (or chunky) in build with a broad chest, strong short legs and fairly large round paws. The tail is comparatively short and thick. The head is massive and round with full cheeks, small ears set far apart on the head and large round eyes. The coat is short and very dense, resilient and firm to the touch.

This is a cat with a very sweet and gentle nature which makes an undemanding pet. Although short-haired, it needs regular grooming and it is important to accustom kittens to combing from an early age.

The British Shorthair is recognized in several feline colors and patterns but not every association allows them all. In the GCCF and CFA, for instance, those colors derived from pointed cats and their variations (seal, lilac, chocolate) are not acceptable. Nor is the pointed pattern allowed.

European Shorthair

The European Shorthair is the indigenous cat of the European continent. Its standards are the same as those of the British Shorthair which it resembles. Specialization has provided many other types of cats which are arguably closely associated with them. For example, the Chartreux and the Russian Blue, while able to trace their beginnings to special ancestors, may be related via the blood of the 'European' shorthair.

In some countries the Albino is recognized as a variety. Unlike other white cats, its color is due to the recessive albino gene, not the dominant white gene, and so its pale blue eyes do not bring an association with deafness.

BRITISH SHORTHAIRS.
1. Blue. 2. Blue kitten; its ghost tabby markings will disappear as it matures. 3. Black. 4. Cream. 5. Black smoke. 6. White orange-eyed. 7. Tortoiseshell and white; black and white bi-colored. 8. Cameo. 9. Black-tipped. 10. Red tabby. 11. Silver tabby. 12. Brown tabby.

Chartreux

A type said to have been bred selectively by Carthusian monks as long ago as the sixteenth century at the monastery near Grenoble famous for its liqueur. It is native to France and was certainly established by 1756 when George Louis Buffon included the Chartreux in his *Histoire Naturelle*. During the 1930s it had its own scientific name bestowed by a French veterinarian who decided that it should be called *Felis catus cartusianorum*.

Typically, the Chartreux has a massive body and build; its head is not round but is heavily jowled and the coat color should appear silvery and have a woolly texture. Known for its characteristic jowls, this cat has leg boning which seems insufficient to support the massive, muscular body. It should have a sweet or open expression, an angry expression being considered a fault.

Like most of the shorthair varieties, the Chartreux is placid and gentle, and an undemanding pet. It comes in only one color — a silvery blue.

American Shorthair

Some American breeders seek to trace this breed back to the Pilgrim Fathers but the history of the American Shorthair as a 'fancy' cat dates from the turn of the century when a pedigreed red tabby was sent from England to the United States to be mated with indigenous short-haired cats. This cat, named Belle, was the first short-haired cat to be registered with the Cat Fanciers' Association. At first the breed was called the Shorthair, then the Domestic Shorthair, but was renamed the American Shorthair in 1966.

Typically a medium to large cat, the American Shorthair is distinctly different from the British cat. It should have a strong muscular body, less square in shape than the British Shorthair, and legs and tail of medium length. The head should be rather oblong, with full cheeks and a squared muzzle. The ears are medium in size with rounded tips and the eyes round and wide with a slight slant at the corners. The coat must be short and thick with a hard texture.

Easy to feed and rear, American Shorthairs are noted for their calm, kind temperament and renowned for their hardiness and hunting ability.

They are recognized in all feline colors and patterns except Himalayan/Siamese and their derivatives.

1 and 3. Chartreux (head and full body).
AMERICAN SHORTHAIRS.
2. Classic tabby.
4. Shaded silver mother and kitten.
5. Brown classic tabby.
6. Silver mackerel tabby.
7. Shaded silver.
8. Silver mackerel tabby kitten.

Exotic Shorthair

During the development of both refined Shorthair breeds and Persian varieties, long-haired and short-haired cats were occasionally mated together to introduce new or desirable genetic factors to an established line. This practice was generally carried out as a single exercise but, during the 1960s, various breeders, with the approval of the board of the CFA, decided to create a breed name for cats of mixed pedigree Shorthair and Persian parentage. They called it the Exotic Shorthair.

Fanciers of this breed consider it to be a short-coated version of the Persian. A cat of extreme 'typiness' but with a coat that is tangle-free and much easier to care for. Typiness here refers to the extreme conformation of the head being produced by Persian and Exotic Shorthair breeders of today. This head is described as being round with large round eyes set well apart, a nose which is short, snub and broad, and with a definite 'break' or indentation just above the nose leather. The coat, which is not as short as that of the typical Shorthair, is very dense, standing well out from the body, and soft in texture.

The show standard for the Exotic calls for a cobby body with a deep chest, short, thick legs and a short tail. The head is round and massive with a broad skull, a short stub nose, full cheeks and a strong chin. The ears are small with round tips and set low on the head with great width between and the eyes are large, full and round.

In temperament the Exotic is very like its Persian forebears, making it a quiet, gentle and placid companion.

The Exotic can be found in most feline colors and patterns but not all associations accept all colors.

American Wirehair

In 1966 a cat lover in Vermont, United States, noticed an anomaly in a litter of farm kittens — one had a strange, sparse and wiry coat. An experienced breeder acquired the unusual kitten and one of its littermates and sent hair samples to a British geneticist for analysis. It was confirmed that the coat was of a different type to anything previously studied in the domestic cat and a breeding programme was initiated.

The original wire-haired cat was a red and white male called Adam. He was first mated to his normal-looking littermate and then to other short-haired cats, and from these beginnings the new breed was born. All American Wirehairs trace their ancestry back to Adam; careful selection of breeding stock has allowed the refinement of the breed over the years. Championship status for the breed was achieved in CFA in 1977, and the show standard requires a medium to large body with medium-length legs and tail. The head is round with prominent cheekbones and a well developed muzzle and chin, medium-sized ears with rounded tips and large round eyes. The unusual coat is of medium length, springy and tight. Individual hairs are crimped, hooked or bent, including the hairs within the ears. The overall appearance of

the coat is more important than the crimping of each hair. The density of the coat leads to the formation of 'ringlets' rather than waves. Curly whiskers are desirable.

All feline colors and patterns are permitted except Himalayan and those showing evidence of hybridization resulting in the chocolate and lavender series and those colors combined with white.

Manx

This is a tailless cat. Manx is the adjective for people and things which come from the Isle of Man in the Irish Sea, with which this cat has long been associated and where a special cattery has been established to ensure the continuance

1. Black smoke Exotic Shorthair.
2. Calico (tortoiseshell and white) American Wirehair.
3. Cream Exotic Shorthair.
4. Red tabby American Wirehair.

1. Odd-eyed white Manx, a rumpy-riser.
2. Red and white Manx, a rumpy.
3. Tabby and white Manx, a stumpy.
4. Cymric.

of the breed. Various legends purport to explain its loss of tail, which is in fact due to a mutant dominant gene. The original mutation must have occurred many years ago however, for Manx cats have been known since the turn of the century; a specialist club for the breed was established in Britain as early as 1901.

Although so long established, Manx cats remain rare, mainly because Manx queens produce small litters, as a direct result of the Manx gene. This gene not only produces the tailless characteristic. It also affects other parts of the cat's body and is semi-lethal. Homozygous Manx (kittens inheriting the tailless gene from both parents) die within the womb at an early stage in their development. The Manx that we see is an heterozygote, with only one gene for taillessness paired with one for a normal tail. This means that Manx cannot breed true and Manx litters often contain kittens with varying sorts of tails. A completely tailless cat is called a Rumpy and this is the true show-type Manx; the Rumpy-riser has a tiny knob where the tail should be; the Stumpy or Stubby has a movable tail stump which may be kinked or curved and the Longy has a short but otherwise normal tail.

Breeders usually cross Manx with normal-tailed Manx offspring in order to ensure a healthy litter.

Manx cats are appealing and lovable and make good pets.

The Manx show standard calls for a short back and extra height in the hindquarters, and it must have a distinctive double coat. The double coat is short and dense with a well-padded quality due to the longer, outer coat and the close, cottony undercoat. Texture of the outer guard hairs is somewhat hard; the appearance is glossy. Some standards describe the Manx as having a hopping rabbit-like gait.

Most associations allow all feline colors and patterns except the Himalayan, or those showing hybridization resulting in the chocolate and lilac series, or these colors combined with white.

Cymric

During the 1960s some American breeders of Manx cats noticed an occasional anomaly in their litters — a kitten with long hair. Rather than discarding these 'faulty' kittens, they decided to work together to attempt to establish a separate breed of long-haired tailless cats and decided to name the breed Cymric (pronounced kum-ric) from the Welsh name for Wales, Cymru.

The breed has gained recognition with several associations throughout the feline world and is very like the Manx from which it is descended, except for its beautiful medium-long coat, tufted ears and toes and face-framing ruff.

Colors are as for the Manx.

Above *Black and white Japanese Bobtail.*

Japanese Bobtail

This breed, with its distinctive tail, has existed in its native Japan for many centuries. It is well established as a family cat and as a symbol of good luck, the most popular color being the *mi-ke* (pronounced mee-kay) which means literally 'three-colored' and has a pattern of black and red patches on a white coat.

The Japanese Bobtail came to the attention of the Western world in 1963 when visiting cat show judges from the United States first handled specimens of the breed. In 1968 an American woman, living in Japan and breeding Bobtails, sent a consignment of three to America, later taking a further 38 cats with her when she returned there to live. The breed rapidly grew in popularity and gained recognition with most American associations.

The Bobtail is an elegant, slender cat, medium in size, with fine bones and long slim legs. The distinctive tail is rather like that of the Stumpy Manx, but it is carried erect and the tail structure is disguised by a pom-pom of fur rather like a chrysanthemum. The triangular head is of medium length and width with high cheekbones and large oval eyes set at a slant and the ears are large, upright and expressive. The Bobtail has an endearing personality and a soft melodic voice. It thrives in family groups and loves human company. It is recognized in most feline colors, with or without white, except for the Himalayan pattern.

These cats are pictured in old Japanese wood block prints. Although established for so long in Japan and also found as household cats in Thailand, Bobtails did not become a 'fancy' cat until they attracted American enthusiasts.

Scottish Fold

The Scottish Folds have ears which do not become erect as they mature. They first appeared in a litter of otherwise normal kittens on a farm in Scotland in 1961. William Ross, the farmer, noticed the folded ears of one tiny animal and further Scottish Folds were bred. The folded ear is due to the action of a single dominant gene — all Scottish Folds must have at least one folded-ear parent. An unfortunate side effect of this genetic make-up is the incidence of thickened tails and limbs and, for this reason, the GCCF in Britain refused to consider registration or recognition of the Scottish Fold, effectively banning their breeding.

Below *Red and white and tortoiseshell and white Japanese Bobtails.*

1. Scottish Fold (left) with a prick-
eared cat.
2. Brown tabby Scottish Fold.
3. American Curl kittens.
4. Snowshoe.

2

1

Many robust kittens were produced which had perfect bone structure however, and most of these were exported to the United States where the CFA granted full Championship status to the breed in 1978. The CA of Britain, formed in 1982, accepted the Scottish Fold for show purposes and registration, thus allowing Scottish Folds to be shown in their native land.

The Scottish Fold is of medium size with a rounded body and slender legs and tail. The head is rounded with a firm chin and jaw and distinct whisker pads. The eyes are large, wide and expressive, the nose short with a gentle curve. The ears are folded forward and downward; small and tightly folded ears are preferred to larger, loosely folded ones and the ears should be set cap-like on the head.

All feline colors and patterns are permitted except Himalayan and those colors showing evidence of hybridization resulting in the chocolate and lavender series, or those colors with white.

American Curl

A recent mutation is that of the American Curl, a cat whose ears are folded vertically instead of horizontally as in the Scottish fold. Appearing in all colors and coat lengths, this cat's distinctive curled ears give it a somewhat surprised or quizzical expression. Breeders are working to perfect an agreed upon standard and are busy trying to fulfill requirements for provisional acceptance which is an important step toward eventual Championship status. The alert, upright-standing curled ears feel rigid and are formed of cartilage.

Snowshoe

First bred in the United States, the Snowshoe combines the heftiness of the American Short-hair with the body length of the Oriental. It is an intelligent, well-balanced cat with a sparkling personality, and loves human company.

3

4

The Snowshoe's long body is strong and well muscled, the legs of medium bone with compact, oval paws and the tail is thick at the base, tapering slightly towards the tip. The head is triangular with large, pointed ears and large, oval eyes, which should be a bright, sparkling blue. The coat pattern is basically Himalayan or Siamese — with a pale coat and darker colored points, but in this breed the paws are white, as in the Birman cat. Any recognized points color is allowed.

Rex Cats

Curly-coated breeds of cat are known as rex, a term first used to describe a similar coat in the rabbit. There are two distinct breeds, known as the *Cornish Rex* and the *Devon Rex*, after the English counties in which the mutations were first recognized. The two types result from two different genes.

The Cornish Rex, first discovered in 1950, has a curly, plush coat caused by a mutant gene which inhibits the production of normal guard hairs and, in some cases, of awn hairs also. It is bred with an elegant, lithe body and a 'Roman' nose.

The Devon Rex, which appeared ten years later, has a very short, wavy coat which also lacks guard hairs, but the two breeds are quite distinct and not compatible when mated. The Devon Rex is of accentuated 'foreign' type and has a unique, pixie-like head with large, often tufted, ears.

Pre-dating the first English-born curly kitten was a cat born in a litter of feral felines at a hospital in Germany in 1946. The interest aroused by the Cornish Rex caused some German breeders to work with their own rex breed and,

Above right *Blue Devon Rex.*
Below *Blue Cornish Rex.*

in 1960, exports were made from Germany to the United States where they were found to be genetically compatible with Cornish Rex imported from Britain. A curled kitten also appeared in Oregon, United States, and one from a litter of farm cats in Verona, New York, in 1966 became the first of the breed now known as the American Wirehair.

In Britain both the Cornish Rex and the Devon Rex were recognized as separate breeds and given Championship status in 1967 although they were not accepted in the United States as two breeds until 1979. In Europe FIFe followed Britain's lead in recognizing the existence of two distinct rex genes but still use the name of German Rex in some cases.

Both types of Rex make intelligent, affectionate and rather extroverted pets. They do not shed their coats and are therefore very easy to groom by hand-stroking and the occasional use of a comb.

Rex have been bred in many colors. In Britain the Cornish can be of any color, the Devon of any except bi-colors. The American standard excludes lavender (lilac) and chocolate and the Siamese/Himalayan pattern. However, pointed-patterned rex are widely bred under the unofficial name Si-Rex in many countries, and in the United States are now accepted for the Championship bench.

Sphynx

The first Sphynx cat appeared as a spontaneous mutation in Ontario, Canada, in 1966. One kitten of a litter born to an ordinary black and white domestic cat was found to be completely hairless and with an unusual body conformation and a pixie-like head.

The Sphynx is unique in several ways besides its hairlessness and conformation. It sits in such a way as to avoid letting its body areas touch a surface, drawing its hind legs together to form a little 'seat', and it often stands with a foreleg lifted.

Handling a Sphynx is a unique experience as it often has a very short and almost invisible down on the body. The body itself feels rather hot and somewhat clammy.

The Sphynx standard calls for a long, hard and muscular body, barrel-like chest and a long, slender neck. The tail is long and tapered and the legs long and slim, with dainty, oval paws. The head is slightly longer than it is wide, with a whisker break and a 'stop' or change of angle in the profile.

Sphynx can be any of the colors acceptable for Manx and Rex cats. This breed is not recognized by all organizations — some refusing it because of difficulties identified in breeding studies in Canada.

Top *Blue silver tabby Devon Rex.*
Above *Chocolate tortoiseshell smoke Cornish Rex.*
Right *Sphynx.*

THE LONG-HAIRED CATS

Modern long-haired cats are the descendants of two distinctly different types taken to Europe during the sixteenth century. Naturalist Nicholas-Claude Fabri de Peiresc took cats from Angora (now known as Ankara), in Turkey, to France. These were described by his contemporaries as 'ash-colored, dun and speckled cats, beautiful to behold'. They had coats of long, silky hair, tall ears and long noses and were of light build. The cats were bred and some of their offspring taken to England, where they were known as French Cats. Later, heavier long-coated cats arrived in Europe from Persia (now Iran) and the two types were mated quite indiscriminately. By the end of the eighteenth century the longer-coated Persian style of cat had gained in popularity over the longer-bodied, sparser-coated Angora type of long-haired cat.

Charles H. Ross, writing in 1868 in a book which preceded the first cat shows, provided a fine record of the early fancy cats. He describes the Angora as

'a very beautiful variety, with silvery hair of fine silken texture, generally longest on the neck, but also long on the tail. Some are yellowish, and others olive approaching the colour of the lion; but they are all delicate creatures and of gentle dispositions.'

The Persian cat he describes as

'a variety with hair very long and very silky; perhaps more so than that of the Angora; it is however differently coloured, being of a fine uniform gray on the upper part with the texture of the fur as soft as silk and the lustre glossy; the color fades off on the lower parts of the sides and fades, or nearly does so, on the belly.'

In another book, *The Domestic Cat*, published in 1876, Dr Gordon Stables called the long-haired breed Asian Cats and described their coloring as similar to that of European or Western cats and made particular note of their small, round, sweet faces.

An early judge at cat shows, John Jennings, wrote of Russian, French, Chinese and Indian long-haired cats and decried the fact that the faces of the Persians were getting shorter.

It was not until 18 years after the first Crystal Palace Cat Show of 1871 that standards of excellence were made official. These published standards of points made firm distinctions between the early breeds of long-haired cats. The Persian was required to have a fine, silky and very soft coat, the Angora was to be woollier and with a tail like the brush of a fox, while the Russian needed to be even woollier than the Angora and to have a shorter tail with a tassel-like tip.

Since those early days a wide range of varieties of long-haired cats has evolved, each with its own approved standard of points by which it is judged at shows.

Long-haired cats can be delightful pets but it must be remembered that they need daily grooming to keep their long, flowing coats free from knots. The owner of a long-haired cat must be prepared to undertake this regular task. Some breeds also need bathing, especially before shows; so a potential show kitten should be selected for its calm, even temperament as well as perfect health and beauty.

Angora (Turkish Angora)

So much emphasis was placed on the Persian type by the Cat Fancy that the Angora became extinct outside its native land and was not revived as a breed until after World War Two.

During the 1950s and 1960s cats from Turkey were imported into Britain, Scandinavia and North America and formed the foundation stock for the development of a revived breed of Angora cats in Britain and Turkish Angora cats in Europe and North America.

In the United States the Turkish Angora was granted full Championship status in some associations in the early 1970s, some bodies allowing a range of colors, some only white. Now, as in Europe, most colors are accepted by all.

Today's Turkish Angora has a long sinuous body, small to medium wedge-shaped head, wide at the top with a definite taper toward the chin. The ears are wide at the base, long, pointed and tufted, and are set high on the head. The coat is long and silky and free from the woolly under-coat found in the Persian, making the Angora easier to groom and keep free from knots and tangles.

Turkish (Turkish Van or Van)

The fascinating cat known as the Turkish in Britain, and the Turkish Van or Van in North America and some other countries, comes from the Lake Van region of Turkey. In the 1950s it was introduced to the rest of the world by Laura Lushington. During her travels in the Lake Van area she noticed some unusual long-coated cats which were basically white with some distinct auburn markings. They were affectionate and playful, very active and hardy and had a strange affinity with water: they liked to dabble their paws in pools and to swim in the icy waters of Lake Van. Miss Lushington made several trips to Turkey, taking home carefully selected cats to undergo six months' quarantine in Britain before starting on the long road of breeding programs needed to obtain recognition in 1969.

The Turkish (Van) has a long muscular body, long legs and tail and a strong head of medium length and width, topped with large, upright ears. The large round eyes are wide set and should be light amber in color with pink eye rims. The basic coat color is chalk-white, the tail should be completely colored and there should be colored markings on the face, placed so as to leave a white blaze and white ears. Colored markings are permitted on the body but these must be small and irregularly placed. The nose leather and paw pads should be pink. The only colors recognized are Red (Auburn) and Cream.

Persian or Longhair Cats

Today a wonderful range of Persian or Longhair cats is exhibited for these stocky, long-coated cats have been among the most popular of show cats for many years. The first Persians arrived in the West from Persia during the sixteenth century.

They soon became popular and, over the years, the type was refined by careful breeding and more and more colors and patterns evolved to give the diversity known today.

Persian cats are renowned for the stockiness of their build. The cat is medium to large, equally massive across the shoulders and the rump, with short, thick legs and large round paws. The tail is short and carried low. The short, thick neck supports a massive round head with a broad skull, short snub nose with 'break' and tiny, wide-set, round-tipped ears. The eyes are large, round and lustrous and must be of the correct color to complement the coat.

The coat of the Persian is long and has a thick undercoat. The texture is very fine and the length is constant all over the body, including the shoulders, except for the ruff which is immense, framing the face and continuing as a frill between the cat's forelegs. The hair is also very long on the tail forming a full brush; there are tufts on the ears and between the toes.

Persian cats are generally placid and gentle. The queens make good mothers and the cats are quite undemanding, except that the coat requires regular thorough grooming to prevent tangles and matting.

Persian cats are recognized in almost the whole range of solid and mixed colors and patterns, including the color range patterns of the Turkish Van.

Below *Seal point Colourpoint (Himalayan) kitten.*
Bottom *Persian (Longhair) lilac.*

PERSIAN LONGHAIRS.
1. Black smoke. 2 Shaded Cameo. 3. Cream. 4. Blue. 5. Shaded silver. 6. Red and white bi-color. 7. Black. 8. Golden-shaded. 9. Chinchilla.

1

2

3

4

PERSIAN LONGHAIRS.
1. A litter of tipped cats that ranged from chinchilla to Smoke.
2. Shaded cameo. 3. Red self. 4. Harlequin tortoiseshell.
5. Black. 6. Black and white bi-color. 7. Blue tortoisehshell and
white (dilute calico). 8. Chocolate. 9. Pewter. 10. Seal
tortoiseshell tabbypoint (Colourpoint)

5

6

7

8

9

10

1

2

3

4

5

Colourpoint Longhair (Himalayan)

This breed is truly Persian in conformation but with the pattern and coloring typical of the Siamese. These cats were deliberately developed by breeders in the United States and in Britain from matings between Persians and Siamese in the 1920s, followed by careful and selective crossing and back crossing of the offspring. It took many years of such careful breeding to produce the typical cats seen on the show benches of today. A book of breeds published in 1931 by the Cat Club of Paris pictures a Himalayan type cat which they refer to as 'Persan-Siamoise'.

The Colourpoint (or Himalayan as it is more usually known in North America where Colorpoint – without the 'u' – is the name for a color range of Siamese-type cats) has a chunky body with short thick legs and large round paws. The tail is short and carried low and the head is round and massive with a short stub nose, tiny round-tipped ears and large round eyes.

The coat is long and thick and stands away from the body. The toes and ears are tufted, a full ruff frames the face and continues as a frill between the front legs and the tail is thick and brush-like.

The Colourpoint/Himalayan is a quiet but lively and interesting pet as well as a satisfying show cat. This breed has small litters of cream-white, fluffy kittens, the points' color beginning to come through gradually after four or five days. Recognized in all the Siamese and most Colorpoint Shorthair colors, all varieties must have blue eyes. The CFA now recognizes the Himalayan as a color variety of the Persian.

Peke-faced Persian

This cat is a very extreme type of the Persian cat recognized by only a few associations. Others have probably refused recognition because the foreshortened muzzle can cause problems with the cat's tear ducts and respiration. Breeders have to be extremely careful not to perpetuate any such problems but the recognized strains are now claimed to be free of these difficulties.

The Peke-faced Persian is similar in conformation to the Persian and has the same luxuriant fur. The difference lies in the flattened face, very like that of the Pekingese dog from which the breed takes its name. A totally different head bone structure gives it high set ears and a distinctively wrinkled muzzle.

The Peke-faced is recognized *only* in Red and Red Tabby.

Maine Coon

Native to the State of Maine in the United States and sometimes called the American Longhair, the Maine Coon has been known as a true breed for more than a hundred years. It was popular in the late nineteenth century, excelling as a working farm cat and also taking prizes at early

6

COLOURPOINTS (HIMALAYAN).
1. Seal point. 2. Lilac point.
3. Cream point. 4. Seal tabby point.
5. Blue point and Cream point.
6. Chocolate tortoiseshell point.
7. Peke-faced Persian. 8. Peke-faced Persian.

7

8

1

2

exhibitions held in conjunction with state and county fairs. A tabby Coon was Best in Show at the Madison Square Gardens Cat Show of 1895 but then, with the arrival of several breeds imported from Europe, the Maine Coon's popularity declined.

In 1953 the Central Maine Coon Cat Club was established to promote the breed and, by 1967, a standard was drawn up and accepted by some of the American registering bodies. In 1976 the International Society for the Preservation of the Maine Coon was formed and the Cat Fanciers' Association finally accepted the breed and granted Championship status.

The Maine Coon has a unique, endearing and gentle personality. It is quite a large cat but without any coarseness of bone. The body is long and well-proportioned, with a broad chest, strong neck, sturdy legs and round, tufted paws. The head is of medium width and length, with high cheekbones and large, wide-set eyes, which may be gold, copper or green, except in the pure white Maine Coon which has either blue or odd-colored eyes. The coat is long and quite heavy, shorter on the shoulders, but long and silky on the sides and flanks with a full ruff framing the face. The long, plume-like tail provides the finishing touch.

The Maine Coon is accepted in most feline colors and patterns, except those derivative from pointed colors and pointed colors themselves.

Norwegian Forest Cat

Known as the Norsk Skaukatt in its native Norway, the origin of this breed is shrouded in mystery and folklore. It is referred to in Norse mythology and in fairy tales published in the middle of the nineteenth century. It was in the 1930s, however, that a group of breeders gathered together some hardy, semi-wild farm cats and set about establishing a true pedigreed breed, embodying all the desired traits for the cat best

suited to the country's rather inhospitable climate. The breed gained in popularity during the 1970s and was granted Championship status in FIFe in 1977.

The ideal show cat is very similar to the Maine Coon in appearance except in head shape and coat. The Norwegian head is shorter, more triangular and has a somewhat straight profile. The coat is of greater density and is thicker than that of its longer-headed, well-muzzled, silkier-coated American Main Coon 'cousin'. The Forest Cat must have a double coat. The woolly under-coat keeps the body warm, while the medium-length hanging top coat resists rain and snow. The tail is full and bushy and the cat sports a full ruff framing the face.

Cats of this breed are intelligent, cautious, excellent hunters and exceptionally good at climbing. They are strong and very hardy, playful and particularly independent. Most colors are permitted in the Norwegian Forest Cat.

1. Red tabby and white Maine Coon. 2. Brown tabby and white Maine Coon. 3. Blue tabby and white Norwegian Forest Cat. 4. Birman. 5. Blue-cream point Birman kitten. 6. Red point Birman. 7. Seal tortoiseshell point Birman. 8. Seal point Birman.

3

Birman

This striking breed is thought to have originated in Southeast Asia where it is said to have been a temple cat.

The Birman was developed in France and became successful until World War Two, which reduced numbers to just two individuals. It was some years before the breed was again viable. In the early 1960s some Birmans were exported from France to England and soon gained popularity, achieving recognition in 1966. From England the cats were imported into the United States and gained recognition in CFA in 1967.

The Birman is not so cobby as the Persian, although it has heavy bone and is a substantial cat. It is longer in the body and the head than the Persian and has a longer muzzle and larger ears. The coat is long and silky, with a brush-like tail and it has Himalayan markings on the points, except for the four paws which are white. The white gloves are required on all four feet. Those in the front form a line running straight across the front paw just at the 'ankle' in the perfect specimen, while those on the rear paws extend up the back of the hock and are called 'laces'. Ideally, the laces end in a point or inverted 'V' and extend half to three-quarters of the way up the back. As in all Himalayan-patterned breeds, the eyes are blue. The temperament of the Birman falls halfway between that of the placid Persian and the extrovert Siamese. It is an affectionate and very inquisitive cat with a good personality. The females mature early and prove excellent mothers.

Seal-, Blue-, Chocolate- and Lilac-Point are recognized in most associations; some also allow Red- (Flame-), Tortoiseshell- and Tabby- (Lynx-) Point.

Ragdoll

There was much controversy over this breed until recent years, for it was originally suggested that the Ragdolls (developed from a litter of a cat injured in a road accident) had a peculiar limp quality (hence the name) and were unable to feel pain. It now seems clear that they are not insensitive, a quality which would have made it difficult for them to live any kind of life without risking serious injury.

Ragdoll varieties exported from the United States caught the public imagination and dedicated breeders worked hard to produce cats of outstanding type and coloring for the show bench. Today the Ragdoll is recognized in three patterns and the usual range of Himalayan points colors. The patterns are 'colorpoint', when the cat has points on all its extremities and no white; 'mitted' when it has points plus white on paws and under the body; and 'bi-color' when it has points plus white on the head, body and legs.

All Ragdolls should have blue eyes. They are large cats with strong bone but not cobby like the Persian. They have a noble head with a long nose and wide-set ears. The coat is profuse but silky and comparatively easy to keep well groomed.

Ragdolls are inquisitive and lively and make good companions. The breed is not accepted by all Associations.

Above *Ragdoll kittens.*

Below *Ragdoll.*

FOREIGN AND ORIENTAL CATS

Almost all the 'Foreign' breeds are short-haired cats, although some long-haired varieties have been developed from them. Some do have links with the countries from which they take their names, but European and North American breeders have been responsible for most of the varieties as they are known today.

The Foreign group all tend towards much leaner bodies than the longhairs and other short-haired types, and have fine bones and rather narrow heads. To their admirers they have an elegance beyond that of other cats, and they frequently seem to demand more contact and attention from their humans. However, their sleek coats, even in the long-haired forms, require less grooming than the Persian type of cat. Claims that they are more intelligent than other breeds would be hotly contested by fanciers of rivals — intelligence is an attribute of an individual not a type.

The whole group is often referred to as 'Foreign Shorthairs' but this can lead to some confusion since this is also used as a name for cats of Siamese type but without the pointed pattern which form part of this larger group.

Russian Blue

This is a breed that stands alone. It is a short-coated blue of foreign type but its standard of points ensures that it remains a unique breed.

The Russian Blue has a somewhat obscure history. It was first known as the Archangel Blue and was said to have been taken to Britain by sailors returning from the Baltic port of Archangel. At the turn of the century it was common to lump all of the blue shorthairs into one class, regardless of type, and the sleek, fine-boned Russians were beaten in popularity by the chunky Blue British Shorthairs. Only in 1912 were separate classes established for the two types.

Although breeders worked hard to promote the Russian Blue in the early years of its development, the breed suffered a major setback during World War Two when it became difficult to feed and breed cats in Britain. After the war, when stock was scarce, Russian cats were mated with Siamese to increase the gene pool. The Foreign Blue kittens resulting from these matings lacked the distinctive plush coat of the Russian, and it was not until 1965 that breeders made a concerted effort to re-establish the true Russian type and coat. A new standard of points was produced and careful breeding programs instituted using English and Swedish lines.

The modern Russian must have the special coat of short, thick double fur which can be stroked both ways without exposing the blue skin. A medium shade of blue is preferred, with the hairs having a silvered appearance at the tips. The head is unique, being a short wedge in shape with a flat skull and a straight forehead and nose. In Britain the standard calls for the large ears to be placed upright on the head. In the United States associations the ears should be set wide apart — that is to say, as much on the side as on the top of the head. The head is distinctive in that it presents the most flat planes of any breed; from the front there are six distinctive flat planes forming a hexagon; in profile, there are more flat planes, a flat forehead, a straight nose and a flat level underjaw. All standards agree that the eyes should be vivid green and set wide apart but the British require them to be almond-shaped while the Americans prefer them rounded.

The Russian Blue is a delightful cat with a quiet voice and a loving temperament. It is easy to care for and, although it does crave the company of humans and other pets, is not as demanding as some of the other Foreign cats.

Black Russian and **White Russian** cats are also being bred and are recognized in Australia and New Zealand.

Russian Blue.

Korat

Known for centuries in its native Thailand as the Si-Sawat, the Korat is said to bring good luck to Thais who own them. This rare and beautiful cat, which was named after the high region known as the Korat Plateau, has retained most of the characteristics of an ancestor illustrated in the Cat Book Poems, a manuscript dating back to the thirteenth century. In this a painting is accompanied by the description:

'the cat *Mal-ed* has a body color like *Doklao*; the hairs are smooth with roots like clouds and tips like silver; the eyes shine like dewdrops on a lotus leaf.'

Mal-ed means seed and refers to the seed of a Thai plant called the Look Sawat, which has a silvery-gray fruit, slightly tinged with green. *Dok* means flower and *Lao* is a plant with silver-tipped flowers. Si-Sawat then is a compound word referring to the Korat's mingled colors of a silver-gray coat and light green eyes.

At the National Cat Club's London Show of 1896 a Korat brought from Siam was entered as a Siamese Cat but was disqualified as the judges expected all Siamese to be fawn with dark brown points. It did not reappear in the show world until 1959, when a breeding pair of Korats was imported into the United States, to be followed by further cats and the formation of a breed club in 1965. The Korat was accepted by most American associations in 1966 and by the remainder in 1969. Korats were first taken from the United States to Britain in 1972.

The Korat is neither as svelte as a Siamese nor as cobby as a Shorthair, but it is hard and muscular, with slender legs and a tapered tail of medium length. Its heart-shaped head is topped by large round ears, set rather high on the head, and the large and luminous eyes may be green or have a very slight amber cast.

The coat is single-layered, of short glossy hair which lies close to the body. It is silver-blue in color and appears to be tipped with silver as it catches the light, an effect caused by less clumping of the color factor at the end of the hair shaft.

Siamese

The Siamese type of cat was established in Thailand many centuries ago. Portraits of the *Vichien Mas* in the ancient Thai manuscripts known as the Cat Book Poems show a cat like the modern breed, with a light coat marked with darker extremities, but with the color only on the ears, paws, tail and just around the nose and whisker pads.

It is fairly well established that cats from the Royal Court of Siam were taken to Britain in 1884 and to America, by diplomatic families and by permission of the Thais, but they were by

then already known in Britain and had been exhibited at Harrison Weir's first Cat Show in 1871.

The German traveler and naturalist Simon Pallas reported seeing a cat with a pointed pattern coat — though of generally darker coloring — on a journey west of the Caspian Sea in 1793 and published an engraving of it. It appears a very solid-looking cat compared with modern Siamese, but so do those in pictures of cats exhibited early in this century, and the dark coloring compared with the Cat Book Poem type could be explained by climatic differences — the color of the Siamese coat is affected by temperature.

Over the years breeders and judges have favored more extreme types, with the faces of Siamese cats becoming more pointed. Today's cat should have a long wedge-shaped head that narrows to a fine muzzle, with large pricked ears, wide at the base, which follow and advance the line of the head, and almond-shaped eyes that slope upwards and outwards. The body is long and svelte with slim legs set on oval feet and a long, tapering tail.

Above Chocolate point Siamese.
Left Seal tabby- (lynx-) point Siamese.

Above Siamese cats illustrated in the Thai Cat Book Poems have very limited points, due perhaps to local climate.
Below left Lilac tortie point Siamese.
Below Blue point Siamese.

Top An engraving of the cat seen by Simon Pallas in 1793.
Above The type of Siamese exhibited at shows early this century was much more round-faced than the modern cat.

Above Fawn tabby point Siamese.
Below left Cream point Siamese.
Below right Seal point tortoiseshell Siamese.

The first cats in the West were the dilute form of black known as Seal Point. Their striking appearance ensured attention and interest. These early cats often had kinked tails and squints (crossed-eyes) and at first it was thought that these were natural to the breed — supposedly ancient Siamese legends were recounted to give them a romantic origin — but both would be considered faults in a modern show cat.

The Siamese soon became popular in the United States and was shown at Madison Square Gardens in 1909. American breeders have tended to aim for a particularly long head but some who prefer the older type have recently begun a return to a cat looking like the earlier, less extreme form than the modern show cat.

American cats have often achieved a much greater degree of contrast between points and body color in their darker cats, due partly to their careful selection for breeding and partly to a tendency to live at a generally higher ambient temperature.

Many of the early imports of seal-pointed cats carried other dilute and recessive genes in their make-up and in following years blue-pointed and chocolate- pointed kittens occurred. At first the various registering bodies refused to accept the different colors, considering them 'sports', but eventually the science of genetics was applied to coat coloration in the cat and the rules of inheritance backed up the breeders' claims, allowing the Blue-Point and Chocolate-Point to be accepted for breeding and the show ring. Eventually when blue- and chocolate-pointed cats were mated their offspring produced the dilute form of chocolate known as lilac and the

Lilac-Point (Lavender-Point) came into being. In some associations, Lilac-Point is known as Frost Point.

Not content with the four naturally-evolved colors in their Siamese, some breeders decided to introduce the sex-linked red color and, although it took several years of selective breeding, back-crossing and effort to gain approval, Red-Point, Cream-Point and the whole range of Tortoiseshell-Points were eventually accepted and given Championship status. However, since out-cross to other breeds such as American Short-hairs was required, they were not always classed as Siamese (see below).

One or two Siamese queens made their own mating arrangements and eventually some Siamese-shaped tabby kittens took the fancy of some breeders. One female accidentally found a half-Siamese tabby mate and in her litter she surprised her owner, and the cat fancy in general, by producing the first tabby-pointed Siamese. These kittens were considered so attractive that a breeding program was set up to develop them under the name of Shadow-Point. The name was later changed to Lynx-Point, which is still favored in some associations, but changed again to Tabby-Point in others. Later, when Red-Point and Tabby-Point Siamese lines were mixed, Tabby/Tortie- or Torbie-Points were produced in all the main coat colors.

Most American registration bodies separate the red and tabby color lines from the other Siamese, grouping them as a separate breed under the name Colorpoint Shorthairs — not to be confused with Colourpoints, which is the British name for what Americans call Himalayans or the

Left *Chocolate tabby point Siamese.*
Below *Balinese tabby- (lynx-) point.*
Bottom *Seal point Balinese.*

Pointed Persians. Siamese have also been used to produce solid colored and patterned cats with green eyes (or blue in the case of whites) which are known as Oriental Shorthairs or Foreign Shorthairs.

Colorpoint

Those American registration bodies which do not permit any other than the original four solid color points to be considered as part of the Siamese breed give them the name Colorpoint. They include points in tortoiseshell, blue-cream, and lilac-cream and lynx-point (tabby-point) in the whole range of colors.

In every respect other than the patterning of their points these cats look like the Siamese and have the same qualities.

Balinese

For many years long-coated kittens had appeared in litters of Siamese of certain blood lines. Their long hair barred them from show classes and they were kept only as pets. Eventually, in the 1940s, two American breeders decided to develop such cats as a separate breed. Because of their svelte shape, dainty features and graceful movements, reminiscent of the dancers of Bali, the name Balinese was chosen. The breed gained recognition with the CFA in 1970 in the four basic Siamese colors: Seal, Blue, Chocolate and Lilac. By 1980, further points colors were also accepted — but under the breed name Javanese.

The Balinese resembles a Siamese in every way except for its long silky coat, which lies close to the body, and the beautiful plumed tail. All varieties have blue eyes. The coat is free from any woolly undercoat and is therefore easy to keep well-groomed and tangle-free.

They are intelligent and playful, affectionate and rather demanding. They object to being left alone for long, but get on well with other cats and dogs.

1. Blue tabby Javanese (New Zealand).
2. Brown Javanese (New Zealand).
3. White Oriental (Foreign) Shorthair.
4. Cinnamon Oriental (Foreign) Shorthair.

Javanese

The red- and tabby-based colors of the Balinese — the long-haired equivalents of the Colorpoints — are not accepted by many American associations under the name Balinese but are known as Javanese. In all respects except color they are identical to the Balinese.

In New Zealand, where the red and lynx- or tabby-point varieties are accepted as Balinese, spotted and self-coated forms of the Balinese are recognized under the name Javanese.

Oriental Shorthairs (Foreign Shorthairs)

The Siamese cats seen during their early days in the Cat Fancy included some which were colored all over, instead of having the color restricted to the points. These cats also lacked the blue eye color of the pointed Siamese. A rather muddled

state of affairs existed until the end of the 1920s with two dissimilar cats going under the same name. The Siamese Cat Club of Britain then formally announced that henceforth only blue-eyed Siamese would be eligible for show classes.

Non-pointed cats then faded from the limelight, although the occasional all-black or all-blue cat of good oriental conformation made news in the contemporary cat press.

In 1952 a British breeder who crossed her Siamese with black short-haired cats, in the hope of producing a Siamese with truly black points, was thrilled, as she wrote to the Siamese Cat Club *Newsletter*, to produce 'a beautiful little *brown* kitten. It is male, Siamese in shape, with a nice long tail and nicely shaped eyes.' This cat, Elmtower Bronze Idol, was the first Havana or Oriental Chocolate Cat, although when the variety was eventually given GCCF recognition in 1958 it was under the name Chestnut Brown Foreign Shorthair and only later was it changed back to the Havana.

In 1962 another breeder set out to produce a blue-eyed all-white cat and this, under the name Foreign White, and the Foreign Lilac, resulting from the use of lilac-points in the development of the Chestnut Brown, were both recognized in Britain in 1978. The Foreign Black (a 'self' seal-point) was added four years later. In both these breeding programs, and those for red, tortie and tabby Siamese, other solid kittens had appeared and now a whole range of attractive coats on a Siamese body have been created and recognized by many associations around the world.

With the exception of the startling blue eyes of the White, these are all green-eyed though like the Siamese in other respects. In personality too they resemble the Siamese — rather demanding of time and attention, and extremely generous with their devotion to their owners. Extrovert and agile, the Oriental, whatever its color, makes a delightful, intelligent pet. Its short, fine coat is very easy to keep in good condition with the minimum of grooming.

ORIENTAL (FOREIGN).
1. *Shorthair blue.*
2. *Shorthair lilac tortoiseshell.*
3. *Shorthair cinnamon tabby.*
4. *Shorthair ebony.*
5. *Shorthair cream and red tabby.*

Havana Brown

Cats produced in the British Havana breeding program — which eventually created the Chestnut Brown Foreign Shorthair – were of only moderately Siamese type and were taken to the United States in the mid-1950s. No outcrossing was allowed and these developed a distinctly different breed from what became the British type. It was recognized in 1959 as the Havana Brown, with standards based on those for the Russian Blue, not the Siamese type.

The Havana Brown should be a rich warm mahogany brown, nose leather brown with a rosy cast. Its body, legs and tail are all of medium length. The head is slightly longer than it is wide with a distinct change in slope or 'stop' on the nose between the eyes instead of the smooth Siamese profile, and a definite whisker break. The oval eyes should be green but chartreuse shades are acceptable.

The Lavender Foreign Shorthair is a more dilute color form, created by adding the blue dilution of the Russian Blue and recognized by the ACFA in the United States. It should not be confused with the British Foreign Lilac, which is of Siamese type.

Burmese

Although similar looking cats appear in the Thai Cat Book Poems paintings, all modern Burmese can trace their ancestry back to a Siamese hybrid female named Wong Mau, with solid body color but discernible darker points, who was taken from Rangoon to the United States in 1930. At first this attractive cat was mated to Siamese males, then her offspring were mated together and back-crossed to Wong Mau herself. Three types of kittens were produced — some Siamese, some like Wong Mau, a type now deliberately bred as Tonkinese, and some much darker and with less distinct points which were the first true Burmese cats. They were officially recognized in 1936 by the CFA — the first pedigree breed to have been developed completely in the United States.

In America the Burmese has become a substantial cat with a round head, full face and rounded ears. Outcrosses to Siamese were made because of the shortage of Burmese and for this reason the CFA suspended registration from 1947 to 1953, although other bodies continued

1. Havana Brown kittens. 2. Havana Brown.
3. Burmese Blue (British type). 4. Burmese chocolate (British type). 5. Burmese sable (British type). 6. Burmese cream (British type).
7. Burmese red (British type). 8. Burmese sable (American type). 9. Tortie tabby Tiffany.

to accept it. About this time cats were exported to Europe and the type recognized in Britain in 1952 was much more Siamese in appearance. In Britain (and in Europe, Australia, New Zealand and other countries which follow the British standard) a cat of modified 'foreign' type is called for, medium in size, hard and muscular with slender legs and a straight tail of medium length. The head should be slightly rounded on top with wide-set, medium-sized ears that tilt slightly forward. The cheekbones are wide, giving a shortened wedge shape. The nose has a distinct break in the profile and the chin is firm and determined. The large lustrous eyes show a slightly oriental slant and should be golden yellow in color.

The Burmese in America maintains a more rounded head and the eyes are rounded too, following the conformation of the original Wong Mau. Although in many respects the breed is similar on both sides of the Atlantic the heads are distinctly different.

A number of color varieties have been created. At one time the CFA recognized only the original Brown (or Sable) as a true Burmese. Most other associations also accepted the Blue, but the CFA gave it a different name, the Malayan, which could also be colored Champagne and Platinum. Today they recognize all as Burmese in two divisions, Sable and Dilute; the Dilute Division containing the colors blue, champagne and platinum. Chocolate and Lilac were originally developed in America but the reds, creams and tortoiseshells were largely British creations and are not accepted in America.

The short, fine and glossy coat of the Burmese requires little grooming but this breed is very affectionate and does not like to be left alone, enjoying the company of other cats and of humans.

The Tiffany is a long-haired version of the Burmese and not generally recognized on the show bench.

Malayan

This is the name used by some American associations for cats matching the Burmese standard for type but in the color range Champagne (Chocolate), Platinum (Lilac) — and Blue as well. Coats tend to be paler than in other breeds due to a dilution factor in their genetic make-up. They have the same character as Burmese. In the CFA these cats compete as the Dilute Division of Burmese.

Tiffany

This breed is Burmese in type and coloring but has a beautiful coat of long silky hair. In the United States the Tiffany was developed from long-coated cats which appeared in litters of normal Burmese, but in Britain they came from the Burmilla breeding program and have been refined by backcrosses to Burmese of very good type.

Colors are as for the Burmese.

Tonkinese

The Tonkinese is a hybrid of Siamese and Burmese and shows characteristics of both parents. A mating between a Siamese and a Burmese produces all Tonkinese kittens, whereas mating two Tonkinese produces, on average, two Tonkinese kittens to one Burmese and one Siamese.

Tonkinese have dark points which merge gradually into the body color which is intermediate between the pale Siamese and the dark Burmese coloring. Tonkinese eye color is blue-green or turquoise, never blue or yellow. This is a cat of medium size, alert, active and muscular in appearance. The body is of medium length with fairly slim legs and oval paws; the tail is medium to long with a slightly rounded tip. The head is a modified Siamese/Burmese wedge with high cheekbones and wide ears of medium size. The eyes are almond-shaped but more open than those of the typical Siamese. The coat is medium-short, fine, soft and silky and close-lying. In the mature cat it should be rich and even in color, slightly lighter under the body and with densely marked points. Kittens may have lighter body color because this can take up to 16 months to reach its adult hue.

The Tonkinese is friendly and affectionate with a mischievous, inquisitive air. It is generally good with other cats, dogs and children. It is less vocal than the Siamese but its coat is just as easy to keep in superb condition.

Bombay

The Bombay was developed in the United States from a sable Burmese and a black American Shorthair. This cross produced jet black kittens with the type and hardy constitution of the shorthair combined with the sleek coat and distinctive head of the American-style Burmese. Further breeding lines were started using only genetically black stock, eventually producing a cat resembling a black American-style Burmese which was granted Championship status by the CFA in 1976. Pioneers of the breed thought it looked like a miniature Indian black panther and chose Bombay as the breed name.

The Bombay is a muscular cat of medium size, neither too compact nor too rangy. The head should be fairly large and pleasantly rounded without any flat planes but with a distinct nose break and a firm chin. The ears are of medium size, wide at the base, with rounded tips, set to tilt slightly forward on the head and wide apart. The wide-set eyes are large and round and may be any shade of gold to copper, the greater the depth and brilliance the better. The short, satin-like coat has a reflective sheen which makes the Bombay look more intensely black than any other feline variety. This is a 'black only' breed.

Above left *Seal point Tonkinese.*
Left *Bombay*

Abyssinian

The most famous of all the ticked tabby, or agouti, breeds is the Abyssinian, a cat which has been selectively bred for many years, allowing the reduction of the incidence of natural tabby barring normally found on the cheeks, neck, tail and underbody. Today's show standard Abyssinian has been relieved of all unwanted tabby bars, leaving a clear glowing ticked coat, rather like that of a Belgian Hare.

An Abyssinian cat was taken from Ethiopia to England in 1868 but there is no evidence that the breed descends from this individual. Recognized for shows in 1882, they were known under many names, including the Russian, Spanish, Hare, Bunny and Ticked Cat. It was once thought that it resulted from a cross between a cat and a wild rabbit.

The modern Abyssinian is a well-established and popular breed, known throughout the world. It is a lithe and sinuous cat of medium size, but not so svelte as the Siamese. The requirements for head shape differ in different countries but it has a rather heart-shaped face with rounded planes on a modified wedge-shaped head with large, wide-set ears, often tufted at the tips, and large almond-shaped expressive eyes of gold-green. It has long slender legs with dainty paws and the body is balanced by a fairly long, tapering tail. Although it is fine-boned, the Abyssinian does not look frail or delicate.

Abyssinian cats are quiet and gentle with easy-care coats. They seem to cope well with confinement to the home and so make good pets for people without gardens.

In America the Abyssinian is recognized in the original form known as Ruddy (or Usual) with

1. Sorrel Abyssinian.
2. Silver Abyssinian.
3. Lilac Abyssinian.
4. Sorrel Abyssinian kitten.
5. Ruddy Abyssinian.

black or dark brown ticking on a rich brown fur, and in Red (Sorrel) which is a warm red ticked with chocolate brown and blue, a warm soft blue-gray ticked with various shades of slate blue with an ivory undercoat. In Britain blue, chocolate, lilac, cream, silver and the various tortoiseshell and tabby variations on these colors have all been accepted. In CFA, the Fawn Abyssinian is seeking Championship recognition and is currently seeking a color standard approval. The Silver Abyssinian has been refined to a beautiful state in New Zealand where Abyssinian breeders have worked long and hard on this challenging color.

1. Abyssinian kittens. From left to right: lilac, ruddy or usual, blue, sorrel.
2. Ruddy Somali.
3. Ruddy Somali kittens.

Somali

In litters of Abyssinian kittens some breeders discovered the uninvited arrival of a few with long coats. At first these 'throw-outs' were given away to be neutered pets; then a group was formed to develop the long-coated Abyssinians as a separate breed. Breeding programs were started throughout the world from original stock from the United States, Australia and New Zealand and breeders were generous in allowing their cats to be exported and exchanged for the benefit of the new breed which, by general agreement, was called the Somali.

In conformation the Somali is very like the Abyssinian. The type called for differs slightly between associations — for example, American standards often require a shorter, more rounded head than those of Europe. The Somali has the ticked coat of the Abyssinian but the fur is much longer as well as softer and silkier, and there are more bands of color on each hair. Colors are as in the Abyssinian.

Ocicat

The Ocicat is a hybrid breed developed in the United States from Abyssinian, Siamese and American Shorthair. The result is a large well-spotted cat with a resemblance to a young ocelot, hence its attractive name.

The body is muscular, large but lithe, with a complex spotted coat pattern of darker spots on a lighter ground. All ocicats may have any eye color except blue. The original coloring of dark chestnut brown markings on a beige coat is known as Dark Chestnut; milk chocolate markings on creamy beige are Light Chestnut; Silver and Bronze varieties or also recognized. In total, 12 color variations have gained Championship recognition in CFA. The colors are Blue, Blue Silver, Chocolate, Chocolate Silver, Cinnamon, Cinnamon Silver, Fawn, Fawn Silver, Lavender, Lavender Silver, Silver and Tawny (Brown Spotted Tabby). A very distinctive cat, the ocicat is a large, well-spotted agouti cat of moderate type which displays the look of an athletic animal. It is well-muscled and solid, graceful and lithe yet has a fullness of body and chest.

Spotted Mist

The Spotted Mist, the first new breed to be developed in Australia, evolved from first crosses between Burmese and Abyssinian, with the addition of some domestic tabby. A medium-sized and moderately 'foreign' type, the body should be firm and muscular with a broad chest, strong legs and neat oval paws. The tail is long and thick with minimal taper. The broad head has a firm chin, well-developed whisker pads and large wide-based ears set well apart and tilted slightly forwards. The large lustrous eyes are very expressive and may be any shade of green from chartreuse to ultramarine. The short fine and close-lying coat is easy to keep in good condition. It is clearly and delicately spotted against a misty ground color while the legs and tail are ringed and the face lined as in other tabby varieties. Cats of this variety are said to be particularly affectionate.

The Spotted Mist has been bred in a range of colors expected from cats with Burmese ancestry and, after ten years' careful breeding, was recognized in Australia, the country of its creation.

Egyptian Mau

The Egyptian Mau was bred in the United States and should not be confused with the cats of the same name bred experimentally in Britain during the 1960s and now known as Oriental Tabbies. The Mau is similar in build to the Abyssinian and the foundation stock for the breed was brought to America from Egypt via Rome in 1953, although the breed did not gain recognition until 1968.

The Mau (which is the ancient Egyptian word for cat and can also mean 'to see') is a cat of medium size, muscular and graceful, with well-proportioned legs and small oval paws. The medium-length tail is slightly tapered. The head forms a slightly rounded wedge, showing gentle contours from all angles. The ears are medium to large and the eyes large and almond shaped with a slight slant towards the ears, neither round nor oriental. The fine silky coat is of medium

1 and 2. Ocicats.
3. Silver Egyptian Mau.
4. Spotted Mist.
5. Silver Egyptian Mau.

length and must exhibit the desired Mau pattern. This requires good contrast between pale ground color and deeper markings, forehead barred with a typical 'M' and frown marks going over the head and neck and breaking into spots on the spine, then forming a dorsal stripe towards the tail, which is banded; the cheeks are barred with lines from the eyes to the base of the ears; the chest has one or more necklaces, the upper legs are barred and the shoulders have bars breaking into spots, with similar markings on the haunches. The torso is clearly spotted and the underbody has 'vest button' spots. Eye color is always gooseberry green.

The Mau is recognized in Silver (charcoal markings on pale silver); Bronze (dark brown on light bronze); and Smoke (jet black on charcoal gray with silver undercoat).

Burmilla

A chance meeting between a Chinchilla male and a lilac Burmese female produced the first litter of Burmilla kittens, captivating creatures with type partway between a British Shorthair and a Burmese, large green eyes and short dense silvered coats. The Burmilla was quickly established by a dedicated small band of breeders and has proved a popular pet as well as a stunning show cat.

The Burmilla standard calls for an elegant, lithe but muscular medium length body, with a straight back, slim legs with neat oval paws and a medium to long tail with a round tip.

The head is gently rounded with medium to large ears, set moderately apart and tilted slightly forward. The eyes are large and set well apart, with a round lower lid and a straight upper lid. They may be any shade of green.

This is a cat with a playful temperament and its gentle nature makes it an excellent mother.

Ground color may be silver or golden with an evenly-shaded or tipped mantle, denser along the spine and gradually decreasing along the flanks

and may be Black or its Burmese dilute form Sepia, Blue, Chocolate, Lilac, Caramel, Beige, Red, Cream or Apricot (only in Sepia is the dilution differentiated). The underparts should be as silver as possible (light tan in the Golden). Legs should be slightly ringed on the upper part, pad to wrist (hock) in the color of the shading or tipping and the paws silver with pads matching the tipping. The tail has distinct rings and tip in the color of shading or tipping. The face is pencilled around the eyes, nose and lips with an 'M' on the forehead and traces of tabby markings. The nose tip is terracotta, outlined with the tipping color.

Burmoire

This variety was produced by matings between Burmilla and Burmese cats. It should resemble the Burmese in type and coat texture but the coat pattern and coloration should be exactly as that specified in the standard for the Oriental Smoke series. Such cats have colored markings on a silver base coat, giving a rippling effect rather like that of watered silk. The color range is as for the Burmilla.

Asian Tabby

This breed is also the result of matings between Burmilla and Burmese cats. The Asian Tabby is a cat of Burmese type and coat texture but with the coat pattern of the Oriental Ticked Tabby. The color range is as for the Oriental Ticked Tabby.

Singapura

The Singapura was developed from cats discovered in Singapore and taken to the United States. Tommy Meadow, the breed's founder, drew up

a careful breeding program and her work has been rewarded by the production of an attractive viable breed with an enormous aesthetic appeal.

The Singapura is a small to medium shorthair, moderately stocky and muscular in build, with heavy legs tapering to small oval paws. The tail is of medium length with a blunt tip. The head has a rounded skull and a definite whisker break, a muzzle of medium length with a blunt nose and a well-developed chin. The ears are large and slightly pointed and the eyes are large and almond shaped, held wide open and hazel-green or yellow in color.

The Singapura's coat is very short and fine, each hair having at least two bands of dark brown ticking, separated by bands of warm old ivory, light next to the skin and dark at the tip; the overall impression is of a sepia-colored cat. The tail tip is dark and the color extends along the tail and onto the base of the spine. Muzzle, chest, chin and stomach are the color of unbleached muslin, with salmon tones to the ears and the bridge of the nose. Nose leather is pale to dark salmon, outlined with dark brown, paw pads rosy brown and eye rims dark brown.

Singapuras are now being exported to Britain and Japan. They are very friendly cats and easy to keep in peak condition.

Seychellois Shorthair

This striking cat is the result of a breeding program registered with the Cat Association of Britain in 1988. It is of medium size and oriental conformation. It has a long svelte body, with an elegant neck and long slim legs with small, oval paws. The head is wedge-shaped with very large pointed ears, the eyes of almond shape, oriental set and preferably blue in color.

The coat is short, fine and silky and predominantly white with splashes of any color or combination of colors on the head, legs and body. The tail is colored. Markings are classified into three groups:

Seychellois Neuviéme: nearly all white with colored tail and tiny colored markings on the head.
Seychellois Huitiéme: mainly white with colored tail and splashes of color on the head and legs.
Seychellois Septiéme: white with colored tail and splashes of color on the head, legs and body.

Seychellois Longhair

Identical to the Seychellois Shorthair in all but coat length which is medium long with a longer ruff. It has a full plumed tail and tufts on the ear points.

Bengali

This cat is an attempt by an American breeder, Jean Mill, to duplicate in a domestic cat the pattern, color and facial characteristics of the Leopard Cat of Asia. It was developed from crosses with Leopard Cats which produced females (male hybrids proved sterile) which were then mated with a red feral domestic cat, with brown rosettes on its fur, found living in the rhinoceros compound in Delhi Zoo, and a brown spotted tabby from a Los Angeles cat shelter.

THE CAT OF THE FUTURE

Other breeds which have been produced and which may eventually be recognized by the world's show bench are such cats as the California Spangle — a spotted breed given notoriety by the Hollywood store Nieman Marcus — and the Himbur (a Burmese X Himalayan cross). These challenging combinations demonstrate the continued search for beauty on the part of dedicated cat breeders throughout the world.

THE LIFE OF CATS

STUDYING THE CATS

Aristotle does not have much to say about the cat family in his *Natural History*, written in the fourth century BC, but at least he wrote from observation. Unfortunately when Pliny expanded it in Roman times he added all kinds of travelers' tales. His work became the basis for the *Physiologus*, probably written in Alexandria, which became the standard natural history encyclopedia for centuries after.

When medieval monks, the scholars of the Middle Ages, wrote and illuminated their bestiaries they drew on these ancient sources. Not natural histories in a scientific sense but 'a kind of naturalist's scrapbook' as Terence White described them, bestiaries are intended to display the amazing variety of God's creation. The monks took everything on trust — fact and fantasy — writing of animals they had not studied and often had not seen, although when they drew the domestic cat which shared their lives they could not help but have been aware of its most obvious behavior.

Later centuries brought more empirical attitudes and in the eighteenth century voyages of exploration, such as those of Captain Cook, often carried naturalists to collect specimens and artists to record new animals and plants. Most famously, in 1831, young Charles Darwin set sail on HMS *Beagle*. The voyage did not take him to lion or tiger country but, in his published *Journal*, he remarks on the introduced cats which became a plague on St Helena and reports on the jaguar in South America. Most of his information is secondhand from local people but he was shown jaguar scratch markings on trees, which he compares to the domestic cat's on furniture, and found many of their tracks on the islands in the mouth of the Parana River. Strangely, he writes of cats gone wild in the rocky hills near Buenos Aires as 'altered into a large and fierce animal'.

Were these really feral cats or were they one of the small South American species?

Such naturalists did not have the opportunity to make extensive, long-term studies of an animal in its habitat. Much nineteenth-century research relied on zoo specimens and skins and skeletons taken back for museum collections. It was the big-game hunter who had more opportunity to learn about the cats and who provided valuable information on behavior, but hunting made animals, already difficult to locate, even more secretive when man was near.

In recent years our knowledge of the cat family has been expanding. The establishment of wildlife reserves and sanctuaries and bans on hunting have begun to reduce some animals' fear of people. Leopards, for instance, were long known to be common in East Africa but because of their stealth and extremely efficient camouflage were very rarely seen. Now those in the reserves and parks often show an indifference to motor cars which enables visitors to see them more frequently. Even in forested territory, where sightings of the cat family were comparatively rare, park wardens and researchers have been able to observe cat behavior more closely than had previously been possible. Tigers had often been observed in pairs and zoologist George Schaller reported group gatherings, like the night-time meetings also recorded for groups of domestic cats (see page 158). In Ranthambore Tiger Reserve, in 1986–8 Valmik Thapar and Reserve director Fateh Singh studied three families of tigers in which the males joined females in hunting and happily played with their cubs. In Khama in 1989 Belinda Wright saw a family group of mother and cubs, together with an older cub from a previous litter, accompanied by a huge mature male.

Sophisticated equipment which allows zoologists to record behavior and follow movements is expanding knowledge all the time, but it is obviously easier to study the animals of the open grasslands of Africa than those species which live in forests. Among the smaller species, especially, there are still cats about which very little is known.

Captive animals in safari parks and zoos give another opportunity for study, though it cannot be assumed that animals there will necessarily behave as they do in their native habitats in the wild.

In the last decade a number of researchers have turned their attention to the study of both farm and feral domestic cats and cats in laboratories.

Scientific experiments require data to be collected from reproducible, comparative situations coupled with controls. These can only be precisely set up in laboratory situations. Such conditions must inevitably have their effect on animals and, like those under which animals are kept in zoos, cannot be considered an accurate model of life either in the wild or in the home. Nevertheless, such precise observations and patient field work by dedicated zoologists and ethnologists have dramatically increased the body of knowledge about feline behavior.

Many things which had been the subject of unconfirmed reports have now been scientifically

Previous page A Cat Fight in a Larder *by Paulos de Vos (1595–1678), in the Prado, Madrid.*

Below *Illuminations from a twelfth-century copy of a bestiary illustrate some of the bestiarist's beliefs:* **(left)** *Sick lions eat monkeys to cure themselves. Lions spare the prostrate and allow captives to return to their own country. They are frightened of cockerels, especially white ones.* **(right)** *They like to walk on mountain tops. They sleep with eyes open (here a female with three unanimated cubs on her back). The male breathes life into cubs, which they believed were born inanimate.*

recorded and photographed so that we can now see them for ourselves on our television screens. As we learn much more about some species we become increasingly aware of the diversity of behavior, not only between species but also according to geographical distribution. Whereas, before, a single observation of an idiosyncratic individual may have colored our understanding of the whole species we must now see this as only a variation from a wide range of behavioral possibilities.

Generalizations about behavior are therefore suspect and scientists will often disagree about the way in which observations should be interpreted. Pet owners who have studied their own cats will be aware that although there are many times when they have concurred with someone else's interpretation of a particular kind of behavior, there are others when their own observation suggests a different explanation.

What follows reflects the incomplete understanding that we have today. For instance, the development of the domestic kitten has been the subject of a number of detailed scientific studies in the last two decades but, although it is likely that development in other members of the cat family will be very similar there is no body of research to prove it and no knowledge at all

about some species. There are many ways in which the development and behavior of the various cats differ. Even within the same species individuals can occupy very varied habitats and have evolved different life styles. Our knowledge of the behavior of one of the cats may guide us in understanding some of the others but, as some of the differences described here show, it would be wrong to assume that something described for the lion is applicable to the margay or even to the tiger and our patchwork of knowledge is always subject to reinterpretation. There is still much to learn about the lives of the members of the cat family.

Left *Checking newly-attached radio collar. So long as the battery lasts the collar will transmit a signal which makes it possible to track the cheetah's movements.*

Below *Careful observation of your own pet can give a deeper understanding of feline ecology and behavior.*

KITTENHOOD

At birth

Kittens and cubs are blind and helpless when they are born. The lion cub's eyes are sometimes open, though not yet functional, but the domestic kitten's eyes are closed and its ears folded down. Reacting to its mother's warmth a kitten seems to push itself forward, but the newborn cat is not using its legs which are not yet strong enough to support the body, though its claws, which are not yet retractable do help to grip the surface beneath. First the muscles on one side of the body are contracted, then the other. This makes it twist first one way then the other, its head swinging from side to side and the wriggling movement carrying the kitten forward. Often a mother cat will start this pattern by licking down each side of the spine in turn. The sense of smell helps guide the kitten to a nipple and the swaying head eventually comes into contact — leading with the chin with the head kept raised to keep the nostrils clear — and so it begins to suckle.

The earliest of the litter may try to suckle while the others are being born or none may start until all the births are finished but it should be no more than an hour or so before they are all sucking away. Although it sometimes takes them a little while to get the hang of it, they soon develop an efficient technique. If any kittens fail to make their own way to the nipple, mother will guide them with a little nuzzling or licking and draw them back to her with a paw if they move away.

After a little initial competition with their littermates as to who sucks where, domestic cat kittens will settle down within the first two days with each kitten associated with one particular nipple and to that one it always returns. It has been suggested that this reduces the wear and tear on the mammary tissue because the kittens do not fight over them, though as they get older, and more likely to do damage this attachment becomes less strong. The rearmost teats produce a greater milk flow and it is the stronger kittens who generally establish claim to them, adding further to their advantage. Weaker kittens may still suck there if they get the chance but will vacate them when their 'owner' comes. The kitten's own smell identifies its own particular nipple and all but the very weakest cats maintain their territorial claim.

If a mother is not well fed and has given birth to a large litter this teat territoriality can mean that the weaker kittens may not get enough nourishment to survive but ensures that the stronger ones have the advantage and increases their chances.

This first milk, known as colostrum, produced only on the first few days after the kittens are born, not only contains a rich supply of protein and minerals but also passes on antibodies which protect the kittens from infection. Orphan or rejected kittens, who miss out on this, start life at a considerable disadvantage.

The newborn kitten will use its paws to push the fur away from a teat and press on the skin around it, making it easier to grasp. This first milk flows quite fast enough to satisfy the tiny kitten but in a day or so it will be using a similar motion, pummeling around the nipple with its paws, to increase the flow. You can often see the gesture repeated in a contented adult domestic cat on a comfortable lap, kneading against a jersey with its front paws and probably salivating at the same time as though it feels back in those secure and blissful days of being suckled.

As each kitten has its fill, it releases its hold on the nipple and slips down to fall into a deep sleep. Sometimes it seems to be asleep even before it shuts its mouth and its tiny pink tongue is left protruding slightly, curled as it was to grip the teat and moving a little as though it were sucking still.

For the first two days after giving birth most mothers seldom leave their kittens, except perhaps to drink and to pass wastes. House cats, used to a regular feeding pattern, may welcome nearby food and water, but for the wild animal there is no chance of going off to hunt at this time. Eating the placentas as the kittens are delivered gives the mother some sustenance and they probably contain vital vitamins and a hormone, oxytocin, which encourages her to release milk.

After the first couple of days mother will leave her young for short periods and the kittens will huddle in the nest to keep warm. Piled together, each tries to get into a comfortable position, chin resting on a brother's or sister's back and cozily surrounded without being crushed. As they stir in their sleep they move about. One, waking, finds he has slipped to the bottom with the others piling on top of him, extricates himself and climbs back up again to the top of the heap. No sooner is he settled than a sister extricates herself and another rearrangement begins.

When the mother cat returns she will begin vigorously to wash the kittens and then lie with her body curled around them to encourage them

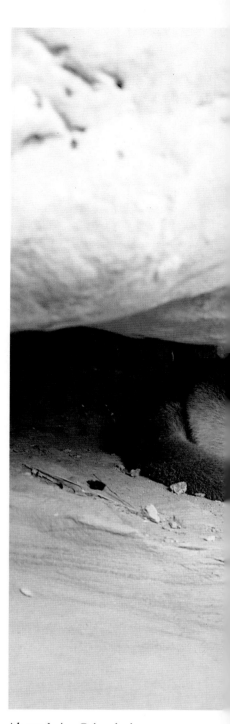

Above In her Colorado den, a cougar mother grooms her three-week-old cubs.
Below Newborn Birman kittens.

Below *A newborn cheetah cub has long dark fur, quite unlike its adult coat.*

Below *This leopard cub, born at Tiger Haven, Duddwha, is only two days old; its ears are still down and its eyes are not properly open.*

to wake and to feed. Until weaning starts, kittens will spend about a third of their time feeding and, at first, most of the rest asleep. Since they will not necessarily all be awake and feeding at the same time the mother may spend well over half her time meeting their successive demands for food.

The newborn of all the cat species have the same foreshortened faces and large paws and show their close evolutionary relationship more strongly than the adults. Lion cubs are usually heavily spotted, like the leopards and other spotted cats, and tiger cubs look like tabby kittens. In fact both spotted and striped patterns are forms of the same genetic background and are the original pattern for all domestic cats. They are often visible in kittens which will later be self-colored. Siamese and similar coats, however, are not apparent at birth, and their tabby heritage is hidden by a genetic albinism; the darker points only gradually emerge, though their coloring can be predicted from the nose leather of the maturing kitten.

The various species, as would be expected, range widely in size. While a domestic kitten will

weigh only 3–5 oz (80–140 g) a lion cub will be nearly three times as heavy. The larger cats will suckle for considerably longer and be much older before they begin their independent lives.

Awakening to the world

Lion cubs' eyes that are closed at birth may take up to a week to open, as do tiger cubs, while the longest in opening are probably those of the Sand Cat which may take two weeks. Domestic kittens vary from five to ten days; the Siamese and other Foreign breeds usually being the earliest to open — they tend to be precocious in everything! (Exceptionally, a domestic kitten's eyes may open much earlier or even at birth.) It may be another week after the eyes have opened before their sight is fully functional. All domestic cats are born with blue eyes and it will be about three months before they change to their adult colors.

There is often a sticky discharge around the unopened eyes which the mother will lick away. If it persists once they have opened and seals the

Mothers will carry their young to a new den if they think predators or other dangers pose a threat.

Cat mothers carry their young by the loose skin on the scruff of the neck, gripping it between the teeth firmly enough to hold the kitten's weight but without harming it. The kitten becomes totally relaxed when held in this way, the body usually curling slightly, which helps to avoid dragging it on the ground.

lids together again, this may indicate infection and require treatment.

The mother will wash her kittens frequently, not only to keep them clean but also to stimulate defecation and urination, eating wastes or removing them from the nest area. Licking down the belly also aids a kitten's digestion. A kitten who strays will almost always start to cry and its high-pitched calls immediately alert the mother. While it is too small to find its own way back, she will retrieve it and carry it back to the nest. The nest area is impregnated with a strong scent by discharges from the mother, during and after birth. This remains and helps to guide kittens back to the nest. While owners may like to clean up and replace bedding after a birth they should not clean the area too thoroughly or this signal could be lost.

If the nest site is disturbed, by natural causes such as flood or in the case of farm cats, for instance, by shifting hay out of a barn, or just by what seemed a quiet and secluded garage being brought back into use, the mother may have to move her kittens. If predators come too close she may also look for a safer place to settle them in. Even lion and tiger cubs, left alone when mother is hunting, could be vulnerable and domestic kittens have been carried off by foxes.

Cubs and kittens are carried from one place to another by the loose skin on the scruff of the neck, which the mother grips between her teeth just firmly enough to hold the weight but not enough to do any damage. Although a nape bite is one of the most common methods by which felines kill their prey, accidental injuries are extremely rare. An automatic inhibiting mechanism seems to operate which prevents the cat from fully closing its jaws. A kitten grasped in this way offers no resistance but relaxes and curls up slightly, making it easier to carry clear of the ground. With a growing animal this may not be enough, in which case its relaxation probably minimizes the damage as it gets bumped along.

Since the others must be left unguarded while she is carrying one kitten, this is a time when they are very vulnerable to predators. Should her route be barred — for instance by the closing of a shed door when she has not transferred all the litter — she may be unable to reach an isolated kitten before its temperature has fallen too low to survive. Although even day-old domestic kittens can recognize temperature differences and will move closer to a source of warmth, their bodies do not begin to regulate their own temperature until they are about three weeks old and it may be a month longer before they have developed the full mammalian mechanisms for temperature control. They are consequently very susceptible to the loss of maternal and sibling heat and exposure to cold conditions, though such exposure during the first few days of life apparently hastens the development of temperature regulation.

By about two and a half weeks old kittens will be crawling about their nest with their ears sticking up in the erect adult position (except for the recently developed Scottish Fold domestic breed). By about the third week they are getting steadier on their feet and beginning to develop their first or 'milk' teeth. Until this time suckling will usually be initiated by the mother, but now the kittens begin to take the initiative. The domestic cat mother certainly seems less eager to give milk, probably because the kittens' teeth begin to grip her nipples, but also as the first stage of encouraging the kittens to independence.

Soon the cubs or kittens are beginning to explore outside the nest. Their senses have developed considerably in their first weeks of life. Studies of the domestic cat have shown that the sense of smell is nearly mature by three weeks old. They have orientation to natural sounds in about two weeks and almost adult responses by four. It may take three weeks before they are able to interpret visual information sufficiently to use it to locate and go to their mother and sometimes as long as a month before they can use vision to negotiate obstacles. Vision is still impaired by eye fluids which do not clear completely until about five weeks of age; it is over two months before they are as fully sighted as adults.

Physical development of the domestic kitten

Some animals, the gazelle for instance, are able to stand and walk, even run, within moments of birth, but for cats, like humans, developing strength and control is a slow process. Timings are approximate and may vary considerably.

At Birth A newborn kitten wriggles along, its limbs at its sides and unable to support it.

Day 5 Legs, shoulders and pelvis strong enough to support the body. It is more stable but cannot yet walk.

Day 12 Front legs can support a sitting position, hind legs can prop body up when static.

Days 17–20 The first tottering steps improve as it learns to maintain balance as the weight shifts from one leg to another.

Day 21 It can raise a front paw while sitting and balance while it scratches an ear with a back paw. It is walking well but still occasionally stumbles.

Day 23 It can carry its weight in a squatting position to urinate and defecate. It can stretch up with its front paws and may even climb up a piece of furniture or a log.

36 hours

5 days

19 days

28 days

12 weeks

Kitten development
At birth *a domestic kitten weighs only 3–5 oz (80–140 g), the eyes are closed, the ears folded and the umbilical cord still attached.*

By the fifth day *the remains of the umbilical cord shrivel and fall off, then the eyes begin to open, although this will not be complete until the eighth or even thirteenth day. All kittens begin with blue eyes; if the adult color is different this begins to change at about twelve weeks old.*

At two and a half weeks *the kitten begins to crawl. Its ears are almost erect and it may even be cutting its first teeth. Within another few days it can stand and may begin to lap and take its first solid food.*

At between four and five weeks old *it will be moving quite well, coming to a bowl to feed from a steady standing position. It will have grown to a weight of about 1 lb (450 g), will be playing with its siblings and beginning to groom itself.*

By eight weeks *a kitten will have a full set of teeth and should be fully weaned, though it will probably still try to suckle if it gets the chance. A month later its second teeth begin to push through. Point color in Siamese will have become clear, though it will continue to develop, and coat texture will become firmer. Longhaired cats will not develop the typical full coat until after their first molt. Twelve weeks old is an appropriate age for a kitten to move to a new home.*

By the time they are three weeks old, the increasingly mobile kittens of domestic cats may try to follow their mother a little way as she goes off on more frequent expeditions. (Big cats' cubs take longer growing up.) As they learn to control and coordinate their limbs and explore the sensory and physical world around the nest they will pounce and bounce, run, jump and stumble. At first most of their activity centres on siblings and their mother; play-fighting develops into a regular rough and tumble but despite the flashing new teeth and claws they rarely inflict any injury, for the same restraining mechanism that enables their mother to carry them by the neck comes into operation. Kittens at this age begin to groom each other and learn the patterns of behavior for a friendly greeting. They rarely show aggression to any approach from the front for attacks usually come from behind.

As they develop better coordination between eye and limb control they begin to show an ability to chase after and catch small moving objects. This becomes an increasingly important part of play from about two months old.

The mother cat no longer curls up and encourages her kittens to suckle — it is they who demand to be fed now. She will sit a short distance away or even find a high vantage point from which to keep an eye on them without being pestered.

Learning about life

In the wild, responsibility for preparing young felines for adult life and teaching them the skills that they will need to survive is usually the sole responsibility of their mother. Many of the mechanisms appear to be inherent, for laboratory tests have shown that electrical stimuli to the brain can produce such actions as pouncing, hitting, grasping, pulling down, biting, kicking with the back legs, tossing and catching. These appear to come to maturity without any need for lessons or particular experience. However, kittens certainly do learn a great deal just from seeing their mother or other cats perform certain actions. Encouragement and rebuke seem to be part of the maternal relationship and activities such as using a litter tray, or voiding away from the nest area are a matter of definite demonstration.

Choice of prey and food preferences appear, from laboratory tests, to be very much influenced by those of the mother or by those of which they have experience. At weaning kittens will follow their mother's choice, even when that is a food not normally considered the typical cat's diet: in one test, for instance, where mothers had been trained to eat mashed banana or mashed potatoes, their kittens ate these in preference to meat pellets even when their mother was not present to copy.

The kitten develops its abilities through play. The earliest games of the domestic cat appear to be centred on actions and postures that will eventually play an important part in the social interaction of the species: backs will be arched and fur stand on end (especially the hairs upon

Above *Cougar kittens romping in the snow.*

Left *Play-fighting Somali kittens. The exposed belly leaves the submissive kitten vulnerable, but would also allow it to deliver a blow with its back legs if the other persisted in the attack.*

Left and opposite *Domestic kittens learn through play, investigating the environment, and from their mothers and other family members.*

going on. One chases another and then, in the middle of beating it up, will suddenly stop and ask to be chased itself.

Then the games begin to change. Instead of chases there will be a quiet and stealthy approach along the ground, and control of objects with the paws develops, including biffing something along from paw to paw like a soccer player dribbling a ball. Kittens start to experiment with using their teeth to bite and will wait in ambush to pounce on a sibling or a leaf that stirs or even adopt a total pretence and catch imaginary prey conjured from thin air. The emphasis has changed from the interaction between cat and cat to the development of hunting skills.

First prey

During the fifth week of her kittens' life. a mother who is herself a hunter will begin to bring prey back to the nest. First the prey will be dead and the kittens allowed to inspect it and to play with it before the mother eats it. She will encourage the kittens to eat some too.

A lioness does not drag a whole carcass back to her den at this stage but will bring chunks of meat to the cubs. When hunting she may be away for much longer periods than the smaller cats and lion cubs seem to be able to wait for as much as two days between meals. If local prey is very scarce she may have to lead her cubs to a new den in better stocked territory, but this can take a heavy toll on cubs. Studies of nomadic

Above *Chasing mother's tail makes a splendid game for a young lion cub.*

the tail) when the kitten is suddenly surprised, or wants to surprise. Sometimes, before it has learned to jump on anything, a kitten just jumps straight upwards on all four legs. It will rear up on its hind legs and reach out with the front ones. Soon there are all kinds of play struggles

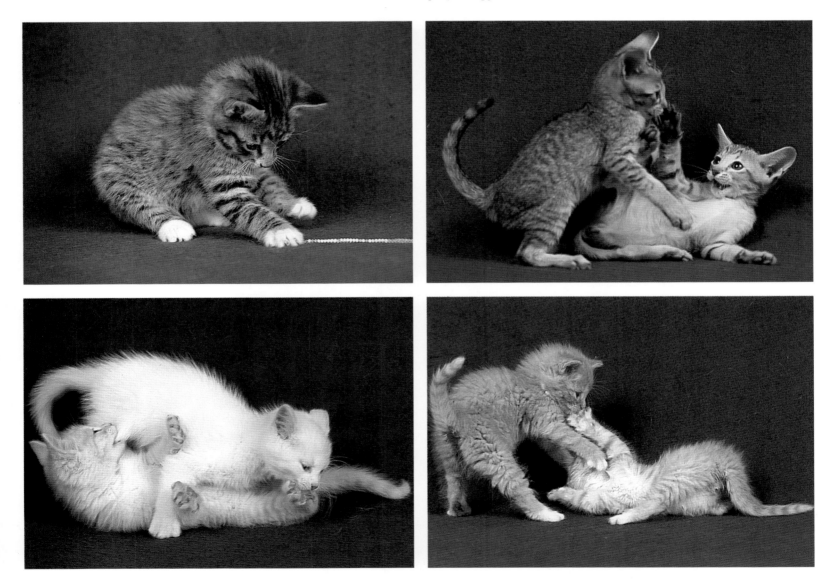

lionesses that belong to no settled pride show that they rarely rear cubs successfully.

Later, lion cubs will follow their mother to the hunt as spectators, but domestic cats, using the neck hold instead of the killing bite, bring live prey back to their kittens. If the kittens fail to catch the mouse or other prey she will prevent its escape. Kittens not only learn how to hunt but also learn what animals make suitable prey and to associate hunting with food. They also learn how to place the killing bite.

It requires a very strong stimulus to trigger the instinct to kill and for a kitten this seems to be provided by competition with its mother and siblings. It may also be one of the reasons why cats are often seen to 'play' with their victims, releasing a mouse they have caught and then catching it again, perhaps several times, or tossing it in the air and then catching it. This prolongation of the catching process probably helps build up the stimulus to deliver the fatal neck bite, though it could also be an example of the way in which domestic cats have retained juvenile behavior through domestication. It seems likely that if cats do not learn both how to kill and to associate prey-catching with eating before they reach about five months old, although they may become efficient hunters they either never attempt to kill or fail to do it cleanly. This may be why many pet cats will catch and eat a fly or spider — which are available prey in almost every home but can be eaten without first having to be killed — but even if they succeed in catching a bird make no attempt to eat it. Although movement away from them is likely to trigger a chase reaction in any feline, they will not necessarily attempt to do more than hold the object of the chase and then release it to chase again.

Above *Kittens soon learn to use mouths as well as paws. Many enjoy playing retrieval games.*
Right *'Dribbling' a walnut, a Siamese kitten becomes an accomplished soccer player.*
Left *Learning to hunt is all a matter of using your eyes and nose, and moving very carefully.*
Below *Cheetah cubs explore the world with their mother, but she will be very lucky if she manages to raise this whole litter to maturity.*
Below right *Fully weaned, kittens now share their mother's food.*

Above Leopard begin to follow their mother from about three months, safer than being left in the den. This cub, at five months, may have just begun to make small kills itself, but the impala they are now taking to a secure place was killed by the mother.

Left A cat carries a rabbit back to her kittens.

Below Sister lionesses take their cubs out together in the Masai Mara National Reserve in Kenya.

Growing up

Most pet cat kittens leave their mothers when they are about eight to twelve weeks old and move to a new home. It is possible that existing cats in the new household may accept and look after them to some degree but most future learning will come from experience and observation of other cats rather than from purposeful demonstration. Human provision of food, shelter and cossetting may preserve some juvenile characteristics in the adult cat but in dealing with strange cats and the world outside a kitten is on its own.

Feral domestic cats, or those in households where mothers are allowed to keep their kittens, maintain maternal behaviour for much longer, even bringing back food for kittens that have already become fully mature. If they continue to breed, however, their preoccupations are likely to be with new litters and a daughter will be treated more like a sister. Female groups of 'aunts'

often help each other at births and in raising kittens and if they give birth at about the same time kittens may be suckled by aunts as well as mothers. If newborn kittens suckle immediately from an aunt with a slightly older litter they could miss the important colostrum from their mother, so it is likely that they would suckle from their mother first. Among lions, which also practice group rearing, a mother usually leaves the pride to give birth in isolation and the colostrum period will have passed before cubs meet their aunts.

Neutered toms may stay as part of a household or a feral group, where they too have occasionally been known to help in births and kitten rearing, but a fully grown entire male is not likely to be tolerated by a resident tom cat, though sometimes it is the established male who moves on, allowing the grown kitten to take over both the old tom's territory and his mother and sisters as 'his' females.

Among the more solitary species families seem to split up before the young have reached maturity. In the case of the European Wildcat this is at about five months old, though males do not show signs of sexual maturity until four or five months later and females are a year old before they first come into oestrus. Lynx, on the other hand, stay with their mother until chased off by suitor males at the beginning of the next mating season. Lynx siblings often stay together as a group for some months more before going off to find individual territories; they take much longer to become sexually mature: 21 months for females and 33 months for males. Cheetah usually leave their mother between 15 and 17 months but may stay with her until they are two years old, by which time they have already reached maturity. With them too, the litter may stay together for a time as a hunting group.

Cougar cubs also stay with their mothers well past the time when they can hunt for themselves, sometimes until they are nearly two, and reach sexual maturity when they are three. Jaguar cubs stay together as a family until they are two years old, the male sometimes helping feed them when they are too young to hunt. They probably do not breed until they are three. Leopard males have also been seen dragging food back to the family, which stays together from 18 months to two years, although young are efficient hunters earlier and young males often roam off on their own. They start to breed at two and a half to three years old.

In East Africa, on the plains of the Serengeti, a lioness may rejoin her pride as soon as her cubs are sufficiently mobile to follow her safely, or team up with new lionesses, though some lionesses remain solitary. Lion cubs are not weaned until they are six months old and do not start taking a serious interest in hunting until they are about ten months old; their earlier attempts are more likely to reveal the hunters to the prey than be of help to their mothers.

If cubs are not killed or driven away by incoming adult males, they will stay with their mother until maturity, when male cubs will leave the pride. Female cubs may stay even when mature, increasing the size of their family pride.

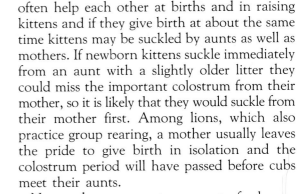

Opposite *The carrying grip is firm but not so tight as to cause pain or injure the kitten.*

Below *When sisters stay together in a core territory, 'aunties' help look after kittens.*

Above *A small crocodile is a challenging opponent to two young lions, though big cats can sometimes become skilled at dealing with these beasts.*
Right *Domestic kittens may go to new homes when they are eight or ten weeks old but they are not ready to fend for themselves at such an early age. Care by their new owners helps to create the domestic relationship and the continuing juvenile behavior which is usually evident in domestic pets.*

COMMUNICATION AND CONFRONTATION

Top *The claw marks of a tiger on a tree in Bandhogarh National Park inform other tigers of its presence. Scent from the paw pads is deposited at the same time as the scratch is made.*
Above *Domestic cats will also claw-mark territory, a different action from scratching by which they simply exercise their claws and detach old claw tips.*

Below *Spraying, leaving a particularly pungent odor, is much more noticeable to most humans than other scent signals. The rigid posture of the cat, who usually directs the jet against a vertical surface, clearly distinguishes it from ordinary urination.*
Below right *To communicate with humans domestic cats often use 'meows' which are not part of the conspecific vocabulary. The peremptory call of a cat that finds food or attention not offered at the expected time is unmistakable in its meaning.*

Feline communication, like that of all animals including ourselves — although people are not always conscious of the signals that they may give — is a combination of vocal, visual, tactile and olfactory messages. Some messages are methods of marking a cat's territory. They include scratching of surfaces such as trees, spraying with urine mixed with secretions from scent glands, and leaving feces in prominent places. Although cats are commonly thought to bury their scats after defecation, research has shown that in the wild this is unusual. Burying has usually been interpreted as a means of hiding the evidence of an animal's presence from potential predators, but if an animal wants to advertise its occupation of a territory this is one way to do it. Researchers have discovered that even domestic cats tend to bury feces only in proximity to their main living area. Similarly, many people think that only male cats spray, but this is a common female practice too and appears to be a sign of confidence as well as an advertisement of sexual condition. It is not the same as simple urination, which is directed downwards, but is usually done against a vertical surface and accompanied by a quivering of the tail. House cats may perform this quivering gesture in the home with no spray being released and they will usually refrain from spraying their own eating places.

Cats tend to avoid an area sprayed by a more dominant cat if the mark is fresh. In shared territory domestic cats interpret a fresh mark as an indication that the area is currently occupied and avoid confrontations. Scent markers that are more than four hours old are usually ignored. Wild species and free-ranging domestic cats with defended territories will regularly spray their boundaries to warn others of their occupation.

Feelings of insecurity, which may be caused by the introduction of another cat into the house, or even a new boyfriend or girlfriend taking attention a pet has come to consider its due, may initiate spraying from a cat which has previously not done so indoors. New objects may also be marked when they are brought into the home. Cats who spray in front of an opponent are trying to show off their self-confidence and strength, and the winner will often spray after a fight. Neutering usually reduces the desire to spray and when performed before sexual maturity will usually forestall it altogether.

Scent markers are also produced by rubbing against an object, a person or another cat, bringing it into contact with secretions from scent glands on the chin, temples and base of the tail. The body contact between family groups and colonies establishes a group scent identity by which members of the group are recognized as friends. When you stroke your cat you are probably exchanging scent marks — at least as far as your cat is concerned.

Vocalization

Cats clearly communicate vocally. The snarls and spits of rage or annoyance, the cry of the female domestic cat in oestrus and the gentle coaxing mew with which the male courts her, the roar of the lion, announcing his presence over a wide territory, and the chirruping sounds with which mothers call to kittens are all easily understandable even to human ears. It is much more difficult to comprehend the range of other sounds the cat family make and the way they use them. There are considerable variations between the calls of different species, the broadest being the ability to purr or roar.

The vocalization of domestic cats has been most studied. They make at least 13 vowel

sounds by muscle tension in mouth, throat, face and lips, and seven or eight consonants by closing and shaping the mouth to alter the resonance. Marvin Clark, a blind musician whose hearing was ultra-sensitive, believed that he could distinguish 100 different sounds in the cat's vocabulary and New York researcher Dr Mildred Moelk identified three main groups of sounds: murmurs, calls and cries.

Murmurs, sounds produced with the mouth closed, include regular purring, which usually indicates pleasure — the rougher the purr the greater the pleasure — but can also be a sign of distress. The difference is more easily recognized from circumstance than sound although a very observant owner may detect a difference in an individual cat. A smooth, high-pitched purr used with humans seems to be an indication of anticipation and approval when the cat sees you about to do something — get food, prepare a favourite game — that it will enjoy, or to say, perhaps, 'I want some too.' A short purr on an inward breath with a trilled 'r' — *mrrr* — is used in greeting. A longer murmur, beginning with a 'uh' sound and with a tenser mouth is used as a call, varying from plea to command according to its tone and a longer *mrrrraow* is a particularly coaxing 'please'. There is also a short-inhaled murmur, dropping in pitch, *mhhng* which is used as an acknowledgment that you have realized or have done what it wants.

Calls, vowel sounds made as the mouth slowly closes, as in the familiar *meow*, range from begging, through demands to complaints to sounds indicating worry and bewilderment. The initial warning growl also falls in this group but when reinforced falls in the next.

Cries, made with mouth and jaw open and tensed vocal muscles, include the full growl, snarl, hiss, spit and a drawn-out wail of anger or dispute, the mating call and a low-pitched, wavering cry of protest which is a first stage warning to stop doing or making it do something it dislikes.

Some sounds, such as the greeting murmur, are used mainly in cat-person conversation, while very soft murmurs are directed usually by a

mother cat to her kittens. Paul Leyhausen identified a particular version of the high pitched gurgle-like greeting which was used by mother cats to draw their kittens' attention to prey she brings back to the nest. A sound close to that of greeting is used to indicate a mouse, but a louder version approaching a scream is used when the prey is a rat and kittens respond accordingly with much more caution.

Mother cats use a particular chirrup to call kittens back to the nest.

Body language

As with any animal — including ourselves — gesture and body posture can frequently tell as much and, to those who do not understand the vocal 'language', often very much more about responses and intentions. We have learned to suppress some of these give-away signs in an effort to conceal our feelings but we never succeed in hiding them all. In a cat they are very easy to recognize. They follow a similar broad pattern throughout the cat family. The body language of the domestic cat, described below, has parallels in the other cat species.

Below left *When cats which know each other meet, they usually make contact first through the nose and whiskers and then pass beside each other. Kittens may gently rub flank to flank with the tail curving towards the other but as they get older they rub the cheek against the length of the body, engaging scent glands on the side of the head, which mark the other cat. In this way a whole litter, or a colony (including human members) acquires a family smell that aids identification.*

Below *Two tigers greet each other in exactly the same way as friendly domestic cats.*

A cat walking with its tail held high and probably curving at the tip is a confident cat, and this is a friendly greeting.

Below *The response to a threat includes erecting the guard hairs. The tail usually responds first but if the insecurity increases, the body fur also rises. This has the effect of making the cat look bigger and more intimidating, so may reduce any threat if it comes from another animal.*

Below right *A cat which exposes its vulnerable belly is either totally confident, like this sleeping lion, or making a big gesture of non-aggression, so that rolling on the ground often becomes an offer to play or a preliminary sexual invitation.*

Everyone knows the arched back of the 'angry' domestic cat. But it is not quite as simple as that. In fact angry is not really the correct interpretation and the stance is the result of a mixture of conflicting reactions. The cat is annoyed or threatened by something against which it begins to advance in order to attack or intimidate it. At the same time it recognizes a threat and the front part of the cat begins to retreat from it, the conflicting movements producing the arched back. The result can be correctly interpreted as a 'defensive threat'. Of course, there are occasions when a cat arching its back is simply having a yawn and a stretch. The 'angry' look is usually emphasized by the fur, or at least part of it, standing away from the body, especially the tail.

When any mammal is frightened its fur stands on end, and this is especially noticeable in the domestic cat. People are usually only conscious of a prickling on the scalp and back of the neck but the mechanism is the same. It makes the outline of the animal much bigger, so that it appears more powerful and intimidating to an opponent. Fearsome though it may look, the erected fur is a sign not of confidence but of fear; you will often see a cat streaking for cover with a tail fluffed out like a bottle-brush.

The direct opposite of the cat enlarging itself is the cat shrinking back to look as small as possible, making a smaller target and at the same time showing less of its vulnerable underbelly.

A cat that rolls over onto its back is showing the greatest relaxation and non-threat. It is the position in which a kitten has its abdomen washed and digestion stimulated by its mother's licking — but beware, it is also an extreme defensive posture for it frees the hindlegs from supporting the body. Anyone who takes advantage of this situation can be dealt powerful raking blows by the claws of the rear feet.

Tail position is another clear indicator of the way a cat is feeling. An upright tail, usually with the tip curled slightly forward, indicates a fully confident cat and is a sign of friendly greeting. A lashing tail is a gesture of temper and frustration but a flicking tip is often the accompaniment of intense concentration.

The head and face reveal a great deal about a cat's mood. Position of ears and whiskers and the dilation or enlargement of the pupils are the most easily noticed elements, but the twitching of the nose and the position of the lips can also add to the messages conveyed. Some owners claim that their cats actually smile, though this is an anthropomorphic rather than a scientific interpretation. An owner may be able to interpret a happy face but cats do not literally smile! A purr is a much safer indication of a happy cat. Ear and head positions not only show mood but also indicate exactly where a cat's attention is focused.

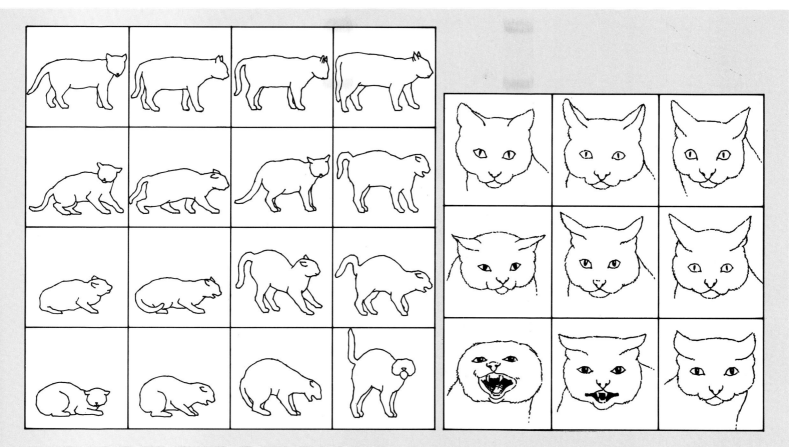

Feline body language

Above left *A cat's body language in a confrontation reflects the complexity of the conflicting feelings which such situations arouse and presents a mixture of offensive and defensive indicators with a great range of possibilities. Here, as originally presented by Dr Paul Leyhausen, is a range of combinations. The top left presentation shows a relaxed animal feeling neither mood. The top row, moving right, shows increasing preparedness to attack; moving down the left column shows growing readiness to defend. The other positions show the relative combination of these feelings as one or other becomes more intense; bottom right shows the greatest intensification of both, with the arched-back stance.*

Above right *To complicate the interpretation of confrontational body language the face and head may indicate a different level of mood from the body signs. The face is usually quicker to react than other parts — and sometimes one ear may even contradict the other. Ears are particularly significant, the greater the aggression the more of the back of the ear is displayed; the stronger the defensive intention, the more the ears are lowered, the larger the pupils become and the more likely the cat is to snarl or spit. This presentation, also after Leyhausen, follows the same arrangement as that of the whole body.*

Left and below *In a conspecific confrontation cats will go through a succession of maneuvers to determine who should give way, and although a paw may lash out one or other will usually give way before it escalates into a full-scale fight. Occasionally however, especially if an intruder refuses to retire from a cat's core territory and the defender feels forced to take positive action, it may develop into a savage battle.*

Territorial behavior

Although most of the cat family are considered to be territorial their wide range of sizes and habitats produces much variation between species, and even within a species local conditions can lead to notable differences. Although a majority are thought to be solitary animals after they reach maturity, sibling adults in some species may stay together before establishing individual territories. Cheetahs may hunt together and tigers are among those which have been observed in family groups; however, the lion and the domestic cat are the only species that form larger groups sharing territories.

Cats usually occupy a central area, which females especially will defend against outsiders, as well as a wider home range which may overlap with that of others. Male territories are much larger than those of females and may embrace several of them.

The size of territory will be closely linked to an animal's size and needs. Where prey is very plentiful an area can support a denser population and territories will probably be smaller, though competition from other species must also be taken into account. Domestic cats, or other species that can scavenge food scraps, can live in much greater density with territories reduced to that of comparably-sized browsing plant eaters, and very much less when they are consistently fed by humans.

A few animals break the territorial pattern. Some lions on the Serengeti plains have no permanent territories but follow the great migrating herds of wildebeest, zebra and gazelle over an area of up to 1500 sq miles (4000 sq km). Others, such as the Cougar in Idaho, while more strictly territorial, do move to higher slopes in summer and fall and return to the valleys in winter and spring, following their ungulate (hoofed) prey. Lynx, and possibly other non-tropical species, operate over a larger range in winter, when prey are more difficult to find, and very adverse conditions may also force migration on an animal. A lynx marked in North Minnesota in November 1974 was trapped in Ontario, Canada, 300 miles (480 km) away two years later.

The Iriomote Cat, which is considered the most primitive of all the cats, is believed to be strictly territorial, as may be its close relatives the Leopard, Fishing, Flat-headed and Rusty-spotted Cats. The desert-living cats appear to be very widely spaced while the extinct lions of the North African desert are said to have lived in monogamous pairs, each of which occupied an oasis or waterhole, a pattern which seems to be duplicated in the Namibian Kalahari desert. It is possible that pairs of Snow Leopards may also share the same range. Young male Cheetahs frequently form temporary hunting groups but, although they tend to avoid other groups and they regularly mark the areas they are currently using, there seems to be no evidence of territorial defense.

Leopards will usually defend their territory against any other of the same sex, although males have occasionally been seen staying with their mate and cubs and even taking food back to the family. Bobcat females maintain almost exclusive territories and breeding Ocelot females do not overlap. While in Nepal and Central India there is no overlap between territories of female tigers, those of females elsewhere are sometimes shared and their territorial imperative is weak.

The lion pride

In addition to the migratory populations and desert family groups at waterholes, lions' social structures have shown considerable variation. The basic unit is the pride but its composition differs in different places.

In the Gir Forest of India, where the pride consists of two males with three or four females and their cubs, the adults probably form a permanent nucleus, their young going off to form new groupings or to fill gaps in other groups. In the semi-desert of south-western Africa a single male and only one or two mates form another possibly permanent unit, for the pickings are less and cannot support a larger group.

In Botswana, where the semi-desert of the Kalahari has dependable annual rains, prides of one to three males and twice that number of females are formed at the beginning of the rainy season. Females may mate before the pride is formed and come and go freely. With the coming of the dry season, when prey becomes scarce and scattered it is difficult to make sufficient kills in an area small enough for the pride to stay together so it breaks up, individuals ranging widely in the search for food.

In the savanna lands of Zaire and Uganda two or three males form a pride with three to five females and stay with them for six years or more, the whole of their reproductive lives. Further east, from Kenya down to the Transvaal, prides are frequently larger, from two to five males and five to 20 females, sometimes more. Males here have a shorter pride life, usually only two or three years before they are driven out by younger stronger lions at their peak.

Sometimes a pride does not stay as a central group but is fragmented into several smaller ones, sharing and defending the same territory and excluding others. This spreads predation over a wider area.

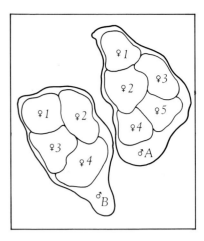

Territorial patterns depend upon both terrain and prey availability. With tigers in Nepal and Central India and with leopards in Sri Lanka female territories tend to be contiguous and several are overlapped by those of a single male. The males have a wider area than all the females put together, allowing separate hunting territory and not overlapping with those of other males. Elsewhere female ranges sometimes do overlap and even where they do not occasional social contact occurs outside mating and cub-rearing times.

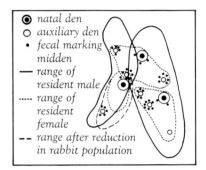

○ natal den
○ auxiliary den
• fecal marking midden
— range of resident male
···· range of resident female
-- range after reduction in rabbit population

Male bobcats have ranges which frequently overlap, although they are so large that meetings probably seldom occur. They enclose those of two or more females who use a number of dens, which can often be discovered through the fecal heaps which are placed around them.

Opposite A jaguar may range a territory of 200 sq miles (500 sq km).

Below A pride of lions on the plains of Namibia.

Occasionally a single male will be associated with several groups of females. One observed in Nairobi National Park in 1973 visited four separate, all-female prides, within which there appeared to be a hierarchy with a dominant female, who remained so even when the male was present though she gave him precedence when it came to eating from a kill.

Young males often form a small group, hunting together as they gain experience and strength. Females, after leaving the pride to give birth, may team up with other female loners. Sometimes mixed groups are formed.

In all the savanna lands of eastern Africa there are many nomadic groups and individuals looking for territories; in the Serengeti more than half the lions live without their own territories, wandering through the plains between and around pride lands and 'poaching' on their edges. Such conditions do not provide the stability and support that pride sisters can give, and although many lionesses still breed, they have less success in rearing cubs. Since males can only be certain of breeding success within a pride, they will always be looking for opportunities where they, alone or in a group, can drive the males from an existing pride and take over their role.

Pride takeovers

The resident males have a considerable investment in the cubs of the pride and will fight fiercely to protect them. However, when a challenge comes from stronger lions or a larger group, the instinct for personal survival usually makes the weaker lions back down and the conflict does not reach a point where the weapons of tooth and claw are used with full lethal force. After a chase, which shows up the weaker forces, confrontations usually lead to capitulation and the loser is allowed to depart unmolested.

The females take no part in the males' conflicts, although female-only groups can be forceful in keeping other lionesses out of their territory and will draw together and advance aggressively on the approach of a solitary lion. Loners need to be excluded because a single lion rarely manages to hold on to a pride and his cubs would have little chance of survival, as explained below, while an outsider female would start a different (and unwanted) maternal line from that shared by the pride and make extra demands on the resources of the territory.

If the incoming males win, and displace the pride lion or lions, they will chase off any immature males without wounding them, but then systematically set about killing all the younger cubs. This drastic behavior is necessary if the purpose of their victory — to sire cubs — is to be successful. So long as the females are with young cubs they will not come into season, and the lions would have to wait perhaps a year or more before mating, which would leave little time for their own cubs to mature before they too might fall before the challenge of new incoming males. Having lost their cubs the females also have the imperative to reproduce again and appear to come into season within a matter of

Life in an East African pride

Male lions do not 'form a pride' in any active sense, they only *join* a pride, for the basis of any resident pride is a group of females, usually close relations, sisters, daughters and granddaughters. The territory belongs to them and is occupied for many years. While their female offspring may be absorbed into the pride, male cubs, though they may stay with the pride until they are four years old and fully mature before leaving in search of a mate, are usually driven off earlier during a pride takeover.

When a lioness returns to the pride with her cubs her sisters will assist in rearing them, for cubs will take milk from lionesses other than their mother. Cubs are not weaned until they are six or seven months old, but as lionesses, if they are not pregnant or in milk, come on heat every three months throughout the year, there are always 'wet nurses' available.

Hunting is mainly the job of the lionesses. They provide the food while the males provide defense against other males, protecting the territory, the cubs they sire and the females against predators and other males. Although pride males rarely hunt, they are given precedence at the kill and allowed to feed first. In a large pride the cubs may not be able to fight their way in to feed until the adults are replete. This struggle probably helps to toughen them up but a cub may be killed by a heavy blow as it is pushed back. In times when food is scarce cubs may starve. However, since it takes less time to produce new cubs than for an animal to grow to maturity, this is the most efficient way of ensuring that the fittest survive. Away from food, both females and males can be very tolerant and playful with their own cubs and those of others in the pride.

Top left *Pride structure may vary but lionesses are always the basis.*

Above *Lions are tolerant of their own offspring, except when in competition for food.*

Centre left *'Aunties' share in the care and rearing of the cubs*

Bottom left *A lioness defends her pride.*

Bottom centre *Lion marking pride territory in the Kalahari Desert.*

Left *An incoming male will kill young cubs to ensure his own breeding chances.*

days. Nervously they approach the males and soon are often flirting outrageously with their cubs' killers, but they do not conceive.

The new males may have won this battle, but how effective are they going to be at defending the territory and how satisfactory as mates? In the following weeks they get a chance to show their mettle and, if they maintain their position, new bonds are formed. After three months the lionesses start to become pregnant and in six months new cubs are being born.

The pride structure ensures a continuity of the genetic line through the closely related females of the pride, with a periodic influx of new male genes. The males have the opportunity to fertilize a number of females. The female grouping makes for more efficient hunting strategies and enables them to exclude single, males who alone would not be an effective defense against intruders. A group of males is more likely to be successful in securing time for all the cubs to mature. Females will help support an injured or ailing sister and tend her cubs, but a weak male is no use to them and his replacement is accepted.

The pride system makes sense where a large territory needs to be held — difficult for an individual — and where group-hunting strategies can be used against large prey animals, so that one kill can feed many. Such cooperation in hunting and defense and joint rearing of young is not practicable when prey is too small to share or, though large, is too scarce to support a group. Among the rest of the cat family it is only with domestic cats that such large-scale socialization develops and then on rather different principles.

Social life in the domestic cat

The close relatives of the domestic cat, the African and the European Wildcats, are both solitary-living species. Their prey are usually small and easier to hunt alone and there is no evidence that either ever live in groups. It follows that the natural condition of the domestic cat, were it living wild, would be a solitary one and this often seems to be the case with feral animals. However, there are many instances of large and small colonies of cats who share core areas or at least overlapping territories.

The ranges of solitary females tend to overlap in relationship to the availability of the food supplies. Where there are colonies these are mainly related to a concentrated food supply, usually from a human source whether deliberately or incidentally provided. For instance, farm buildings may provide a concentration of easily available small rodents, but there may also be a supply of farm and household scraps regularly made available or which may be scavenged. A colony of cats which were studied in a Japanese fishing village had access to dumps of fish waste and there are many cases of urban cats being regularly fed by individuals in city parks and squares or on industrial locations.

Like lion prides, colonies seem to be based on extended families of closely related females, large colonies being made up of several separate matrilinear groups that probably have a

dominant male who will be linked with one particular group but who will usually range more widely. Immature males or those that accept a subservient situation and do not attempt to challenge the dominant male remain within the group. To breed, a subservient male must either wait until the group's dominant tom is ranging elsewhere — most include several groups within their territory — or go roaming himself in search of a female group without a male.

In a colony of 81 cats in the Piazza Vittorio Emanuele, in Rome, researchers observed from 8 to 20 of the 'resident' males attempting to mate with each female during her period of oestrus — two-thirds of the available adult males in some cases. In this case males totalled nearly half the cats regularly in the square, but since any cat present for more than ten percent of the days studied was classed as resident it is possible that males over a wider area may have included a focus of so many females regularly within their range because of the mating opportunities offered. Unfortunately the records do not indicate whether some of the males were subservient and made no attempt to mate or whether they all had equal opportunities.

A dominance system also operates amongst colony females, probably based on prior claim. Members of a colony of cats in Fitzroy Square, in central London, which was fed nightly by a cat-lover, used always to give precedence to one small white cat if she moved towards the food plate where they were eating, even though many of them were bigger, younger and stronger cats. She was a kind of matriarch — mother, grandmother or aunt of most of the other cats. She never showed any sign of aggression to the others. They simply gave way to her.

An established female that is aging or ailing may have to relinquish part of her territory, but siblings are unlikely to allow it to be forced out of the core area where most of the females' territories overlap. Subservient females often have to adopt territories and locate their nests beyond the area of the other females, though, as part of the group, still permitted to overlap the food source and feed there.

An artificial colony

At Mutsugoro's Animal Kingdom, in eastern Hokkaido, Japan, lives what is probably the world's largest single group of cats. Their shared territory is a large shed and a summer outdoor run. It is not a natural colony but originated in various unwanted and stray cats, some of them deliberately abandoned outside the Animal Kingdom, which is a private animal sanctuary run by the zoologist and writer Masanori Hata (Mutsugoro). At first more than 30 cats shared Mutsugoro's home, never allowed out because they were likely to be savaged and probably killed by the Kingdom's free-running twenty-odd dogs which had not been trained to accept them. Their later home was larger but still a strictly

Feral cats maintain a territorial distance between members of the colony.

enclosed environment. In such unnatural conditions some aspects of cat behavior became very apparent but, as with confined zoo and laboratory animals (or city-dwelling humans), the artificial proximities may have produced neuroses and distortions which are not applicable to cats in general.

Toms were not neutered, for they did not want to extinguish the colony by neutering them all and anything less would still have left a mate for all the females; consequently females were spayed to keep the population in control once it had reached 120.

The British zoologist Jeremy Angel was in charge of the cats when the initial colony of 33 was transferred from their various locations in different parts of the family house to their new cat sheds. He has described how they seemed terrified of their large new environment and skulked in dark corners. Gradually, and probably in response to the need to urinate, they emerged one by one to make use of the tubs of sawdust placed around as litter boxes. Even cats who had previously played and slept together now seemed to try to avoid any contact, though one or two confrontations did take place.

Within 24 hours the more juvenile cats were confidently established in their new surroundings and, though some more timid cats stayed wherever they had retreated, an increasing number of extremely vocal spats between toms developed into three days of confrontation, some of it directed against females. Angel, who considers intersexual hostility rare in cats, saw this as a reflection of the considerable fear and tension resulting from being thrust into a new location.

Gradually the conflicts became less intense. Angel noticed that the strongest toms tended to avoid any encounters with weaker ones which might have led to a confrontation. When the colony was well established cats appeared to check whether passageways and other confrontation points were occupied before using them. They would even round corners of furniture very widely so that they were not suddenly face to face with another cat. Fights seemed to be personal matters between cats which did not like each other, rather than territorial affairs, though there was some defense of favourite places.

Since food was regularly provided for them all there was no need to defend a hunting ground, but 'first come first served' seemed to be the rule when any cat had settled in a particular spot. While the density of population meant that they all shared the same territory this 'mobile territoriality', as Jeremy Angel calls it, apparently gave the occupying cat the same authority that a territory owner usually gains even over a superior animal entering it. New adults introduced into the colony were not attacked by the established animals, although the newcomers themselves often seemed petrified at facing so many unknown cats.

Though a hierarchy developed it seemed to be more of a stratification into a group of more dominant cats and a group of less forceful ones than an individual pecking order, fights usually being within each group and the lower-ranking toms having fewer battles. In fact, where food was concerned, lesser cats left the food bowls earlier rather than the stronger ones eating first. Paul Leyhausen, on the other hand, found boss-cats definitely hogging food bowls in his experiments.

For a time, one particularly belligerent tom did top the hierarchy at Animal Kingdom, terrorizing even the oldest tom who was the last to give way to him, though later the roles were reversed. This bully cat seemed unable to develop the tolerance needed for so many cats to live in the same enclosure in what was effectively a non-territorial environment.

At the bottom of the hierarchy there were a number of cats who became pariahs, so frequently attacked by the other cats that they became frightened to leave the refuges they found for themselves except when the other cats were sleeping. They were the victims mainly of lower ranking toms, but occasionally of senior toms and females. For most of them this was to be a temporary situation; gradually the other cats would begin to ignore them and they would eventually become accepted.

Jeremy Angel suggests that these timid cats, by running away if confrontation threatened, became a prey substitute, for any rodents or other prey that appeared were soon caught.

Exceptional though this large captive colony was, in some ways it probably magnified the conditions faced by the typical city cat or suburban pet having to share a home range with many other cats.

Territories of domestic pets

The house and garden of the average home provide a much smaller territory than that over which most wild cats would range, yet to go beyond them might well intrude upon the territory of another cat, let alone those areas which may be occupied by dogs.

Domestic pets seem to treat their human household as though they are a conspecific family or colony sharing a territory, though accepting small personal areas within that shared home ground — whether it is a person's or a cat's favorite chair or the establishment of the china cabinet as being the territory, perhaps, of the people who take things in and out of it. The territorial boundaries may be established by human usage. The cat does not see the front railings or the garden hedge as being boundary markers but registers the human occupancy by family 'use' of the area: not just by where you lie to sunbathe or sit to read but part of the side-

Above right Indian Summer, *a painting by Ryozo Kohira. House cats establish personal claims to favorite spots.*
Below right *Island cats on Mykonos in Greece.*
Below *Access and precedence may cause dispute but rights of way are frequently acknowledged on a time-share basis. Rubbing and spray-making show when another cat last passed.*

walk that you sweep, the place where you clean the car, the flower bed that you weed, the hedge you trim, perhaps even a regular walk to the store or the mailbox at the corner.

A pet cat, with all its needs provided by its owners, has no pressing need to hunt and can survive therefore in very restricted territory — even a very small apartment with no outside access. It may well extend its range beyond the apparent territory of its humans but it is likely to tolerate sharing these areas with other cats. If its family has a large garden it may not even claim all of it (though this may be influenced by the fact that the family do not regularly use much of it either). It may not use all of it itself, keeping to particular routes and favorite places — especially spots where the cat can sun itself — and will defend slightly less of the territory than it uses.

Even indoors there seem to be favored routes and areas that are rarely or never used. One cat, for instance, who regularly used the whole of a T-shaped kitchen counter for access to a boiler top and to keep an eye on all kitchen activity, always returned to the same spot to jump up and down from it, even when clearly aiming for its own food on floor level which was nearer the other end. In the garden, the same cat, whilst making use of almost everywhere else at some time, was never seen to explore one flower border, except for the exceptional occasion when she chased a retreating intruder across it. Any cat owner will be able to observe similar behavior.

Females, especially those with kittens, are much more likely to defend their territory than males, who range more widely. Those in very great proximity, but not of the same household, such as cats living in terraced houses with very small gardens, may be so close as to claim all available space as a defended core area and very little overlap will then occur between them.

In the center of big cities, where there are no private gardens, domestic pets may have no clear outdoor territory (except perhaps a roof or window ledge) and have to fit around the existing territories of feral cats.

On average, males — whether suburban or city — are like countryside and feral cats in having territories which usually enclose those of several females and about ten times larger than those of females in the area.

Any new pet cat may make its first expedition outside only to discover that other cats have already claimed every inch right up to the doorstep. It must then win itself a territory by challenging other cats and forcing them to retreat and surrender territory to it, or at least to withdraw their defended zones and treat this as joint terrain.

The geography of cat territories may not necessarily be contiguous. A cat unable to gain more than a foothold in its own backyard could take over one left unclaimed several doors away, the route to get there being shared ground where other cats will allow the newcomer to pass.

As in the Japanese Animal Kingdom colony, cats may keep an eye open for other cats and avoid confrontation by not taking a route along

'Ownership' of a roof may have nothing to do with the territory beneath it.

'Keep off, this place is mine.'

Chinning leaves scent marks on the surfaces the cat rubs against.

Below Twisting the tail around an object as a cat goes by also leaves a scent mark.

Right and below *House cats share their core territory with people, and those from different homes tend to have adjoining rather than overlapping ranges, although there may be some common access routes.*

Opposite *Every cat has its favorite place.*

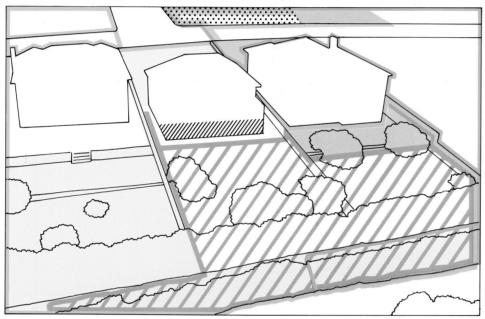

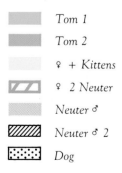

	Tom 1
	Tom 2
	♀ + Kittens
	♀ 2 Neuter
	Neuter ♂
	Neuter ♂ 2
	Dog

a wall or down a path where another cat is already sunning itself, but if the occupant is in transit they will simply wait until the way is clear. Indeed, it seems that cats often work on a time-share principle so that they never clash over the use of a particular place. This will often be the case among cats of the same household or may operate in a slightly different way so that the cat with the strongest prerogative lays claim first, allowing other cats to join him or her after a short period of exercising prior rights. For instance, one cat who claimed the right to be first upon her owner's bed each night, allowed a sibling to join her only when the light went out, even though he was quite free to use the bed during the day and they would usually be found curled up there together if left in the house on their own.

Feral city cats

City-dwelling feral cats do not have people with which to form a family group but form their own, usually (as already described) based on a matri-linear relationship and with a shared central territory based on a food supply.

Institutional buildings, such as hospitals, and industrial sites often have areas of little-used land which provide relatively undisturbed locations for colonies to become established. These may be encouraged for the role they play in vermin control. Excavated archaeological sites to which the public does not have access, fenced-off areas with electrical substations and all kinds of other enclosed areas may be a base for large or small colonies where they are protected both from people and from marauding dogs.

Roger Tabor, who made a study of city feral cats, pointed out that the railings of the basement areas of the houses of London squares, as well as those enclosing many of the squares' central gardens also create protected places; even if a dog gives chase and can squeeze between them it will be so much slower in doing so, giving a cat plenty of opportunity to flee to safety.

Night 'clubbing'

In areas with a fairly high density of domestic cats which are not kept indoors at night an intriguing phenomenon has been observed by Paul Leyhausen and other 'cat-watchers'. Cats congregate together, usually on a piece of ground or a rooftop outside the personal home range of any single cat. They are not drawn together by a female on heat and there is usually no sign of disputation. They groom each other, make vocal exchanges and appear to be engaged in social activity much like people at a party. Before dawn the 'club' breaks up and they all return to their own homes. George Schaller has observed similar activity among a group of tigers.

In recent years we have begun to understand a lot more about cat behavior but this activity still remains one of the many mysteries.

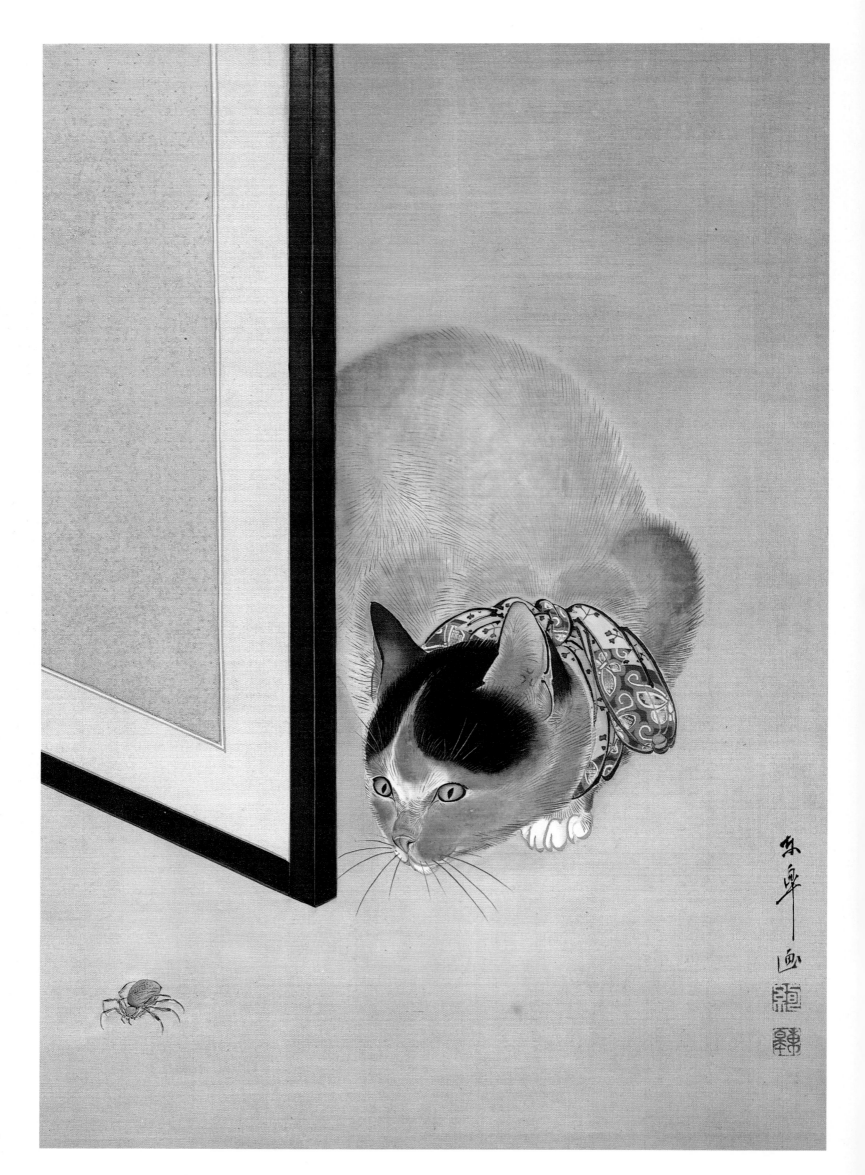

HUNTING PATTERNS

The play of kittens and cubs rehearses many of the actions which find practical application in the hunting field, though they need their mother's example and plenty of practice to become efficient predators. By watching domestic kittens trying out their skills or by playing with an adult pet you can observe in microcosm the hunting repertoire of the smaller cats and much of the behavior of the big cats too.

Quite apart from species differences, individual animals will develop particular skills related to particular prey. Not many domestic cats, for instance, are proficient at catching birds, except chicks which fall out of the nest, or fledglings which make an unintended landing and are slow to get into the air again. Those few that regularly do catch birds may, however, be very good at it, using techniques more like those of the Serval for whom birds make up a large part of its prey.

The smaller cats

Because young reared without knowledge of other species appear, at first, to treat all animals they meet as though they were other cats, the mothers of kittens reared in the wild, and even some domestic pets, will bring living prey to their kittens. Domestic cats who normally never hunt may also do so when they have a litter; not because of the need for food, which is already provided by their owner, but in response to an hereditary need to train their young.

In the early stages of development kittens will not notice another animal if it is still. If it moves slowly they may see it and advance to investigate it by sniffing, but if it moves towards them they are likely to be more hesitant and may even retreat. The larger the animal and the faster it moves the more likely a kitten is to take flight. They will generally only begin to give chase when an animal moves away from them and moves fairly quickly. If it moves off at an angle from them this seems to trigger a more positive response.

It takes a cat some time to learn to recognize motionless animals as prey and to identify the sounds and cries made by suitable prey found in their territory. With experience, their sensitivity at higher wavelengths enables them to distinguish all kinds of squeaks and rustlings which are beyond the range of the human ear. Even a kitten too young to see properly will react to scratching sounds and high pitched calls and you can always attract a cat's attention by making such noises. Experienced cats can locate nearby prey by sound alone.

Cats show an excellent memory for place and will return with great accuracy to check out a spot where they have found prey, even after a considerable time lapse. They will use vantage points for reconnoitring and exploit available cover, keeping the body low in order to reduce their profile when moving over an exposed flat surface. Often they will wait in ambush by a rodent hole or a route frequented by prey. A pet cat will often choose to hide around the corner of a sofa or under a chair, or even dive for cover behind a curtain, as you trail a piece of string for it, preferring to pounce when the string comes within range rather than chase it in the open.

Watching beside a hole, a cat does not spring on a mouse the moment it emerges lest it might too easily escape back into the hole again. It will wait while its victim checks its surroundings and moves away from safety. Then it pounces. The watchful cat, concentrating on prey, lies with its body hunched, the hind soles flat on the ground and the front paws drawn back below the shoulders. The tail may be stretched out or curled around the body but its tip usually twitches slightly. The head is forward with the ears erect and focused and the whiskers are spread wide.

Sometimes, when a cat knows a small animal is inside a hole, it will use a paw to scoop it out.

When stalking prey a cat will usually move freely in well spaced cover, slowly and cautiously where it might be seen or heard. It will survey the lie of the land at each corner, or as new terrain comes into vision, and utilize camouflage, shadow and contour.

If you are watching a hunting cat from a window or other vantage point you may see it halting to take stock of the situation, sniffing for new scent signals, ears pricked for the slightest rustle and all clearly exposed to your view; but it is not you the cat is hunting. From the prey's position the cat will only be noticed by the very alert.

Once it has located its prey the cat will advance with even more caution. Notice how it will sometimes freeze in mid-movement, perhaps aware that it might have been heard, even though it seems noiseless to a human observer, or perhaps because the prey has looked in its direction. The one thing it seems unable to suppress is the

Opposite *A cat hunting a spider. Painted on silk by Japanese artist Toko (1868–1911). Many cats become efficient spider catchers and seem to find them a delicious addition to their diet.*
Below *Still life with cat and mouse by an unknown English artist c.1820.*

excited twitching of the tail tip. It has been suggested that this may be a way of concentrating its victim's attention on one point and ignoring the rest of the cat. It certainly seems to diffuse the tension, allowing the rest of the body to be kept in strict control.

The cat advances, one stage at a time, trying to reach the cover closest to the prey before revealing itself. A dash across open ground will alert it, necessitating a gallop from the cat and a leap to secure its quarry and giving it a better chance of escape. Such a dash is much more likely in an animal which itself is feeling vulnerable; no cat wastes time in hiding if it can make its escape up a tree or to some other haven.

Having reached the point closest to the prey the cat adopts the watching stance described above, then prepares to spring. Its hind legs will move further back, the heels lifted to transfer the weight to the toes and the rear feet alternately treading the ground as it gets more agitated, a movement that can be seen greatly exaggerated in kittens. In long grass or where there is some other obstruction the cat may make a high leap onto the animal, but usually it will land at the side of its prey, the final spring being a body movement with the hind feet staying firmly on the ground, giving the cat stability and the ability to correct direction if its quarry takes evasive action. Even when jumping down on prey from above, the smaller cats will usually land beside it first. To drop down on a soft body would mean landing on an unstable surface and make it more difficult to allow for movement. Nonetheless, kittens often try this, especially when ambushing siblings, and it is a technique that may be used by some of the arboreal cat species.

The kill

On its final spring a cat may deliver a killing bite directly to the back of the neck, severing or crushing the spinal cord, bringing death almost instantaneously. Alternatively it may hold its victim down with a paw before administering the bite, or use its paw to pull the creature towards its mouth to bite it.

Above A hunting cat stalks carefully, making the most of cover and, keeping a low profile, gets as close as possible to its prey before making a spring.
Left A kitten's chances of catching a bird are slight unless a chick falls from the nest or an inexperienced fledgling has problems taking flight.
Opposite top In urban situations, especially during the day when rodents are in their dens, birds offer a continuing interest, however unsuccessful a cat may be.
Opposite centre A serval leaps onto prey it has located by faint sounds in the grass.
Opposite below A Greek island cat catches a lizard — a change from begging scraps from tourists.

With larger prey (domestic cats and wild cats will rarely tackle anything larger than a rabbit, and then usually only immature or injured specimens) a blow with a paw to stun or knock the animal over is usually struck from behind and at an angle across the back and shoulder. The head is then brought down to bite immediately forward of the paw on the nape in short-necked prey, or at the base of the neck near the shoulder for long-necked prey, such as pigeons, which stretch out their necks as they try to escape. Sometimes a cat will then release the prey and take another bite, carefully placing it by sight. The larger *Felis* and the Cheetah may bite first in the shoulder area and then use both paws to pull the prey up to the mouth to deliver the fatal bite. Alternatively, they may use the big cat's technique of suffocation.

A very small creature, such as an insect, may be gobbled up straight into the mouth without any attempt to kill it first, though sometimes it may be trapped under a paw or caught between both front paws held together. Flying insects may be swatted with a paw or caught in the mouth. Cats can be extremely accurate in catching such comparatively small creatures. Bumblebees, which are larger and usually slower than most insects, seem to be favorites with some cats, who seem unconcerned by a sting on the chin or paw. Most cats learn to avoid bees and wasps after being stung once or twice which is just as well, since a sting on the tongue or inside the mouth could produce a swelling causing breathing problems and needing veterinary treatment.

Sometimes a cat that has failed to catch an insect — and the cat's expression frequently registers its disappointment when this happens — may carefully take a hopeful look beneath a paw in case it did succeed after all. One neutered tom, though a genuinely good fly hunter, would sometimes pretend he had caught one when its buzzing stopped and look extremely crestfallen if anyone was still watching him when the buzzing started up again.

Playing with prey

Cats will often 'play' with their prey. A small rodent will sometimes be released without being killed and then repeatedly recaptured. As Christopher Smart puts it in his poem *Jubilate Agno* in the famous section about his cat Jeoffrey

For when he takes his prey he plays with it to give it a chance.
For one mouse in seven escapes his dallying . . . .

But Jeoffrey is not giving the mouse a sporting chance, nor is he being deliverately cruel; both are anthropomorphic interpretations. A considerable degree of excitement must be generated in the cat before it will kill, and there is strong indication that the nape bite is learned rather than innate behavior. Here you *may* see parallels with the way in which soldiers have to be 'psyched up' to engage in direct combat. A kitten has to overcome its trepidation at the unknown behavior of what could be a dangerous creature. Support is provided by littermates but increasing

Above *Although adept at catching flying insects, this cat only once caught more than one bird a year — and always fledglings.*
Above right *Appearing from nowhere on a Mediterranean beach, this cat soon found a new friend to share its meal.*
Right *A serval playing with the body of a rat, discharging the tension built up during the hunt.*

boldness can also be the result of the escalating excitement of both play and struggle. The anxious kitten releases the prey, probably out of fear, its movement stimulates the 'chase-attack' response and it repeats this action until it has worked itself up sufficiently to make the kill. This behavior can persist in the adult cat even when it has become an experienced killer. With easy prey it helps increase the tension; with large prey it may also help to tire the prey, reducing its ability to defend itself.

A cat will sometimes also 'play' with the carcass of an animal it has killed. This usually occurs when the hunter, perhaps because of a long wait or a difficult struggle, has built up a high level of excitement. This cannot be immediately dissipated and the cat may throw the prey in the air, repeatedly catching it and performing what looks like a 'victory dance', to release the pent up tension.

Even when the tension has not reached a level to require such release a cat will not usually begin to eat immediately after a kill but will look around, perhaps even walk away, often taking time out to groom itself. If the killing bite is

inhibited, becoming more like the carrying grip, prey may be unharmed. If they do not struggle — and small animals usually keep still — a cat may put down the motionless victim thinking it dead, giving it a chance to escape while the cat's attention is elsewhere.

The majority of cats will prefer to take dead prey to somewhere with cover before they eat and, where there is none, will stop and look around, even in a familiar and secure place. They do not want the creature that they have worked so hard to kill to be taken from them by a scavenger.

European and Asian small cats, and the Lynx and Bobcat in North America, will gnaw at small birds as they are, feathers and all, but birds from blackbird-size upwards they will attempt to pluck first, using an upward jerk of their heads to pull out the feathers. The other New World cats are thought to pluck all sizes. To loosen the feathers, cats shake the bird vigorously in the mouth in an action similar to that used by dogs to kill prey, but with cats the prey is already dead. They will shake a rat in the same way if they have difficulty in biting it open, just as the big cats shake large pieces of meat to loosen them from the bones, before eating from the point held for the shaking.

The smaller cats almost always start eating a carcass at the head, rapidly moving the nose to and fro along the body, almost certainly checking the lie of the fur, scales or feathers with their whiskers (and sometimes misinterpreting the wing-joint of a bird as the point to start). Eating in this direction enables them to swallow with the lie of the fur, scales or feathers.

Some of the larger *Felis* species bite through the head of larger quarry, often ignoring it when it has fallen off. They may grasp pieces of meat between the pads and claws of the front paws while tearing off flesh with their teeth. Big cats may hold a chunk down with one paw, but small cats seldom seem to do this, though some use it as a way of anchoring a bone. They will eat in a crouching posture, shearing off strips of flesh which begin to slide down the gullet even as they

are being cut. The tongue will rasp meat off bones. Cats often look as though they are eating sideways. They do so because they have to get flesh back into the corner of the mouth to reach the cutting surfaces of the carnassial teeth.

Mother cats take prey back to the nest for their kittens and, understandably, may continue the habit even when they do not have a litter — but why do domestic males occasionally take prey home, sometimes leaving it as a 'present' for humans? This behavior has not been satisfactorily explained. It has been suggested that it is because the cat does not know what to do with prey surplus to its needs, even that it is a persistence of ancient Egyptian training of cats to retrieve. More plausibly, it may indicate a greater degree of socialization than is usually attributed to the small cats. In cat colonies, admittedly often made up of genetically related individuals, other cats may take prey which has been carried back, if the captor puts it down, and prey-sharing may be part of the small cat behavior pattern just as it is with the species that hunt together.

Hunting alone

Most cats are opportunistic hunters, taking available prey when they come across it and scavenging too, if they find carrion or food thrown or put out by humans. They may develop particular tastes or skills based either on the food on which they were reared on or personal aptitudes.

Domestic cats usually hunt alone, although there is a record of kittens following and watching their mother hunting. Even when cats from the same home or colony are hunting in the same field they do so independently, even though they may keep an eye on the others' activity. The prey caught by the smaller cats is usually too small to share, so group activity is not motivated.

Some have been observed quite methodically investigating a potential hunting ground in a

This page and opposite below
Cats are efficient scavengers — and thieves.

regular pattern but there does not seem to be any great variation in technique.

In Alaska, young lynx have been seen out with their mother but, although by fanning out over a wider distance they may act as beaters, starting up hare, and learning some skills in the process, the real chase and kill is usually by the mother.

Cougar, the largest of the 'lesser' cats, have been seen chasing a deer, one on either side and another behind, and some collaboration among family groups may occur in other species.

Rabbits and burrow-living birds are sometimes hunted actually in their burrows, as well as by ambushing the entrance. On Macquarie Island, south-east of New Zealand, cats methodically checked out rabbit warrens and on Marion Island, in the sub-antarctic, they would take antarctic prions and petrels from the tunnels of their burrows. On islands where there are no mammal predators the introduction of cats, or other carnivores, can unbalance the ecology, even leading to the extinction of other species, as has happened in many places, including such large territories as New Zealand.

Jaguarundis take small animals from guinea pigs to small deer but seem to prefer catching birds. Swiss naturalist J.R. Rengger, writing 160 years ago, described tethering a hen on a string near a hedge where he knew a jaguarundi was hidden, to see how it got its prey:

'After a short while its head poked out from between the bromeliads, first here, then there, peering around carefully to make sure there was no danger. It then tried to approach the bird without being seen, its body kept close to the ground and scarcely moving the blades of grass as it stalked. When within six or eight feet of its victim the jaguarundi slightly contracted its body and with a well-aimed leap, got the bird by the neck or head in its teeth and immediately tried to drag it back into cover. It did not twitch its tail as much as other cats I have seen when it was stalking. It can often be seen near houses, watching domestic fowl from among the shrubbery.'

Although chicks may be taken from the nest there is no evidence of any of the cat family discovering birds' eggs as a useful diet supplement. Jaguar, however, have been recorded taking turtle eggs.

Fishing

Cats with access to garden ponds often spend a great deal of time watching the fish in them. Probably relatively few become efficient anglers but clutching claws could cause the fish damage and lead to infections, so it is worth designing ponds so that cats cannot dip a paw into the water to flip fish out. There have been a number of reports of very successful fishing cats. One Scottish country pet would regularly hook fish off the angler's line onto the bank to save the use of a gaff net, and an exceptional cat that lived at Plymouth naval base in the 1820s used to dive into the sea to catch its dinner. In Paris there is a street named *Rue du Chat qui Pêche*, but

The Snowshoe Hare is the main prey of the North American lynx.

Cats and birds

Bird lovers concerned about feline predation should remember that most domestic cats are not good bird-catchers. Since 75 percent of young birds die anyway without affecting the population balance those young or weak birds taken by cats are probably saved from a more painful end through starvation.

The pattern of wait and watch before pouncing and of making a landing beside the prey operates against successful hunting of birds, which often have a chance to take off into the air. Domestic cats who succeed in catching birds have usually learned to suppress the pattern; others frequently give up all attempts to catch them for even the preliminary stalking procedure with its watchful halts means that their bird may have flown before they can launch the attack. Some domestic cats, however, develop the techniques of the Serval and Caracal and will chase and leap after birds, catching them in flight with their claws or batting them down with a paw.

On islands where there have been no previous land predators, the introduction of cats, or any other mammal carnivore can be devastating. On Stephens Island, New Zealand, in 1894, the lighthouse keeper's cat brought home 16 specimens of a previously unknown species of bird, the Stephens Island Wren *Xenicus lyalli*. Having presented ornithology with a new discovery, within the year that single cat had also made the bird extinct. There are other cases of endemic species disappearing and many where local populations have been eliminated.

Some owners claim to have taught their cats not to catch birds. However, this seems unlikely and, for any free-ranging cat, can only mean that it has been discouraged from bringing them home. Hunting is natural behavior which persists even when a cat is well fed and has no need to find its own food; birds are a cat's natural, though not usually its most important, prey. Pet owners worried about bird-predation can probably reduce it by belling their cats (on a proper elasticized collar). Because their success rate is so poor, many cats give up even attempting to catch birds.

Indoor pets often react to birds outside the window. A cat seeing a bird (or even a fly or butterfly) out of reach will often watch it carefully, uttering a strange staccato chatter which seems specific to this situation. Is it a response of excitement or frustration? It sounds very like a threatening boast of what the cat would do if only it could get at the bird, though that must probably be dismissed as an anthropomorphic interpretation!

A feral cat on Santa Cruz in the Galapagos Islands. The introduction of cats and other domestic animals had serious effects on the delicately balanced ecology of these isolated islands.
Left *A Japanese domestic cat, which has adopted techniques like those of the Caracal, takes on the challenge of a sea eagle, much bigger than itself. Some cats, especially kittens, conscious of threat from predatory birds, take cover if a large bird hovers overhead.*

Although cats will watch fish for hours, waiting for the chance to scoop one from the water, few become skilled anglers.

whether this was an actual cat which fished the Seine or the name is a corruption of *pécher* (to sin) is uncertain. What is certain is that for some cats it is *not true* that 'The cat likes fish but will not wet its feet' and cats that are proficient anglers will teach their kittens how to fish.

The big cats

The big cats, *Panthera* species, can all be efficient solitary hunters but the ungulates (antelope, deer, and similar creatures) which form a major part of their prey provide a larger meal and make prey-sharing a more practical proposition than it is for the smaller cats. It is easier for a group of cats to separate an individual from a large herd than to rely on finding an animal already grazing away from the main group or straggling behind because weakness or suckling young are slowing it down.

Cases of two individuals joining forces to attack the same animal, or of one driving prey towards the other, have been observed among snow leopards and tigers, but the most frequent and the most sophisticated cooperation is among the lion prides of East Africa.

How lions hunt

In the Gir Forest male lions frequently make the kill but in Africa the hunters of the lion pride will usually be a group of lionesses. They may include some lions, but pride males largely leave hunting to the females, reserving their own energies for defending their territory. On sighting a likely herd of antelope or zebra, a large East African hunting party at Amboseli or in the

Right *A stalking lioness advances with her ears flattened and nose raised so that the spine, neck and head profile is almost level.*
Below right *A lioness suffocates a wildebeest by gripping its throat.*

Serengeti will set off either together, or at short intervals, in the direction of the potential prey. As they get closer they slow their advance and begin a more careful approach, most of them spreading out in a semi-circle around the herd, with a few taking up positions forward of it.

For a successful attack a lioness needs to get within quite close range for, although a lion may reach 37 mph (60 mph) for short bursts, in a chase most of its hoofed prey can soon outrun it. Although it has no obvious camouflage pattern the color of the lion's coat makes it difficult to spot and stealth will allow it to get within range. A hunting lioness advances with ears flattened outwards and nose raised so that spine, neck and head form an almost level profile, except for a lump at the shoulder, making her much less noticeable. With a large hunting team, however, it is part of the strategy that the 'beaters' are observed.

At first a group of antelopes give little attention to the predators, even though they have registered that the lions are there, for they are too far away to be an immediate threat. As the hunters approach, the antelopes take flight, bringing them close to the ambush party who now rush out, each taking an individual they have already picked out. Some score near misses but one antelope may be pulled down. With larger prey more than one lioness would probably attack the same animal. The lioness does not deliver the spinal *coup de grace* of the smaller cats but grips the throat between its jaws, throttling the animal as the other members of the pride join her to share the kill.

Even two predators working together will have an enormous advantage. They can pick out two possible victims or, taking a single buffalo for instance, they can make it face each in turn to defend itself with its horns, giving the other a chance to get in to make a successful attack. Victims are carefully selected as being those most vulnerable. The young and inexperienced, mothers who may be slowed down by trying to protect their young, animals hampered by lameness or injury — all will make easier prey.

Working alone, a lion will have stealthily to approach as close as possible, then make a dash, or wait in ambush until prey graze within range or until some other threat drives them near. If the attack is not immediately successful lions will rarely keep up the chase for more than a hundred yards or so and will usually give up earlier.

The animal who makes the kill in a group attack seldom begins eating immediately. It may withdraw some distance away and be the last of the adults to eat.

If male lions are present, they will be first to feed. A male arriving after others have started eating may drive the lionesses and their young away. In times when kills are few, cubs are the last to get a chance to eat, and may even starve.

Two lionesses close in on a gazelle.

Adults can always breed again but for the cubs there could still be many hazards ahead before they are able to raise young of their own so, by the hard logic of species survival, the preservation of their young lives has less value.

Other prey

When antelope and deer are not plentiful lions will turn to other prey. In certain areas various kinds of pig become the major species, and giraffe are also occasionally taken. Young hippos, vulnerable if they stray from their mothers, are favorites in some places and even young elephant are occasionally attacked; but lions will also take any small mammals they come across, birds and even locusts and termites. Crocodiles and snakes have also been taken and fish are sometimes scooped out of shallow water. Lions will take advantage of other animals' kills, have no compunction about eating carrion and even scavenge around settlements, as well as taking domestic animals where they are not well guarded.

Asian lions and tigers

The lions of the Gir Forest, tigers and the other big cats of Asia do not have access to great herds like those of East Africa, though predation on domestic cattle does provide comparatively easy prey in some areas. Whilst pride lions may be lucky enough to make one successful kill in four attempts, their success rate is usually considerably less. George Schaller estimated that tigers preying upon deer in the Khana Reserve in India made only one successful kill for 20 attempts that failed.

Tigers adopt a hunting technique of stalking prey in a manner much like that described for the smaller cats, though active hunting is more usual than ambush. They need to get within a range of about 66 ft (20 m) before they can

launch an attack, which is usually made from the side or rear. Though probably making its dash in a series of great bounds, a tiger does not generally spring upon the prey through the air but makes the final attack with its hind feet on the ground, attempting to seize the animal about the shoulders, neck or back. The impact of the charge may knock the animal off its feet or a blow from a paw just throw it off balance, but the tiger's weight will pull it down. Once down, the most usual way in which the kill is made is a throat bite from the side or front, asphyxiating the animal.

The carcass is then taken to dense cover, carried in the mouth or dragged if the animal is large. A small animal will be eaten in one meal but larger prey will provide food for several days, the tiger staying by the kill to feed at leisure.

Tigers in Manchuria, preying upon wild pigs, exploited the terrain by mounting ambush on a cliff or overhang where they were likely to pass and leaping down upon them, killing them by crushing the neck vertebrae.

Leopards and jaguars

Leopards, the most widespread member of the cat family, often occur in the same habitats as both lions and tigers, for they are highly adaptable in their hunting behavior. They prey on smaller mammals than those their larger relatives usually choose, using similar techniques to those of the tiger; leopards are particularly accomplished stalkers, having considerable success with birds. They employ the nape bite on small animals such as baboons and young gazelle or when jumping down on a victim from a tree, but may use the throat bite on slightly larger prey.

Good climbers, leopards will take animals in trees, or after panicking them into jumping to the ground. To prevent a carcass being stolen by other predators, leopards will carry it up into a tree, holding it by the neck in their teeth as

Clockwise from top *(1) Three lionesses attack a giraffe calf in the Masai Mara. The mother's hooves could deliver a crippling blow but she cannot take on all three at once and they have separated her calf from her. (2) A tiger drives vultures from its kill. Hyenas and other scavengers not only try to share the pickings but sometimes succeed in driving off the hunter. However, a leopard will rarely contest a lion which tries to steal its kill. (3) A tiger makes a monkey kill. (4) A horse attacked by a lion, an engraving by George Stubbs (1724–1806). When, aged 30, he was visiting Italy, the painter is said to have seen an escaped lion devouring a horse. Other authorities claim it was a piece of sculpture, not a real attack, that put this image into his mind. However, it remained with him for the rest of his life and was the subject of several paintings. (5) A Serengeti lion, perplexed by an encounter with a Grey Cobra. Some cats are skilled at killing snakes and include them in their prey.*

Right *A leopard caches its kill in a tree, out of reach of most scavengers. Caracal have also been known to lodge their kill in the fork of a tree.*

they climb. There they cache it in a fork and eat it carefully so that no major pieces fall to the ground.

A jaguar will also occasionally take animals such as sloths and sleeping birds in trees but hunts mainly on the ground, the capybara being its major prey. Living near waterways, it takes coypus, otters and other riverine creatures, such as frogs, turtles, even cayman and fish, flicking them out onto the bank with a paw. Amazonian Indians report that it 'angles' by twitching its tail in the water to attract the fish.

The Cheetah

The Cheetah takes smaller animals than the big cats and its physique is adapted to a different hunting strategy from all the others because it is such a specialized sprinter. It lives in open country and, although it will take advantage of what cover is available, it may have to hunt where there is very little. It adopts a stalking technique very similar to the other cats but with its coat pattern breaking up its shape, and careful control of its movements, it can still remain unnoticed, even as it approaches without cover, until perhaps within a hundred yards of its target. However, when the intended victims do see it they will flee much sooner than they would from a lion. They know they need to be that much further ahead of this particular enemy.

From as far off as a hundred yards, cheetahs can rush in at high speed — they hold the land speed record for any living creature — advancing in long and rapid strides until they can close in and strike the victim down with a forepaw or by colliding with it. They kill by a strangling bite on the throat, which may have to be maintained for several minutes before the animal is dead. To make this easier to hold without affecting their own breathing, the cheetah's upper canine teeth have specially small roots so that they do not restrict the nasal passage, giving this cat a greater capacity to take in air.

Female cheetah live and hunt alone, except when they are caring for their cubs, but males often form small groups, sometimes holding joint territory and sometimes travelling as nomads hunting together.

Cheetah can run faster than their prey, but they cannot keep going for so long. If a victim manages to change direction and elude them, or the cheetah fails to make contact with a blow, the prey may be able to get ahead as its pursuer begins to tire. After making a kill, or exerting itself without success, a cheetah may need as much as half an hour to recover, but first, if possible, it will drag the carcass into cover where it is less likely to be seen by thieves and scavengers.

Cheetah often lose their kills to large cats, vultures and hyenas. They tend to hunt later in the morning and earlier in the afternoon than leopards and lions, which reduces immediate competition, but this means they are more likely to be seen by vultures, the circling of which can bring other scavengers to the spot. Vultures have been known to drive cheetah away from their kill.

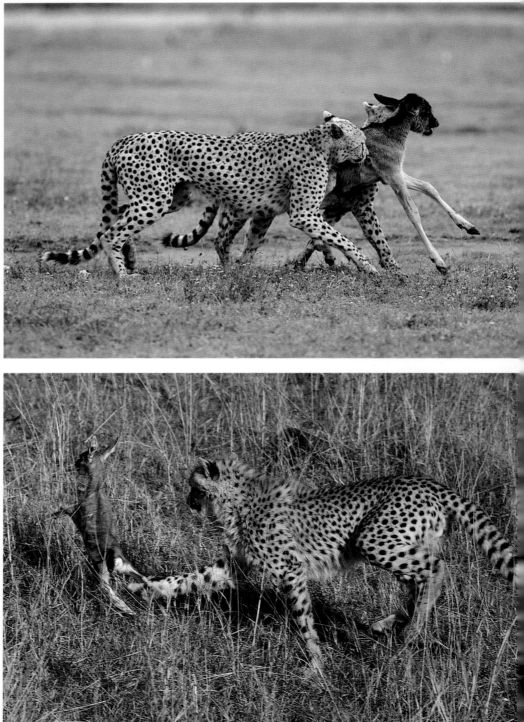

Clockwise from top opposite

A jaguar diving for fish.

A cheetah tries to drive vultures from its kill.

A female cheetah watches her cubs stalking wildebeest.

A cheetah plays with a baby Thomson's gazelle before despatching it.

A pair of male cheetah close in on a wildebeest calf.

DOMESTIC DIFFERENCES

The physical changes in the cat which have been brought about by domestication are few compared with those in dogs or draft and farm animals, for it is only recently that breeders have begun to distort its natural form by producing the more extreme types of Siamese and Peke-faced cats and perpetuating mutations such as the Manx and Drop-eared cats. Breeders' selection for particular characteristics, such as the long hair of the Persian cats, would probably be a disadvantage in the wild and the extremely placid Ragdolls are clearly unsuited to an independent existence. It is to be hoped for the cats' sake, that no such developments will take place as the distortions of dog breeding, which have produced animals unable to give birth naturally in breeds such as the Bulldog, and the breathing problems of many Pugs and Pekinese. Respiratory and tear duct difficulties have already occurred in the very flat-faced cats. Although there is strong feeling among many cat lovers, especially in Britain, against the development of these extreme types, they are very popular with others. This means that breeders must take great care not to create animals with anatomical features that produce health problems.

Fortunately the only major physical change in our cats is a slightly longer digestive tract than in the wild animal, a development which occurs in most species when they are domesticated. That does not affect the animal's life. What will affect it are the environment, interference with rearing, and conditions imposed by its breeders and owners. Wild animals kept in captivity in zoos are acknowledged to develop all kinds of psychological and sexual problems, yet people consider domestic cats are ideally suited to be pets. They have the reputation of being a solitary species which does not need space to be happy and fits perfectly in the small modern home, purring away to show how contented they are. Nevertheless owners should always remember the cat's origins and natural behavior and respect them.

Above *Cardboard boxes, whichever way up, always attract cats. They provide a place in which to hide, to jump in and out off and an excuse for rivalry.*

Right *Cats like high places from which they can observe the world.*
Below *Cats find little difficulty in helping themselves to dry cat chow.*

Right *A paper bag or a newspaper provides a lot of fun.*

Some species of cats, including domestic cats, are not always solitary but live in family groups and have wider conspecific interaction. Many have a strong sense of territory and that territory can be extensive when space allows. Farm cats can match this kind of life without great difficulty. Many domestic pets, free to roam outdoors, can establish a larger range, hunt and socialize, so far as local densities permit. The cat with restricted or no access to the outside world is limited in the extent to which it can live that kind of life. However, pet keeping always involves a measure of adaptation to an 'artificial' environment.

Imprinting, the development of awareness of and attraction to their own species (or sometimes a mistaken identification with another when not reared by their own kind), occurs in the domestic cat more slowly than in species which have to be mobile from birth. Socialization with other

Left *A window from which to watch the world go by makes life more interesting for any cat.*
Below *An eighteenth-century enamel snuff or pastille box. The spaniel here looks playful but the cats have claws extended, eyes wide and ears held back in a strong defensive threat — this game has gone too far. Even the near cat's tail seems to be lashing as though it has lost its patience. Domestic pets usually get on well, especially if they grow up together. Very often a cat tends to bully a larger dog.*

species, and especially with humans, is developed most strongly when a kitten is 2–7 weeks old. Kittens which are handled by people at this age, fondled, stroked and talked to, are more likely to become people-oriented. Their overall development also seems to be somewhat accelerated. If the mothers are present when their kittens are handled, and are themselves confident with people, the kitten-person bonding will be stronger. If other species are present (and equally accepted by the mother) the kitten will accept them as though they were conspecific, even prey animals often being treated as though they were cats.

Later, close contact at a period of great stress, such as when a cat is nursed through illness, can sometimes also induce behavior similar to imprinting, the animal perhaps even following a person about when possible. Stress appears to affect the brain in a way which recreates the conditions under which imprinting occurs most strongly.

Socialization with people is essential for a pet cat that is not going to have the opportunity to pursue a free feline life. Sensitivity to cats is equally essential on the part of the people involved for interspecific relationship to work. We tend to be less adept at interpreting and understanding cats than they are at understanding us, but an awareness of basic feline communications systems will help.

Although a domestic pet will not need to hunt for its food, the behavior link with hunting will still be present. While such opportunities as do occur for genuine hunting may be taken, the cat will turn much of this behavior into play. This will be reinforced by the pattern, observed in most domesticated animals, of juvenile features being retained into adulthood, produced partly by the continuing pseudo-parental role of the

person providing food, grooming, reassurance and other care.

Play is one way in which zoo animals relieve their boredom. It occurs in adulthood in many species in the wild, but wild cats' time and energies are mainly taken up with hunting, reproduction and rearing young, and what is left is more frequently spent resting. In the house cat play replaces much of the other activity and, without it, life could become very dull indeed.

Other cats and other pets in the household will improve the quality of some cat's lives, but it will usually be easier to introduce a kitten into a household where there are other established pets than to bring in adult animals. Most have a caring reaction to young creatures, much like that on which most of our own pet keeping is initially based. Very shy, over-possessive or unsocialized animals will not find it easy adapting

Below *The warm bonnet of a car is a favorite place for a nap.*

to another. Establishing a new arrival may take time and, even then, produce no more than an acceptance on sufferance.

Cats will often invent their own games and invite people to play them. They may prefer to play a particular game with one member of a household and the game partner will not necessarily be the person who feeds them or whose lap they prefer. Individual cats may be keener on petting than play or vice versa, a preference not always easy to discern in kittens, though it could be an important factor to a person selecting a pet.

To parallel behavior in the wild the indoor cat will want places in which to conceal itself, and enjoy being able to jump and climb, and gain a view from high places like the top of a bookcase or out of a window. Although it may adapt to the restriction of life in a single room or a city bedsitter, the cat will prefer access to a variety of spaces to create a more interesting range. A cat who has the freedom of an entire house may spend different segments of the day in the same sequence of different places. When visitors (human or animal) appear the cat may come out to welcome or inspect the intruders but will often disappear into hiding if it feels outnumbered, emerging when they leave to check out each part of the house in turn to ensure no interloper still remains on its territory.

Domestic cats tend to have a longer life span than those in the wild, even without the benefits of veterinary help. Castrated males live longer than undoctored toms and castration before puberty tends to extend life further (although it also appears to be linked with a higher incidence of death from leukemia). Neutering (altering) does not affect hunting activity and does not necessarily prevent spraying (about ten per cent still spray) but it will reduce the cats' roaming and fighting inclinations.

Above *Ladders are easily negotiable going up, but coming down, like descending trees, is sometimes more of a problem.*
Right *Cats reared with animals of prey species tend to treat them as their own kind. Other members of the same species, however, may still be seen as prey, and if this happens there could be dangerous confusion if the 'family' should start a chase.*
Below *A cat does not have to belong to a circus to develop specialist skills. Many enjoy being carried sitting on a shoulder or wrapped around a neck. A bicycle adds to the fun but this is not something to do on a public highway where if the cat jumped off it could get run over. It is sensible to put a leash on a cat which is taken out in the street, but that could be dangerous on a bicycle.*
Below right *A smooth-rolling billiard ball that can be sent ricocheting around the table makes a splendid toy, but claws are not good for the baize.*

PERPETUATING THE SPECIES

Reproduction in the cat family follows the typical mammalian pattern, but there are many small differences both between and within species, probably caused by the climate and food availability, both of which would affect the potential for successfully raising young.

In warmer countries there seems to be no specific breeding season and kittens and cubs may be born during any month. In higher latitudes mating is in the early part of the year, January through March in the north, although with the European Wildcat it has been suggested that there may also be a second litter later in the year. Domestic cats could certainly produce three litters a year, though to permit a pet to do so would not be in the cat's best interest. Various experts have declared particular mating seasons for domestic cats: February, June and October in western Europe, January through September in the northern United States, two

weeks either side of the end of January and the end of July in north Africa — but many cat owners could testify from their own experience how inaccurate such generalizations are.

In practice, season depends on the individual cat as much as on the conditions in which it lives. A warm home, regular and plentiful food and a sense of being cared for may provide a trigger to enable confident mating all year round, but the number of daylight hours — extended by artificial lighting for the domestic pet — is probably the most important influence. Some breeds, notably the Siamese and others of 'foreign' type, often seem to be very frequently in season, though this may only be because they tend to be more noisy and demonstrative and to have cat-centred owners who are more likely to notice.

Unlike some other mammals, the female cat does not have a regular monthly cycle when she periodically releases unfertilized eggs. In the human female there is a recurrent cycle of 28 days all the year round. In domestic cats the cycle is about 21 days, though it appears to vary considerably between cats and may be seasonal. In colonies of feral cats (and among the females of a lion pride) a tendency to synchronization of the cycle among group members has been noticed, a pattern also seen in groups of women. This could create advantages in that with a number of litters being born at the same time communal care and defense of small kittens would be made easier. It could also reduce fighting between males over particular females, with the result that they could then spend more time and energy in copulation.

The breeding cycle

The breeding cycle begins with a period, known as the anoestrus, the infertile phase when the body is preparing for the coming stages and the female is totally uninterested in overtures from tom cats. As the body begins to prepare for mating, a stage known as pro-oestrus, the cat begins to rub herself against things. Within a day she is rubbing against almost everything she encounters, particularly with her head and neck. At this point she may allow a tom to come near her and may show some positive interest in him, but she will not permit any real intimacies.

Toms know the female is coming into season because she produces pheromones, scent signals, produced by glands which add them to the urine and a vaginal secretion. This sweetish smell, not unlike that of the human female, but specific to the cat, is easily identifiable by toms and strong enough to be detected by some humans, at least when they are handling the cat. Urination or body contact will leave signs about her territory but the scent is far carrying. Even if the cat is not allowed outdoors toms soon seem to turn up from nowhere.

Female felines have no qualms about letting the world know when they are in season, calling loudly to attract the local males.
Right *A queen on heat needs careful watching and firmly closed doors and windows if she is not to escape and mate.*

Check every opening. This queen climbed a louvered window to make her escape.

Below *At first a lioness rebuffs an impatient male.*
Below right *When the lioness accepts him, the male grips her neck between his teeth.*
Opposite below *At the moment of ejaculation the lion gives a roar. After mating the lioness rolls on the ground.*

The female now begins to roll around on the ground, lying on her back and wriggling in front of a tom or someone she likes, probably purring, clenching and unclenching her paws and rubbing her head and neck against any vertical surface with which her rolls bring her in contact. She may allow a tom to approach to smell her and even to lick her head and vulva.

Pro-oestrus behavior may last only a day or as long as three days before the female is ready to allow a tom to take the courtship further. Although a little heavy stroking from a human friend may be welcomed, if an inexperienced tom attempts a mating at this stage she will probably turn on him, hissing and spitting. It is not always in fights with other males that tom cats gain their battle scars.

The cycle now moves into its third stage, oestrus, or heat as it is sometimes called. This is the period when the female is sexually receptive. The follicles which produce her ova swell and are ready to release them.

By now she will have begun to make quiet deep-throated calls that grow louder as her condition intensifies; with most females these calls progress from a moan into a howl. Siamese cats have a reputation for being particularly vocal, especially if they are confined indoors, while Russian Blue breeders often lament the lack of outward signs of oestrus. There are no hard and fast rules — one deaf blue-eyed white Persian produced a literally china-shattering howl! The male answers her calls, or announces his arrival outside the house, with gentle purrs and chirrupings to initiate his courtship.

If several toms appear — and they probably will — they may adopt aggressive postures or do battle. Whether they are actually fighting over her or fighting because they are invading another tom's territory to reach her is debatable, for the female will not necessarily accept the winning male and will probably mate with more than one of her suitors.

With the solitary wild cat species battles over a female do not seem to occur, for transient males may be allowed to pass through unmolested, so long as they do not make a challenge for the territory. In the lion pride the males do not dispute mating rights. It is not necessarily the dominant male who mates first. The first lion to court and be accepted by a lioness is unmolested, though the other lions in the pride may well mate with her later.

When F.K. Werner was studying lynx in the Carpathians he observed males occupying a definite mating territory as 'masters' of mating sites, similar to the 'stands' of deer bucks, which other males did not approach. Here females competed for the male's attention. This has not been supported by other researchers who report seeing several males competing for one female and fighting over her.

The mating

An experienced tom cat will wait until the female shows signs of being ready to accept him before he attempts to mount her. Their courtship will make her more excited and if toms spray around the area or even over her, their scent increases her stimulation. She crouches with her body against the floor and her hind quarters raised and begins to tread up and down with her front paws, her tail raised and swung to one side. She makes soft, inviting little noises. After, perhaps, some exploratory rubbing and licking, the tom will step across her body and lick, then bite, her neck. Grasping it in his teeth, as a mother cat carries a kitten, he quietens the female. The tom straddles her, often treading up and down with his rear legs on her back which she raises into the copulatory position known as lordosis. He arches his body and she treads with her hind limbs to bring his penis into line with her vagina and he then enters her.

Intromission consists of only a few pelvic thrusts before ejaculation, a matter of only five or ten seconds, only about four minutes in total having elapsed since he gripped her neck.

When the male ejaculates the female makes a loud and piercing cry and pulls away. She may

turn on the male spitting and scratching if he does not keep his distance. She then rapidly washes her vagina before rolling vigorously on her back and purring, while the male washes his paws and penis at a safe distance from her.

Copulation stimulates the release of a hormone which causes ripe follicles in the ovary to burst open, releasing their eggs. This process, known as induced ovulation, occurs in rabbits as well as cats but differs from most mammals which release eggs automatically as part of their menstrual cycle.

The female's scream is often described as one of pain; once it was said to be caused by the tom having semen 'of fire'. A more scientific explanation is that because the tom's penis is covered with projections which increase in size to become horny spines when the male's hormone level is high, these barbs cause pain on withdrawal. Over fifty years ago, however, a Californian researcher carried out an experiment on the cause of ovulation in which he used a smooth glass rod tapering to a rounded point as a simulacrum penis to stimulate a cat in oestrus. He pressed the rod against the sides of the vaginal passage with no response. The cat made the characteristic cry only when it was pushed directly towards the cervix. The cry was not caused by withdrawal and the instrument used had a smooth surface with no barbs or spines.

Then why does the cat turn on her mate, and indulge in the routine of washing and rolling immediately after copulation? Perhaps because this rolling plays some essential part in assisting the hormonal changes which produce ovulation (as indeed may the stimulus of the tom's barbed penis), or the passage of the sperm and subsequent fertilization, although how we do not know.

After a time, the female will be ready to copulate again, often indicating her readiness by giving the male a light tap with her paw or approaching and rubbing her partner. Usually the domestic cat will not encourage the tom again for about half an hour, although some may wait three times as long and others be ready after only

about ten minutes. In some other cat species matings may be even more frequent.

Mating with the same tom may continue until his energy begins to wane, when, if there are others waiting, he will be succeeded by another male. If there is only one male, mating may continue on and off over a period of up to two or three full days. The pair will often curl up to sleep together and indulge in affectionate displays of mutual grooming as they are resting. If a cat is not mated the oestrus period will continue for longer than when mating takes place.

The Cougar seems to be on heat for about eight days, with as many as 12 couplings each day, though pairs have been reported spending as long as two weeks together in courtship before the female has been stimulated sufficiently to mate.

Lionesses usually stay on heat for about four days, though two in Dresden zoo once continued mating for eight days with 360 couplings counted! The love-making of the big cats follows the same pattern as that of the small cats but tends to be rather less noisy and violent.

Top left *The lordosis position, an indication that the queen is ready to accept copulation.*
Top right *The tom grips the scruff of the queen's neck with his teeth, then positions himself on her back, treading with his hind feet preparatory to intromission.*
Above *After mating the tom will usually lick his penis. This is covered with backward-pointing barbs which stimulate the queen as he withdraws.*

The hormones which mating releases not only start ovulation but also all the other processes, including the production of another hormone, progesterone, which prepares the uterus to receive the eggs and sets off all the other changes brought about by pregnancy. For this reason, if a cat is artificially stimulated, she may show some signs of apparent pregnancy, even though she has not actually been mated.

The eggs are not released until 24–26 hours after the first mating. This is one reason for repeated mating. It also means that if there are several male partners the same litter can include kittens from different fathers.

If a female is not mated during oestrus the follicles of the ovary will shrink back after a few days until the beginning of a new cycle restimulates them.

Deliberately preventing a cat from mating for long periods can lead to problems such as the development of ovarian cysts, which can produce abnormal levels of female hormones thereby interfering with conception. Artificial stimulation does not have this effect and may be a better course than just shutting her in if you want a cat to breed in the future but have reasons for not letting her breed at the time. Some pedigree owners use a vasectomied tom in this situation to cause ovulation and postpone a proper mating until the following oestrus.

There is a cooling off period, known as metoestrus, lasting up to another day, during which the female cat may allow a tom to mount her but not to copulate. She will often follow the procedure through as far as the stage of treading with her back feet ready for insertion of the penis, then turn on him. Her condition then returns to anoestrus, with no interest in sexual advances.

Pregnancy

Gestation periods vary among members of the cat family and may differ between individuals by several days. In the domestic cat, although within a month of fertilization the foetuses will develop into almost complete miniature kittens an inch (25 mm) long, there is, at first, little noticeable outward change. After about 16 days the nipples may become pink and enlarged, especially if it

is a first pregnancy, though this can also occur after an unfertilized mating. An experienced person may be able to feel the kittens as pea-size lumps within the uterus at about the 21st day and as individual kittens a week later, after which they cannot be felt individually until about the 7th week. However, it is best to leave this to the vet as untrained hands could cause injury.

There will not be any noticeable abdominal swelling until the fifth or sixth week of pregnancy in the domestic cat and some go almost their full term before it would be noticeable to strangers that they are pregnant. A small litter will obviously show less than a large one. Apart from eating more, and therefore having to hunt more in the wild, the mother-to-be will behave as normal until the weight of kittens begins to restrict her movement. This may not be until the ninth and final week in most domestic cats. Among the big cats, especially, the kittens may hamper hunting near the end of pregnancy and only easier prey be attempted, though hunger may force more strenuous activity.

About two weeks before kittens are due the domestic cat looks for somewhere sheltered to give birth. Most wild species will find something like a small cave or deep cover; pets should be offered a suitable box so that they do not choose some inaccessible corner.

GESTATION PERIODS IN FELINE SPECIES

All timings are approximate. There is considerable variation in some species and for some of the smaller cats the period has not been satisfactorily established.

Domestic cat	65 days
Wildcat	68 days (less in Africa)
Jungle Cat	66 days
Caracal	70–78 days
Serval	about 75 days
Black-footed Cat	63–68 days
Sand Cat	63 days
Leopard Cat	about 56 days
Fishing Cat	63 days
Lynx	60–74 days
Bobcat	60–63 days
Cougar	90–96 days
Margay Tiger Cat	74 days
Jaguarundi	63–70 days
Lion	100–119 days
Leopard	90–105 days
Tiger	103 days
Snow Leopard	98–103 days
Jaguar	93–110 days
Clouded Leopard	85–90 days
Cheetah	91–95 days

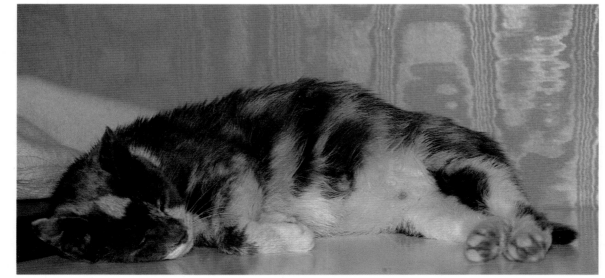

Left 'Pinking up' is the first clear sign that a cat is pregnant if the embryos have not been felt growing. It occurs about three weeks after mating in the domestic cat.
Above Some cats do not become noticeably distended until the pregnancy is well advanced.

Right *Fertilization occurs 24–36 hours after mating, when three to six eggs are released by the ovaries. The implantation of the embryo occurs about two weeks after mating. At first a yolk sac provides nutrients until the placenta and umbilical cord develop to provide direct support from the mother by about the 22nd day. Meanwhile a backbone has formed and the limbs are beginning to appear. By the end of four weeks from fertilization all the organs are present and the embryo has become a fetus. A week later its growth will probably become noticeable as a swelling in the mother's belly. Growth is now rapid. From about six weeks it is likely to double in size before birth at nine weeks.*

Overleaf *Giving birth is only the beginning of kitten rearing — there are weeks of care ahead.*

Birth

Exact length of pregnancy can vary by several days within a species, influenced perhaps by food availability and other conditions, and in the case of domestic pets, if a favorite person is not present, the cat may delay birth until their arrival. Indications that a queen is coming to full term include all sorts of erratic behavior: circling about apparently searching for something, suddenly stopping what she is doing to indulge in excessive licking of herself, rushing off to the litter tray to urinate and then being surprised when she doesn't, shredding things with her claws. First-time mothers are likely to be more erratic than others but this stage, if noticed at all, will generally not last longer than one day.

In the first stage of labour the cat will retire to her nest and begin to breathe more quickly, possibly panting a little as she breathes through her mouth as well as normally through the nose, and purring. In the second stage contractions of the abdomen begin, at very long intervals at first but eventually about every half minute. Eventually the vaginal opening begins to enlarge and the amniotic sac, the fluid-filled membrane containing the kitten or cub, begins to emerge.

Most feline births proceed with no complications. As each new life emerges the mother makes sure that the sac is broken and licks her kitten

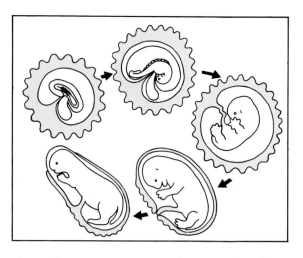

clean, the same action stimulating its breathing. Then she severs the umbilical cord.

The placenta, or afterbirth, through which food and oxygen have been supplied to the embryo, is usually passed out at the next contraction (unless there is only one between identical twins) and is eaten by the mother. This practice both reduces the risk of attracting predators to the birth and provides valuable nourishment for the mother before she is able to leave her litter. At intervals one birth follows another, each kitten or cub making its way to a nipple and beginning to suck. The demanding task of feeding and rearing a new litter has begun. The cycle of life has been repeated.

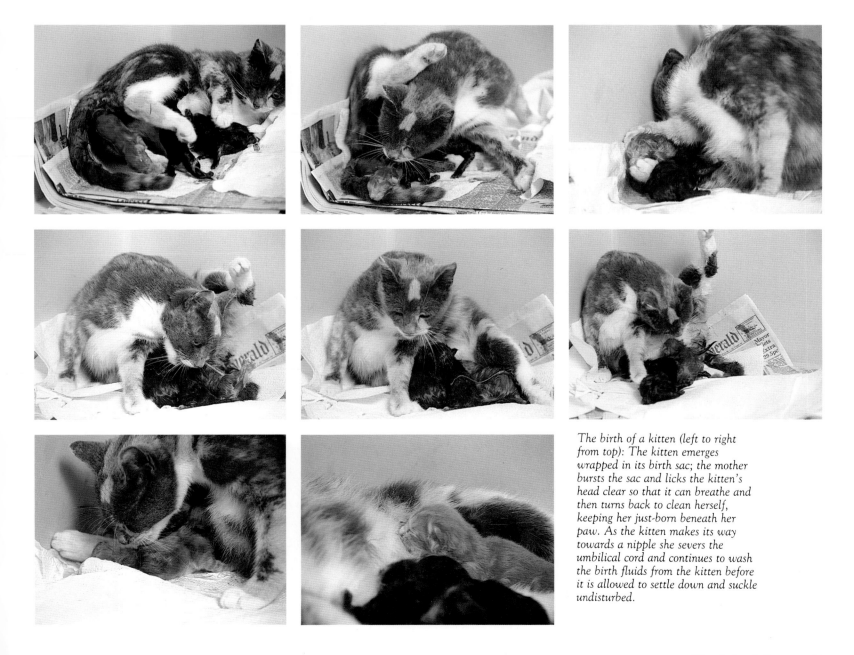

The birth of a kitten (left to right from top): The kitten emerges wrapped in its birth sac; the mother bursts the sac and licks the kitten's head clear so that it can breathe and then turns back to clean herself, keeping her just-born beneath her paw. As the kitten makes its way towards a nipple she severs the umbilical cord and continues to wash the birth fluids from the kitten before it is allowed to settle down and suckle undisturbed.

CATS AND PEOPLE

CATS IN ANCIENT TIMES

Previous page *Mr and Mrs Clark and Percy by David Hockney. Celia Birtwell (Mrs Clark) has pointed out that Hockney misidentified the cat. This is another of their cats.*

Above *An impression from an Assyrian cylinder seal of 1350–1000BC shows the hero Gilgamesh with a vanquished lion.*
Right *Samson, the Israelite lion hero, in a woodcut by Albrecht Dürer (1471–1528).*

Above *These lion-headed creatures are not demons but Ugallos, protective spirits which guarded the royal palace at Nineveh (645–635BC).*

Below *A big cat, painted on the wall of a cave at Niaux in France by prehistoric people. No sabre-tooth cats appear in prehistoric art and all the potential lions are shown without manes, including one at Les Cambarelles, which is quite definitely male.*

When humans first appeared upon the scene the cat family was already established as the dominant carnivores over much of the Earth. At first, the relationship with the big cats was one of hunters and prey, with the big cats as the hunters. Sometimes prehistoric humans would get the chance to scavenge from cat kills. Bushmen of southern Africa in comparatively recent times described following lions to scavenge the remains of the lions' meal but they would not attempt to kill the lion, for indeed that would remove their provider.

When people learned to make and use tools and weapons they were able to defend themselves against attack and so deliberately hunt. Some of the world's earliest heroes were lion-killers. Gilgamesh, King of Uruk, the hero of Sumerian, Babylonian and Assyrian cultures, slew the lions which guarded the passes of Mount Mashu which led to paradise. Although there are more apparently significant victories in the epic poem that tells his story, it is with lions that he is most frequently depicted in sculptures and seal reliefs.

Samson, the Israelite champion, as the King James's version of the Bible puts it, 'rent' the lion 'as he would have rent a kid, and he had nothing in his hand.' Heracles, the Greek hero, killed ferocious lions that were attacking flocks on the slopes of Mount Kithairon. When, after killing his wife and children in a fit of madness induced by the goddess Hera, the Delphian oracle instructed him to perform his famous Twelve Labors to expiate his guilt, the first Labor was to exterminate the Nemean Lion. This beast, which lived on the mountainside outside the city of Nemea, between Corinth and Argos in the Peloponnesos, had skin impregnable to weapons. Unable to pierce its body with his arrows or spears Heracles had to grapple with it hand to claw until he succeeded in throttling it. Thereafter, the hero himself wore the lion's skin, making him invulnerable to weapons, and he is usually depicted clad in it.

For some tribal societies in Africa, where in historical times lions have been more common than in Europe and the Middle East, the killing of a lion used to be an essential stage in the passage to manhood.

It seems that very early, people singled out the lion as the most formidable of animals and the 'king of beasts'. Vanquishing a lion gave particular prestige. We do not know how lions came to be a symbol of human monarchy. Perhaps the wearing of lion pelt trophies by hero-leaders gave them symbolic status or maybe a parallel was drawn between the wielders of animal and human power: in the ancient Hindu *Atharva Veda* the king is compared to a mighty lion.

Baked clay tablets dating from 5500 BC show that the lion was by then well established as a 'royal beast'. They refer to the transport of captured lions being sent to an Akkadian king at Mari. The organization of royal lion hunts became a feature of several later cultures, a symbolic playing out of the hero's role.

On the sides of caves at Niaux, in France, and at other sites, prehistoric people painted what appear to be cave lions. Their purpose is obscure. Most cave paintings show deer, bison and mammoths, animals which were hunted for food and clothing. Could these lion pictures have a cult significance? It is the bull which seems to be the dominant animal symbol in the earliest known civilizations, not the lion. The bull was the major symbol of power and virility at Çatal Hüyük, the neolithic city discovered in Turkey, and the subject of cults in Mesopotamia, Egypt and Crete, through to the Mithraic rites of the Roman legions. Its image lingers in the *arenas* of Spain and Mexico. But the lion, the leopard and eventually the cat all join it in the Egyptian pantheon and in the Mesopotamian cultures too the feline began to rival and perhaps surpass the taurine cults. While cattle became increasingly domesticated the cats continue to be a universal symbol of the wild power of nature.

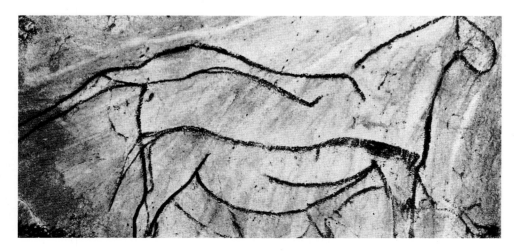

At Catal Hüyük there are leopard figures in relief on the wall of what appears to be a shrine. Modeled in plaster with the heads projecting well out from the wall they have been painted many times, a thin white layer of plaster applied before each renewal, their spots sometimes rendered as floral rosettes, sometimes as geometric forms. Perhaps they featured in a particular festival and the coat of plaster deconsecrated them until its next celebration. Among figures found at the same site are a number which show a female accompanied by leopards, including one which has been interpreted as showing childbirth in which the goddess's arms each rests on a leopard's head. One figure shows a man astride a leopard, others a man riding a bull, but it seems that leopards were particularly associated with the goddess, and that she was the city's most important deity.

Ishtar (or Innin as she was originally called in Uruk, then in later centuries, Astarte) goddess of Gilgamesh, of Uruk, the Akkadians and other Middle Eastern cultures, was often depicted standing on a lion's back and was said to travel in a chariot drawn by seven lions. Lions in glazed brick lined the approaches to the Ishtar gate of ancient Babylon and huge lion figures flanked the entrance to her temple at Nimrud. Lions also stand as guardians at the gate of the Hittite capital of Hattusas. Nergal, lord of the underworld, another Babylonian god, took lion form.

The lion image continued to be important in the Middle East and featured in architecture and objects such as a famous drinking cup from Babylon. A stone lion was chosen by Alexander the Great as a memorial to his lover Hephaiston, erected in Persia at Ectabana. The lion became an important symbol to the Parthians, representing fire both in the worship of Mithras and later,

when Zoroastrianism became the dominant faith in Persia. With the coming of the Arabs, bringing Islam, the new religion adopted some of the old symbols, including the lion which became the guardian of water and thus a symbol of life itself. Its form is used for water spouts, fountains and bath house fittings (the Persian word *shir* means both lion and tap) as well as being a protective guardian flanking entrances to buildings and on door fittings. Right through to the Shahs of the twentieth century the lion continued to be used as a symbol of authority and courage, and as a monument to fallen soldiers and martyrs of the Middle East. Down the centuries the lion has served as a potent symbol of power and empire throughout the world.

The gods of ancient Egypt

Images of lions were used as symbols of power early in Egypt's history. On a slate palette used for mixing cosmetics and dating back to 3100 BC, two lions are shown with long necks that intertwine. They probably represent the joining of the kingdoms of the Upper and the Lower Nile. A slightly earlier palette shows a lion, probably representing King Narmer, or Menes as he is also known, seizing his enemies during the conquest of the north by the south which led to the unification of Egypt and the establishment of the first dynasty of rulers.

Five hundred years later, Chephren (or Khafre) is represented with the body and power of a lion in what must be the world's best-known sculpture — the famous Sphinx at Giza, outside Cairo. Later Egyptians saw this as a representation of the sun god, but by then Egyptian pharaohs were

Above left *The fountain in the Court of the Lions at the Alhambra in Granada. Moorish Spain followed the Islamic tradition of linking lions with water.*

Above *Heracles, the Greek hero, with the Nemean lion, portrayed in flowers as a well dressing at Youlgreave, Derbyshire, where such decorations are an annual custom.*

Below *A rug woven in the nineteenth century in the Fars province of Iran, where lions have for centuries been a traditional decoration of these rugs for tents, the designs sometimes realistic but often very stylized.*

themselves considered gods and the lion and other members of the cat family were not just symbols but forms in which many of their most important deities might appear.

The ancient Egyptian civilization lasted so long and involved such a large number of deities that it is difficult to be certain whether the same gods remained in different forms or whether they were gradually replaced by new objects of worship. As in most early cultures, animals and a mother figure seem to form the original pantheon. Later, probably early in the historic period, many were anthropomorphized and represented with human bodies, though they frequently retained their identifying animal heads, local deities perhaps more often keeping complete animal forms.

In the Late Dynastic Period (1085-332 BC) cults of gods in animal form were widely revived. To people used to the simplified and monotheistic religions of today the apparent change of form and name and the overlapping of responsibilities and powers among the gods of ancient Egypt may appear confusing, but they have their parallels in the different avatars in which the Hindu gods appear, and even Roman Catholic adherents of Christianity will be familiar with a variety of titles by which the Virgin Mary is known, each associated with an appearance at a particular place or a particular attribute of the Virgin.

The lion was one of the shapes in which the Sun God was depicted, a god who in the first mythologies was known as Ra, sometimes represented as a hawk-headed lion, and a lion shape might be taken by each of the three daughters of the Sun: Tefnet, Sekhmet and Bast. Bast (or Bastet or Pasht) later became identified with the domestic cat and Ra himself is shown as a cat in some circumstances. Astarte, too, appears in Egypt, represented by a cat from about 1000 BC.

Tefnet and her brother-husband Shu were worshipped in lion form at Leonopolis and Heliopolis. They were the 'celestial lions', gods of moisture and air who held up the sky (their daughter Nut) to separate it from the earth (their son Geb).

Sekhmet, a lion-headed goddess, was sometimes thought of as an aspect of the cow goddess Hathor, creator and nourisher of the world, protector of women, daughter of Ra and either wife or mother of Horus. As a form of Hathor, and at the same time the eye of Ra, she took her lion form to massacre men who rebelled against Ra. The sun god was concerned that in her fury she would exterminate every man and woman and begged her to stop, but she refused. To save those people still alive, Ra spread across the scene of destruction 7000 jugs containing a magic potion made from beer and pomegranate juice and Sekhmet, thirsty from the effort of killing, mistook this for human blood and drank it until she became too drunk to go on with her slaughter. To appease her a similar brew was prepared each year on her feast day.

In Memphis Sekhmet was the wife of Ptah, the patron of craftsmen. She was the protector of the pharaoh, mistress of the deserts and patron

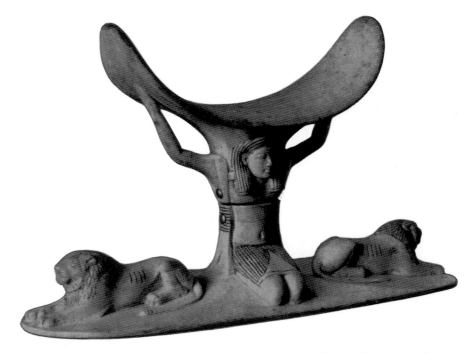

of doctors, for she brought both diseases and cures. Her name means 'the powerful' and in both her forms she could be terrible, bringing destruction to the enemies of Ra.

Aker, the early god of the earth, was depicted as a lion with two heads. His worshippers believed that at night, when the disc of the sun disappeared behind the mountains of the west, the sun had been swallowed by one of Aker's heads and passed inside his body — that is, through the earth — until at dawn it came out through the other mouth and appeared over the mountains to the east. Later, when Geb became god of the earth, Aker became associated with the underworld and was represented as a black lion.

Nefertum (meaning Atum the Younger, another incarnation of the sun at dawn), the son of Sekhmet and Ptah is often shown standing on a crouched lion and sometimes with a lion's head, like his mother's. Mut, a mother and sky goddess, who parallels Hathor, is sometimes given a lion's head. So too is Renenet, goddess of suckling and nourishment and sometimes a harvest goddess, though she is usually depicted as a snake-headed woman. Wadjet, or Buto, a snake goddess and protector of Lower Egypt, whose cult centre was the city named after her in the Delta, has also been shown with a lion's head, often with a sun disc and snake above it. Mafdet, a panther goddess, protected against snakes and scorpions. Sekhanit, the goddess of scribes and writing, is shown wearing a leopard skin, Apademak was a lion-headed god taken over

A headrest from the tomb of Tutankhamun shows Shu in human form with two lions representing the horizons of the east and west — yesterday and tomorrow, replacing the idea of earlier sun-swallowing Aker. The lions also represent the 'celestial lion' forms of Shu and Tefnet.

Left The sun god Ra slays Apophis, the serpent of the dark, beginning the dawn of each new day, Illustration in a 3200-year-old copy of the Egyptian Book of the Dead.

from the Sudanese, Pakhet a lion-goddess worshipped near Beni Hassan and Shezmu, butcher and cook to the gods and bringer of wine and perfumes, took lion form as his popularity increased.

The lioness Men'et was the nurse of Horus, a grim-looking lion called Mihos was worshipped as the son of Ra and Bast at Leonopolis and also had a temple at Bubastis, and the lioness Mehet was worshipped at This, while at Heliopolis they had a lion-headed goddess known as Menehet.

Bes, the ugly, dwarf-like god of marriage, music and dancing, guardian of sleep and bringer of sweet dreams who appeared at births, usually wore a leopard or lion skin but is sometimes given complete lion form. He was not a state deity so had no big temple, but was a popular household god and many children were named after him.

The south wind was represented with either the head or the body of a lion, in reference to its burning character, and there are pictures on monuments from prehistoric times and on magic wands of the Middle Kingdom which show a strange lion or leopard god of unknown name with a long and twisting neck.

The Pharoah's big cats

A lapiz blue glass inset below the eye on the heads of felines which support a funerary bed from Tutankhamun's tomb perhaps identifies them as cheetahs, though a slight ruff hints at lions. From quite early times the royal throne was sometimes depicted borne by two lions, which seem to have been associated with kingship. Tutankhamun's own throne is carried on lions' legs and feet and embellished with two lion heads. Two further beds from the same tomb have as their supporters a cow (representing Hathor and Nut) and the hippopotamus-headed Tueris, but two other cats, probably leopards, carried

Above *Leopards carrying figures of Tutankhamun on their backs, as they were discovered on the opening of the pharoah's tomb.*

Above right *An Egyptian bronze of lion-headed Wadjet.*

Right *Leopards were probably believed to play some role in transporting the pharoah through the underworld.*

Below right *A carved relief of the goddess Sekhmet, at Komombo in Upper Egypt.*

Below left *Tutankhamun's throne, supported on lions' feet and embellished with lions' heads.*

statuettes of Tutankhamun on their backs. In three other tombs similar leopards were found with mortices cut in their backs, presumably also to carry statuettes. A wall painting shows a lion carrying a statuette of a pharaoh on its back. Stone slabs on which the dead, both animal and human, were prepared for mummification have also been found with lions carved on their sides as symbolic supports and are also shown in paintings. It would seem that the big cats played some kind of role in conducting dead kings and the sacred animals to the underworld.

The worship of Bast

At Bubastis, a city of the Nile delta, the leading local deity was Bast, or Bastet. At first she was a lion-headed goddess but later the domestic cat became her sacred animal. She was thought of as the wife or daughter of the sun god and also as the wife of Ptah so, understandably, in lion form, she has sometimes been confused with Sekhmet, or seen as the Big Cat and Little Cat forms of the same deity. Bast's associations were with happiness and the warmth of the sun and she loved pleasure and dancing.

About 950 BC Bubastis ('the house of Bast') became the national capital and Bast a goddess revered throughout the kingdom. She is usually represented as a cat-headed woman, often holding a sistrum (a musical instrument like a wire rattle that is also associated with Hathor), with which she would beat out the rhythm, or a semi-circular aegis (a shield or protective amulet), decorated with a lioness's head. Further up the Nile, near Beni Hassan, she was revered in a secondary form under the name Pekhet.

We do not know why the lion gave place to the cat. Perhaps the cat was seen as a symbolic lion and it was obviously much easier to raise within the temple precincts. Cats were certainly kept as sacred animals at Bubastis, just as appropriate animals were kept in the temples of other gods. They were carefully watched by the priests and their behavior interpreted as the way in which the goddess would convey her wishes or warnings. Care of the sacred animals was a special honor which descended from father to son.

When an Egyptian wished to make a vow or request a favor of the god or goddess to which the animal was dedicated, he would partly shave the head of his child (the amount shaved depended on the nature of the vow or request) and then weigh the clippings. An equivalent weight of silver was presented to the guardian who would then prepare an appropriate amount of fish and give it to his sacred charges.

The Greek historian Herodotus, whose *History* supplied that information, thought that the annual festival at Bubastis was the most important and most zealously celebrated of all the religious festivals of Egypt. He writes of visitors in great numbers, 700,000 of them, not counting children, who sailed there down the Nile in a high-spirited indulgent holiday mood. Men and women traveled in the same boat making music all the way. Some of the women

Above *A figure of Bast, flanked by two cats, dating from the fourth century BC. In one hand she shakes a rattle-like sistrum, in the other she holds an aegis, a ceremonial basket decorated with a feline head.*
Below *A bronze cat of the Saite Period (663–525 BC) with a collar incised around the shoulder and a scarab on the crown of the head. It is typical of the many cat figures found at temple sites which were associated with the cult of Bast and which were often presented as votive offerings.*

carried sistrums, the metal rattles which were an attribute of Bast, making a noise like jangling maracas, while many of the men played flutes. Those without instruments would sing and clap the rhythm with their hands. Every time they passed a riverside town they would bring the boat close to the bank and, while some continued to

Mummification

The mummification process for cats and other small animals was not so elaborate as that for humans. Kittens appear to have been simply dipped into a solution of preservative chemicals and then wrapped in linen, with the result that all that remains of them is a bundle of dust and fragmented bones.

Adult cats of owners who could afford it were more elaborately treated, although, with the exception of the sacred bulls of Apis, few animals were given the full mummification treatment used for people. In human mummification the internal organs were removed and preserved separately, the space they occupied often being filled with sand to maintain shape. In the case of cats the corpse was first dehydrated and preserved by applying natron, a naturally occurring compound of sodium carbonate and sodium bicarbonate. After the chemical processes were complete the animal was arranged with the rear legs brought up in a sitting posture, the front paws stretched straight down and the tail brought forward to lie against the belly. It was then wound in a sheet of linen and over that carefully bandaged. The final outer covering of cloth, palm or papyrus leaves of two colors was sometimes interwoven in a geometrical pattern, perhaps intended as a stylized presentation of the pattern of the fur. The head covering was modeled naturistically, with cloth or palm leaves sewn on to form alert, upright ears and markings or discs of colored cloth reproducing eyes, nose and mouth.

make music, others would joke and jeer at the expense of the townsfolk, standing up and dancing, or lifting up their skirts to expose themselves and flash or moon at the people on the bank.

When devotees at last reached Bubastis the festival involved not only the celebration of many sacrifices but also an enormous amount of drinking — more wine being consumed than during the whole of the rest of the year. Since Bast was a goddess of fertility — and the domestic cat has always had a reputation for its sexuality — we can imagine that there was a great deal of promiscuity and licentiousness.

The city, like many others along the Nile, was raised on higher ground, created out of the earth removed long before during the digging of canals. Herodotus says it was raised higher than other cities, but in the centre the ground level was retained and in this hollow, looked down on by the surrounding city, was Bast's great temple.

Though there were larger and more costly temples, Herodotus thought none was more attractive than this of Bast. Channels cut through from the Nile brought water almost all around it, but were separated by the entrance way. These channels were 100 ft (30 m) wide and

shaded by trees. A broad paved road, 660 yards (600 m) long, led from the city market place to the temple gate. The entrance building was over 36 ft (10 m) high and decorated with finely executed figures 6 cubits (10 ft/3 m) tall. The outer wall, which was of stone and also carved with figures, extended about 220 yards (200 m) along each side. Inside, a grove of very large trees was planted around the temple-house that contained the image of the goddess. Excavations have confirmed the main points of Herodotus' description.

Above left *An Egyptian bronze votive figure with inlaid electrum eyes, 26th Dynasty 644–525* BC. *The inscription asks Bast for life on behalf of Iufaa, son of Jjed Djehuty.*
Above *Another bronze of the Late Period (712–332* BC).
Far left *Pharoah Nekhthoreb making an offering before Bast, a wall carving in her temple, from the 1889 excavation report.*

The wrapped mummy was then placed inside a mummy case or funerary box of wood or bronze, sometimes perhaps a pottery jar, like those in which thousands of hawks were found at Saqqara. The mummy case might be in the shape of a seated cat, often painted and sometimes with a head of bronze or wood painted to suggest metal. One in the British Museum has the body painted white to represent bandages and a green-painted head.

In 1890 over 300,000 embalmed cats were discovered buried in underground galleries at Beni Hassan. The archaeologists were not then very interested in cats and most of them — 24 tons of mummies — were shipped to Liverpool and sold as agricultural fertilizer, so an opportunity to make a species study which could have thrown light on the origin of the domestic cat was lost.

Strangely, when Bubastis itself was excavated in 1889 the archaeologists reported no catacombs lined with mummified cats. They found only brick-lined pits filled with the ashes and burned bones of huge numbers of cats. Near each pit was the furnace in which the animals had been burned. Scattered haphazardly among the debris were votive statuettes of cats and a few small fragments of gold paper which may have been from a mummy case. Were these cats burned when originally deposited or was this some later destruction by members of a later cult, early Christians perhaps who did not

revere the cat? But if the latter were the case why should the trouble be taken to line pits with brick?

X-rays of a collection of unopened cat mummies which were presented to the Natural History Museum in London by Sir Flinders Petrie have shown many of their necks to have been broken. Contrary to the laws that are said to have protected cats in Egypt, they seem to have been deliberately killed. Nearly half of the mummies examined had died before they were four months old and nearly all the rest were less than eighteen months.

Was an offering of a mummified cat required by the postulant for some cure or favor, creating a market for animals specially bred and sold by the temple to meet the demand for votive offerings? These particular mummies date from the Ptolomeic period, 330–30 BC, and are no proof that such practices occurred in earlier times. However, at Saqqarà, millions of ibis and hawk mummies have been found and, since killing them was a crime, and collecting naturally dead birds in the wild could hardly have produced these numbers, it seems likely that they were specially bred as offerings.

Above *A cat mummy from Abydos, dating from the Roman period, after 30* BC. *The cloth head cover is sewn into a naturalistic shape and painted; the body outer covering of interwoven strips of cloth may be intended to suggest a patterned coat.*
Left *A bronze coffin for a mummified cat, inscribed with a prayer to Bast.*

Right *Although the Egyptians duly revered the cat they were not without a sense of humor. This satirical papyrus, made by Theban scribes about 100 BC, shows cats acting as nursemaid and servants to baby and Lady Rat.*
Opposite *Egyptian Mau — the modern breed developed to re-create the cat of ancient Egypt.*

Cats in the home

A cat cult seems to have been established long before cats became domesticated. Perhaps the keeping of sacred animals in the temple led to their being kept in houses. Herodotus implies that several kinds of sacred animals were kept in people's homes, but he does not specify which ones. There were dogs, of course, for they had been domesticated long before by prehistoric hunters. A later Greek writer, Eilen, claimed that the Egyptians kept house snakes which would obey their owners at a snap of the fingers, and certainly baboons were kept as pets. But did Egyptians really ride on crocodiles as Pliny seems to have believed? It has even been claimed that lions were tamed and taught to fight as part of ancient armies.

When were cats first domesticated? The remains of a cat were found at Jericho in strata dating from about 6700 BC, but, although in a city, they are almost certainly those of a wild cat. One discovered at Harappa in the Indus Valley, dating from 2000 BC, could be domestic but there is no firm evidence until about 1600 BC by which time cats were well established in Egyptian homes.

The Egyptian feline goddess, Mafdet, a snake-killer and protector of the pharaoh in the royal palace, appears in magic formulas carved on pyramid chambers of the Fifth and Sixth Dynasties (before 2280 BC), but there is no indication that cats were domesticated so early. Even in later times, it does not seem that real cats were kept as snake-catchers. As in India it is more likely that a house snake was used to keep other snakes away and mongooses (ichneumon, another

animal treated as sacred) were more likely to be snake catchers, although there are plenty of examples of cats attacking snakes and their fondness for chasing string does seem to suggest a connection.

More importantly, a snake could represent both good and evil in Egyptian religious symbolism. Linked with Buto-Wadjet as the protector of the pharaoh and as the uraeus, the serpent on the pharaoh's headdress, it was clearly good, but there was also the serpent Apophis, symbol of darkness and arch enemy of Ra, who at time of eclipse devoured the ship of the sun in which Ra sailed through the sky each day and who gained power every night only to be vanquished by Ra and his defenders every morning. Two papyri in the British Museum have paintings showing the head of the serpent being cut off by a cat. The Egyptologist Sir Ernest Budge identified this cat as Ra himself.

Protective amulets in the shape of cats or cats' heads seem to date some kind of cat cult back to at least the Sixth Dynasty. In a tomb at Abydos dating from the Twelfth Dynasty (1991–1786 BC) Sir Flinders Petrie discovered 'seventeen skeletons of cats and, in the offering recess, a row of the roughest little offering pots.' The number of cat amulets and charms found from the Seventeenth Dynasty (1650–1567 BC) shows a considerable increase and sometimes they are linked with the name of Bast. These are evidence of Egyptian familiarity with cats but not proof of domestication. The skeletons may be temple cats but they could be wild animals.

More positive evidence of domestication appears in wall paintings which show cats in clearly domestic situations. In the tomb of the harbormaster May and his wife Tui at Thebes, dating from 1450 BC, there is a painting of a ginger-colored cat beneath the chair on which Tui sits. It wears a collar and its lead is tied to a leg of the chair. There are several cats depicted in Theban tombs. One ginger cat, in a tomb of 1400 BC, sits under a lady's chair at a feast. In the tomb of the sculptor Ipuy, of the same date, a kitten sits on Ipuy's lap, pulling at his sleeve, while another with a silver ring in its ear, is underneath the chair of his wife. In a later tomb, from the reign of Rameses II (1292–1225 BC) yet another cat eats a bone beneath its mistress's chair.

It is possible that the earliest of these could be tamed wild cats, but it would certainly seem that cats had become regular pets and were being conditioned to share their lives with humans. On the other hand it has also been suggested that these cats sitting under chairs are not real cats at all but symbols that the wife or other lady below whom they sit will continue to be available for intercourse with the deceased — but that cannot account for cats like the one on Ipuy's lap.

Other tomb paintings show that they could be more than pets. In the tomb of the sculptor Nebamun a cat is shown beneath the chair of a banquet guest, but there is another in a painting of a scene on the marshes of the Nile delta. The deceased man is out hunting wildfowl. In one hand he holds the legs of three birds he has already caught and in the other he brandishes

Herodotus' description of the temple at Bubastis was confirmed by excavation, but what are we to make of his reports of the following cat behavior?

'The number of domestic animals in Egypt ... would be still greater were it not for what befalls the cats. Because the females, when they have kittened, no longer seek the company of the males, these last, to obtain their companionship once more, practice a curious artifice. They seize the kittens, carry them off and kill them, but do not eat them afterwards. Upon this the females, being deprived of their young and longing to supply their place, seek the males once more, since they are particularly fond of their offspring.'

There are similarities here with the behavior of male lions taking over a pride in East Africa today. Had Herodotus heard something of the kind and misapplied the information? However, there seems no explanation at all for another of his reports: 'On every occasion of a fire in Egypt the strangest prodigy occurs with the cats. The inhabitants allow the fire to rage as it pleases, while they stand about at intervals and watch these animals which, slipping by men or else jumping over them rush headlong into the flames. When this happens the Egyptians are in deep affliction.'

Above *The paintings in the tomb of sculptor Nebamun (c. 1400 BC) not only show a cat beneath a chair, but also one balanced on a papyrus stem in the marshes of the Nile delta where the deceased is wildfowling. The cat has two birds clasped in its claws and another in its teeth. Is it assisting as a retriever of the birds Nebamun has struck down with the throwing stick he wields in his left hand?*

Below *Other paintings of cats out hunting in the marshes include one in the tomb of Menes, at Thebes, and this from the tomb of Nacht in the Valley of the Nobles at Luxor where the cat seems to be waiting for the birds to fall, while throwing-sticks fly through the air above it.*

a throwing stick. Precariously balanced on a papyrus stem is a lively tabby cat with one duck in its mouth and two more held down by its paws. Two more tomb paintings show very similar scenes. The inference is that by 1400 BC Egyptian wildfowlers were using cats to flush out birds and as hunting auxiliaries, perhaps even training them to retrieve.

Animals of the sacred species were protected by law in Egypt. Killing one of them was a very serious crime; to deliberately do so carried the death penalty. Even accidentally killing a hawk or ibis meant death, though in the case of a cat this was commuted to a heavy fine. When a family cat did die, the whole household went into mourning and shaved off their eyebrows. It is likely that it was then mummified and it might be taken or sent to Bubastis for burial. Herodotus thought all cats were buried there but cat burials have also been found at the temple at Beni Hassan, at Saqqara and at other sites.

In 525 BC, the Persian King Cambyses defeated the Egyptian army at Pelusium, a city at the extreme east of the Nile delta, and made Egypt a Persian province. He is said to have gained his victory by ordering his soldiers each to find a cat and to carry it as or on their shield as they advanced, while in front of them they drove all the other cats that they could find. The Egyptians, fearful of harming any of these sacred animals, were unable to offer any resistance.

There seems to be no firm historical evidence to support that story, but other nations were certainly aware of the Egyptian attitude to cats. A Greek comic poet from Rhodes has one of his characters tell an Egyptian 'If you see a sick cat you weep for it. As far as I'm concerned. I'll happily kill it for its skin.'

According to Diodorus Siculus, a Greek historian of the first century BC, Egyptians were so frightened of being blamed for the death of a cat that, if they came across a dead one, they would run off shouting lamentations and protestations that it was already dead when they found it. He confirms the value put upon a cat's life in his account of a Roman embassy which was sent to Egypt to negotiate a treaty at the time of Ptolemy Auyletes, father of the famous Cleopatra. When one of the Romans accidentally killed a cat, crowds soon surrounded the house where he was staying and demanded he be punished.

Plutarch later remarked upon the care with which the Egyptians mated their cats for compatible character. If owners chose breeding partners, they must have exerted considerable control over the lives of their much-loved pets.

The lion continues as a potent symbol in the classical world.
Left *Greek stater coined in electrum on Miletos c.575 BC.* **Centre** *An Ionian stater of c.580 BC.*
Right *This Greek tetradrachma shows a lion attacking a bull.*

Domestic cats in the classical world

Egyptians guarded their cats jealously and none were supposed to leave Egypt. Agents were even sent to other countries to buy and repatriate cats that had been smuggled out. Nowhere else in the classical world did cats become particularly important, either as cult objects or pets, but in time they did become established overseas.

A little ivory carving of an open-mouthed cat, dating from about 1700 BC, was found in Israel; about 1600 BC a painter included a cat stalking a pheasant in a fresco at Hagia Triada, in Crete and a terracotta cat head was found at Palaikastro at the eastern end of the island, dating from about 200 years later. Two inlaid daggers found at Mycenae show cats hunting among papyrus reeds, similar to some found in the tomb of the Egyptian Queen Aahotep (1600 BC) and a subject familiar from the later tomb paintings. These artifacts provide evidence of contact with Egyptian culture rather than of local domestic cats but by the middle of the first millennium BC there is an increasing amount of visual evidence of the cat as a domestic animal in the Greek world.

Several fables involving cats have been attributed to Aesop, Greek author of moral stories in which animals are used to satirize human characteristics. He died in 546 BC so, if he really wrote them and they are not later additions to his work, cats by then must have been familiar animals in Greece.

The depiction of a cat on some Greek coins is not of domestic significance but a number of paintings on Greek pottery found at Greek settlements in southern Italy show cats lying along a person's forearm or people with a cat reaching up towards a bird. Most intriguing, perhaps is a carving on the side of the base of a statue which shows a cat almost nose to nose with a dog, both on leads held by young men. Most beautiful is a funerary stele from Salamis showing a young man holding a bird and accompanied by a slaveboy and a cat which must have been much loved to earn a place on his memorial — though sadly the cat's head has been broken away.

The lion terrace at Delos. The stylized form of these figures in Naxian marble is similar to lions in cycladic pottery of the same date — about the second half of the seventh century BC. They are all male and have their heads turned towards the east; they were possibly intended as guardians of the area sacred to Leto, who gave birth to Apollo on this island.

Right *A funerary steel of an ephebos 430-420 BC, found on Salamis. In one hand the young man holds a bird; the other reaches to a cage (the bars of which would have been painted); and above his slave there sits a slim and elegant cat.*
Below *A relief on a statue base found built into the Themistoclean wall, near the Athens Keramicos. It is usually interpreted as a group of young men inciting a cat and dog to fight. However, although the cat has its back partly arched and a paw out ready to deliver a swipe if the dog takes any liberties, the dog has paws out, head down and tail up — a posture that usually indicates an invitation to play.*

A mosaic found at Pompeii shows the sort of spotted cat already seen in Egyptian wall paintings.

Although some of Aesop's fables show the cat as the enemy of mice, the Greeks do not seem to have placed any value on cats for vermin control. The mongoose or some kind of ferret or weasel (confusingly called gali, also later used for cat) was given that role. However, a line in a poem by a third-century BC Sicilian Greek declares:

'all cats like a cushioned couch'

which suggests that by that date cats were popular pets already known in the Greek colonies on the island.

Five hundred years later, an agricultural treatise by Palladius recommends cats for protecting gardens from moles and mice. By then cats were quite common as pets, known not only in Rome but in its outlying provinces; their bones have been found in the remains of Roman villas in Britain. They gained mention in Pliny's *Natural History*, written in AD 77, where the author comments on their 'silent stealth' when hunting birds and on 'how slyly they will sit and watch and then dart out upon a mouse.' However most Latin texts refer to them in connection with Egypt.

It may have been the fashion for exotic religions which aroused interest in cats in imperial times. At Portici, near Naples, a painting was discovered showing a priest of the Egyptian goddess Isis and a woman with a sistrum worshipping a cat. At Pompeii a mosaic shows a cat carrying off a chicken and, more tragically, a woman found entombed in the lava was still holding a cat in her arms.

Imperial pets

It was not only the little cats from Egypt that the Romans kept as pets. A number of the emperors had big cats in their households. The mad Caligula had a pet lion, Nero a pet tiger (perhaps actually a cheetah) which he called Phoebe, which sat beside him at table, and Caracalla had a lion called Acinaces which joined him at mealtimes and in his bedchamber. Heliogabalus used to enjoy driving a chariot drawn by four lions or tigers and used to play frightening tricks on people with lions and other beasts whose claws and teeth had been extracted — not so safe even then, for a playful pat from a lion's paw could bowl you over! These emperors, who also saw themselves as gods, must have thought it fitting to be masters of the King of Beasts. Their pets were pampered, their manes dusted with gold and their necks decked with jewels; but when they grew old or became bad tempered they probably ended up as hunters or hunted in the arena.

Lions and Christians

The Romans began to keep wild animal collections during the third century BC, but it was not until 185 BC that Marcus Fulvius Nobilior, returning from a campaign in Greece, introduced the hunting and killing of lions as a spectacle in the Roman amphitheaters. For 40 years these were only occasional 'entertainments' but then they became more frequent. The praetor Lucius Sulla, having received a present of lions from the king of Mauretania, provided 100 to be killed in the arena. Pompey gave a show in the circus Maximus featuring 600 lions and lionesses, as well as 20 elephants and the first rhinoceros ever seen in Rome. Julius Caesar presented 400 lions and the first giraffe. After the opening of the Colosseum in AD 80, when 5000 animals died in the inaugural show, the demand for wild beasts was enormous. At one time there were 11,000 wild animals held in the imperial forest reserves to the south of Rome. Hunting of lions to send to Italy, and for the amphitheaters in the African provinces themselves, is thought to

In a Roman mosaic from Paphos in Cyprus, Dionysus is depicted in a chariot drawn by a leopard.

have played an important part in the disappearance of the lion from North Africa.

The *venationes*, as the hunting spectacles were called, were sometimes staged in settings that contrived to turn the circus or arena into a newly created wood of transplanted trees or on occasion the machinery of the Colosseum was used to make the forest appear to rise from the ground. The smooth walls of the podium wall gave no purchase for an animal's claws but, for extra safety when such dangerous animals as the big cats were involved, a system of rollers continually moved across the walls to dislodge any foothold and nets were strung to prevent the cats leaping upward.

From simulated hunts the *venationes* developed into battles between different kinds of animals or between men and beasts, and then into the massacre of defenseless victims by animals who were starved or specially trained to attack.

If animals refused to leave their cages they were driven out by burning straw. Frightened by the noise of the crowds or disinterested in making a kill, they did not always provide the 'sport' the Romans wanted. On one occasion more than a hundred lions were massacred without offering any resistance.

Lions and tigers were not only trained to be man-eaters, a number were taught circus-type tricks as well. These tamed animals included tigers whom their trainers would kiss and lions who would chase and catch a hare but carry it gently in their jaws so that it survived without a scratch.

Above *A Roman* venator *transfixes a leopard on the iron point of his hunting spear. His only protection is the leather bands around his legs and sewn onto his tunic. A detail from a mosaic now in the Galleria Borghese, Rome.*

Left *Christian martyrs face the lions in a Roman amphitheater. At the Colosseum the beasts were kept in the basement and raised on lifts to arena level. It would be against the natural instinct of a lion to dash out into the bright sunshine of the arena, and the sound of the crowd would have been as frightening to the lion as the lion was to its potential prey. The condemned, who were sometimes tied to a stake, were recommended to gesticulate to attract the animal's attention. Death came more quickly with a blow from one of the big cats than from smaller carnivores which might literally tear a living person to pieces. Sometimes executions were worked up into dramatic scenarios with the victim being presented as Orpheus or some other person killed by animals.*

Left *In later years the* venatori *were given armor like that of the gladiators in this scene from the film Quo Vadis.*

Caligula and Nero are said to have supplemented their pets' diets with the occasional human victim as a private entertainment but death in the venationes was usually the fate of the lowest grades of criminals, known therefore as *bestiarii*, the early Christian martyrs among them.

Rome was not the only civilization to adopt such barbaric practices. Several oriental kings punished malefactors in this way and hungry cougars are said to have been kept to act as executioners for the Incas.

The spread of the domestic cat

Apart from the animals in menageries the only wild felines in Europe in post-classical times were the Lynx and the small Wildcat, both of which were hunted for their skins, or for sport, but the domestic cat spread from the Mediterranean to the far corners of the Roman Empire and beyond. At first it was probably a curiosity or an exotic pet, later it became valued as a rodent catcher. House mice and rats were not originally European animals; they spread in the wake of human settlement, culminating in the influx of rats from the Middle East taken back to Europe by the ships of the Crusaders. Seamen welcomed a cat aboard ship to keep down the rats, and their cats, in turn, helped spread the cat around the world and eventually across to the Americas.

Studies of the dominance of certain colors and patterns in different cat populations led researcher N.B. Todd to suggest that the sex-linked red color originated in the orient and was carried, perhaps by Viking longships, to Britain, Brittany and parts of Scandinavia while the blotched tabby pattern, which seems to have developed in Britain in the tenth century, was carried by trading vessels up the valleys of the Seine and Rhône.

Wider afield, some people have claimed that domestic cats had already reached China by 2000 BC but this seems unlikely. The earliest confirmed Indian reference to domestic cats dates from about 200 BC. There are fables concerning cats in the *Rayamana* and *Mahabharata*, Indian sacred epics, originally dating from before 500 BC, but they could be later interpolations. It seems likely that cats would have reached China later than India, and from China, thence to Japan.

In some parts of Europe there is little archaeological evidence of cats in the post-Roman period but in Saxon Britain the cat appears to have been a familiar domestic animal, valued as a mouser. In the mid-tenth century the Welsh King Hywel Dda decreed a set of laws specifically relating to the cat and a century earlier Henry I of Saxony set the fine for anyone who killed an adult cat at 60 bushels of corn. By this date the cat appears to have been accepted as a protector of the grain.

Cats appear in the decoration of a number of medieval manuscripts; Celtic monks seem to have been particularly fond of them. One Irish monk, working as a manuscript copyist in the ninth century, wrote a delightful poem in Irish about a cat companion, comparing their two lives:

> I and Pangur Ban my cat
> 'Tis a like task we are at;
> Hunting mice is his delight
> Hunting words I sit all night ...

Cats occasionally appear in the carving of capitals and other architectural features of medieval churches and in the decoration of church furniture, especially on monastic misericords, the little ledges on the underside of seats on which monks were allowed to prop themselves during the night-time offices.

The rules drawn up for anchoresses (female hermits) in the thirteenth century allowed them one cat as their only companion and no other animals.

Pope Gregory the Great, when he retired from the papacy to monastic life in 604, also had a pet cat but not every churchman was a cat lover; some remembered its association with pagan worship. After several centuries in which the popularity and appreciation of the value of the cat increased, the Church in Europe became its persecutor.

Left *It was claimed that at one spectacle a lion stopped and licked the feet of its intended victim, a runaway slave called Androcles. When a leopard was sent into the arena, the lion killed it. When questioned the slave told how, when hiding in a cave, a lion came to him with an injured paw, apparently asking for help. He pulled out a thorn embedded in the flesh and thereafter the lion stayed with him, bringing back food from its kills. Later Androcles was captured and by chance had met 'his' lion in the arena. Both slave and lion were given their freedom. A scene from the film version of Bernard Shaw's play based on the story.*

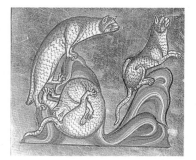

Above *Cats from the thirteenth century Harleian Bestiary and the Aberdeen Bestiary c.1200. Cats in very similar poses to the Aberdeen three also appear in a near contemporary manuscript in the Bodleian library.*
Left *A cat with a crossbow attacks the castle of the rats, one of a series of battles between the two which decorate a fifteenth-century Book of Hours.*

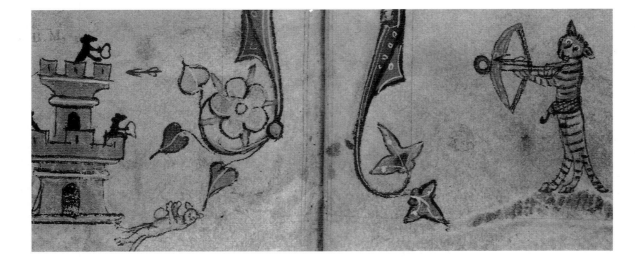

Extracts from the Laws of Hywel Dda

The value of a kitten from the night it is kittened until it shall open its eyes is one legal penny and from that time until it shall kill mice, two legal pence, after it shall kill mice, four legal pence and so it always remains. Her qualities are to see, to hear, to kill mice, to have her claws entire, and to rear and not to devour her kittens. If she is bought and be deficient in any one of those qualities, let one third of her worth be returned.

Royal mousers were more valuable:
If anyone kills a cat that guards a house and a barn of the King, or steals it, it is to be held with its head to the ground and its tail up (the ground being swept) and clean wheate is to be poured about it until the tip of its tail be hidden — that is its worth.

Pet cats were on a different scale. They were valued at one pound if they belonged to the king, half that if the owner was a *breyer* (a class of freeman) and only a penny if owned by a *taeog* (a class of farmer).

The laws particularly specify that owners must pay for damage a cat might do by mousing in a flax crop; flax was valuable for making linen.

Above *A cat playing a fiddle and a goat playing a lute, carved on a misericord in Hereford Cathedral, England. The cat and the fiddle, a popular subject when this was carved in the fourteenth century, is the name of numerous inns and is often said to be a corruption of either* Le Chat Fidéle (The Faithful Cat) *or* Caton le Fidéle — *possibly a governor of Calais at the time of Mary Tudor, too late to account for medieval carvings. Kit is an old name for a small fiddle, played for dances, and sounds like a more plausible link with cats.*

Left *An Irish poem was written* To Pangur Ban, my White Cat *in a commonplace book at St Paul's monastery at Reichau over a thousand years ago.*

WITCHCRAFT, MAGIC AND PERSECUTION

Above *The goddess Freyja, drawn by two white cats, in the Kattewoensday procession at Ypres.*

Below right *This stone traditionally marks where Dick Whittington heard Bow Bells calling him back to London.*

Above right *For many years this desiccated cat hung above the bar of Dirty Dick's tavern in London's Bishopsgate. It was discovered in the foundations of the building when repairs were being carried out. The burial of a cat in the structure of a building may have been more than a charm against rats. Human sacrifice and the use of blood and hair in mortar was once a way of ensuring a structure's safety. The modern custom of burying coins and other tokens is a symbolic survival of such propitiatory magic. This cat has now disappeared; it was stolen in 1987.*

The Romans of the Imperial period were attracted by exotic religions and some took up the Egyptian cult of Bast, whom they identified with their Diana (the Greek Artemis), the hunter goddess of the moon, linking the night-prowling cat with her. In later centuries Diana became identified with Hecate, originally another Greek moon goddess, but later associated with the underworld, with enchantment, and thus regarded as the chief of witches.

In northern Europe the Wildcat and the Lynx — and by association the domestic cat — were linked with Freyja, the Viking goddess of female mysteries, fertility and wealth who was credited with introducing wizardry among the gods. She was chief among the *disir*, a group of female cult figures linked with both human reproduction and agricultural yield. Some traditions had her chariot drawn by cats and cats appear to have been involved in her worship. In the complexity of Teutonic beliefs she is sometimes confused with Odin's wife or thought to be the leader of the Valkyries, who were originally demons of carnage.

In Ireland a cat-headed god appears to have been worshipped in the first century AD and a huge black cat — the King of Cats, called Iruscan — who lived in a cave at Knowth in Meath, appears in Irish folklore, with a Christian version describing its killing by St Ciaran.

In China a fertility god, Li Chou, was worshipped in cat form and offered sacrifices at an orgiastic festival at the end of harvest. Elsewhere, the cat itself might be the sacrifice: it was once a widespread custom for a cat to be killed as the last sheaf of corn was reaped. In *The Golden Bough* Sir James Frazer describes how, in France and Germany, well-fed cats were garlanded with flowers and ritually eaten on the first day of harvest.

In the Ardennes, on the first Sunday of Lent, cats were burned in or roasted over a fire which had to be lit by the last person to be married. Shepherds drove their flocks through the smoke to protect them from witchcraft in the coming year and everyone sang and danced — the livelier the dance the better would be the coming crop.

At Briançon, in Dauphiné, a cat was decorated with flowers, ribbons and ears of corn at the beginning of harvest; if any of the reapers cut themselves the cat was made to lick the wound.

In eastern Europe a cat was buried alive in a field of corn to ensure a good harvest, and in part of France a kitten buried in the ground was thought to prevent the growth of weeds. At least as late as the eighteenth century a cat buried in the foundations or built into the wall of a building was used in many places as a form of magic to keep rats away.

In the eyes of many Christian churchmen the cat was closely connected with pagan cults and most sought to ignore it. Nevertheless cats became associated with some of the Christian

saints. St Martha, who lived in the first century AD was said to have had a cat as a companion but others were given a cat as a symbol of their attributes for, like the gods of the pagan world, saints were often associated with particular responsibilities. The second century St Agatha, who included weather among her concerns (as did some of the earlier cat figures), was said to appear as an angry cat to chastise women who worked on her saint's day; she is still known as Santo Gato in the Pyrenées. St Gertrude of Nivelles, seventh-century patroness of gardeners, widows, travelers — and cats — was often shown with a cat companion; St Ives (eleventh century), patron of lawyers, was shown with a cat as a symbol of justice; and the Virgin Mary, symbol of motherhood also inherited the cat of the pagan fertility goddesses.

In Aix-en-Provence, during the Middle Ages, a strange ceremony was performed each Corpus Christi Day in which a tom cat was displayed, wrapped like a baby in tight swaddling bands, then, according to some accounts, publicly burned at exactly noon. Links with fire and sun seem obvious. Could the priests have been trying to overlay a pagan fertility rite with some Christian significance, the cat serving as some sort of proxy for Christ's own sacrifice?

Magic cats

In southern France there was a wide belief in magician cats, known as *matagots*. They were thought to bring prosperity to a home where they were loved and cared for. Some eastern traditions also see the cat as a bringer of luck or fortune.

The most famous of *matagots* to English speakers is the cat belonging to Dick Whittington, three times Lord Mayor of London early in the fifteenth century, who was said to owe his fortune to it. A poor boy from Gloucestershire, Dick walked to London, where he had heard the streets were 'paved with gold', in search of fame and fortune. As the modern version has it, he found work as a scullion and got a cat to keep down rats where he slept. Then when his fellow servants all invested in a trading voyage of their master's, Dick ventured all he had — the cat. Despairing of success he set off to walk back to his village but, resting on Highgate Hill, overlooking London, he heard the bells of the city seeming to call 'Turn again, Whittington, Lord Mayor of London' and went back.

When the ship returned he found that it had traded at an island overrun with rats. These Puss had vanquished and been rewarded with a princely fortune for her owner who was able to set himself up as a leading merchant.

Although portraits of Lord Mayor Whittington show him with a cat they all date from long after his death in 1423 and the legend has

been explained by saying that the cat was actually a catboat — a one-masted vessel used for coal and timber — which made him a fortune trading in coal between Newcastle and London, or alternatively an *achat* (a purchase), but the tale is actually a version of one told much earlier in Italy, and before that in Persia.

The *matagot* turns up in another traditional tale, best known in the version told by Charles Perrault in his fairytale collection as *Le Maître Chat, ou Le Chat Botté* (The Teacher Cat, or Puss-in-Boots) though it dates back much earlier and may have an Arabic or Sanskrit origin.

Puss-in-Boots is a clever trickster and con-man and a reminder of the double nature and contradictions often inherent in interpretations of the cat. The cat became a symbol of domesticity, caring motherhood and home comforts yet, at the same time, of the mysteries of the night, of rampant and promiscuous sexuality and sharp-clawed aggression. To those who do not know cats very well — and sometimes even when one does — they can seem unpredictable, untrust-

Above *Dick Whittington offers his cat for his employer's venture (top). The cat rids an eastern potentate's palace of rats (below). Woodcuts from* The History of Sir Richard Whittington *published about 1770.*
Left *According to popular legend Sir Richard Whittington, Lord Mayor of London, was made rich by his cat. This engraving, based on an earlier portrait of the famous Dick, is said to have originally shown him in a traditional pose with his hand resting on a skull, but the image was re-cut and a cat inserted to attract a wide popular sale.*
Below left *Dick and his cat now delight British children as one of the popular stories told in pantomimes each Christmas.*

worthy even. They match the male-centred attitudes of the medieval Christian Church towards women which contrasted the purity of the Virgin Mary with the original sin attributable to Eve. It is significant that 'catty' suggests unpleasant characteristics and that brothels are known as 'cat-houses' to North Americans. The cat, however tame, can still lead a secret double life in the wild. Its independence cocks a snook at dogmatic authoritarianism. Perhaps it is not surprising that when medieval churchmen sought to extinguish pagan practices they saw the cat, the animal of the mother goddess, as a useful symbol of evil.

Cat persecutions

In the twelfth- and thirteenth-century persecution of the Waldensian and Albigensian sects, when great numbers were massacred as heretics, one of the crimes of which they were accused was participating in rites involving cats. In 1233 Pope Gregory IX declared that heretics worshipped the devil in the form of a black tom cat, giving authority to an idea already widely held. Feeling against the cat was probably especially whipped up by the Church to counter a revival of the cult of Freyja in the Rhineland in the mid-thirteenth century. When, at the beginning of the fourteenth century Pope Clement V decided to suppress the order of Knights Templar as part of papal policy, the charges levied against them included accusations of homosexuality and worship of the devil in the form of a black tom cat. At just the time when the cat would have been of great value in controlling the rats which spread the Black Death, the bubonic plague which decimated Europe in the fourteenth century, it was most vilified and destroyed.

A French book known as the *L'Evangile du Diable* (The Devil's Bible) declared

> 'Only fools do not know that all cats have a pact with the Devil ... Why do cats sleep, or feign sleep, all day long, by the fire in winter or in the sun in summer? Clearly their task is to keep watch on the barns and stable through the night, to see all, to hear all. It is easy to see why the Evil Spirits, warned just in time, always manage to disappear before we can see them.'

In many places the Church encouraged ceremonies in which cats were deliberately and cruelly killed. They probably had their origins in pagan rites which were now reoriented against the cat to fit the new orthodoxy and clearly identify it with the devil. In Paris a fire was lit in the Place de Grève each St John's Day and a barrel or sack of cats hung over it to be ritually burned, thereby ridding the city of evil. The King of France often watched or lit the fire and afterwards people took home some of the ashes to bring them luck. One year, the boy who became Louis XIII persuaded his father Henry IV to reprieve the animals from burning, but this did not end the practice. Louis XIV was the last king to take part, in 1648. At Ypres, on the second Sunday of May, there was also an annual ceremony in which live cats were thrown from

the belfry of the city hall — a cruel tradition which went on until 1817.

At Metz, in 1344 there was an outbreak of St Vitus' Dance. A knight arrived at the peak of the epidemic and took lodgings in the town. As he was about to fall asleep, he saw a huge black cat sitting staring at him. He made the sign of the cross and drew his sword, at which the cat hissed blasphemies and disappeared. Next morning not one citizen twitched or pranced. The knight was convinced the cat had been the devil and the city fathers agreed. They too organized a public burning of cats. For the next 400 years a great bonfire was built on the anniversary of the knight's experience and 13 cats burned in an iron cage.

At the end of 1484 Pope Innocent VIII issued a bull intensifying the rooting out of those who 'abandoned themselves to devils' or conjured spells and charms. Until the thirteenth century

Above, top to bottom The Adventures of Puss in Boots: *Puss warning reapers of the king's approach; Puss catching a mouse; Puss showing in the king and princess. Illustrations from a version of this story published in New York in the early nineteenth century.*

Above right *A cat found in Cheapside, 'habited like a priest'. An engraving for* Fox's Book of Martyrs.

Below *A sixteenth-century window in the church of St Gervais in Paris includes a portrait of a spotted cat beside the donors. Is this a valued pet rather than a symbol?*

Below right *This engraving of Adam and Eve by Albrecht Dürer, made in 1504, almost certainly intends some symbolic meaning in its choice of animals. The lower four creatures are often said to represent the different humors of man but the placing of the cat, with its tail curled around the foot of Eve, suggests that it stands in for the devil and his influence on woman, while the mouse represents the weakness and vulnerability of man.*

the Church had officially considered the power of witches imaginary; now it took it seriously and for the next four centuries witches were added to the victims of the Inquisition, thousands losing their lives, especially in France and the German states.

In Paris in the 1730s there was a massacre of cats quite separate from these ritual persecutions. It was sparked off by young men apprenticed to a Paris printer. Frustrated in all their attempts to get better conditions from their master, they began it by catching the printer's wife's pampered pet, whose life seemed so much easier than their own. From this it escalated into a great slaughter of pet cats in protest at social conditions and the exploitation by human 'fat cats' of the working people.

Witchcraft and metamorphoses

England had no regular cat ceremonies but was not without its cruelties. In 1559 the coronation procession of Protestant Elizabeth I included an effigy of the pope which was finally consumed on a bonfire. Trapped inside its wicker frame were live cats who 'squalled in a hideous manner as soon as they felt the fire,' cries which were described as 'the language of the devils within the body of the Holy Father'. This was cruelty simply for effect with no magical significance, but by the end of Elizabeth's reign, and especially in that of her successor, James I, not only the cat but anyone who owned one might have been in danger for there was a surge of interest and belief in witchcraft in Britain.

James, already James VI of Scotland, was fascinated by witchcraft. He wrote a book on the subject called *Daemonologie* and personally interrogated accused witches at his Edinburgh palace of Holyrood House. One group confessed in 1590 that the Earl of Bothwell had asked them to contrive the king's death. Agnes Tompson told how

'at the time His Majesty was in Denmark she ... took a cat and christened it, and afterward bound to each part of that cat the chiefest parts of a dead man, and several joints of his body; and that in the night following, the said cat was conveyed in riddles or sieves ... and so left ... right before the town of Leith in Scotland. This done, there did arise such a tempest in the sea as a greater hath not been seen; which tempest was the cause of perishing of a boat or vessel coming ... to the town of Leith.... And furthermore, the said witch declared, His Majesty had never come safely from the sea if his faith had not prevailed above their intentions.'

The king's interest possibly encouraged a greater number of prosecutions but his investigations seem to have undermined his own belief in the supernatural, or at least made him eager to expose counterfeit bewitchment and prevent innocent people being prosecuted.

In Britain, people believed that witches had a 'familiar', a supernatural servant which often took the form of a small animal — a cat, dog, toad, rabbit or something not so identifiable. Cats were not the most commonly named in witchcraft investigations but they are the ones that have remained strongest in the popular imagination. Anyone who has a loved pet knows how intimate that relationship can be. It is not difficult to understand how easy it was, at a time when most people found life too hard to lavish affection on an animal, for a man or woman seen cuddling or talking to a pet to be accused of witchcraft. There are many examples in reports of witch trials.

In 1582, eight-year-old Thomas Rabbet of St Osyth in Essex gave evidence that his mother had

'four several spirits, the one called Tiffin, the other Titty, the third Piggin and the fourth Jack, and being asked of what colours they were, saith that Titty is like a little grey cat, Tiffin is like white lamb, Piggin is black, like a toad, and Jack is black, like a cat. And he saith, he hath seen his mother at times to give them beer to drink, and of a white loaf or cake to eat; and saith that in the night-time the said spirits will come to his mother and suck blood of her upon her arms and other places of her body.'

Elizabeth Southern, accused with others in Lancashire in 1612, admitted to a familiar called Tibb who appeared as a black cat, a boy, a brown dog or a hare.

In 1618 Ellen Green, a Leicestershire witch, told in her confession how another witch, called Joan Willimot, had come to her and persuaded her

'to forsake God and betake her to the Devil, and she would give her two spirits, to which she gave her consent; and thereupon ... called two spirits, one in the likeness of a kitlin [kitten] and the other of a moldiwarp [mole]. The first the said

Willimot called 'Puss!', the other 'Hiss, hiss!', and they presently came to her, and she departing left them with this examinate; and they leaped on her shoulder, and the kitlin sucked under her right ear on her neck and the moldiwarp on the left side in the like place. After they sucked her, she sent the kitlin to a baker ... who had called her 'Witch' and stricken her, and bade the said spirit go and bewitch him to death.'

It was commonly thought that a witch suckled familiars or that, vampire-like, they drank her blood. People even believed that witches had an extra nipple somewhere on their bodies for this purpose; and finding a wart or cyst might be considered proof of this. Since cats like to sleep on beds and will even creep under the covers, it is not difficult to see how this could be distorted by malicious minds.

When Joan Flower was tried for bewitching the Earl of Rutland's family in 1618, her daughter testified that she was sent to take something belonging to the Earl's son Henry and when she brought a glove her mother

'stroked Rutterkin her cat with it, after it was dipped in hot water, and so pricked it often; after which Henry Lord Roos fell sick within a week ...'

She also described similar spells with Rutterkin against other members of the family but when she tried to bewitch the Earl's daughter Katherine by rubbing a piece of her handkerchief on the cat's belly

'Rutterkin whined and cried 'Mew!', whereupon she said that Rutterkin had no power over the Lady Katherine to hurt her.'

Other trial records and contemporary pamphlets tell similar stories but they were not always accepted as convincing proof. The powerful Fairfax family of Yorkshire accused a company of witches of bewitching their children, but they failed to secure a conviction, despite detailed evidence that one woman, Jennet Dibble, had a familiar 'in the shape of a great

black cat called Gibbe, which hath attended her now above forty years'. Quite a life span for a domestic cat!

In England, unlike Scotland and continental Europe, torture was not officially allowed to extract confessions, though witches were 'pricked' with a bodkin (a needle-pointed dagger) to see if any sore, unhealed places on their bodies, especially on the breasts and private parts, were the devil's mark (which would be insensitive to pain). Sometimes a bodkin in which the point retracted into the handle helped to fake evidence.

At the time of the Civil War between King and Parliament, in 1645, Matthew Hopkins, self-styled Witch Finder General, did use torture. He stripped and trussed up suspects and had them watched to see if they were visited by familiars or 'imps' — even a spider might be interpreted as an imp — walking them continually to keep them awake through several nights and always asking questions framed to produce apparently incriminating answers. A special parliamentary commission ended Hopkins' activities but in two years he and his assistant were responsible for the hanging or burning of nearly 300 witches.

Above *Three witches, from a contemporary broadsheet about their trial. Their familiars include a dog, owl and rat as well as Puss.*

Above *Aubrey Beardsley's illustration of the Black Cat in Edgar Allan Poe's horror story.*
Below *Francisco de Goya (1746–1828) linked cats with witches and demons in several of the etchings he published as Los Caprichos including the three reproduced here.*

their magic accused them, but in 1662 Isobel Gowdie of Morayshire in Scotland went to the authorities voluntarily and gave a detailed confession that she was a witch, something not even her own husband had suspected. She claimed to have the power to change her shape, using this spell to turn into a cat:

I shall goe intill ane catt,
With sorrow, and sych, and a blak shott;
And I shall goe in the Divellis nam,
Ay guhill I com hom againe.

To turn back again she said:

Cat, catt, God send the a blak shott,
I am in a cattis likness just now,
But I sal be in a womanis likness ewin now.
Catt, catt, God send thee a blak shott.

While the idea of the familiar spirit was strong in Britain, in continental Europe the belief in the ability of a witch or warlock to change shape was dominant. The folklore of the world is full of tales of people, usually women, who turn into cats or vice versa. Discovery is usually because an injury inflicted upon the cat remains an injury when she turns back into a woman.

An American version from the Ozark Mountains relates the tale of a man taking on a bet to sleep in a place said to be used by witches. He takes plenty of whisky to keep him company and when, by midnight, nothing has happened he is getting very drunk. Just as he is falling asleep a huge cat appears, howling and spitting. As it comes to attack him he fires his pistol. He hears a female scream but his candle is knocked over, though before being plunged into darkness he thinks he sees a bleeding human foot. Next day there is nothing to be seen, but he hears that a woman close by has accidentally shot her foot off and died from loss of blood.

A Norwegian version tells of a miller whose mill has twice been burned down, both times on the eve of Pentecost. The third year he keeps watch, taking care to draw a magic circle around himself for protection, and sees a group of cats appear. They light a fire and above it heat a pot of pitch. As they swing the pot to spill the molten pitch into the fire and spread the flame he cries out. The leader of the witches tries to pull him out of his magic circle but he draws his knife and hacks off her paw. She and the coven flee and the mill is saved but next morning, to his horror, he finds his own wife's hand has been severed at the wrist.

There are also stories of wives who take cat form to steal out at night and visit lovers, while one of Aesop's fables, warning against an ill-match, when love blinds the eye of the beholder, tells of a young man enamored of a beautiful cat, who is turned into a woman for him.

A Japanese traditional tale, linked with the Nabe'shima family, tells of a vampire cat that killed a prince's favourite, O Toyo, buried her body and took her shape to suck the prince's blood without detection until one of the prince's soldiers kept himself awake by plunging a dagger into his thigh so that the pain would help him resist the cat's sleep-inducing spells. Her nightly visits ceased and when the prince began to regain

Above *Witch Finder Matthew Hopkins with two witches and their familiars. The frontispiece to* Discovery of Witches, 1647. *The last hanging for witchcraft in England was in 1686, the last indictment in 1717, and in 1736 previous witchcraft laws were replaced by one which punished those who brought accusations of witchcraft.*

Opposite *The actor Onoye Kikugorö as a witch cat in a play based on stories of the 53 post stations on the Tokaido road. This woodblock print of 1852 was designed by Utagawa Kunisada.* **Below** *An 1847 print by Utagawa Kuniyoshi of a dancing cat demon in a scene from the same play.*

Even at the height of that witchhunt there were sceptics, including the Puritan parson John Gaule who published a collection of sermons on witchcraft in 1646 in which he declared that

'Every old woman with a wrinkled face, a hairy lip, a squint eye, a spindle in her hand, and a cat or dog by her side, is not only suspected but pronounced a witch.'

The persecution crossed the Atlantic to the New World, where its most famous outbreak was at Salem, Massachusetts, in 1692. In all 150 were accused of being witches in the Salem trials. Fifty were acquitted, 13 hanged, one pressed to death, and one died in jail but a change in the rules of evidence prevented more hangings.

Cotton Mather, Puritan preacher and one of the founders of Yale University, reported the trials in his *Wonders of the Invisible World*. At the trial of Susanna Martin he records that Robert Downer testified that when the defendant had been prosecuted some years before he had told her that he believed she was a witch. She had then threatened him 'that some she-devil would shortly fetch him away.' The following night, when he was in bed,

'there came in at the Window the likeness of a Cat, which fell upon him, took fast hold of his throat, lay on him a considerable while, and almost killed him.'

Remembering Susanna's threat he cried out 'Avoid, Thou She-Devil. In the Name of God the Father, the Son, and the Holy Ghost, Avoid! whereupon it left him, leap'd on the Floor, and flew out at the Window.'

Most witches were brought to trial when someone who believed they had suffered from

strength, the soldier, convinced she was some evil spirit, set out to kill her and to escape she turned back into a cat.

The big cats

It is not only the domestic cat that can be a 'were-cat'. In Malaysia and Indonesia people used to believe that there were men (rather than the cat-women of European superstition) who turned into tigers, either spontaneously or through some spell, and tigers which could assume human form. The hunter and conservationist Jim Corbett reported a belief in parts of India that man-eaters were men who turned themselves into tigers. These were either sadhus (a kind of holy man) who had developed an appetite for human flesh or thieves who took the jewels and valuables of the victims. He cites one case of a sadhu who was only saved from lynching because he was arrested and while he was closely guarded by the police the killings still went on.

It is claimed that ritual murders by secret societies were sometimes made to look like the work of man-eaters complete with spoor marked by specially carved wood. 'Leopard men' societies in West Africa and 'Lion men' in East Africa have been well documented. Their rituals may have involved oaths linked with the cats, but much closer links were involved where a tribal clan or an individual identified with an animal (not necessarily one of the cats). A member of the Lion Clan among the Akamba people of East Africa, for instance, would not kill a lion unless it actually attacked him or his cattle and was not allowed to take a lion's skin.

Early this century Swedish anthropologist Gerhard Lindblom witnessed one of his porters take meat out to a lion he heard calling. The man was a member of the Lion Clan and thought it his duty to share food with a hungry kinsman who was probably old and unable to hunt well.

In both north-eastern India and West Africa blood-brotherhood with a totem animal is some-

times practised. A leopard, for instance is trapped and then bled through a small incision so that its blood can be mingled with that of its human 'brother' or perhaps drunk. These rituals are secret but it has been suggested that the animal may be partially drugged by inhaling the smoke from burning herbs to keep it calm. Scarification on the face may also be a sympathetic symbol to suggest the feline whiskers.

The idea of transmigration of the spirit of a man into one of the big cats occurs in many cultures. Some Chinese believed that because tigers carry the character 王 on their forehead, this showed that each was an important person reincarnated in this form to atone for his or his forefather's sins. Some African peoples thought that their rulers were reincarnated as lions or leopards, so consequently would try to avoid killing them.

In one part of north-eastern India, according to an Indian Army officer writing early this

In one of Aesop's fables a young man in love with his cat begs Venus to help him, and the cat in his arms becomes a beautiful woman — but on their wedding night a mouse scurries by and, responding to her feline instincts, she leaps after it, disappointing her lover and offending the goddess with this profanation of the rights of love. She is immediately turned back into a cat.

Below left *A Japanese woodblock print of the vampire cat of the Nabeshimas killing O Toyo.*

Below *A pair of leopards made from ivory and decorated with copper disks and inlaid glass eyes, made for the Oba of Benin and now the property of HM Queen Elizabeth II. They are thought to be based on leopard figures used as water holders for ritual ablutions.*

A Benin bronze leopard mask, worn on the hip at the crossing of the kilt in the ceremonial dress of the Oba. The Benin ruler kept a menagerie of specially captured leopards. Their numbers perhaps strengthened the qualities of courage, strength and cunning which they symbolized and which were considered necessary attributes of a chief.
Below For an initiation rite of the Bapende tribe in Zaire the young men's dress represents lions.

century, anyone who killed a tiger was supposed to perform a ceremony known as *ai* in which he dressed as a woman and placed flints in the tiger's mouth, while eating eggs himself. He then solemnly apologized to the tiger and made three cuts in its head. This would ensure that the tiger's ghost would not haunt him. In Sumatra local people were even known to go to places where Europeans had set traps for tigers and explain to any that could hear that they were not responsible. If they were forced to kill a man-eater they would attempt to catch it first so that they could say how sorry they were that its behavior made it necessary for them to kill it and to ask its forgiveness before they did so.

In central India the Gonds used to worship a tiger god which represented the spirit of the wild. They built a house for him in the forest and believed that in the shape of a great white tiger he would protect them and their livestock by chasing off other beasts.

In China a white tiger, Bach-ho, was the spirit of the west and Ta-sheng, the Guardian or Great Spirit was often painted in tiger form on the walls of houses. In Chinese art the tiger is usually a symbol of the wind and often set against the dragon, which is rain. In Korea, too, the tiger features in mythology, folk art and folk tales.

In the past, few Chinese could have seen a real lion, there have been none in China in historical times, but it was nevertheless a frequent guardian of temples and palaces and represented in life by the imperial lion-dog, which we know as the Pekinese. To the Chinese exotic things are thought to bring good luck, which is why the lion dance is performed on festive occasions and especially at New Year.

When real tigers were killed in China their flesh fetched higher prices from apothecaries than from butchers, for a whole range of powders and pills were made from various parts of the body, from eyeballs to genitals. Whether their effects were medical or magical, people believed in them and also that one of a tiger's whiskers, worn as a charm, would give a man power over women.

Such medical applications also extend to India where tiger's fat in particular is thought to have particular efficacy as a cure for a variety of ills, echoed in the use of the name Tiger Balm for a well-known ointment from Hong Kong, used for the treatment of muscle aches and as a general panacea. In Africa lion's fat is also considered an effective treatment for earache, rheumatism and other ailments.

In Europe the domestic cat furnished similar additions to the pharmacopoeia. The uses listed in William Salmon's *The Compleat English Physician* (1693) range from the application of a cat's flesh to ease hemorrhoidal pain to the use of ash from its burned head to cure blindness and powdered dung mixed with mustard seed, onion juice and bear's grease to cure baldness.

Only a century ago there was still a firm belief in some parts of the United States that shingles and various other afflictions could be cured by applying the freshly removed skin of a cat and in Kansas the wearing of the skin of a black cat was thought to cure rheumatism, a similar belief to that which still stimulates a trade in cat skins in West Germany.

Above *Lion statues flank a stairway in the Forbidden City in Beijing.*
Above right *A lion dance at a festival in Hong Kong. The lion is brought to life by a ritual painting of the eyeballs with ink.*
Right *Chinese bronze tiger figure from fifth to third centuries* BC.
Far right *A bronze vessel for ritual offerings, made in the Shang period, fourteenth to twelfth centuries* BC, *shows a tiger protecting a man.*
Below *Eighteenth century Chinese watercolors of characters from a story or an opera. The animals symbolize their personal attributes: a former brigand, now a general, with a tiger; another general with a lion; a priest with a wildcat.*

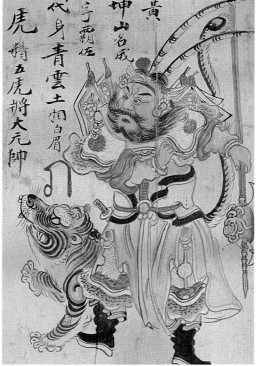

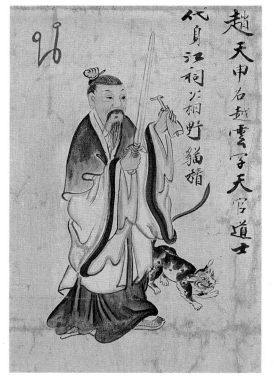

THE DOMESTIC CAT IN THE FAR EAST

The nobility and good fortune associated with the lion and tiger in China were not entirely shared by their smaller relatives. In China, and later in Japan, the cat held a rather ambivalent position, often being associated as much with evil and the occult as in medieval Europe, or at least considered an exploitive trickster, though this did not stop it from also being a valued pet.

Cats in China

At the end of the sixth century some members of the Emperor's family were accused of using cat spirits against the Empress, and people owning 'cat-spectres' were banished to the outer regions of the empire. But cats were not all bad. They were recognised as valuable in vermin control, and the fertility god Li Chou, worshipped by peasant farmers, appears to have been some sort of feline divine ratter. In paintings of the

Above *Well-fed cats being offered for the table in China about 1840.* **Right** *Kittens are still sold in Quinping market as a feature of the Cantonese cuisine.*

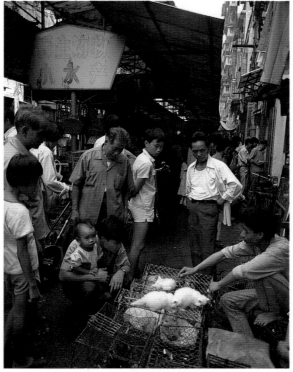

Sung Dynasty (960–1279), when the first known examples of cats appear in Chinese art, they are frequently included in portraits of the children of noble families, so clearly they had great prestige. Their ability to see in the dark was believed to mean that they could spot evil forces abroad at night and give protection from them. Paintings and pottery figures of cats, some made so that lights could be placed in the eyes, were also used to frighten spirits and to scare off rats, but although cats are sometimes pictured chasing butterflies they do not seem to have been painted as mousers or hunters in Chinese art.

Less happily for the cat, it joined all sorts of other animals as part of Chinese cuisine, especially in the south where, northern Chinese say, the Cantonese eat 'anything with four legs except tables, and anything that flies except aeroplanes'. Even today, cats, sometimes including tiger and clouded leopard, can still be purchased for the table in some Chinese markets. But before western cat lovers recoil in horror, they should perhaps think of the rabbits, lambs and other animals that are also kept as pets and still end up in the cooking pot, quite apart from the stock animals they eat, and they should also remember that there is a long Buddhist tradition of vegetarianism in China.

Cats in Japan

Cats probably reached Japan via China. The first known Japanese reference to a cat is in a ghost story written in 705 which describes the ghost of a man from Kyushu Island appearing to his son in cat form.

Soon after the Emperor Kōkō ascended the throne in 884 he was presented with a cat from China. His successor Udā described it in his diary, commenting on its soundless step and mice-catching abilities that quite outclassed those of other cats, and remarked that it seemed to understand what people said. Although the comparison with other cats suggests that they were already known they seem to have remained a rarity. A century later, Emperor Ichijo was presented with a cat from Korea. In 999 one of a litter of kittens so pleased him that it was given its own maid and the title of a court lady of fifth rank. Watching it wearing a red collar and chasing a piece of thread, he was charmed by its sensuality. Cats became the highly prized and pampered pets of the courtiers and nobility. Painted and sculpted cats had to do the job of protecting rice from mice and rats without any help from their living models.

It was not until a law passed in the seventeenth century which ordered that cats should be set free from their leashes and should no longer be sold or even given as presents, that they were able to take up their traditional role. However, this did not stop the spreading of tales of witches that could turn into cats and of demons in cat form.

A devil cat or *nekomata* could often be recognized by its bifurcated tail, and since it was considered the source of the cat's supernatural powers, it is said that tails were often cut off kittens to prevent them from turning into demons. Could this have had any influence on the development of the bobtailed type of cat which has been known for centuries in Japan? Docking would have no effect on genes but if people preferred a cat that looked already docked, it may have led to selection of those kittens in which it randomly occurred in order to develop such a strain. Because Japan cut itself off from contact with the outside world for many centuries, this national type, like the Manx, would have had more chance to develop.

Although it is only recently that pet cats have again become fashionable in Japan, the Japanese have always shown a healthy respect for the clever cat. The *mi-ke* type, a three-coloured cat like the tortoiseshell and white calicos of western breeds, is thought to bring good luck. Sailors were particularly keen to have one aboard for they believed they could both warn of approaching storms and scare off storm demons.

One Japanese cat, known as the *maneki-neko* (inviting or beckoning cat) can been seen in pottery or other figures as a good luck talisman in many homes and even welcoming people into shops. It is the cat associated with the Gōtokuji Temple, in what is now a western suburb of Tokyo. The temple is famous as the burial place of the general Ii Naosuke, a warrior of the Edo period, and for its ancient trees, but especially for this beckoning cat.

Once a very impoverished shrine, it was tended by a poor monk who had a cat with whom he shared his food and which he loved as though it were his child. Things were so bad that he even asked the cat to help. One summer evening a party of samurai came by, tired after a day out hawking. Their leader came in and told the monk that as they were passing they saw a cat raising its paw and beckoning to them, inviting them to come in. It had made them curious, but they were tired and would like to rest. The monk offered them his hospitality and the traditional tea ceremony and spoke to them of uplifting religious matters. Meanwhile, the sky clouded over and there was a great thunderstorm.

When they were ready to leave, the samurai introduced himself as a follower of Lord Ii Naotaka of Huikone. 'Your cat's invitation must have been a miracle from some god that enabled us to avoid the storm and benefit from your sermon. We will return,' he said.

He did return, and many others also came as pilgrims bringing offerings because they had heard of the beckoning cat and the sermon given by the monk. The Ii family chose this temple as their burial place and its fortunes changed entirely. People began to call it the cat shrine. When the monk's cat died he buried it there with many prayers for its soul and later, sculpted and modeled in its beckoning pose, its image became a common feature of Japanese life. The *maneki-neko* is thought to bring good luck, to keep homes safe, to make a business prosper and to grant wishes to those who are worthy and call on it in their prayers.

The temple has now become a shrine and burial place for cats to which people bring offerings and come to pray for their own cats' souls.

While Americans often refer to a brothel as a 'cat-house', linking the supposed promiscuity of the cat with prostitution, the Japanese refer to geishas as cats as a compliment because, like the supernatural cats, they could bewitch men with their charms.

But cats did not have to be supernatural to bewitch the artists of Japan. They appear in many Japanese paintings and woodblock prints, including those of Utamaro and Hi roshige, often as the companion of 'beauties'. They are celebrated most in the work of Ichiyusai Kuniyoshi (1796–1861), especially that done about 1840. As well as pets with their mistresses, domestic scenes in which they play, steal fish or sleep on a cushion, and witch cats in scenes from the Kabuki theatre, he produced a number of satires showing cats as people, actors' portraits which caricature them as cats, a print with cats cleverly arranged to form the characters *una-ma-ōzu* for the word meaning catfish, and another for *u-na-qi* (eel) — both with the creatures shown caught in net cartouches to emphasize the point. There is also a triptych of 53 different cat groups in entirely natural poses representing the stations on the Tokaido road.

There were more cats than students in Kuniyoshi's studio, as a sketch by a pupil named Kyosai shows; one snuggled in his kimono and others all over the place.

A century later, Tsuguharu Fujita, a Japanese artist working mainly in Paris, also became well known for his studies of cats and, like Kuniyoshi, included them in a number of self portraits. Japanese artists continue to show a special feeling for the cat.

Siamese and Burmese cats

Unlike many breeds of cats, the Siamese and the Birman do have real associations with the countries for which they are named. It is possible that the Siamese did not originate in Thailand, and they are not common there today, but they were certainly kept in the ancient capital of Ayudha and had a special place in the royal court. A set of manuscript scrolls, known as the Cat Book Poems, which were preserved in the Thai National Library and date from before the sack of Ayudha by Burmese invaders in 1676, show typical pointed cats like the modern Siamese and describe them as having black tails, feet and ears against white fur, though the color extended only a very short way up the leg and with much lighter masks. The Poems document the good and bad luck patterns of cats and also shows *Si-Sawats*, known to the west as Korats, which are more common in Thailand today, and the copper-brown cat the scroll identifies as the *Sopalak*, which some believe to be the modern Burmese.

Cats were kept in temples and there was a belief among Buddhists that when a person of great spiritual advancement died, their soul would enter the body of a cat until, on the death of the cat, the soul would ascend to heaven. The

belief was clearly linked with the ritual entombment of a cat in burials of members of the Thai royal family. A small hole was left in the roof so that the cat could escape. When it emerged, the priests knew that the soul of the prince or monarch had passed into the body of the cat. At Thai coronations, as recently as the 1920s, a cat was included in the coronation procession to enable the former king to witness the installation of his successor.

The Burmese breed in the west is descended from one cat that is said to have come from Rangoon in 1930 but the Cat-Book Poems suggest that it, too, was a long-established type. A legend set in times even earlier than the Buddha purports to explain the origin of the pattern of the Birman cat. At a temple of Lao-Tsun, where a blue-eyed golden goddess called Tsun-Kyan-Kse was worshipped, there were 100 pure white cats who lived with the priests. One night invaders from Thailand approached the temple and the priests gathered to invoke the goddess's help. As they knelt before her their elderly chief priest, Mun-Ha, died. As his spirit left him, his own favourite cat leaped on to his head. The priests watched in amazement as the cat's white fur changed to the gold of the goddess, its eyes became sapphire blue like hers and its ears and feet took on the color of fertile brown earth, except where they touched the old priest's silver hair and retained the white of purity. As Mun-Ha's soul entered the cat, the animal turned to face the approaching Thais, rousing the other priests to defend and save their temple. Next morning every one of the temple cats had taken on the sacred colors of the goddess. Seven days later, Mun-Ha's cat was dead.

You do not have to believe the story, any more than you should credit those invented to explain crossed-eyes or kinked tails which used to occur in Siamese cats. Equally unauthenticated are claims that the modern Birman breed descends from a pair of cats presented to French soldiers who helped to defend another temple of Lao-Tsun during a rebellion in 1919.

Opposite from top to bottom: *A Japanese painting of a roaring tiger by Mori Tessan (1775–1841); the* maneki-neko *or beckoning cat, a popular Japanese good luck figure which brought fortune to the Gotokuji Temple; the entrance to the Gotokuji temple; beside a shrine at the Gotokuji temple are votive offerings in the form of the* maneki-neko. *Strings of paper cranes are hung to the right, each an offering of prayer for the owner's cat.*
Top right *Japanese Bobtails are common in Tokyo streets.*
Right *A Japanese veterinarian treats a cat with a form of acupuncture.*
Below *These Japanese practitioners believe that cats can benefit from yoga and place them in appropriate positions.*

Overleaf *Burmese kittens.*

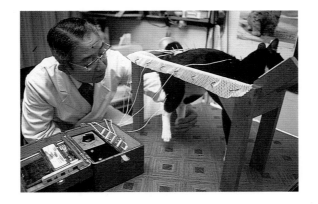

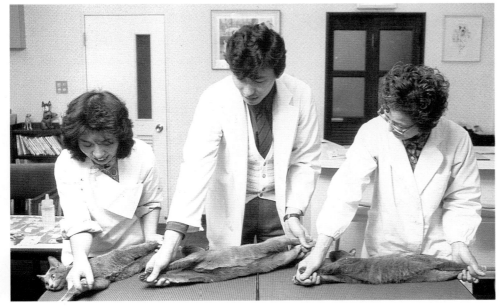

CATS IN LATIN AMERICA

Domestic cats did not reach the Americas until after the arrival of Europeans but the jaguar and other cats of the New World had their place in the pantheon and mythologies of its cultures. Beliefs among Amerindian peoples include the concept of medicine men turning into jaguars after death and the idea of the jaguar as a malevolent spirit against whom a warrior was powerless.

In Argentina the cougar earned the name *amigo del christiano* (the Christian's friend) from an event said to have taken place in 1536. When the Spanish conquerors at Buenos Aires were surrounded by Indians and near starving, a young girl slipped through the besiegers in search of food. She lost her way and took shelter in a cave used by a cougar and her cubs. Instead of attacking, the cats looked after her (as in so many

European tales of wolves and children) but when she was eventually found and returned to Buenos Aires she was accused of treachery and siding with the Indians. Her punishment was to be chained to a tree and left to be eaten by wild beasts but when a party went out to recover her remains for burial they found her still alive and a female cougar defending her from a circle of other hungry-looking cougars and jaguars. Seeing this as some sign of grace the governor pardoned her.

The protective powers of the big cats certainly did not save the native peoples who worshipped them from the onslaught of conquering Europeans brandishing the Christian cross. How many gold and silver cats were melted down by the conquistadors we can never know, but some relics of the pre-Colombian cults do survive. Deep in the Central American jungle, in what is now Guatemala, was discovered the Mayan

1. A gold jaguar figure from the Simü culture of Colombia.

2. A stone jaguar figure found in the region of Escuintla in Guatemala.

3. Aztec warriors belonged to the orders of Eagles and of Jaguars. The Jaguar knights wore a skin with the head forming their helmet, here shown in stylized form in the Codex Nutall.

4. An Inca K'eru, a wooden drinking vessel, in the shape of a jaguar's head.

5. A feline head in gold.

6. A golden receptacle from the Mochica Culture in the form of a sacred cougar, perhaps for some ritual use. The tongue is decorated with a human face, the ear pendants are ceremonial knives and the body and tail are embossed with rows of double-headed snakes.

7. A fifteenth-century Incan pottery vessel in the form of a jaguar eating its victim.

8. A squatting jaguar on part of a frieze on the pyramid temple of Kukulcan at Chichen Itza. A secret stair led to the room in which a red jaguar throne was found.

centre of Tikal with its great Jaguar Temple. At Monte Alban, in Mexico, the Zapotecs worshipped their jaguar god Cosijo, at Chichen Itza a solid red-painted jaguar throne for the use of a high Mayan-Toltec dignitary was found within the 'castillo' and the walls of the pyramid temple of Kukulcan are decorated with sitting jaguars.

At Tula there is a frieze of prowling jaguars below another frieze of eagles. Similar motifs appear on a great wooden drum discovered at Malinalco, a later Aztec site whose buildings date from the fifteenth century. Eagles and jaguars were the symbols of the two great orders of warrior knights of the Aztec culture. The principal building at Malinalco, hewn from the solid rock, is guarded by cougars. Inside, the natural walls of a circular chamber are carved with eagles and cougar heads. The Jaguar knights wore jaguar skins as uniforms, the head as a sort of helmet and in Ochpaniztli, the month that coincided

with the end of August and the beginning of September, they paraded with the Eagles in an annual military review.

In Peru in the sixth century BC the Chavin people of the northern highlands were worshipping a cougar god which their artists represented in a very stylized form, and the later Paracas culture of the southern coastal region embroidered cougar demons on the wrapping cloths for their dead.

Cat cults existed throughout the American cultures relating to the animals the people knew. They appear in their art in the shapes and decoration of both ritual and everyday objects, worked in wood and stone and precious metals. Sometimes they are easily recognizable but sometimes so highly abstracted as to be discernible only to those trained in reading pre-Colombian forms.

The members of the cat family do not appear ever to have been hunted as a major source of food but the wearing of their skins goes back to the earliest times and probably acquired a ritual or ceremonial meaning, for it seems often to be associated with priests or people of rank. Although in the Middle Ages cat skins were used as trimmings, and later those of lynx and other Canadian species may have found their way among the beaver fur traded by the Hudson's Bay Company, it is only in comparatively recent times that a major trade in cat skins has developed.

In Africa a Masai youth, after his initiation, had to seek out a male lion and kill it single-handed before he could become a *moran*, or warrior, a practice long-since banned. In the early empires of Egypt and Mesopotamia the hunting of big cats became a sport reserved for kings and noblemen. This symbolic acting out of the protector hero role, emulating that of Gilgamesh and Heracles, is recorded in claims like that of the Pharaoh Amenophis III (1405–1367 BC) to have killed 102 savage lions in the first decade of his reign, or of the Assyrian Tiglath-pileser I (745–727 BC) to have 'killed 120 lions on foot with great courage, and brought down 800 lions with my javelin from my chariot'. Assurbanipal (668–626 BC) recorded that he had overcome great numbers of lions which 'shake the mountain with their roars' and to have

> 'penetrated their hiding places and destroyed their lairs. For my royal amusement I have caught the Desert King by his tail, and on the instruction of my helpers, the Gods Nusib and Nergal, I have split his head with my two-headed sword.'

However true such claims may once have been, the Assyrian Great Kings did not necessarily go out into the desert to hunt the lion. Hunting had by then become a highly organized sport. Assurbanipal might claim to have killed 450 lions and 620 other animals in a single hunt but his ridding the land of lions was a flamboyant royal metaphor. The reliefs on the walls of his palace at Nineveh show that his lions were usually captured, or even specially bred, just for the hunt.

The Mesopotamian lions were much smaller than the animal of the African plains (the bas-relief presentations probably exaggerate their size), making it easier for the Assyrians to tackle them at close range. These massive hunts, and the capture of animals for them, greatly reduced local populations, though they survived in the Middle East until eventually wiped out by nineteenth-century hunters.

In post-classical times there were no big cats left in Europe to be hunted but there were lynx and wildcats. With the development of the royal forests of medieval kings they joined the boar, hare, deer and other animals which provided sport for royal hunting parties or those granted licenses to kill beasts of the chase; such animals were considered the property of the Crown and not for every common man and serf to kill. Cat fur was used for trimming garments and is mentioned as the most costly kind of clothing permitted to nuns and abbesses under twelfth-century ecclesiastical sumptuary rules.

The verderers, whose job was to maintain Forest Law, protected both the woodland and the wildlife to ensure that there was plenty of game to hunt. When religious attitudes began to turn against the cat this still gave the wild (and

*Scenes from Assurbanipal's lion hunt, carved on the walls of his palace at Nineveh. Lions were taken to the hunting ground in cages, the attendants who released them protected by their own cage on top (**upper right**). Assurbanipal, from his chariot and on foot slays lions with arrow and spear. The dead are carried ceremonially from the field and placed before an altar where the king pours libations over them (**lower right**).*

Sit lęuibus cattos canibus sectantur agrestes   Arbore deijciunt vel acutę cuspidis hasta.

feral) cat within forest boundaries some protection, but they were thought equally satanic. At the beginning of the fifteenth century Edward, Duke of York, making an English translation of an earlier treatise on hunting by the Comte de Foix, added material on hunting in England. He declared that

> 'of wildcats ... every hunter in England knows ... their falseness and malice. If any beast has the devil's spirit in him without doubt it is the cat, both the wild and the tame.'

With the development of grouse- and pheasant-shooting on big estates in the eighteenth and nineteenth centuries, gamekeepers in areas where wildcats still survived saw them as a threat to their birds and sought to exterminate them along with other 'vermin'. Charles St John, a Victorian 'sportsman' noted that they were being 'exterpated' in the Scottish Highlands and commented on the fierce fight they put up when cornered, or approached when trapped, and how difficult they were to kill. 'If a tame cat has nine lives,' he considered, 'a wild cat must have a dozen.'

Not even the domestic cat escapes his censure. 'There is no animal more destructive than the common house-cat, when she takes to hunting in the woods,' he declared.

> 'In this case they should always be destroyed ... once they have learned to prefer hares and rabbits to rats and mice, they are sure to hunt the larger animals only. I believe, however, that by cropping their ears close to the head, cats may be kept from hunting, as they cannot bear the dew and rain to enter these sensitive organs.'

In fact, although wildcats do sometimes kill mountain hares, grouse and even roe deer fawns on occasion, diet studies based on stomach contents of European cats show that their prey is mostly small rodents such as voles and woodmice.

World War Two temporarily put an end to hunting for sport and gave species like the wildcat a chance to recover. Since then there have been programs to reintroduce Lynx in some parts of Europe where they had become extinct.

In India the Emperor Ashoka, who ruled in the third century BC when Buddhism spread through most of the sub-continent, issued an edict protecting all wildlife except for certain species which were required for food. Under later invaders, sport-hunting of big cats again became a popular royal pastime, especially after the Moghul conquest, and with the introduction of firearms in the fifteenth century, the decrease in the tiger population perhaps began.

The *shikar*, or hunting party, became a favourite diversion of officers and administrators of the East India Company and the succeeding British Raj. It was a real test of courage to face a savage beast with spear and knife, but when the hunter fired with a rifled-barreled weapon from the safety of a howdah on an elephant's back or from a *machan* (a platform set up in a tree, below which a goat or other bait was tethered to attract the tiger) it seems that the only real danger was to the beaters who drove the game towards the guns.

Despite the huge numbers of tigers slaughtered in the mid-nineteenth century — and some Maharajahs claimed to have personally killed

Hunting forest cats, from an eighteeenth-century book by Pieter Bol and Joseph Galleus in the Florence National Library.

King George V, Emperor of India, on shikar in Nepal.

Left *George V and Maharajah Sir Chandra Shamsei Jang with a tiger kill.*

Tiger hunting from a machan *in the 1900s. The tiger has been attracted by a tethered bait.*

more than a thousand — there still seemed to be an inexhaustible supply. They were frequently seen and, though they helped to control the deer, pigs and monkeys which raided crops, they took their toll of domestic livestock as well. In Bengal alone, in the 1860s, tigers were also said to have claimed over 2000 human lives a year.

By the 1920s and 1930s, though 'bagging' a tiger might be every young sportsman's ambition, the tigerskin trophy became so commonplace that it lost its importance as a status symbol, in India at least. Real hunters gained more pleasure from the tracking and stalking than from the kill itself, and it became a point of honor to kill outright and not to leave a wounded animal, not only because it would suffer, but also because it was much more likely to become a man-eater.

Tracking and executing man-eaters became a job for the most accomplished hunters. Preeminent among them was Jim Corbett, author of several books on hunting, who became an expert on the tiger and, later, a leading conservationist. One of the Republic of India's national parks is now named after him.

In southern Africa, where European colonization began in 1652, vast areas remained largely uninhabited, penetrated only by a handful of white explorers who might also hunt big-game when the opportunity arose. It was the Boer Voortrekers, moving north in 1836 to establish themselves inland away from British domination, who began the onslaught on African animals.

Clearing the territory for agriculture and killing predators to protect livestock had a much more disastrous effect than the game hunters of the nineteenth century, such as the famous Albert Selous. Between them farmers and hunters eliminated some African animals altogether and greatly reduced the range of others, including lions.

Early in the present century a new type of big-game hunter appeared on the scene, emulating a widely publicized East African trip made by

Theodore Roosevelt, ex-president of the United States. Setting out from Nairobi in 1909 with 500 African porters and tons of equipment on what was described as a 'scientific expedition', Roosevelt managed to kill a huge number of animals. Despite his entourage he did actually hunt, the highlight being lion-spearing on foot and much of the attraction lying in 'the spirit of the wilderness ... the hardy life of the open' and 'the awful glory of the sunrise and sunset in the wide spaces of the earth, unworn by Man' as well as 'in the thrill of the fight with dangerous game'.

'Teddy' Roosevelt sometimes traveled on a bench fixed over the cowcatcher of a locomotive and it was in this way that the young Winston Churchill made a 16-hour journey from Mombasa to Nairobi, shooting at the lions and other game as he steamed past.

One hunter rode out from Nairobi after lion with a pack of hounds, blowing on a silver hunting horn and shouting 'Tally-ho!'. Another eccentric used to lasso lion and rhino and then parade them through the town.

The decades between the two World Wars were the years of the 'champagne safari' when rich men would hunt by motor car, their lions being found for them so that all they had to do was fire the rifle before lying back in a hammock to enjoy the creature comforts provided by the safari organizers. They returned with a fine set of trophies as proof of their machismo, much to the scorn of the old-style hunter.

In 1887 the Boone and Crockett Club was founded in the United States to promote hunting as a sport which was perceived as a way of developing confidence, self-reliance and all kinds of manly virtues associated with the great outdoors. This was the spirit of the old hunter who had a respect for and understanding of his prey. Many of them were among the originators of the conservation movement. The effete pseudohunter was little more than a big-game murderer.

MENAGERIES AND ZOOS

People have always been fascinated by the strange and the exotic. Unusual animals, and potentially dangerous ones especially, attract interest in themselves, quite apart from being kept as pets or used in the arena or the circus.

The sacred animals in Egyptian temples were not exotics, though lions were not usually seen in the highly populated areas of the Nile valley, and would have been viewed by worshippers with interest. By 1000 BC, however, the Chinese emperor Wen Wang had made an animal collection, in an enclosure 1500 acres (600 hectares) in size, which he called the Ling-Yu — the Garden of Intelligence. At about the same time the biblical King Solomon was also keeping animals. So did later Middle Eastern kings, such as Assurbanipal and Nebuchadnezzar, and some Greek city states also had collections. The Garden of Intelligence presumably had some scientific purpose but other early collections seem to have been mainly for spectacle until about the time of Alexander the Great, who sent back to Greece interesting animals captured on his campaigns at a time when his ex-tutor Aristotle was making a systematic classification of living creatures and writing his *Natural History*.

The Roman world had zoos as well as animals kept for the arena but, after the disintegration of the Roman empire, little is heard of animal-keeping until, in the eighth century, the Frankish emperor Charlemagne began a collection of exotic species for which other rulers sent him presents of wild animals, including a lion which arrived as a gift from the Emir of Cairo.

Royal and state menageries

At the beginning of the twelfth century, Henry I of England had a collection of animals, possibly begun by his father William the Conqueror. Kept at his palace of Woodstock, near Oxford, it included lions, leopards and lynxes. Two centuries later Henry III moved it to the Tower of London. It then included three splendid leopards sent as a present by Frederick II, Holy Roman Emperor, in 1235 in token of the three leopards of England which appeared on the royal arms. When, in the same year, Henry's sister Isabella married Frederick, she found him an even greater enthusiast for wild animals than her brother. Their wedding procession included lions, panthers and cheetahs (for which he also ran a hunting training school).

Under Edward II, the sheriffs of London had to supply a quarter of a sheep and three sous a day to feed a lion in the Tower, sixpence to feed a leopard and three-halfpence for the keeper's diet. Under Edward III the cost had gone up to two shillings and one penny for 'one lion, one leopard and two cat lions' and twelve sous for their attendants, but over the following century the Tower lions died and were not replaced although the menagerie continued.

In France, Philip IV (Philip the Fair), had lions in his menagerie and Philip VI had a collection at the Louvre while the exiled popes set up a lion house at Avignon.

In the Netherlands, a fourteenth-century Count of Holland kept lions in a menagerie at The Hague. The city of Amsterdam kept a collection of lions as a symbol of the independence

Above right *In this carving on the walls of Assurbanipal's palace at Nineveh, a tame lion roams free with musicians in an Assyrian 'Paradise' or pleasure garden.*

Right *In early zoos, and sadly in many menageries today, big cats were kept closely confined in cages.*

achieved in its municipal constitution in 1340 and at a castle in Ghent (where at one time a lion was tied up near the entrance gate in the role of watchdog) four lions were kept. Their feeding and care was contracted out to the local butcher for a small fee and the right to charge visitors to see them.

At his castle at Cintra Alfonso V, king of Portugal, maintained a menagerie made up of animals brought back from his wars in Africa. He often sent gifts of lions as tokens of friendship to other rulers. He may have sent one — he certainly sent monkeys — to René of Anjou, whose menagerie became famous throughout Europe. When René's daughter Margaret married the English king Henry VI in 1445, one of his courtiers gave her a lion as a wedding present, whereupon the animal enclosures at the Tower of London were rebuilt and the collection enlarged. The animals' cages and keepers' quarters were in and around a fortification known as the Lion Tower (now demolished) where British monarchs maintained a menagerie until 1831.

Queen Margaret, who led armies both for and against her husband during the Wars of the Roses, earning Shakespeare's description 'a tiger's heart wrapped in a woman's hide', staged combats of lions against tigers to amuse her court.

Rome had a lion pit near the Capitol from the thirteenth century until 1414, when the last remaining lion was destroyed after it escaped and killed a child, and various Italian noblemen also established animal collections. Foremost was probably the menagerie of the city of Florence, built up by the Medicis, which Lorenzo 'the Magnificent' made the pride of the city. Another Medici, Pope Leo X, set up a menagerie at the Vatican.

Florence looked after its lions well. In 1459 there was an attempt to stage a spectacle like the Roman *venationes* in the blocked-off Piazza della Signoria, but the 20 lions involved were so well fed that after wandering around for a while they lay down in a shady corner. At another attempt at a similar spectacle in 1514, which included hunting leopards (cheetah), two lions were supposed to be the star turn. One did kill a couple of dogs that charged up to it but no others came

to harass it. Neither lion had the least interest in chasing after animals; they wanted rather to escape from the noise of the enormous crowd.

The Florentine lions were originally kept in the Piazza San Giovanni but were moved in the fourteenth century to a menagerie at the Piazza della Signoria, until Duke Cosimo I found their smell too obnoxious and they were moved away from his palace to a site now marked by the Via dei Leoni.

Across the Atlantic, in Mexico in 1519, the conquistador Cortes found a menagerie which formed part of the palace of Montezuma and housed a collection of animals so large that it required 300 keepers. Here the jaguars and ocelots were sometimes fed the bodies of human victims sacrificed in the Aztec temples.

In Europe the popularity of menageries fluctuated. In France there was a resurgence of interest when Louis XIV developed a passion for animals and built a small zoo in the gardens at Versailles. In London the collection under the Commonwealth included six lions in 1657 and in 1708 there were 11 lions, two leopards and a tiger. Despite new acquisitions in the next half-century, and additional collections at Windsor and at Kew, by 1822 there were no big cats at all at the Tower. By the end of the eighteenth century the Florentine collection and the Portuguese royal menagerie no longer existed, although the Prince of Orange still had a menagerie at Loo when French armies swept into the Netherlands during the Revolutionary Wars.

The first 'zoos'

The first claim to be a truly public zoo goes to the Austrian Imperial Menagerie originally founded at the Schönbrunn Palace in Vienna in 1752 and opened to the public in 1765, while in 1775 a zoo was founded in the Royal Park in Madrid. In 1793 a public zoological collection was created in the Jardin des Plantes in Paris from the animals of the previous royal collection at Versailles, joined later by the survivors of the Dutch menagerie. Here a real scientific study could be made of living animals.

Visitors to the Tower of London had always been permitted to view the lions for a small fee and from an all time low in 1822 of only 'the grizzly bear, an elephant and one or two birds', the appointment of Alfred Cops as Keeper saw the collection built up again, with two new lion cubs in 1823. Three years later, prompted partly by the scientific interest in and general popularity of the Paris collection, the Zoological Society of London was founded. In 1828 it opened its own collection in the Zoological Gardens at Regent's Park and gained royal patronage. In 1830 William IV presented all the animals from Windsor to the Zoological Society and the following year divided the collection at the Tower between Regent's Park and a new zoo opening in Dublin (where the first recorded lion cubs to be bred and reared in captivity were born 21 years later). Two other English zoos soon followed: Bristol and Belle View, Manchester, both opening in 1836. Amsterdam opened a zoo in 1838, Berlin in 1844,

the offshoot of one at Potsdam, but it was not until 1899 that New York gained its first zoo in the Bronx.

Over the following decades Londoners began to shorten 'Zoological Gardens' to the more convenient term 'zoo' by which such collections have popularly been known since.

Housing the animals

In the early public zoos specimens were kept in cages designed to protect the public from attack and give them a good view of the animals. Often they were indoors, especially with species from warmer lands, but as experience and under-

Above *Heavy planting, a varied terrain and water, all help to create a more natural environment for the tigers at San Diego Zoo in California. Visitors are kept safely separate from the animals but have a good vantage point from which to observe them.*

Above right *The 'lion glens' and other open habitats created by Carl Hagenbeck offered animals greater freedom. However, in recent years their drawbacks have been recognized and more stimulating environments are being created.*

Safari park lions are not allowed to hunt live prey but are fed meat from protective cages.

standing of the needs of different species grew, attitudes to housing and presentation began to change. It was found that, after acclimatization, exercise and space were usually more important to keeping an animal healthy than providing it with heated indoor housing. It was also realized that some species from tropical climates could adjust to temperate winters.

One of the first people to organize a zoo in this way was Carl Hagenbeck of Hamburg, who became one of the world's largest animal dealers, owner of a circus and director of one of Europe's great zoos. His favorites were the big cats and he wanted to present them so that visitors could see them in something approaching a natural environment. Instead of cages he planned ditches and moats to prevent the animals escaping, and built artificial cliffs, caves and panoramas to suggest their native habitat. At his Tierpark (Zoo) at Stellingen, near Hamburg, set up in 1848, he built an artificial 'glen' to house his carnivores, with an inner den where they could retire for shelter or privacy. Here his lions and tigers exercised in all weathers, sun and snow, and they adapted to the colder climate by growing thicker fur.

Hagenbeck seems to have had a very close rapport with his animals, maintained even after long separation. One instance, which he gives in his autobiography, concerned a tiger which, after developing an eye condition that made it nearly blind, was nursed by him daily until completely recovered. The tiger and its mate were sold to Berlin zoo but, to the end of its life, it recognized Hagenbeck whenever he visited.

'He would always fall into the most violent excitement on hearing my voice in the distance; and when I came up he would purr like a cat, and was never satisfied till I had gone into the cage and spent some little time with him.'

At the Bronx Zoo, in New York, two lions and a tiger who, long before, had been in his care became attentive as soon as he approached their den. They

'stared at me like a human being who saw a familiar face but could not put a name

to it. But the moment I called out the names by which I used to address them in Hamburg they sprang up and ran to the bars, purring loudly when I stroked and caressed them.'

One old lion he had known for 18 years, although in pain, lay down calmly when ordered to do so by Hagenbeck and allowed him to cut and extract claws that had grown too long, curving and entering the flesh. Owners of domestic cats may sometimes be able to inspire such confidence in their pets and Hagenbeck believed that all carnivores, if caught young and treated properly could be brought up as domestic pets, saying

'their so-called wild nature does not break out unless something happens to put the animals in a rage; and this, after all, is just the same with domestic animals.'

In time, other zoos emulated Hagenbeck's concepts and began to take them further, but today there are still many animals kept in cages, and sometimes in very stark and sterile surroundings. Given the unnatural conditions of keeping any animal away from its natural habitat, zookeepers have sometimes balanced the risks of parasites and infection against naturalness and concluded that this was the best zoo solution. For some species, including the cat family, it has often been possible to extend their exercise space and provide a variety of environment, on a small scale in city zoos and a larger one at country zoos, such as the Zoological Society of London's Whipsnade branch in the Berkshire countryside. In neither, however, is it possible for a lion or lynx to lead a natural life, hunting wild prey in a territory that matches its surroundings to the wild.

Safari parks

The first 'safari parks' were an attempt partially to provide a more natural environment. A breakthrough in the presentation of big cats to the general public, the concept originated with British circus owner Jimmy Chipperfield, who sought to create on a smaller scale something similar to the experience of the game reserves of Africa where tourists can observe wildlife in its natural state. His plan was to create an enclosure in which it would be possible for lions to live in a more natural way so that visitors could drive through and observe their behavior close at hand, staying within their cars and keeping the windows closed to avoid the risk of any accident.

Chipperfield found an ally in the Marquis of Bath, owner of Longleat House, an Elizabethan mansion with extensive parkland, part of which could be surrounded by high and secure fences to enclose the animals. The scheme was not unequivocally welcomed but its success with the public led to the Chipperfield family's organizing ten other safari parks around the world and the idea being extensively copied.

Unknown to Jimmy Chipperfield, and at about the same time, the administration of Tama Zoological Park, in Japan, had a similar idea which pushed forward more rapidly and opened a year

before Longleat was ready. The system at Tama differed in that the enclosure was an artificial area within an existing zoo. Because visitors there drive around in a specially armored bus they lose a little of the proximity to the animals felt in the Chipperfield-style safari parks.

Starting with only lions in 1966, Longleat now has a very comprehensive collection of large wild animals which includes white rhinos, African elephants, giraffes, zebras, sea lions, hippos, various antelopes, gorillas, a large group of monkeys, and Bengal tigers — one the only white tiger currently in Britain. All those kept in large groups breed prolifically, except the elephants and gorillas, and perhaps they too will breed in future.

Safari parks may give an impression of real wildlife to the visitor but in essence the animals are living an artificial life and their freedom is limited. Lions have the opportunity to form prides and to chose their mates, so that breeding is more natural, but they are animals reared from birth with their food provided and with medical attention always at hand. Being well fed they have no need to hunt and no live prey animals are provided for them. Lions do not by nature exert themselves unnecessarily, so such animals exhibit only a part of their natural life style and their behavior is modified by the conditions under which they live.

The future of zoos

The entire concept of zoos and captive animals has been heavily criticized in recent years. At one time zoos provided the opportunity for scientific study of animals but today the basic needs of identification and classification have largely been met. Since sophisticated techniques now exist to study animals in the wild and it is acknowledged that zoo animals, because of the artificial circumstances in which they live, do not display totally natural behavior — and often show definite signs of psychosis — what argument can there be for the existence of zoos?

One of the main reasons for the creation of modern zoos was educational, but now animals can be seen magnificently filmed in their natural habitat with commentaries by skilled zoologists explaining their behavior. Air travel has made it easy for those who can afford it to reach distant places, and a branch of the tourist industry is now devoted to taking people on expeditions and safaris to see the world's flora and fauna in its natural setting. With all this, is there still a role for zoos?

In fact there are still many things that can only be discovered by close and consistent monitoring of animals under controlled conditions, and zoos remain the only places where the majority of people are likely to see living wild animal species at close quarters. They continue to have a valuable scientific and educational role. They also play an important part in conservation by offering facilities for captive breeding of rare species which can then be released into the wild. Captive breeding preserves a larger gene pool for those species which have become so restricted in their habitat that numbers are lower than desirable for the continuation of healthy stock. Also, where suitable habitats no longer exist, zoos provide a modern Ark in which species can be maintained so that, if those habitats can be recreated, there will still be the appropriate animals to enjoy them. Zoos do not offer the ideal environment for animals but, without them, some animals would disappear altogether.

Lions can adapt to temperate living conditions and even enjoy a gambol in light snow, but when winter conditions are severe they require protection and are provided with housing.

At Woburn Wildlife Kingdom, England, as at all safari parks, the animals have right of way.

The earliest human philosophies and theologies saw men and women as a part of nature. Gods and spirits of places often took animal form or animal attributes. In some cultures that oneness with nature still survives. The Hindu believes that life passes through a series of divine incarnations from fish to mammals and that man is integrally linked to all creation, the Buddhist, committed to non-violence, believes that any harm done to the spirits and forces of the natural world will damage all, including ourselves, and North American Indian culture presents man as the fellow, not the master, of other life.

This has not been true of the three religions which grew from the semitic tribes of the Middle East: Judaism, Christianity and Islam; all share the teachings of the Hebrew book of Genesis which gave man 'dominion over the fish of the sea, and over the fowl of the air, and over the cattle, and over all the earth and over every creeping thing that creepeth upon the earth.' This, coupled with the idea developed by Plato and Aristotle of a 'Chain of Being' in which all creatures, except man, are placed in a fixed hierarchy of creation, led people of the Western cultures to think that the natural world was for man's convenience and selfish exploitation. The

beginnings of a questioning of that attitude date perhaps from the publication of Charles Darwin's *Origin of Species* in 1859.

At a conference in Assisi in 1986, to celebrate the 25th anniversary of the World Wide Fund for Nature, Jewish, Christian and Islamic leaders underlined an interpretation of 'dominion' — in the context of Genesis — as meaning not a right to exploit but rather of 'responsibility for', of stewardship, and joined with Hindu and Muslim leaders to call for a responsible attitude towards the natural world. But the current concern for conservation and protection of the environment is a very recent development.

The origins of the modern movement can be seen in the appeals by artist-explorer George Catlin who, as early as 1833, was lobbying for national parks to preserve the landscapes, animals *and man* of the American West. In *Walden, or Life in the Woods* (1854) Henry David Thoreau wrote of people's spiritual need of the wilderness. Magazines such as *Harpers* began to publish articles on nature and its preservation which awakened the interest of East Coast Americans. In 1864 the Yosemite Valley, California, was designated for preservation and in 1872 the Yellowstone area of north-west Wyoming became the first of the United States National Parks. Yet, at the same time, the buffalo was being wiped out on the North American plains. Significantly Yellowstone is the only place where an original population still survives.

The humane societies

If concern was not, as yet, for wildlife preservation, people were beginning to feel some responsibility for the treatment of the domestic animals that they exploited. Richard Martin, a Dublin-born landowner who earned the nickname 'Humanity' Martin from the Prince Regent, felt so strongly that he campaigned for the first 'preventive act against the cruel and unjust treatment of animals', which was eventually passed by the British Parliament in 1822.

Two years later at a meeting at Old Slaughter's Coffee House, in London's St Martin's Lane, the world's first animal protection society was formed by Martin, Quaker MP Foxwell Buxton, William Wilberforce (the anti-slaver) and the Rev. Arthur Broome, who became its first Secretary. The young Princess Victoria became its Patron and, when she became Queen in 1837, it became the Royal Society for the Prevention of Cruelty to Animals (RSPCA). The French Société Protectrice des Animaux was established in 1845; the American Society for the Prevention of Cruelty to Animals in 1866; the American Humane Association in 1877, and others followed in various countries of the world.

The humane societies, together with other bodies such as the People's Dispensary for Sick

Opposite *The first conservationists? Noah's Ark, painted by Miskin, a leading artist at the court of the Mogul Emperor Akbar. Adam may have been given dominion over the animals but the story of the Ark gives Jews, Christians and Moslems a clear example of their duty to protect and preserve their fellow creatures.*
Below *The First Phase of Cruelty by William Hogarth (1697-1764). Among the animals being tortured is a cat with two balloons attached which has been cast out of an attic window, two tied hanging from a post and one in the foreground being set upon by a dog.*

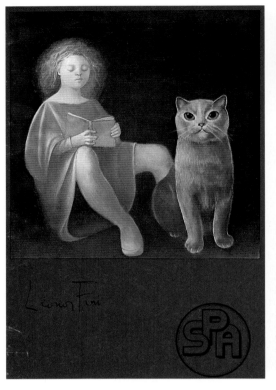

Top left *A poster for the French animal protection society uses a painting by Leonor Fini.*
Top centre *It took the RSPCA and Staffordshire Fire Brigade to rescue this kitten which got stuck up a tree.*
Above *A Parisian group protest against a scheme to exterminate the feral cats of the city, proclaiming that all cats living in France were 'part of the national ecology'.*
Above right *New Zealand RSPCA and Dutch posters (**top right**) encourage the neutering of cats.*
Right *A sticker for the Société Protectrice des Animaux young people's section.*
Far right *A National Petwatch poster draws attention to the use of cat pelts by furriers.*

Animals (founded in 1917), the Blue Cross (1897), the Cats' Protection League (1927), the Feline Advisory Bureau (1958) and the many other animal welfare bodies around the world, all serve their individual purposes. But together they perform a valuable service for all cats; they fight for animal rights, prosecute people who abuse animals, provide or support veterinary services for those who cannot afford private veterinary fees, conduct or finance research into cat disease, behavior and genetics, run refuges for strays, place unwanted cats with new owners, run neutering programmes for feral cats and play a major role in educating the public in better animal welfare. Sadly they are also forced to accept the role of executioner for thousands of unwanted cats and kittens every year.

Several of these organizations concern themselves only with cats, others with all domestic animals, but in recent years the RSPCA, in particular, has been concerning itself not just with the welfare of individual animals but with animal species in general, and with wildlife as well as with domesticated animals and pets. It has always had a role in protecting zoo and performing animals but the increasing threat to wildlife and the cruelties of the wildlife trade led to a change of attitude, marked by the opening of an animal hostel at London Airport. In 1960 the Society set up a Wildlife Committee and it now has a separate Wildlife Department within the organization. Its aims now converge with those of the animal conservation bodies.

The conservation movement

A landmark in what we would now call the conservation movement came in 1890 when William Hornaday, chief taxidermist of the United States National Museum, launched a campaign to save the buffalo.

> 'We are weary,' he wrote, 'of witnessing the greed, selfishness and cruelty of "Civilised" man towards the wild creatures of the earth. We are sick of tales of slaughter and pictures of carnage.'

One influential supporter of such initiatives was Theodore Roosevelt. He appointed a Conservation Committee to assess natural resources, followed in 1909 by a National Conservation Conference, and a world conference was also planned, though dropped when he retired from the Presidency. Roosevelt was an enthusiastic game hunter, and largely responsible for the fashion for African safaris among the wealthy. In this way, he was typical of the blood-sport enthusiasts who, through their hobby of killing animals, gained an understanding of the needs of their prey and were among the first to realize the way in which species were disappearing.

In London in 1903, a group of hunters formed the Society for the Preservation of the Wild Fauna of the Empire, known today as the Fauna and Flora Preservation Society. They gained the nickname 'the Penitent Butchers'. By then Canada, Australia, New Zealand and South Africa had already begun to create National Parks, the Kruger National Park (originally estab-

lished as the Sabi Game Reserve in 1898) in the Transvaal preserving territory for the African cats. In the following decades some European parks were created. So some minimal habitats were preserved, but the killing still continued.

In Africa the 'sportsman' was uncontrolled but in India, from 1880, game laws and the control of the Forest Service set the territory over which an individual could shoot and the number of game that could be taken.

In 1934 the International Office for the Protection of Nature (OIPN) was founded in Brussels and in 1956 this eventually became the International Union for Conservation of Nature and Natural Resources (IUCN). In 1961 this scientific organization was joined by the World Wildlife Fund (now the World Wide Fund for Nature — WWF) which raises money for conservation and plays a major role in educating public awareness of the issues. Many of the other groups which have since been formed to fight for conservation and the environment are able to adopt a more militant approach than these international bodies,

Above The Cat's Wedding. A *display created by taxidermist Walter Potter for his Museum of Curiosity, set up at Bramber, Sussex, in 1861, and now at Jamaica Inn on Bodmin Moor. The museum assures visitors that these kittens and the 37 in the companion* Kittens' Tea and Croquet Party *were not killed just to make these scenes. However, as Harrison Weir complained in the 1880s, many kittens were killed to make stuffed toys for mid-Victorian children and later to make ornaments to clip onto picture frames and mirrors. It is fortunate for today's kittens that people now prefer cartoon cats for such novelties.*

Top left *A kitten in a New Zealand RSPCA centre.*

Top right *Strays in a British PDSA sanatorium in need of a new home.*

Above *Illegal hunters still kill animals for their skins. These Ocelot and Margay pelts were photographed on offer in Brazil but the problem exists in many countries, especially where people live at subsistence level and poaching can provide a far greater income than legitimate employment.*

Right *Not all cat species are fully protected. Hunting is still permitted for Bobcat and Lynx in North America and trapping continues for the fur industry. Each year 70,000 bobcats are trapped, often in steel-jawed gin traps like this, in a photograph issued by the anti-fur trade body 'Lynx'. Such traps have been outlawed in England since 1954 and in Scotland since 1973, although their manufacture is still permitted, so that the law (even in Britain) may well be flaunted.*

which must work closely with national governments. They range from Greenpeace, with a commitment to the total environment, to Lynx, which campaigns specifically against the fur trade and the cruelty it involves.

Despite the vast numbers of big cats taken by white hunters and the maharajahs in Africa and India, the major cause of animal losses has been the clearing of land and removal of game by the advancing settlers. While the African elephant was slaughtered wholesale for its ivory, there was no great international trade in cat family pelts prior to World War Two.

Manchurian hunters had long found a market for tiger skins and parts through mainly Chinese traders but, in the 1950s, striped and spotted furs became fashionable clothing among the world's wealthy and prices sky-rocketed. A possible tiger population in India of 40,000 at the beginning of the twentieth century (though most Indian naturalists consider this estimate too high) dropped to about 4000 by 1946, according to an estimate by Jim Corbett. By 1967 it was down to less than 3000. In South America, 15,000

Convention on International Trade in Endangered Species

CITES provides a worldwide system of controls on international commerce in wild animals and plants, in whole or in part. It identifies and lists species needing protection in three categories. Participating countries are responsible for issuing permits and licences for any trade or movement that is allowed in them:

Appendix I Species threatened with extinction by trade. No permit is issued except for strictly scientific purposes.

Appendix II Species liable to be endangered by trade if not strictly regulated. Trade is monitored and must be properly documented. If trade threatens to become incompatible with survival the Parties may transfer species to Appendix I.

Appendix III Species which individual countries wish to protect, even though they may be common elsewhere, for which that country needs the cooperation of others in enforcement of trade controls.

The IUCN Species Survival Commission established the Trade Record Analysis of Fauna and Flora in Commerce (TRAFFIC), with a network of offices in several countries, with the Wildlife Trade Monitoring Unit (WTMU) in Cambridge, England. Signatories to CITES all reserve the right to permit trade in certain species and, of course, they may impose stricter regulations within their own territories.

By the beginning of 1990 there were 104 countries which had adhered to CITES. They included the major producing and importing countries but the effectiveness of the convention was greatly reduced by defective national legislation and poor enforcement.

Despite international agreements and local protection measures there are still some cat species legally hunted and sold as well as poachers who take wildlife for the smugglers' illegal market.

ocelot skins were exported from the port of Iquitos in 1966 alone. The threat now came not from the holiday safari but from commercial hunters, though the bagging of a tiger whose skin was worth $1000 was an added attraction for the 'sportsman'.

For the tigers protection finally came after an epoch-making General Assembly of the IUCN in Delhi in 1969, which helped to increase concern for other cats. Public outcry led to the retreat of spotted fur fashions in the 1970s, though they still retain an appeal to some of the unthinking affluent.

Many countries now began to establish reserves to protect their wildlife and to pass protection laws. However, although national parks and reserves can be established and hunting prohibited or officially controlled, so long as there is more money to be made from skins or other animal products than from the normal occupations open to local people — if there is work for them at all — there will be those who will flout the rules and risk punishment to supply the trade demand. Hunting controls were clearly not enough. The demand had to be removed or at least reduced. That could only be done by international cooperation to control the trade. In 1960, attempts began to establish an international convention to control wildlife trade. It took 13 years to agree a final draft and not until 1975 did the Convention on International Trade in Endangered Species of Wild Flora and Fauna (CITES) come into effect, ratified by only ten nations.

Trade in the domestic cat

Not only wild species are in danger from the hunter. Professional thieves are known to be stealing domestic pets in Britain, the United States, Australia and other countries. Some are thought to be sold to unscrupulous restauranteurs and many to skin merchants, as this National Petwatch poster points out.

Cat fur has been used as a garment trimming for hundreds of years and the domestic cat has been widely used as a laboratory animal. But the domestic cat is not an endangered species; the opposite is true. There are far too many cats looking for homes as well as feral cats breeding unchecked.

It is undeniable that experiments on cats have brought knowledge of benefit to people, and to other cats, which could not have been obtained in any other way, but many totally unnecessary and often cruel experiments on animals are conducted for various kinds of research or for the testing of yet another cosmetic which could be pursued by other methods. In Britain, for instance, new pesticides and some pharmaceuticals are still *required by law* to be given the LD50 test; this means they are to be applied repeatedly to animals until they kill a percentage of test subjects. There are a number of animal rights organizations which campaign against such testing and against other abuse of animals.

Such practices can only be ended by pressing for legislation against them and refusing to purchase products which have caused suffering either in testing or manufacture.

Less publicized has been an illicit trade in domestic animals which are trapped or stolen for sale to laboratories or for their pelts. National Petwatch, a British organization that has been monitoring cat disappearances for some years, has plotted 'black spots' where large numbers of cats disappear and where gangs of thieves appear to be operating. There are many reports of people seen picking up cats at night and taking them away.

This is not just a British concern. Similar large-scale cat thefts have been reported from Australia, the United States (especially California) and Japan, where cat skins are used to make the traditional musical instrument the *shamisen*, although its manufacturers claim that most skins originate in countries where cats are eaten.

It may be pure sentimentality to dislike the idea of a skin or carcass being used for some practical purpose after death, and there are pet owners who have their animals stuffed, have skeletons mounted or who like the idea of making something from their fur. A popular English children's book writer, for instance, had a much-loved pet stuffed and turned into a pajama case. Any pet owners to whom this would be distasteful should either make their own burial or cremation arrangements or ask whoever is responsible to sign an assurance on the manner of disposal.

PETS NOT PELTS!

WAS THIS ONCE YOUR PET?

A major investigation by National PETWATCH in early 1985 revealed that the vast majority of dead cats are not disposed of by incineration - but go to skin merchants.

The pelts are passed to London furriers where they are either processed ready for export to West Germany and other countries where there are flourishing markets for cat skin garments or they are sent directly to firms such as Steingraf who claim that these pelts - Medicat - ward off arthritis, rheumatism and slipped discs.

The demand for pelts is so great that cats are now being stolen, usually by colour, to supplement these supplies.

NATIONAL PETWATCH   P.O. BOX 16   BRIGHOUSE   WEST YORKSHIRE   HD6 1DS

CONSERVATION

Conservation issues cannot be viewed in isolation. For many years concerned people have been warning that resources were being over-exploited, pollution was getting out of control and our world was being destroyed. At last, perhaps too late, the message is beginning to get through, although many governments and businesses seem only to pay lip service to conservation aims and fail to take effective action.

Over the centuries, the developed nations have destroyed much of their own environment and exploited that of other countries. There is little logic in their censuring the Third World for doing the same, especially when they are still drawing short-term social and economic advantages from that new exploitation and when their own economies are still creating most of the pollution. A change at the consumer level might help to bring about some real change. Each individual's waste of resources and unnecessary consumption increases the problem and is not cancelled out by a contribution to the World Wide Fund for Nature.

In recent years there have been many successes in the conservation battle and some losses have been avoided, but others still multiply. The fight to save the cat family may represent in microcosm the wider struggle for the world. Its problems and issues, repeated and magnified, now affect all our lives.

Conservation for domestic breeds

Domestic as well as wild species can come under threat of extinction. For a long time the Angora cat was absent from the domestic scene and a special breeding programme was established at Ankara Zoo to ensure that it would survive. Similarly there is a breeding establishment on the Isle of Man to ensure that the Manx cat does not disappear.

While some breeds may go out of fashion, others are so modified by changes in breeders' taste that a distinctly different type develops — which is why some cat lovers in the United States are seeking to re-establish the original Siamese type alongside the extreme wedge-shaped cat of the modern American show bench.

A modern safari party on elephants in Bandhogarh National Park, India.

Wildlife reserves

The Royal Forests and Game Reserves of centuries past were areas in which a variety of animals could not be hunted or trapped by ordinary people. Grazing, forestry or agriculture were forbidden or controlled and officials policed and punished any offenders. They were set up to maintain a source of animals for kings, queens, eminent ecclesiatics and licensed noblemen to hunt, and to protect resources with economic value for the benefit of the Crown. In England, for instance, one function was to ensure the supply of wood from which to build the ships of the Royal Navy.

A modern wildlife reserve must have similar controls and, though it is for the preservation of the species, not the pleasure of a nobility, to the indigenous people it may often seem to have been created for others at their expense, much as the king's forests did to a medieval peasant. Today, however, the poacher does not merely steal game from the king's kitchen; he endangers the survival of the animals themselves. The outlaw is no Robin Hood righting wrongs and redistributing incomes in a more egalitarian way but, except for some subsistence poaching for meat in some tribal areas, he is a tool of an exploitive commercial enterprise, one strand in an international web of smuggling and illegal trade.

There are other, more important differences as well. The medieval Royal Forest was maintained for deer and other animals of venery. Natural predators were eliminated and prey populations built up to provide more quarry for the hunter. If big cats had not already disappeared from medieval Europe they would have been deliberately wiped out.

Even managing a park for trees and deer has its conflicts and we now realize that a wildlife reserve, even one set up initially to protect a

Real and fake safaris

Signing CITES covers trade but does not necessarily protect animals within a country where a particular species may not be considered endangered. In South Africa, for instance, it is only in government wildlife reserves that the cats are protected (apart from any culling to control overpopulation). Landowners may still shoot lions and other game on their own property and there are many private reserves where game, including lions and leopards, can be hunted on a limited scale if a permit is obtained to do so. Private game farms now occupy about four times more land than those managed as public parks and reserves and game conservation is to a large extent sponsored by hunters' fees — an argument for hunting which is often put forward in other territories.

Although the Professional Hunters' Association of South Africa considers that for an animal to be a properly hunted trophy it must be free to breed and feed naturally and have a sporting chance of evading the hunter, with hunting banned in so many other territories there have been instances of bogus 'safaris'. To the disgust of the professional hunters it was discovered in 1957 that lions and cheetahs reared in captivity were being released in an enclosure to be shot from the safety of a vehicle by tourist 'hunters', who paid R4,000 for the opportunity to do so. In 1988 an American trophy hunter's application to import a tiger skin revealed that two Bengal Tigers bought from a zoo had been shot on a Vryburg game farm in 1983.

Texan environmentalists were also shocked to discover, in 1988, that specially bred lions were being hunted at the Wallisville Reservoir. To imitate the exploits of the Assyrian kings (though with modern arms) hunters paid fees ranging from $3500 for a young lion reducing to $2500 for an older lion that had lost its teeth. The organizer was fined for running a commercial venture on government land without permission, for breaking litter laws by abandoning a carcass and for not getting the correct permit for some taxidermy — but the hunts are perfectly legal provided the hunt is on private land and the organizer is careful not to break other laws.

Below *Tourists in East Africa get a close-up of a leopard and her cubs.* **Bottom** *The odd behavior of a photographer in a car-mounted mobile 'hide' attracts the attention of a lioness.*

single endangered species, must protect the whole ecology.

A wildlife reserve, apart from those for the protection of plants or creatures with very small territories, can rarely be effectively enclosed, except by natural boundaries. It may be home for part of the year to migratory animals whose routes must be left open. If food becomes scarce or territories are all occupied animals may move out to new territories nearby.

The often conflicting interests of wildlife, local inhabitants, scientists, visitors and national economy must be balanced. In both India and Africa it has been suggested that, in places where once endangered animals have locally increased in numbers and culling becomes necessary, there should be a limited return to hunting by commercial shikars. This could provide much-needed work and income and show local people that reserves do make an economic contribution to their welfare. Similar suggestions are made for the limited exploitation of animal products. The problem is that allowing some legal sales of products from protected species makes it much more difficult to keep illegally obtained products out of the market. The proposers of such policies say that a total ban forces prices up, making poaching and smuggling more viable, and that present policies involve the destruction of confiscated products which could be sold to raise money to improve the fight against the poachers.

Despite legal protection, animals are still being hunted to extinction. Several subspecies of tiger have been lost in recent years, and illegal hunting in Sumatra makes another loss likely. However, India's Project Tiger shows what can be accomplished by a determined government, and also illustrates some typical problems raised by conservation and attempts at their solutions.

A tiger in the Bandhogarh National Park, India, set up as part of Project Tiger.

Return to the wild

Pioneers in the release of big cats back into the wild were George and Joy Adamson with Elsa, an orphaned lion cub, hand-reared from a few days old. Despite her close relationship with them, she was eventually established in the wild, though retaining an attachment so that she brought her cubs to their camp. Sadly, when only five years old, Elsa died of a parasitic infection and the Adamsons had to adopt her cubs in their turn before releasing them again.

These were only the first of the Adamsons' releases. Joy successfully released a cheetah, Pippa and, after the filming of the Elsa story as *Born Free* George set out to rehabilitate lions used in it, including Boy, a former mascot of the Scots Guards in Africa. Then Christian, a circus-born lion sold as a pet by Harrods store in London (when it was still legal to do so) and for a time resident of Kings Road, Chelsea, was sent to Africa to be trained for release.

Although successfully released, Boy later had to be shot when he attacked and killed

one of Adamson's assistants, but there were many other successes. Before his murder by poachers in 1989 George Adamson had been responsible for training 300 lions for the wild.

Others who pioneered the training for release of big cats raised by people include Norman Carr with lions in Africa and Arjan 'Billy' Singh who has successfully released leopards, a tiger and a Fishing Cat in India.

George Adamson in his study.

The Sumatran Tiger: Illegal slaughter

Although the Sumatran Tiger has been fully protected by law since 1972, in 1988 it was reported that only about 800 still survived and that they were being killed illegally at a rate of about 100 each year for the fur trade and medicine markets. How soon will it follow the Javan and Bali tigers into extinction?

The forests of Sumatra are under great environmental pressure. Government-organized mass immigration for resettlement in Sumatra to reduce overpopulation in Java and Bali is placing new pressure on the environment. Heavy exploitation of the forests for logging and slash and burn techniques of farming are reducing habitat. Wide tracks opened up by the loggers have been adopted as easy routes by tigers who patrol their large territories with regularity. This makes it easier for trappers to predict when and where to set their sprung snares, often placing them where a track narrows or two tracks join.

When a trapped animal is found it is shot with a home-made rifle, firing bullets made from melted toothpaste tubes and other available sources of lead, and using powder from match heads.

Depressed markets and falling prices for rubber have left many tappers without an income and about a dozen men have turned to tiger-trapping on a regular basis — a desperate measure for they receive only $100–$150 (US$160–240) per skin. From this they have to bribe forest wardens and others, but wardens are paid too little to resist this supplementary income, which makes their work meaningless and ineffective.

Although providing the official framework for protection of the tiger, government policy and the international commodity markets both work against it, while the destruction of habitat also threatens the long-term resources of the land.

Sumatran Tiger. Will they survive only in zoos?

"Project Tiger"

"The State shall endeavour to protect and improve the environment and to safeguard the forests and wildlife of the country."
Extract from the Constitution of the Indian Union (Bharat).

In 1971, when tiger numbers had fallen to about 2000, WWF launched its Operation Tiger, which quickly gained the support of the governments of India, Nepal and Bangladesh. Except in Burma, tiger hunting was banned. Some WWF aid also went to Thailand and Indonesia, although they had no specific tiger program. CITES signatories were bound neither to import nor to export tiger skins.

In 1973 Indira Gandhi, then Prime Minister of India, launched India's own *Project Tiger*, originally for six years but still continuing with support from the WWF. The Indian central government funds all the nonrecurring costs on approved works and half the recurring expenditure, State governments fund the rest.

There were about 1800 tigers in India when the project started, about one-sixth of them in reserves. Action was begun in nine key areas and habitats aiming at the maintenance of a viable tiger population, the rehabilitation of habitat and the preservation of areas of biological importance for the benefit of the people. By 1987 a census reported 1141 tigers in reserves and a total population of over 4000. New reserves now total 17 Tiger Reserves in 12 States covering 16,150 sq miles (26,000 sq km) of forest.

In total India has 275 national parks and wildlife reserves and has ratified all the main international conservation conventions. Her record shames many other nations and owes a great deal to the late Mrs Gandhi's original enthusiasm.

Each tiger reserve consists of a core area, where wildlife is totally protected, and a surrounding

A tiger with cubs in the Bandhogarh National Park, India.

Billy Singh with Harriet, an orphaned leopard he bottle-reared and released to the jungle at three years of age. She mated with a wild leopard and for the first few weeks looked after her two cubs in a tree house built by Singh before moving them to a natural lair in the jungle. With the monsoon rains the rising river threatened her lair and she reappeared at Singh's farmhouse with her cubs and raised them in the kitchen before vanishing back into the jungle when the floods retreated.
Below *A young tiger, Tara, follows Billy Singh. This tiger was later released into the wild as part of Singh's rehabilitation program but his critics claimed that she became a man-eater.*

buffer area in which grazing, and the collection of bamboo, thatching grass, wild fruits and roots and fuel wood may be permitted. Local people are employed in the construction of patrol roads and watchtowers and other work in the reserve and benefit from the development of water sources created for the wildlife. In some cases people have been resettled away from the reserve and provided with ploughed land and village amenities such as wells, clinics and temples.

If cattle are grazed in the buffer zone some losses to tigers, who find them easy prey, are inevitable, although this is more common with the lions of the Gir Forest. Compensation is paid to the owner, provided that the carcass is produced in evidence.

In two reserves, Dudhwa National Park, in the north of Uttar Pradesh, and in the Sundarbans on the Ganges delta, there has been serious conflict between people and tigers. There is always risk if someone blunders into a tiger's den, especially if it is a mother with cubs, but tigers are rarely habitual man-eaters. At Dudhwa, however, the killing of 95 people by tigers over a period of only five years led to calls for a return to tiger hunting, which could be very lucrative with hunters prepared to pay thousands of dollars for the 'privilege' of killing a single tiger.

Investigation showed that villagers were using the buffer zone to an extent that invited confrontation. Many of the victims had been killed when crouching to defecate or stooping to cut grass, presenting an appearance less obviously human than a standing man and more like that of the usual prey animals. Sugar cane, which is very like the bamboo thickets and high grasses in which tigers rest up during the day, had been planted right up to the edges of the core forest area. This brought tigers out into the buffer zone and close to settlements. Deer also wandered out of the reserve and tigers followed them.

Human lives lost are a tragic way of confirming the importance of proper buffer zones. Arjan 'Billy' Singh, the conservationist whose Tiger Haven abuts the reserve, has fought for many years to get people to accept that by offering controlled feeding of meat or easy kills man-eaters can be 'reformed' and will give up attacking people. One notable success was a tiger which came to be known from its distinctive pugmarks as 'Long-toes'; she had killed four people, the last a man who had unwittingly intruded on her den. After being fed 32 meals which were gradually reduced in quantity, at five-day intervals, she stopped prowling outside the park and kept to a diet of wild herbivores. However, this was a healthy tiger, well able to catch prey. It would not be possible to retrain an incapacitated animal.

Arjan Singh reared leopard and tiger cubs, and a fishing cat, and rehabilitated them in the wild from Tiger Haven. His technique has been to provide food until they have acquired the skills to kill their own. There has been controversy over Tara, one of his released tigers, which Dudhwa officials alleged had become a man-eater because she still lacked those skills. Reserve officials report shooting her, but Singh claims this was another tiger and that he has seen Tara since.

Singh has been active in pressing the conservationist case (he was awarded the WWF's gold medal) and this has sometimes brought him into conflict with other interests. Wider political implications cannot be avoided when fighting the conservation battle.

Swiss lynx

Swiss Lynx have been successfully reintroduced in parts of Sweden and Switzerland and released in the Vosges mountains in France and the Böhmer Forest of Czechoslovakia. There are proposals to reintroduce them in the Massif Central of France, the Abruzzo National Park in Italy and near Innsbruck in Austria as funds and lynx from breeding programmes become available. There has, however, been serious controversy in Switzerland where the first releases were made in 1971. Shepherds complain of predation on their sheep, which are not guarded because for a century there have been no large predators to attack them. If they can prove their animals have been lost to lynx they receive compensation at rates agreed between the government and the sheep-owners.

Hunters allege that lynx are killing too many roe deer and chamois. With the current lynx population of 50–100 they could be taking 3000–6000 a year. It sounds an alarming total but to put it in perspective, it must be realized that three times as many are killed on roads and more than 50 lynx annually have been killed by cars, by hunters or found dead for unknown reasons.

In areas closed to hunting, large chamois and roe deer populations developed. These have been rapidly depleted with the arrival of the lynx who found them easy prey because they were not used to predators. Swiss biologist Urs Breitenmoser, who with Heinrich Haller has trapped 20 lynx and fitted them with radio collars to study their movements, feels sure that prey populations will readapt. Lynx populations have decreased in the areas they first occupied. He hopes this means that as prey populations drop the lynx will need larger territories and move outwards, but Breitenmoser says it is still too early to judge the impact of the reintroduction of the lynx.

The Sundarbans

The Sundarbans is a great expanse of mangrove forest and swamp that stretches across the border between India and Bangladesh for 6250 sq miles (10,000 sq km). The Sundarbans have a long history of man-eating tigers (records go back at least to 1660) with the huge number of 1046 lives lost in 1902. In recent years there have been about 50 annual killings in the combined Indian and Bangladeshi Sundarbans.

No one now lives within the area of the Indian Tiger Reserve itself and few tigers move outwards to inhabited areas. Those that have show no sign of attacking human prey but several of them have been captured and removed to Calcutta Zoo. The core area is accessible only to Reserve staff and scientists, and permits are required to enter the buffer zone. The fishermen, honey collectors and wood gatherers who traditionally use the area are banned from key areas during the breeding period, when tigers are more likely to attack, and permits to collect *Phoenix paludosa* for thatch have not been issued since 1979, because it forms the tiger's favourite den.

Man-eating may come about because a tiger, especially if injured or under pressure to feed its cubs, is short of food and finds people easy prey. To counter this and discourage attacks on livestock and villages on the perimeter, pigs have been released into the forest when tigers have roamed near the borders.

Researcher Kalyan Chakrabarti found man-eating unrelated to tiger density, as indicated by their pugmarks; the most highly populated area came only fifth in victim numbers. He did find a link between aggression and salinity; 20 percent of casualties have been in areas of pure *Ceriops* growth, where soil and water are at maximum salinity. As a result new rainwater pools have been constructed.

Most kills have been made at 7–8am or 3–5pm, which are within usual periods of tiger activity. Attacks appear to peak just before and after full and new moons as though there is a element of periodicity.

Tigers will swim out and pull people from boats, often so quietly and efficiently that their presence is unknown until the plop of the body into the water is heard. Attacks on land are usually from behind and on the right nape of the neck. For this reason it has been recommended that people carry a strong stick of *Ceriops* wood on the right shoulder. Fiberglass armor covering head, nape and chest, with iron spikes on a back piece has been developed and no one wearing this has been attacked. Simpler, but so far effective, has been a face mask worn on the back of the head. Wearers have reported seeing tigers following them for many hours but not attacking, while several wearers fell victim when they temporarily took off their masks.

An entrance to the Sundarbans Tiger Reserve on the delta of the Ganges. Special measures have been necessary in this reserve to counter persistent man-eating.

Below left *Electrified dummies dressed in old clothes which retain a human scent were an experiment to discourage tigers from attacking people. When first introduced spoor marks showed that tigers which attacked them subsequently kept clear. Batteries must be frequently replaced to keep them effective. Recently some tigers seem to have been undeterred. Has this conditioning failed?*
Below centre *A fishing boat electrified to deter tigers from boarding or trying to pull fishermen overboard.*
Below *Tigers habitually attack from the rear and face masks worn on the back of the head seem to be successful in deterring them, though some local people fear that tigers are too intelligent to be deceived in this way for long.*

Above *Towser, born in the still house of Scotland's oldest operational distillery in 1963, worked right up to his death in 1986 catching an average of three mice a day — achieving a world record total of over 28,899 mice according to the* Guinness Book of Records.

Below *The pictorial story of a stowaway aboard ship. A ship's cat reported in an issue of the* Graphic *published in London in 1883.*

WORKING CATS

Except for the period in which it became the subject of persecution for its supposed occult and devilish connections, 'the harmless, necessary cat', as Shakespeare called it, earned a place on farms and in houses as a rat and mouse catcher. It has been encouraged to stay by supplementary feeding and the shelter provided by barns or homes and its numbers are kept in check by removal of surplus kittens, or more recently by neutering.

In storehouses and factories, government departments, museums and many kinds of public buildings cats have done a similar job. Their function has often been recognized by an official position on the payroll, or at least a specific allowance made for their keep. Elsewhere they have been looked after by cat-loving members of the staff who have befriended them. Many individual cats have not only been good workers but also established favorites with human members of the workforce, popular with visitors and even becoming celebrities in their own right.

In large outdoor complexes, where there may be many cats, they often live as feral animals with human contact mainly through auxiliary feeding, but they can still do a useful job of rodent control.

Champion of all mousers was Towser, who was on the staff of Scotland's oldest whisky distillery. From 1963 until his death in 1987 he was credited with catching 28,899 mice! His successor, young Mr Toddy, hardly had a chance to notch up any score at all before he was kidnapped in 1988. There is still a reward on offer for his safe return. Another Scottish rodent operative is Smudge, a paid up member of Branch 29 of the General, Municipal, Boilermakers and Allied Trades Union, who works at the Glasgow People's Palace (now a museum) on Glasgow Green.

Below *Towser's successor, Mr Toddy.*

1

2

3

6

4

5

7

1. Tiddles was another famous cat, responsible for the night patrol of London's Paddington station. His core territory was the ladies' lavatory where he turned up as a bedraggled kitten in 1970 and was taken in by June Watson, who ran the facilities. She is seen here showing off Tiddles and his press cuttings to a visitor. He became extremely popular, ladies calling in just to see him — out of bounds, of course, to other gents — and add to his collection saucer for animal charities. His basket and corner was lavishly decorated for special occasions and the Silver Jubilee display in 1977 gained him international attention and a flood of extra mail for fan club secretary June to answer. Once, for a treat, June took him home with her but it was not to his liking and he was obviously delighted to go back to Paddington. Well fed and cared for, Tiddles weighed in at 33 lb (15 kg) before he died in 1983.

2. Stable cat is another time-honored occupation. Cats often have an excellent rapport with horses, most famously one who became the special friend of the Godolphin Arabian (also known as Godolphin Barb) and who, in 1731, founded one of the three famous lineages of thoroughbreds.

3. Ale, rather than the hard stuff, is the responsibility of Biggles at the Plough and Sail Inn at Snape.

4. Cats have found work in all manner of places. Farm cat might be considered the nearest to a freelance occupation.

5. Christmas is appropriately named for a cat in employment with the clergy.

6. Egyptian grain stores may have played a role in the early stages of domestication and a traditional windmill certainly needs a cat.

7. Oriental temple cats used to keep rats from sacred scrolls and books and have an honorable successor in this librarian cat.

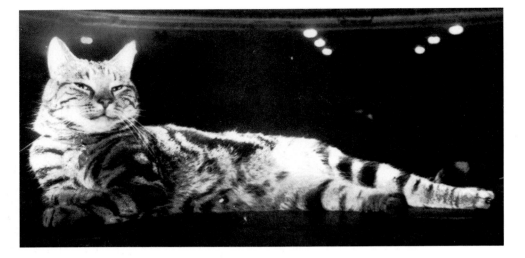

Beerbohm, a theatre cat in the tradition of T.S. Eliot's.

Nini, resident at a coffee house in Venice towards the end of the last century as an attraction to custom, had a visitors' book in which popes and kings signed their names, and Giuseppe Verdi entered a few bars of *La Traviata*.

Tommy, the post office cat, of Hartford, Connecticut, learned a number of tricks and performed them at a postmen's benefit concert, while Blackie, of London's Post Office Headquarters from 1972–84 was the last of a line that stretched back to 1868. His pay had doubled from a pound to two pounds per week by the time he died.

Royal Navy ships often had a cat, but since the introduction of strict quarantine laws the practice has had to end, though shore establishments continue to employ them. Charlie, service number C1111115, held a Navy pay book and was on duty at the shore base at Chatham when he was run over at only one year old in 1981. He was given a full military funeral. The base was closed soon after so he had no successor.

The Home Office in London's Whitehall, however, had a succession of cats from 1883 onwards, all called Peter and always black; that is, until 1964 when a black Manx got the job whose sex meant that she had to be called Peta. At five shillings a day she was earning much more than the Post Office's Blackie when she was retired in 1974. Sadly, along with much else in Britain, rodent control in the Civil Service seems to have been 'privatised' in the 1980s under Prime Minister Thatcher and good working cats have had to make way for commercial companies who rely on poisons rather than hunting skills, a backward step ecologically.

Hamlet, the cat of the Algonquin Hotel, New York, probably thought himself too much of a celebrity to do his own rat catching. Many well-known people tried to cash in on his fame by being photographed with him. He died in 1982 but there have been two successors, Hamlet II and Hamlet III.

Most famous of museum cats was Mike, who for 20 years stationed himself at the gates of the British Museum. He was introduced to Sir Ernest Wallis Budge, Keeper of the Egyptian Department (with its mummified cats) in 1909, when just a kitten, by Black Jack, a local cat that voluntarily took on the job of Reading Room cat under the great dome of the museum's library. Sir Ernest, the only person other than the gatekeeper who was allowed to pet him, published a 165-page obituary after Mike's demise and several other scholars also commemorated him in verse.

Right The Palace Guards *by Rudolph Ernst, dated 1890. Not as romantic a notion as it looks. Oriental potentates did keep tamed big cats and the Emperor Haile Selassie of Ethiopia had lions roaming around his palace.*

Right Cheetah and Stag with Two Indians *painted by George Stubbs in 1765. The cheetah was taken to England by Sir George Pigot. He presented it to George III, who in turn gave it to his brother the Duke of Cumberland. The background shows Windsor Park where it was sent to hunt deer, but without success.*

Hunting with cats

It is not only the rodent-catching domestic cat that has been put to work. The Egyptians apparently used their cats as retrievers. When Marco Polo and his uncles made their famous journey across Asia in the thirteenth century Marco saw 'small leopards and lynxes, (actually cheetahs and caracals) and what he called lions, though since they had stripes they were probably tigers, being used like hunting dogs.

Kublai Khan, the Mongol founder of the Yu'an dynasty of China, whose empire stretched from Turkey to the Pacific, had enclosed game parks, similar to those of the Assyrians, stocked with deer and other animals which he hunted with hawks and with trained cheetahs which were 'mounted pillion behind their keepers: ready, at the word of command, to give chase to a deer or antelope.'

The 'lions' which had 'a thick, glossy coat marked with bands of black, white and red,' must surely have been tigers. They were used for hunting boar, wild oxen and bears. To help control the ferocity of the tigers when released each was trained to live with a small dog.

Cheetahs, or 'hunting leopards' had been trained for centuries. A Mesopotamian seal dating from earlier than 2000 BC appears to show a cheetah on a leash and with a hood over its head.' There are hunting cheetahs shown in Egyptian tomb and temple art and both the Assyrians and the Minoans are thought to have used them.

Crusaders saw cheetahs used for sport in Syria and Palestine and later hunting packs were established at some European courts, such as that of the Emperor Frederick II. In the fifteenth century the Dukes of Ferrara and Milan each had hunting packs. A Ferrara cheetah, trained to go after hares, was presented to Louis XI of France and, after Louis XII conquered Milan, the Sforza pack was taken back to France where the king hunted with them at Chateau d'Amboise. Louis' successors, Francis I and Henry II also hunted with cheetahs.

Indian miniatures, painted to illuminate a record of the reign of the Mogul emperor Akbar (1542-1605), depict cheetah being captured in traps and scenes which show clearly how they were used for hunting.

Hunting or coursing with cheetah did not survive in Europe, despite an attempt to revive it by Leopold of Austria around 1700. It remained a popular sport with some eastern rulers up to recent times; the Gaekwar of Baroda kept a pack and the Maharajah of Kolhapur maintained a large stable, importing animals from Kenya. These were trained to chase buck and, it was claimed, to kill only males, which have darker coats, to encourage which their food was brought by men in dark clothes while their regular attendants wore light colors. They lived in a large dormitory, each with its own platform bed, and except when hunting, or being fed or exercised had a black mask tied over their eyes. They were taken to hunt by car or truck and released to course after black buck to amuse the Maharajah and his friends. If they struck down a female they

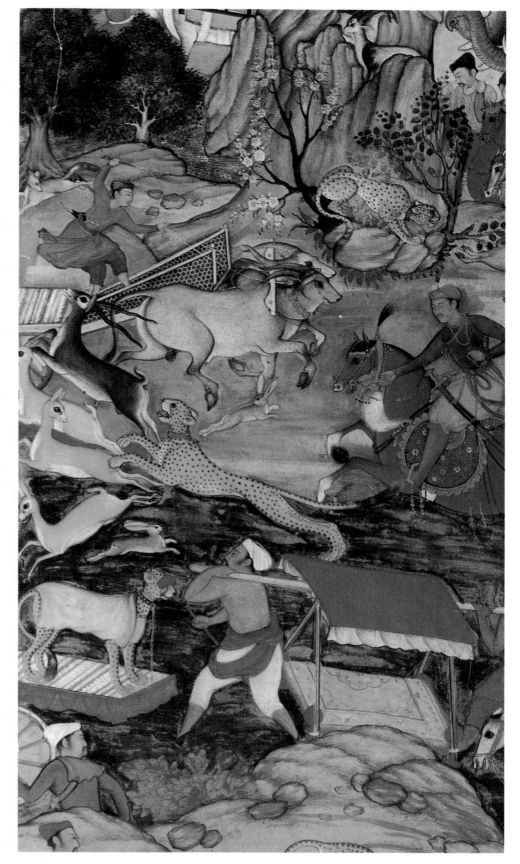

An illustration from the Akbar Nama *painted about 1590. Cheetah were taken to the hunting ground on litters, their eyes covered with a hood, like a falcon's, then transferred to ride pillion behind their keeper. They would be sent after quarry like coursing hounds and, having struck it down, would wait for their master to come and complete the kill. Akbar's flattering chronicler, Abu Fazil, records that the Emperor trained some cheetah himself — and more quickly than was usual. On one hunt a particular cheetah called Najan followed a deer across a ravine, making a leap of 70 ft (21 m) to the astonishment of all who saw. Akbar gave this animal the rank of 'Chief of Cheetahs' and ordered that he should be given the honor of a drum being beaten before him.*

were punished by having the carcass taken from them, but they were allowed to eat some of each male kill before the venison was removed to the Maharajah's kitchens.

The Maharajah also tried to train leopards to hunt, but without success.

JOHN AUSTIN

Respectfully invites the Nobility, Gentry, and the Public,
to view his Collection of

ANIMALS
OF
OPPOSITE NATURES
LIVING IN ONE CAGE,
WHICH ARE SHOWN ON
Waterloo Bridge, Mondays, Wednesdays, and Fridays;
AND ON
Southwark Bridge, Tuesdays, Thursdays, and Saturdays.

The Proprietor begs leave to inform the Public, that for nineteen years it has been his constant study and employment to train animals of opposite natures and birds of various kinds to live together in peace and contentment. Any person viewing this collection will perceive that the time has not been uselessly employed, and must be greatly surprised at the extraordinary effect here produced by habit and gentle discipline, when he sees cats, rats, and mice, in company with hawks, pigeons, owls, and other birds; likewise rabbits, guinea pigs, and squirrels, living on terms of friendship with them in the same cage. In this collection, revengeful passions are not known; the weak are without fear, and the strong without the desire to injure; the rats and mice go to sleep under the cats; rabbits and pigeons playfully contend for a lock of hay; birds sometimes perch on the head of a cat, eat, and frequently rest for the night there;—as one family, they feed out of the same dish, and are so harmless, that children may take the mice in their hands, and play with them in perfect safety. The birds being set at liberty, take flight, but soon return and rejoin their curious companions; in a word, this is one of the rarest curiosities ever seen, and well worthy the attention of the Public.

Above *A nineteenth-century advertisement for a trained cat show.*
Below right *Eight cats, their heads and paws poking through holes, make the sounds of this cat organ. From the keyboard a peg-legged devil directs a choir of demonic animals. This print by seventeenth-century artist Franz van der Wyngaert links the cat organ with witchcraft but such associations are not necessarily implied.*
Above right *These much happier singing cats, in a sixteenth-century print, appear to be performing a round or fugue, each with its score for 'Mi miaou'. The advertisement above announces: Boarding pupils taken here and the master comes to perform in town.*

The capture and taming of animals has always involved an element of training to make them fit into a human environment and to make them controllable, especially necessary with those members of the cat family which are potentially dangerous. Everyone who has a domestic cat as a pet imposes on it a pattern of behavior which is not that of the wild cat. It is only one stage further to teach a cat some games or tricks and to exploit it as an entertainer.

Although Roman animal trainers had big cats performing in the *venationes* of classical times, and some were trained to pull chariots for Imperial appearances, they would have been difficult and dangerous animals for traveling entertainers to take from fair to fair when roads were poor and transportation primitive. Although dancing bears were taken from place to place there is no evidence of big cats being presented until more recent times.

Musical cats

Domestic cats, except for the temporary novelty of imported types, attracted little attention in themselves but were among the many animals which were made to perform for popular spectacles. When the future Philip II of Spain visited Brussels in 1594, as Prince of Castille, a cart with an 'organ of cats' formed part of a procession in his honor. About 20 cats, chosen according to the pitch of their voices, were shut up in boxes, too small to allow any movement, with their tails hanging out through holes. Cords tied to the tails were connected to organ pedals and a tame bear was used to press the organ keys which tightened the strings to pull the tails and make the cats cry out.

A cat organ is illustrated in Gaspard Schott's *Magia universalis* of 1657 and another seventeenth-century print by Franz van der Wyngaert shows a devil conducting a choir of demonic animals from the keyboard of a similar cat piano. Such contrivances were seen in Paris in 1753 and Prague in 1773 and Champfleury

describes one in which the keys drove sharp spikes into the cats at the base of their tails.

Some people continued to find such things amusing. A print published in 1883 illustrates a 'cat piano' that must have relied upon similar kinds of cruelty, though since these cats are shown in open boxes it is perhaps more surprising that they kept quiet than that they screamed on cue.

A sixteenth-century French engraving presents a much happier picture of cats in a performance that combines the physical and the vocal, in which they are under no physical restraint.

Cat concerts or 'Miaulique' Shows (as a booth at Saint Germain announced them) seem to have been a feature of some eighteenth-century fairs, while a trainer called Bisset put on what he called a 'Cats' Opera' at a hall near London's Haymarket in 1758.

Trained cats

Cats can be reared with mice and birds so that they do not treat each other as predator and prey. They have been exhibited as curiosities by street entertainers with mice and birds sitting on a cat's head or being carried in its mouth. Training a cat to give a performance is much more difficult. Cats may invent their own virtuoso display and perform it at their whim but, though you may be able to teach them tricks, to get them to perform to order is another matter.

American writer Agnes Repplier described a visit to the Folies-Bergère in Paris early this century when an animal trainer presented a troupe of poodles, monkeys and a cat in which

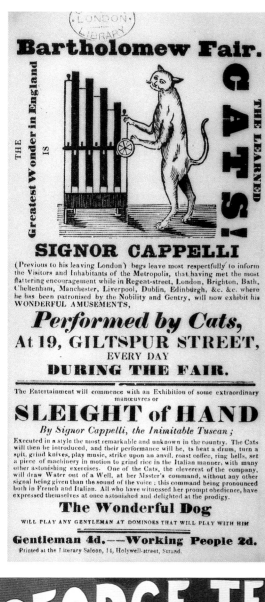

the cat jumped through a hoop, balanced on a rubber ball, came down a ladder on her ball, played a fiddle and then stood on her head. However, on the night that Miss Repplier saw the show, the cat gave up after balancing the ball, retired to the top of the ladder to wash herself and settled down to sleep, totally ignoring the entreaties of her trainer. A friend who went to another performance thought that the cat was there only as decoration for, when she saw the show, the cat struck out at the monkeys and then merely sat on the ladder and watched!

Signor Cappelli, from Tuscany, toured Europe showing his family of 'learned cats', which he had taught to perform all kinds of mechanical activities from roasting coffee to sharpening knives. He visited London in 1829 and 1832 and the *Literary Gazette* declared that the cats'

'restoration to rational functions is the best proof we have yet met with of the progress of education and the march of mind'.

One cannot help but wonder why!

Toward the end of the century Harrison Weir saw an act in which cats began by running across the stage on cue, leapt over a variety of obstacles and topped this by walking a tightrope on which white rats, then mice and birds, were placed at intervals, naturally without harming them. One or two

'stopped and cosseted one or more of the white rats, two of which rode triumphantly on the back of a large black cat'.

The cats Weir saw were probably George Techow's famous nineteenth-century troupe of

Left *Handbill for Signor Cappelli's 1832 performances in London.* **Below** *Poster for George Techow's cat troupe which played variety theaters and vaudevilles at the end of the nineteenth century.*

performing cats. They could jump through hoops of fire, balance on their front paws and do all the kinds of tricks Weir describes. Techow claimed that a stray was easier to teach than well-cared-for cats:

'half-starved ... forced to defend himself from foes and to snatch his living where he can, [he] has his perceptive faculties enlarged. I cannot teach a kitten. I take them from a year or two or three years old, and train them three years longer before it is safe to put them on the stage with confidence in their performing the tricks they may have mastered.'

Herr Techow may not have been very scientific in his brain cell theory but he clearly understood the need to invest a great deal of time and patience to achieve success.

Circus acts

Circus and variety acts with domestic cats are very rare today, perhaps because success is so hard to achieve, but Yuri Kouklachev, star of the Moscow State Circus, is a modern cat trainer. 'Patience and care are the secret,' he says. 'I noticed that cats are more alive at night so I began to play with them then, gain their confidence and begin to teach them simple tricks.' He also says that it takes three years to train cats in an act which includes jumping over obstacles, doing 'handstands' and playing chess.

Modern circuses, as opposed to those of Rome and Byzantium, had their origin in the equestrian displays given in Lambeth, London, in 1768 by Philip Astley, a former Sergeant Major in the British Army, who turned trick rider. The name came into use four years later when the Royal Circus was opened in Blackfriars Road in competition with Astley's, only half a mile away in Westminster Bridge Road. The idea was soon copied in France, Russia and, in 1793, in the United States at Philadelphia and New York.

An American, T.A. van Amburgh is said to have been the first to introduce a wild animal or 'jungle' act along with the acrobats and horses, though it is not certain exactly when. Both 1820 and 1833 are given as dates when he appeared entering a cage with jungle animals. The innovation is sometimes credited to another great circus manager, the Italian Antonio Franconi, but he seems to have made only an isolated appearance and not to have presented a regular act. Amburgh, the high point of whose act was to put his head into a lion's mouth, made his New York debut at the Zoological Institute, not in fact an educational institution but a pompous name to give respectability to a circus show.

Wild animal acts developed along different lines in Europe and America. The American style emphasized the savagery of the animals, generating excitement as the pistol-firing, whip-cracking trainer risked his life by pitting his will against that of roaring animals. European taste was for an act which emphasized the skill of the trainer and the obedience of the animals, though retaining enough of their wildness to add an extra frisson of danger.

Above *A nineteenth-century naive painting of a big cat trainer with an unusual litter of ligons. Does this record a real mating between circus animals?*

Opposite *The great American showman, P.T. Barnum, who founded The Greatest Show on Earth, joined with J.A. Bailey in creating the Barnum and Bailey Circus in 1881.*

Below *One of the feline stars of the Moscow State Circus with trainer Yuri Kouklachev.*

Henri Martin, a trainer from Marseilles, presented dramas in which he and his lions played a major part. His three-act *The Lions of Mysore* was so popular that he retired on the profits and went to live in the Netherlands where he helped to found the Amsterdam Zoo.

German animal collector and zoo director Carl Hagenbeck was also fascinated by animal training. He was horrified by the techniques involving cruel whips and red-hot irons which he saw some trainers use to control their animals and believed that a gentle training based on trust and kindness would be equally effective. He established a circus in 1887 and employed a trainer who would follow methods he approved, based on a system of rewards and punishments. He began the experiment by training dogs and then went on to training lions. Starting off with 21 big cats he decided that only four of them showed any aptitude as performers.

Mary Chipperfield, the internationally famous British animal trainer (whose father started the Safari Park at Longleat), develops a very close relationship with her animals. She has hand-raised many of her performers in her own home. She believes that the easiest big cats to train for performance are those that are born in captivity and hand-reared. All the animals she trains today have been captive-born in zoos, safari parks and circuses.

Some trainers have utilized the animals' natural aggression in their training, inciting the lions and tigers to 'come on' at them, but Mary Chipperfield uses the inducement of a titbit of meat on the end of a stick to bring them forward. For instance, if she wanted them to step from one

Right *Playbill for a performance by T.A. van Amburgh at Astleys in 1838.*
Opposite *Big cat trainers were a major attraction of the great international circuses at the turn of the century.*

rostrum to another, she would first place a rostrum between her and the cat and then encourage it to advance. Then she would add a second rostrum for the animal to climb. To get an animal to leap from one rostrum to another she first taught it to walk across the two, then moved the rostra apart a little at a time, until the walk became first a jump and then a leap.

With the big cats training does not begin until the animals have reached the end of cubhood. With tigers that means about 18 months old, when they are most curious to learn. The routine is developed slowly and each day's session follows the same basic pattern.

One lion, Marquis, which Mary had reared from a cub, she even managed to teach to ride on the back of her Spanish stallion, Jarro. An

Left Mary Chipperfield with the young Marquis, hand-reared at Longleat. The rejected cub of one of Longleat's first lions, he later become head of one of the Longleat prides. He was father and grandfather of many cubs before his death at the age of 19.

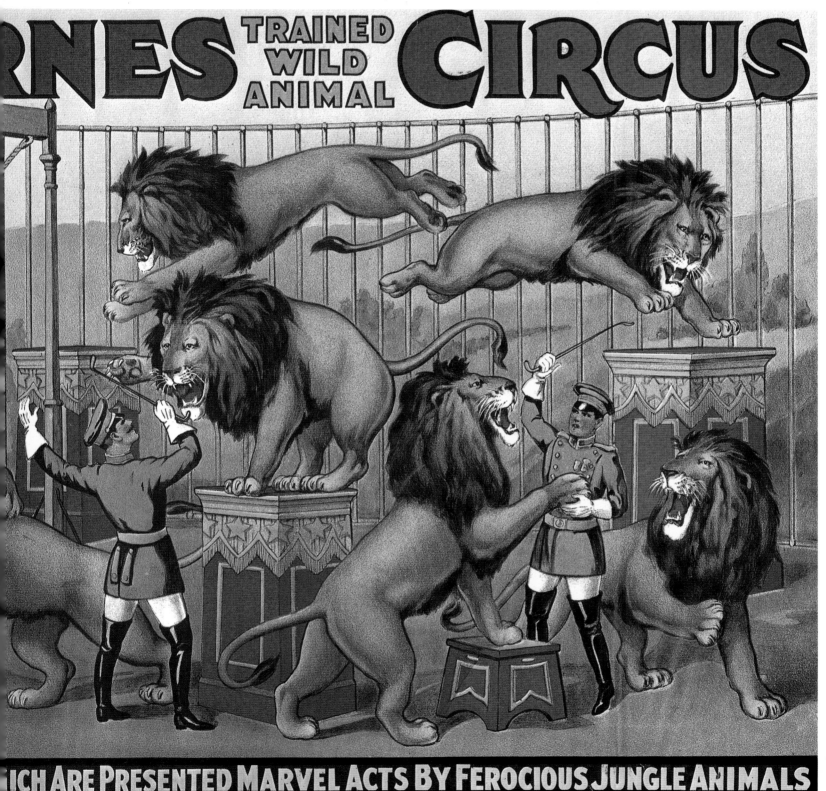

RNES TRAINED WILD ANIMAL CIRCUS

ICH ARE PRESENTED MARVEL ACTS BY FEROCIOUS JUNGLE ANIMALS

amazing achievement given the natural fear which horses have of a predator leaping on their backs. First she started taking the lion with her when she went to groom the stallion in his stable. Later she left the lion chained in the stable for long periods, close enough for the two animals to get used to each other but without being able to touch. Meanwhile she trained Jarro to accept dogs leaping on his back, gradually increasing the size of the dog, while Marquis was trained to climb on circus rostra and to jump from one pedestal to another. When the lion had got used to jumping on a pedestal the same height as Jarro's back the horse was substituted — and Marquis became a jockey!

Mary has worked with animals all her life and seems to have a natural command over them, an authority that is absolutely necessary if she is to maintain control in the circus ring. Outside the ring she can be totally relaxed with them. She used to regularly swim with her tiger Sukie and it is clear that she and her animals have a close affection for each other.

Many people now feel that there is no place for animal acts in circuses. They find such performances demeaning to the animal, believe it wrong to make an animal do something that is not part of its natural behavior and feel that training involves both fear and cruelty. The confinement necessary for a traveling show and even the housing of a permanent circus certainly imposes unnatural constraints, and the creation of natural environments as in progressive zoos is impracticable. On the other hand if animals are confined, as Mary Chipperfield points out,
'training gives them exercise and directed play fills some of the gap left when they do not have to hunt for prey and do not have the freedom to invent their own group games with other animals.'

While trainers with such a genuine love of animals in the Hagenbeck tradition would never consciously be cruel to them, organizations such as the RSPCA point out that the way in which big cats often respond to commands during a performance, slinking across the ring with belly close to the ground, sometimes snarling and with ears flattened, is itself characteristic of a frightened animal.

As with all animal rights issues it is difficult to see an ethical difference between teaching a horse to become a mount or haulage animal, disciplining a cat to suit a pet owner's life style and teaching a big cat tricks. If there are valid reasons for keeping an animal captive, then teaching it tricks and games is certainly one way of trying to avoid the bad effects of restraint and boredom.

Top *Mary Chipperfield training her tiger Bengal. She begins training big cats at about 18 months old. She has trained many kinds of animals, including 30 domestic cats which had to walk in a line down a village street in the film of Doctor Dolittle.*
Above *Mary Chipperfield performing with her tigers at the Blackpool Tower Circus. She spends a lot of time sitting and feeding them in order to discover their different characters and aptitudes. She can then use them to advantage in her act for, like humans, each is a distinct individual. In her experience, females make the best jumpers and she keeps the big, heavy males for slower tricks such as walking, lying down and rolling over.*

Teaching your own cat tricks

Few domestic cats are amenable to being taught tricks and not everyone would agree with George Techow that it is best to wait until they are grown up before attempting to teach them. Basic training in how you wish the cat to behave in your home should certainly be done as early as possible.

Cats play for their own amusement, not to ingratiate themselves with owners, and are less likely than dogs to learn tricks. However, if you can devise a game that the cat really enjoys, something like retrieving or a form of chase, you may find it initiating the action. Similarly, a cat may well invent a novel way of getting your attention. Pulling a pen out of your hand, blocking the movement of a typewriter carriage or just sitting on the book you are reading are typical ploys when they feel you have been putting other pursuits above their interests.

Try to make anything you want to teach your cat grow from some existing natural activity. If you want your cat to jump

through a hoop or balance on a see-saw you are going to need a lot of patience and will need to build up to it one stage at a time. Start off with the hoop or see-saw plank on the floor. Play a game the cat already likes or offer it a titbit to make it walk to you through the hoop or along the plank; just holding a favorite food morsel in front of it may work. Pulling a piece of string is more likely to make it wait and pounce.

Once the first action is well established, slightly raise the hoop on a support or tilt the plank slightly while still keeping it rigid; gradually increase the jump or angle. Try placing the hoop on a chair the cat is already used to jumping up to, or lean the plank against one. Eventually hold the hoop up in the air or place the plank on a pivot. You may need to go back to near floor level again and gradually raise the height. Always begin each stage of the learning process with actions that the cat has already added it its repertoire.

Cats of stage and screen

Training cats to repeat well learned tricks is one thing. Getting them to respond within the dramatic situation of a stage play can be much more difficult which is why they are rarely required to do more than run on or off or curl up quietly. Filmed drama is able to make more demands for the action only has to be got right once and there can be many tries, although, as anyone who saw Truffaut's *Day for Night* will remember even getting a kitten to lap from a jug of cream can prove frustrating!

Food baits, scent trails and sound signals can all be used to direct an animal into particular actions. For *Born Free* George Adamson became live 'bait' for the film cubs to stalk and leap on but their closeness to him triggered inhibiting responses when their muzzles touched his neck. To create one confrontation two lionesses were separately encouraged to treat a particular rock platform as their own territory so that they would dispute it when released there together.

There have been movies such as the Japanese *I am a Cat* (1975), depicting humans filmed from the cat's point of view, and others with people peripheral to the story such as *The Adventures of Chatran* (1986) and Disney's *The Incredible Journey* (1963). There have been horror movies with demon cats or people turning into cats.

Movie animals have their own version of the 'Oscar' and several of the winners have been cats. *Rhubarb* (1951) won the first Picture Animal Top Star Award (PATSY) from the American Humane Association for its feline star. Cat in

Breakfast at Tiffany's (1962) and Tonto in *Harry and Tonto* (1985) have been other winners. Morris, who won in 1973, was the star of Nine Lives pet food commercials and famous throughout America. His British counterpart was Arthur, star in Spiller's Kattomeat commercials. The original Morris and Arthur both had successors. Another cat well known from advertising was Solomon, a Chinchilla who promoted Kosset carpets for many years and also had roles in James Bond movies.

The first cat movie star was Felix, a cartoon cat who made his debut in 1922 (although George Herriman's *Krazy Kat* strip had also been transferred to film in 1916). There have been many cartoon cats since, including Tom with his mouse sidekick Jerry (who appeared in 154 shorts and in live-action movies with Gene Kelly and Esther Williams), Sylvester, with canary Tweety Pie, Top Cat, the streetwise television star, and the X-rated Fritz! Feature length cartoons have had feline villains, such as the cat in Disney's *Pinocchio*, and heroes like the title kitten in the same studio's recent *Oliver and Company*, a feline version of *Oliver Twist*. Top of the cat cartoons, perhaps, was Disney's 1970 *Aristocats*, but there are bound to be many more.

Oddest of screen cats perhaps is 'Cat' in the *Red Dwarf* television series. The ship's cat of a space ship, only survivor of its species after earth has been destroyed; he has evolved into a humanoid 'hip-cat' though still with feline instincts.

Below *The 1951 remake of the early Christian epic* Quo Vadis *was a field day for the animal handlers. Here the Colosseum lions are seen off set.*
Below right *In a scene from* Quo Vadis *Robert Taylor pours a drink for Patricia Laffan's Empress Poppea, never seen without her pair of cheetahs.*

Left *Ray Milland and Jan Sterling with Rhubarb in Rhubarb, a comedy about a ginger alley cat to whom a millionaire left his money. The film was 'held together by the splendid performance of the disdainful feline in the title role' according to movie pundit Leslie Halliwell.*

Below *Paul Mazursky's Harry and Tonto was a touching story of an elderly widower evicted from his New York home, who treks to Chicago with his cat. Art Carney, splendid as Harry, was well-matched by his feline co-star.*

Right *Cat is abandoned by Holly Golightly towards the end of Blake Edwards movie version of* Breakfast at Tiffanys, *starring Audrey Hepburn and George Peppard.*

Below *The Cowardly Lion (Bert Lahr), Dorothy (Judy Garland), the Tin Man (Jack Haley) and the Scarecrow (Ray Bolger) in Mervyn Le Roy's film version of* The Wizard of Oz.

Above *Cat (Danny John Jules), the hip-cat evolved from the space ship's ordinary feline, in Paul Jackson Production's popular television space-comedy series* Red Dwarf.

Right and below right *Katherine Hepburn and Cary Grant in Howard Hawk's* Bringing up Baby — *baby is the leopard!*

Below *Cats have had their share of horror movies too. Things got much worse than this for Gayle Hunnicutt in* Eye of the Cat.

Right *Kim Novak and Pyewacket the cat in Richard Qine's screen version of John van Druten's witchcraft comedy* Bell, Book and Candle.

Far right *A gentle-looking Chinchilla Persian cat points up the evil of Herman Bloefeld (Donald Pleasance) in the James Bond movie* You Only Live Twice. *The same cat, called Solomon, also featured with the villain Charles Gray in* Diamonds are Forever.

CARTOON CATS

Which were the first cartoon cats? They were around long before the animated film. Do the comic drawings of ancient Egypt count or the cats in the margins of medieval manuscripts? Cat-mad Louis Wain's anthropomorphic cats are shown in humorous situations and occasionally used for political comment. The big cats have often featured in political cartoon as representatives of imperial powers, while a New Zealand politician was regularly portrayed as a tom cat.

The Rainbow, Britain's first children's comic magazine, featured a colony of Wain-like cats in 1914, but by then Herriman had already created Krazy Kat, forerunner of a number of strip-cartoon characters in both juvenile and adult publications.

Outstanding among modern cartoonists, all of whose cats maintain an essential feline nature, are Frenchman Siné, Sven Hartman and Thomas Hartner with their Jacob, America's Saul Steinberg, Bernard Kliban and Jim Davis (with his anarchic fat cat Garfield), and the inimitable British artist Ronald Searle.

There have been many cartoon successors to Krazy Cat and Felix, including Tom, the cat half of Tom and Jerry (**below**) and Jim Davis's much-loved cat Garfield (**left**); also comic book Corky and the creations of Searle, Kliban, Watterson, Bentley and Joliffe (**opposite below**).

Left George Herriman's Felix, the first cartoon cat created as a newspaper strip in 1910, transferred to the movies in 1916.

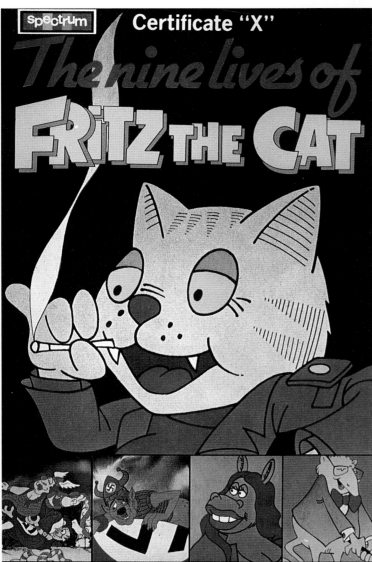

Fritz, created by Robert Crumb, was seen in an underground magazine before his sexually explicit behavior gave this movie the first X-rating for a cartoon film.

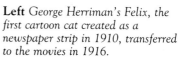

Louis Wain, who became president of the National Cat Club in 1890 drew cat show studies for magazines as well as the remarkable output of humorous cats in human situations with which he made his reputation.

CAT LOVERS — AND OTHERS

There are people who are allergic to cats. Fine particles of cat fur and dander, carried in the air, often set off a reaction similar to hay fever. The sufferers deserve our sympathy, especially if they are fond of cats. There are also those who, much less logically, fear cats. They are sufficiently common to have been given the name *ailurophobes*, although the Greek *ailuros* (waving ones) may have meant another animal and not a cat with its waving tail.

Most famous of ailurophobes was probably Napoleon. One story tells how an aide-de-camp rushed to answer the Emperor's cries for help and found him half dressed, dripping with perspiration and thrusting his sword again and again into a tapestry behind which a cat was hiding. The British World War One general Earl Kitchener was another military man who was afraid of cats.

Then there are those who just hate cats. General Dwight D. Eisenhower, the United States President and Allied Supreme Commander in Europe during World War Two, could not stand them. His orders to his household staff at Gettysburg were that cats should be shot on sight.

Many horrible things have been, and still are, done without even the 'excuses' of the religious persecutors of the past, from dipping cats in kerosene and setting them alight and playing football with a living cat as a ball, to the cruelty of the sentimental who abandon unwanted kittens to die because they cannot bear the thought of having them deliberately 'put to sleep'. Sadly, there are still millions of cases for the animal welfare societies to handle, man's (and woman's) inhumanity to cats echoes people's inhumanity to people. But even during the dark centuries when cats were the object of official persecution there were those who loved and cared for them.

The roll-call of ailurophiles or felinophiles (take your pick of long words for cat lovers) includes many famous and prestigious people: prelates and presidents, poets and painters, philosophers and mathematicians; and millions and millions of unsung people like us who have discovered how much a cat can add to the enjoyment of life.

Cardinal Richelieu playing with his kittens as drawn by Victor Adam for Fournier's Animaux Historiques.

Churchmen's cats

Like their sixth-century predecessor Gregory the Great, Popes Gregory XV (1621–23), Leo XII (1823–29) and Pius IX (1846–78) all had a great fondness for cats. Pope Pius had a cat which used to sit on a chair facing him at dinner, quietly and patiently waiting while the pontiff ate before being served his own food by the Pope himself, a ritual that many cat owners share. Pope Leo bequeathed his cat to the French statesman the Vicomte de Chateaubriand, who recorded that:

'My companion is a large grey and red cat, striped with black. He was born in the Vatican, in the loggia of Raphael. Leo the Twelfth reared him on a fold of his white robe, where I used to look at him with envy when, as ambassador, I was received in audience. The successor of St Peter being dead, I inherited the bereaved animal. He is called Micetto, and surnamed 'the Pope's cat,' enjoying in that regard much consideration from pious souls. I endeavour to soften his exile, and help him to forget the Sistine Chapel, and the vast dome of Saint Peter's where, far from earth, he was wont to take his daily promenade.'

History records a number of eminent clerics who were cat enthusiasts including Cardinal Thomas Wolsey, Chancellor of England under Henry VIII before the Reformation. He is said to have had his cat beside him when he sat in judgment.

William Laud, Archbishop of Canterbury (impeached and beheaded by Parliament in 1645) was also fond of cats. He was given some of the first 'Cyprus-catts' (tabbies) to be imported into Britain in 1638, according to John Aubrey, an antiquarian of the time. Since Edward Topsell illustrates a striped tabby in his book of 1607 these were probably the first of the 'classic' or 'blotched' tabby pattern, although Aubrey says common English cats were previously white with bluish patching.

Laud's contemporary, Cardinal Richelieu, principal minister of Louis XIII and for many years virtual ruler of France, delighted in having kittens around him, playing with them when he arose and before he went to bed. In *Les Chats* Champfleury, writing two centuries later, says Richelieu only liked them young and prankish and sent them away when three months old to be replaced by new ones. Nevertheless he had a room fitted up as a cattery with two attendants, so perhaps the rejected pets were still well looked after, for when he died he left a pension for the current 14 cats and for their keepers so that they would continue to care for them. Sadly for the cats, however, Richelieu had been so hated that his animals suffered for his unpopularity and instead of living in the luxury he had planned for them, they were killed by Swiss mercenaries.

An earlier French cat apologist, Paradis de Moncrif, described Jean Baptiste Colbert, Richelieu's successor as chief minister under Louis XIV, as always having kittens playing about his office, which made Champfleury wonder if that author had confused the two men in his story. While both these cat lovers were in power in France, the brutal St John's Day cat killings continued.

King Louis XV had a white cat which used to come to his bedroom every morning. Fortunately his queen, Marie Lecznska, had a passion for cats, but one of his courtiers, the Duc

de Noailles was terrified of them. So great was his fear that once when the king crept up behind him, grasped his neck and gave a savage miaow, the poor duke fainted right away and proved so difficult to bring round that for a time it was feared that he had died of fright!

Mohammed and the cat

Muslim tradition reminds believers of the care and consideration which they should show to innocent animals in the story of a cat which used to visit Mohammed in the house where he lived. He gave it his affection and when the cat asked for water while he was performing his ablutions, the Prophet interrupted the sacred ritual to take a bowl and gave it some. On one occasion it had curled up to sleep beside him and, when the time came for prayer, Mohammed realized it was on the edge of his garment. Rather than disturb it, he cut the cloth and crept away. The Prophet was not alone in his liking for cats; one of his companions was so fond of them that Mohammed gave him the name by which he has ever since been known — Abu-Khurairha (father of cats).

The Archbishop's Desdemona

Some people ban their cats from the dining room and thus avoid the problem faced by more indulgent cat-owners. That problem is teaching them to behave, for however patient a cat may be in ambush, it finds restraint that much more difficult when it sees a titbit flash from the plate into *your* mouth. If only cats could all be as well trained as those of the nineteenth-century Archbishop of Taranto at Naples. One visitor, Lady Morgan, to whom he apologized for his passion for cats and for not excluding them, described how

'between the first and second courses, the door opened, and several enormously large and beautiful Angora cats were introduced by the names of Pantalone, Desdemona, Otello, etc. They took their places on chairs near the tables, and were as silent, as quiet, as motionless, and as well behaved as the

Angora cat.

most *bon-ton* table in London could require. On the Bishop requesting one of the chaplains to help the Signora Desdemona, the butler stepped to his lordship, and observed, "My lord, la Signora Desdemona will prefer waiting for the roasts." '

Politicians' cats

A liking for cats ranges across political creeds and party affiliations. The British World War Two leader Winston Churchill and the Soviet revolutionary leader Lenin were both cat lovers. So was Jeremy Bentham, the eighteenth-century economist and political theorist, who had a cat which he fed on macaroni at his table. He called him John Langbourne when a kitten, gave him a knighthood as he grew up, and when he reached a sedate maturity retitled him the Reverend Sir John Langbourne, Doctor of Divinity!

Raymond Poincaré, president of France during World War One, was an enthusiast for the Siamese breeds; his favourite cat would sleep on his left arm as he sat at his desk writing with the other. 'The cat,' he considered,

'is witty, he has nerve, he knows precisely how to do the right thing at the right time. He is impulsive and light-hearted and knows the value of a well-phrased quip. He gets himself out of the most difficult situations by a pirouette.... I have never seen him embarrassed. When faced with a problem he chooses from two solutions with amazing speed, selecting that which is not only suited to his interests and point of view but also that which is elegant and gracious.'

French premier Léon Blum also had a Siamese at the Elysée Palace and one of his predecessors, Georges Clémenceau, owned a Blue Persian.

American presidents have been cat lovers too. During the Civil War, when Abraham Lincoln was visiting the camp of General Grant he found three half-frozen cats and promptly adopted them. Theodore Roosevelt was not only interested in the larger members of the species. He named one kitten after Tom Quartz, a cat in Mark Twain's *Roughing It*, and had a cat called Slippers which used to attend White House dinners and state occasions. Calvin Coolidge, 30th president of the United States, had a cat called Timmie and a canary called Caruso that used to walk up and down on Timmie's back and settle down between his front paws when the cat lay down.

Adlai Stevenson did not make it to the presidency but certainly won the support of cat-lovers in 1949 when, as Governor of Illinois, he spoke out against a bill which would have made it a public nuisance for a cat to go outside its owner's property, except on a leash. The proposed legislation originated in a wish to protect certain bird species, but as Stevenson said,

'The problem of cat versus bird is as old as time. If we attempt to resolve it by legislation, who knows but what we may be called upon to take sides as well in the age-old problems of dog versus cat, bird versus bird, or even bird versus worm.'

Ten Downing Street, the official home of the British Prime Minister, has had a succession of resident cats. During the 1920s and early 1930s it was Abanazar. Then, when Winston Churchill became Prime Minister in 1940, he took his black cat, Nelson, with him to Number Ten

Top *Winston Churchill's marmalade cat, Jock, in residence at Chartwell.*
Above *Kaspar, the 3ft-high (90 cm) cat carved by Basil Ionides for London's Savoy Hotel in the 1920s to prevent bad luck when a table has 13 guests. Sitting on a chair with a napkin round his neck before a full place setting, he is served a complete meal, course by course. At meetings of The Other Club, on strict instructions of its founder, Winston Churchill, he has attended every session since 1927.*
Above left *Australian Prime Minister Bob Hawke shares his breakfast with his cat.*
Left *Wilberforce, the Downing Street cat. Police on duty had instructions to let him in the moment he arrived.*

A delegation of rats and mice approach this cat with a petition. An engraving by Wenceslaus Hollar (1707–77) to illustrate the Aesop's fable which William Langland also used to satirize John of Gaunt and fourteenth-century politics.

Labour Prime Minister Harold Wilson took Nemo, the family Siamese, with him when he moved into Downing Street in 1964. There was no cat at Number Ten after he moved back to the family home in 1970, when Edward Heath became Prime Minister, but vermin problems in the house demanded action and in 1973 a black and white kitten called Wilberforce was selected from the RSPCA refuge at Hounslow to take up official residence as the Office Manager's cat, with an appropriate allowance as civil servant mouser. He served under four prime ministers until retired by Mrs Thatcher in 1986. He then went to live in Essex with the retired caretaker of Number Ten and died in 1988, aged 15.

There was no scratching at the door or waiting to be let in for Wilberforce. The policeman on duty at the front door had instructions to ring the door bell whenever he arrived. Even when Harold Wilson resumed the Premiership he ruled supreme, for the Wilsons decided to remain at their private house, so there was no conflict with their own cats, and Nemo, sadly had already died.

THE LITERARY CAT

Cats themselves may have no political affiliations but English poet William Langland used a cat to represent the power of the Establishment in a poem that played its part in launching an early attempt at a popular uprising — the fourteenth-century Peasant's Revolt which was finally precipitated by attempts to levy a poll tax which was punitive to the poor. In the prologue to *Piers Plowman* Langland takes the popular medieval fable of the belling of the cat and uses it to represent the political situation of the time. A council of rats and mice, representing the English Commons, meet to discuss their safety and in particular what to do about a great cat (probably representing John of Gaunt) who plays with them as he chooses. They would protest but fear reprisals. One elegant rat, who has seen the rich men of London, with chains about their necks, going everywhere and causing trouble, suggests that if they had bells on their chains men could hear them coming 'and awey renne'. If the cat could be belled in the same way they would be warned of it. The council agrees, a bell is bought and hung upon a collar — but no rat will volunteer to put it around the cat's neck. Then a shrewd mouse comes forward and declares: 'Even if we killed the cat, another like him would come and scratch us.'

The fable is an old one found in several European cultures and probably first appeared in collections of Aesop's *Fables*. It is included in Pieter Brueghel the Elder's painting illustrating proverbs of the Netherlands.

The lion, too, has had a role in folk tales and fables but, except as a danger to be hunted or overcome and as characters in a few more recent children's stories, the wild cats have not featured importantly in literature. The domestic cat seems to have attracted many writers from the ancient Greek poet Agathias down to such modern poets as Ted Hughes and Stevie Smith. Petrarch's love

where a place was reserved at the dining table and a chair kept for him in the Cabinet Room next to the PM. He probably slept on Churchill's bed and was often seen there when Winston was working in bed in the morning. 'That cat is doing more for the war effort than you are,' Churchill told one of his staff. 'He acts as a hot-water bottle and saves fuel, power and energy!'

In 1953, when Churchill was again in Downing Street, a kitten turned up on the doorstep and was taken in. Churchill, who had just recovered from a second stroke, made a speech to the Conservative Party Conference at Margate on that day and, pleased with his performance, decided it was the cat that had brought him luck and named it Margate! On his 88th birthday Churchill was presented with his last cat, which he called Jock (after the friend who gave it). It lived at Chartwell, his country house, and became popular with visitors when the house was opened to the public after the great man's death. Sir Winston provided for Jock's board and lodgings in his will and stipulated that a marmalade cat should be in 'comfortable residence' at the house for ever. When Jock died, in 1975, his successor inherited his name as well as his home.

Drawing by Theophile Steinlen from his 'story without words' The Awful End of a Goldfish.

Right An engraving of Thomas Carlyle with a cat.

Above Sir Walter Scott at Abbotsford with his cat Hinse and his bloodhound engraved by R. Bell after the painting by Sir John Watson Gordon. Acquired about 1812, Hinse used to dominate Scott's dogs. Washington Irving commented 'This sage grimalkin was a favorite of both master and mistress, and slept at night in their room ... sitting in state in Scott's armchair, and occasionally stationing himself on a chair beside the door, as if to review his subjects as they passed, giving each dog a cuff beside the ears as he went by'. After 15 years of bossing the household Hinse was killed by a young bloodhound called Nimrod who snapped back a bit too hard.

Right A self-portrait of the Scottish artist John Kay (1742-1826) with his favorite cat, thought to be the largest in Scotland at that time.

for his cat seems to have been more real than his idealized love for Laura, and who would think that Kingsley Amis, despite the fact that cats give him hay fever, works with a beautiful white-furred, blue-eyed cat named Sarah on his lap. Aldous Huxley advised any aspiring 'psychological novelist' to get a pair of cats, preferably Siamese, and 'mark, learn, and inwardly digest the lessons about human nature which they teach'. Many writers and artists have both included cats in their work and been great enthusiasts for them. So too, have countless unknown people, but it is those who have found fame, in whatever sphere, whose pets also tend to find permanent record. Nevertheless, in Michael Joseph's *Cat's Company* and numerous other celebrations of the cat you can find tales of many 'unknown' cats recorded.

Some of the earliest surviving cat poetry censures it as a bird-killer — Agathias threatens to take its life in revenge — and this remains a subject through the centuries, though Erasmus Darwin, the evolutionist's grandfather, chose to celebrate the predator in *The Freebooter*:

Cats I scorn, who, sleek and fat,
Shiver at the Norway rat.
Rough and hardy, bold and free,
Be the cat that's made for me;
He whose nervous paw can take
My lady's lap dog by the neck;
With furious hiss attack the hen,
And snatch a chicken from the pen.

The tenth-century Arab poet Ibn Alalaf Alnaharwany mourns the hunter within another favourite form — the feline epitaph — in a poem about a cat shot as she was robbing a dove-cote:

Why, why was pigeon's flesh so nice
That thoughtless cats should love it thus?
Hadst thou but lived on rats and mice
Thou hadst been living still, poor Puss.

Samuel Johnson, in his *Dictionary* of 1755, defined the cat as 'a domestic animal that catches mice, commonly reckoned by naturalists the lowest order of the leonine species'. That entry hardly reflects the great affection in which Dr Johnson held his own cats. His biographer and amanuensis, James Boswell (who could not abide cats) describes how the lexicographer would go out to buy oysters for one cat called Hodge, and reports how, on his admiring Hodge scrambling up his master's chest one day, Johnson observed

' "I have had cats whom I liked better than this," then, as if perceiving Hodge to be out of countenance, adding, "but he is a very fine cat, a very fine cat indeed." '

Johnson befriended Christopher Smart, a poet who developed religious mania and was committed to Bedlam Asylum. There, a cat became Smart's companion. To it he devotes a long and beautiful section of his strange poem *Jubilate Agno*: 'Consider my cat Jeoffry' which celebrates the domestic cat as wonderfully as his younger contemporary William Blake captured the tiger in his famous poem, *The Tiger*.

William Cowper was another eighteenth century poet who celebrated the cat, as did Thomas Gray, John Gay, and in the nineteenth century

John Keats, William Wordsworth, Alfred Tennyson, Algernon Swinburne, Robert Southey, Joanna Baillie and others.

Charles Dickens had a cat who once snuffed out a candle with his paw to make the novelist stop writing and give him attention. William Thackeray's household had a family of strays which they named after Dickens' characters. Walter Scott, originally mainly a 'dog man', had a cat called Hinse who in later years became his constant companion. Matthew Arnold's cat, Atossa, would walk across his desk pushing the end of his pen with her teeth, but he still thought her ways were beautiful, even though she was always waiting for a chance to pounce on the family canary. He put her in his poems. It was Mark Twain, however, who made the definitive statement that 'A home without a cat, and a well-fed, well-petted and properly revered cat, may be a perfect home, *perhaps*, but how can it prove its title?'

Other British and American writers who loved cats include Thomas Carlyle, Henry James, Thomas Hardy, Edgar Allan Poe (whose sinister fictional cats certainly are not portraits of his own tortoiseshell Catarina), Frances Hodgson Burnett (who exhibited at New York's first cat show), Lafcadio Hearn and a host of other names.

Lewis Carroll's Alice has a cat called Dinah, mentioned several times in *Alice's Adventures in Wonderland*, who is also featured, with her two kittens, in the first and last chapters of *Through the Looking Glass*. And one of the most famous of the *Wonderland* characters is the disappearing Cheshire Cat who declares, '*I* growl when I'm pleased, and wag my tail when I'm angry. Therefore I'm mad,' before fading away to a grin. That

Top Matthew Arnold's Atossa, sketched by Sir Laurence Alma-Tadema.
Below left One of the best-loved poems in the English language: The Tiger by William Blake (1757–1827), as illustrated and printed by him in Songs of Experience.
Below Sir John Tenniel's original illustration of the Cheshire Cat in Alice's Adventures in Wonderland.

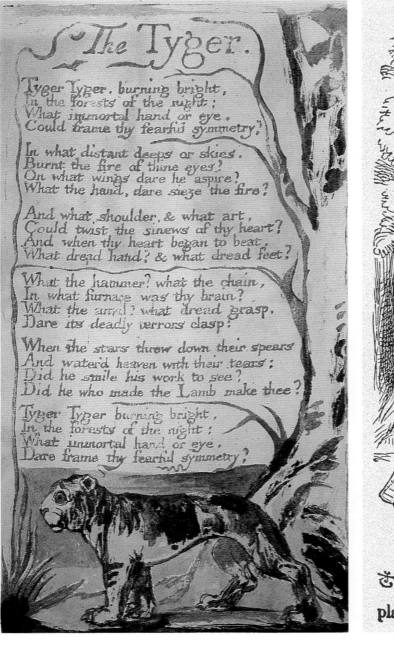

"Well, then," the Cat went on, "you see a dog growls when it's angry, and wags its tail when it's pleased. Now *I* growl when I'm pleased, and wag my tail when I'm angry. Therefore I'm mad."

"*I* call it purring, not growling," said Alice.

"Call it what you like," said the Cat. "Do you play croquet with the Queen to-day?"

Guy de Maupassant, Victor Hugo, Prosper Merimée, Emile Zola, Joris Karl Huysmans, and Anatole France were all devoted to their pets and wrote about cats in their work. Honoré de Balzac wrote a charming story, *Peines de Coeur d'une Chatte Anglaise*, which is a delightful comment on differences in amorous pursuits on both sides of La Manche told through the character of cats. Théophile Gautier, whose house was full of cats, wrote a book about them, *La Nature chez Elle et la Menagerie Intime*. Charles Baudelaire, whom Gautier described as adoring his cats which 'wander about the house with velvet tread, like the genius of the place, or come and sit upon the table near the writer, keeping company with his thought', wrote several poems about cats, including three in *Fleurs du Mal*. Pierre Loti wrote a life of two of his cats, Hippolyte Taine wrote 12 sonnets to cats — and the list could be continued.

Twentieth-century verse and fiction has continued to feature cats, from the stories of Colette who as well as being devoted to cats, for a time had a pet ocelot, to the writings of Jean Cocteau and Jean Paul Sartre, from the Russian imagist Sergei Esenin to W.B. Yeats, and from T.S. Eliot's somewhat anthropomorphic, but witty and delightful *Old Possum's Book of Practical Cats*, now turned into an internationally successfully long-running musical *Cats* by Andrew Lloyd Webber, to the understanding and keen observation of George MacBeth's *Fourteen Ways of Touching The Peter*.

In Japan early in the century Kinnosuke Natsume published his multi-volume *I am a Cat*. More recently Paul Gallico adopted a feline voice for poems and in his well-known *The Silent Meow*, while Don Marquis used a cockroach, archy, to tell his verse tales of the alley cat queen mehitabel. Hector Munro ('Saki'), who wrote *Tobermory*, a story of a talking cat, particularly loved cats and when in the Military Police in Burma kept a tiger kitten. Tennessee Williams told the strange story of Nitchevo in *The Male-*

other great artist and nonsense writer, Edward Lear, invented the Runcible Cat, the Seven young Cats that chased the Clangle-Wangle and the famous Pussy-cat that went off with the Owl in a beautiful pea-green boat. Lear was devoted to his own cat Foss and left many amusing sketches of him.

Heinrich Heine wrote many poems about cats and for a time shared a garret at his uncle's house with a fat Angora; while another German poet, Joseph Victor von Scheffel, made a tom cat a major character in his *Der Trompeter von Säkkingen* and E.T.A. Hoffman wrote in the first person as his favorite cat called Murr. However, it is the French writers of the nineteenth century who seem to have been particularly felinophile, in contrast to the seventeenth century when Paradis de Moncrif's *Les Chats* was greeted with ridicule by the literary establishment. Champfleury's 1870 book with the same title went through many editions.

Far left *Portrait of Pierre Loti by Henri Rousseau, possibly painted from a newspaper photograph, for the two men are not known to have met, though it has also been suggested that the title was the invention of the picture's first owner.*
Left *Edouard Manet drew these rooftop caterwaulers for Champfleury's book* Les Chats.
Below *Ernest Hemingway with one of his cats at Finca Vigia, his Cuban home. At one time there were 25 cats living in the house. Hemingway crossed Cuban cats with Angoras to produce what he considered a new breed.*

diction and Truman Capote gave Cat an important role in *Breakfast at Tiffany's*. Karel Câpek, Olivia Manning, Compton Mackenzie, Ernest Hemingway, Walter de la Mare all belong among the felinophiles. Doris Lessing has often given cats a place in her work, and shows a particular understanding of them, but it may surprise the fans of thriller writer Patricia Highsmith to find one of her stories is a tale of a successful murder by a cat, while Giles Gordon's *The Jealous One* makes a cat the gun-toting perpetrator of a *crime passionnel*. Raymond Chandler had a black Persian named Taki which he used to call his 'feline secretary' because she tried to sleep on his papers when he was trying to write.

To these more important literary figures must be added journalists like Derek Tangye and Beverley Nichols, publisher Michael Joseph and many others who have written popular books about their own cats and their experiences with

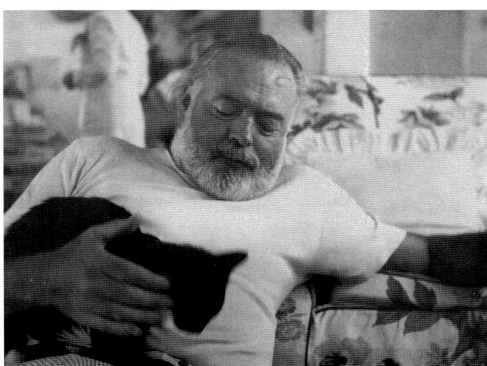

Far left *Colette always seems to have had a cat. They appear in several of her books and there are a pair of Siamese in her libretto for Ravel's opera* L'Enfant et les Sortiléges. *She herself became a cat for one of her stage performances:* La Chatte Amoureuse *in 1912.*
Left *French writer and film director Jean Cocteau with one of his Siamese cats.*

A.A. Milne's Tigger, the lion in C.S. Lewis's *The Lion, the Witch and the Wardrobe* and other Narnia stories (which also include a not very worthy cat) and Frank Baum's Cowardly Lion in *The Wizard of Oz*, all of whom have found their way on to stage and screen to join the mock-savage lion of Pyramus and Thisbe in Shakespeare's *A Midsummer Night's Dream* and the fairy-tale pussies of pantomime.

Andrew Lloyd Webber is not the only composer to have been inspired by cats. Hans Werner Henze has written an opera based on Balzac's *Loves of an English Cat* (with a libretto by Edward Bond). In the seventeenth century a number of composers wrote popular pieces that imitated the sound of cats and other animals and, early in this century, there was a popular one-step dance tune called *Me-ow*, in which the band vocalized the appropriate cat cries. Much better known however is the *Duetto Buffo deii due Gatti* of Gioacchino Rossini in which two female singers serenade each other with variations on the word me-ow. There is another cat duet in Maurice Ravel's *L'Enfant et les Sortilèges* (libretto by Colette) and there is a pas de deux for two fairy-tale cats in Pyotr Tchaikovsky's *Sleeping Beauty* in which the orchestra not only suggests their calls but also a very definite 'spit'. Igor Stravinsky gives the clarinet a purring theme in his *Berceuses du Chat* and, although the work is not otherwise imitative, the songs have a feline feeling. He also made a setting of Lear's *Owl and the Pussycat*.

In *Peter and the Wolf* Serge Prokofiev gives the cat a sprightly theme with which we can identify her all through the work. Domenico Scarlatti's *Cat Fugue* has the distinction, not of sounding like a cat, but of having the original theme reputedly composed by Scarlatti's own pet walking across the keyboard.

Above *The Scarecrow, the Tin Man, Dorothy, Toto and the Cowardly Lion wearing their green spectacles in Oz. One of W.W. Denslow's illustrations for L. Frank Baum's classic children's tale* The Wizard of Oz.

Above right *Beatrix Potter wrote and illustrated her stories of Tom Kitten.*

Below *Cats are extremely popular characters for children's books and have inspired some superb stories in many languages and fine illustrations.*

them, as well as an increasing number of zoologists and animal behaviorists as scientific interest has turned towards the study of the cat.

Since Lear's time there have been an increasing number of children's stories about such cats of character as Beatrix Potter's Tom Kitten, Simpkin and other cats, Kathleen Hale's *Orlando, the Marmalade Cat* and Dr Seuss's *Cat in the Hat*, and contemporary writers and artists such as Graham Oakley, Nicola Bailey and Posy Simmonds, with her ghost cat *Fred*, have all created cat protagonists.

The wild members of the cat family have been well recorded in the memoirs of big-game hunters and natural history books but they have not made much impact on world literature, though the leopard on the peak of Kilimanjaro is perhaps well known from Ernest Hemingway's short story *The Snows of Kilimanjaro*. Outside the creatures of fable few wild cats have achieved fictional fame, with the notable exceptions of the

CATS IN ART

Felines appear in cave paintings and as gods or emblems of gods and of power in religious and cult objects and images through the centuries. Lions appear as guardians, symbols of strength or of strength overcome, and as the attributes of saints as well as early gods.

The domestic cat appears in bestiaries and in light-hearted decorations in the margins of manuscripts and carved on the capitals of columns, misericords and stalls in churches, sometimes recalling cats in fables and several times shown playing a fiddle. Because of the Church's past hostility to cats it is possible that its appearance in Christian religious art may represent evil and the devil, or in some paintings

be symbolically linked with the treachery of Judas. Nonetheless, an early fourteenth-century fresco at Assisi suggests a cat in a natural kitchen scene, even though it is placed next to a depiction of Christ's Last Supper. Cats find their way into paintings of the Annunciation of the Virgin, of the Holy Family and of domestic episodes from the Bible, including pictures by Leonardo da Vinci, Tintoretto, Titian, Rubens, Barocci and Veronese.

Veneziano Domenichino tucks a cat in beside a dwarf under the edge of his trompe l'oeil tapestry of *Apollo killing the Cyclops*; Pintoricchio places a cat playing with a ball right in the foreground of his *Return of Ulysees* and also puts a white cat in a *Visitation of the Virgin*. Hieronymus Bosch includes a number of cats in his allegories and fantasies, as do the Brueghel family in their pictures (including a delightful blue-gray looking down in Jan's *Adoration of the Magi*) but it is in the later Dutch interiors that the cat begins to

The Dinner at Emaeus *by Jacopo da Ponte (c.1510–92) known as Bassano, in the Archbishop's chapel at Bassano. This cat appears in several paintings by members of the da Ponte family and was almost certainly a family pet.*

be more regularly featured, sometimes in the act of stealing off with something from the kitchen as in Nicolaes Maes' *A Sleeping Maid*, while his great teacher Rembrandt occasionally depicts a cat, including one in an etching of a Madonna and Child.

There are seventeenth-century engravings of cats by Wenceslaus Hollar, Francis Barlow and Cornelius Visscher. In the eighteenth century cats appear in the work of Giovanni Tiepolo, Jean-Baptiste Chardin, François Desportes, Antoine Watteau, Jean Fragonard, Jean-Baptiste Greuze and Jean-Baptiste Oudry. Cats more frequently find a place as companions in portraits.

Left *Detail from an Annunciation by Federico Barocci (c.1535–1612) in Urbino cathedral. This delightful realistic study surely reflects the good attributes of the cat, unlike the cat in Lotto's Annunciation.*
Below *Illustration for Goethe's version of Reineke Fuchs (Reynard the Fox) by Wilhelm von Kaulbach (1805–74). Cat and Tiger stand on King Lion's right.*

Left *Detail from* The Last Supper *by Pietro Lorenzetti (active 1320–45) in the lower basilica at Assisi. Last Supper paintings sometimes include a cat which the composition associates with Judas, a symbolic link between the betrayer and the devil. But this kitchen, set next to the room in which the meal is taking place, seems to be a natural scene with no sinister implication.*

Opposite *Cat studies by Leonardo da Vinci (1452–1519) in the Royal Library at Windsor. Some of the forms appear to have evolved into big cats and one has become a dragon. A number of cat sketches also survive which were made by Leonardo in preparation for his Madonna and Child with a Cat, showing Jesus playing with it and struggling to stop it escaping from his arms.*

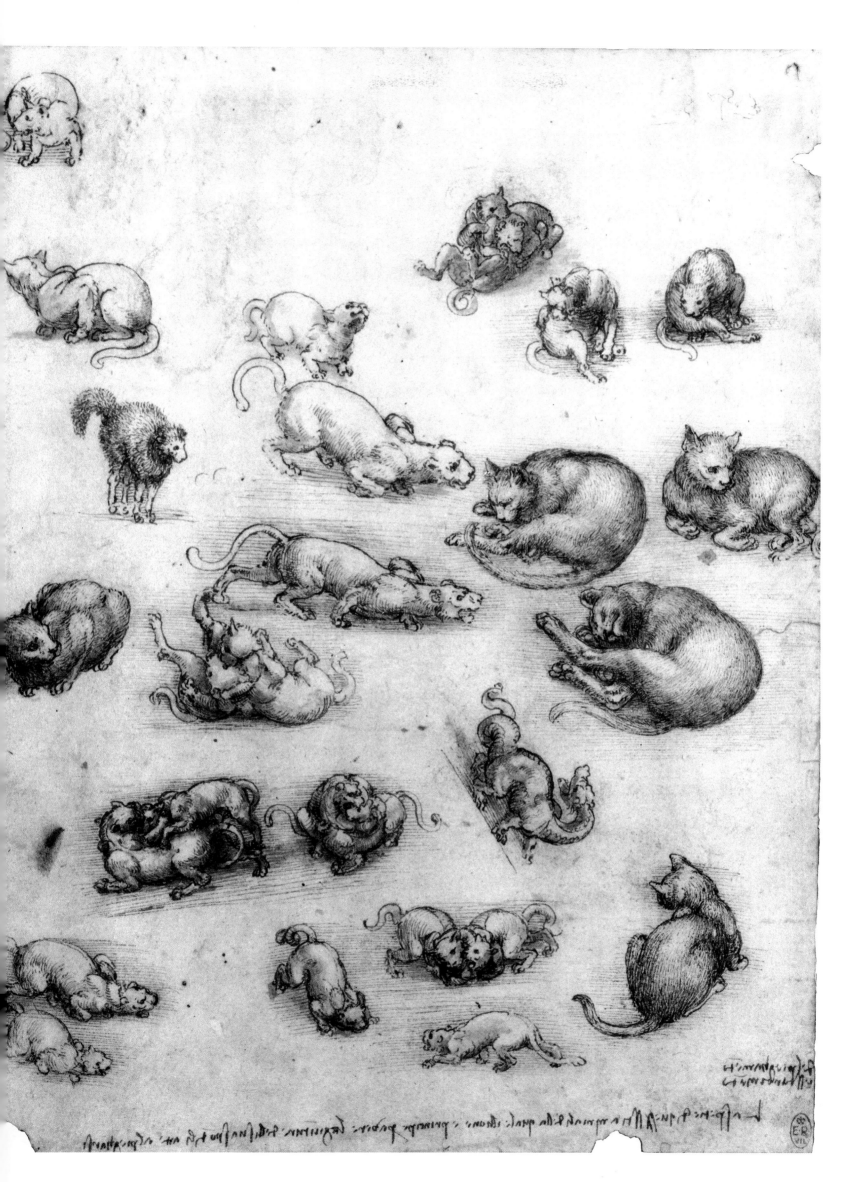

Among the best are William Hogarth's picture of the Graham children, Jean-Baptiste Perronneau's *Girl with a Kitten*, Joseph Wright's *Dressing the Kitten*, Nathaniel Hone's portrait of actress Katherine Fisher (which puns upon her name by including a kitten fishing into a bowl of goldfish) and Goya's portrait of young Don Manuel, son of Count Altamira which has three cats watching his pet magpie. George Stubbs painted a portrait of *Miss Anne White's Kitten* in 1790 and included in his paintings of *The Godolphin Arabian* a cat which was said to have shared its stable and watched over the famous racehorse when it died. He painted no other domestic cats but did some superb studies of the larger members of the cat family.

Nineteenth-century children's portraits painted by traveling artists frequently feature cats and occasionally the cats are portrayed alone.

Cats crop up in woodcuts and engravings of Thomas Bewick, George Cruikshank and later illustrators Gustave Doré and Grandville (Jean Isadore Gérard) and it was through engravings of his work that Gottfried Mind of Basle became best known. This artist, who gained the contemporary soubriquet of 'the Raphael of Cats', was besotted with them, sitting still for hours rather than disturb his favorite Minette and her kittens when they settled on his lap and shoulders. He

Top Interior with a Mother and child *by Jan Baptist Weenix (1621–63?)*
Above left Peasant Family in an Interior, *possibly by Louis Le Nain (c.1593–1648) though it could be by one of his two brothers since even their signed pictures carry no initials and are undated. Their pictures include a number of peasant groups with cats.*
Above Dressing the Kitten *by Joseph Wright (1734–97), usually known as Wright of Derby, a specialist in lighting effects, here thrown by the candle masked by the foreground arm.*
Left *Oil sketches of a kitten by François Desportes (1661–1723).*

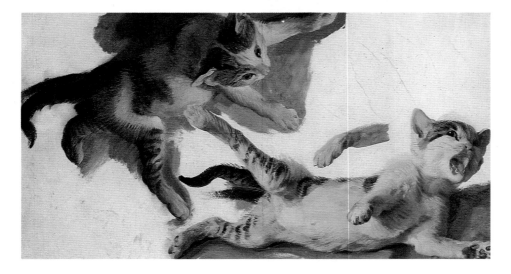

Left *Lion and lioness painted in enamel on copper by George Stubbs in 1770.*
Below *Lion Lying in a Pass by Eugéne Delacroix (1798–1863), who painted a number of cats, as well as his better-known wildlife studies.*
Bottom *Mother Cat with Three Kittens, watercolor by Gottfried Mind (1767–1874), often called Der Katzen Raphael, although from the evidence of this picture, he never properly studied the iris of a kitten's eye. As he worked, Minette, his favorite cat, sat by him or on his lap while kittens draped themselves on his shoulders. In 1809 the authorities of Berne, where he made his home, ordered the destruction of its cats because of a suspected outbreak of rabies. Mind hid and saved Minette but was heartbroken by the execution of 800 of the city's cats.*

was the first painter to make a speciality of portraits of cats themselves, rather than of their owners.

Dutch-born Henriette Ronner succeeded him as *the* cat specialist. Her work is often crude, a little wooden, and usually too sentimental for today's taste, but her best work can catch the vitality of cats and kittens. British Louis Wain was another artist who became obsessed with cats. Most of his work dresses cats up as anthropomorphic images to comment on his fellow men but in later life, as his mind disintegrated and he entered an asylum, his images do capture the wild vitality of cats before dissolving further into the psychedelic patterns of classic schizophrenia.

Théophile Steinlen, also Swiss born, though he lived and worked in Paris, where his house became known as 'Cat's Corner', was famous for his posters and graphic work presenting cats, including a series of *Images sans Paroles*, a form of story strip showing cats' adventures with balls of wool, raiding fish bowls and similar escapades.

French artists Jean Ingres, Théodore Géricault and Eugéne Delacroix all sketched cats and the last two painted some magnificent lions. Edouard Manet did illustrations for Champfleury's book and put a black cat on the bed in his *Olympia*,

Above A Bit of Cheese *by Henriette Ronner (1821–1909).*
Below *A page of cat sketches by Theodore Gericault (1791–1824).*

1. A poster for a tea and coffee company produced about 1899 by Théophile Steinlen (1859–1923). 2. A silver-gilt tankard in the shape of a panther, made in London about 1600, one of a pair acquired by the Russian Tsar in 1629. The heads form a removable lid. 3. A seventeenth-century gunner's breastplate in the armory of the Hermitage in Leningrad. 4. A purpurine figure of a cat, produced by the Fabergé workshop about 1900. 5. Poster by Henri de Toulouse-Lautrec (1864–1901) promoting English singer May Belfort, who became briefly famous at the Moulin Rouge in Paris for the song Daddy wouldn't buy me a bow-wow... 6. A pair of leopards in biscuit porcelain, just over 40 in (1 m) long, made for export in China in the Kangxi period (1662–1722). 7. A decoration for a menu by Toulouse-Lautrec.

Top Surprise. *Henri Rousseau (1844–1910) painted this rain-lashed jungle scene in 1891.*
Above Cat and Kittens *painted by an unknown American artist c.1872–83. Cats were a popular subject for American naive painters and traveling portraitists who often included them in children's portraits.*
Right Boy with a Cat, *an early painting by Pierre-Auguste Renoir (1841–1919).*

Auguste Renoir and Pierre Bonnard included cats in several portraits. Henri Rousseau included a cat in the portrait usually identified as Pierre Loti as well as painting a group of pictures with large jungle cats. Picasso painted one in a portrait of Jacqueline and a savage *Cat with a bird*, and English artist Gwen John, living in France with a house full of cats, painted them often. Paris-based Japanese artist Tsuguharu Fujita was another cat specialist, often including them in self-portraits as well as painting them alone. Franz Marc also made a number of cat studies and Vanessa Bell, Dora Carrington (whose home with Lytton Strachey had many much-loved cats) and William Nicholson (who portrayed Churchill's Jock) were all enthusiasts in a line which includes many contemporary artists including the deliberately naive work of Martin Leman and the glorious cartoons and lithographs of Ronald Searle.

Top *A woodcut by Raoul Dufy (1877–1953) as a bookplate for Guillaume Apollinare.*
Above right Cat Looking at Fields at Asakusa, *a colored woodblock by Andō Hiroshige (1797–1858). A white bobtailed cat gazes out at Mount Fuji in the distance.*
Right Aholah *by Tsuguharu Fujita (1886–1968), a Japanese artist working mainly in Paris who made many studies of cats. He often included them in self-portraits.*
Above Cat Voyage *by Ryozo Kohira, a contemporary Japanese painter also working in Europe.*

Kittens Dec 10-25 1944 :
Changi Jail, C.P'nt.   Ronald Searle.

Left *Royal Cats, a series of figures in a modern interpretation of the traditional Imari style made by the Royal Crown Derby Porcelain Company. From left to right: Abyssinian, Siamese, Burmese, Russian, Egyptian and Persian.*

Opposite *Sketches of kittens made in 1944 by Ronald Searle in Changi Gaol, the infamous prisoner-of-war camp, where he was held by the Japanese during World War Two. Searle drew the kittens several times during the days when they were being fattened up to become the starving prisoners' Christmas dinner. He recounts in To the Kwai and Back that they were 'gently fried to give us a memorable meal'.*

Below *A selection of the 'Great Cat' gems designed and made in the 1940s and 50s by Cartier for the Duchess of Windsor. They were the inspiration of Jeanne Toussaint, close companion of Louis Cartier (who called her 'Panther'). She conferred closely with the Duchess on many jewelry projects.*

Top *Five pound coin produced by the British Royal Mint when Victoria became queen in 1837.*

Above *Gold two mohurs coin issued by the East India Company in 1835.*

Right *The British royal arms, shown here in the form used by Charles I, features several lions. One crowned lion is a supporter and in the blazon the first and fourth quarters show the three lions of England quartered with the lilies of France, which was still claimed as an English possession. The second quarter shows the rampant lion of Scotland, and even the harp for Ireland in the third quarter is given a lion's head for decoration.*

Below from left to right *The village sign of Old Catton, using a rebus: cat + barrel (or tun) = Catton; a lion's head as a royal symbol on a railway carriage made for Queen Victoria; the blazon of Christopher Columbus which includes the castle and lion from the Spanish royal arms of the time.*

THE SIGN OF THE CAT

In addition to their symbolism in art and religion, images of cats, both big and small, have been widely used in heraldry, signs and in advertising. Since 1144, when Henry of Saxony incorporated the lion in his arms, people and nations have used the big cats in their arms or as bearers. The shields and banners of the Middle Ages were emblazoned with lions and leopards. Venice carved the winged lion of St Mark on fortresses all over her empire and, later, the British lion represented Britannia's power. Scotland and Spain displayed a lion rampant and English kings three leopards (the correct heraldic name for lions passant guardant).

Vandals and Suevi carried a black cat emblem into battle and the United States Tank corps, the 85th Division of the American Expeditionary Forces in World War One, adopted a wild cat as their insignia, painted on their tanks, worn as shoulder flashes and used in recruiting posters. Other US Army units have also used cat emblems and several squadrons of the British Royal Air Force have feline badges: a cheetah for the 51st, a tiger for the 74th and a leopard for the 230th Squadron.

Cats appear in several personal coats of arms: the German Katzen family with a silver cat holding a rat on an azure ground, the Neapolitan Della Gattas with a fine cat couchant on its crest, the Chetaldi of Limoges with two silver cats on azure, while in Scotland Clan Mackintosh, with wildcats as bearers and on its helm as well as a rampant lion quartering, is only one of many feline heraldic symbols. Cats appear above the arms of the Royal Burgh of Dornoch and across the top of those of Inverness District Council.

Among company badges few can be better known than Metro-Goldwyn-Mayer's roaring lion, Leo, parodied in Mary Tyler Moore's mewing kitten, or the badge of Jaguar Cars. The

Top left The Red Lion is a popular name for a tavern but you will find many White Lions too.
Top right Cats appear on a number of inn signs, but this one is much less familiar than the Cat and the Fiddle.
Above The winged lion of St Mark, the evangelist, was adopted by the City of Venice as its symbol and appears on Venetian buildings and fortifications throughout their old possessions but nowhere more impressively than here, on the clocktower in St Mark's Square in the heart of Venice.
Far left The arms of the City of Coventry feature a cat, signifying watchfulness, as their crest.
Left The arms of the Royal Burgh of Dornoch. Local wildcats appear in the arms of several Scottish places and families.

Exxon Oil Company has for many years exploited the powerful image of the tiger in its advertising. In contrast, cuddly Persians have been used to suggest the comfort of carpets, the coziness of home in hundreds of press advertisements and commercials, while the elegant orientals have been used to emphasize the sexiness of perfumes or sheer stockings. The pet food industry, too, has used all the skills of the filmmaker to present captivating cats in commercials to convince us that each product is going to make our own pet happier and healthier than that of its competitors.

Inns, restaurants, cafes and discotheques have appropriated the cat — black, white, marmalade or with a fiddle; red lions, white lions and golden lions. Cigarettes, chocolate bars, stationery, patent medicines, book publishers, security firms, railroads, all kinds of products and services have used members of the cat family as brand names to exploit the associations with speed, strength, authority, beauty or domesticity associated with them. The British Egg Marketing Board even used to stamp eggs with a 'lion mark' as an indication of approved quality!

Above *Several United States military units feature cats on their badges, including a gun-toting tom cat and Felix with a grenade, while the 17th Bombardment Squadron and 79th Tactical Fighter Squadron of the Air Force both use tigers.*

Right *Cards from around the world: the business card for a New York State seedsman; a Brussels shop selling and repairing umbrellas; 1943 Dutch postcard; 1911 British birthday card; photographic postcard of the 1950s.*

Sleep like a Kitten on ~ CHESAPEAKE and OHIO LINES

THE GEORGE WASHINGTON ♡ THE SPORTSMAN ♡ THE F.F.V. ♡ THE FINEST FLEET OF AIR CONDITIONED TRAINS IN THE WORLD

Clockwise from bottom right *A Venezuelan politician calls himself El Tigre and uses a tiger as his symbol. The jaguar is often known as 'el tigre' in South America but the Asian tiger is painted here; a World War One recruiting poster used the Imperial lion to inspire British patriotism; a black cat chosen as the brand name for a coffee; Chessie, probably the most famous cat in United States advertising, was mascot of the Chesapeake and Ohio Railway; the Esso tiger became the advertising symbol in many countries for the Exxon Oil Company; Tiger Balm was chosen as the name for the Chinese medicated ointment because the tiger was seen as a symbol of strength and held in high esteem and reverence; a leaping jaguar once crowned Jaguar car bonnets. Removed, like other projecting automobile mascots because it could cause injury in an accident, it remains the company logo.*

koffie ZWARTE KAT

TIGER

JAGUAR

THE EMPIRE NEEDS MEN!

THE OVERSEAS STATES

All answer the call.
Helped by the YOUNG LIONS
The OLD LION defies his Foes
ENLIST NOW.

EL TIGRE
EL PRESIDENTE NUEVO
VOTA VERDE

Cats on postage stamps

Wild animals of the cat family have been popular subjects for stamp designs ever since the first Malayan tiger stamp was issued in 1891. The domestic cat was not depicted on a stamp until 1930, but since then the universal appeal of pet cats has resulted in their appearance on hundreds of stamps from countries all over the world.

THE OTHER SIDE OF THE COIN

There can be no doubt about the love that people can have for their cats but what do they get in return? It is difficult even to consider the question without being accused of being sentimentally anthropomorphic. The dog is a pack animal that learns its place in the hierarchy and can exhibit loyalty, defense of its human pack and human property and a sometimes fawning gratitude, but the cat is usually described as being an independent opportunist. The very characteristics of having a mind of its own, of resourcefulness (deceitfulness, low cunning, thievery, as its critics might say), its refusal to always fit in with human wishes and convenience, its insistence on being an equal — all these appeal as much to many who love cats as its beauty, grace, soft fur, warm presence and comforting purr. How often do owners feel that they are there only for the cat's convenience? Though cats will sometimes offer a kind of 'cupboard love' they are just as likely to make demands as rights. A dog accepts a subservient role as part of membership of the pack and, if its human fails to play the role of dominant leader, that relationship can become unmanageable. The cat requires at least an equal contract, or some would say one on its own terms.

The sixteenth-century French writer and philosopher, Michel Eyquem de Montaigne wondered 'when my cat and I entertain each other with mutual apish tricks, as playing with a garter, who knows but I make my cat more sport than she makes me? Shall I conclude her simple, that has her time to begin or refuse to play as freely as I myself have? Nay, who knows but that it is a defect of my not understanding her language (for doubtless cats talk and reason with one another) that we agree no better? And who knows but that she pities me for being no wiser than to play with her, and laughs and censures my folly for making sport with her, when we two play together?'

So, what does the cat owner get out of the relationship? Is it returned affection? Rubbing their bodies against us may be to demonstrate they care, or merely a proprietorial marking process. But why then should they do it against a stranger in the street? On the other hand those cats that have sought out their people over a long distance rather than adopt another home, must have had some special feeling for them.

Cats, especially Siamese, may sometimes intervene vocally in a domestic quarrel, though it could be no more than a request to stop disturbing them; and, indeed, they are more likely to disappear in the face of anger lest it be vented in their direction. Many owners, when alone, have found their cats acting with obvious concern when they have been sad or ill in bed. This could be a response to signals transmitted by the owner which make the cat feel the need of reassurance and it is actually demanding rather than giving attention but, if the owner feels it the comforting gesture of a loving friend, then the effect will be the same. Do you really believe that a cat who gently licks the tears from your eye can only be attracted by the salt?

Even those who neither own a cat nor are owned by one will acknowledge the cat family's aesthetic beauty and the sensual texture of the feline fur, both the source of enormous pleasure.

Many people will suggest that allowing a child to keep a pet will help to develop a sense of responsibility through having to care for it, and a cat is less demanding than a dog in that it is unlikely to need to be walked or bathed. But a pet animal can offer much more to a child and, just as importantly, meets exactly the same needs in an adult owner.

A cat can be a confidante to whom you can safely tell the deepest secret. It will never laugh at what you tell him or her and certainly never spill the beans to any other people. The animal's need of you can increase self-esteem, and its interaction with you offer the reassurance of something unchanged by problems in society outside. It permits a degree of physical contact and a display of physical affection, a response which is often inhibited between people. Simply stroking a cat has a calming and relaxing effect which can relieve tensions.

With the single, the homosexual, the childless couple or those whose children have left home, a pet has often been identified as a child substitute. There is an element of truth in this for human nature needs to give nurturing love and care. It should not be at the expense of human contact but, where social attitudes prevent that affection from being displayed, this can be a valuable release, and a way of awakening those responses in people in whom such feelings have been repressed.

Companionship for the lonely and isolated is only the most obvious element. Both medical doctors and psychiatrists now recognize the motivating effect a pet can have in helping people who are recovering from surgery or illness, in rehabilitating the psychologically damaged, in restoring purpose to those who have begun to feel useless to, or abandoned by, society. In homes for the elderly, hospitals, rehabilitation centres and even prisons, the introduction of pet animals has been shown to have very beneficial effects.

A cat is not necessarily the animal to chose for a therapeutic role. A budgerigar or canary may be more suitable for those who are unable to offer more than minimum care, or a dog for those who must be motivated to take exercise or to go outdoors, and doctors and therapists must take such things into consideration. They must allow for the emotional upheaval which would be caused by the death of a short-lived animal, the concern someone who knows that they are going to die may have for the animal's future care. They must match pet to patient. The success of such initiatives clearly demonstrates the important and positive role which pets play in our lives and, for those of us who favor cats, provides some explanation perhaps of why we find them so important.

Above *A pet shrine at Kamakura in Japan, where people make offerings for cats' souls and cats themselves seem to remember their ancestors.*
Right *Pet-keeping has been used to develop responsibility and strengthen self-esteem. In prisons it has proved therapeutic and at Lorton prison in Virginia the experiment in 'zootherapy' began by allowing inmates to care for the feral cats roaming around the jail. Now a variety of animals (but not dogs) are permitted and veterinarians give weekly lectures on animal medicine.*
Opposite *Who could resist this lovely Abyssinian kitten?*
Following spread *Abyssinian kittens.*

Practical friends

There are plenty of instances where cats have made more than a psychological contribution to their owner's lives. Many animals seem more sensitive than people to the faint tremors that may precede an earthquake. Cats have been observed as becoming very agitated, drawing back their ears, meowing and trembling. They may try to leave the danger zone and have, by their action or by positive pleading, got their owners outside and away from the worst danger. Similar prescience of air-raids before warnings have been sounded have been reported. Again the air vibrations created by airplanes, especially masses of bombers, may be sensed by the cat. Cats have also been reported to have been able to distinguish between friendly and enemy aircraft so that their owners knew early when to take to the shelters. That cats could tell the difference is not surprising — many people could distinguish between the sound made by British- or German-built engines during World War Two. But had cats really learned to associate one sound rather than the other with falling bombs? Perhaps they learned because their owners displayed more agitation at one sound when it became audible to them.

Sailors used to interpret sudden, unusual activity in their ship's cat as warning of a coming gale. Since gales would be preceded by a change in atmospheric pressure it is understandable that the cat would detect this, though the corresponding increased activity is not so readily explained.

One famous instance of a direct cat benefactor with no indication of self-interest occurred at the Tower of London. During the dynastic struggles between Lancaster and York in the fifteenth century Henry Wyatt, thrown into prison by Richard III, was a captive in that grim fortress where he had previously been Governor. As he lay in a dungeon without bed for comfort or covers to keep out the cold, he was befriended by a cat which found her way in to him. She not only snuggled up to keep him warm but went out and brought him pigeons which she killed to supplement the tiny ration of food he was allowed. Later, in 1532, his portrait was painted with the cat in a style suggesting Holbein.

It was also at the Tower that the Earl of Southampton's pet cat sought him out in 1601 (see page 44).

During the long and gruelling siege of Stalingrad (now renamed Volgograd) during World War Two a cat called Mourka proved itself not only helpful but heroic, forming a vital link by carrying messages concerning gun emplacements from a group of Soviet scouts back to their company headquarters.

But most of us expect neither heroism, weather forecasting, nor any other practical skills from our household pets. There are, perhaps, even those who would prefer that the cat's natural abilities as rodent predator should be forgotten. They do not require a cat to have any practical purpose, provided that it can produce a purr to reassure them that at least all's well in someone's world.

CARING FOR CATS

KEEPING A CAT

Your responsibilities

Keeping a pet of any kind is a considerable undertaking. In the case of a domestic cat it can mean a commitment to as many as twenty years' responsibility for another life, and demands a serious assessment of your own suitability and willingness to accept that responsibility before you take on the job.

The appeal of an attractive little kitten can be very strong and the cost of a few cans of cat food seems a negligible consideration — but multiply that cost by the number of mealtimes in a year, add veterinary bills, a regular supply of litter for a cat that lives indoors, boarding charges if you have to leave your pet in a cattery when you go away and many other incidental expenses. They soon mount up. The cost is not only financial; you need *time* to provide food and water, buy food, clean feeding bowls and litter trays, take the cat to the vet, nurse it when sick, groom it, play games with it and consider its needs — every day of the year. Arrangements need to be made for its care when you are away from home. In short your cat's welfare must be considered in nearly all the decisions affecting your own life.

None of us knows what lies twenty years ahead, but we can look at the life style we expect in the immediate future and consider whether it encompasses the demands of cat ownership. Anyone whose career involves postings abroad may find themselves transferred to a country where quarantine regulations make it impossible to take an animal with them unless it first spends a long period in quarantine, a traumatic experience for both pets and people quite apart from the expense. Long haul airline flight crew, rock musicians, commercial travelers — in fact anyone whose work takes them away for days at a time — is ill-placed to be a caring owner unless there are others in their household prepared to share the responsibilities. Young people who expect to leave home to go to school or university or are planning to back-pack around the world would be irresponsible to embark on cat ownership unless the pet is a welcomed acquisition of the whole family. Indeed, whoever the nominal owner is, a pet should always be acceptable to all the people with whom it has to live.

Consider *why* you want a pet. Is a cat the best animal to fit your needs? A dog will make a better companion for walks, a gerbil means a much shorter commitment, a goldfish demands the minimum of care.

The responsibilities of looking after an animal should never be imposed on others. Giving a cat or kitten as a present is not a good idea unless you are absolutely certain that the recipient both wants it *and* is able to take care of it. Never give an animal as a surprise, because preparations must be made for its arrival. Never give a kitten to a child (however eager he or she may be to have one) without first making sure that the parents are keen on the idea and will take the ultimate responsibility for its care.

This may sound like very obvious advice but all too often it is ignored. Every year thousands of cats, rejected once the owner's first enthusiasm for them has passed, have to be destroyed by animal organizations. If such people can be dissuaded from keeping pets any amount of repetition is worthwhile.

Cat or kitten?

Most people who decide to keep a cat think primarily of acquiring a kitten but, although there is a great deal of pleasure to be gained from being involved as a kitten grows and develops, there are always grown cats looking for homes, perhaps because their owners have died or for some reason are no longer able to care for them. There are thousands of unwanted and abandoned cats and strays, both young and old which, if they are lucky, end up in animal refuges. Giving one of them a home will save its life and should be a first thought if you are not set on a particular breed. Even then you may find just what you are looking for, except that stray cats don't carry their pedigree papers with them. You may even find yourself adopted by a stray who decides to move in with you; but in that case do make an effort to ensure that there is not some frantic owner looking for it!

Older cats may take a little longer to adjust to a new home and may have developed habits which will be difficult to change, but it is just as rewarding to gain the confidence of a cat which has been badly treated and lost its trust in people as it is to play with a tiny kitten. In London 50 percent of the seemingly feral tom cats picked up by cat welfare workers for neutering or treatment prove to be tame, no matter how bad their state or how belligerent their attitude.

For some people a mature cat may indeed be the best choice. It will not require feeding so frequently, so it does not matter that you are out during the day, it will be more likely to curl up on your lap than demand constant games and less likely to jump all over the place knocking over valued possessions or rushing around under the feet of an older person whose mobility is impaired.

Choosing a cat or kitten

Researchers have discovered that the majority of people choose a cat for its appearance, especially its color. Some breeders claim that cats with a blue coat tend to have gentle temperaments and most people would agree that Persian cats are often less lively than shorthairs and oriental breeds more interactive with people, but there is often more difference between the character of individual cats than there is between breeds. There does appear to be some genetic element to personality: studies of kittens born of sisters and raised under the same conditions gave evidence of temperamental differences reflecting their paternity. A particular pedigree breeding line may pass on personality traits and many breeders do take temperament into account when planning matings. The environment and rearing of cats from the same home could also tend to

Find out which is your nearest humane society cat refuge. There are many kittens like these who desperately need homes if their lives are not to be curtailed.

reproduce a particular temperament. How much the characteristics associated with some individual breeds owe to genetic features and how much to nurture and environment is unknown.

Breed characteristics, as described in 'Domestic Varieties' section can be some guide as to the suitability of a kitten but you might gain a better picture from the behavior of the mother cat and other relatives at the breeder's cattery or the owner's home. If you are choosing a grown-up cat its character will already be established. It is possible that less appealing features could be modified, but that requires time and patience. With a kitten, observation will enable you to assess its physical condition but is not always a reliable guide to the way it will develop in another environment. Sibling competition can produce activity that may be lacking without that stimulus.

Some breeds of cat can be very expensive to buy (especially if they have very good pedigrees) but kittens that do not quite match up to the standards of future show champions are usually sold as pets at much lower prices. If you are interested only in a pet, make that quite clear. Apart from offering you a less expensive kitten the breeder may not want to sell a potential champion to someone who does not want to show or breed. If you have no strong feelings about a particular breed and you do not know of kittens looking for a home then adopt a cat from a cat refuge.

Do not choose a breed from books and photographs. Go to a cat show and look at real cats. Take the opportunity to talk to breeders and owners to learn more about a breed and make contact with a potential source from which to buy. Your local veterinarian may also be able to recommend a breeder. You may be able to buy from a pet shop, but then you will not be able to see a kitten in relation to its mother and background. Some breeders who live out of town or are too busy to see individual clients may sell only through a store, but most dispose of their best kittens privately and many are adamant that kittens should *never* be sold through stores. Some stores do not keep cats on the premises but will obtain one for you, perhaps arranging a preliminary visit to the cattery to choose a kitten and then fixing everything so that you can collect it from the store when it is old enough to leave its mother.

If your choice is a rare or very popular breed, you may find there is a waiting list for kittens. A visit to the cattery will then give you an opportunity to see its general standards and find out more about the breed; perhaps a particular breeding line will be recommended as having the kind of character you want. If you are only looking for a pet kitten which lacks the physical perfection demanded for show champions may be available more quickly.

If you have no other pets at home, and especially if there is no one in the house all day or you go out a great deal, consider having two kittens. It will mean two mouths to feed but they will keep each other company and play together, making life much more interesting for them and making up for the attention you are not able to give. Look out for a pair that already seem attached to each other if you are getting them from the same cattery.

Selecting a kitten

Don't buy from a cattery that looks unhygienic and badly run and try to resist the urge to look after a weak and sickly looking kitten. There is no point in saddling yourself with unnecessary

These kittens, put out for sale on an Athens pavement, are evidence of a growing fashion for cats as pets in Greece, where previously most were barely tolerated scavengers. Dealers who sell cats under such conditions should not be encouraged.

A well-run breeding cattery can give you confidence when choosing kittens.

problems and veterinary bills (and the ensuing heartbreak if things go seriously wrong) when there are plenty of healthy cats available, though loving care and attention can work wonders so that even the rejected runt of a litter has a chance.

Ask to handle the kittens. Provided that you have not been in contact with cats from which you might pass on disease, the breeder should allow this. Find out how much contact they have already had with people. Take a very careful look at the kitten you have your eye on *and* its mother and siblings.

If *any* of a supposedly healthy litter seem ill or dirty you would be wise to reject the entire litter and look for another breeder. Even the best catteries cannot escape occasional health problems, but a responsible breeder will warn you about them and be unhappy about letting you take an animal until any problems have been cured, and will guarantee the kittens' good health for several weeks.

In any large litter some kittens will be smaller than the others. The smallest, the 'runt', may have received less food and maternal attention than the rest of the litter and even been bullied by its siblings. It may not be so robust as its fellows and unsuited as a working cat but, apart from an initial timidity, there is no reason why it should not be a healthy pet. Size is only important if you intend to show and are looking for fine examples of the breed.

Choose a kitten that is playful and inquisitive, not one that reacts nervously to any noise or sudden movement or one that spits and scratches at any approach. However, be warned that a very bold cat may prove a bossy one and be difficult to discipline.

In the end, any choice is very personal and subjective. Color and appearance will be important if you are looking for a pedigree show cat and we all respond differently to particular behavior and personality. You may well find that a particular kitten has chosen you and be hard put to refuse it. If possible, don't base your choice

Wild species as pets

There is plenty of evidence that individual members of a variety of feline species, when reared from cub and kittenhood, can form close associations with some people. However, there is a big difference between Elsa growing up on an African wildlife reserve or Billy Singh's leopards at Tiger Haven and a non-domestic species kept as a pet. Even the relatively small Ocelot and Margay, which have been kept as house pets by some North Americans, need constant handling to remain good-natured, will attempt to eat all kinds of things from curtains to electric cables and scratch their way into anything and everything, cost you a considerable sum to feed and you could not go away, even for a weekend, without there being someone with whom they were equally familiar, for boarding catteries do not accept them. Neither they nor

on one visit only. Return on another occasion, preferably at a slightly different time of day. The kitten that was sleeping off its lunch may now prove to be the liveliest and you will have a chance to see them all in a different mood.

Most cat breeders care greatly that their kittens go to good homes. They often make a sale not only on the understanding that you have the right to return the kitten if a veterinarian finds anything wrong with it (which should always be a condition of sale) but, if you find problems in keeping it would rather have you take it back so that a more suitable owner can be found.

Male or female

Unless you intend to breed, sex is not especially important because, in the interests of all, it is best to have a pet cat neutered or spayed when it reaches the appropriate age. Stud males do not make good household pets and an entire male will probably spray not only in your house and garden but in those of your neighbors too which will make neither him nor you very popular. He will also father kittens on local breeding females, increasing the number of kittens whether they are wanted or not.

Even if all the local pet owners have responsibly neutered their toms there is always the

any other of the wild species is suited to a home environment. Capture for their fur and for the pet trade has made these endangered species. They now come under CITES regulations and it would not be possible legally to obtain one to keep as a pet.

National or local laws control the keeping of dangerous or endangered animals and it is extremely difficult to obtain the necessary permits. Their space requirements, cost of upkeep and the secure enclosures you would need to construct mean that only zoos, establishments breeding species to replenish endangered populations or professional animal trainers can provide the facilities necessary. If you live in an area where there are indigenous cat species and discover cubs or kitten that you know to be orphaned, seek professional help. Young left on their own are not necessarily abandoned and should only be treated as orphans if you have proof their mother is dead.

possibility of an unneutered feral tom ranging the neighborhood and impregnating queens. If you do not want to breed from a female then she should be spayed; even an indoor-living female will try to get out when in season and not just through doors and windows.

You may want your cat to have kittens, and sharing in the birth and rearing of a litter can give a great deal of pleasure. Some owners feel

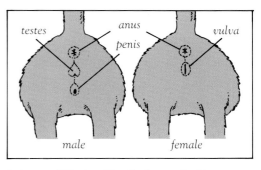

It is more difficult to identify the sex of a kitten than that of an adult cat. Viewed from the back — you may have to lift the tail out of the way — the anus and vulva of the female are close together like a dotted 'i'. In the male the round opening in which the penis is hidden is set lower, separated by the scrotum, which will not usually become apparent until the testicles develop several weeks later.

Points to look for when choosing a healthy kitten

Fur should be in good condition, glossy and free of any powdery deposits (which could indicate a bad skin condition) and of the black specks of flea droppings. When you handle the cat you should feel no hard or scabby patches of skin under the fur. Look out for any scaly areas or fur loss, especially on the head, which could be due to fungus such as ringworm.
Eyes should be bright and follow everything with lively interest. Like us, all cats may develop a little deposit in the corner of the eye which is easily wiped clean but there should be no signs of any runny discharge. The nictitating membrane (third eyelid) should be retracted.
Nose should be clean and not runny.
Ears should be free of any gummy discharge or

the brown specks that indicate an ear mite infestation.
Anus Check for signs of diarrhea or segments of tapeworm (which look like grains of rice); at the same time check on the kitten's sex, even the experts occasionally make a mistake!
Belly should feel rubbery when you hold a kitten, not hard or flabby. If it seems blown-up then it may be infected with roundworms.
Movement should be well coordinated with no sign of lameness. If a kitten leans to one side or keeps shaking its head look out for ear infestation. If it constantly scratches itself beware of fleas.
Note: Although you may choose a kitten when it is younger, do *not* take it from its mother until it is at least eight weeks old.

that their cat should experience motherhood and allow at least one litter to be born before she is spayed. If you do not mind what the resulting kittens will be, allow the cat to mate freely with the local toms, but if you find them unsuitable, or have a pedigree cat you want to breed, then you will have to keep her shut indoors from the very first sign that she is coming on heat. Windows, including louvers, must be firmly closed, no doors left open which give access outdoors and all other apertures blocked off.

Providing for the newcomer

If you are buying from a pet shop you may be able to take a kitten away with you, in which case all the preparations described below will have to be undertaken beforehand or effected with the utmost speed!

In most cases, when you have seen kittens at the breeder's you will have to wait until they are old enough to leave their mother before you can take them home. No kitten should be separated from its mother until it has been fully weaned, unless there are exceptional medical reasons for doing so, and it should be at least eight weeks old before going to its new home. The kitten then has a full chance of normal development as part of the litter and the mother will be approaching the stage when she begins to distance herself from her young and will be less stressed at losing them. Under British law (the Pet Animals Act) no shop may sell kittens under eight weeks old — twelve weeks for pedigree animals.

Equipment

Feral cats may still have to scavenge and curl up wherever they can to find cover from the elements, but the domestic cat is now catered for by a whole industry specifically directed towards satisfying its every need. Some of the toys and trappings are irrelevant to the real welfare of cats but quite a lot of the purpose-built items are not only easier to use than the substitutes to be found around the home but often less expensive. The first essentials are a carrying basket, a litter box, food and water bowls and a collar with identity tag. You will also need a bed, scratching post and toys, though they need not be purpose-made and can be improvised from materials you already have. Your list should include a brush and comb for grooming.

Carrying basket An essential for transporting a cat home, visits to the vet and any other journeys. Never carry a cat in your arms outside the home. A sudden fright or distraction and it may be out of your grasp and out of sight (or under a truck wheel) in moments.

The simplest carriers are collapsible cardboard boxes with ventilation holes, constructed with carrying handles which keep the container closed against pressure from inside. Often available from veterinary surgeries as well as pet stores, they are cheap and easily stored flat. They do the job efficiently for occasional use but will not stand up to frequent soakings in bad weather or by incontinent cats. On a long journey a determined cat may scratch or chew its way through the cardboard and, if the box is not correctly assembled a heavy cat could fall out through the bottom. Except in a real emergency, do not use an ordinary cardboard box as a carrier; you will have your work cut out keeping the cat in it.

Wicker is a traditional basket material, fairly easy to clean and disinfect, providing ventilation and some privacy and not unattractive to have about the house, but fiberglass and plastic-covered wire are even more hygienic. Some types

A carrier is absolutely essential when taking a cat to the vet or on any journey. A top-opening carrier makes it easier to lift a cat in and out. With an end-opening type (and with an uninjured cat) up-end it to lower the cat in.

are available with built-in water bowls and other fittings. An open wire cage, however, gives no protection from weather, other animals' sneezes or intrusive human fingers. They are really only suitable for journeys by car and not for veterinarians' crowded waiting rooms.

Newspaper, toweling or a piece of blanket in the bottom will make the carrier more comfortable, and newspaper up the sides and/or a cloth placed over the top will give some protection from drafts in a wire mesh type.

Many carriers open on the narrow side, which often has bars so that the cat can see out and you in. Although it allows the carrying handles to be firmly fixed on top it can be extremely difficult to remove a resistant cat from this kind of carrier. A top opening makes it much easier to put the cat in and take it out. The weight may have to be carried through the hinge and closures of the lid but the convenience is worth the heavier wear at these points.

Litter box Every cat needs a toilet tray or litter box when it first moves into a new home and if you do not allow your cat free access to the outdoors it will be a permanent fixture. Any container big enough for the cat to squat in and with sides about 3 in (7.5 cm) high can be used with sand, sawdust, peat or newspaper to absorb

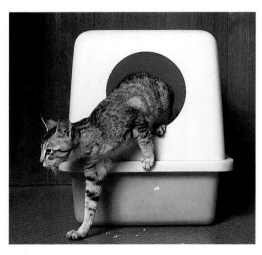

Litter boxes range from simple trays to types with disposable liners, drainage sumps and other elaborations. A plastic cover with an aperture for the cat to enter will stop litter from being scattered all around.

the waste. However, these materials may not disguise its scent and will require frequent changing. Commercial cat litter, usually fuller's earth or some other absorbent clay, though synthetic materials are also used, is more expensive but more efficient and hygienic. The small bags stocked by many supermarkets are a very uneconomic purchase. Large bags are much better value. Pet suppliers will often deliver regularly to your door; you may find them advertising in the local press or on the information board in your vet's waiting room.

To begin with, try to obtain the litter which the breeder or previous owner uses so that it will be familiar to the cat. If you prefer another kind, change when your cat has become accustomed to the litter tray in the place where it is kept.

Pet stores have tough plastic trays which are cheap and easy to clean. Some have disposable plastic liners to enclose them. Those with a high cover prevent the cat from scattering litter around and help contain any odor not absorbed.

Bowls For health reasons do not use family food bowls for pet food and water; wash cats' dishes separately from family dishes. Special pet bowls are most easily distinguished, and plastic containers shaped so that cats will not spill them are cheap and easily available. There are also sophisticated food and water dispensers which will keep food covered when the cat is not eating or automatically issue dried cat food and water so that it is always fresh. Most cats will learn to use them fairly rapidly but they are not suitable for new kittens. They are comparatively expensive and more difficult to clean but could prove useful to owners who find it difficult to serve food at regular times.

Collars Every cat should have a collar carrying an identity disc or a cylinder containing a slip of paper with owner's name, address and telephone number. Never allow a cat outdoors without it. The collar must have an elastic section so that if it should ever get caught on a nail, twig or other projection, it will stretch and allow the cat to free itself. Collars are no protection against thieves but the idea of tattooing an identifying number, increasingly recommended for dogs, is more difficult to carry out on a cat whose fur gives a more general covering. The most recent identification method is by the insertion of a tiny silicon chip beneath the skin carrying encoded information which can be read by a special scanner. Such a system linked with registration and the equipment of a registration organization, police forces and other involved bodies with a special scanner to read the chip would give absolute proof of ownership and ensure that cats who had lost their collars could be returned to their owners without risk of being put down as unwanted strays. However, a simple identification tag on a collar is an easy way to enable individuals to trace an owner.

When you buy the collar get a leash as well. You may be able to train the cat to it and it will make it easier to control if traveling.

Bedding A cat will happily choose its own place to sleep but if you do not want it to be in your favorite armchair, on your bed or on the central heating boiler, give it a bed of its own. All kinds of beds are available from wicker baskets to bean-bag nests, little houses with built-in heating units or beds that form part of complete environments with a sort of cat adventure playground. But most cats love ordinary cardboard boxes; leave an empty one around and a cat will almost certainly jump into it. Line it with newspaper and some soft bedding. Cut down one side to give easy access for kittens. or place the box on its side to make a cave-like den.

Scratching post Essential for cats that do not go outside and sensible in any home to avoid damage to furniture and furnishings. It can be a natural log, a hessian- or carpet-covered post (preferably choose a coarse fabric unlike any elsewhere in the house) or a commercially-produced pad or pillar on a firm base or fixed to floor or wall. Cats need to scratch to remove worn covering from claws and to stretch and exercise their limbs.

A scratching post, preferably offering a coarse texture different from any of your furnishings, will save them from possible destruction. It may be freestanding on a stable base, or a panel attached to an upright surface, or even to the floor, if that is how your cat likes to scratch. Show the cat how to use it by demonstration and by putting its claws up to the post in a scratching motion.

Toys Pet shops and markets stock all kinds of toys from catnip-stuffed mice to balls on springs that pop in and out of holes. Cats will play with anything which they can chase, pat, toss or pounce upon. A crumpled piece of paper, a table tennis ball, a cotton reel (spool) dangling on a string, a sheet of newspaper to dive beneath, a large paper bag or carrier, are among their favorites. Best of all is a piece of string with a tireless human at the other end! Be careful not to leave a threaded needle about as a kitten may chew the thread and get the needle stuck in its mouth, or even swallow it. Do not offer cats toys with detachable eyes that they might swallow or any coated with toxic paints. Kittens will tear toys to pieces and chew them even more than young children do. Avoid foam rubber or plastic fillings which they might chew and swallow and be prepared for them to find — and steal — their own toys: a raffia coaster, dishwashing pad and small pieces of clothing, from underwear to socks, are typical of what one cat likes to acquire; with a flick of the paw she can throw them in the air. *Never* allow cats or kittens to play with rubber bands or plastic packaging which could require surgery for removal if swallowed.

Kitten comforts The first time a kitten is on its own you can offer a little comfort by making sure that its bed is warm. Special electric heating pads are available but an ordinary rubber hot-water bottle (or even a brick heated in the oven), can be effective. Wrap it in a towel to diffuse its heat more slowly. An old-fashioned wind-up clock that ticks, tucked under the bedding to give a pulse like its mother's heartbeat, is often thought to help bridge those first days of being alone. If you use an alarm clock, make sure that the alarm is off or it might prove a frightener rather than a comforter!

Preparations

So you have equipped yourself with the items you will need. What more is necessary before you bring your new cat or kitten home? First plan when that will be. Do not choose a day when you have other commitments. Leaving behind mother, siblings, and everything it has known for a strange new world is a traumatic experience for a kitten. If you have already gained its confidence, you can help a great deal by being a reassuring presence in the period of settling in. Left to its own devices, it could get into difficulties when it plucks up courage to explore its new home or even cause damage by knocking things over or soiling carpets. Warn everyone in the household to keep disturbance to the minimum and discourage any visitors. Friends may be anxious to see the new kitten but they must wait until it has settled in. Make sure children appreciate that they must be very gentle, at first waiting for the kitten or cat to come to them and not rushing to pick it up or trying to make it play.

Decide where you are going to put the cat's bed. Choose a quiet, draft-free place (check at floor level yourself) away from the routes which are in constant use. Fix places for litter tray and food where they will not be in your way. You will probably want to have the tray tidily tucked away, but it must still be somewhere fairly near the cat's food and water and convenient to you for changing. If you have a covered litter tray they could all go in the same area. Even the best of cats will sometimes pull food out of its bowl and a big bone will not fit in it anyway so spread newspaper to protect the floor from spills — or better, a piece of thick polythene or a plastic mat which is easily wiped down.

Now make an inspection of your home. Are there any places that you do *not* want the cat to go. Though it may be able to weave a delicate path among your valued ornaments and crystal, it cannot see from below what is on a table or shelf before it jumps up. It is not unknown for a cat which feels it is not getting enough attention to deliberately push an ornament off the mantel-shelf and it is probably wise to make a rule that it should not jump up on to tables or cupboards or kitchen surfaces where food is prepared. You should certainly discourage it from leaping on a hot cooker where it might do itself some injury. You may decide it is best to keep some rooms strictly out of bounds. If rules are to be kept, you must impose them from the start and not allow things to a captivating new kitten that you may wish to ban later. But be warned — cats are inquisitive and they like high places, so you cannot always expect them to toe the line if you are not around.

Take a look around your home from a cat's point of view. There is a warm and cozy space inside that tumble-drier which you left with the door ajar; there is an appetizing scent of fish scraps coming from the kitchen waste bin; there is certainly something tasty cooking on the stove and a refrigerator always has food inside. That open fire is warm and it is tempting to go closer, the electric cable looks just like a piece of string to play with and an open drawer is an invitation to jump inside and snuggle up among the soft clothes inside. Bleaches, household detergents, paints and insecticides can all be toxic to cats, so make sure you close cupboards. Do not leave sharp knives where cats could play with them, objects resting over table edges where they could be toppled or cords hanging temptingly. Note that several kinds of house plants are poisonous, including azaleas, poinsettia and philodendrons. To discourage a cat from nibbling them, grow a special pot of grass for it (especially if it cannot get outside to find its own).

These are not problems that you have to face all at once for, on its arrival, you should not let the cat range through the house. Choose one room for it to explore and feel safe in first. Temporarily, put bed, litter tray and food there, even though more permanent locations will be elsewhere. Make sure everyone knows which room is chosen and when you expect to be home so that nothing dangerous is left in it. Any other household animals can be kept well away and ask humans to keep clear too until the cat has begun to feel secure.

Last, but not least, get some food and, regardless of what you hope to feed the cat on later, find out the diet and mealtimes the cat has been accustomed to, and try to match them, gradually making changes as the cat settles in.

Collecting the new cat

Collect your new companion yourself. Do not give the job to someone else. You have to gain the cat's confidence and offer some sort of reassurance during the separation from its family and introduction to a new home. You also need the opportunity to sort out any last problems with the breeder or previous owner. If it is a pedigree cat, make sure that you have the pedigree documentation and, if you intend to breed or show, that the cat is registered and the ownership transferred to you. If this has not already been done, get full instructions on how to do it. Check whether the cat has had any vaccinations and request the appropriate certificates if it has. You should already have full details of its current diet.

If there is anything that you feel unsure about — grooming, giving a pill, the address of the local breed society or just how to hold a cat — this is your chance to ask the breeder personally. A demonstration is often a much better way of learning than trying to follow instructions in a book.

Do you know the proper way to hold a cat? Mother cats carry their kittens by the scruff of the neck, holding them in their teeth. You may pick up young kittens by gripping them in the same place, but put your other hand beneath the kitten to support its body as soon as you have lifted if from the ground. However, this is not the ideal way to pick up any kitten or older cat, let alone carry it, though it is a useful hold for restraining a cat or grabbing one that panics and is about to bolt (if it doesn't bite you first).

Lift a grown cat by putting one hand beneath the body and lifting behind the forelegs, cupping

The correct way to hold a cat.

the other hand beneath the rump as you lift. The best way to carry it is on the crook of your arm or held against your body. If its main weight is carried on one forearm, its front paws resting on the other, that still leaves a hand free to stop the cat from slipping or jumping down. However, provided the cat is firmly, but not tightly held and its weight supported, there may be other positions that your cat prefers — sitting on your forearm for instance while stretched against your body with its front paws over your shoulder. Some even like being cradled like a baby, belly upmost, especially if it is tickled , but they are exceptions and this position does leave claws free to strike a raking blow across your face if the cat becomes frightened or annoyed!

Before you settle the kitten in its basket, make sure that you have all the necessary document-ation, the breeder's address and telephone number and the veterinarian's address and phone number in case you need any urgent advice. Many breeders will be interested in the cat's future progress, and some give a batch of ready stamped and addressed postcards to purchasers of new kittens to encourage them to send regular reports on them.

Make sure the carrier is firmly closed and check all the fastenings as you cannot risk an escape on the way home. On a long journey talk to the cat at first. When it seems comfortable ignore it and hope it goes to sleep. On a short trip you can reassure it from time to time, especially if you are changing from one form of transport to another, waiting at a roadside or on a railroad platform where there is a lot of frightening noise. If traveling by car try to get someone else to drive so that you can give your attention to the cat.

Inside a car or taxi you might even allow the cat out of the basket and on your lap, but only if all windows are closed and it is already wearing a collar and a lead. It is essential that you have control over it at all times. A cat can easily distract or interfere with the driver, get under the pedals or in the way of other controls. Make sure it is safely back in the basket with the fastenings closed before you open the car door.

Arrival

Take the carrier or basket straight to the room chosen as the first place for the cat to get to know. Shut the door and then open the basket. If the cat does not jump out of its own accord, lift it out gently. It may want to explore but if caution outweighs inquisitiveness, carry it over to the litter tray — it may need it after its journey. Make sure it knows that food, milk and water are there but do not press it to eat or drink. It needs to reassure itself about its surroundings first. If it settles down to wash you will know it is feeling much more sure of itself. Now you might offer a game with a piece of string or it might prefer some gentle stroking or be so tired by the excitement that it just wants a nap, perhaps jumping back into the basket if it is not already curled up on your lap. When it sleeps you can lay it gently in its bed. Now is the time to switch on the bed warmer or slip in the wrapped hot-water bottle and the ticking clock. Do not allow the bottle to get stone cold before replacing it or it will have the opposite effect to that intended. Once the kitten is used to being on its own you can dispense with both.

Meeting the household

Introduce other members of the household one at a time. There is no harm in allowing children in to have a peek while the cat is asleep but give it plenty of time to adjust to each new person.

If it is difficult to convince people that they must be patient it will probably be even harder, if you have other pets, to convince them that they should not charge in to meet the newcomer and maybe chase it straight out again. First you have to try to make the resident cat or dog understand that the new kitten belongs. One way that usually works is the trick used by shepherds to get a ewe to adopt an orphaned lamb: make it smell right. If you already have a cat, rub the kitten's coat with some soiled litter from that cat's litter box. With a dog you might use the bedding from its basket or something else well impregnated with its smell. Ideally do this even before you take the kitten into the house. This may well be enough to allay their fears and make them see the newcomer as a companion rather than a threat.

It is the older pet that now needs attention and reassurance. Give it plenty and let it come back into the room with you to meet the new one. Both may bristle with apprehension, but that is no reason for you to worry; in fact try not to do so for any tension on your part will transmit itself to the animals. The strangeness of the newcomer will probably inhibit the other animal from attacking and the kitten will probably adopt a suitably submissive posture and be accepted. You may even find it being given a good wash! Occasionally, the established pet is the one that appears terrified. Then you will just have to wait for the two of them to get used to each other.

Most animals have a benevolent attitude towards infants, but when the new cat is already adult it may be more difficult to integrate. You may have to accept a situation of somewhat intolerant compromise. Make sure that you, and other members of the household, give just as much attention to the established pets as before so that they don't feel their noses have been put out of joint, even though they have to tolerate sharing the very heart of their home territory. There will be plenty of time to enjoy the new arrival when a *modus vivendi* has been established. You may find you end up with a precocious kitten bossing a dog ten times its size. *Warning:* Never expect an established cat to share its food bowl. One each is the rule.

Exploring the home

Once the newcomer appears to be secure in its immediate surroundings it can explore further afield. It may be eager to do so after only a couple of hours or maybe not until next day. Never try to rush it and be prepared for it to be several days, or even longer, before old and new pets are

A cat flap will give your pet access in and out but get one that can be locked shut for occasions when you need to keep the cat indoors. Some flaps have magnetic catches, released by a complementary magnet on the cat's collar.

ready to share their territory. Before you let it investigate a new room make sure that all the other doors and windows there are closed. Do not let it go outside. This must wait both until it is totally established and until vaccinations have had time to take effect. In some areas traffic and other hazards make it unsafe ever to let a cat outdoors, except on a lead.

Keep to the rules you have made about anywhere that is out of bounds. Even if you seem to hear a plaintive mew outside your bedroom door the whole night long, if you have decided you do not want the cat sleeping there, do not lose your resolve by allowing it in. You cannot expect the cat to keep your rules if you begin to break them yourself. Rules must *never* be broken, and remember that cats make rules and develop expectations too. A litter-trained cat that 'forgets' its training is usually doing it to attract your attention and in protest at your not keeping some part of the bargain, or because it is ill.

Vaccinations

Even if you have a certificate to show that a kitten has received vaccinations for panleukopenia (feline enteritis) and feline viral respiratory diseases (cat flu and snuffles) it may require a second shot depending on the age at which the first one was given. If it has not had either this should be arranged for as soon as possible. The cat should not be allowed out for two weeks after the injection; ideally it should also be kept isolated from other cats in the house but this is not always possible.

At the same time as its vaccinations, the vet can make a check on the cat's general health and condition (a wise practice even if it has had its shots) and you can discuss the future neutering of the kitten if you do not intend to breed. Vets vary in the age which they think most suitable for castration and speying.

Veterinarians

If there is more than one vet within reach, how do you choose? Every vet should do his or her best for any animal and is expected to have a knowledge of cats but some are more used to dealing with large farm animals while others have a practice specializing mainly in domestic pets. Breeders and other cat owners may recommend a particular practitioner but if you have no contacts in a neighborhood you may have to take pot luck with local listings. Even within a practice you may find one partner more interested in cats than the others, or your cat may seem more inclined to trust one particular individual. Do not judge vets on how charming they are to you, watch how they behave with your animals.

Some fashionable veterinary practices do make a lot of money and many pet owners have a rather nasty surprise when they get the bill for specialized or complicated treatment, hospitaliz-ation or surgery but, when compared with what the comparable bills would be for private treat-ment for a person, they seem much less expensive. Most vets charge a basic fee for every visit to the surgery, more if they come to visit you, plus separate charges for particular treatments, drugs etc. A reputable vet will provide you with a scale of charges or an estimate for a particular pro-cedure. You can always shop around. It is possible to take out medical insurance for pets and with a young animal this is probably worthwhile; the rates can be more expensive if you start when an animal is several years old. It will not cover spaying or castration and a small fixed amount for any course of treatment may still be the responsibility of the owner.

Some animal welfare societies run free clinics, or charge reduced fees to those who cannot afford to go to a private vet; however, there may not be one near where you live. Veterinary schools also usually run a clinic with a lower scale of fees for those in need.

Vets' training and skill enables them to deduce a great deal from handling and looking at an animal but, since the animal cannot answer their questions directly, they are dependent upon the owner to explain exactly what has happened, to describe the onset of symptoms and the animal's reactions. The owner is the person who knows the cat best, who can most readily recognize changes in behavior or observe the development of physical symptoms. It is important that you keep a look out for any changes in behavior as well as any signs of injury or illness; this is something which should become an automatic part of regular grooming sessions.

Keep a diary of your cat's normal behavior, noting any significant changes, and you will have a useful record of his or her progress which will be valuable to your vet if something goes wrong. You will also need to observe and report on any reactions in a cat which is undergoing treatment.

Feeding your cat

Kittens need frequent feeding: four or five meals a day until they are about six months old, reducing to three by nine months and two, morning and evening, for adult cats. Breeding females will need feeding up to four times daily because they cannot eat enough at one time to meet their needs. Quantities will vary according to age, size and individual. Always give the same diet and number of meals a new cat or kitten is used to. Changes can be made once it has settled in, but gradually or they may lead to diarrhea or refusal to eat.

Dried and semi-moist commercial foods contain less moisture than canned or fresh food and their bulk will be correspondingly less. Quantities recommended by manufacturers give a rough guide, though they may err on the generous side. The best guide is the cat itself. If a fully-grown cat eats well, and maintains weight and health but leaves some food on the plate, you can slowly reduce the amount you feed. If it is always demanding more but puts on weight it is just greedy and you should cut down the intake. The accompanying table gives an approximate guide for different kinds of foods.

If a cat refuses a perfectly good meal yet seems otherwise in good health it may simply be because it knows you have something it likes better for your own dinner. Do not substitute something else. The occasional day of fasting will not do a mature cat any harm. In the wild cats often go without a meal if prey is difficult to find.

Commercial cat foods

Commercially-produced pet foods are now a multi-billion dollar industry and the big companies' research departments have developed foods that are carefully balanced to meet all a cat's dietary needs. Whether presented as canned meat, semi-moist pellets in foil bags or as dry food they are a very convenient way of feeding a pet and those produced by reputable companies are nutritionally better than the fine steak that some doting owners serve their pets; they include essential vitamins and minerals which are lacking in muscle meat.

Special kitten formulae are also available.

When dry cat foods were first introduced they were blamed for the occurrence of urinary blockages. The manufacturers have since changed their mineral content and increased the amount of salt to encourage the cat to drink more and produce an acid level in which the crystals that create the blockage cannot form. Provided cats fed on these foods drink plenty of water they are now considered safe; but it is most important that the cat is drinking. Such foods have a shelf life of about six months, will keep after opening if kept dry, and if they are left down all day do not attract flies as canned or fresh food may. Some cats show a preference for their crunchy texture. The semi-moist pellets do not seem to find favor with so many cats but canned foods seem acceptable to all. Individual cats may show strong preferences for particular brands or flavors. Uneaten canned or semi-moist food should be discarded when the next mealtime arrives, and in very hot or fly-troubled places, uneaten food should be removed a couple of hours after serving.

There are pet foods on the market which consist entirely of meat or fish with no added supplements to supply the other nutrients the cat needs. Check the ingredients listed on the can; if this is the cat's sole diet you should ask your vet's advice on giving missing vitamins or minerals.

Although commercial dog foods are usually a little cheaper than cat food, do not economize by feeding them. Dog food usually contains more vegetable matter and is *not* correctly balanced for a cat's needs. Cats need a diet twice as rich in protein as that which dogs require. Many animals can make their own vitamin A and convert the

fatty acid called lineolic found in vegetable as well as animal fats, into the form their body needs. Cats cannot; they need a ready-made supply obtained from animal fat, which also provides a good source of vitamins D and E.

Vegetarian mixtures are now available from some specialist suppliers but those prepared for cats (unlike the mixtures for dogs) do not form a complete diet and a proportion of meat is still required, though research may lead to some alternative in the future.

Most cats seem to like some variety in their diet and you should ring the changes, including some fresh as well as commercial foods, even if your cat clearly prefers a particular brand and flavor. There is always a possibility that the recipe may be changed or local stores stop stocking a particular line.

Always have fresh, clean water available for your cat. This is essential, even if you offer your cat milk as well. Although many cats and all kittens enjoy milk — and few can resist cream — some adult cats reject it. After weaning, as they mature, quite a lot of cats have difficulty in digesting milk, which produces flatulence and diarrhea.

Another supplement which cats seem to need (although it is not clear what good it does them) is grass. Nearly all cats are seen to eat it occasionally and some develop a passion for it. Although its dietary role is uncertain it acts as an emetic to help cats bring up balls of fur swallowed when grooming themselves and probably adds roughage. A cat without access to grass will often eat the leaves of similar-looking plants which will simply make it sick. Leave an untrimmed piece of lawn or let a few clumps grow in the garden, or for an indoor cat grow some in a pot. Pet shops often have pre-sown pots, often of cocksfoot (*Dactylis glomerata*) or rye grass which seem to be favorite species.

Cats are not able to detoxify their bodies and pass out poisons as readily as humans and some other animals. Aspirin, for instance, can be dangerous, as can many types of food preservatives including benzoic acid. See Poisons, page 305.

Fresh foods

Before the easy availability of convenient canned food most domestic cats lived mainly on unwanted parts of carcasses, table scraps and other leftovers. Exactly what, might vary considerably from one place to another. Fish heads, lights (lungs) and other offal might be the staple in Britain but Japanese cats are fed rice and miso soup (miso provides the protein usually obtained from meat), perhaps with a sprinkling of dried fish flakes or small whole fish.

Cats are carnivorous but they can digest vegetables and cereals if they are cooked; they provide useful bulk but should not exceed about one-fifth of the total volume. Some cats refuse them totally, even when cunningly disguised with meat and gravy. They may be fooled by suitably flavored and textured vegetable protein but the dedicated vegetarian owner must remember that a cat is a carnivore. Convincing a cat that it must not scavenge meat or catch its own birds, rodents or fish is likely to prove difficult. Cats instinctively snap up the occasional spider or butterfly and will chase mice and birds, even if they never connect catching with eating them. The true vegetarian cat does not exist.

Fresh food must be varied; too much of one thing, all fish for instance, can lead to problems.

Cook meat and fish to kill germs. Always well-cook pork which is more likely to carry tapeworm larvae. As in human diets, however, any cooking

| Type of Cat | Average Weight | Calories per day | Canned Food | | Semi-Moist Food 300 calories per 100 g (3½ oz) | Dry Food 330 calories per 100 g (3½ oz) |
			Kitten food 120 calories per 100 g (3½ oz)	Cat food 75 calories per 100 g (3½ oz)		
Kitten 2 months	0.7kg (1½ lb)	160	130g (4½ oz)	210 g (7½ oz)	55g (2oz)	50g (1½ oz)
3 months	1.2kg (2½ lb)	240	200g (7oz)	320g (11oz)	80g (3oz)	70g (2½ oz)
6 months	1.8kg (4lb)	350	290g (10oz)	460g (16oz)	120g (4oz)	105g (3½ oz)
Adult 1 year	3.2kg (7lb)	400		530g (18oz)	135g (5oz)	120g (4oz)

Quantities are approximate. Individual animals may need as much as 25% more or less than those indicated.

A lactating queen may need three to four times the normal amount at the peak of her lactation.

It is recommended that kittens are fed a proper kitten food or that an adult food is supplemented. Adult foods do not always contain sufficient nutrients for a growing kitten.

destroys some of the nutritional content of food. Muscle meat and boned fish both lack vitamin A and calcium, which must come from other sources. Meat is deficient in iodine and too much liver builds up harmful surpluses of vitamin A and causes a painful bone disease. An excessive amount of oily fish or of horsemeat can make the cat lose vitamin E. For specific problems see page 319.

Wild cats gnaw raw bones. This helps to keep teeth free from tartar and domestic cats seem to enjoy them; some will even crunch small bones. Butchered bones, however, are sometimes splintered and the thin slivers can be dangerous, while cooked bones, especially stewed ones can become soft and get stuck on teeth which pierce them. Never give cats bones from chickens or other fowl. The answer seems to be feed large knuckle bones, and fish bones (especially when pressure cooked), but keep an eye open for splinters, small pieces that might get swallowed and stick in the throat and always watch out for any problems. For removing bones that get stuck see page 304.

If a cat which is not fed a balanced commercial food does not drink milk or crunch bones it may need calcium supplements.

Eggs are an excellent source of protein, fat and vitamins, and beaten egg can be served raw. Many cats prefer them boiled and chopped with other food or scrambled, though others will not touch them.

Cheese, especially strong-smelling kinds, can become a passion with some cats and is often recommended as a way of persuading cats that are off their food to feed. Cats that don't drink milk may eat it, but some will reject cheese of any kind.

Individual cats, like humans, can develop unusual tastes. Many do not like any of the commercially produced cat treat 'candies', but relish asparagus tips, french beans (whole not sliced), fried mushrooms, bacon rinds, hamburgers, marshmallows, breakfast cereals and pond fish flakes and pellets. Some people feed dried cat food to carp so perhaps the last is not surprising: both contain dry fish products. One female even developed a penchant for dry sherry and was delighted when offered some very dry champagne at a party. She soon became unsteady on her feet but if she had a hangover did not relate cause and effect for she continued to try to steal the occasional tipple. Alcohol, however, like all drugs, is dangerous and should never be given to cats. If they must get 'high' then limit it to playing with catnip-stuffed mice or sniffing and rolling around the plant itself, *Nepetna cataria* or similar plants, such as *mataba*, which seem to send Japanese cats into seventh heaven.

The scent of catmint and similar plants gives some cats particular pleasure.

Almost every cat seems to love lobster and prawns, even if they are not very keen on fish, and you will easily discover your own cat's special favorite food. There is no harm in indulging a cat occasionally, but do not encourage it to be faddy. You will only be making problems for the future.

Grooming

Most kittens learn to wash themselves before they leave their mother, apart from a few exceptions that are happy to let their fellows do it for them. Among short-haired cats failure to keep themselves clean is usually an indication of ill health. The breeding of long-haired cats, however, has made their job a very difficult one. A Persian cat living a normal feline life can get very soiled and really does need help. A daily brushing is essential. With shorthairs it is not so vital but, once it has got used to the procedure, the cat will enjoy regular grooming which will keep your home from being smothered in discarded fur!

Start grooming early in kittenhood. A mature cat unused to it may be very uncooperative at first but most cats enjoy the attention and the sensation.

For longhairs many experts use only a metal comb and do not brush. Any brush should be natural bristle, rather than wire or plastic, which can tug fur out at the roots, or nylon, which will produce static electricity. Choose a comb with both wide and close-set teeth, or use two combs. For most shorthairs a rubber brush (like a pad with rubber knobs) is often recommended, but for Rex, which lack guard hairs, use a very soft brush. Some people use a soft toothbrush for grooming facial fur.

The most comfortable place for grooming is on a table top, although, if you insist, you can kneel down on the floor! Spread a sheet of paper or white plastic to catch any fur and dirt you may remove. Newspaper is not ideal, partly because the newsprint may come off on the cats' paws but mainly because it makes it difficult to see the dirt which may fall out. The paper makes it easy to dispose of the dirt and easier to check for parasites. You may prefer to groom in the garden or on your lap, but try to do it frequently on a sheet as a parasite check. If you are not sure whether black specks are dirt or flea droppings, press a damp cloth on them; flea droppings will leave a blood-colored smudge.

Begin grooming with an overall inspection for cuts, scratches, abscesses, broken teeth, build-up of tartar, development of gingivitis and skin problems. Pay particular attention to the ears, anus, claws, the space between the toes and to the pads of the feet.

Most scratches heal very rapidly without attention but even small injuries from fights or snags on nails, wire netting, etc. can turn nasty if ignored, especially when a wound heals leaving dirt inside. Clean the eyes with a soft cloth dampened with water. Wipe down and toward the nose and then outwards.

At least once a week, use cotton buds on sticks to clean the ears. (Do not poke them in but wipe them around the outer ear. Never use them on the eyes.) Moisten them with a little baby oil or surgical spirit (rubbing alcohol). If the ears smell unpleasant or there is a dirty brown fluid-like build-up of wax, these are signs of ear mites, but a little golden wax in the ear canal is normal and healthy.

If claws have grown too long because they do not get enough wear on hard surfaces, they should be trimmed with nail clippers, not scissors — the kind of clippers that are similar to sprung

wire cutters are the easiest to use. If long claws are left, they can start to curve back into the paw so do not ignore them. Take great care not to cut into the live part (or quick) of the claw. Hold the paw in one hand and gently squeeze the claw sheath so that the claw projects. Note the area suffused with blood and keep well clear of this with the clippers. Get your vet or an experienced owner to show you how to do this *before* you attempt to do it on your own.

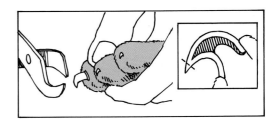

When trimming claws take care not cut into the quick.

Long-haired cats Comb, first with the open teeth and then with the fine, beginning with the legs and then the flanks and back. In general, work upwards from the underparts and from front to back. If tangles are too dense for the open-toothed comb or your fingers to free them, a skewer or knitting needle may do the job. At worst you may have to resort to scissors (use round-ended not pointed ones) but this is something which frequent grooming will avoid. Oily stains from the sebaceous glands can be reduced by using talcum powder to remove the grease but 'stud tail' (excessive staining along the upper side of the tail which occurs with some entire males) needs special attention.

Ask an experienced breeder or your vet to show you how to regularly bathe to eliminate the problem. Occasionally dry shampoo with talc or proprietary powders. Dust them into the coat and rub into the fur right down to the roots before combing out. Remnants of pale powders left in the coats of dark-colored cats may look like dandruff so, for appearance sake, use bran. Warm it in the oven, tip into a box or tray, and then place the cat on top to make this job easier.

Next, brush in the same sequence, from front to back, which will help the fur to stand up and away from the body and raise the ruff around the neck to frame the face. In some breeds the tail will need special attention. Maine Coon Cats, Turkish Van Cats and Angoras should be groomed in a similar way to shorthairs, but daily.

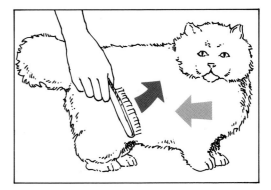

On long-haired cats work upwards and from front to back.

Short-haired cats Comb and brush horizontally, from front to back. Some cats, especially Siamese, really enjoy quite vigorous brushing in all directions or an all-over massage with the fingertips just like the stimulating scalp massage you probably have at your hairdresser's. However, this is not a treatment for show cats whose appearance is so important. In temperature-dependent colors (the 'pointed' cats) excessive brushing is said to darken the coat. Shorthairs require much less grooming and are more able to cope on their own. Vigorous but careful stroking with the lie of the coat will help remove dead hairs, especially after a massage or when a cat is molting heavily at the onset of summer. Indoor life encourages heavier year-round molting than in the wild cats so grooming will help to reduce fur balls and the amount of fur left on your furnishings.

Add an extra gloss to a short-hair coat by a rub with a pad of velvet or chamois leather, or with an old piece of nylon stocking pulled over the brush. Brush with the coat, not against it.

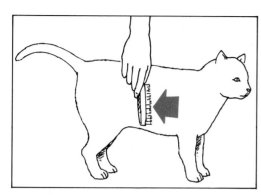

On short-haired cats work horizontally from front to back.

Wet Shampoos It is not often that a cat needs a wet bath but exhibitors often like to wash cats before shows and any cat may need one for medical reasons or if its coat is contaminated with grease. Do not expect a cat to like it at first and, if you think regular bathing is likely to be its lot, make sure that you give it a wash well before it is six months old. Older cats seem to find it even more of an ordeal if they have not become accustomed to the process.

Expect a struggle so, if possible, get someone to help you. If you know your cat hates being washed do not let it see your preparations. You do not want a fight or a flight before you even begin.

Do not use a shampoo made for human adults. Very mild baby shampoos are acceptable but there are some which are specially formulated for cats. Do not try to do the job in a bathtub which will mean bending over the cat. Use the kitchen sink or a large washbowl. Fill it about 4 in (10 cm) deep and test the temperature with your elbow, as for a baby's bath. Put the cat into the water, holding it very firmly! Wet its head first and then the rest of the body, scooping water up with a plastic pot or beaker. Avoid water trickling into the ears. Apply shampoo and work up a lather, keeping it away from the cat's eyes. Pull the plug and rinse with a hand-held shower or have another bowl of clean water ready for rinsing. In the case of a medicated shampoo, check the manufacturers' instructions or those given by your vet. Most give a specific time to leave on before a thorough rinse to remove all traces.

Dry a longhair by blotting with a towel (rubbing will tangle the coat), then comb. With shorthairs rub vigorously in all directions with a rough towel and then brush. Use a hair-dryer if the cat will tolerate it. Get it used to the hair-dryer in advance when you are using it yourself; first the noise, then the air jet, but do not bring it very close and keep it on warm but not full heat. Never play the air jet on the eyes or into the ears. A blotting and careful combing will help speed up drying whenever a cat gets wet, either soaked by a downpour or an accidental dip.

Small areas of contamination with paint, tar or other obnoxious substances on the coat or paws can sometimes be removed by rapidly washing the area with a little washing-up detergent. If firmly attached, loosen by swabbing with olive oil or similar cooking oils (or by dipping a paw into it). Always rinse thoroughly afterwards.

Training your cat

Training can never start too early and by the time a kitten comes into your care it should already have received quite a lot of instruction from its mother. Teaching a cat is a matter of patience and determination, and success depends on a system of reward rather than punishment. Unfortunately the domestic cat has no natural urge to accept and obey a leader, unlike the dog, whose instinct is to be subservient within a pack. If you are lucky, a young kitten, seeing you as a kind of mother substitute, may give you some of the obedience which the mother cat received, but although a top cat frequently emerges in cat colonies, the independent cat tends to be ego-centric. You must win its cooperation.

Training has two aspects: discouraging unsuitable behavior and teaching a cat to do the things you want it to do. Punishment is not a valid measure apart from the gentlest reproof. Cats are relatively easily bruised and should *never* be struck. Pain should have no role in education for animal or human. A light tap on the nose or a thump from a rolled up newspaper close to but not touching the animal are as far as you should go, but it is better if you can try to disassociate reproof from yourself. In that way good behavior may not depend upon you being there to enforce it. A water pistol (or a plastic bottle with a nozzle similar to those used for washing-up liquids) will let you squirt water from a short distance. Whether physical or verbal, discouragement must occur when the misdemeanor takes place. It is no use later, when you discover it, for the cat will associate reproof with what it is doing then. Once the lesson is learned, however, a cat may be well aware when it has broken the rules and be careful to avoid you when the crime is discovered.

A word of warning: a playful cat may decide that avoiding that rolled up paper when it jumps on the table to make you slap it down is a splendid game, especially if you show any sign of finding it amusing. A cat's resourcefulness, physical skills and cunning are part of its attraction but do not let that temper your disapproval. Cats are very responsive to mood and tone of voice. A firm 'no' is often the only admonishment they need. They will recognize displeasure but if you are obviously amused at the same time as you are telling them off you can hardly expect them to believe you are really annoyed.

Keep games and approval as rewards for doing the right thing and try always to make your reactions unmistakable. A stroke, a tickle under the chin, a massage on the nape of the neck — you will soon discover the things your cat enjoys, quite apart from the occasional tidbits, which are excellent reinforcement tools.

Toilet training A kitten's mother will almost certainly have taught it to use a litter tray. All you need do is show it where it is or at most put the kitten in and move its paws in a digging motion. You do much the same to teach an untrained kitten, but then you must keep an eye open for the moment when the youngster balances with its rear end clear of the ground ready to urinate or defecate. That is when, moving smoothly and gently so that it does not panic, as a fright would only precipitate urination, you should pick it up quickly and place it in the tray. There are bound to be a few accidents at first,

but it will soon get the idea. Clean any soiled spots thoroughly; swabbing with vinegar disguises any remaining smell and cats seem to dislike it. Commercial deodorants are also available and some are very effective. If the place is not cleaned, the cat will go there again. If you find this happening regularly in the same spot, place the litter tray there for a time, then, once the cat has started using it, gradually transfer it, between visits, to its permanent location.

Do not rub a cat's nose on a soiled patch or chastise it after the event. Once it has got used to a tray, a cat's soiling elsewhere suggests a urinary disorder or other illness, or a bout of diarrhea if it looks as though the cat did not reach the tray in time. Before you rush off to the vet, however, check out the tray. If it needs changing, the cat may simply have found it too dirty to use; some cats tolerate only a comparatively low level of soiling, and some will deliberately soil elsewhere as a gesture of protest.

All cats need to be litter-trained, even if you intend to allow them outdoors when they are older. There may well be times when illness, oestrus or a move to a new home may mean that you have to keep them indoors. Once taught, it will be easier to get them to accept a tray again.

Even when allowed outdoors, many cats will continue to use the tray and, unless they are always free to come in and out, you should keep one for use when they are locked in. Encouraging them to use the earth outside will save the trouble and expense of changing litter though neither you nor your neighbors will be very happy if they dig their latrines just where seedlings are sprouting in the border. If there is no heavy traffic or other dangers out of doors and you are prepared to take a chance with your flowers, encourage them to transfer to outside by putting the litter tray in the garden. You may need to do it in stages if the area you want them to use is some way from the house. Obviously they need somewhere they can dig. At first go on changing the litter, but when you feel the new location is accepted, remove the tray and leave a pile of litter, reducing replenishment until none is needed.

Spraying Spraying is not limited to males. Wildcat females tend to spray more than toms but domestic females rarely spray indoors unless under great stress. You cannot stop it in entire males, though you can discourage them from using particular places by the water jet technique if you catch them in the act, or by serving their food near places where they spray because they usually prefer to do so away from feeding areas. However, they will still go on spraying elsewhere and, even if you manage to prevent it in your house you, and probably your neighbors, will not only have to put up with plants or shrubs being damaged by frequent sprays of urine but with places which smell so strongly that they are unapproachable. Toms may enter other homes, especially where there are entire females, and spray there too! However much respect one has for an animal's natural way of life, this kind of intrusion is quite unacceptable. If you and your cat are to be friends with your neighbors this is another strong argument for castration, which should be performed before the tom reaches the age to begin spray marking or it may continue to do so even after neutering. Cats which are kept for stud will not be allowed to roam and confining them in their own housing localizes the problem.

Scratching Whenever a kitten or new cat claws and scratches carpet, furniture, drapes, wall-covering or anything else it can damage, take it immediately to the scratching point you have provided — a post, panel, log or old piece of furniture. If the cat tends to use a horizontal surface, fix your panel on the floor; if vertical then follow that preference. An unconfined cat may prefer to use somewhere out of doors and choose a tree or fence where the damage will not be serious.

One ploy, if a cat begins to scratch a particular upholstered chair, is to take a piece of the same or similar fabric and lay it over the area the cat has clawed, keeping it in position by placing a book on top so that, when the cat scratches, the book will fall and act as a deterrent. In this way, the cat does not associate the falling book with you but with its scratching. Beware, however, this may backfire and be treated as a game!

Out of bounds Preventing a cat from jumping on to tables, work surfaces or other places, stopping it from playing with electric wires and enforcing other general rules for its safety and your convenience, must rely on the general discouragement and reward techniques.

Naming and calling Choose a name which is distinctive and easy for the cat to recognize when you call it. A pedigree cat may have an official name on its certificate but you may want something simpler for everyday. A kitten will usually learn its name quite quickly, but an older cat, especially a stray who may already have learned to respond to a given name, may take longer. Always use the name when you are doing things the cat likes, especially when offering food or stroking it. Avoid using the name when you are annoyed by its behavior and trying to correct it; in such circumstances just say 'bad cat' or something similar. If a cat associates its name with pleasant things it is far more likely to come to you when called. At first only call a cat when it is going to want to come to you. Do not try calling it when it is eating, has just had a meal or is turning around to settle down for a snooze. In those circumstances it is not disposed to pay you much attention.

Going out Cats are creatures of habit and regular routines. They expect meals at regular times. If you go out to work or have a set pattern to your day, they will soon adjust to it. They will soon learn when they have to return if they are not to be shut out of the house. However, if you are irregular in your day, or simply want to give your cat added freedom, you might consider a cat door or cat 'flap'. There are a number of types which can be set into a hole in the wall, a door panel or even a window pane. The best kinds will be designed so that they open freely from both sides but do not admit drafts when not in use. The drawback of a cat flap is that other cats may come through it too, though there are some kinds with electromagnetic locks which limit use to cats wearing the appropriate magnet on their collars. Unfortunately magnets only have two poles so, if your neighbors use the same kind of flap, 50 percent of them will have the appropriate 'key'.

Teach cats to use a flap by keeping it fully open at first. Then, when they have used it a couple of times, wedge it slightly ajar so that they can easily identify the opening on their return. Remove the wedge and see if they have learned their lesson. If they call to be let in swing the flap to remind them.

Games and skills

A cat can be conditioned by association with the benefits or disadvantages that the required behavior brings. That is sufficient when you are dealing with dos and don'ts concerning its natural activities, but that is not really learning, which is based on observation and discovery. Some cats can be enormously clever at working things out, though with what may seem inconsistency to us. For instance, an owner that had spent a considerable amount of time on his knees by a door slightly ajar, unsuccessfully trying to show a cat that by hooking a paw around its edge it could be opened further, saw it moments later reaching up to try to turn the handle. That is the way it had seen humans usually open the door, not this hands and knees business — too bad that in pressing on the handle it was also shutting the door more firmly! Cats do not miss much but they make their own connections, not necessarily the same as ours.

Cats will often develop their own idiosyncratic games, which will usually be clearly linked to some kind of natural behavior — chasing, catching, carrying — and by exploiting such instinctive actions you can encourage a cat to become a retriever or develop other skills for which you recognize a potential. A cat is just as likely to teach you a game as the other way round, and it may establish a routine of games at certain times — a game of hide-and-seek for instance before you go to bed. Such games will be to the cat's own rules. The hiding places may always be the same and, if you are too slow at discovery, your cat may pop out to call you! Like kitten chases, this is a game of 'let's pretend'.

Walking on a leash

How often do you see a cat out on a leash? Cats may prefer to hunt and roam alone rather than follow the pack but there are plenty of them who will tag along with friends and follow them on a walk. Nevertheless, training cats to walk on a leash seems to daunt the majority of owners. It is worth some effort, especially if you live where there is heavy traffic or if you are away from home a lot. Think of the advantage of being able to take your cat for exercise or of being able to have it accompany you to the office or on holiday and enjoy outings with you.

An ordinary collar may put too much strain on the cat's neck if you use a leash. A proper harness which goes behind the cat's front legs as well as around the neck is preferable. Often called a 'figure of eight' harness, the cat cannot wriggle out or choke itself by pulling. First get the cat used to wearing the harness for a few minutes each day, then attach a string or cord and let it get used to that for a few days too. Then start holding the other end of the string and try to get the cat to walk a little way, calling it towards you. Always slacken off the cord if the cat pulls away at the beginning; the leash should not be associated with restraint. When you have obtained some cooperation swap the cord for the proper leash.

All the preliminary training should be in the house or garden where the cat feels confidently at home. You can then start taking it for short walks outdoors, and then gradually introduce it to traffic and other noises and distractions.

Although cats can produce bursts of great speed and energy they cannot sustain effort as long as humans, so do not expect a cat to keep up over a long distance. Many will happily sit on your shoulder or lie draped around your neck and this is a convenient way of carrying them when they begin to tire. Keep hold of the attached leash so that you always have the cat under control.

Even if you do not succeed in teaching your pet to walk on a leash you will still find it invaluable for restraining a cat when you have to take it to the vet or on a journey.

Traveling with a cat

The dangers of having a cat loose in the car have already been mentioned — so don't! With a leash-trained cat it may be perfectly safe to walk down to the shops with it sitting on your shoulders but for any trip by bus, car, train or boat, use the carrying basket. Even if you think you can handle the cat without it, the transport company may have regulations that require a particular type of cat carrier or reserve the right not to carry animals at all. It is always worth checking before planning a journey to see whether the company will carry animals on the service you propose to use and exactly what their requirements are. On a train you may have to leave the cat in the luggage van, so check whether it will be possible for you to visit. Airlines may require animals to be in a pressurized container and carried in the cargo hold, although some permit a cat to travel in a special container placed beneath passenger seating.

For a long journey, you will need to make provision for toilet needs; also drinking water if it is likely to last more than six hours. In a private car or traveling in the luggage van you could take a litter tray, bowl and water with you; otherwise they will have to be in the carrier. Although cats are not as susceptible to travel sickness as dogs, as a safety measure it is wiser not to feed a cat immediately before traveling. It may object to going without a meal but that will be more comfortable for you — and it — if it becomes ill. If you know a cat to be prone to sickness or to be extremely nervous, your vet may agree to administering a tranquilizer.

Unaccompanied journeys

Make sure that the cat is labeled with both the destination and name of the person or organization collecting at the other end, and with your own, complete with addresses and telephone numbers. Check that the collection arrangements are clearly understood. For air travel you may need to deliver the cat to the cargo section several hours before take-off. For a journey of more than 24 hours (or 12 in the case of kittens) the cat will also need to be provided with food. If it will accept dry or semi-moist kinds they will be much more convenient. In the case of interconnecting flights, the airline will usually handle the transfer and check the cat's condition at each transfer. Airlines do not usually accept very young kittens unaccompanied.

Vacations

If you have a permanent vacation home, you can take your cat with you. It already feels secure with you so it will not take long to adapt to its vacation territory, but never risk letting it roam free until you are quite sure it has settled in and that neither road traffic nor predators — hawks, owls, foxes, coyotes, etc. — make free-ranging dangerous. Unless you are absolutely confident that a cat will come when called, keep it indoors from the mealtime preceding your time for returning home.

Some hotels welcome pets with visitors, but unless a cat is leash-trained, it may have to stay in your room. More practical for most people is to arrange for a cat-sitter, or someone to feed the cat regularly, look after it and spend a little time with it. Make sure that they are well aware of your pet's routine and needs, have the vet's number and can contact you if necessary.

If you cannot get your cat looked after at home, a boarding cattery is the answer. You may need to book cattery accommodation well in advance, especially for busy vacation periods. Visit before you make a booking to ensure that the place is clean and well run and has appropriate veterinary back-up. You will need to prove that your cat has had the necessary vaccinations. If a cat requires special diet or medication, this should be explained.

With a young cat, even if you have a cat-sitter available, boarding may be advisable as young cats usually adapt more easily than older ones and will get accustomed to the idea for the future. Elderly cats who have never been away from home can be upset by suddenly being uprooted and separated from family and territory.

Cats and the law

The laws concerning cats differ from country to country and even from state to state. Cats are often covered by legislation against cruelty to animals but owners are not usually responsible for their cats' actions since, free-ranging, they are not under their control. However, if they cause injury or damage in circumstances which the owner could easily have prevented or has deliberately encouraged, that owner may be liable for damages.

There is not usually any requirement for drivers and others to report accidents involving cats. They do, however, count as property in terms of theft.

International and interstate travel

Many countries will not permit the import of a cat without a health certificate issued by a veterinarian within a limited period before departure and may also require export documents and a proof of rabies vaccination. A medical certificate is required when crossing the border into certain States of the United States.

Quarantine

The most important legislation which affects pet owners concerns movement into areas that are free of rabies and have strict quarantine regulations, principally the United Kingdom and Eire, Australia, New Zealand and Hawaii. In some other countries (and in some of the United States), rabies injections are recommended or mandatory, but in those mentioned, no risk whatever is allowed of animals introducing the disease. Not even a cat living on a visiting boat may come ashore. Animals entering these countries must spend six months or longer under observation in special quarantine catteries where pens are spaced to prevent cross-infection. If they are rabies-free at the end of this period, they may join their owners. Pet owners are usually allowed to visit the cattery to see them during their isolation but often not allowed to enter or approach close to pens. In fact, many believe that visits only upset the cats. In Hawaii, however, visits are recommended and owners are even allowed to groom their quarantined pets, despite the risk of rabies transmission which this contact allows.

Quarantine is at the owners' cost and quite expensive but it cannot be avoided. A cat smuggled, or even accidentally taken into these countries may be destroyed. Regulations differ and should be checked.

Six months in quarantine is a long period and obviously not to be considered unless you are moving to another country permanently; even then you might consider finding the cat a new home rather than have it and you go through the experience of quarantine.

BREEDING

Planning for kittens

If you have a female cat you may want to allow her to have kittens, for sharing the birth and rearing of a litter can be a delightful experience, but first consider very carefully the problems of finding them homes or of adding them to your own household. If you have a cat of a popular breed with a good pedigree and can match her with another, you may find a good demand for her kittens, but do not imagine it is an easy way to turn a profit. Breeding is an expensive and time-consuming hobby that demands dedication to the cats. It will cost you something in stud fees, in addition to the expense of rearing kittens and any veterinary bills that may be necessary. Stud owners may require proof that the cat is free from feline leukemia and AIDS and these tests can be expensive.

The best way of going about breeding a pedigree cat is to join a Cat Club, buy a registered kitten and follow the guidance of experienced breeders. Many of them will be reluctant to sell a high-quality cat to anyone not registered as a breeder and will insist on purchasers signing a contract to spay or neuter a cat which is bought as a pet. If you have an ordinary house cat you will still face the cost of rearing the kittens but the boyfriend will come for nothing — just let her out of the door when she is in season.

However, this would be very irresponsible; there are far too many unwanted kittens already. If you do not want another half-dozen kittens yourself, or already know of homes eager to take them, producing more is a bad idea. Spaying is a good one.

Even if you are sure you want the kittens, consider the possibilities. Have you seen the local dominant tom? Do you want your kittens to look like that, or have that kind of personality? If you don't, you will find that breeders of pedigree cats rarely permit their stud toms to serve non-pedigree females. You may even know someone with an attractive, gentle-natured tom and be able to pay a house visit, but the chances are pretty slim, for responsible people do not usually keep entire toms as pets.

If your cat is unspayed and free to wander you may have no choice in the matter for if you are unfamiliar with the signs she may have mated even before you realize she is on heat. Some females mature very early, especially Siamese who sometimes first 'call' (come into oestrus) as young as six months, sometimes even four. You will understand why it is called 'calling' as soon as you hear her. If you do recognise the signs and keep her in, you will probably find all the local male talent lined up outside so you can easily assess the potential fathers before you take your chance. Missing a mating on her first season will not do her any harm. Breeders do not usually mate their cats this early and in fact they seldom conceive at this 'warm-up' call. However, do not let this happen repeatedly. If you want your cat to mate later but for some reason not yet, she can be artificially made to ovulate and end her oestrus, coming into season again three to four weeks later, or for longer periods could be put 'on the pill', although this could upset her cycle for months. In either case, this is a matter for your vet. If you find yourself deciding on more than one 'postponement' think again and decide to have her spayed.

If you are mating a pedigree female — and once into the world of breeders you had better start calling her a 'queen', the usual term for a breeding female cat — then you have to choose an appropriate stud. Apart from being the right breed you may want to ensure that there is no tendency towards any bad points present in your cat as far as breed standards go, and that the stud has qualities which will compensate for any weaknesses in the queen's conformation 'type' as the Fancy terms it.

If you got your cat direct from a breeder she or he will probably be happy to advise you. The Breed Society will also be able to put you in touch with suitable stud owners. Some studs have a reputation for being particularly suitable for virgin or 'maiden' queens; others are noted as being prepotent, that is, throwing superior 'type' progeny again and again.

Ideally you should visit first to satisfy yourself of the cattery's standards and the quality of the stud. You should certainly make all the arrangements well in advance of when you wish to mate your cat. It is not easy to predict exactly when a cat will come 'on heat' so you cannot make a firm booking, especially if it is a young cat and you have not yet established the usual frequency of her calling. Each queen has a pattern to her calling, both the number of days and the timing of her cycle which make subsequent oestrus easier to forecast. Agree all details in advance so that arrangements can be finalized very quickly when she does come on heat.

The stud house should be secure, spotlessly clean and comfortably equipped, with an outdoor run, if the climate is suitable, but certainly with a recreation area and good ventilation. It should include separate quarters for the queen, though she may not always want to retire to them, and it should be away from other cats if part of a larger cattery.

You will have to pay a stud fee, which may be inclusive or have various other expenses added to it. If you think it is expensive be thankful that you do not own a racehorse. The stud owner has to provide and run the premises, thoroughly clean and disinfect the stud house and run between every visitor, and will be feeding your cat and overseeing the whole process, as well as having the expense of a valuable stud and his upkeep. They are also risking the possibility of injury to their stud from your cat. The cost may be higher if the stud is an important champion.

If you have a good quality queen the stud owner may be prepared to arrange a mating in return for the choice of a kitten from the litter. If you enter into this kind of arrangement make sure that all the details are agreed in a written contract so that there can be no future dispute.

The stud owner will want to see your cat's pedigree and you will be expected to provide proof that the queen has had still valid inoculations for feline infectious enteritis and respiratory viral infections. Some stud owners may also want a certificate attesting that she is clear of feline leukemia and cat AIDS. In return you are entitled to receive similar assurances concerning the stud. Stud owners sometimes ask for very recent vaccinations, which may increase the antibodies a mother can pass on to kittens in her colostrum. It is up to you to ensure that your cat is free of fleas and worms, and suitable treatments should be given in time to be completed before her expected 'call'. Some breeders prefer a queen's claws to be trimmed to lessen the risk of injury to the stud or themselves if she is nervous.

If the owner thinks there is any sign of illness in your cat when it arrives a vet may be consulted and the mating then called off if there is anything wrong. Such care is necessary because contact not only places the stud at risk (and his owner's investment in him) but all the future females who come to visit.

If there is no sign of your cat coming on heat when the date of your booking arrives you will of course let the stud owner know, so that another queen can be accepted instead if the stud is asked for. As soon as you recognise the first signs of your queen coming on heat you must ensure that your home is secure and she cannot get out through any door, window or other opening to find her own tom. Then immediately inform the stud owner. If you are lucky the stud will be free, but even if there is another queen in residence you can arrange to take your cat as soon as possible. A queen will usually stay at least two days and often longer, depending on when the pair are introduced. If the stud is still occupied you will have to wait, and the owner will also need 24 hours to clean and prepare the stud house and rest the tom. Since your cat's oestrus will continue for several days if she is not mated, this will seldom be a problem.

The mating

Before being introduced to the stud cat, your queen will be given a chance to acclimatize herself in her own part of the housing. A first-timer may take a while to settle in; an experienced mother will set about inspecting the talent straight away. Only after the cats have made it clear that they are well disposed towards each other will the gate between their quarters be opened. Courtship and mating will then usually proceed as described in the section on 'The Life of Cats'. The stud owner will be on hand to ensure that neither harms the other and to check that mating takes place. A round-the-clock watch does not have to be kept but it is usual to ensure that at least three observed matings take place — although there is the rare cat that refuses to mate when there are people watching. Practice varies as to whether the queen is put back in her own quarters after the first mating or whether the pair are allowed to run together as soon as they have made friends.

Sometimes a tom or a queen refuses to have anything to do with the other. Occasionally a young maiden queen may need to be stroked and artificially stimulated before she is aroused enough to accept the tom, or be so nervous that she has to be held while the stud mounts her. The odd cat needs a very long period of fraternization. These problems are seldom encountered.

Another possibility, but only if the journey to the stud is a very long one (or the queen has had to wait her turn) is that she stops calling before she gets there. Then it is a matter of 'try next time' and, if the cat is part of an important breeding program, it may be worth boarding the queen at the stud cattery until her next call to be quite sure it does not happen again. Similarly, if translocation caused a great upheaval, a queen will remain with the stud owner until it is quite certain that she is pregnant.

When repeated matings have been confirmed and you collect your queen, make sure that you have a copy of the stud cat's pedigree and make arrangements to obtain any forms necessary for registering the kittens later. You may also be given a certificate of mating. When you get your cat home keep her securely indoors for the next week; she may still be in oestrus and if she can get out to another tom may present you with his kittens instead of the ones you want!

When you groom her keep a lookout for fleas and tapeworms. Even the best stud owner could have been unlucky with a previous visitor but not found any sign of parasites before your cat arrived.

If conception has been achieved the signs will gradually appear as described in 'The Life of Cats'. If not, the signs will probably be much more noticeable — your cat calling again in three or four weeks' time.

Caring for the pregnant queen

At first the mother-to-be requires no special care. She may sleep a little more and she will certainly need more food. If she has been used to just an evening meal start giving her breakfast too. Towards the end of pregnancy it will be easier if her stomach does not have to deal with too much at one feeding so get her used to smaller more frequent meals now. You may have to start her off with a few treats if she does not like the idea of breakfast before you substitute more routine food. Quantity depends on her size and how active she was before. A small and not very active cat may need nearly twice as much food by the end of her pregnancy, so if she asks for food you should give it. A balanced diet is usually all a healthy queen requires but sometimes vitamin or mineral supplements may be advantageous. You may want your vet to confirm pregnancy at about the sixteenth day so this would be the time to find out about any supplements and check on how much to feed.

Your cat will carry on life as normal, which is probably one reason why few cats have any problems in having kittens. Unlike most other domestic animals, from dogs to cows, the cat's body has not been distorted by controlled breeding and chemical interference; birth remains more natural. Never give a pregnant cat any drugs or vaccinations, except in an emergency and with veterinary approval, for they could harm the kittens. When grooming, keep checking for fleas; you do not want the kittens to start off with an infestation. Pick the fleas off if you can. If you have to powder or spray for fleas, thoroughly brush out the treatment and do not risk giving it near the date the kittens are expected.

Choose a suitable place and prepare a kittening box. This should be about 2 ft (60 cm) square and 20 in (50 cm) deep. Make it of wood or use a cardboard box. Cut an opening on one side for the mother to come and go, but not so low that the kittens can climb out. Line the box with plenty of newspaper. If it has a top, which will help keep out drafts, it should be hinged or removable so that you can see inside and help the cat if necessary. At least seven days before you expect the kittens set it in a warm place, away from bright light and disturbance but easily accessible. If she does not find it for herself, place her in it occasionally to identify it as hers. Tearing up the paper inside can be taken as a sign of her approval but not all cats do it. If she persists in looking for somewhere else to have the kittens and seems to have chosen another place

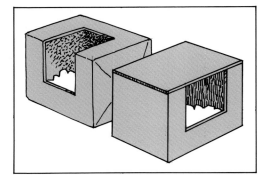

Two styles of kittening box.

that would still be accessible put the box there. If it is in an awkward corner try to block it and keep cupboards and drawers closed so that she does not pick on one of them.

As soon as she starts looking for a nest you should keep her in the house. Most cats like to be near their humans but some could choose to hide away outside. This means that you need to reintroduce her to a litter tray if she no longer uses one.

By now the weight of the kittens may be affecting her mobility. If it is a big litter she may have trouble cleaning her rear end. Gently wash the anus and vulva for her with warm water and pat them dry. The nipples may begin to produce a little milk which dries around them so wash them gently too. Usually the hair thins out around the nipples but in a long-haired cat it may help to trim it away slightly from around the nipples, the back legs and the vagina. Some cats also suffer slightly from constipation in the last stages of pregnancy. A little oily fish, such as pilchard, will help or, if it persists, a spoonful of cod liver oil, olive oil or medicinal liquid paraffin (mineral oil, not kerosene) can be given.

Make sure the birth room is warm, ideally about 72°F (22°C). If it is in a cold place, a low power infra-red lamp above the box or a well insulated and waterproofed heating pad beneath it should keep an even temperature.

Birth

Changes in behavior, increasing displays of affection, alternate squatting and scratching, frequent unsuccessful attempts to urinate, vomiting up a meal soon after eating it (out of excitement or because her contractions are beginning), heavy purring and/or panting — these are all indications that birth may be imminent. They may be so brief that you do not notice them or they may persist for 24 hours. There will be a clear discharge from the vulva, perhaps as much as two days beforehand. If it is pus-like or smells foul it is an indication that something is wrong and you should consult your vet immediately. It is worth getting in touch with him or her anyway so that you know where to make contact in the unlikely event of there being problems.

Add a towel or blanket to the kittening box and be prepared to be around all night. Perhaps your cat will prefer to be left alone, but many feel happier to have their humans close and some will even delay giving birth until you are there. If you are going to stand by and play midwife give your hands a good scrub (but *not* with carbolic, which is harmful to cats) and have ready some cottonwool swabs, pieces of clean rough toweling, and petroleum jelly. Optional extras are some sharp surgical scissors, alcohol or an antiseptic suitable for cats and a spool of thread. Another box with a hot-water bottle in it covered by a piece of towel may be useful if you have to take any kittens from the mother.

The process of labor will usually proceed without any help from you. If, on delivering a kitten, your cat fails to lick it clear of the amniotic sac within a minute of delivery you should clean the kitten for her, but give her a chance to do so first, though she may ignore it if she is delivering another kitten in quick succession. Often the sac will break as it arrives, but if it has not, feel gently for the kitten's head and tear the sack with your fingers to free it and peel the membrane away. Wipe fluid and mucus clear of the mouth and nostrils and massage the kitten with a piece of towel to start it breathing.

If the umbilical cord has not broken, sever it by gripping it close to the kitten's body with the fingers of one hand and with the other hand, about 2–3 in (5–7.5 cm) further along, press the index finger against one side of it and then rub the thumb nail across it from side to side until it parts. Done in this way it will rarely bleed. If you prefer to use scissors, first tie thread around the cord between the kitten and where you intend to cut. Take care not to pull on the cord or you could cause a hernia. Then sterilize the scissors and cut at about 2 in (5 cm) from the kitten. However, the mother usually manages all these operations herself.

If a kitten is not breathing swing it up and down (see illustration). If this does not clear its air passages and start it breathing, apply artificial respiration. Cover both nose and mouth with your lips and breathe in short gentle puffs. Do not blow hard, a kitten's lungs are *tiny*.

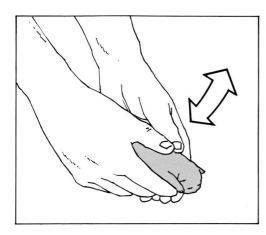

As each kitten is born, check that the placenta follows; occasionally one may be retained inside the mother, decay and cause infection. If this happens call the vet who will give her an injection to promote the expelling of the retained placenta.

If a cat appears to have difficulty in delivery do not interfere until you are quite sure it cannot cope on its own. A little verbal reassurance and gentle stroking of her belly may calm her if she is getting agitated. A delivery can be quite slow with long pauses after each kitten emerges. If it is coming out head first the cat's licking will probably break the sac and free its head to breathe and just a little more patience is required. A 'rear first' delivery — a real breech birth, with the legs still inside, not just feet and tail coming first — will be difficult because of the greater width. It may help for the cat to have something to push her hind paws against; if she is too far from the side of the box give her your hand to push against. A delivery with one leg out and one leg in can be more difficult.

If you have decided assistance is necessary, liberally coat a little finger with petroleum jelly (or medicinal paraffin) and gently push the kitten back before lubricating the vaginal wall and drawing the kitten out. If the cat is exhausted from her efforts and has really given up with the kitten half out, use a piece of rough toweling to grasp it firmly and pull it gently upwards first, then downwards, attempting to synchronize your movements with the mother's contractions if she continues pushing.

Most births go very smoothly. Even a real breech birth should cause no alarm, though if a little gentle help does not succeed you should call your vet. You should definitely seek professional help if a cat has strong contractions for more than an hour without producing any kittens; if a kitten is presented for more than 15 minutes; if the mother seems distressed and exhausted; or if her contractions grow weaker when there are clearly other kittens to be born,

especially if more than three hours have elapsed since a delivery.

If you need to remove kittens while giving the mother attention, or care for kittens you are dealing with, the second box with its hot-water bottle comes into use. However, kittens should quickly be returned to mother as their suckling will maintain her instinctive maternal behavior. If she has had to be operated upon you must watch that while still partly anesthetized she does not roll on top of them, or attack them in the confusion of coming round.

If all kittens are stillborn this may indicate an infection of the womb. A deformed or half formed fetus among the births may indicate that the cat was originally carrying too large a litter and her body had put the process in reverse, reabsorbing some of the fetuses. If this process starts after the skeleton has formed and hardened it will result in a partially formed fetus being expelled.

Orphans and rejects

In the rare case of accident to the mother, rejection of a runt in a large litter or exclusion of a weak kitten by its siblings, you may have to intervene. Hand-rearing is difficult, arduous and requires round-the-clock availability to be successful. The best solution is fostering on another lactating female who may have lost all or some of her own kittens. Rubbing the kitten with a little milk squeezed from the foster mother's nipples is likely to increase its acceptance. Sometimes other small mammals will also accept a kitten and feed it with their own offspring.

Cat litters are normally four to six kittens and large enough to allow for many not to reach adulthood in the wild, so the occasional kitten born dead or too weak to survive will not usually worry a mother who is busy with others, although you should consult your vet in case there is any problem with the mother. If it is a large litter, ask the vet's advice on how many the cat can raise without undue strain. The rest should be given a painless death (euthanasia) unless you are willing and able to hand-rear them.

Hand-reared kittens must be kept warm: 90°F (32°C) on the first day and 85°F (29°C) for the next week, after which the temperature can gradually be reduced to about 70°F (21°C) by four weeks. You can regulate temperature by changing the height at which an infra-red bulb is suspended over the box.

You will have to groom and clean the kittens, using a damp coarse towel to simulate the mother's tongue and cotton wool around the face and anus. Massage from head to tail on the abdomen to stimulate digestion, and urination. They may not pass feces for the first few days (there is no need to worry until day five) but defecation can be stimulated by massaging the anus with cottonwool dipped in a little light oil (medicinal liquid paraffin).

Feeding is difficult. Special milk powders designed for kittens are available but as a temporary measure use either baby milk powder made up at twice the human concentration or unsweetened evaporated milk diluted with one part boiling water to three of concentrate. Cow's milk does not have enough protein for cats. Your vet will be able to advise you on how often and how much to feed. Serve it at about 100°F (38°C). Do not attempt to spoon it down their throats, they must suckle it. Special feeding bottles are available which will simply require you to place the teat in the kitten's mouth, but as a temporary measure use an eye dropper or a syringe and *very* gently squeeze out a little at a

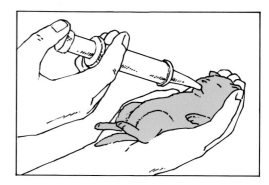

time for them to suck. Do not force it into their mouths or it could go down the wrong way and drown them. If nothing like that is available twist a piece of clean cloth, thoroughly washed to ensure there is no detergent or bleach in it, and dip it in the milk to be sucked on.

If you sit with a coarse towel on your lap it will both keep you clean and give the kitten something to grip. Support the kitten in your palm, head between your finger and thumb and give milk with the other hand. If it does not attempt to suck, dab a little on its mouth. If it gulps down too much and chokes, lift the tail end to bring up air. To burp a kitten do not pat its back, as with a human baby, but massage its abdomen.

If a kitten develops any sore spots or 'nappy rash' soothe them with an antiseptic cream, but check with your vet that it is mild enough for use with kittens.

If kittens are unable to suckle from their mother they miss getting important antibodies against disease which are present in her first milk, or colostrum as it is properly called, which protect them from many feline diseases in their early life. They are therefore much more susceptible to infection. Your veterinarian may suggest giving them a course of inoculations at four or five weeks of age, earlier than is usual for most kittens.

'Fading' kittens

Sometimes an originally healthy litter begins to lose its vitality, moving lethargically, its strong voices becoming weak. This can happen two or three days or about ten days after birth. Because the kittens are not suckling much you may think the mother has no milk and indeed find her teats seem dry when you squeeze them gently. This is not usually a failure of milk supply, but the nipples have become blocked with dry milk. Bathing them with warm water will get the milk flowing again but you may still have difficulty in getting the kittens to suck. You may be able to keep them going by feeding them with a syringe but the chances are slight. In this condition, known as the 'fading kitten syndrome' and not fully understood, the whole litter is likely to become rapidly weaker until respiration and temperature become so low that they die.

Post-natal problems

A slight discharge of clean blood from the vagina for about a week after kittening need not cause concern but if there is a brown viscous discharge, usually accompanied by fever and the cat shows abdominal pain when handled, this probably indicates a retained placenta (see above). Symptoms usually occur about three days after giving birth and demand immediate veterinary attention. Antibiotics and hormones can usually sort things out but if not dealt with rapidly a complete hysterectomy may be necessary. You may well have to raise the litter yourself!

Other things to look out for are lack of interest in the litter, excessive thirst and vomiting; these may indicate an infection of the uterus. Rejection of suckling kittens can also be due to mastitis, an infection of the milk glands which may produce a gray/brown discharge. Although in a very mild case gentle squeezing may clear the blockage in a nipple, antibiotics may be necessary, and since infected milk could harm the kittens, hand-rearing may be necessary for a time.

If the mother's breathing becomes abnormally rapid and she is very nervous with dilated pupils and possibly muscular tremors and difficulty in walking this may be milk fever, also known as eclampsia or lactation tetany (see page 315).

Rearing the kittens

With a normal healthy litter your job will be to see that the mother is properly provided for — she will need more food to make the milk for those hungry mouths — and to keep the place safe for the kittens. If it is difficult to ensure that there is nothing dangerous in the room and that they do not wander outside, a baby's play-pen can be useful, provided it has side mesh that the kittens cannot climb through; you may have to put cardboard up the sides when they get big enough to climb!

Make sure the litter tray is within easy reach for mother, and handy for her to teach the kittens to use it. You can help if you see them start to dig. Put them in it after every meal, for feeding stimulates defecation.

Once the kittens' eyes are open make sure that they do not become resealed by the slightly gummy discharge which may be produced for the next few days, wiping it away with a damp cloth if necessary, though mother will probably do this job herself along with giving them all the other care they need and starting to teach them as they grow older.

At about three weeks old, when they begin to show their first teeth, you can offer them canned kitten food and a little egg yolk beaten up in milk. If commercially produced kitten food is not available you can use baby foods made up to about twice the concentration used for babies, but talk to your vet about quantities and mixtures.

If you are lucky kittens may begin to start eating from their mother's food dish and at this point you might start introducing some proprietary canned kitten food.

Remember that kitten stomachs are small, only about the size of a walnut at six weeks, so they need small meals, often — five at intervals through the day is ideal. Check that it is they, not mother, that are taking the food and that they are all eating. Mother herself will discourage them from suckling as they get older either by lying so that it is more difficult to reach her nipples or by simply leaving them alone more often.

Do not bring every visitor in to look at them and remind children that the kittens are very tiny and not yet ready to play games. From about four weeks, however, they should begin to be accustomed to human handling and given a little gentle grooming, especially if they are of long-haired type. With a good mother they will not need it but it will get them accustomed to the idea. When mother begins to get tired of their constant pestering you can begin to play games with them; in the first few weeks leave everything to her to carry out the normal rearing processes described in 'The Life of Cats'.

If she feels you are interfering too much, if they wander too far or for some reason she thinks they are in danger, she may carry them back to the nest or even take them off and hide them somewhere.

If you are hand-rearing kittens you will have to do everything, so the sooner you can get them onto solid food the better, but do not attempt to do so before the fifteenth day. If you are only raising part of the litter try to get mother to accept them back as soon as they and the others are partly weaned. Rub them with a little of her milk or urine to make them smell less of you and more of her. She will then be able to give them the lessons in cat life that you cannot.

Finding new homes

A hand-reared kitten that is fully weaned could go to a new home from about six weeks old. Encourage the new owner to visit, play with it and handle it on several occasions beforehand so that the kitten can become familiar with a new source of security. Normally, however, a kitten should not leave a healthy mother until it is *at least eight weeks old*, unless there is some powerful overriding consideration. From seven to ten weeks mother cats usually begin to distance themselves from their kittens, though they still keep a close eye on them and rush to protect them at any sign of danger. If kittens are taken away one at a time she will not become particularly upset at their going, though she may spend a day looking for the last one after it leaves. Owners are likely to find the parting much more traumatic if they have raised the kittens.

Finding homes is not always easy, for you will want them to be good ones. Do not press friends and neighbors into taking kittens, they must be really wanted. If you ended up with a larger family than you intended, that is a responsibility you accepted when you decided to allow your cat to breed. If they are pedigree kittens the stud owner may well know of people who are looking for kittens of the breed. Your vet may know of others who are looking for kittens and will probably be happy to put a notice up in his surgery. People whose cats have died and want a new one certainly understand the responsibilities that ownership involves.

Pedigree kittens with a carefully matched parentage may be in demand and fetch high prices but do not expect to make money out of breeding kittens. If you add up all the costs and attention involved you are unlikely to make a profit even with a kitten of championship stock, but you will have shared a thrilling and beautiful experience. Even the most ordinary mixed-breed house cat will be just as precious to you after that, its life just as valuable. Do not just give it away. Ask for a token payment, to be given to one of the animal welfare organizations if you like; it may make new owners approach their responsibilities more seriously. Offer to take the kitten back if it is returned within a short period as that may save it from being abandoned. Many breeders ask for a cat to be returned to them if circumstances at any time force an owner to give it up. They caused it to be born and accept final responsibility for it.

Make sure the new owner has a proper carrying basket or box and has prepared for the kitten's arrival. Give them all the information on diet and care that you needed when you first obtained your cat. Do not forget to supply a copy of the kitten's pedigree, if it has one, and explain how it can be registered.

Playful, inquisitive, but a little apprehensive, a kitten embarks on life in a new home.

THE ELDERLY CAT

A well cared-for cat lives to 15 or even 20 years if not struck down by accident or disease, much longer than most dogs. It is impossible to sensibly compare its age with the human span for while cats mature much more rapidly than people, if they have lively and interesting lives they go for many years showing little sign of aging. A twelve-year-old will not be as continually demanding as a kitten and will be more settled into a routine but will still be eager to play a game with you, especially if you have a regularly appointed time, and just as appreciative of affection. An older cat will probably be less tolerant of disruption, may disappear when there are strange visitors, be more annoyed if its meals are late — in fact, behave like any other creature of habit.

If it has been boss cat of the neighborhood an aging cat may have to face a loss of sovereignty, especially if some tough young newcomer has moved in nearby, which can produce both a more aggressive defense of its core territory and a greater timidity at the unknown. Most noticeable will be the changes in a breeding female. From about eight years the number in a queen's

litter will grow fewer and by about 12 she may not conceive at all, though toms are potent for considerably longer. In both cases neutering and retirement to a less demanding life before that stage is reached is recommended.

Physical signs of aging are usually a little graying around the nose and sometimes elsewhere in the coat, a slight loss of weight (unless they are overfed) and a tendency to a slightly lazier life. Major weight loss is a sign of something wrong and should be investigated. The elderly cat is more susceptible to cat flu and other respiratory infections and some of the body mechanisms become less efficient. Sight and hearing, like our own, deteriorate with advancing age. Constipation may be a problem and require diet modification. Tartar build-up on teeth may cause gingivitis and more frequent scaling is necessary, and if a cat loses its teeth you may have to cut up food for it. Tumors, both benign and cancerous, are relatively common and any growth or lump should be investigated. Arthritis and heart disease are less common than in dogs or humans but chronic kidney disease is frequent as cats reach advanced years and most cats are prone to it if they live long enough.

From age ten or 12 you should take even an apparently healthy cat for a veterinary check-up more frequently than for its booster inoculations — at least every year and preferably every six months as it gets older. Inevitably you are likely to have more veterinary bills with an elderly cat, but you took on that obligation long ago.

Euthanasia If a cat has a chronic and incurable condition you will have to try to assess the quality of its life. There comes a time when either the cat itself gives up the struggle or becomes so severely ill that it would be cruel to allow its pain to continue, but there are many situations when suitable care can ensure that a cat can still enjoy life. Cats that are deaf or blind can often still lead amazingly agile lives. But if the cat is in great distress and nothing can be done, or if the treat-

ment itself is very painful and success is doubtful, and in certain circumstances when treatment is far beyond an owner's means and the after-care more demanding than they could handle, the wisest decision will be to bring the cat's life to a painless end.

Euthanasia is now carried out by a simple injection of an instantly lethal drug into a vein. Beyond the initial prick of the needle the cat feels nothing and your vet will probably allow you to hold it to the last if you wish.

Making the decision to end another life is a difficult one to take but the decision has to be your own. A vet can give you advice on the cat's condition but cannot tell you what to do or when. A cat responds to its current state, rather than comparing it with how fit it used to be and will accept limitations of mobility, perhaps even a certain level of pain, as the new norm. You may be very conscious that it is failing; it may be more aware of the love and attention you are giving it. Few owners could clearly say whether the final decision is made because their bond with the animal enables them to know when the cat itself has had enough or whether it is their own reaction to its pain but, however sad, making it and helping your cat to a peaceful end is your ultimate caring action.

Disposal You may be happy to leave it to your vet to dispose of your pet's remains. If you are anxious that they should be incinerated and no use made of the body for fur or manufacture secure his or her assurance — any responsible vet will give you a signed statement if you wish it. On the other hand you may consider that the corpse is just a corpse and not mind what use is made of it. Some people like to have their pet stuffed, or even have something made from the skin. They see the beauty in a skull or skeleton and may wish to preserve it. Others find such ideas extremely distasteful.

Local law may allow burial in your own garden, in which case the grave should be at least three

At one time a dozen years was thought a good age for a cat but better care and veterinary skills now see many living much longer. This tortoisehell and white was 18½. Towser, the champion mouser (page 238) reached 24. The oldest on record was Puss, a tabby tom from Devonshire, England, who lived to 36!

feet (90 cm) deep. Or you may wish to have a separate cremation; your vet will probably be able to put you in contact with a service who will collect the cat from the surgery and return the ashes to you. In some places pet funeral parlors offer more elaborate services with ceremonies, tributes, burial plots and memorials according to your taste and pocket.

Whether you commemorate your cat with a rose bush in the garden, by endowing a surgery in a free veterinary clinic or putting a coin in the collecting box on animal charity days, the happy time you have spent together will be an enduring memory.

Overleaf *White Persian (Longhair).*

THE HEALTHY CAT

Maintaining good health is a balancing act, with the cat's body resistance on the one side and various diseases on the other. To maintain this balance arrange vaccinations for the common virus diseases, assist with grooming where necessary, provide access to areas where the cat can exercise, give a sufficient and properly balanced diet and ensure the cat does not become fat, protect it from physical dangers, and keep its food utensils and environment as clean as possible.

Causes of ill health

Stress can lower a cat's natural resistance to infection. Stresses include changing homes, boarding, traveling, showing, excessive heat or cold, or even the administration of certain drugs. A queen is under greater stress when she is on heat, and during late pregnancy, kittening or lactation. Individual cats may be more easily affected by stress, particularly Siamese and Orientals.

Infections may be caused by viruses, bacteria, fungi, yeasts, or parasites. These can be picked up by inhalation into the lungs, through the mouth, by direct contact with the skin, or via insect or other bites. A cat may lack sufficient immunity to a particular type of infection, or large doses can overwhelm normally adequate defenses.

Non-infectious causes of ill health include allergies, faulty diet, hormonal disorders, inherited defects, injury, malfunctions of body organs such as can occur in heart or kidney disease, old age degeneration, poisoning and tumors.

Signs of ill health

As the owner you can detect your cat's problems early. You will usually be the first to see anything wrong or feel something abnormal when handling it. Look for one or more of the following eleven key groups of signs:

1. **Pain and fever.** *Pain* is one of the earliest signs of disease. Detecting when a cat is in pain and locating the area from which the pain arises can help to determine the cause. The animal may be restless, continually get up and down, or cry, or it may remain still and be silent. It may favor the painful part, such as carrying an injured leg, moving its head as little as possible if its neck hurts, or keeping its abdomen tensed if it has a painful bowel condition. Pain from skin, muscle or bone damage is often easier to detect and locate than that from deeper structures such as internal organs, or the brain or spinal cord.
Fever is a rise in body temperature following infection, but a rise (hyperthermia) can also be due to other causes such as heatstroke. The quickest way to detect fever is to take your cat's temperature. Fever may also be accompanied by an increase in the rate of the heart beat and pulse.

2. **Behavior change.** One of the earliest signs of a problem may be a subtle change in your cat's personality or behavior: not being in the usual place at the usual time; spending more time sleeping; becoming more active; grooming, licking, biting or scratching excessively.

Taking your cat's temperature

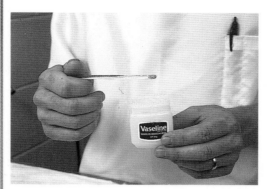

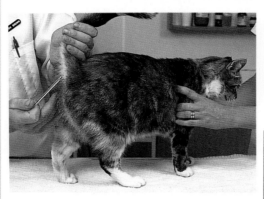

Get someone to hold the cat. Use a stub-ended thermometer, lubricate the bulb with liquid paraffin, petroleum jelly or vegetable oil, and insert it about ¾ in (2 cm) into the rectum. Leave for about one minute, then withdraw, wipe and read. Normal temperature is about 101°F (38.6°C); anything over 102.5°F (39°C) could indicate a fever.

Measuring your cat's heart rate and pulse

To feel the heart beat place one or two fingers on the chest just behind and level with the elbow. The best place to feel the pulse is in the femoral artery in the groin. Count the number of beats over a period of one minute. A cat's normal heart rate is 110-140 beats per minute, but can vary widely between individuals. Minor stress such as traveling, cat shows or veterinary examination can cause an increase. Under severe stress or illness the rate may reach 300 or more.

Checking lameness

To determine the particular part of the leg that is injured gently take hold of it. Starting at the claws and working upwards, *gently* press all over the limb checking for pain or swelling. At the same time flex and extend each joint, starting with the claws and working upwards, and note your cat's reactions.

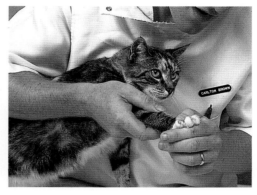

3. **Body control and movement.** Lameness is one of the most common signs of a muscle, tendon or bone problem, but can also be caused by nerve damage. An affected limb is often favored, carried or dragged. But signs of painful movement may be more subtle, such as the cat stopping habits like begging for food or jumping on a favorite chair. Note any loss of balance.

4. **Breathing and voice.** Note any labored breathing, coughing, sneezing or wheezing, and any change in voice.

5. **Defecation and urination.** Look for changes in the consistency of the feces such as diarrhea or constipation; straining; increased frequency; the presence of blood.

6. **Discharge.** Under this heading come runny eyes, and discharge from ears, nose, skin, anus or vagina.

7. **Ear, eye, hearing and sight.** Signs include changes in pupil size, discoloration, abnormal eye movements and lack of response to sounds or visual stimuli.

8. **Eating, drinking, mouth and gums.** Observe any loss or increase in appetite; difficulty in chewing or swallowing; eating or drinking more or less than usual; regurgitating or vomiting food; dribbling; or inflammation of mouth or gums.

9. **Skin/fur.** Watch out for changes to the fur and skin: the coat becoming dull or matted; hair loss (alopecia); dandruff, scabs or inflamed areas.
Four things can help an owner or vet to decide the possible cause of a skin condition:

(a) **The amount and pattern of hair loss (alopecia).**
Outdoor cats, especially those in cold climates, normally shed twice a year. Indoor cats may shed continuously. Shedding may also occur during stress or disease since at that time more hairs enter the resting stage. Alopecia is an abnormal, partial or complete loss of hair that may or may

not occur in association with a skin condition. It may occur in only one particular-spot, or affect part or the whole of the body. The loss may be temporary, with hair regrowth, or permanent. Hair may be lost because it falls out (shedding), or because of physical removal by scratching, chewing, licking or rubbing.

(b) **The presence or absence of itching (pruritis) and dermatitis.**
Pruritis is an irritation in the skin or a sensation that elicits the desire to scratch. It is one of the most common signs associated with skin disease. It may occur in conjunction with skin lesions or not. If it occurs *before* signs of a skin rash the cause is more likely to be an allergy.

The itching usually provokes a scratching, chewing, or licking response, which in turn causes hair loss, broken brittle hairs, a dull coat, and areas of excessive pigmentation. Self-trauma results in inflammation (dermatitis, commonly called eczema) which leads to more irritation. This is called the itch-scratch cycle. Ulcers may appear, and bacteria or fungi often invade the inflamed skin. Affected cats often withdraw from social contact with other pets or owners. General irritability and personality change may occur.

(c) **The speed of onset.**
A sudden occurrence is more likely to be caused by skin parasites, a gradual onset by a hormonal problem, an allergy or a tumor.

(d) **The time of year.**
Many skin diseases have a seasonal basis. For example fleas and flea-bite dermatitis occur more in summer, whereas inhalant dermatitis from pollens is more often seen in spring and autumn. An allergy to house dust or food will be non-seasonal.

10. **Swelling.** Not always visible, but may be detected by running a hand over the cat's body. A painless and extensive swelling that pits on pressure indicates edema, which usually occurs in the lower limbs or under the chest or belly and is caused by the accumulation of tissue fluid under the skin.

Localized swelling with pain suggests an abscess, sting or bite, dislocation or a fracture.

11. **Weight loss or dehydration.** These signs may develop gradually and not readily be noticed. Dehydration causes a loss of skin elasticity: when the skin is pulled away from the body it does not immediately return to its original position.

When to call the vet

Get veterinary advice immediately if a cat is:
* partly or completely unconscious
* in a state of shock, or hemorrhaging
* thought to have had access to poisons or been bitten by a snake or spider
* uncoordinated, falling over, or partly or completely paralysed
* obviously injured
* vomiting frequently or has had severe diarrhea for several hours

Your vet would rather answer a false alarm than be called in too late. For a less urgent problem make it a rule to seek advice early rather than late. You can always talk to a vet or vet nurse over the telephone if you are worried or unsure what to do.

Handling, and administration of medicines

Before trying to do anything place the cat on a firm table or bench with a non-slip surface. If possible get someone to hold it for you as shown. Don't hold it by the scruff of the neck.

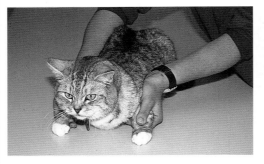

Tablets

Raise the head and use your fingernail to pull the lower jaw open as shown. Place the tablet over the back of the tongue, using a pencil if necessary to push it down.

Liquids

Use a syringe whenever possible, otherwise a teaspoon. Raise the head. Instil liquid carefully into the gap behind the canine tooth, or into the cheek pouch, and keep the head raised until it has been swallowed.

Ear preparations

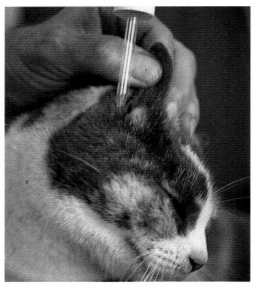

Warm the preparation to room or body temperature. Administer carefully, then massage the base of the ear gently for several minutes. It takes 5–10 minutes for most preparations to act. When released the cat will shake its head, loosening debris which can be wiped away with cotton wool or gauze. Do not insert cotton buds deep into the ear canal or you may cause damage.

Eye preparations

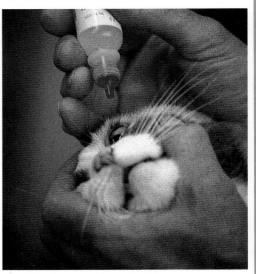

Raise the head and turn it slightly as shown. Place drops or ointment into the outside corner of the eye and allow to flow over the eyeball before releasing the cat.

Nursing a sick cat

Because of their nature many cats can make difficult patients, and where nursing is required it may be better to carry it out at a veterinary hospital rather than at home. However, some illnesses require home nursing by the owner, and in such cases specific instructions will be given by the veterinarian. The following basic principles usually apply, but each cat's individuality should be taken into account:

• give TLC (tender loving care). Most cats respond to it. But at the same time respect your cat's wishes and don't overdo it.
• give the cat the peace and quiet it wants, and/or the family or human contact that will make it happier and more contented. Don't allow children to stress the animal.
• if required, isolate it from other animals.
• give it clean, warm, comfortable surroundings.
• assist with grooming and cleaning where necessary.
• offer strong-smelling foods that will stimulate appetite, but check with your vet before offering liver or heart.
• maintain an adequate supply of fluids, either by mouth or by injection.

FIRST AID AND EMERGENCY CARE

Action in emergency

Your objectives are to
• prevent the cat's condition from deteriorating further
• alleviate its suffering and provide comfort
• protect its injuries from further damage
• avoid being scratched or bitten.
You must be
• calm and efficient
• able to take emergency action yourself

- able to give orders to, or take instruction from, others.

You should
- get someone to arrange for veterinary assistance while you carry out any life-saving procedures
- switch off any power supply that could endanger you or the cat
- approach the cat quietly and cautiously, and if it is conscious try to calm and soothe it
- remove anything that might aggravate its condition, providing that by so doing you don't make matters worse. Remove any collar the cat is wearing
- clear the cat's airway by removing any obstruction in the mouth or throat, but try to avoid being bitten
- keep the cat's head level or slightly down to prevent blood, saliva or vomit causing choking
- apply artificial respiration or cardiac massage if necessary
- stop any serious external bleeding using finger pressure, a pressure bandage or a temporary tourniquet
- if possible, and using the greatest care, transfer the cat to a safe place in a dark, quiet area, and/or confine it in a cage
- assess whether it is suffering from shock or internal bleeding, and treat accordingly
- keep it moderately warm by covering in a towel or blanket, but do not apply heat
- get it checked by a vet as soon as possible.

Artificial respiration

Perform this immediately if a cat stops breathing or is suffering from asphyxia (see below). Remove any obvious cause, and the cat's collar if worn. If the cat has drowned or is choking first swing it by the hind legs (refer **Drowning**). Lay the cat on its side with the head slightly lower than the rest of the body to allow any fluids to drain out. Wipe away any fluid blocking the nostrils. Open the mouth, pull out the tongue to open up the airway, inspect the throat and remove any visible obstruction. Use something to prop the mouth open, such as a cotton spool between the upper and lower canine teeth, with the teeth entering the hole in each end.

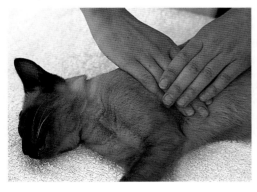

Unless there is severe injury or a penetrating chest wound place the palm of one hand over the chest just behind the elbow, the other palm on top, then press firmly but gently and quickly release. Repeat every 5 seconds, checking regularly to see if the cat is breathing on its own and that the heart is beating. Another method is to hold the cat by the thighs and swing it vigorously in a wide arc about 10 times. In cases where there is a serious chest injury use mouth to nose resuscitation. Close the cat's mouth, place your lips over the cat's nose and blow directly into its nostrils. Repeat this every 2 or 3 seconds. If the cat's heart is beating continue artificial respiration for as long as necessary or until veterinary help is obtained. If the heart is not beating and veterinary

help is not just a few minutes away, try heart massage (refer below). Even if this is not successful continue artificial respiration for at least 10 minutes before giving up.

Heart massage

This must be done properly and only if the heart really has stopped. Place the fingers and thumb on each side of the chest from below, then squeeze firmly and quickly several times. Check for a heart beat, if necessary repeat. Intersperse with artificial respiration.

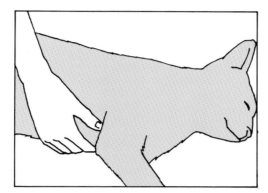

Bandaging

Cats don't like being bandaged and will usually remove one, possibly aggravating the original condition. Only apply a bandage in cases of emergency, or when recommended by a vet.

A bandage is used to provide: *support* for an injured limb (with or without a splint); *protection* to cover a wound and keep a dressing in place; *pressure* to help stop bleeding, slow down the circulation of poison or reduce tissue swelling.

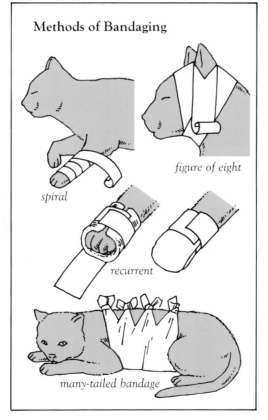

Methods of Bandaging

spiral

figure of eight

recurrent

many-tailed bandage

The spiral. For support, pressure or protection of the lower limbs and tail.
Figure of eight. For support and protection of the elbow or hock joints, and the top of the head.
Recurrent. For protection of the paws or tail.
Many-tailed bandage. For protection of the back or the belly.
Tube bandage is useful for bandaging the ends of limbs.

Splints can be used at the scene of an accident to restrict movement and provide temporary rest, support and pain relief for a damaged limb or tail. *WARNING: Inexpert application of a temporary splint could make an injury worse. If in doubt, merely restrict the cat's movement by wrapping it in a blanket and/or placing it in a cage or box.*

Use a straight piece of wood, plastic or thick cardboard, cut to the right length and width. Make sure that the splint is long enough to immobilise the joints immediately above and below the fracture site. If bone is protruding through the skin (compound fracture) apply a clean dressing to the wound before splinting. Carefully bandage the limb (not too tightly), fully enclosing the foot. Then apply a thick layer of cotton wool. Apply the splint, and bandage in place. With a compound fracture avoid bandaging directly over the damaged site.

Instead of a splint you can just use the thick layer of cotton wool bandaged over the affected area making sure that the joints above and below are included.

The Elizabethan collar is applied to prevent a cat from licking or biting at a dressing or wound.

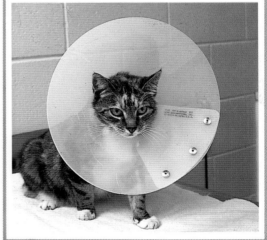

Common Problems

Abscess. Abscesses are a common skin problem, and usually due to bacterial infection from a bite (commonly from a cat, but sometimes from a snake or other animal). Most common in entire males following a fight, they often occur on the side of the face, limbs, base of the tail and back. The main signs are localized swelling and pain, and the cat may lose its appetite and develop a fever. Evidence of puncture wounds may be seen.

If an abscess bursts, the cat will usually keep it clean by licking. If it hasn't burst, bathe the affected area with saline solution (2 tsp salt per pint of water, 10 gm per litre) or epsom salts in warm water (1 ounce or 2 tbsp per pint, 40 gm per litre) to bring the abscess to a head. If it does not burst within 24 hours it may need lancing. In emergency this can be done by the owner using a sharp knife or razor blade, but is best done by a vet. The opening must be made *at the lowest point* of the swelling so that the pus can drain away, and kept open for as long as possible. A vet will usually suture a tube in to act as a drain. The abscess should be irrigated with an antiseptic solution such as cetrimide (Savlon) or an antibiotic. If an affected cat becomes off color and has a fever then consult a vet, who may prescribe antibiotics to control the infection.

Where the skin is tense and an abscess cannot form an infected wound can result in diffuse inflammation tracking underneath the skin (cellulitis). The main sign is hypersensitivity or pain over a wide area. Treatment can include the application of a hot compress for 15 minutes 2–3 times daily, together with antibiotics.

Asphyxia. Unconsciousness caused by lack of oxygen reaching the brain. Causes include being shut in an unventilated space, smoke or carbon monoxide inhalation, choking, strangulation (cat collar caught on a projection), drowning, a penetrating chest wound causing collapse of the lungs, or paralysis of the chest muscles following electrocution. In all cases immediately commence the correct method of artificial respiration (see above) and get veterinary help as soon as possible.

Bleeding. Severe loss of blood can quickly lead to shock (see below) and death, so take immediate action to stop it. *External bleeding* can be seen and dealt with. Arterial blood is bright red and tends to spurt out. Use finger or thumb pressure on the side of the wound nearest the heart, but if unsure apply pressure with finger or thumb directly over the bleeding point, and continue to do so until you can get veterinary help. Only use a tourniquet if you cannot stop the bleeding by other methods, and release it for a few minutes every ten minutes or you may cause gangrene. Venous blood is dark and usually oozes out. Use finger pressure on the side of the wound furthest from the heart until you can apply a pressure pad made from cloth bound firmly over the wound. Capillary bleeding from small blood vessels can be stopped by a pressure pad or by the application of an ice pack. *Internal bleeding* cannot be seen or controlled by the owner, but signs include pale or white gums and shallow rapid breathing. Since these are also symptomatic of shock it may be difficult to tell the difference, but take the initial steps to treat for shock and get immediate veterinary help.

Broken claws. A claw may break level with or just above the quick. Remove the broken part using nail clippers. A break involving the quick is very painful and bleeds, and you may need to get veterinary advice. Several torn or broken claws, especially on the hind legs, indicate that the cat has been in a road accident or near miss. The damage occurs as the cat frantically digs in its claws to get leverage to run.

Burns and scalds. Treatment for *thermal burns* (dry heat) and *scalds* (moist heat) is similar. Immediately apply cold water, ideally at about 40°F (4°C). Cool it with ice or an item from the deep freeze. Apply to the affected area for at least 10 minutes to reduce pain and swelling. Keep the

area clean and free from infection. An antihistamine cream will help to reduce swelling, and an antiseptic cream prevent infection. If the skin has broken get veterinary advice. In severe cases the cat will need urgent treatment for shock. *Electrical burns* to the lips and tongue can occur when a young cat or kitten bites through the live cord of an electrical appliance. Refer *Electrocution*. *Chemical burns* to the skin are usually caused by a strong alkali such as household bleach, or an acid. Water-based substances should be washed off with large amounts of water, oil-based substances with mild soap and water. Use vegetable oil to remove kerosene. Refer *Poisoning*. It can take hours or even days before signs of chemical burns are visible. Refer also *Sunburn*.

Choking. May be due to an insect sting (refer *Stings and bites*), an object stuck in the throat, or inhalation of fluid. If you can't remove the object or the cause is fluid inhalation, vigorously swing the cat (refer *Drowning*). If unsuccessful, apply artificial respiration.

Convulsions or fits. In most cases these only last a few seconds, but occasionally may go on for a minute or more. Because there is a possibility of being bitten or scratched while trying to handle the cat in that state, it is best to leave the cat alone until it recovers. It should only be handled if it is likely to injure itself, in which case place a large towel or blanket over it, scoop the animal up, and place it quickly in a quiet, darkened room or corner. Once the cat recovers it will probably seek such a place of its own accord.

Dehydration. Usually follows prolonged diarrhea or vomiting, or chronic kidney disease. In minor cases fluids can be given by mouth. Severe dehydration can affect blood circulation and cause shock, and properly balanced saline fluids must be given by subcutaneous and/or intravenous injection.

Drowning. Usually the result of a cat falling into a pool or tank from which it cannot escape. To drain water from the lungs grasp the cat by the hind legs above the hocks and swing firmly forwards and backwards between the legs, or from side to side or in an arc. Check the breathing and heart, and if necessary apply artificial respiration by chest pressure.

Electrocution. This commonly occurs when a kitten or young cat bites through a live electrical cord, and is often fatal. *Switch off the current before trying to assist.* Apply heart massage and/or artificial respiration, then get veterinary help.

Exposure. Refer *Hypothermia*.

Falls. Cats can survive falls from quite remarkable heights, but when injury occurs it often involves the head. The jaw may be broken, either mid-line or to one side. The roof of the mouth (hard palate) may be split. Injury may also occur to the nose. Other bones in the body may be broken and the cat may be suffering from shock. Carry out the basic emergency drill recommended above, then get veterinary help.

Fits. Refer *Convulsions*.

Foreign bodies. *Objects in the mouth and digestive system*. A bone or other object lodged on or between the teeth or across the roof of the mouth causes pawing and dribbling. It may be possible to dislodge it using a pencil or blunt instrument, restraining the cat and opening its mouth as shown. A cat that chews the bait on a fish hook may get the hook lodged in its gum or tongue, or through the cheek. Cats have been known to swallow corks

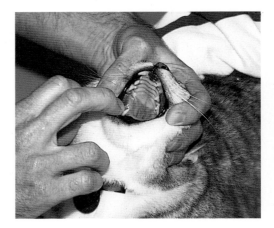

cellophane wrappers, tinfoil balls, rubber bands, string or yarn, and pieces of material, plastic or metal from cat toys. A needle (usually threaded) may lodge in the throat or be swallowed and get stuck further down, and veterinary help is usually needed. If you see a piece of thread protruding from your cat's mouth or anus it may have a needle on the end, so don't pull on it. An object stuck in the back of the throat causes gagging or choking (refer *Choking*), and an anaesthetic will probably be necessary for removal.

Objects lodged further down in the esophagus, stomach or intestine cause signs that vary according to the site and type of obstruction. They include loss of appetite, regurgitation, vomiting, diarrhea or constipation. Surgery is usually necessary.

Objects in the ear. Usually a grass seed. If visible moisten the canal with liquid paraffin or vegetable oil and try to gently pull the seed out using a pair of tweezers. Make sure you get all the seed out, as it can break off. In many cases the cat won't let you do this or the 'arrow head' shape of the seed makes it too difficult to remove, so you should get veterinary help as soon as possible.

Objects in the eye. Usually a grass seed, which often lodges behind the third eyelid causing extreme pain and irritation. The cat paws at the eye. Immediately apply anaesthetic eye drops and get the cat to a vet. Removal should not be attempted by the owner unless veterinary help is not available. Chemicals accidentally entering the eye should be washed out with copious amounts of clean water before taking the cat to a vet.

Fractures. Depending on the site of the fracture a temporary splint or support can sometimes help to minimise further damage and make the cat more comfortable until veterinary help can be obtained (refer *Bandaging*, page 303). But inexpert handling can make the damage worse, so if in doubt leave well alone. It is best to lift the cat by sliding it onto a blanket or towel. This is particularly important if a spinal injury is suspected, when a piece of board or thick cardboard should also be used to keep the spine fully supported. Fractures to the lower limbs can be supported with a bandage.

Frostbite. Usually affects the tips or margins of the ears, and repeated exposure of these parts to very cold conditions can result in them darkening and eventually sloughing. On rare occasions the feet or tail may be involved. The affected parts should be thawed out slowly at a temperature of about 104°F (40°C). If necessary treat for shock, then get veterinary advice.

Hyperthermia. Usually occurs when a cat is shut or trapped inside a hot enclosed area such as a parked car (heatstroke), or has been sleeping in hot sun (sunstroke). The cat is no longer able to control its body temperature which can rise to over 106°F (41°C). Signs are rapid breathing, loud open-mouthed panting, weakness, staggering and incoordination, collapse, and semiconsciousness. Treatment is to immediately cool the cat down by sponging or dunking in a cold water bath, then drying with a fan. A cold-water enema (½ oz or 15 ml) is very effective but usually not possible for the owner to carry out unless the cat is semi-conscious.

Hypothermia. Excessive lowering of body temperature, usually as a result of shock (refer below) or exposure to wet or cold conditions. Newborn kittens that become isolated from their mother are very susceptible. At first there is shivering, but as the body temperature continues to drop the animal becomes unconscious. Treatment of exposure is to provide warmth but not excessive heat, and a bath of warm water 104°F (40°C) is ideal.

Shock. Can be caused by bleeding (refer above), dehydration (refer above), an allergic reaction to stings or bites, or toxicity following severe damage to body tissues by burns or scalds. It can also occur following fright, severe pain, exposure to cold (refer **Hypothermia**), and starvation. Most cases follow an accident or injury. There is reduced flow of blood in many parts of the body, particularly the skin and gums, while the body tries to maintain an adequate supply to essential organs such as the liver, heart and lungs, and brain. Signs reflect the severity. Inadequate blood to the brain leaves the cat semi-conscious or comatose, while not enough to the heart and lungs causes a rapid heart beat with a feeble pulse, and rapid, shallow breathing. The pupils are usually dilated, the eyes appear glazed and vision is affected. The gums and tongue are pale, a bluish-white color, and feel cold and clammy. The body feels cold (especially the paws), and the cat may be shivering. Muscle relaxation can result in lack of control over bowel and bladder. The cat may vomit.

Shock is potentially life-threatening, so take steps to minimise its effects while seeking professional help. If the cat is on a cold or wet surface, and you judge it too dangerous to move it, put newspapers, a towel or a blanket underneath. Otherwise move the cat to a quiet place of safety, place it in a head-down position at about 30 degrees to horizontal, cover it with a blanket and keep it warmed to the temperature of its surroundings. If the cat is wet, dry it off with a towel. You can use a hair dryer but don't let the cat get too warm or this will increase the blood flow to the skin and reduce the amount reaching the vital organs, making things worse. Keep the cat as quiet as possible. If it wishes to drink give it warm water or milk with glucose. Don't try to force liquid down, and don't give liquids if it is vomiting or unconscious.

Stings and bites. *Insect stings* are most common in young cats that are play hunting, and most result in pain and swelling. Stings on the foot pad cause temporary lameness, those in the mouth cause pawing and dribbling. If you can see the sting remove it with tweezers. Stings on the skin or foot pad can be bathed with methylated spirits or vinegar, then treated with an antihistamine cream. In many cases the cat will remove the sting itself and treatment is unnecessary. Occasionally there may be a severe reaction including vomiting and muscle spasms, or the sting may be in the throat causing severe swelling and choking. Treat such cases as a veterinary emergency.

Snakebite most commonly occurs on or near the head. Non-venomous snakes leave a U-shaped series of marks. Their bites can become infected with bacteria so the area should be cleaned with hydrogen peroxide and an antibiotic ointment applied. Venomous snakes leave two distinct puncture wounds. These are usually difficult to see unless the fur is shaved. Signs of poisoning depend on the variety of snake. Bites by elapid snakes (which include Australian species and the American coral snake) cause dilated pupils, breathing difficulty, distress, depression and generalised weakness or paralysis. Viper bites cause tissue necrosis at the site of the bite. Treatment is designed to slow the spread of venom until the appropriate antivenin can be administered. Keep the cat as still as possible. For bites on the head or body apply ice packs to reduce the circulation. If the bite is on a leg apply a pressure bandage over the whole area, or a tourniquet above the bite which must be released and reapplied every 10 minutes. Making an incision over the wound to allow the escape of blood and venom is not recommended. Wherever possible get the cat to a vet. Owners living in more remote areas are advised to keep an antivenin kit of choice in their first aid box.

Spider bite can be a problem in some parts of the world such as North America and Australia. Species include the black widow, brown spider, funnel web, red back and red-legged widow. When bitten a cat often leaps into the air and cries out. There is usually severe pain and swelling, and many bites leave a wound that takes a long time to heal. Bites from highly poisonous spiders result in acute illness with muscle spasms and require urgent veterinary treatment. There are no specific antidotes.

Tick bite fever occurs in the warm coastal regions of Australia. Signs occur about 4–5 days after infestation and include a change of voice followed by incoordination, gradual paralysis and possibly death. Owners of cats living in affected areas should check their animals daily, looking particularly around the head, neck and shoulders. A tick can be killed by applying a cotton bud soaked in acetone (nail polish remover), alcohol or methylated spirits, then carefully removed by gripping it as close to the skin as possible with fine tweezers. Do not squeeze the tick or you may cause the injection of more toxin. If the tick is removed too roughly and the head is left in the skin it may cause a small abscess.

Sunburn. Refer *Ear*, page 313.

Sunstroke. Refer *Hyperthermia*, page 304.

Travel sickness. Refer page 309.

Unconsciousness (coma). To check if a cat is unconscious shine a light, such as a torch, into its eyes. Normally the pupils will constrict, but if the cat is unconscious they will be dilated and won't react. Touching the eyelids at the corner of the eye will usually cause a conscious cat to blink, but cause no reaction in an unconscious one. Other signs include loss of muscle control or paralysis, but sometimes spasm and muscle rigidity can occur, as can convulsions causing violent and irregular movements of the limbs.

Wounds. Types are incised (glass, sharp knife), lacerated (tears from barbed wire, car accident) or puncture (thorn, fish hook). Minor cuts and lacerations can usually be left for the cat to lick clean, but if necessary can be bathed with a solution of cetrimide (Savlon). Antiseptic or antibiotic ointments are only effective if the cat cannot lick them off. If healing does not occur see your vet. Bites and scratches are invariably infected and unless minor and superficial they should *not* be left untreated. Puncture wounds from teeth or thorns should be bathed regularly to keep them open and prevent abscess formation. Deep or extensive wounds usually need veterinary treatment and possibly stitching, so first control bleeding, then cover the wound to protect against further infection and get the cat to your vet.

Poisons and poisoning

Cats are more sensitive than other pets to many chemicals commonly used in the home and workshop. Poisoning can occur through swallowing or licking off the fur, or by absorption through the skin or pads. *Chemical burns* to the skin can be caused by acids, alkalis, phenols and petroleum products. Keep all chemicals, paints, sprays and other potential poisons properly sealed in a locked cupboard.

Common signs of poisoning include *digestive signs* such as abdominal pain, diarrhea or vomiting; *nervous signs* such as excitement, incoordination, muscle tremors or convulsions; and *respiratory signs* such as difficulty in breathing. In the later stages many affected animals show severe weakness and depression. All these signs are common to other major problems, and poisoning should only be suspected and home treatment initiated when a cat is known to have had contact with a poisonous substance or there is strong circumstantial evidence. Where the particular compound is known take the specific measure listed below, and if seeking veterinary help take the packet or label with you.

Immediate action

Swallowed poisons. The cat may or may not vomit afterwards. *Don't give an emetic if the cat has swallowed acids, caustics or petroleum products, or it isn't fully conscious or able to swallow.* Under any other circumstances, induce vomiting by giving an emetic (refer list).

Chemicals on the skin. These must be washed off as soon as possible. For most chemicals use large amounts of water or dunk the animal in a bath. For petroleum products and turpentine use vegetable oil or margarine, then wash with a mild soap. Refer *Common household items*, page 306.

Useful emetics from the kitchen cupboard

1. Give one teaspoon (5 ml) of 10 volume (3%) hydrogen peroxide solution.
2. Dissolve a tablespoon of bicarbonate of soda in quarter cup of water, give 1–2 teaspoons (5–10 ml).
3. Dissolve 1 tablespoon of salt in half cup water, give 2 teaspoons (10 ml).
4. Place half a teaspoonful of salt on the back of the tongue.
5. Put a finger-nail sized crystal of washing soda down the cat's throat.

Liquids can be given by spoon or syringe.

Common pesticides and herbicides

Alphachloralose is used to kill rodents and repel birds, but may also kill birds. A cat eating a dead bird may become poisoned. Signs are depression, loss of balance, difficulty in breathing, cold extremities (hypothermia) and collapse. Give an emetic, maintain normal body temperature and provide rest and quiet. The chances of recovery are fair.

Anticoagulants such as Warfarin, Drat and similar products cause spontaneous hemorrhages and death from internal bleeding. Cats may eat the bait directly or rodents containing the poison. It usually takes 5–10 days before fatal hemorrhage occurs. Signs include pallor, labored breathing, weakness and prostration. Pinpoint hemorrhages may appear on the gums, and there may be bloody diarrhea. Veterinary treatment is essential and involves sedation, blood transfusion and the administration of Vitamin K or its synthetic equivalent.

Arsenic may be found in herbicides, rodenticides, and ant or cockroach baits. Signs include restlessness, vomiting, bloody diarrhea, abdominal pain. Give an emetic, then milk, then see your vet urgently. The antidote is dimercaprol (BAL).

Metaldehyde is widely used in slug and snail baits, but most have been reformulated to make them much less attractive to pets. Signs include incoordination, muscle tremors, vomiting, diarrhea, rapid breathing, salivation, convulsions. Give an emetic and get veterinary help. Convulsions must be controlled with tranquilizers or barbiturate anaesthetics.

Organochlorines (chlorinated hydrocarbons) are now restricted in use and cases of poisoning are fewer. Compounds include BHC, chlordane, DDT, Dieldrin, Lindane, methoxychlor and toxophene. Signs include hypersensitivity and behavioral changes, dribbling and muscle spasm. There is no specific antidote. Wash any compound off the coat, give an emetic if swallowed. *Don't* give milk. Get veterinary help.

Organophosphates are used as insecticides in certain worm and flea remedies including flea collars. Compounds include carbamate, diazinon, dichlorvos, fenthion, malathion, and trichlorfon. The main sign of overdose or poisoning is weakness. Others include dribbling, diarrhea, muscular twitching and incoordination. Wash any remaining substance off the coat, and get a vet to administer atropine sulphate by injection as soon as possible. Don't give sedatives or purgatives.

Phosphorus is used for control of rats, also rabbits and opossums. Signs include vomiting and bloody diarrhea. There may be apparent recovery followed later by jaundice, convulsions, coma and death. Give 2 tsp (10 ml) olive oil and get veterinary assistance. The outlook is poor.

Strychnine poisoning may be malicious or follow eating of baits or animals killed by strychnine. Signs include hypersensitivity, muscle twitching and spasm. Death usually occurs in a few hours. Give an emetic and get the cat to a vet who will give injections to control muscle spasms. The outlook is good with prompt treatment.

Sodium fluoroacetate (1080) is used in some areas for opossum, rat and rabbit control, and cats are sometimes affected by eating poisoned carcasses. Signs include rapid breathing, seizures and prostration. Give an emetic, get to the vet as soon as possible. Poisoning is usually fatal.

Poisoning by animals

Blue tail lizard poisoning occurs in the southeastern United States. When caught the lizard may shed its tail, which is then eaten. Signs are agitation, dribbling, vomiting, and incoordination. Give an emetic and get veterinary advice.

Toad poisoning results from a venom secreted by the skin glands that is rapidly absorbed into a cat's system when the toad is held in its mouth. The venom from the common toad (*Bufo bufo*) causes a transitory irritation and salivation, and treatment is not necessary. The cane toad (*Bufo marinus*) secretes about 15 times more venom than the common toad and poisoning can be more serious. Signs include reddening and swelling inside the mouth, dribbling lasting for several hours, severe abdominal pain, continuous vomiting, rapid breathing and incoordination. There is no home treatment and veterinary help should be obtained. Refer also **Stings and bites**, page 305.

Common household items

Acetominophen is contained in the commonly used analgesics Paracetamol and Tylenol. Two 325 grain tablets can cause poisoning in a cat. The main sign is cyanosis (blue color of the gums). Give an emetic and get veterinary help.

Acids spilled on the coat should be washed off with large amounts of water, or the cat can be dunked in a bath. If licked off the coat and swallowed *don't induce vomiting*. To help to neutralize the acid give half a cup of 5% solution of bicarbonate of soda, milk of magnesia, neat evaporated milk or milk, then get veterinary help.

Alkalis such as bleaches, cleaners and solvents spilt on the skin should be washed off with large amounts of water or the cat dunked in a bath. If licked off the coat and swallowed, *don't induce vomiting*. Give vinegar/water 1/4, lemon juice or neat evaporated milk to neutralise and get veterinary help.

Aspirin poisoning usually occurs because a cat has been given an overdose. Before giving your cat aspirin consult your vet because the correct dosage should only be given every third day. A single 5 grain (324 mg) tablet given to a 2 kg cat is the equivalent of giving a 70 kg human 35 tablets. Baby aspirin contains only 1.25 gr (80 mg), and a cat can be given half a tablet every third day. Signs of poisoning include incoordination, loss of balance and vomiting. Give an emetic, then milk, then get veterinary help if needed.

Detergents may cause skin irritation if used for bathing a cat, and frothing at the mouth and vomiting if licked off the coat. Thoroughly rinse off the skin, then rewash with mild soap. Make it a rule not to use detergents or carbolic soaps for bathing cats.

Ethylene glycol is a common constituent of antifreeze that cats appear to find palatable. Poisonings are most frequent during the winter months and signs include vomiting, incoordination and depression. Get the cat to a vet. The treatment is ethyl alcohol (ethanol) by injection. An untreated cat may develop kidney failure.

House and garden plants that are potentially poisonous are rarely eaten but cats may occasionally chew at certain house plants when bored. Examples include sheep laurel and mountain laurel used for floral decoration in North America, azaleas, chrysanthemum, diefenbachia (dumb cane), ivy, philodendron, and poinsettias. In most cases the signs include vomiting, diarrhea or nervous symptoms. Pine needles from Christmas trees and the water from the base both contain irritant tar products. If consumed by a cat the main symptoms are vomiting and diarrhea.

Lead poisoning is now rare. Signs are vomiting and stomach pain followed by nervous symptoms. Give an emetic and immediately take the cat to a vet who will administer the antidote, calcium EDTA.

Paint is usually not toxic when spilt on the fur. *Don't use turpentine* to remove it, but allow it to dry, then comb it out or cut off the affected hair.

Petroleum products (kerosene, petrol, oil, grease) can burn the skin and cause photosensitisation (inflammation when exposed to sunlight), and if licked off can cause lip or tongue ulcers. Wash off with vegetable oil, then mild soap, then rinse. If swallowed they can cause long-term liver or kidney problems. Administer two tablespoons of vegetable oil or liquid paraffin and get veterinary advice.

Phenols are contained in many household disinfectants and cleaners such as Jeyes fluid and Lysol, in creosote, and in some treated sawdust. Contact with the skin can cause severe irritation and the chemical should be washed off the coat using plenty of water followed by a shampoo. If swallowed phenols can cause severe vomiting and diarrhea, nervous signs and coma, so immediately administer vegetable oil or evaporated milk, then give an emetic, then get veterinary advice.

Tar stuck to the fur or skin can be softened with vegetable oil or margarine and removed by washing with a mild shampoo followed by thorough rinsing.

Turpentine can cause severe skin irritation. Apply vegetable oil, wash off with mild soap, then rinse.

FELINE IMMUNODEFICIENCY VIRUS (FIV)

The cause of feline AIDS, and first isolated in 1987. Retrospective studies showed it to have been present in many countries for anything from 15 to 20 years, and it undoubtedly has been around for a lot longer. FIV belongs to the same family as the virus that causes AIDS in humans, but there is no evidence that FIV can infect people.

The main effect of FIV is immuno-suppression. An affected cat's immune system is unable to react effectively to any infection that it picks up, leaving it more or less defenseless. But FIV can also cause tumors and/or disease of the nervous system.

The significance of the discovery of FIV is that it could be behind many of the symptoms and conditions in cats for which scientists have so far been unable to find a definite cause, such as inflammatory conditions of the mouth and certain chronic urinary and skin infections.

Signs are variable, and related to both the initial viral infection and secondary (mainly bacterial) infections that may follow. Initially a cat may merely appear off color and disinterested in food, but very soon secondary infections cause varying signs, most commonly stomatitis and gingivitis, loss of weight, chronic nasal discharge (rhinitis), chronic diarrhea and chronic skin disease. The cat is more likely to contract infections such as feline infectious anemia, demodectic mange and toxoplasmosis. The cat's inability to fight these infections usually results in chronic illness and, if euthanasia is not carried out, death.

The virus does not appear to be sexually transmitted, or to pass from a queen to her unborn offspring. The main method of transmission is thought to be through cat bites, because the virus is present in small quantities in the saliva of affected cats and the disease is more common in free-ranging or feral toms.

Commercial blood testing kits are available to detect the FIV antibodies which most cats develop. But a few cats don't produce antibodies and will test negative. The prevalence of the disease varies from area to area and country to country. About 1–2% of clinically normal cats show a positive test, but not all of these will go on to develop a full-blown infection. Those that do may not show signs for months or even years. In surveys of cats that have signs suggestive of FIV anything from 14% to 89% have proved positive, the incidence reflecting the area or country that they come from, and to some extent their life style, since the highest incidence has been found in outdoor male cats.

Research is in progress to develop effective vaccines and drugs to combat FIV.

THE NOSE AND RESPIRATORY SYSTEM

The normal cat breathes through its nose, unlike the dog which is a habitual mouth breather, and open-mouth breathing in the cat is usually a sign of stress, exhaustion or respiratory disease. Because the nose is the principal route through which air is taken into the cat's lungs it has four very important protective functions. Its lining (mucosa) is covered in a layer of mucus and richly supplied with blood vessels which help to control loss of body heat. They also increase or decrease the temperature of inspired air to that of the body before it reaches the lungs. Passage of air through the nose increases its humidity to almost 100%, while during quiet breathing the sticky mucus on the nasal mucosa removes about 95% of inhaled dust particles or droplets containing viruses.

Because the cat's nose plays such an important role in breathing, anything that reduces the effectiveness of the nasal mucosa will therefore expose the respiratory system to potential damage or infection.

A cat's normal breathing rate is about 30 breaths per minute and a rate much greater than this should be considered abnormal.

Signs of respiratory problems include nasal discharge and inflammation (rhinitis), sneezing, coughing, dribbling (salivation), painful or difficult breathing which is often associated with open-mouth breathing, and rapid breathing.

Bronchial asthma. Caused by a spasm of the bronchial muscles resulting in a narrowing of the air passages. The major signs are labored breathing and sneezing, and a dry cough. The cat may breathe open-mouthed or gasp for breath, the greatest difficulty being in exhaling the air rather than inhaling it. The causes are not clear, but may include allergy to pollens or house dust. Treatment is with corticosteroids and drugs to dilate the bronchi, and try to find and eliminate any allergic cause. Long-term treatment may be necessary in some cases.

Bronchitis. Inflammation of the bronchi, which results in the secretion of thick mucus into the air space. Usually caused by bacteria or viruses, other causes include allergy and parasites. The main sign is a harsh cough. Treatment usually includes antibiotics to control bacterial infection which almost always ensues. Drugs can be given to break down the thick mucus and dilate the bronchi to assist breathing. Good home nursing will help, as may humidifiers.

Cat 'flu. A common term for feline respiratory disease.

Cryptococcosis. A chronic respiratory infection caused by a yeast-like fungus called *Cryptococcus*. Signs include nasal discharge, sneezing and snuffling. Affected cats may be listless, lose weight, and develop a fever. Treatment often fails. A skin form of the disease can cause skin nodules. Other fungi can also cause respiratory infections, but these are rare.

Feline pneumonitis. Caused by the organism *Chlamydia psittaci*, an early symptom is watering of the eye. This is soon followed by a nasal discharge that becomes thick and pussy, and the cat starts sneezing. The condition responds well to treatment with tetracycline antibiotics, but recovered cats appear not to develop a lasting immunity and may become reinfected. Vaccination programs have been tried but do not seem to have provided complete protection.

Feline respiratory disease (upper respiratory disease, URD). The two major diseases in this complex are caused by viruses, and both can be prevented by a vaccination programme started at 9–12 weeks of age and continued annually throughout life. One virus causes *feline viral rhinotracheitis (FVR)*, the other causes *feline calicivirus infection (FCV)*. Both viruses are widespread throughout the world and they are probably of equal importance in causing the disease, accounting for about 80% of all 'cat 'flu' cases. Once the virus infection has become established bacteria usually become secondary invaders. The main signs are fever, sneezing, dribbling, conjunctivitis, and discharges from the nose and eyes (refer *Eye*, page 313) which become thick and yellow. There is often a cough. The disease can last for 1–3 weeks, but FCV is typically milder than FVR, running a course of 7–10 days, and one characteristic symptom is ulceration of the tongue, sometimes the paws. A characteristic of FVR is inflammation of the cornea of the eye (refer *Keratitis, Eye*, page 314). Treatment for both conditions is supportive, with nursing and adequate fluids. Antibiotics will treat any secondary bacterial infection.

Many cats contract respiratory disease without the owner being aware of it. In a British survey of 1500 clinically healthy cats before vaccination 40% of colony cats, 25% of cats at shows and 8% of single household pets were shedding virus. Infection is more common in colony cats than individual household pets because conditions are ideal for the disease to persist and many recovered cats can be symptomless carriers of the disease. At least 80% of FVR-recovered cats shed virus intermittently in the secretions from their nose or mouth. This shedding is most likely about 1 week after stress (boarding, showing, mating or corticosteroid treatment), and shedding then continues for about 2 weeks. FCV is excreted more or less continuously by carriers, and this may continue for as little as a month or be lifelong. Shedders can be detected by swabbing and culture.

In breeding or boarding catteries infection is often introduced by a clinically normal carrier cat. Once established (endemic) in a breeding cattery the disease is usually seen in the acute form in young kittens once their passive immunity (derived from their mother) is lost. Older cats may show chronic or recurrent nose and eye discharges and sinusitis. The disease can be controlled by good management and an annual vaccination programme, although there may be occasional breakdowns.

Upper respiratory infection can also be caused by the organism *Mycoplasma*, but its effects are usually confined to the eye.

Hemothorax. Blood in the chest cavity. Usually the result of an accident or poisoning by an anticoagulant poison such as Warfarin or Drat. The main signs are respiratory distress and varying degrees of anemia and shock.

Laryngeal spasm. This results in intermittent bouts of paroxysmal coughing and wheezing, accompanied by difficulty in breathing. The cat crouches down with its head extended forwards. Episodes last for only a minute or two, and range in frequency from several times a day to less than once a week. Between episodes the cat appears quite normal. The cause is not known. Immediate relief can usually be achieved simply by giving the cat a teaspoon (5 ml) of water. The condition is not life-threatening and may resolve itself after a week or two. Veterinary treatment for severe cases includes antibiotics and corticosteroids.

Laryngitis. Inflammation of the larynx is uncommon in cats, and usually associated with feline respiratory disease (refer above), especially FVR. Sometimes it can result from a tumor. The major sign is a partial or complete loss of voice.

Lungworms. These occur in most countries in the world, and in the early stages of infection or during a heavy infestation partially blocking the bronchi an affected cat may develop a cough. Veterinary treatment is essential, and usually involves an injection.

Pleurisy. Inflammation of the pleura lining the lungs and inside of the chest. This can occur through infection tracking from the lungs, because of a tumor, or following an accident or a penetrating wound of the chest. Infectious causes include bacteria, viruses, fungi or parasites, and signs of breathing difficulty may take a long time to show up.

Pneumonia. Inflammation of the lungs, most commonly caused by feline respiratory viruses, sometimes by bacteria. Migrating roundworm larvae and adults, or lungworms, may also be an underlying cause. The main sign is labored breathing, with or without a cough. Pneumonia is a serious disease that requires veterinary treatment and careful home nursing. Bacterial infections can be controlled by antibiotics.

Pneumothorax. Caused by air entering the chest cavity and causing partial collapse of one or both lungs. Usually the result of an accident causing a penetrating wound or a broken rib.

Rhinitis. Inflammation within the nasal cavity. The most common causes are the feline respiratory viruses, feline pneumonitis, or foreign bodies. It is also a common sign of infection with feline AIDS (FIV)

Sinusitis. Inflammation of one or both sinuses can follow upper respiratory disease or be caused by an injury such as a penetrating bite wound and the introduction of bacterial or fungal infection. On rare occasions it can be caused by a tumor. The main sign is a nasal discharge. Treatment includes antibiotics, corticosteroids, or surgery depending on the cause.

Tumors. Tumors of the lung or breathing passages are uncommon. The main sign is difficult or labored breathing. Treatment depends on the type of tumor and its site.

THE MOUTH

Common signs associated with disease of the mouth include loss of appetite, bad breath, difficulty in swallowing or chewing, inflammation of the mouth (stomatitis) and gums (gingivitis), salivation or dribbling, and tartar formation.

Cleft palate. This sometimes occurs as a genetic defect in newly born kittens. It has also been reported in kittens born to a queen suffering from iodine deficiency. It may occur alone or associated with harelip. The main sign is regurgitation of milk through the nose while the kitten is suckling.

Dental problems. As cats get old their teeth become worn or lost, usually both, but tooth decay (caries) is uncommon. Signs of a tooth problem often include clawing at the mouth, difficulty in eating or refusing food.

Occasionally a tooth is chipped or broken in an accident, but treatment is only necessary if the root canal is exposed. Take your vet's advice if such a problem arises.

Dental calculus (tartar) is common in older cats and those fed soft food. It usually affects the areas closest to the salivary ducts, on the outside of the molars and pre-molars, and on the inside of the incisors. It is formed of minerals (mainly calcium hydroxyapatite) and bacterial plaque (bacteria mixed with salivary protein), and eventually causes lipping close to the gum under which bacteria can become established and cause inflammation of the gum (gingivitis) and/or around the tooth root (periodontitis).

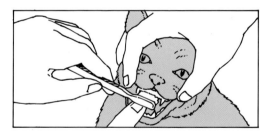

Dental calculus can be removed by scaling, and antibiotics should be given to control any bacterial infection. Preventive measures include feeding some uncut meat or dry food in the diet, and regular cleaning of the cat's teeth with a toothbrush.

Mouth infection. Various injuries, bacteria, fungi and viruses can cause inflammation and infection of the mouth (stomatitis), which usually involves the gums (gingivitis), especially in the angle between the upper and lower jaws, and the tongue (glossitis). Signs include bad breath, dribbling (salivation), loss of appetite and pain, and the gums may be inflamed or bleeding.

Acute stomatitis may result from trauma, a foreign body such as a fish bone, fish hook, or needle, or the viruses that cause feline respiratory disease (FCV and FVR). It is particularly common with FCV, some strains of which cause ulcers on the surface of the tongue, hard palate or around the nostrils, and the stomatitis can last for 2–3 weeks.

Chronic stomatitis is often associated with bacterial, viral or fungal infections, although why it starts is not always entirely clear. In some cases it is caused by dental problems (refer above), but in others it may be triggered by a breakdown in the body's immune system, such as can happen during infection with feline leukemia virus or feline AIDS.

Treatment for mouth infections depends on the underlying cause, but usually includes antibiotics to combat the bacteria or fungi that are often involved as secondary invaders.

Pharyngitis. Inflammation of the pharynx, commonly associated with feline respiratory disease. Signs include retching and general oral disease. Treatment is for the underlying cause.

Ranula. A swelling under the tongue caused by a blocked salivary duct. Treatment is by surgery.

Reddening of the gums (gum hyperemia). This looks rather like a red line. It is not due to inflammation (gingivitis) but caused by an increased amount of blood in the gum margin. It is common in kittens and not a problem. In older cats diets high in vitamin A (e.g. liver) can lead to gum hyperemia and tooth changes, and treatment is often unrewarding although antibiotics may help.

Rodent ulcer. Also known as eosinophilic granuloma, this condition affects adult cats and commences on the upper lip margin, either midline or opposite the top of the canine tooth on one or both sides. It forms a reddish-brown ulcer with a raised border. There is usually no pain or irritation. The cause is unknown. Biopsy is recommended. Treatment includes anti-inflammatory drugs such as corticosteroids, and cryosurgery.

Tumors. A benign tumor called an epulis causes a swelling on the gum but rarely needs to be removed. Cancer of the lip (squamous cell carcinoma) is more common in white cats and associated with the exposure of unpigmented skin to strong sunlight. It requires veterinary treatment, usually by cautery. A similar condition can affect the ear (refer *Sunburn*, page 313).

Wounds. Those near the lips and mouth, or on the side of the face, are generally caused by fighting, usually infected, and may abscess. For treatment refer *First aid*, page 305

THE DIGESTIVE SYSTEM

Common signs associated with disease of the digestive system include loss of appetite, regurgitation of food, vomiting, jaundice, diarrhea or constipation and excessive thirst. But remember that vomiting and/or diarrhea can be caused by disease of another body system.

Anal abscess. Situated one either side of the anus, the anal sacs store a pungent fluid secreted by the anal glands. During defecation a little of this fluid is squeezed out through the anal ducts and coats the feces, acting as a scent mark. Blockage of one or both ducts causes swelling and discomfort. Infection can then enter causing an abscess that makes defecation painful and leads to constipation. Conversely, chronic constipation can result in the glands not being emptied, the contents drying out, and bacterial infection getting in. An anal abscess requires draining and antibiotic treatment, but a simple blockage can be relieved by manual expression. Ask your vet to show you how to do it without getting the pungent contents all over you.

Ascites. Accumulation of fluid in the abdomen, which may cause it to swell. It occurs with the 'wet' form of feline infectious peritonitis (refer

below), and with some kidney, liver or heart problems.

Diabetes. There are two types of diabetes. The most common, *diabetes mellitus* or sugar diabetes, is caused by lack of insulin secreted from the pancreas and occurs mainly in middle-aged or elderly cats. Signs are excessive thirst and urination, but the latter may be difficult to detect. Most affected cats have an enlarged liver. A urine test showing glucose in urine and a blood test showing a high blood glucose level after fasting will confirm the disease. The cat should be hospitalized until the correct dose of insulin has been established, then the owner can give the necessary once or twice daily subcutaneous injections. Diet should be high in protein and low in fat and carbohydrate, preferably in canned form.

Diabetes insipidus is rare, and caused by the lack of a hormone produced in the pituitary gland in the brain that controls the removal of excess water from the urine as it is produced in the kidneys. Affected cats excrete large amounts of very weak urine, and drink excessive amounts of water. Veterinary treatment is possible.

Enteritis. Inflammation of the intestines. The most common causes are dietary or due to an immune-mediated reaction by the cat's body (refer **Malabsorption** below). *Salmonella* bacteria, a common cause of enteritis in animals and humans, may infect cats whose resistance is lowered by other disease, especially FIV or FeLV. Occasionally kittens can be affected in catteries where hygiene is poor. Because *Salmonella* species can be infectious to humans affected cats and kittens should be considered a potential human hazard. Mild enteritis with diarrhea in newborn or very young kittens may be caused by feline enteric coronavirus (FECV), first described in the early 1980s and related to, but quite different from, the virus causing feline infectious peritonitis (refer below). Ubiquitous, it is spread by fecal contamination of food and prey. There is no specific treatment but antibiotics will help to control secondary bacterial infection. The major virus disease that causes enteritis, feline panleukopenia (feline enteritis), is discussed under a separate heading below. Low-grade viral infection may occur, one sign being protrusion of the third eyelid.

Feline infectious peritonitis (FIP). This virus infection may be fairly widespread but only a few cats develop signs, more commonly those under 3 years old. Occasionally litters of kittens may be affected. It often occurs in cats from catteries infected with FeLV. Initial signs are fever, lethargy and loss of appetite. From there the disease can gradually develop into one of two forms. The 'wet' form results in a build up of fluid in the abdomen (ascites), which can become grossly distended. There is anemia and weight loss. Respiratory symptoms develop in about one in every five cases. The 'dry' form causes variable nervous signs such as incoordination, fits, deafness and paralysis, and other problems such as inflammation of the iris of the eye (iritis), retinal degeneration and blindness, and chronic kidney disease. The outlook is usually hopeless, and euthanasia is generally advised.

Feline panleukopenia (FPL). Also known as feline infectious enteritis (FIE), this highly infectious virus disease occurs worldwide, mainly affecting young cats. Infection can be spread by almost any route, including direct contact, contaminated bedding, food dishes, hands or clothing, and through flea bites. The virus survives in the environment for long periods and unvaccinated cats should not be introduced into a cattery or household where the infection has occurred. Signs are variable, depending on age and ability to deal with the infection. Kittens infected before birth can suffer brain damage, and by the time they are 3 weeks old and starting to walk they typically stagger and fall over. There is no treatment. In other kittens and older cats the disease will show as a severe illness lasting 3–7 days. An affected cat has a fever, is depressed and won't eat. It starts vomiting and then develops severe diarrhea, both of which cause severe dehydration. It will often sit by its water bowl but rarely drink. Abdominal pain causes it to cry out. Many affected cats develop symptoms of shock, and up to half of them may die. In some kittens under 6 months old the disease may be extremely acute and the only sign may be sudden death. Adult cats with adequate resistance may show few signs of illness, and recover. Acute cases require emergency veterinary treatment that includes blood transfusions and fluid therapy containing essential nutrients. Intensive nursing is required from the owner. Various combined vaccines are available for protection against FPL and some other virus diseases. All kittens should be vaccinated, commencing at 9–12 weeks of age with a booster about 4 weeks later. Depending on where a cat lives it should receive a booster every one or two years.

Hairball. The swallowing of hair and its retention in the stomach with subsequent vomiting is a normal process, especially in long-haired cats during the period of maximum shedding. Hair that is not vomited up is usually passed on through the bowel. Accumulation of hair in the stomach can eventually lead to the formation of a large mass, which partly fills the stomach. The result is that the cat cannot eat very much food at one time, so it feeds little and often yet may still appear hungry or lose weight. Hair passed through the digestive system may also form an obstruction in the colon, leading to chronic constipation. Treatment for hairball is to give two teaspoons of liquid paraffin daily with the food for a few days. Regular grooming will help to prevent hairball formation.

Hyperthyroidism. This is one of the major causes of chronic weight loss in the older cat. Signs are associated with an increase in the cat's metabolic rate. There is progressive weight loss despite a normal or increased (occasionally ravenous) appetite. The cat shows a marked change in temperament and is hyperactive and excitable. It may pace constantly, unable to properly rest or sleep, and groom itself excessively. The coat is often dull and scurfy (seborrhea), and the nails grow excessively long. There is often diarrhea or frequent passage of bulky stools, heartbeat is rapid and irregular, and affected cats usually have an abnormally high body temperature (hyperthermia). Excessive thirst and vomiting may also be seen. Treatment is usually a combination of drugs and the surgical removal of the thyroids.

Liver disease. Inflammation of the liver is known as hepatitis. Problems affecting the liver are not uncommon in cats, but because it has extensive reserves of tissue signs may only show up after there has been a large amount of damage. Common signs are loss of appetite, loss of weight, depression, jaundice, or the passing of soft, greasy, yellow feces. Tumors are the most common cause of liver disease, but bacteria, viruses or various toxic chemicals including treated sawdust or wood shavings can also be responsible. Liver abscess may cause death in newborn kittens, and is caused by bacterial infection tracking up from the navel. A chronic liver disease that may be associated with the body's immune system is seen typically in cats under 5 years old, possibly more often in long-hairs. The most common sign is a mild jaundice. Some affected cats lose their appetite, but many remain bright and eat well. Treatment with corticosteroids may be of help. Fatty liver (the accumulation of fat within the liver) can result from a variety of causes, including nutritional problems and diabetes mellitus. An unusual liver disease reported in North America seems to occur only in older cats that are obese, and may be due to a nutritional cause or a malfunction of the body's metabolism. An affected cat refuses to eat, usually following some stress such as boarding or surgery, and this may continue for a long time. The cat loses weight, is depressed and lethargic, vomits, develops jaundice and becomes weak. Brain and nerve problems develop, and there may be muscle twitching and behavioral changes. Without appropriate treatment the outlook is poor. An early diagnosis is essential, followed by intensive nursing.

Malabsorption. Inability of the intestines to absorb all the digested food. It may be caused by an immune-mediated body reaction, damage to the intestinal wall following enteritis or severe worm infestation, or certain types of tumor. A common sign is the passage of large amounts of soft or watery feces. A fecal test confirms that the pancreas has produced sufficient enzymes and the food has been properly digested. Veterinary advice is essential, and treatment involves feeding a high-quality diet and eliminating any stress factors.

Pancreatic disease. The pancreas produces two secretions: insulin, essential for the process by which body cells get energy from glucose and a lack of which results in diabetes mellitus; and a mixture of digestive enzymes that is secreted into the small intestine and mixed with the food. There are specific enzymes for protein, carbohydrate or fat. Insufficient production or secretion of these enzymes (pancreatic insufficiency) results in food, particularly fat, not being fully digested and becoming very fluid. In the large intestine this forms an ideal medium for bacterial growth causing an intermittent or chronic diarrhea with soft or liquid, putty-colored feces in which fat globules may be visible. The cat does not get enough nutrients, so loses weight. Veterinary tests can quickly confirm the condition. Treatment includes feeding a diet low in protein and omitting certain types of fat and carbohydrate. Feeding pancreatic extract can help replace some of the missing enzymes. Refer also **Malabsorption**.

Stricture. A narrowing of the digestive system caused by a deformity of the esophagus or stomach. Food unable to pass through the affected area accumulates and causes distension. Projectile vomiting, in which vomit is emitted with a great deal of force, occurs anything from half an hour to several hours after eating. Obstruction of the junction between the stomach and the small intestine (pyloric stenosis) is especially common in Siamese. Treatment is surgery to correct the deformity. Obstruction by a foreign body can cause similar symptoms.

Travel sickness. Mainly caused by the rhythmic, up and down movements that affect a cat's inner ear (refer **Ear**, page 312), but sights and even smells can also be factors. Affected cats should be fasted before a short trip, or fed a light, fat-free meal about two hours before a long one. A tranquilizer can be given in tablet form about an hour before departure. The effect lasts up to 6 hours. An injection will act more quickly but last a shorter time. Side effects of sedation include protrusion of the third eyelid and weakness or incoordination. Tranquilized cats are less able to control their body temperature and are more likely to suffer from heat stroke. Cats prone to epilepsy should not be given tranquilizers without veterinary consultation.

Most cats can be acclimatised to traveling. Place the cat in a covered carrying cage or box with adequate ventilation, and put it in the front of the vehicle where the ride is smoother. Start with short trips, then gradually lengthen them. Avoid bumpy roads and travel at a constant speed. Most cats soon adjust.

Tuberculosis. This is now uncommon but should be mentioned because of its potential danger to humans. The commonest source of infection for cats is infected milk, but in Australia and New Zealand the opossum (*Trichosurus vulpecula*) carries the disease and can pass it on to cats. Lesions may develop in the skin causing ulceration and an infectious discharge, but more commonly are confined to the lymph glands in the throat or intestine. The main sign of throat infection is difficulty in swallowing, while that of intestinal tuberculosis is a progressive weight loss. Treatment is often possible, but where there is danger to human health, such as with skin lesions, euthanasia is usually recommended.

Tumors. Lymphosarcoma is a malignant tumor that is often caused by the feline leukemia virus, and in older cats it frequently involves the intestines. Other types of tumor can also affect the bowel. Common signs include diarrhea, gradual weight loss and intermittent vomiting. Some tumors may be operable or respond to chemotherapy, but many are discovered too late for the cat to be cured.

INTERNAL PARASITES

Kittens and young cats are generally more susceptible to parasitic infections than older ones. Good nutrition plays an important role in the development of immunity.

Worms and flukes

Hookworms. (*Ancylostoma* or *Uncinaria* species.) On rare occasions kittens can be infected in the uterus before birth. After birth infective hookworm larvae present on damp infected ground can enter the body by burrowing through the skin, or they may be eaten in contaminated food. Hookworms usually cause greatest damage because of blood sucking. They attach to the bowel wall and secrete an anticoagulant. After a time they move on to a new site, leaving the damaged area to bleed. So the main signs of hookworm infection are anemia and weight loss. Some cats show no signs of infection, but a routine laboratory fecal examination will detect the eggs. Some roundworm treatments are effective against hookworm, others are not. Ask your vet which to use.

Liver flukes. Various types of fluke occur throughout the world and most are of little importance. But one species is considered the most important disease of cats in the Bahamas, and also occurs in Florida.

Roundworms. Some species of roundworm live in the stomach, others in the intestine. They usually grow to about 3 in (75 mm) long, but can reach twice that length. Common intestinal roundworms in cats are *Toxocara cati, Toxascaris leonina,* and *Toxocara mystax*. The first two are also common in dogs. The stomach worm *Ollulanus tricuspis* is more common in cats in Australia and now the subject of attention in North America.

Kittens are commonly infected by larvae contained in their mother's first milk or by eating roundworm eggs stuck to the fur or skin around her nipples, or to their own fur. In small numbers roundworms do little harm, but large infections can cause damage to the lining of the intestine and prevent the proper digestion of food. Affected kittens develop a distended (pot) belly, fail to gain weight, and may become anemic.

Adult cats can become infected by eating roundworm eggs either directly or contained in the bodies of prey, but worms are usually a problem only in adult cats already suffering from some other form of debility. The eggs of several roundworm species can infect humans, and young children are particularly at risk. The eggs develop into larvae that migrate through the liver and other parts of the body, causing damage, and can reach the eye or the brain. These larvae do not develop into adult worms. Children should be told to wash their hands after playing with kittens.

To minimise infection to cats and humans treat queens at mating. Use a drug recommended by your vet. Treat kittens at about 4 weeks old, then every 2 weeks until about 5 months, then every 6 to 8 weeks until a year old. Adult cats that roam and hunt should be treated every 3 or 4 months, indoor cats once a year. Your vet will advise you what is best for your area.

Tapeworms. *Dipylidium caninum* has fleas as its intermediate host and is often found in household cats. Rarely, it can infect children who eat fleas containing its larvae. *Hydatigera taeniaformis,* whose intermediate hosts are rodents (mainly rats and mice), is more common in free-ranging cats. The dog tapeworm *Taenia pisiformis* can be contracted by a cat if it eats rabbit viscera. The most common sign of tapeworm infection is the occasional appearance of a tapeworm segment through the anus, or stuck to the surrounding fur like a flattened grain of cooked rice. Another sign is protrusion of the third eyelid (haw). Most tapeworms rarely cause a problem in healthy cats, but may cause a dull coat and loss of condition in the young, old or debilitated. In Australia the tapeworm *Spirometra erinacei* can cause severe enteritis and anemia in young animals. Various worming remedies are available, but flea control is also important.

Threadworms (*Strongyloides* species) and **Whipworms** (*Trichuris* species). Very common and rarely cause problems, but are becoming more important in parts of Australia and the United States.

Protozoan infections

Coccidiosis. An intestinal infection caused by one of several species of protozoan parasite, usually a disease of young cats. Signs depend on the severity of the infection, ranging from none to severe diarrhea and eventual death. Treatment includes sulphonamides and where necessary fluid therapy to combat dehydration.

Toxoplasmosis. Caused by the protozoan parasite, *Toxoplasma gondii,* which commonly infects many species of animal and can be transmitted to humans. Up to half of pet cats get infected, most at around 3–6 months of age, and during the following week or two they excrete hundreds of millions of oocysts in their feces. After a few days these become infectious, and under the right conditions can remain so for more than a year.

Most infected cats show no signs of illness. In those that do the disease can be acute or chronic. Acute infection is more common in young cats and signs include loss of appetite, breathing difficulty, fever, jaundice, or diarrhea and vomiting over a period of about two weeks. The chronic form is more likely to occur in older cats and can last for months. Initially there may be fever, with vomiting and diarrhea, and labored breathing. Later, as the infection spreads to other organs in the cat's body, other signs may develop relating to the area affected. These include nervous signs such as fits, retinal degeneration leading to blindness, anemia, and irregular heart beat or signs of heart failure. A pregnant queen may abort or give birth to kittens that are weak or die. Treatment of such infected cats is not usually recommended because of the public health risk, but drugs are available from a vet if required.

Human infection is extremely common and mainly arises from one of two sources. Almost all meat contains *toxoplasma* oocysts and people can become infected by eating it raw or inadequately cooked, or by failing to wash their hands after handling it. The second source is from a cat's feces, with which adult humans may come into contact while emptying litter trays or handling soil when gardening. Children can be infected while playing in sand pits to which cats have access.

In many countries more than half of people over 40 years old show evidence of having had the disease, while in some more than 90% of the population has been infected. Most humans show no signs at all, but in some, particularly children, the disease is similar to mild flu, with fever, tiredness, muscle pains and swollen glands. Once recovered, humans and animals are usually resistant to further infection.

It is to pregnant women that toxoplasmosis poses the most important danger. In women infected for the first time during pregnancy the disease can cause abortion (miscarriage) or stillbirth. Their babies have a 40% chance of being infected in the womb, and about 1 in 6 of these will be born affected in some way. Figures quoted for Europe suggest that about 3% of all babies born show some form of deformity caused by toxoplasmosis ranging from blindness to various degrees of mental retardation.

To reduce the chances of contracting toxoplasmosis pregnant women should take the following precautions:

- don't get a new cat or kitten during pregnancy.
- feed all cats in the household on commercially prepared foods or thoroughly cook all meat.
- wear gloves when gardening.
- if possible, get someone else to do the emptying and disinfection of litter trays. If not, empty them daily, before the oocysts become infective, and wear gloves when doing so. Do not put the feces into the garden.
- cover children's sandpits when not in use, and don't let cats use them for toileting.
- wear gloves when handling raw meat, or wash hands afterwards.
- don't eat undercooked or raw meat.

THE SKIN

Of all the body systems the skin is the one most commonly involved in veterinary problems, accounting for more than one out of every five cases presented to the average small animal veterinary practice. Certain breeds may be more prone to particular skin problems, but the incidence usually varies from country to country because of the different gene pools.

Acne. Mainly affects the chin region. Hair follicles become blocked with blackheads due to excessive secretion of sebum. The cause is unknown, but may be hormonal or inherited. It may possibly be due to failure to clean the chin properly, and this in turn can be associated with lameness or pain in one foreleg which makes it almost impossible for the cat to clean its chin. As with human acne the object is to control rather than cure, washing the area with 2.5% benzoyl peroxide shampoo. Acne can be complicated by bacterial infection which causes inflammation of the hair follicle (folliculitis). This needs treatment with antibiotics.

Allergies. The most common is *flea-bite allergy,* caused by a reaction to flea saliva (refer *Fleas* below). It often causes a miliary dermatitis (refer *Dermatitis* below). Self-mutilation often results in severe skin damage, infection and ulceration which should be treated by a vet. The original cause, fleas, must also be eliminated. *Mosquito-bite allergy* has been reported from Queensland, Australia. It is more common in the summer, and can cause similar signs to flea-bites. *Food allergy dermatitis* is considered uncommon by some authorities, but others suggest that it accounts for up to 10% of all skin allergy cases. Signs usually develop before 9 months of age. The most common is itching, with a miliary dermatitis and hair loss around the face, head, neck and shoulders. Foods implicated include fish products and cow's milk. Since the offending allergens are found in most commercial diets, merely changing brands is rarely effective. Confirmation is by feeding an elimination diet prescribed by a vet. *Drug or chemical allergy* may be caused by any compound. Antibiotics of the penicillin group, tetracycline or gentamycin are often implicated. Other allergens include dichlorvos (used in some flea treatments), chlorinated hydrocarbons (found in some ear preparations), and FeLV antiserum. *Flea-collar dermatitis* is an allergic reaction to the chemicals contained in a cat's flea collar. Signs are reddening, itching, scaling or crusting of the neck where the collar lies, and some hair loss. Treatment is to remove the collar. Some cats are even allergic to certain vitamins. Common signs include itching, nettle rash (urticaria), and loss of hair. Identifying the cause usually needs veterinary help. *Allergic inhalent dermatitis* is considered to be an inherited condition, and is caused by allergens such as house dust and pollens from flowering plants. Veterinary advice will be needed if this condition occurs.

Bacterial infections. Cats are less prone to bacterial infections of the skin than dogs, possibly due to their meticulous cleaning habits. A cat that does not or cannot groom itself is much more likely to be affected. Bacteria can invade the skin and hair follicles causing inflammation and pus formation, a condition called pyoderma. It is usually secondary to self-inflicted trauma following irritation such as flea bites, and veterinary treatment with antibiotics is essential. Refer also *Abcess*, page 303, *Acne*, page 310.

Cryptococcosis. The fungus *Cryptococcus neoformans* frequently infects cats. It usually causes sneezing and snuffling, but can also cause skin nodules (lumps). By the time these are discovered the disease has usually been progressing for a long time and can be very difficult to cure. The fungus can infect humans, but cat-human transmission does not appear to be common.

Dermatitis (eczema). Inflammation of the skin, a common reaction to many skin problems and often aggravated by self-mutilation and infection. *Miliary dermatitis (miliary eczema)* is a skin reaction with large numbers of small, inflamed, itchy spots that develop a crust or scab on them. These have a characteristic distribution over the head and ears, top of the neck, lower part of the back, the back and inside of the thighs, and the belly. It is most often the result of flea-bite allergy, food allergy, fungal infections other than ringworm, or *Cheyletiella* mite infection (refer *Mites*), and the underlying cause should be treated. In about one case in six there is no obvious cause, and hormone therapy may help. This usually needs to be continued for the rest of the cat's life.

Excessive psychologic shedding. May occur in spring and autumn in outdoor cats. There is a generalised loss of undercoat, but the guard hairs remain and cannot easily be pulled out. Treatment is not necessary.

Feline leprosy. Usually caused by mycobacteria which cause painless lesions in the fat under the skin. The best treatment is surgery, but failing that the drug used to treat human leprosy, dapsone, can be given by mouth. Other drugs may also be effective.

Fleas. These parasites are the most common cause of skin problems in cats. They spend most of their time off the host, jumping on only to feed and breed. Eggs are laid on the skin or in the environment. Optimal conditions for fleas are 70–80% humidity and a temperature range of 65–95°F (18–35°C), and homes in tropical and subtropical areas provide ideal conditions throughout the year. In colder climates flea problems reach their highest incidence during the summer, and their lowest during winter. Although in winter the indoor temperature in a home may be within the ideal range, particularly in houses that are centrally heated, the humidity is not usually high enough.

The life cycle takes as little as 2 weeks or more than a year, depending on the environmental conditions. Flea larvae feed on adult flea fecal casts, dried blood, feces and eggs of the tapeworm *Dipylidium caninum*, for which they act as an intermediate host. (Refer *Internal Parasites*, page 310.)

Flea bites usually cause irritation or allergy. A cat may show signs of hypersensitivity to flea saliva after only a few bites. All dermatitis resulting from flea infestation probably has an allergic basis.

To check for fleas, place the cat on clean white paper and rub or brush the fur against the lie. Flea dirts will usually fall onto the paper and appear as dark specks. When moistened, the blood contained in them causes red streaks or stains on the paper. Remember that even if there are no flea dirts, fleas could still be the cause of a particular irritation or dermatitis.

Treat all cats and dogs in the household. Different products are recommended for different climates and countries. Many of them need to be used regularly, as often as twice a week, to fully control the flea problem. Some are safe for use on kittens and young cats, some are not. Products include spot treatment, rinses or shampoos, aerosol or pump sprays, powders and flea collars. Some contain biological chemicals such as methoprene which delays the hatching of flea eggs and interrupts the life cycle of the flea at the larval stage preventing pupation and causing death. Two main types of flea collar are available. Those that produce an insecticidal vapor should be used with caution and not on sick cats, whereas those that have microfined particles of insecticide that work their way through the coat have fewer side effects. Most flea collars are effective for 5 months or more. Some may not be fully effective in endemic flea areas, but may be useful where fleas are not too much of a problem. Some can cause allergy (refer *Allergies*). Herbal flea collars use substances such as pennyroyal mint oil and eucalyptus oil to repel fleas rather than kill them, and are effective for at least 10 weeks. Whatever your preference, use only products that are recommended for cats, and if in doubt ask your vet which to use. There is no scientific evidence for the claim that feeding thiamine (vitamin B1) prevents flea infestation.

Treating the environment is as important as treating the cat. Inside the house you should vacuum at least once a week, concentrating on cracks and crevices, and then burn the contents or vacuum flea powder into them. Sprays and foggers ('bombs') containing biological chemicals such as methoprene are very effective if used as directed.

It is more difficult to control fleas outside, but concrete yards and commonly frequented sleeping places can be sprayed with malathion or carbamate every fortnight.

Chemicals used for flea control

There is a general move away from the more toxic insecticides. Compounds belonging to the organophosphorus group (organophosphates) generally have a narrow safety margin and if overdosed or used on susceptible cats they can cause toxicity. (Refer *Poisons and poisoning*, page 305). Carbamates, such as propoxur or carbaryl, are less toxic but should not be used on kittens under 8 weeks old. Insecticides belonging to the botanical group, such as pyrethrins and pyrethroids, rotenone, and citronella, are gaining in popularity, as are biological chemicals such as methoprene.

Fly strike. In neglected cats, especially matted longhairs, or debilitated animals, flies may lay eggs onto the skin. These hatch into maggots that cause severe inflammation which is soon followed by bacterial infection. Old cats that cannot clean themselves properly should be checked regularly. Matted hair must be clipped off and the area washed off with a safe insecticide (refer panel) and an antiseptic solution. In many cases veterinary advice or treatment is needed.

Hematoma. Swelling of the skin caused by bleeding from a broken blood vessel. Most frequently affects an ear (refer *Ear*, page 312).

Hormonal alopecia. This is sometimes seen in neutered shorthair cats. Of those affected 90% are males. Hair loss occurs in the groin, the back and inner aspect of the thighs, and the belly. Lesions are usually found in similar areas on each side of the body (bilaterally symmetrical). There is diffuse thinning, particularly of the primary hairs, which are easily removed from their follicle. This is in contrast to psychogenic alopecia/dermatitis (see below). There are no parasites or primary skin lesions. The exact cause is uncertain, but because cases respond to sex hormone therapy it is thought to be due to an imbalance or lack of sex hormones, and more likely to occur if the cat has been neutered at an early age. Cases also respond to treatment with thyroid hormone, but affected cats do not have a thyroid deficiency. Hair regrowth takes up to 3 months, and in many cases will occur without treatment.

Inherited skin conditions. *Albinism* is a rare, congenital, recessive trait. Partial albinism is linked to deafness in domestic short-haired cats. *Alopecia universalis* causes baldness, but some facial hairs and whiskers are left. Examples are bred as Sphynx or Canadian hairless cats. Their skin feels oily and has an unpleasant odor caused by the accumulation of fatty secretions on the skin surface. This must be removed by weekly bathing. *Hypotrichosis* is a rare disease that occurs in Siamese and Devon Rex cats. Affected kittens have soft, downy hair that falls out within 2 weeks of birth. Some hair regrowth may occur, but by 6 months of age the cat is almost bald and, like the Sphynx cats, has an oily, seborrheic skin.

Insect stings and bites. Refer *First Aid*, page 305.

Granuloma. *Lick granuloma* is a raised, wet, swollen area that is extremely irritant and continuously licked by the cat. It is usually in a place readily accessible to the cat's tongue, such as the groin, the inside of the hind legs, or the belly. Veterinary treatment is essential. Corticosteroids are usually used to control irritation, and long-acting injections have proved very effective in curing the condition. *Linear Granuloma* appears as raised, pinkish-yellow skin nodules. In one form of the disease they occur mainly in the mouth. Another form, on the back of the thigh, is more common in cats under a year old. Lesions often resolve spontaneously. The cause is unknown. Treatment is as for lick granuloma.

Mites. The common name for mite infestation is mange. *Notoedric mange* is caused by the burrowing mite *Notoedres cati*, and usually results in lesions on the head and neck. There is reddening of the skin (erythema), and scale and crust formation. The mite's life cycle of 2–3 weeks is spent entirely on the host. The condition is now uncommon, but mentioned here because it is highly contagious to other animals and people. Treatment requires weekly applications of prescribed drugs for about 3–4 weeks. *Demodectic mange* is uncommon. Lesions usually occur around the eyes, less often on the forelegs, but a more generalized form may occur. The most common sign is scaling of the skin. One form of the disease causes severe itching and requires veterinary treatment, the other may regress without treatment. *Otodectic mange* is usually confined to the ear canal (refer *Ear*, page 313) but can sometimes spread onto the head and body. Free-living mites can also cause head and ear problems, and the species *Cheyletiella* is responsible for a disease known as *cheyletiellosis*. The mite infests many different species of animal and spends its entire 5-week life cycle on its host, living on the skin surface. The most common sign is dandruff (scale formation with fine white flakes), especially on the upper part of the back. The condition may progress to seborrhea or miliary dermatitis. The mite is contagious and may infest people and other animals in the household. Most cases occur in cattery situations and young animals. One survey of long-haired cat breed catteries revealed that almost two-thirds of them had cats with *Cheyletiella* infection. Treatment is with any of the standard insecticides recommended for cats.

Psychogenic alopecia/dermatitis. A condition in which hair loss, sometimes accompanied by dermatitis, is caused by excessive licking and grooming. It is fairly common, especially in short-hair breeds of a more nervous disposition such as Siamese, Burmese and Abyssinians. The cause may be psychological, due to boredom, or anxiety from a change of home or the arrival of another cat or a baby in the household. Food allergy has been incriminated in some cases, others may be a reaction to nerve or muscle pain. The excessive licking may not be noticed because the owner considers it normal or the cat does it out of view. The main sign is partial hair loss, often symmetrical with quite clear stripes along the back. Other areas affected are the flanks, groin, the back and inside of the thighs, and the belly.

Close examination shows the hairs have been bitten or licked down to a fine stubble, as if the cat had been shaved. The hairs are not easily removed from their follicles, as they are in hormonal alopecia (refer above). In most cases the skin is normal and not inflamed, but sometimes dermatitis is present, and this can lead to ulceration. Treatment includes behavior modification, treating any underlying itching (pruritis) or modifying mood using tranquilizers, sedatives or hormones.

Ringworm. A common fungal infection which can prove a problem in catteries. *Microsporum canis* causes 98% of cases. Lesions usually appear as discrete spots with a circular, expanding border mainly on the face, ears, or towards the ends of the limbs. They may or may not cause itching (pruritis). Hair stubble occurs in the affected part because the fungus weakens the hair shaft causing it to break just above skin level. On rare occasions ringworm may become more generalized over the head and ears, chest and limbs. Lesions may be symmetrical, with excessive pigmentation and scaling. Many cats are symptomless carriers. It is contagious to other animals and humans. Diagnosis is by microscopic examination of affected hair, ultra-violet light fluorescence, and culture. Ringworm is frequently a self-limiting disease, running a course of 1–6 months. The most commonly recommended treatment is with griseofulvin tablets for about 6 weeks, and a variety of lotions or creams is also available from a vet.

Seborrhea. There are two forms of this condition, but in cats the dry form (seborrhea sicca) is the most common. The coat appears dry and there is general scaling and dandruff. There is usually no itching or inflammation. Common underlying causes are malnutrition, intestinal parasites, or mite infestation, and these should be treated first. Daily supplementation of the diet with small amounts of vegetable and animal fat (about half a teaspoon of each) will usually help. A rarer 'wet' form occurs in which the skin apears oily or greasy.

Stud tail. A skin condition most common in sexually active males, but also seen in other cats. Persians and Siamese seem to be more often affected, but the apparently higher incidence in pure bred cats may be simply that their owners notice it more. Signs are scaling, waxiness and blackheads (comidomes) on the top of the tail

near its base. No therapy is required unless for cosmetic reasons.

Ticks. These mainly infest farm livestock and only incidentally get onto cats. In temperate climates they are more active during the summer. They suck blood, and once engorged drop off. There are two main types, soft-shelled and hard-shelled. The most important soft-shelled tick is the spinous ear tick (refer *Ear*, page 313). There are several species of hard-shelled tick, most of which cause little more than a passing irritation. However the saliva of one *Ixodes* species in the warm coastal regions of Australia contains a toxin that can cause gradual paralysis and even death. (For removal, refer *Tick bite*, page 305).

Tumors. The most common skin tumor is the *squamous cell carcinoma*, which is malignant. It commonly occurs on the nose or the pinna of the ear (refer *Sunburn, Ear*, page 313). Most affected cats are over 5 years old, but ages range from 1 to 17 years. Multiple nodules in young cats and solitary nodules in older cats are often caused by *fibrosarcomas*. Most are located on the head and limbs. About half of these cats will be affected by a mutant of the feline leukemia virus (FeLV), and on blood testing will be FeLV positive. Several other types of skin tumor, benign or malignant, can occur in cats. Most tumors are malignant and secondary tumors in other organs (metastases) are common. Surgery should be carried out as soon as possible, and cats treated early may survive another 4–5 years. The longer the delay the less the life expectancy.

Wounds. Refer *First aid*, page 305.

THE EAR

Ear problems are common in cats and can be potentially serious because infection can spread down the ear canal, through the ear drum and on into the middle and inner ear. They should be treated promptly using specially formulated veterinary preparations which assist the removal of wax, pus and other debris, and disinfect the ear canal. For the method of administration refer page 302).

Common signs of ear disease include reddening, swelling, or the formation of crusts or scabs on the pinna; ear twitching, rubbing or scratching involving one or both ears; head shaking or tilting; ear discharge and/or odor; pain; circling; and personality changes. Because of nerve connections to the brain and other parts of the body disease of the middle or inner ear can affect hearing, balance and orientation, and cause nausea and vomiting.

Abscess. Infection within the pinna is uncommon, usually the result of a cat fight or scratching, and causes pus formation, swelling and pain. It should be drained by a vet. Refer also *Hematoma*.

Canker. Refer *Mite infections*.

Congenital/inherited deafness. A few cats are born deaf. In some white cats deafness results from degeneration of structures in the inner ear that commences a few days after birth. It is usually associated with white cats with blue eyes, and in those with only one blue eye deafness may affect only the ear on that side. Long-haired cats

are more likely to be affected than short-haired. Both sexes are affected.

About one in five white cats is deaf, but the incidence in a litter sired by a deaf parent will be about 80%. There is no treatment, but affected cats can live normally although they are more prone to accidents.

Ear canal infections. Inflammation of the ear canal (otitis externa) is usually a sequel to irritation or infection. In about two out of three cases the cause is a *bacterial infection*, often complicated by the presence of fungi and/or yeasts. In about one-third of cases the original cause is ear mite infestation, from which bacterial infection may follow. *Bacterial infection* is more common in young cats under one year old, and the prevalence drops off markedly from 7 years of age on. In many cases both ears are affected. The cat scratches at them and shakes its head. The pinna and ear canal become inflamed, swollen and painful, and a discharge commences that eventually becomes more fluid and foul smelling. Some affected cats show periodic irritability, go off their food, and vomit.

Fungal infection of the ear canal is more common in young cats, and often complicated with bacterial infection. It can also result from prolonged treatment with ear drops containing antibiotics that do not kill fungi or yeasts.

Ear infections require veterinary attention because they cause severe pain and there is a danger of infection spreading through the ear drum. Bacteria, fungi and yeasts require different treatments, and swabbing and culture will identify the type of infection. Your vet may prescribe antibiotic injections or tablets as well as a topical preparation.

Grass seed. If a grass seed lodges in the ear canal it causes extreme pain and irritation. For treatment refer *First aid*, page 304.

Hematoma. Swelling of the pinna, usually confined to one side only. Once thought to be caused by trauma following a cat fight or constant scratching with the hind claws, recent opinion suggests a body reaction, possibly to ear mite bites. Whatever the cause the result is swelling caused by an accumulation of blood-stained fluid between the cartilage and the skin. It usually requires veterinary attention to remove the fluid, then local treatment with corticosteroids. If left untreated the ear may become distorted (cauliflower ear). Any underlying infection of the ear canal must also be treated.

Inner ear disease. Inflammation of the inner ear (otitis interna) also involves the main nerve connecting the ear to the brain. Many signs are similar to ear canal infection (otitis externa). In addition there is often loss of equilibrium causing the cat to circle around or fall over, and there may be disorientation. Sometimes an affected cat will crouch down and remain immobile. Other signs are hearing loss and uncontrolled movements of the eyeball (nystagmus).

Causes include infection, injury, meningitis, allergy, cancer and congenital defects, or senile degeneration in old cats.

Middle ear disease. Infection and inflammation of the middle ear and ear drum (otitis media) can arise from infection ascending up the Eustachian tube, entering through a perforated ear drum, or arriving via the blood stream. It is a painful condition. The cat often holds its head down and to the affected side (head tilt). Other signs may include personality change, restlessness and insomnia, nausea and vomiting, pain on manipulation of the head or jaw, and fever. In severe cases the cat may develop convulsions. Veterinary treatment is essential, and commonly involves antibiotics and pain killers combined with corticosteroids to reduce the inflammation.

Mite infections. *Ear mite infection (canker)* is common and caused by the mite *Otodectes cynotis*. Early signs are scratching and the accumulation of thick, dark brown wax in the ear canal. As the condition progresses there is a strong odor, and if left untreated bacterial and other infections can occur. First wash out the ear canal with liquid paraffin or olive oil to remove as much as possible of the waxy accumulation, then apply a prescribed insecticide solution. This kills adult mites but not their eggs, which hatch out about 10 days after laying, so treatment must be continued over a period of at least three weeks. Continuous application of ear drops can alter the natural secretion of wax (cerumen), dry out the ear canal and promote inflammation and bacterial infection, so it is usual to apply drops for about four days and then allow about four days' rest, repeating this regime at least three times. Ear mites are contagious, so always treat both ears, and all other cats and dogs in the household.

Grass mites or *harvest mites* can cause grass itch, in which reddish, crusted lesions up to ¾ in (2 cm) diameter form on the pinna. The small reddish-orange mites can usually be seen, and particularly affect the cleft on the lateral edge of the pinna but may also invade the ear canal.

Mange mites, particularly the burrowing mite *Notoedres cati* can cause irritation, scabs and crusted lesions on the pinna and in the ear canal.

Old age changes. As a cat gets old degeneration of the brain and structures of the middle and inner ear can lead to deafness. Because this occurs gradually it can be difficult to detect and diagnosis relies heavily on the owner's observations. Signs include failure to move the ears and turn the head to pick up sounds, changes in behavior or patterns of sleep or play, failure to come when called or wandering around as though lost. Hearing tests conducted by vets include reaction to a sudden handclap, tuning forks, ultrasonic testing with a dog whistle, and reaction to natural sounds such as birds or other cats. Affected cats are usually able to adjust although they may be more prone to accidents or injury.

Sunburn. Reddening of the ear tips and margins, with flaking and scaling, is commonly seen in white cats suffering from sunburn (solar dermatitis). Signs of severe damage may not appear for years. Eventually scabs develop, under which are sores that bleed profusely if the scabs are removed. The condition can progress to a malignant cancer. Treatment should be undertaken as soon as the condition is noticed. The cat should be kept out of strong sunlight, and sunscreen lotions or creams used. Because the condition results from a lack of protective pigments in the skin, regular use of a non-toxic felt marker pen or tattooing by a vet can help. Once the cancer has started, freezing (cryosurgery), X-ray therapy or surgical amputation may be necessary.

Ticks. The ear canal may be inhabited by the parasitic larval and nymphal stages of the *spinous ear tick*, found mostly in the south-west United States. Treatment is with prescribed ear drops. *Sheep ticks* may lodge on the surface of the pinna, or even in the ear canal itself. For removal refer **Tick bite fever**, page 305).

Tumors. Benign (non-cancerous) tumors are usually associated with the wax-producing glands and more likely to occur in old cats with chronic ear disease. They can completely block the ear canal and usually require surgery. Small fleshy growths called polyps can also occur.

Vestibular syndrome. An unusual condition that can affect cats of all ages. It seems to occur more often in spring and autumn, and at night. Affected cats have a head tilt and fall to the side. They show severe nystagmus (abnormal eye movement) and are usually very disorientated and distressed. Some vomit. Sometimes the affected cat lies flat on the ground, which could indicate that both ears are affected. No treatment seems to be of any help, but cage confinement is recommended in the early stages. Most cats improve in a few hours and can walk with a stagger in 4–5 days. Balance is usually regained after about 8–10 days, and full recovery usually occurs within 3–6 weeks. On rare occasions a cat may show permanent signs of damage, or suffer another episode.

THE EYE

Most eye problems are caused by infection or injury. The cat's rapid blink reflex usually protects the eyeball during cat fights, confining any damage to the eyelids or third eyelid.

The eye's natural reaction to irritation is an increase in tear production (lacrimation), so watering of the eye and inflammation of the conjunctiva (conjunctivitis) are often the first signs of an eye problem. Others include blinking, partial or complete closure of the eye, abnormal sensitivity and discomfort to light (photophobia), protrusion of the third eyelid (haw), cloudiness on the cornea, and dilation or constriction of the pupil.

Minor eye conditions such as temporary irritation from dust or dirt can be treated at home with saline or veterinary eye drops. The method of administration is shown on page 302.

WARNING: Apart from clean water, saline or mineral oil, never place anything in the eye that has not been specially formulated for use in the cat. Any eye disease or injury should be regarded as potentially serious. Except for minor problems all home treatment should be accompanied by veterinary advice.

Allergy. Uncommon. The main signs are sudden watering from both eyes with or without conjunctivitis, but otherwise the cat appears normal. Veterinary help will be needed to determine the exact cause and prescribe the correct treatment.

Black spot (mummification). A hard, raised, brown-black plaque that gradually develops on the cornea and may cause watering and discomfort. Unique to cats, it may be an inherited condition and is more common in Persians, Colourpoints (Himalayans) and Siamese. It may require surgical removal.

Cataract. Cloudiness or opacity of the lens. Unilateral cataract (one eye only) is often caused by trauma. Bilateral cataract (both eyes) is uncommon, and usually congenital or associated with diabetes.

Corneal ulcer. An important possible sequel to keratitis (see below), damage by a foreign body and feline viral rhinotracheitis. Healing can be very slow, and the condition requires veterinary treatment including antibiotics. If the cornea perforates, part of the iris may wash forward, plug the hole, and become permanently attached preventing normal constriction and dilation of the pupil.

Ectropion. Turning out of an eyelid, almost always associated with the formation of scar tissue following an injury. The result is an overflow of tears, and correction is by surgery.

Entropion. Turning in of an eyelid. Usually inherited and more commonly seen in Persians. The inturning usually occurs towards the outer edge of the lower eyelid. The hairs along the edge of the inturned lid rub against the cornea, causing irritation and watering of the eye. Eye drops or ointments will alleviate the problem but for a permanent cure surgery is required.

Eye worm. In some parts of the United States the eye worm *Thelazia californiensis* causes conjunctivitis and a thick discharge. Veterinary treatment is by injection of the drug ivermectin.

Glaucoma. Swelling of the eyeball with a fixed, dilated pupil. Caused by reduced drainage of the fluid within the eyeball and an increase in pressure. Causes include inflammation of the iris (iritis), bleeding, and cancer caused by feline leukemia. Usually seen in older cats it is often insidious in onset leading to a chronic and painful condition accompanied by a change in color of the cornea to reddish-blue ('red-eye' or 'blue-eye'). Veterinary surgery may relieve the signs but the condition is not curable. Removal of the eye may be recommended to relieve the pain and enable the cat to live a more normal life. Apparent enlargement of the eyeball can be caused by an abscess or tumor behind the eye which forces it forward.

Haw. The name commonly given to conditions in which the third eyelid protrudes, affecting one or both eyes. Causes include feline dysautonomia, Horner's syndrome, tetanus, chronic bowel infections caused by parasites or viruses, and the administration of sedatives.

Horner's syndrome. This results from trauma causing damage to certain nerve pathways to the eye. The affected eye has a constricted pupil and is slightly withdrawn into the socket causing the third eyelid to protrude across the eye. Vision is not affected. The condition does not usually require treatment but may be permanent.

Infections. Inflammation and reddening of the margin of the eyelid (blepharitis) often results from bacterial infection following cat fights. Treatment is with antibiotic eye ointment or drops, and/or tablets or injections. The bacterium *Chlamydia psittaci* can cause conjunctivitis in cats of all ages, usually affecting one eye first and the other a week or so later. It may also cause upper respiratory signs (refer **Feline pneumonitis,** page 307). Treatment is with antibiotic eyedrops. Vaccination may prove beneficial and should be discussed with your vet. A less severe infection may be caused by two types of *Mycoplasma*, and by the yeast *Cryptococcus*. The viruses causing feline respiratory disease also cause eye infection. The treatment of eye infections depends on the cause, but usually includes antibiotic eye ointments or drops which may or may not contain corticosteroids.

Injuries. Damage to the cornea can occur following a fight or accident (refer **Keratitis**). Severe trauma such as a road accident can cause an eyeball to be forced from its socket and trapped outside the eyelids. Action is to immediately protect the eye from further damage, keep it moist with clean water, eye drops or mineral oil, and get immediate veterinary assistance. Occasionally chemicals and objects such as grass seeds can enter the eye. The latter usually lodge behind the third eyelid or between the eyeball and lower lid. The main signs are a partially or completely closed weeping eye, at which the cat may paw, and severe pain. For treatment refer **Foreign bodies**, page 304).

Keratitis. Inflammation of the cornea, usually the result of injury or infection and commonly associated with feline viral rhinotracheitis. Early signs include cloudiness or opacity, and if untreated infection can lead to corneal ulceration (see above). 'Dry eye' or keratitis sicca results from a condition in which tear formation is greatly reduced or absent. In all cases of keratitis veterinary treatment should be obtained.

Old age changes. Blindness may occur as part of the aging process. Because it occurs gradually many household cats learn to adjust to failing eyesight and live happy and healthy lives even when totally blind.

Squint. More common in Siamese cats, and thought to be associated with an abnormal development of the pathways taken by the nerve fibers that supply the eye. It is not harmful and there is no treatment.

Retinal degeneration. Gradual destruction of the cells of the retina, leading to partial or total blindness. It can be an inherited condition in Abyssinians. Infectious causes include feline infectious peritonitis, toxoplasmosis, and crypto-coccosis, and treatment may prove difficult. It may also be due to a deficiency of the nutrient taurine, in which case early detection and treatment can prove successful.

Tear canal blockage/deformity. This will result in an overflow of tears. Temporary blockage may occur while an eye is inflamed or infected, and treatment for the infection will usually cure the tear canal problem. Permanent deformity or blockage is common in cats that have been bred with very flattened faces, such as Persians and Exotics, and the chronic overflow of tears causes tear staining of the fur.

Union of the upper and lower eyelids. Normal in most newborn kittens during the first 8–12 days of life, or during the first few days in Siamese and Orientals. Delayed opening beyond 14 days is usually due to a minor infection underneath the lids, which should be gently separated and antibiotic eye drops or ointment instilled. If in doubt get veterinary advice.

Uveitis. Inflammation of the iris of the eye and its associated structures resulting in constriction of the pupil which appears red or cloudy. The most common cause is immuno-mediated (a reaction by the cat's immune system). Others include trauma; bacterial, viral or fungal infections; and toxoplasmosis. Treatment depends on the cause but often includes corticosteroids.

THE URINARY SYSTEM

As cats age many of their organs start to deteriorate. The kidney is one of them, and chronic kidney disease is one of the most frequent causes of ill health in old cats. But kidney and bladder conditions also occur in younger animals, and cat owners should know how to recognize them and what action to take.

Signs associated with chronic kidney disease are excessive thirst and urination, loss of appetite, depression, weight loss, bad breath, inflammation of the gums (gingivitis) and mouth (stomatitis) and vomiting. Several of those signs may also occur with diabetes mellitus (sugar diabetes). The most common signs of bladder problems are straining, pain during urination, and blood in the urine (hematuria).

Acute kidney disease. This is uncommon. It can be caused by toxic substances, such as when a cat swallows anti-freeze (ethylene glycol) (refer **Poisoning**, page 305) or after the administration of certain antibiotics. It can also occur following rapid deterioration during chronic kidney disease. The signs include severe depression, loss of appetite, vomiting and dehydration. Veterinary treatment is essential, and the outlook is poor.

Chronic kidney disease (chronic renal failure). This is the most common type of kidney problem in cats, and commonly called 'end-stage kidneys'. As kidney function deteriorates it becomes more difficult for the cat to eliminate all the waste products from its body. To compensate for this the kidneys produce greater amounts of more dilute urine. This in turn means a greater loss of fluid from the body, for which the cat compensates by drinking more. So one of the earliest signs of kidney disease is excessive drinking, although this may not be noticed by the owner. As the condition progresses further the kidneys are unable to eliminate all the waste products in the urine, so the body uses other methods. One of these is to secrete urea, a product of protein digestion, through the saliva. Bacteria in the mouth react with this to produce ammonia, which causes bad breath (halitosis). Other body disturbances include leaching of calcium from the bones. In the jaw bone this can result in teeth becoming loose and falling out. Limb bones can become more brittle and likely to fracture.

Chronic kidney failure can be a sequel to a variety of disease processes, as well as the result of old age deterioration. Bacterial infection of the kidney can cause a condition known as pye-lonephritis, which may be relatively important as a cause of end-stage kidney failure. The 'dry' form of feline infectious peritonitis and another kidney condition called glomerulonephritis may also lead to chronic renal failure. Cancer of the kidney is very rare. An uncommon congenital condition leading to kidney failure has been reported in longhairs and Abyssinian cats.

Veterinary diagnosis of chronic kidney disease is based on the signs, a clinical examination and blood and urine tests. There is no treatment, but a number of steps can be taken to reduce the impact of the disease. It is essential to maintain the cat's fluid intake, if necessary by injection, and to control secondary problems such as mouth infections or other disease processes. The cat should receive a low-protein diet containing protein of high quality such as chicken or fish.

Commercial kidney diets are generally available. Because B vitamins are soluble in water and easily lost in the urine, additional amounts will help. Anabolic steroids (hormones) prescribed by a vet will help to stop tissue breakdown. The outlook is poor, but some cats live on for many years. It is important to protect the cat from illnesses or stresses that would normally be considered trivial, but in this situation can have a severe effect.

Cystitis. Inflammation of the bladder, with or without bacterial infection, most commonly associated with the feline urological syndrome (refer below). Cystitis caused by a bladder worm has been recorded in Australia.

Feline urological syndrome (FUS). This is the most important lower urinary system condition in the cat because of its common occurrence and potentially serious nature. Affected cats are likely to be young, neutered, slightly overweight, and take little exercise. In the female it results in cystitis and one of the earliest signs is an increased frequency of urination, but with only a small amount of urine (often blood-stained) being passed each time. Instead of using its litter tray the cat may urinate in other parts of the house. Otherwise it may be bright and continue to eat, and not be excessively thirsty. Sometimes an affected cat vomits or has a fever.

In the male the signs are similar but accompanying the cystitis there may be a complete or partial blockage of the urethra with crystals of struvite (magnesium ammonium phosphate hexahydrate), one of the earliest signs of which is frequent licking of the penis which may be seen protruding from its sheath. The cat adopts a classic posture and strains as it frequently attempts to urinate, which may lead the owner to think that it is constipated. Any urine passed may be blood-stained. Feeling the bladder reveals that it is hard, and distended to about the size of an orange. Early treatment is essential, as rupture of the bladder has been known to occur. Cats that have only a partial obstruction and remain untreated may become depressed and dehydrated.

The first thing that a vet must do is relieve the obstruction. This is usually achieved by careful washing out (lavage) of the crystals blocking the urethra. Antibiotics may be needed to treat any bacterial infection.

The precise cause of FUS is still a matter for debate, but there is no association between FUS and the breed of cat or its age at neutering. Whether dry cat foods play a role in the disease is not clear. Fluid intake has been shown to be an important factor in the disease, and cats that eat mostly dry food may consume up to 30% less water than those that eat moist foods. FUS was once thought to be linked to a high magnesium content in certain diets, but this theory is no longer held. It is now thought that a prime factor in the disease is the production of an alkaline urine, for it has been shown that struvite crystals only form in the latter. Cats are carnivorous, and their natural diet rich in animal protein results in an acid urine with a pH between 5 and 6 (pH 7 is neutral, anything higher is alkaline). Most dry cat foods contain 40–50% vegetable matter which tends to produce an alkaline urine with a pH between 7 and 8. So factors that affect the pH of the urine are more important than other postulated causes. Many dry cat foods now contain urinary acidifiers such as ammonium chloride to produce an acid urine, and most have added salt to make the cat thirsty and increase its water intake. The long-term effects of these additions have yet to be determined.

There is no proof of an infectious cause, although bacteria or viruses might sometimes predispose to FUS or invade the bladder after the condition has commenced. The incidence in the general population is probably less than 1%, but in cats attended at vet clinics it was once up to 10%. It is probably on the decrease, possibly following the changes that have occurred in the composition of commercial dry foods.

Dietary management is useful for preventing the disease or following treatment because it is relatively easy to achieve, and a high-calorie diet that produces an acid urine is recommended for recovered cats.

Nephrotic syndrome. Occurs in young cats, resulting in a loss of protein via the kidneys and urine. The underlying cause is not fully understood. Signs include edema (tissue swelling) under the chest and belly and the lower part of the legs. Affected cats often appear bright, but some develop diarrhea or depression. A urine test demonstrates high levels of protein in the urine. The disease is seldom curable. Veterinary treatment includes giving diuretics to increase the amount of urine passed and reduce the edema, a high-protein diet, and confining in a cage to rest.

Urinary incontinence. Frequent or constant involuntary urination due to a loss of voluntary control. Causes include old age, damage to the nerve supply from spinal injury following an accident, and cancer of the bladder. Veterinary advice should be sought. Incontinence caused by injury often resolves gradually over a period of several weeks, but in the early stages it may be necessary to assist the cat by gently expressing its bladder. This will also help to prevent cystitis. Your vet will show you how to do it.

THE REPRODUCTIVE SYSTEM

Failure to breed is the common sign of a reproductive problem in both sexes. In the female other signs such as nymphomania, straining, abnormal discharge from the vulva or mammary swelling are associated with problems during oestrus, pregnancy, birth or rearing.

Abortion. A common complication, early abortion may not be noticed because the queen sometimes eats the fetuses and associated discharges. Kittens born before 8 weeks of gestation are unlikely to survive. Births from 56–60 days are considered premature but survival is possible. Non-infectious causes include trauma, nutritional imbalances, physical abnormalities of the genital system, concurrent illness, and psychologic disturbances in response to stress and hormone deficiencies. Repeated abortions at about the same stage in gestation are generally of hormonal origin, and the problem usually responds to treatment with progesterone started 7 days before the usual time of abortion and continued until 7 days after the expected date of parturition. Infectious causes include bacteria, and the viruses that cause respiratory disease, feline leukemia, and feline infectious peritonitis. Drugs can be used to cause abortion and prevent pregnancy due to mismating. Some must be given within 24 hours of

mating, others can be given up to 40 days after. Consult your vet.

Birth problems. Scar tissue from previous births, serious illness during pregnancy, and even age and size can affect the normal birth process. *Uterine inertia* occurs when the uterine muscle fails to contract properly and expel the fetus. It is more common in queens that have previously given birth, in older, more obese cats, and in long-haired breeds. It may also occur following a long and difficult birth. Stroking the dorsal vaginal wall with a finger may help to prolong contractions and hasten passage of the next kitten. Treatment is by subcutaneous injection of oxytocin, often combined with intravenous injection of 10% calcium gluconate. *Uterine prolapse* sometimes occurs during or after birth, and replacement requires urgent veterinary attention. Bathe the prolapsed portion with warm water or liquid paraffin to keep it moist, then protect it by covering with a clean cloth until veterinary help is obtained. **Uterine ruptures** may occur following trauma in late pregnancy, or immediately prior to or during birth. The cat may develop shock, or there may be few signs other than abdominal discomfort or failure to produce the expected kittens. In such cases surgical treatment is required. In some cats there are no obvious signs and the rupture is only discovered during routine spaying. *Obstruction* to the normal passage of a kitten may occur because of a deformity in the shape or size of the queen's pelvis or the kitten, an abnormal presentation, or inadequate lubrication due to loss of birth fluids. For the latter carefully instil 5–10 ml of liquid paraffin to assist lubrication. It can be difficult to grasp a partly born kitten to gently pull it out, but using a piece of dry gauze may help. Caesarian section is indicated where a queen is unable to give birth normally. If the problem is known beforehand an elective operation may be carried out at about 63 days or when the queen enters labor. Sometimes the rapid delivery of two or more kittens can result in an umbilical cord becoming wrapped around some part of one individual. Often the queen does not attempt to sever the cord, which should be released or severed quickly to avoid damage to the kitten (for method refer page 296). *Vulval discharge* after birth is normally slight and lasts for about 3–5 days. It is usually cleaned away by the queen and not visible. A dark red or brown discharge may be due to retained fetal membranes. The queen's body temperature should be checked and any infection treated by a veterinary surgeon. Refer also **Endometritis; Vaginitis** below. *Hemorrhage* sometimes occurs after a birth, and the main sign is bleeding from the vulva. If serious it can soon cause shock, collapse and death, and veterinary help should be obtained immediately.

Congenital defects in kittens. Many types of defect can occur, affecting various parts of the body and organs such as the heart. Some may be caused by the administration of drugs during pregnancy. For example, cleft palate has been associated with griseofulvin medication for ringworm. Defects can also occur in conjunction with the *fading kitten syndrome* (refer below). For defects that affect the health and welfare of the kitten euthanasia is recommended.

Eclampsia. Refer *Hypocalcemia.*

Endometritis. Inflammation of the lining of the womb. *Acute endometritis* is potentially dangerous, usually due to a bacterial infection ascending from the cervix, and may occur after oestrus, artificial

insemination, excessive matings, a difficult birth or Caesarian section. It is frequently accompanied by mastitis (see below), and should be suspected if a nursing queen is clearly unwell and neglecting to feed or clean her kittens. Other signs include fever, vomiting, diarrhea, and a smelly vulval discharge. Treatment is with broad-spectrum antibiotics. *Chronic endometritis* is a low-grade infection of the uterus. Often the only sign is the inability of a cat to have a healthy litter. She may have infrequent or irregular oestrus cycles, fail to conceive, abort, give birth to dead kittens, or occasionally raise one or two. The most common cause is a bacterial infection, and if it does not respond to antibiotics the cat should be spayed.

Extra-uterine (ectopic) pregnancy. Development of a fetus outside the womb and attached to the lining (peritoneum) of the abdominal cavity, caused by accidental release of an ovum into the abdominal cavity or rupture of the uterus. By about 4–5 weeks the blood supply to the fetus proves inadequate and it dies and is partly resorbed, but the queen may show no visible signs. Once discovered surgical removal may be recommended. The condition seems to be more common than in the past.

Fading kitten syndrome. A complex problem that includes repeat matings, fetal resorption at 4–6 weeks, abortions during the last half of gestation, stillbirths and congenital malformation. Fading kittens are often born underweight, appear emaciated and fail to nurse. Some appear normal but quickly fade and die after a few days or weeks. The cause is still undetermined but feline infectious peritonitis may play a role. Sometimes kittens become weak through being unable to suckle properly because the queen is unsettled, in which case a move to a quieter, less disturbed environment is all that may be necessary.

False pregnancy. An uncommon condition in which a queen may show normal signs of pregnancy (such as enlargement of the nipples) until about 40–45 days, after which they cease. It may follow an unsuccessful mating or artificial induction of ovulation. No treatment is necessary.

Fetal maceration. Death and decomposition of a fetus. It may follow an abortion in which one or more fetuses have been expelled. The queen may or may not produce a red or purulent vaginal discharge, or appear ill. A macerated fetus may be passed with normal kittens at birth, but sometimes needs surgical removal.

Fetal mummification. The death and slow dehydration of a fetus in the womb. Quite common, and often involves one fetus only while the rest develop normally. There is no sign of infection. The fetus may be either fully resorbed, or expelled at birth.

Hypocalcemia (eclampsia or lactation tetany). A fall in the level of calcium in the blood, caused by depletion of body calcium following heavy lactation, and usually seen in queens with 5 or more kittens and at the time of peak lactation (2–4 weeks). Initial signs are restlessness, failure to eat and loss of balance. Later salivation, panting, fever, vomiting and convulsions may occur, followed by death if left untreated. Treatment consists of the intravenous or subcutaneous injection of a calcium solution and placing the queen in a quiet, darkened room until recovered. To prevent a recurrence kittens over 3 weeks old should be weaned, and younger kittens supplemented with milk formula, hand reared or fostered onto another lactating queen.

Infertility. *Failure to come into season* can be caused by many factors including nutritional deficiency (lack of vitamin A or iodine), insufficient daylight hours, isolation from other queens and males resulting in lack of exposure to pheromones (chemicals in the urine) that help to stimulate the onset of heat, or hormonal problems.

Failure to conceive may be due to a problem in the male or the female. In the former it may be inexperience, aggression, a lack of libido due to protein deficiency, or a reproductive abnormality such as a hormonal imbalance or an undescended testicle or testicles. In the female it may be due to wrong timing, intolerance of the male, lack of proper courtship, poor nutrition, ill health, or endometritis (refer above). Thickening of the uterine lining (endometrial hyperplasia) occurs if a queen is allowed to continually cycle without mating, and there is no fully effective treatment.

Mammary gland problems. *Mastitis* is an inflammation of one or more of the mammary glands, commonly caused by bacterial infection. An affected gland feels warm and looks reddened and swollen. The condition may not be noticed until the kittens show signs of hunger or weakness. The glands nearest the tail are most commonly affected. Treatment includes swabbing with a warm saline solution, and antibiotics for both the queen and the kittens. Mastitis can also occur after about 2–3 weeks due to the trauma of kittens nursing. It may help to trim the kittens' claws, but may be necessary to remove the kittens altogether. Any mammary infection should be treated with antibiotics.

Mammary swelling can occur in some young queens. The glands are painful, turgid, and contain a brownish fluid. The condition is usually associated with ovarian problems and after initial veterinary treatment spaying is advisable. Sometimes the mammary glands closest to the head swell because they are not adequately suckled, perhaps because of inverted nipples. Apply a warm, moist compress and gently massage and express to stimulate milk flow, then encourage the kittens to suckle from them. *Mammary tumors* usually affect the forward pair of mammary glands. More common in females over 10 years old, and entire queens, they require surgical removal.

Ovarian problems. *Ovarian cysts* result in frequent or permanent oestrus (nymphomania), and affected queens may lose weight, become hard to handle, refuse to breed, and become nervous or aggressive. The best treatment is to spay the cat. *Remnants of ovary* may be left after spaying, but not always because of faulty surgical technique. Follicles may then mature and cysts develop. The cat may come into oestrus, and even mate, but will fail to conceive. Treatment is surgical removal of the remnant.

Pyometra. The accumulation of fluid, usually infected, in the uterus. The cause is unknown, but probably a hormone imbalance that causes cysts in the wall of the uterus resulting in thickening. It is most common in queens that have not had any kittens. The cervix may be closed, when no discharge is visible, or open, when there is a visible discharge. Other signs may be few, merely slight loss of appetite and depression. The queen may merely be infertile after repeated matings. In more severe cases however there may be fever, loss of appetite, excessive thirst, vomiting, severe depression, and probably a vulval discharge. Swelling of the abdomen may or may not be noticeable. The ideal treatment is spaying. If the patient is a valuable breeding queen alternative treatments can be tried including drainage of the uterus, but these may not be successful.

Uterine Torsion. This may occur during the last few weeks of pregnancy. Signs are abdominal pain, usually following rough handling or some other activity. The cat may crouch and strain, appear restless, vomit and exhibit early signs of shock. Early veterinary treatment is essential.

Uterine Tumor. Uncommon, because so many females are neutered. Mostly found in queens over 10 years of age. Signs are non-specific but may include excessive thirst and abdominal distension. The treatment is spaying.

Vaginitis. Inflammation of the vagina, most commonly seen in sexually mature cats and generally associated with endometritis (refer above). Causes include excessive mating and physical injury. Feline viral rhinotracheitis virus may also cause vaginal infection. Constant licking and cleaning and reddening of the vulva may be the only signs, as the fastidious cat usually cleans up the accompanying discharge. Veterinary treatment includes flushing the vagina and the use of antibiotics.

THE MUSCLES AND SKELETON

Apart from bruises, wounds and fractures caused by accidents or fighting, problems involving the muscles and skeleton are uncommon. The main signs are pain and swelling around the affected area, and lameness.

Muscle and tendon problems

Hernia. Caused by the protrusion of tissue or organs through a natural opening or break in the muscles of the abdominal wall or diaphragm. Correction requires surgery. *Umbilical hernia* results in a swelling at the navel. It is most commonly seen in kittens, and usually inherited. Depending on size it may require surgery. *Inguinal hernia* is more common in the female, and results from the passage of bowel through the inguinal ring, a natural channel in the abdominal wall. It is characterized by a soft swelling in the groin and requires treatment. *Perineal hernia* is uncommon, usually occurs in older males and is caused by a break in the muscles surrounding the rectum, usually as a result of straining from chronic constipation. The intestine passes through the break to create a swelling around or to one side of the anus. Veterinary advice should be obtained. *Diaphragmatic hernia* sometimes occurs after severe trauma such as a motor vehicle accident, in which rupture of the diaphragm allows abdominal organs to work their way through into the chest and affect heart function and breathing. This type of hernia should be regarded as an emergency, and surgery will be necessary.

Muscle diseases. Conditions called myopathies were once regarded as uncommon in cats, but have attracted more attention in recent years. The most common sign is general muscle weakness. In a myopathy caused by low blood levels of the mineral potassium this weakness is accompanied by muscle pain, crouching and a stilted gait, and the cat flexes its neck with the head downwards. It has been seen more in older cats, and may result from kidney disease which causes an excessive loss of potassium from the body. Treatment with potassium corrects the condition. Poisoning by organophosphate compounds can also cause muscle problems.

Muscle injury/inflammation. Bruising caused by trauma is often difficult to see beneath the fur, but the swelling caused by bleeding in and around the muscle can sometimes be felt, and the associated pain causes the cat to react to being touched in that area. On hairless parts of the body it is possible to see the typical discoloration and change of color from purple-black to a yellow-green that occurs over the course of a few days as blood pigment breaks down. Treatment for bruising is not usually necessary. If bleeding causes the accumulation of blood beneath the skin leading to swelling (hematoma), get veterinary advice. Inflammation of muscle (myositis) or tendon (tendonitis) commonly follows bacterial infection from bite wounds and usually requires treatment with antibiotics.

Bone problems

Arthritis. Inflammation within a joint, which usually follows joint infection, dislocation or trauma, but can also be due to degeneration of the cartilages that cover the ends of the bones. Signs include pain, often accompanied by stiffness or lameness, and the affected joint may feel hot and swollen. An antibiotic should be used for treatment of bacterial infections, but because the joint has no direct blood supply these can be difficult to eliminate.

Bone disease/inflammation. The most common bone diseases are the result of a deficiency of calcium and/or an excess of phosphorus in the diet, or an excess of the vitamins A or D. These are discussed in the section on *Nutritional problems*, page 319. In old cats calcium can be leached from the bones making them weaker and more likely to fracture. Inflammation of bone (osteitis) most commonly follows bacterial infection from bite wounds. Signs include pain, swelling or discomfort around the affected area, and the cat may have a fever. Antibiotics are usually required to combat infection.

Dislocation. This occurs when the bones in a joint are displaced from each other. The most common site is the hip joint, usually dislocated as a result of a road accident. It can be difficult for an owner to distinguish between a dislocation and a fracture, but in either case veterinary advice will be needed. Don't try to splint a suspected dislocation. Simply limit the cat's movement by putting it in a carrying cage and get it to a vet as soon as possible.

Fractures. These are usually classified into four main types. A *greenstick fracture*, as its name implies, results in splitting of the bone but there is no complete break and no displacement. It usually occurs in young cats which have softer bones. A *simple fracture* occurs when a bone is broken into two pieces but there is no penetration of the skin. In a *multiple fracture* the bone is broken into three or more pieces. A *compound fracture* is where some part of the bone protrudes through the skin, and infection can result. The most common types of fracture are a broken lower jaw (usually mid-line) or broken pelvis, usually caused by a motor vehicle accident or a fall, and a broken tail (shut in a closing door).

Immediate action can be taken by the owner to stabilise the injury, treat for shock (refer **First aid**, page 305) and confine movement. Wherever possible the cat should then be treated by a vet to provide pain relief and obtain an accurate diagnosis of the injury. Treatment depends on the type of fracture and its location. A greenstick fracture may be left to heal by itself. A lower jaw fracture is usually wired together, whereas a limb fracture may be put in a cast or have a stainless steel pin or plate inserted. A pelvic fracture is usually left to heal on its own, with the cat confined to a small cage for about two weeks to limit movement. A tail fracture may also be left alone, but if there has been damage to the nerves at the fracture site either the cat can end up in chronic pain or the end of the tail may become paralysed. In such cases the tail may require amputation just above the affected area.

Spinal injury. Usually the result of an accident. Severe trauma or fracture of one or more vertebrae can damage the spinal cord and cause partial or complete paralysis.

Sprains. Caused by the stretching or rupture of the ligaments or capsule surrounding a joint. A simple sprain will usually heal with rest, which the cat will usually impose on itself. A sprain may be difficult to distinguish from a more serious injury, so if the condition does not improve in a few days, or the pain or swelling gets worse, consult a vet.

Tumors. Bone tumors are uncommon and usually occur in older cats, more commonly on the long bones of the legs. The majority are malignant and secondary tumors have often spread into the lungs and other organs before the primary tumor is detected. The chances of recovery are very poor, although amputation of the affected leg may be successful if X-rays show no secondary tumors in the rest of the body.

THE NERVOUS SYSTEM

If badly damaged the cells of the brain, spinal cord and nerves cannot heal, and permanent loss of function can occur. This is why it can be difficult to forecast the outcome of many nervous diseases. Signs of nerve damage vary depending on the part of the system affected. Those indicative of brain damage include behavioral changes, blindness, coma (loss of consciousness), deafness, convulsions (fits), weakness, head pressing or tilting, loss of balance, muscle spasms and tremors, and pain. Other signs include incoordination, changes to the gait, and partial or complete paralysis. Some of these signs occur with middle or inner ear disease (refer **Ear**, page 312).

Brain damage/infection. Trauma to the brain is most commonly caused by a motor vehicle accident or fall, causing various degrees of incoordination or paralysis, blindness, deafness and loss of consciousness. Severe trauma can cause brain hemorrhage and swelling, which can result in death. Urgent veterinary treatment is essential. Brain damage can also be caused by a

stroke. Strokes are uncommon in cats, and most likely to occur in animals over 10 years old through a blood clot blocking an artery in the brain. Signs depend on the area of the brain affected, and range from personality change to dilated pupils, abnormal eye movement (nystagmus), blindness, deafness, mild stupor, incoordination and loss of balance, circling, head tilt, partial or complete paralysis of one side of the body, and unconsciousness. Damage can also result from brain tumors, congenital and genetic defects and thiamine deficiency (refer **Nutritional problems**, page 319). Inflammation of the brain tissue (encephalitis) can follow virus infections such as FIP, FeLV and rabies, bacterial infections, cryptococcosis or toxoplasmosis, or be caused by migrating parasites or larvae.

Epilepsy. This syndrome is uncommon in cats, and in most cases due to brain disease. It usually starts with irregular, small seizures that become more frequent and of longer duration over the next year or so. If your cat has a seizure put it in a dark, quiet place, make sure it is breathing properly, and wait for it to recover. If breathing is difficult or the seizure lasts more than about 5 minutes you should get veterinary help immediately. Epilepsy can be controlled (but not cured) with anticonvulsant drugs. Never give unprescribed tranquilizers to a cat with a history of epilepsy, for some can actually cause seizures.

Feline dysautonomia (Key-Gaskell syndrome). This syndrome was first reported in the United Kingdom in 1982, increased in frequency for a few years, but now occurs only sporadically there and in Europe. More common in cats under 3 years old, its cause is unknown. Signs appear to be associated with nerve dysfunction. Affected cats become dull, lose their appetite and lose weight. Other signs may include dilated pupils, protruding third eyelid, constipation, regurgitation of food, dry mouth and reduced tear production. Some cats appear to be unable to retract their claws properly. Treatment is largely supportive and symptomatic, and includes administration of fluids by mouth or injection, and liquid paraffin for constipation. Drugs can be given to increase the flow of saliva and tears.

Feline hyperesthesia syndrome. This condition seems to be increasing in incidence. It is characterised by a rippling or twitchy skin, usually over the back, tail, flank or pelvis, and appears to be accompanied by hallucinations. The eyes appear glassy, the pupils dilated, and the tail usually swishes. The cat may meow frantically. Episodes may last from a few seconds to several minutes, and occur at regular or irregular intervals or times of day. Between bouts the cat may appear normal or only slightly agitated. The cause is unknown, but affected cats are often loners and naturally nervous or excitable. Various drugs can be used to control it, and environmental changes that reduce stress can also help.

Nerve damage/inflammation. Damage to nerves in the spinal cord can occur from trauma, slipped disc, abscess formation, bone disease or a tumor. Major signs are incoordination, weakness, partial or complete paralysis and pain, but these can also be symptomatic of brain damage or other problems.

Damage to a nerve in one of the limbs is usually caused by trauma from a road accident. If it occurs high up on the forelimb it can cause brachial paralysis, in which sensation is lost below the elbow and the leg is dragged along the ground because the cat cannot raise it. If the trauma occurs lower down it can cause radial

paralysis, which often results in the paw knuckling over and the elbow collapsing at each step. Healing and recovery often occurs but it can take several weeks or months, and most vets wait 6 months before making a final judgment. One or both of the sciatic nerves in the hind legs may be damaged following a fracture of the pelvis. Commonly the affected leg sinks and the paw knuckles over. Depending on the severity of the damage recovery can take from a few days to several months, or not occur at all.

Inflammation of nerve tissue (neuritis) results in abnormal sensations such as flashes of pain, or loss of control of muscles resulting in twitches, tremors or spasms. Causes include trauma, tumor, toxic chemicals, tick bites, bacterial infections, inflammation following virus infections such as FIP or rabies, toxoplasmosis, and abnormal changes in the spinal vertebrae (refer **Vitamin A excess**, page 319).

Rabies. An acute, contagious virus disease that causes nervous symptoms and excitability, and finally paralysis and death. It is endemic in wild animals in many countries of the world, but many island nations have eliminated it or prevented its introduction by enforcing strict quarantine policies.

Cats are usually infected after being bitten by a rabid animal, but other methods of transmission are possible. Cat to cat transmission seems rare, and it is suggested that in the United States the main source of infection is from bats, although skunks and raccoons have also been incriminated. In Europe, where cats have been shown to play a significant role in transmitting the disease to humans, infection is more likely to be from contact with rabid foxes or their wounded prey. Cats affected with rabies usually show what is known as the furious form, passing through a stage during which they become extremely vicious. A few show the dumb or paralytic form in which the attacking phase is absent. It takes any time from 9 to 60 days for the virus to incubate in an affected cat, and once clinical signs appear illness lasts from 1 to 8 days.

There are three recognized stages, the first being one in which the only signs may be a change in behavior with a tendency to hide. Quite a number of affected cats never emerge from hiding and die unseen. But many cats pass through this to a second stage, where in the furious form of the disease there is increasing irritability, or there are periods when they show extreme affection towards the owner interspersed with aimless attacks on animals, people or objects. An infected cat secretes virus in its saliva for about four days, commencing from about one day before signs first start to show, so it is during this period that there is a danger of it transmitting the disease to another animal or a human. In the dumb form of the disease there are no vicious attacks. As the cat enters the third stage its voice becomes hoarse due to gradual paralysis of the larynx, and this is followed by incoordination and a slowly ascending paralysis which eventually kills the cat.

The vaccination of cats against rabies is required by law in parts of some countries and in some American states. In countries where vaccination is optional it is encouraged by most veterinarians. In Britain, Australia and New Zealand general vaccination programmes are not allowed because of the quarantine policy.

Several different brands of vaccine are available. A primary vaccination is given at 3 months, followed by annual boosters.

In areas where rabies occurs an accurate diagnosis must be made when a cat displays signs that could be caused by the disease. Toxoplasmosis, lead poisoning, thiamine deficiency, strychnine or 1080 poisoning, panleukopenia, FIP, FeLV infection and conditions causing severe pain can all produce similar signs, so veterinary advice is essential. A firm diagnosis of rabies can only be made by a post-mortem examination of the brain, so any cat suspected of having rabies must be destroyed as soon as possible and the diagnosis confirmed.

Any person who has been bitten must receive treatment before clinical signs develop, or it will be too late. In most of the United States those who have been bitten by an animal are required by law to report it to the appropriate health authority.

THE CIRCULATORY SYSTEM

Heart conditions

The method of checking the heat and pulse rate is described on page 301.

About one cat in ten will contract some form of heart disease during its lifetime. In their early stages many cases are not detected by the cat's owner. Coughing seldom occurs, and the main signs of unwillingness to exercise and loss of appetite may not be noticed, especially in multi-cat households. A tendency to hide or seek seclusion may be the only initial sign, but as the condition worsens cyanosis may develop, due to lack of oxygen in the blood, causing a bluish-purple discoloration of the gums, conjunctiva and hairless parts of the body.

Congenital heart disease. About one cat in 50 is born with a heart problem, and most die within the first year of life. Abnormalities can affect the heart valves, the septum that separates the right and left sides of the heart ('hole in the heart'), the aorta or other blood vessels leading from the heart. These conditions eventually lead to enlargement of the heart (cardiomegaly) which only becomes apparent when a kitten is 2–6 months old.

Cardiomyopathy. The most common type of heart disease seen in cats, and caused by an abnormality in the heart muscle. It can take two different forms:
1. **Dilated cardiomyopathy** in which there is dilation of the ventricles results in inefficient pumping of the blood around the body, or 'pump failure'. It is caused by a deficiency of the nutrient taurine in the diet, and Siamese and Burmese appear more prone to the chronic form in which a gradual onset of lethargy and lack of appetite may be the only signs noticed by the owner. By the time the cat is noticeably ill it may be already be suffering from the early stages of depression, dehydration, hypothermia and shock. The condition is often associated with aortic embolism (refer **Thromboembolism**). Acute cases can die within 24 hours. The average survival time of many cases is only about one month. Treatment includes supplementation of the diet with taurine, and can be successful if the condition is detected early enough.

2. **Hypertrophic cardiomyopathy** results in the ventricles failing to dilate and fill properly, so that less blood is pumped out on each heart beat. It is more common in older cats and often associated with hyperthyroidism. The onset is often acute, with the cat showing various signs including difficult breathing, lethargy, loss of appetite, or even sudden death. There may be posterior paralysis due to aortic embolism (refer **Thromboembolism**). Treatment must include measures to control the thyroid condition, and may also involve cage rest, a low sodium diet and heart tablets.

Heartworm. The roundworm *Dirofilaria immitis* occurs in certain geographic areas of the world. Larvae are transmitted from one cat to another by the bites of mosquitoes, enter the blood stream and lodge in the right ventricle of the heart and/or the artery leading to the lungs (pulmonary artery). They take about 6 months to become adults and affect heart action and blood circulation to the lungs, and the disease is rarely diagnosed before a cat is 9 months old. Signs range from none to severe breathing difficulty, tissue swelling (edema) or sudden death. Occasionally cats may show nervous signs. Treatment needs careful supervision, for dead worms can fatally block a blood vessel. For some unexplained reason it is seen three times more often in males than in females.

Thromboembolism. Also known as thrombosis. A blood clot forms in the heart, eventually breaks up, and small pieces enter a major artery and partially or completely block it. A common site is the lower part of the aorta at the point where it divides into the two main arteries supplying the legs (iliac arteries), causing the condition known as *aortic thrombosis*. The first sign is often a sudden, hind-leg paralysis and many owners think that their cat has been in an accident because it is often in a state of distress and shock. One or both hind legs feel cold, and the cat has little or no sensation in its hind limbs. There may be no femoral pulse. Initially the condition is very painful and the limb muscles are soft, but a short time later they become very firm and hard. Thromboembolism is often associated with cardiomyopathy (see above). Veterinary advice is essential, but the outlook is poor.

Blood conditions

Blood formation occurs almost exclusively in the bone marrow. A mature red cell usually circulates for about 70 days.

Cat's blood is classified into three groups. About 75% of cats have group A blood, about 25% group B, and less than half of one percent group AB. About half of B group cats react to transfusion with A group blood, so blood typing, which can be done in the practice laboratory, is recommended before transfusion is carried out.

Anemia. A shortage of red blood cells circulating in the blood, reducing the amount of oxygen that it can carry. To compensate the heart pumps harder and the cat breathes more quickly. Signs depend on the severity and include pallor of the gums, lethargy, weakness, loss of appetite, thirst, and dehydration with a loss of skin elasticity. There are three main ways in which anemia can occur:
1. **Decreased red blood cell production.** Causes include a *nutritional deficiency of iron or certain B vitamins*, which can be corrected by a proper diet; *chronic kidney disease* for which veterinary treatment is necessary; and *bone marrow tumors* associated with feline leukemia virus (FeLV) (refer

below) for which veterinary treatment is rarely successful.
2. **Loss of blood.** *Sudden hemorrhage* can occur after an injury or accident, or the bursting of a blood vessel eroded by a tumor. A 2 kg (4.5 lb) cat has about 4½ oz (130 ml) of blood. Signs of anemia are apparent after a 20% loss, which is about 26 ml or little less than 1 ounce. A sudden loss of more than 25% of the total volume, which could easily occur after a serious hemorrhage, will precipitate shock. A blood loss of more than 50% quickly causes death. *Long-term blood loss* caused by chronic disease such as cancer or internal parasitism may not be noticed until a mild to moderate anemia develops.
3. **Increased red blood cell destruction.** This occurs after the administration of certain drugs, particularly acetaminophen or phenacetin (refer **Poisoning**, page 305); and in feline infectious anemia (FIA) and feline leukemia (FeLV) (refer below). The life span of the red blood cells is reduced and their rate of destruction increased, while the bone marrow fails to respond to the resulting shortage.

Feline infectious anemia (FIA). The protozoan parasite *Haemobartonella felis* damages red blood cells causing severe or fatal anemia. Transmission is probably by fleas and ticks, and also through cat bites since the disease is more common in male cats. Newborn kittens can become infected through the queen's milk when suckling. FIA occurs worldwide and is responsible for about 10% of cases in the US, often occurring after virus diseases that affect the immune system, such as FeLV or FIV.

Most infected cats show only a mild anemia and apparently recover, but may relapse if subjected to stress or infected with FeLV or FIV. About one-third develop severe anemia, with typical signs of loss of appetite, lethargy and depression, pallor of gums, jaundice and weight loss. Some have a fever. It can take several months for the disease to run its course. Treatment includes blood transfusions, antibiotics, and iron and vitamin supplements, but there is often a recurrence and only about 50% of cases are successfully treated.

Feline leukemia virus (FeLV). The most common cause of anemia and a major cause of disease in cats. It is often referred to as the feline leukemia complex because of the wide variety of problems it can cause. Many of these are directly related to the virus's cancer-producing activity, others arise from its immuno-suppression activity that makes the affected cat more prone to other infections. Its effects are comparable to those of FIV infection (refer page 306) and the human AIDS virus.

Infection is usually the result of close contact with a cat shedding virus in its saliva, such as occurs during mutual grooming or feeding from the same bowl. An unborn kitten can be infected in the womb.

Most infected cats show no signs. Younger cats are more susceptible, and kittens infected at under 16 weeks are the most likely to become diseased. The severity of infection seems to relate to the dose of virus picked up and the length of time that the kitten is exposed. Colony cats are more likely to be exposed to high doses over a long period, and in a cattery or multi-cat household with endemic FeLV 30%–40% of the cats may have virus in their blood (viremia), and many of the rest will have previously been infected. By contrast only about 5% of free-ranging cats have viremia even though the virus is widely disseminated, because the dose is low and the infection controlled.

Most infected cats are affected for only a few days or weeks and develop antibodies against subsequent re-infection. About half of apparently recovered cats carry virus in their bone marrow, but do not seem to pose a significant risk to others. In some cats the virus lodges in the bone marrow and other organs and multiplies. It then enters and persists in the blood and the cat is very likely to develop a FeLV-related disease. Over half of such cats die within six months.

FeLV infection can cause malignant tumors. In cats under one year old the most common site is the thymus gland in the chest. Signs include loss of weight and difficulty in breathing. Malignant tumors can also form in lymph nodes in other parts of the body. True leukemia (malignant cells circulating in the blood) is uncommon.

FeLV infection can also cause anemia (refer above), and its immuno-suppressive activity can allow a number of other chronic infections, such as feline infectious anemia and feline infectious peritonitis, to develop. Other problems associated with FeLV infection include infertility, fetal resorption, abortion and fading kittens.

Diagnosis is confirmed by the laboratory testing of blood samples, and the outlook for cats with FeLV-related disease is usually hopeless. Since the introduction of a FeLV vaccine a combination of blood testing, vaccination and quarantine has improved the chances of eliminating the disease from cat colonies.

NUTRITIONAL PROBLEMS

A cat is a true carnivore, and to remain healthy it must get certain nutrients that are only available from animal sources. Its diet must also provide all the other nutrients it needs in the right amount and balance, and too little or too much of a particular nutrient may cause ill health. Energy is obtained by digesting protein, fat and carbohydrate: too little can lead to poor growth and performance; too much to the laying down of fat and obesity.

If you feed your cat on properly balanced diets manufactured by reputable companies you should have little to worry about. But if you feed a home-made diet be aware of the potential problems and ensure that the foods you use provide everything your cat needs. Remember that cooking destroys certain vitamins and overcooking can greatly reduce a food's nutritional value. Raw food will provide more nutrients, but may also transmit disease. Also remember that a cat that is able to hunt will obtain many essential vitamins and minerals from its prey (including nutritionally valuable insects) and therefore make up for any minor deficiencies in the diet you feed it.

Problems arising from home-made diets

Biotin deficiency. Egg white contains an enzyme (avidin) that destroys the B vitamin biotin, and in theory a cat fed too much raw egg white could develop biotin deficiency, an early sign of which is a scaly dermatitis. In practice this is unlikely because bacteria in the gut manufacture plenty

of biotin for the cat to use, and a deficiency is only likely if a cat is being treated with antibiotics that kill the bacteria, and is also fed a lot of raw egg white. Egg yolk contains more than enough biotin to counteract the effects of the avidin in the white, so feeding whole egg, or just the yolk, is quite safe. Cooking destroys the avidin but also reduces the egg's nutritional value.

Calcium/phosphorus imbalance. Red meats (such as beef, lamb and pork), white meats (such as chicken and rabbit) and white fish are deficient in calcium and phosphorus, iodine, and vitamins A and D. Oily fish contains some vitamin A and D but still lacks calcium and phosphorus. A growing kitten fed an unbalanced diet consisting principally of these foods is likely to develop a disease (nutritional osteodystrophy) in which calcium is removed from the bones making them brittle. Early signs include irritability and a reluctance to run, jump or play, but later on lameness and obvious bone changes such as inward twisting of the forepaws or even fractures can occur. Treatment with the correct calcium supplements will quickly cure the problem. A simple method of balancing the calcium and phosphorus in meat is to add either ½ tsp (2.5 g) calcium carbonate or 1 tsp (5 g) dicalcium phosphate to every 4 oz (100 g) meat fed. Giving the cat milk won't help much; you would need 600 ml (1 pint) of milk for every 100 g meat to get the same effect. Whole fish, pressure cooked including the bones, is a better balanced food than most other meats.

Fat deficiency. Fat is an important source of energy and provides nutrients called fatty acids, one type of which only occurs in animal fats and is essential for the cat. Fat also acts as a carrier for the fat-soluble vitamins (A,D,E and K). A diet lacking in fat can result in poor growth and reproductive performance, a dull coat and dandruff, and increased susceptibility to infection.

Iodine deficiency. Because meat is deficient in iodine a cat fed mainly a meat diet may develop an iodine deficiency which causes a thyroid deficiency. This condition has long been recognized in the larger cat species kept in zoos, causing poor growth and reproduction, weakness and lethargy, and hair loss over the back, hind legs and tail. But it may also be more common than realized in the domestic variety, especially those kept in breeding establishments. Signs in a queen include fetal resorption, difficulties during parturition, and the production of kittens with congenital defects such as open eyes and cleft palates. Kittens from an affected mother are themselves iodine deficient, and may be weak, grow poorly and appear timid and lethargic, or even fade and die. Treatment is to supplement the diet with iodine, and your vet will give you full details.

Milk intolerance. As they grow up some cats are unable to adequately digest the lactose in milk, others are sensitive to milk protein. In both cases the principal sign is diarrhea. Refer also *Malabsorption*, page 309.

Potassium deficiency. Cats suffering from kidney problems may need more than the recommended level of potassium in their diet. Deficiency causes muscle problems (refer *Muscle diseases*, page 316).

Protein deficiency. This may occur in cats that are neglected or fed poor diets such as manufactured dog food which often has a much lower protein level than cat food. Signs include poor growth and performance and a dull coat. Blind-

ness similar to that caused by taurine deficiency (refer below) can also occur.

Taurine deficiency. The nutrient taurine is found mainly in animal tissues. Cats fed on vegetarian diets or diets low in taurine can develop blindness (refer *Retinal degeneration*, page 314).

Thiamine deficiency. Some types of fish (e.g. herring and sprats) contain an enzyme that destroys the B vitamin thiamine, and if fed raw in large amounts they may cause thiamine deficiency. Signs include loss of balance, downward bending of the head and neck, dilated pupils and convulsions. Treatment is with thiamine. Cooking the fish destroys the enzyme. Thiamine deficiency can also occur through destruction of the vitamin during the cooking of food.

Vitamin A excess. Hypervitaminosis A following the feeding of excessive amounts of raw liver can cause bony changes to the vertebrae (particularly those of the neck) that can cause pain, abnormal gait, and heightened sensitivity to touch. The damage is usually irreversible but some improvement can occur after a correction to the diet.

Vitamin E deficiency. Feeding too much oily fish such as red tuna or fish oil such as cod liver oil, without adequate vitamin E in the diet, can cause a painful inflammation of the fat under the skin called steatitis (yellow fat disease). The condition occurs typically in young adult, overweight cats fed only those types of fish. Signs include the formation of hard, painful lumps under the skin, sensitivity to touch, loss of appetite, fever, and a reluctance to move. Treatment is to change the diet and supplement with vitamin E.

Feeding animals that are ill

A cat that has a fever needs more nutrients and energy: for every 1°C rise in temperature its metabolism increases by 10%. It particularly needs additional protein, B vitamins and trace elements. Because a sick cat will often eat less than usual, or even nothing, it is important that the owner gets enough nourishment into it. Offer fresh food at body temperature, feed little and often, and remove and discard uneaten food after 15 minutes. Use highly digestible components such as high quality animal protein (eggs, meat, cottage cheese), and if feeding cereals cook them first to break down the starch. If using commercial foods use only those that are labelled as being complete. Moist foods are better accepted than dry. If force feeding by stomach tube is necessary your vet will advise you.

Special diets. A cat suffering from heart or kidney disease may benefit from being fed a special diet. In many countries such diets are manufactured, and your vet will tell you what is available or how to make up your own. Cats suffering from heart disease require a low sodium diet, fed little and often. For kidney disease the diet should contain enough water, potassium and sodium to make up for the excessive amounts lost through the kidneys, controlled amounts of vitamin K, adequate energy, and high quality protein which may or may not need to be restricted in quantity. A cat suffering from obesity should be fed a reduced-energy diet recommended by your vet.

SIGNS AND CONDITIONS

The following chart lists many of the common signs that can indicate illness or injury. Against each sign are listed the more common conditions associated with it. The list is not complete and meant as a guide only. Except for minor problems final diagnosis should always be made by a veterinarian.

SIGN	FIRST AID	FIV	NOSE & RESPIRATORY SYSTEM	MOUTH & DIGESTIVE SYSTEM	SKIN	EAR	EYE	URINARY SYSTEM	REPRODUCTIVE SYSTEM	MUSCLES & SKELETON	NERVOUS SYSTEM	BLOOD, HEART & CIRCULATION	NUTRITIONAL PROBLEMS
BEHAVIOR CHANGE depression/lethargy	Poisoning			FIP, Liver disease	FUS			Acute kidney disease, Nephrotic syndrome			Feline dysautonomia	Anemia, Cardiomyopathy, FeLV, FIA	Iodine deficiency (kittens)
disorientation/distress	Accident/injury, Hypothermia					Vestibular syndrome							
excessive grooming/licking					Fleas, Granuloma, Psychogenic alopecia								
temperament change	Accident/injury, Bone disease, Foreign body, Poisoning			Dental problems, FIP, Hyperthyroidism		Middle ear disease		Cystitis, FUS	Eclampsia	Arthritis, Bone disease	Brain damage, FHS, Neuritis, Rabies		Thiamine deficiency
BODY CONTROL/MOVEMENT circling						Inner ear disease					Brain damage, Encephalitis, Rabies		Thiamine deficiency
convulsions/fits	Hypothermia, Poisoning			FIP, Liver disease		Middle/inner ear disease		Acute kidney disease	Eclampsia		Brain damage/infection, Brain tumor, Epilepsy, FHS		
head/neck drooping/pain													Potassium deficiency, Thiamine deficiency, Vitamin A excess
head tilt						Middle/inner ear disease, Vestibular syndrome					Brain damage/infection		
incoordination/loss of balance	Accident/injury, Hyperthermia, Poisoning			FIP, FPL (kittens)		Inner ear disease, Vestibular syndrome			Eclampsia		Brain damage/infection		
lameness					Abscess					Arthritis, Bone disease, Dislocation, Fracture, Muscle injury, Sprain	Nerve damage/inflammation		Calcium imbalance
muscle spasm/tremors	Poisoning, Sting/bite (Spider)								Eclampsia		Brain damage/infection, FHS, Neuritis, Rabies		
paralysis	Accident/injury, Poisoning, Sting/bite (Tick)									Bone disease	Brain damage/infection	Thrombolism	
shivering/cold extremities	Hypothermia, Poisoning, Shock											Cardiomyopathy, Thromboembolism	
unconsciousness/coma	Asphyxia, Electric shock, Hyperthermia, Poisoning, Shock			Diabetes					Eclampsia		Brain damage/infection, Brain tumor, Encephalitis	Cardiomyopathy	
BREATHING/VOICE coughing/retching	Foreign body		Bronchial asthma, Bronchitis, FRD, Laryngeal spasm, Lungworm, Pharyngitis, Pneumonia										
difficult/wheezing	Sting/bite (Snake)		Bronchial asthma, Bronchitis, FRD, Laryngeal spasm, Laryngitis, Pleurisy, Pneumonia, Pneumothorax, Tumor	FIP, Toxoplasmosis						Hernia (diaphragm)		Cardiomyopathy, Heartworm	
panting/rapid	Hyperthermia, Shock, Poisoning (Toad)								Eclampsia			Anemia	
sneezing/snuffling			Fungal infection, FRD, Rhinitis										
DEFECATION/URINATION blood in feces/urine				Colitis				Cystitis, FUS, Tumor					
constipation/straining	Foreign body			Anal abscess, Hairball				Cystitis, FUS					
diarrhea	Foreign body, Poisoning	FIV		Coccidiosis, Enteritis, FIP, FPL, Hyperthyroidism, Internal parasites, Liver disease, Malabsorption, Pancreatic disease, Toxoplasmosis, Tumor									
excessive/frequent urination				Diabetes				Chronic kidney disease, Cystitis, FUS					
DISCHARGE ear/eye	Foreign body	FRD				Ear Canal disease, Tumor	Allergy, Ectropion, Entropion, Eye worm, Infection, Injury, Tear canal						

SYMPTOM	Injury / Poisoning	FIV	Infection / Digestive	Respiratory (FRD)	Skin and Fur	Ear / Hearing	Eye / Sight	Urinary System	Reproductive System	Skeletal / Muscular System	Nervous System	Blood & Circulation	Feeding Problem
vulva									Abortion, Endometritis, Vaginitis				
EAR, EYE, HEARING AND SIGHT													
abnormal eye movement						Middle ear disease							
blindness/cloudy eye	Accident/injury		FIP				Cataract, Glaucoma, Keratitis, Old age, Retinal degeneration				Brain damage/infection		Protein deficiency, Taurine deficiency
deafness						Congenital/inherited inner ear disease, Old age					Brain damage/infection		
protruding 3rd eyelid (haw)			Tapeworm infection, Enteritis (viral)								Feline dysautonomia, Nerve damage		
pupils — dilated	Shock, Poisoning, Stingbite				FHS		Glaucoma				Brain damage/injury, Feline dysautonomia, FHS		Thiamine deficiency
yellow color eye (jaundice)			FIP, Liver disease, Toxoplasmosis										
Refer also DISCHARGE, SWELLING													
FEEDING, MOUTH, GUMS													
bad breath			Dental problems, Mouth infection										
bleeding/inflamed gums	Foreign body, Poisoning	FIV	Dental problems, Mouth infection										
difficulty in eating			Dental problems, Mouth infection							Fractured jaw			
dribbling	Foreign body, Poisoning		Mouth infection										
excessive thirst/appetite			Coccidiosis, Diabetes, FIP, Hyperthyroidism, Tumor					Chronic kidney disease	Pyometra			Anemia, FeLV	
loss of appetite	Foreign body		Dental problems, Hairball, Tumor										
pale/white gums	Hypothermia, Poisoning, Shock		FIP, FPL, Hookworms									Anemia, FeLV, FIA	
regurgitation/vomiting	Foreign body, Poisoning		Cleft palate, Pharyngitis, Stricture, FPL, Hairball, Hyperthyroidism, Toxoplasmosis, Travel sickness, Tumor	FRD				Acute or chronic kidney disease	Endometritis				
tartar formation			Dental problems										
tooth loss			Dental problems										
ulceration on tongue	Poisoning			FRD (FCV)									
yellow gums (jaundice)			FIP, Liver disease, Toxoplasmosis									FIA	
Refer also SWELLING													
SKIN AND FUR													
crusts/scales					Mites								Biotin deficiency
dandruff					Mites, Seborrhea								Fat deficiency
dull, unkempt coat		FIV	Internal parasites										Fat deficiency, Protein deficiency
loss/shedding of hair			Mouth infection		Allergy, Dermatitis, Fleas, Granuloma, Hormonal alopecia, Psychogenic alopecia, Ringworm								Iodine deficiency, Fat deficiency
inflammation/irritation	Stingbite, Poisoning				Dermatitis, Fleas, Granuloma, Mites, Psychogenic alopecia, Ringworm (variable)						FHS		
oily or greasy					Psychogenic alopecia, Seborrhea, Stud tail								
Refer also SWELLING													
SWELLING													
anal			Anal abscess							Perineal hernia			
bone										Fracture, Tumor			
ear/eye						Abscess, Haematoma	Glaucoma						
skin — local	Stingbite	FIV	Epulis		Abscess, Fungal infection, Feline Leprosy, Hematoma, Granuloma, Tuberculosis, Tumor				Mammary gland problem	Muscle bruising/inflammation, Umbilical hernia			
WEIGHT LOSS/DEHYDRATION		FIV	FIP, FPL, Hookworms, Hyperthyroidism, Liver disease, Malabsorption, Pancreatic disease, Tuberculosis					Acute or chronic kidney disease				Anemia, FeLV, FIA	

LEGEND: FD=Feline dysautonomia; FeLV=Feline leukemia virus; FHS=Feline hyperesthesia syndrome; FIA=Feline infectious anemia; FIP=Feline infectious peritonitis; FIV=Feline immunodeficiency virus; FPL=Feline panleukopenia; FRD=Feline respiratory disease; FUS=Feline urological syndrome.

GLOSSARY

Words in *italics* are explained elsewhere in the Glossary.

Agouti Pattern of light and dark bands along individual hairs. Non-agouti cats lose the light bands which become solid color.
Ailurophile A person who loves cats.
Ailurophobe A person who dislikes or is afraid of cats.
Albino Animal lacking pigment in skin and hair and with reduced pigment in eyes which may be pinkish.
Allele One of two or more *genes* found at the same position on a *chromosome* which produce alternative characteristics.
Alter American term for *neuter*.
Anoestrus Time between female's sexually receptive periods.
Awn hair Coarser type of secondary hair with thickened tip.

Barring A striped pattern. A form of tabby marking, a fault when occurring in self-colored cats.
Bi-color Having a white coat patched with a second color.
Blaze Marking (usually white) down centre of forehead to nose.
Blue In describing cat coats a color in the blue-gray range.
Break *See* Stop.
Brindling Hairs of incorrect color scattered among those of correct shade. Sometimes appears in hot weather in cats with usually good coats.

Calico American form of tortoiseshell and white. Some *standards* ask for a cat looking as though it has been dropped in a pail of milk, others require no areas distinctly only white or only patched. There are both red and cream and red and black forms of patching.
Calling Distinct and repeated calls of a female cat in *oestrus*.
Cameo Describes hair with red or cream tipping.
Carnivore Animal which eats only, or almost only meat.
Carnassial Of or designating the upper premolar and first lower molar teeth of *carnivores*, used for tearing flesh.
Chinchilla Fur with only the outermost tip colored and the rest white or pale.
Chromosome Thread-like structure in the nucleus of animal cells which carries genetic material.
Cobby Having a low-lying body on short legs.
Colostrum First milk produced by mother, containing antibodies against diseases.
Conformation Body type of cat: characteristic size and shape of breed (also known as type).

Crepuscular Of, or active during evening twilight or just before dawn.

Digitigrade Walking on the toes.
Dilution Genetic variation producing weaker color.
Dimorphism Having two forms.
Diurnal Of, or active during daytime.
Dominant Characteristic appearing in offspring although inherited from only one parent.
Dorsal Relating to the back or spine.
Double coat Fur with thick, soft undercoat with thick topcoat of long hairs over, as in Manx cat.
Double recessive *Homozygous* for two pairs of recessive *genes*.

Entire Not *neutered*.
Epistasis Effect of some *genes* in concealing or 'masking' presence of others.
Estrus *See* Oestrus.
Euthanasia Painless killing.

Family In *taxonomy* the group into which an order is divided and which in turn is divided into genera (singular *genus*). In the case of cats, the Felidae.
Felid Feline, member of the Cat Family, Felidae, or appertaining to it.
Felinophile A person who loves cats.
Felinophobe A person who dislikes or is afraid of cats.
Feral A once domesticated animal (or its descendants), now living wild. Not a genuinely wild form.
Flehmen Reaction seen when *Jacobson's organ* is being stimulated.
Follicle Cavity in skin from which hair grows; also sac in ovary from which egg develops.
Foreign Describes cat with a fine-boned, elegant body, such as Siamese.
Frost point American term for *lilac* (lavender) point.

Generic Belonging to or in relation to a *genus*.
Genes Parts of body cell which pass on and control all hereditary characteristics.
Genotype Set of *genes* an individual inherits.
Genus Taxonomic zoological group into which a *family* is divided and consisting of one or more *species*. In cats *Felis, Panthera* etc.
Gestation Pregnancy.
Ghost markings Faint *tabby* markings seen in some solid colored cats, especially when young.
Gloves White patches on back of feet, as in Birman cats.
Guard hairs Long, bristly hairs forming the outer coat.

Haw *See* Nictitating membrane.
Heat *Oestrus*, also known as being in season.
Herbivore Animal which eats grass and other plants.

Heterozygous Having a pair of dissimilar *alleles* for a particular characteristic.
Homozygous Having a pair of identical *alleles* for a particular characteristic.
Honey mink An intermediate brown color in the Tonkinese, corresponding to Chocolate.
Hot color Too reddish shade in cream cats.
Hybrid Offspring of mating between one *species* and another or one breed and another.

Imprinting Development of recognition of and identification with members of an animal's own species (or in error of another which it takes to be its mother).
Induced ovulation Release of eggs from ovaries in response to physical stimulation in mating.
Infertile Unable to produce or beget offspring.

Jacobson's organ Sense organ in roof of mouth that responds to chemical stimuli (also known as vomeronasal organ).

Laces White markings rising from paws on back of rear legs, as in Birman cat.
Lavender American term for lilac.
Leather *See* Nose leather.
Ley line A line joining two prominent locations, possibly originally the line of a prehistoric track and thought by many to have the effect of linking natural centers of the earth's power.
Lilac Pale pinkish gray, known in America as Lavender; Lilac point often known in America as *Frost point*.
Liquid paraffin British name for medicinal oil.
Litter Family of kittens born at the same time; also clay granules, etc, used to absorb wastes in a toilet tray.
Lordosis Crouched position of the sexually receptive female.
Lynx point American name for Tabby point.

Marsupial Member of branch of mammal *family* in which live young are born immature and continue development in a pouch.
Mask Darker colored area of face, usually combined with a pattern of contrasting points, as in Siamese cat.
Masking *See* Epistasis.
Melanin Main pigment of skin and hair.
Melanism Having a very dark or black skin and fur, overlying any *species* markings.
Metoestrus The period in the female reproduction cycle immediately following *oestrus*.
Mimicry Occurrence of identical or very similar traits due to different *gene* mutations; also imitation of another *species*, usually as a form of camouflage, as in cheetah cubs.
Mittens White patches on the front of the paws, as in Ragdoll cats.
Modifiers *Polygenes* that change the effect of major *genes*.

Moggie Mongrel cat.

Mongrel Cat of mixed or unknown parentage.

Monotreme Member of the primitive order of egg-laying mammals of Australia and New Guinea.

Mutation Change within a *gene* resulting in a change in inherited characteristics.

Natural mink Name given to dark color of Tonkinese, corresponding to Seal in Siamese cat. It may be a random occurrence or result from exposure to radiation.

Neuter A castrated male or *spayed* female. Known as altered in America.

Nictitating membrane Third eyelid, an opaque membrane which rises from the lower inner corner of each eye under the eyelid, also known as haw.

Nocturnal Of, or active during daytime.

Nominate form The *species* from which the whole *genus* was first named.

Nose leather Exposed skin of nose, not covered by fur.

Odd-eyed Having eyes of different colors.

Oestrus Regularly occurring periods of sexual receptivity. Commonly known as heat or season.

Olfactory mucosa Area of the nose responsible for the detection of smells.

Omnivore Animal which eats meat and plants.

Oriental Cat of *foreign* type; also specifically an Oriental Shorthair.

Ovulation Release of eggs from the follicles.

Ovum (plural ova) Egg cell.

Pads Fleshy cushions on soles of paws.

Papillae Projecting cones of tissue on the surface of the tongue and lining the gut.

Partial dominance When neither of a pair of *alleles* is fully dominant to the other resulting in *heterozygous* individuals showing midway characteristics, as in Tonkinese cat.

Parti-color Composed of two or more distinct colors, as in bi-color, tortoiseshell, tortoiseshell and white cats.

Pectoral girdle Skeletal support to which the front limbs of vertebrates are attached.

Pedigree Genealogical table recording ancestry; also a record of this.

Persian Type now known officially in Britain as Longhair.

Pewter British variation of Shaded Silver, but having orange or copper eyes.

Phenotype Individual's visible physical characteristics, determined by its *genotype*.

Pheromone Chemical signal released by an animal which may influence another's behavior, including sexual and territorial marking scents.

Pinking-up Reddening of nipples.

Pinna The ear flap (can also be used to mean a feather or leaf shape and is another name for the auricle, a chamber in the heart).

Placenta Organ through which the kitten fetus receives nourishment and oxygen and loses wastes and by which it is attached to the lining of the womb.

Platinum American name for *lilac* (lavender) in Burmese cat.

Points Darker colored, contrasting areas on the head, ears, legs and tail, as in Siamese cat.

Polydactyl Having extra toes or fingers.

Polygenes Groups of *genes*, individually small in effect, that together produce well-defined characteristics.

Prepotent The ability of one parent to transmit more characteristics to its offspring than the other parent.

Pro-oestrus The period in the female reproductive cycle immediately preceding *oestrus*.

Queen Un-neutered (unaltered) female, especially one kept for breeding.

Rangy Long-limbed and long-bodied.

Recessive Characteristic passed on from one generation to another but which may not show in the earlier generation.

Recognition Acceptance by a cat association of a *standard* describing a new breed or variety of cat.

Registration Recording of a cat's birth and ancestry with a cat association.

Retractile (Usually of claws) able to be withdrawn into a sheath.

Rustiness Reddish-brown tinge in coat of a black cat, sometimes caused by basking in the sun.

Sable American for the brown, the darkest color in the Burmese cat.

Seal Dark brown of the *points* of the darkest variety of Siamese cat, caused by the *gene* which creates the point pattern.

Season Common name for *oestrus*.

Self or **Self-color** Uniform color of coat, also known as 'Solid.

Shaded Having tips of darker color on pale hairs.

Silver tipped Darker-colored hair tips which give a silver appearance.

Smoke Coat with hairs mostly colored but pale at base.

Socialization Getting used to life with others of the same, or other, *species* and learning appropriate modification of behavior.

Solid *See* Self.

Spaying *Neutering* of a female cat.

Species Basic unit of zoological classification, consisting of individuals distinctly different from other species and which can breed together to produce fertile offspring, e.g. *Felis silvestris* (Wildcat); further divided into subspecies with lesser differences, e.g. *Felis silvestris lybica* (African Wildcat).

Spraying Marking with urine.

Standard or **Standard of points** Description of characteristics required for a recognized variety or breed and the ideal description against which it is judged in shows.

Stop Break in the smooth line of the profile above nose.

Stud Male kept for breeding.

Stud tail Build-up of greasy secretion around the base of the tail, more frequently found in un-*neutered* toms.

Tabby Striped, blotched, spotted or ticked *agouti* pattern.

Tapetum lucidum Reflective layer at the back of the eye.

Taxonomy Scientific classification of living organisms into groups according to similarities of structure and origin, etc.

Ticking Bands of color on a hair. *See* Agouti.

Tipped Having dark color on tips of individual hairs.

Tom Entire (uncastrated) male cat.

Tri-color Made up of three distinct colors.

Type *See* Conformation.

Undercoat Soft hairs lying below the longer hair of cats with double coats.

Ungulate A mammal with hooves.

Van pattern Coat with most of fur white and color on head, tail and sometimes a patch on body.

Vestibular Of a space, forming an entrance, especially to a passage or canal in the body.

Vibrissae Stiffer hairs, including whiskers, which are particularly pressure sensitive.

Vomeronasal organ *See* Jacobson's organ.

BIBLIOGRAPHY

Many popular books which have been published on the domestic cat are not listed here but they are readily available through bookshops and libraries. This short bibliography includes some of the more accessible sources which have been consulted in the preparation of this book and which may be of interest to the general reader.

Adamson, Joy, *Born Free*, Collins-Harvill, London, 1960.
— *Living Free*, Collins, London, 1961.
— *Forever Free*, Collins, London, 1962.

Allaby, Michael & Crawford, Peter, *The Curious Cat*, Michael Joseph, London, 1982.

Bedi, Ramesh & Rajesh, *Indian Wildlife*, Collins, London, 1984.

Bertram, Brian, *Pride of Lions*, Dent, London, 1978; Charles Scribner's Sons, New York, 1978.

Burton, John A. & Pearson, Bruce, *Collins Guide to the Rare Mammals of the World*, Collins, London, 1987.

Clutton-Brock, Juliet, *A Natural History of Domesticated Animals*, Cambridge University Press, 1987.

Corbet, G.B. & Hill, J.E., *A World List of Mammalian Species*, British Museum (Natural History), London, 1980.

Corbett, Jim, *Man Eaters of Kumaon*, Penguin, Harmondsworth, 1979.
— *The Man Eating Leopard of Rudraprayag*, Oxford University Press, London, 1956.

Darnton, R., *The Great Cat Massacre and Other Episodes in French Cultural History*, Allen Lane, London, 1984.

Darwin, Charles, *Journal of Researches into the Natural History and Geology of the Countries Visited during the Voyage of H.M.S. Beagle round the World*, John Murray, London, 1860.

Eaton, Randall L., *The World's Cats*, Wildlife Safari Publications, Portland, Oregon, 1973.
— *The Cheetah*, Krieger, Melbourne, 1974.

Ewer, R.T., *The Carnivores*, Weidenfeld & Nicholson, London, 1973.

Fogel, Bruce, *Interrelations Between People and Pets*, Charles C. Thomas, Springfield, 1981.
— *Pets and Their People*, Collins, London, 1983.

Fox, Michael W., *Understanding Your Cat*, Blond & Briggs, London, 1974.

Grzimek's Animal Life Encyclopedia, Van Nostrand Reinhold, New York, 1984.

Guggisberg, C.A.W., *The Wild Cats of the World*, David & Charles, Newton Abbot, 1975. Covering all the wild species of the cat family, this is a comprehensive single volume for the layman, although the 15 years since publication have seen considerable new research.

Hafez, E.S.E. (ed.), *The Behaviour of Domestic Animals*, Balliére Tindall, London, 1975.

Haltenorth, Theodor, *Die Wildkatze*, Wittenberg Lutherstadt, 1975.

Haltenorth, Theodor & Diller, Helmut, *A Field Guide to the Mammals of Africa including Madagascar*, Collins, London, 1980.

Hart, George, *A Dictionary of Egyptian Gods*, London, 1986.

Herodotus (trs. Macaulay), *The Histories of Herodotus*, Vol II, 1890.

Hole, Christine, *Witchcraft in England*, Batsford, London, 1977.

Imaizumi, Y., *Report on the Iriomote cat project*, Environmental Agency, Tokyo, 1976, 1977 (in Japanese).

Jackman, Brian, *The Marsh Lions*, Elm Tree Books, London, 1982.

Joseph, Michael, *Cat's Company*, Geoffrey Bles, London, 1980.

Kemp-Turnbull, Peter, *The Leopard*, Cape Town, 1967.

Leyhausen, Paul, *Cat Behaviour: The Predatory and Social Behaviour of Domestic and Wild Cats*, Garland STPM Press, New York, 1979.

Lloyd, Joan Barclay, *African animals in Renaissance Literature and Art*, Oxford University Press, Oxford, 1972.

Loxton, Howard, *The Beauty of Big Cats*, Ward Lock, London 1973.
— *Guide to the Cats of the World*, Elsevier-Phaidon, 1975.
— *In Search of Cats*, Excalibur, New York, 1976.
— *Cats*, Collins, London, 1985.
— *Caring for Your Cat*, Black Cat, London, 1989.

Manolson, Frank, *My Cat's in Love*, St Martin's Press, New York, 1970.
— *C is for Cat*, Tandem, London, 1967.

Mather, Cotton, *The Wonders of the Invisible World*, London, 1693.

Mountford, Guy, *Wild India*, Collins, London, 1987.

Naville, H.E., *Bubastis 1887-9*, Egyptian Exploration Fund, 1891.

Necker, Claire, *The Natural History of Cats*, A.S. Barnes, New York, 1970.

Pallas, Peter Simon, *A Naturalist in Russia; Letter from Peter Simon Pallas to Thomas Pennant*, ed. Carol Urness, University of Minneapolis Press, Minneapolis, 1967.

Peel, Edgar & Southern, Pat, *The Trials of the Lancashire Witches*, David & Charles, Newton Abbot, 1969.

Prince Philip, H.R.H. Duke of Edinburgh, *Down to Earth*, Collins, London, 1988.

Rabinowitz, Alan, *Jaguar*, Collins, London, 1987.

Rengger, J.R., *Naturegeschichte der Saugethiere von Paraguay*, Basel, 1830.

Robinson, R., *Genetics for Cat Breeders*, Pergamon Press, Oxford, 1977.

Rudnai, Judith A., *The Social Life of the Lion*, Medical and Technical Press, 1973.

St George, E.A., *A Guide to the Gods of Ancient Egypt*, Spook Press, London, 1987.

Schaller, George, *The Deer and the Tiger*, University of Chicago Press, Chicago, 1967.
— *The Serengeti Lion: a study of predator prey relations*, University of Chicago Press, Chicago, 1972.
— *Serengeti: A Kingdom of Predators*, Knopf, New York, 1972; Collins, London, 1973.

Serpel, James, *In the Company of Animals: a study of human animal relationships*, Basil Blackwell, Oxford, 1986.

Simpson, Frances, *The Book of the Cat*, Cassell, London, 1903.

Singh, Arjan, *Tiger Haven*, Macmillan, London, 1973.
— *Tiger! Tiger!*, Jonathan Cape, London, 1984.

Tabor, Roger, *The Wildlife of the Domestic Cat*, Arrow Books, London, 1983.

Turner, Dennis C. & Bateson, Patrick (eds.), *The Domestic Cat: the biology of its behaviour*, Cambridge University Press, 1988. Based on a Symposium, *Cats '86*, held at the University of Zurich–Irchel in

1986, this collection of papers summarizes research and provides a useful bibliography of scientific papers for anyone who wishes to go into more detail.

Thapar, Valmik, *Tigers — The secret life*, Elm Tree Books, London, 1989.

Tilson, Ronald L. & Seal, Ulysses S. (eds.), *Tigers of the World*, Noys Publications, New Jersey, 1987.

Universities Federation for Animal Welfare, *The Ecology and Control of Feral Cats*, UFAW, Potters Bar, 1981.

Van Vechten, Carl, *The Tiger in the House*, Heinemann, London, 1921.

Weir, Harrison, *Our Cats and All About Them*, London, 1892.

Whyte, Hamish (ed.), *The Scottish Cat*, Aberdeen University Press, 1987.

Scientific Journals

Many scientific journals carry papers on research into the cat family. The following were among those consulted in the writing of this book but readers may trace new material by consulting the *Zoological Record* which each year lists papers under subject headings.

Animal Behaviour
Australian Wildlife Research
Behaviour
Carnivore Genetics Newsletter
Ethology
Indian Forester
Japan Journal of Ecology
Journal of Wildlife Management
Nature
New Zealand Journal of Zoology
Scientific American
South African Journal of Antarctic Research
South African Journal of Wildlife Research
Tigerpaper
Cat News, the twice-yearly newsletter of the Cat Specialist Group of the IUCN Species Survival Commission which carries both scientific and conservation news on the whole cat family, is available to subscribers to the Friends of the Cat Specialist Group at the IUCN address on page 327.

CAT ORGANIZATIONS

Registration bodies

International:

Fédération Internationale Féline (FIFe), Friedrichstrasse 48, 6200 Wiesbaden, German Federal Republic.

United Kingdom:

Governing Council of the Cat Fancy (GCCF), Dovefield, Petworth Road, Witley, Surrey GU8 5QWU.

Cat Association of Britain, Mill House, Lebcombe Regis, Wantage, Oxon OX12 9JD.

North America:

American Cat Association (ACA), 8101 Katherine Ave, Panorama City, CA 91402, USA. America's oldest registry. Today a fairly small organization with many shows in the south-east and south-west.

American Cat Council (ACC), USA. Another small association centered in the south-west which holds shows following a modified version of GCCF's methods, barring exhibitors from the show hall during judging.

American Cat Fanciers' Association (ACFA), P.O. Box 203, Pt Lookout, MO65726, USA. One of three international organizations with affiliated clubs in the USA, Canada and Japan. Very democratically run, it produces a monthly news bulletin, grants club charters and individual memberships.

Canadian Cat Association (CCA), 83–85 Kennedy Rd S., Unit 1805, Brampton, Ontario, L6W 3P3, Canada. The only all-Canadian body, its activities centered mainly in eastern Canada. A quarterly news letter is published in both French and English.

Cat Fanciers' Association (CFA), 1309 Allaire Ave, Ocean, NJ 07712, USA. The youngest of the American bodies, with affiliates in Canada and Japan, it produces a bi-monthly newsletter called *Trend* and an impressive yearbook.

United Cat Federation (UCA), 5510 Ptolemy Way, Mira Loma, CA 91752, USA. Medium-sized body centered in south-west.

Australia:

Feline Association of South Australia, 7 Athelney Ave, Brighton, SA 5048, Australia.

New Zealand:

New Zealand Cat Fancy Inc., P.O. Box 3167, Richmond, Nelson, New Zealand.

Republic of South Africa:

Western Province Cat Club, P.O. Box 3600, Cape Town 8000, RSA.

Animal Welfare and Conservation:

American Anti-Vivisection Society, Suite 204 Noble Plaza, 801 Old York Rd, Jenkintown, PY 19046-1685, USA.

American Humane Association, 9725 East Hampden Ave, Denver, Colorado 80231.

Animaux-Secours, Refuge de l'Espoir, Arthaz (74380), Haute-Savoie, France.

The Blue Cross, 1 Hugh Street, Victoria, London SW1V 1QQ, United Kingdom.

Canadian Society for the Prevention of Cruelty to Animals (CSPCA), 5214 Jean Talon St West, Montreal, Quebec H4P 1X4, Canada.

Cat Action Trust, The Crippetts, Jordens, Beaconsfield, Bucks, United Kingdom.

Cat Protection Society of Queensland, 26 Winsome Rd, Salisbury, Queensland 4107, Australia.

Cat Survival Trust, Marlind Centre, Codicote Road, Welwyn, Herts AL6 9TV, United Kingdom.

Cats Protection League, 20 North St, Horsham, West Sussex RH12 1BN, United Kingdom.

Défense et Protection des Animaux, Refuge de Thernay, La Fermelé, 58160, Imphy, France.

Deutsche Tierfreunde eV, Am Dom 6, D-2800 Bremen, Federal Republic of Germany.

Dutch Society for the Prevention of Cruelty to Animals, Bankastraat 100, 2585E,S, The Hague, Netherlands.

Feline Advisory Bureau, 350 Upper Richmond Rd, Putney, London SW15 6TL, United Kingdom.

Friends of Animals Inc., 11 West 60th St, New York, NY 10023, USA.

Fund for Animals, 200 West 57th St, New York, NY 10019, USA.

Hellenic Animal Welfare Society, 12 Pasteur St, Athens 115-21, Greece.

Humane Society of the US, 2100 L High St, NW, Washington, DC 20037, USA.

Irish Society for the Prevention of Cruelty to Animals, 1 Grand Canal Quay, Dublin 2, Eire IUCN.

IUCN (International Union for the Conservation of Nature, World Conservation Centre, 1196 Gland, Switzerland.

Japan Animal Welfare Society (Tokyo), No 5 Tanisawa Building, 1–38 Moto Azabu 3-Chome, Minato-ku, Tokyo, Japan.

Lynx, P.O. Box 509, Dunmow, Essex CM6 1UH, United Kingdom.

National Anti-Vivisection Society, 51 Harley Street, London W1, United Kingdom.

National Audubon Society, 950 Third Avenue, New York, NY 10022, USA.

National Petwatch, P.O. Box 16, Brighouse, West Yorkshire, HD6 1DS, United Kingdom.

New Zealand Society for the Prevention of Cruelty to Animals Inc., P.O. Box 15-349, 3 Totara Ave, New Lynn, Auckland, New Zealand.

Royal Society for the Prevention of Cruelty to Animals (RSPCA), Causeway, Horsham, West Sussex RH19 1HG, United Kingdom.

Society for the Prevention of Cruelty to Animals, P.O. Box 38035, Johannesburg 2000, RSA.

South African Federation of SPCAs & Affiliated Societies, P.O. Box 82831, Southdale, Johannesburg, Transvaal 2135, RSA.

World Wide Fund for Nature and the Environment (WWF), World Conservation Centre, CH-1196 Gland, Switzerland.

WWF–Australia, Level 17, St Martin's Tower, 31 Market St, Sydney, NSW 2001, Australia.

WWF–Austria (Oesterreichischer Stifterverband fur Naturschutz), Ottakringerstr. 114-116/9, Postfach 1, A-1162 Vienna, Austria.

WWF–Belgium, 608 Chaussée de Waterloo, B-1060 Brussels, Belgium.

WWF–Canada, 60 St Clair Ave East, Suite 201, Toronto, Ontario M4T 1NS, Canada.

WWF–Denmark (Verdensnaturfonden), Osterbrogade 94, DK-2100 Copenhagen O, Denmark.

WWF–Finland, Uudenmaankatu 40, 00120 Helsinki 12, Finland.

WWF–France (Association Française de World Wildlife Fund), 14 rue de la Cure, F-75016, Paris, France.

WWF–Germany (Umweltstiftung WWF-Deutschland), Sophiengrassse 44, D-6000 Frankfurt a/Main 90, Federal Republic of Germany.

WWF–Hong Kong, 1 Battery Path, Central, Hong Kong.

WWF–India, c/o Godrej & Boiyce Mfg Co. Pvt Ltd., Lalbaug, Parel, Bombay 400012, India.

WWF–Italy (Associazione Italiana per il World Wildlife Fund), Via Salaria 290, I-00199, Rome, Italy.

WWF–Japan (Sekai Yaseiseibutsu Kikin Nihon Iinkai), Dae 39 Mori Bldg, 2-4-5 Azabudai, Minato-ku, Tokyo 106, Japan.

WWF–Malaysia, P.O. Box 10769, 50724 Kuala Lumpur, Malaysia.

WWF–Netherlands (Wereld Natuur Fonds), 1e Hageweg 2, Postbus 7, NL-3700 AA Zeist, Netherlands.

WWF–New Zealand, P.O. Box 6237, Wellington, New Zealand.

WWF–Norway, Hegdehaugsveien 22, 0167, Oslo 1, Norway.

WWF–Pakistan, P.O. Box 1312, Lahore, Pakistan.

WWF–South Africa (Southern Africa Nature Foundation), P.O. Box 459, Stellenbosch 7600, RSA.

WWF–Spain (Adena), 6 Santa Engracia, E-Madrid 10, Spain.

WWF–Sweden (Världsnaturfonden), Ulriksdals Slolt, S-171 71 Solna, Sweden.

WWF–Switzerland, Forrlibuckstr. 55, Postfach, 8037 Zurich, Switzerland.

WWF–United Kingdom, Panda House, 11-13 Ockford Rd, Godalming, Surrey GU7 1QU, United Kingdom.

WWF–United States, 1255 23rd St NW, Washington, DC 20037, USA.

INDEX

Where there are six or more page references, **bold** figures indicate major entries.

ILLUSTRATION ACKNOWLEDGMENTS

All photographs are by Graham Meadows except those listed hereunder.

(a) above; (b) below; (c) centre; (l) left; (r) right; (t) top; (m) middle.

Anthony Bannister 15(a)(b), 49(tr), 137(ar), 170(cl), 280(a); Bannister/Stanton 15(b); Bannister/Pickford 77(a).

Ardea/London 374(b), 168(c)(b); Ardea/Bertrand 152(c), 142(b), 173(a); Ardea/Daniels 138(b); Ardea/Ferrero 5, 21(bl); Ardea/Fink 21(br), 54(a), 55(b), 71(b); Ardea/Gohier 65(b), 66(b); Ardea/Gordon 67(a); Ardea/Haagner, 33(a), 173(b); Ardea/McDougall 232; Ardea/Putland 225(a); Ardea/Waller 26(a); Ardea/Warren 65(t).

Ashmolean Museum 259(t).

Associated Newspapers Groups Ltd 240(t).

David Bateman Ltd 278/9.

Bridgeman Art Gallery/Gavin Graham Gallery 161, 268(a), 270(bl).

Bridgeman Art Library 259(bl).

British Museum 198(b)(ac), 218(b), 257.

British Tourist Authority 14(b), 200(ar)(b), 201(b), 225(b); BTA/Calder 187(ar), 275(tl)(tr).

Martin Bruce 153(bl).

A & S Carey 8, 35(bl), 40(br), 61, 63, 64(a)(b), 70(c), 71(a), 74(c), 137(al), 140(tc), 150, 166(a), 167(al)(ar).

Chartwell 256(t).

Christie's 74(t), 175(tr), 189(tr), 195(t) (3 pictures), 210(cl), 212(t), 240(c), 255(tl), 266(c), 267(t), 269 (4 pictures).

Cladonia Resources 125(b), 130(r).

City of Coventry 276(bl).

COI 256(b).

Collection Earl of Buccleuch; by kind permission of His Grace the Duke of Buccleuch 44.

Cuba/Hemingway Museum 261(cr).

Gerald Cubitt 1, 48, 49(tl)(br), 52(l), 55(a), 68(a)(b), 69(b)(tl), 72, 76(b), 135(a), 143(b), 146(t), 178(bl)(br), 179(bl)(br), 234(a), 235(b), 237(a), 238(bl)(bc), 382(br) back jacket (ar).

Dierenbescherming, Holland 228(tr).

DSIR, New Zealand (Marc Ryan), 24(b).

Suzanne Emanuel 16(cbl).

F Ennis 176(b).

Mary Evans Picture Library 211(a). 220(ar), 252(cl), 254.

Exxon 277(mc).

Fitzwilliam Museum 266(b).

E W W Fowler 276 (pics left).

Futile Press/W H Rogers 244(a).

Glenturret Distillery 238(a), 238(br).

Griffiths Institute 189(al)(ar); 192(c).

Guildhall Library 242(al), 243(a).

Carl Hagenbeck Tierpark 224(ar).

Claus & Liselotte Hansmann 243(b).

Sonia Halliday 196(b).

Halliday/Lushington, 33(br), 202/3(b).

Jenny Halstead 13(b); 14(a).

B H Harper/Wildlife Society of Southern Africa 77(b).

Harvard University Art Museums 268(b).

Marc Henrie 99(b), 106(c), 130(l).

Hereford Cathedral 199(t).

Dorothy Holby 96(al)(c), 97(br), 98(cl), 101(tl), 114(b), 116(a)(b), 140(bc).

Michael Holford 186(t), 208(br), 210(cr), 217(b).

Hutchison 189(bl), 189(br), 209(b), 210(tl)(tr); Hutchison/Dörig 217(a); Hutchison/Drader 224(b); Hutchison/Hatt, 23(t); Hutchison/Pemberton 211(b), 275(c); Hutchison Library/Regent, 13(a), 13(c); Hutchison/Scorer 194(b); Hutchison/Smith, 33(bl), 230(a); Hutchison/Goycolea 187(al).

IMITOR, 12(a)(b).

Iveagh Bequest/Priv Coll 266(r).

Paul Jackson 261(br).

Peter Jackson 54(b), 57(a), 62, 70(b), 74(b), 170(cr), 172(a), 237(br).

Vicky Jackson 96(b), 98(b), 101(c), 114(tl), 129(al), 131(c).

Larry Johnson 82(t), 101(b), 126(b).

Kobal Collection 43(al); 197(b), 198(t), 249(l)(r), 250/251 all 9 pictures, 252(br); Kobal/Eon 251(br).

Kohira 156(a), 212(lc)(b), 213(a), 271(bl), 282(t).

Kunsthaus, Zurich 261(tl).

Lynx Magazine 230(b).

Howard Loxton 34(l), 156(br), 163(b), 164(al)(ar)(b), 165(a), 168(a), 174(a), 178(a)(m)(t), 186(c), 191)bl), 195(ac)(bc), 287(tl).

Errol McLeary: all diagrams, maps and line illustrations.

Manchester Art Gallery 240(b).

Mansell Collection 197(c), 206(a), 256(t).

Masahiko Misada 56(b).

Metropolitan Museum of Art, New York 16.

Tony Morrison 76(a), 216(al)(bc).

National Gallery, London 270(a).

National Petwatch 228(br), 231.

Daphne Negus 118(c), 119(cr).

Peter Nolan Lawrence Collection 276(bl)(tc)(cr).

Oeffenlichs Kunstsammlungen, Basle 267(b).

Planet Earth, 23(b); Planet Earth/Matthews 1523(br), 153(br), 163(c); Planet Earth Purdy/Matthews 40(ar), 169; 152(b), 153(c); Planet Earth/Rouse 147 (br); Planet Earth/Scott 172(c).

Potters Museum of Curiosities 229(b).

Robert Pearcy 43(ar), 94(bl), 96(ar), 97(bl), 99(tl), 100(b), 101(t), 102(b), 103(r), 117(b), 124(t), 125(bc), 126(a), 129(ar), 131(r), 283.

Rex Features 234(b), 252(a).

Robinson 206(b), 207.

Roger-Viollet 261(bl)(c).

Royal Commonwealth Society 219(b), 220(al).

Royal Crown Derby 273(t) and back jacket (b).

Royal Library, Windsor 265.

RSPCA 228(tc).

Savoy Hotel 256(cr).

Scala 223, 263, 264(a)(bl); Scala/National Museum of Athens 195(b), 196(a), 197(a); Scala/Museo Civco/Recanti 203(a); Scala/Bib. Nat. Firenze 219(a).

Seaphot/Planet Earth/Ammann 171; Seaphot/Planet Earth/Scott 143(a), 144(c), 170(a), 172(b), 232(a).

Ronald Searle/IWM 272.

Scottish National Port Gallery 258(c).

Smithsonian Institute/Freer Gallery 227.

Society of Antiquaries 274(ar).

Solitaire, 20(a)(br), 40(bl), 45(b), 47, 82(ar), 83, 89(5)(12)(14)(16), 90(20)921), 91, 92/93, 94(tr)(ar)(br), 95(tl)(al)(b), 96(tl), 97(a), 99(ar), 100(a), 102(a), 104, 106(a), 107(b), 108(t)(cl)(r), 109(b), 110(a), 111(ar)(cr), 112(b), 113(c)(b), 114(tr), 118(a), 120(bl)(br), 122(r)(b), 127(ar),

128(t), 129(cr)(br), 131(l), 145, 149(c), 159, 165(br), 182/3, 193, 214/5, 288(b), 289(a), 300.

Sothebys 191(ar), 209(t), 266(t), 268, 273(b).

S.P.A., France 228(tc)(bl).

Frank Spooner Pictures 213(b), 213(c), 228(lc), 239(tl); Frank Spooner Pictures/Gamma/Kurita 166(b), 213(b); Frank Spooner/Gamma/Avvsteen 256(cl); Frank Spooner/Gamma/E. Sander 280(b); Frank Spooner/Gamma/de Hogue 281; Frank Spooner/Gamma/ Bougrin-Dubourg 282(b); Frank Spooner/Kaklatchev 244(b).

Suncoast Pictures 18(br), 176(r).

Survival Anglia/Bartlett 138(a), 151; Survival/Kavanagh 58(a); Survival/Davidson 23(ml), 164 (c); Survival/Deiter Plage 167(br), 170(br), 236(a)(b); Survival/Foote 67(b), 69(a); Survival/Matthews/Purdy 140/141(a), 148(br), 152(t), 232(b); Survival/Plage 32; Survival/Price 137(b); Survival/Root 50; 51; Survival/Wilding 165(bl).

Tate Gallery, London 184/5.

Gordon Taylor 199(a).

Norman Tozer 41, 146(br), 147(t)(bl), 154, 163(t), 174(b), 176(al)(ac)(ar)(cl), 229(ar), 247(a).

Tokyo Zoo 59(al).

Tonecraft 143(bl), 99(c), 149(bl).

Vautier 277(br); Vautier/Caillouet 216(ar); Vautier/Lima Museum 217(l); Vautier/Museo Bruning 216(br).

Victoria & Albert Museum 241, 246(l).

Yale Center for British Art, 16(b).

Ypres Tourist Council 200(al), 204(a).

ZEFA/Bauer 2; ZEFA/Lummer 35(mb), 57(b); ZEFA/Orion Press 58(b); ZEFA/Photo Researcher 30/31, 52(r), 53, 56(a), ZEFA/Revers-Widauer 75; ZEFA/Schellhammer 221(b).

Zoological Society of San Diego 49(ml), 59(ar), 66(a); 70(t), 224(al).

© 1969 Danjaq S.A. All rights reserved 251(br).

Every effort has been made to trace copyright holders. Any person or persons believing themselves to have legitimate copyright claims should contact the publishers.

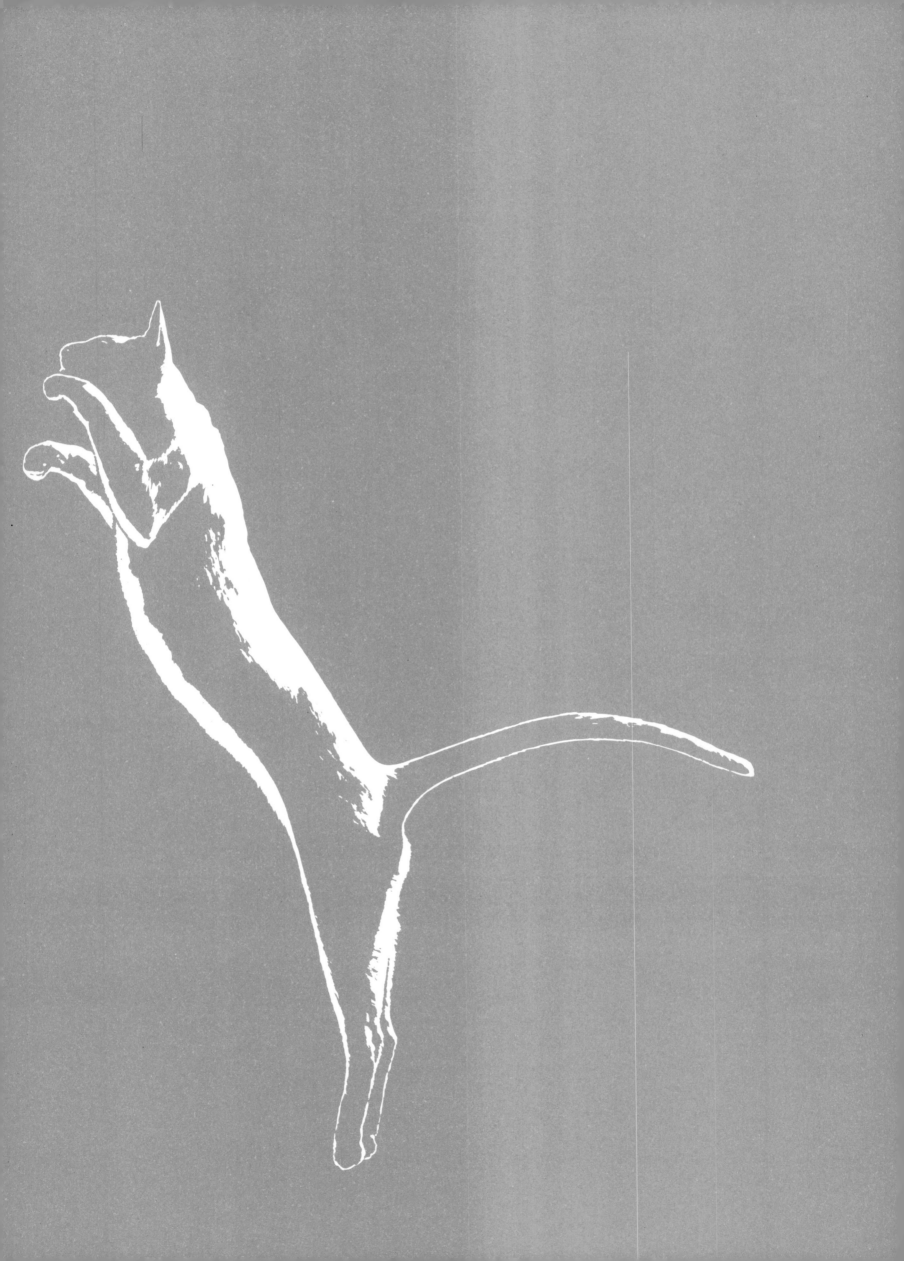